To Rev. Fr. Whelahan ~

From Lennoxtown Pupils
Attending St. Ninian's High
School, Kirkintilloch.
On Occasion of his ~

Sacerdotal Silver Jubilee.

21st January 1942

THE GOSPELS

OF THE

SUNDAYS AND FESTIVALS

VOL. II

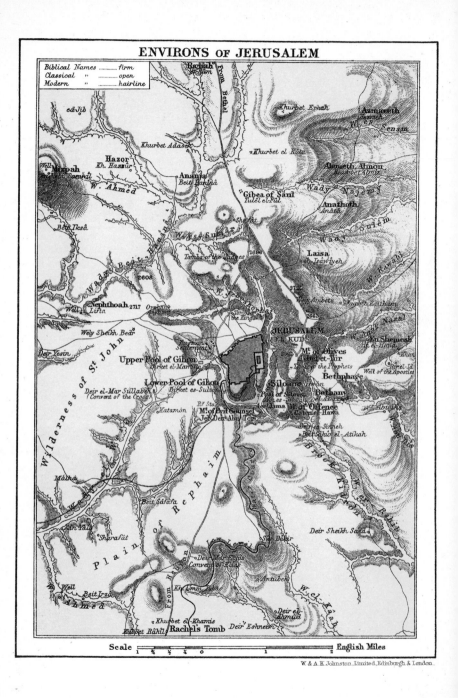

ENVIRONS OF JERUSALEM

Biblical Names .... firm
Classical   .... open
Modern   .... hairline

Scale

English Miles

W. & A. K. Johnston, Limited, Edinburgh & London.

THE GOSPELS

OF THE

SUNDAYS AND FESTIVALS

WITH

AN INTRODUCTION, PARALLEL PASSAGES, NOTES AND MORAL REFLECTIONS

BY

CORNELIUS J. RYAN, D.D.

Canon of the Metropolitan Chapter of Dublin. Formerly Professor of Sacred Scripture and Hebrew, Holy Cross College, Clonliffe

VOL. II

TENTH EDITION

Dublin

M. H. GILL AND SON, LTD.

50 UPPER O'CONNELL STREET

1936

Nihil Obstat :

MATTHAEUS MacMAHON,

Censor Theol. Deput.

Imprimi potest :

✝ EDUARDUS,

Archiepiscopus Dublinensis,

Hiberniæ Primas.

DUBLINI, die 8° Aprilis anno 1924.

Printed and Bound in Ireland at the Press of the Publishers

Contents of the Second Volume.

GOSPELS

OF THE

SUNDAYS AND FESTIVALS.

VOL. II.

PASSION SUNDAY.

I.—TEXTS.

<table>
<tr><td>

GREEK.

JOHN VIII. 46-59.

⁴⁶ Τίς ἐξ ὑμῶν ἐλέγχει με περὶ ἁμαρτίας; εἰ ἀλήθειαν λέγω, διὰ τί ὑμεῖς οὐ πιστεύετέ μοι; ⁴⁷ Ὁ ὢν ἐκ τοῦ θεοῦ, τὰ ῥήματα τοῦ θεοῦ ἀκούει· διὰ τοῦτο ὑμεῖς οὐκ ἀκούετε, ὅτι ἐκ τοῦ θεοῦ οὐκ ἐστέ. ⁴⁸ Ἀπεκρίθησαν οἱ Ἰουδαῖοι, καὶ εἶπαν αὐτῷ· οὐ καλῶς λέγομεν ἡμεῖς, ὅτι σαμαρείτης εἶ σύ, καὶ δαιμόνιον ἔχεις; ⁴⁹ Ἀπεκρίθη Ἰησοῦς· ἐγὼ δαιμόνιον οὐκ ἔχω, ἀλλὰ τιμῶ τὸν πατέρα μου, καὶ ὑμεῖς ἀτιμάζετέ με. ⁵⁰ Ἐγὼ δὲ οὐ ζητῶ τὴν δόξαν μου· ἔστιν ὁ ζητῶν καὶ κρίνων. ⁵¹ Ἀμὴν ἀμὴν λέγω ὑμῖν, ἐάν τις τὸν ἐμὸν λόγον τηρήσῃ, θάνατον οὐ μὴ θεωρήσῃ εἰς τὸν αἰῶνα ⁵² Εἶπον αὐτῷ οἱ Ἰουδαῖοι· νῦν ἐγνώκαμεν ὅτι δαιμόνιον ἔχεις. Ἀβραὰμ ἀπέθανεν καὶ οἱ προφῆται, καὶ σὺ λέγεις· ἐάν τις τὸν λόγον μου τηρήσῃ,

</td><td>

VULGATE.

JOHN VIII. 46-59.

⁴⁶ Quis ex vobis arguet me de peccato? Si veritatem dico vobis, quare non creditis mihi? ⁴⁷ Qui ex Deo est, verba Dei audit. Propterea vos non auditis, quia ex Deo non estis. ⁴⁸ Responderunt ergo Judæi et dixerunt ei : Nonne bene dicimus nos quia Samaritanus es tu, et dæmonium habes? ⁴⁹ Respondit Jesus : Ego dæmonium non habeo ; sed honorifico Patrem meum, et vos inhonorastis me. ⁵⁰ Ego autem non quæro gloriam meam : est qui quærat, et judicet. ⁵¹ Amen amen dico vobis, si quis sermonem meum servaverit, mortem non videbit in æternum. ⁵² Dixerunt ergo Judæi : Nunc cognovimus quia dæmonium habes. Abraham mortuus est, et prophetæ ; et tu dicis : Si quis sermonem meum servaverit, non gustabit mortem in

</td></tr>
</table>

θάνατον οὐ μὴ θεωρήσῃ εἰς τὸν αἰῶνα.
⁵³ Μὴ σὺ μείζων εἶ τοῦ πατρὸς ἡμῶν
Ἀβραάμ, ὅστις ἀπέθανεν; καὶ οἱ προφῆται ἀπέθανον· τίνα σεαυτὸν ποιεῖς;
⁵⁴ Ἀπεκρίθη Ἰησοῦς· ἐὰν ἐγὼ δοξάσω
ἐμαυτόν, ἡ δόξα μου οὐδέν ἐστιν· ἔστιν
ὁ πατήρ μου ὁ δοξάζων με, ὃν ὑμεῖς
λέγετε ὅτι θεὸς ὑμῶν ἐστιν. ⁵⁵ Καὶ οὐκ
ἐγνώκατε αὐτόν. ἐγὼ δὲ οἶδα αὐτόν·
κἂν εἴπω ὅτι οὐκ οἶδα αὐτὸν, ἔσομαι
ὅμοιος ὑμῖν, ψεύστης· ἀλλὰ οἶδα αὐτὸν,
καὶ τὸν λόγον αὐτοῦ τηρῶ. ⁵⁶ Ἀβραὰμ
ὁ πατὴρ ὑμῶν ἠγαλλιάσατο ἵνα ἴδῃ τὴν
ἡμέραν τὴν ἐμήν, καὶ εἶδεν, καὶ ἐχάρη.
⁵⁷ Εἶπον οὖν οἱ Ἰουδαῖοι πρὸς αὐτόν·
πεντήκοντα ἔτη οὔπω ἔχεις, καὶ Ἀβραὰμ
ἑώρακας; ⁵⁸ Εἶπεν αὐτοῖς Ἰησοῦς· ἀμὴν
ἀμὴν λέγω ὑμῖν, πρὶν Ἀβραὰμ γενέσθαι,
ἐγώ εἰμι. ⁵⁹ Ἦραν οὖν λίθους ἵνα βά-
λωσιν ἐπ' αὐτόν. Ἰησοῦς ἐκρύβη, καὶ
ἐξῆλθεν ἐκ τοῦ ἱεροῦ.

æternum. ⁵³ Numquid tu major es patre nostro Abraham, qui mortuus est? et prophetæ mortui sunt. Quem teipsum facis? ⁵⁴ Respondit Jesus : Si ego glorifico meipsum, gloria mea nihil est ; est Pater meus qui glorificat me, quem vos dicitis quia Deus vester est. ⁵⁵ Et non cognovistis eum ; ego autem novi eum. Et si dixero quia non scio eum, ero similis vobis, mendax. Sed scio eum, et sermonem ejus servo. ⁵⁶ Abraham pater vester exsultavit ut videret diem meum : vidit, et gavisus est. ⁵⁷ Dixerunt ergo Judæi ad eum : Quinquaginta annos nondum habes, et Abraham vidisti? ⁵⁸ Dixit eis Jesus : Amen amen dico vobis, antequam Abraham fieret, ego sum. ⁵⁹ Tulerunt ergo lapides ut jacerent in eum ; Jesus autem abscondit se, et exivit de templo.

II.—ENGLISH TRANSLATION.

JOHN VIII. 46-59.

⁴⁶ "Which of you shall convict me of sin ? If I say the truth to you, why do you not believe me ? ⁴⁷ He that is of God, heareth the words of God. Therefore you hear them not, because you are not of God." ⁴⁸ The Jews therefore answered, and said to him : " Do not we say well that thou art a Samaritan, and hast a devil ? " ⁴⁹ Jesus answered : " I have not a devil ; but I honour my Father, and you have dishonoured me. ⁵⁰ But I seek not my own glory : there is one that seeketh and judgeth. ⁵¹ Amen amen I say to you : If any man keep my word, he shall not see death for ever." ⁵² The Jews therefore said : " Now we know that thou hast a devil. Abraham is dead, and the prophets ; and thou sayest : If any man keep my word, he shall not taste death for ever. ⁵³ Art thou greater than our father Abraham, who is dead ? And the prophets are dead. Whom dost thou make thyself ? " ⁵⁴ Jesus answered : " If I glorify myself, my glory is nothing. It is my Father that glorifieth me, of whom you say that he is your God. ⁵⁵ And you have not known him ; but I know him. And if I shall say that I know

him not, I shall be like to you, a liar. But I do know him, and do keep his word. ⁵⁶ Abraham your father rejoiced that he might see my day : he saw it, and was glad." ⁵⁷ The Jews therefore said to him : " Thou art not yet fifty years old, and hast thou seen Abraham ? " ⁵⁸ Jesus said to them : " Amen amen I say to you, before Abraham was made, I am." ⁵⁹ They took up stones, therefore, to cast at him ; but Jesus hid himself, and went out of the temple.

III.—NOTES.

Introductory. From St. John we learn that having for the last time celebrated the Feast of Tabernacles, our Lord was one day teaching in the temple and threatening the Jews for their rejection of the Messiah sent from heaven for their salvation. Touched by grace, some believed in him ; but this was only for the moment. On hearing that, children of Abraham though they were, they needed divine help to free themselves from the slavery of sin, they were filled with indignation at the word, and they received from Christ a severe rebuke for their inconstancy and pride (John viii. 44, 45). The Redeemer did not yet abandon those he came to save, but made another effort to convert his wicked audience. He challenged them to point out in his acts a justification of their unbelief ; he refuted their calumnies ; and he proved his right to their obedience by openly claiming the possession of the essential attributes of God.

He said :—

V. 46. **Which of you shall convict me of sin ? If I say the truth to you, why do you not believe me ?**

In the preceding verse our Lord had asserted without contradiction that he spoke the truth ; here he says : " Which of you shall *convict* me of sin ? " not, " Which of you shall *accuse* me of sin ? " The former they had never been able to do, though they had frequently done the latter. They had laid to his charge the breaking of the sabbath, the eating with sinners, the deceiving and subverting of the people, and the working of miracles by the power of the devil. In making each of these accusations, they had not brought forward even a plausible argument to support their case ; and in every instance they had to retire silenced and confounded. It was to be the same on the present occasion. As an action is to be attributed not to the *nature* of him who performs it but to the *personality* that rules that nature, and as in the Word Incarnate the personality was divine, it was impossible that in Christ there could be the slightest shade of moral imperfection. His divine personality, however, not being admitted by those to whom he spoke, our Lord appealed to the experience of his enemies in proof of his sinlessness ; and having just declared without contradiction the truthfulness of his teaching which was the fulfilment of their prophecies, he thus removed the two possible objections to the reception of his word. Well then might he draw attention to the inexcusable character of their unbelief. He says in effect : —" If admittedly I am sinless, and if admittedly I speak the truth, why do you not believe me?" Not to excuse the unconvinced who throw the blame on God, but to condemn the unbelievers who resist God's grace, Jesus answers his own question thus : —

V. 47. He that is of God, heareth the words of God. Therefore you hear them not, because you are not of God.

The meaning is : " Those who love God and are his adopted children, profit by grace, listen to the words of their Heavenly Father, and diligently execute his will ; you, however, who love not God and are not his children but the children of the devil, you listen not to the words of God, but do in all things the works of your father, the spirit of evil." According to the Apostle, God " will have all men to be saved, and to come to the knowledge of the truth " (1 Tim. ii. 4) ; and man being unable to do this without heavenly assistance, God gives sufficient grace even to the most obdurate sinner. On the other hand, because salvation in the case of adults is not a mere gift, but a prize to be won by co-operation on the part of man, St. Augustine says that God, who created us without ourselves, will not save us without ourselves. Hence at all times, as in the days of St. Paul and St. Timothy, there are to be found those who, with every requisite light and help, " will not endure sound doctrine ; but, having itching ears, they will heap up to themselves teachers according to their own desires ; and they will turn away their hearing from the truth, but will turn unto fables " (2 Tim. iv. 3, 4). So it was with the Jews who had begun to believe in Jesus on this occasion (verse 30), and who now, wilfully closing their eyes to the light, attempted no answer to the purpose, but commenced to indulge in opprobrious language and false accusations. This is clear from the following words : —

V. 48. The Jews, therefore, answered and said to him : Do we not say well that thou art a Samaritan, and hast a devil ?

When the kingdom of Israel (Introduction, pp. cxxxii. seq.) was overthrown by the Assyrians, and most of the people were led away into captivity, some of the remaining inhabitants, who were joined by colonists sent from Assyria, built a temple on Mount Garizim in Samaria, and there united the adoration of idols with the observance of some rites derived from the law of Moses. (See 4 Kings xvii. 29.) This mixed race was regarded by the Jews as profane, schismatical, heretical, enemies of the people of God, violators of the Mosaic law, and semi-idolators with whom not even social intercourse could be kept up. Hence for the Jew, the name of Samaritan summed up in itself all that was opprobrious and vile. Now when our Lord had told his hearers that their works were unworthy of children of Abraham and were inspired by the devil, they in default of an answer, resorted to insult, and charged him with being a Samaritan in his habitual violation of the law, and with being possessed by an evil spirit. They ask: "In our turn do not we habitually say well (καλῶς) in preferring these charges against thee?" By their first accusation they would exclude Christ from the civil community of the chosen people, and by the second, from the worshippers and friends of the true God. (See Stier quoted by Alford.) All interpreters admire the meekness of the reply to this vile and blasphemous insult when

V. 49. Jesus answered: I have not a devil; but I honour my Father, and you have dishonoured me.

In their first charge the Jews did not accuse Christ of being a Samaritan by birth, but of being such by imitating the opposition shown by the Samaritans to the law of Moses and to the religious institutions of the people of God. This was so manifestly false in every sense, that Christ did not deign to give it an answer. Because, however, the second calumny had reference to the source of his miraculous power, and because on being circulated by the teachers of the people, it might prove a stumbling block to the simple, he calmly denied it. "I," said he with emphasis, "have not a devil." He thus clearly distinguished himself from his accusers and implied what he had already stated, viz., that of themselves only was the assertion true. "I," said he in effect, "am not in league with the enemy of God ; on the contrary, in all things I honour that God who is my Father ; and because of this honour which I pay to him, you, his enemies, dishonour me and in me you dishonour him that sent me."

What was to be the consequence of this crime? Jesus answered :

Vv. 50, 51. But I seek not my own glory : there is one that seeketh and judgeth. Amen amen I say to you: If any man keep my word, he shall not see death for ever.

The first verse has this meaning : "It is not my part to defend my honour. There is no need to do so ; for there is one who will vindicate it against the blasphemer and the calumniator" (see Bloomfield). Christ thus threatened the punishment which awaited the obstinate wickedness and wilful blindness of his enemies. Still he would not have them despair, but pointed out to them the means of escape in a penitential acceptance of his heavenly teaching. He did not speak here of the death of the body ; nor did he, who was himself to die, promise to his followers immunity from this lot of all mankind. He merely held out to the penitent believer a hope of avoiding that eternal and spiritual death which is alone worthy of the name.

Closing their eyes still more against the light,

V. 52. The Jews therefore said: Now we know that thou hast a devil. Abraham is dead, and the prophets; and thou sayest: If any man keep my word, he shall not taste death for ever.

These men had wilfully brought upon themselves the malediction spoken of by the prophet Isaias (vi. 9, 10), and more than once referred to by our Lord and by the Apostle St. Paul (Matth. xiii. 14; Mark iv. 12; Luke viii. 10; John xii. 40; Acts xxviii. 26; Rom. xi. 8): " Go, and thou shalt say to this people: Hearing hear, and understand not, and see the vision and know it not. Blind the heart of this people, and make their ears heavy, and shut their eyes; lest they see with their eyes, and hear with their ears, and understand with their heart, and be converted, and I heal them." Perversely taking our Lord to refer to the exemption of his disciples from the death of the body, the Jews replied that the fact of his possession by the devil, which before was probable, was now certain. They gave their reason, saying: " If Abraham and the prophets—the greatest servants of God—have died, how can you assert that those who keep your word shall be exempted from this common lot? "

As is the custom of persons carried away by anger, the Jews continued their insulting language and repeated their question thus in other terms:

V. 53. Art thou greater than our father Abraham, who is dead? And the prophets are dead. Whom dost thou make thyself?

The argument might have been expressed more strongly thus: " Art thou greater than God whose holiest servants—Abraham and the prophets—have died? " To the prejudiced and angry audience, however, it seemed a sufficiently great extravagance that Jesus had dared to claim a superiority to the founder of their race and to the inspired ministers of their religion. St. Gregory remarks: " Poterant etiam dicere: Numquid tu major es Deo cujus sermonem qui audierunt mortui sunt? Sed non dicunt hoc, quia etiam Abrahâ minorem eum aestimabant " (St. Greg. Hom. 54).

In reply to the question: " Whom dost thou make thyself?"

V. 54. Jesus answered: If I glorify myself, my glory is nothing. It is my Father that glorifieth me, of whom you say that he is your God.

In these meekly spoken words, our Lord wished to bring before his hearers the unreasonable character of their opposition to him and to his mission ; and he claimed their assent to his doctrine, not because it was the word of a man however blameless, but because in the miracles he himself had worked, that doctrine was attested by One who was his Father by nature, and whom they professed to honour as their God. He represented to them, in other words, that their conduct would not have been so manifestly impious if they had impugned his authority as Man unsupported by the clear and repeated testimony of God whose legate he was.

In the present circumstances there was no excuse for this unbelief ; but though there was no excuse, Christ gave an explanation of this wickedness when saying :

V. 55. And you have not known him ; but I know him. And if I shall say that I know him not, I shall be like to you, a liar. But I do know him, and do keep his word.

The Jews were said not to know God, because they had not that loving knowledge of their Creator to which all speculative knowledge should lead. Speaking of this two-fold knowledge, St. John writes : " By this we know that we have known him, if we keep his commandments. He who saith that he knoweth him and keepeth not his commandments is a liar, and the truth is not in him ; but whoever keepeth his word, in him in very deed the charity of God is perfected " (1 John ii. 3-5). This criterion Jesus invites them to apply to himself, when for the *third time in the same verse* asserting his knowledge of God the Father, he says : " I do know him, and do keep his word," or execute his holy will.

Having thus replied to the second question : " Whom dost thou make thyself," Christ now answers that in which the Jews ask if he be greater than their father Abraham. He says :—

V. 56. Abraham your father rejoiced that he might see my day : he saw it, and was glad.

The " day " of Christ was the time of his coming and his life on earth spent in the great work of the Redemption of the world. The mystery of the Incarnation, made known in its details by revelation, was the comfort of the patriarchs, of the prophets, and of the many just under the Old Law. In the words of Isaias, these prayed : " Drop down dew, ye heavens, from above, and let the clouds rain the Just : let the earth be opened and bud forth a Saviour " (Isaias xlv. 8). All desired to see the prediction of Christ's coming fulfilled, but it was not given to all while on earth to see its fulfilment. " All these died according to faith," said the Apostle, " not having received the promises, but beholding them afar off, and saluting them, and confessing that they are pilgrims and strangers on the earth " (Heb. xi. 13). Nay more, until Christ descended into Limbo.

and " preached to those spirits that were in prison " (1 Peter iii. 19), all did not know that the gracious work was done. Speaking of the condition of things even during his public life, Christ said to his disciples : " I say to you that many prophets and kings have desired to see the things that you see, and have not seen them ; and to hear the things that you hear, and have not heard them " (Luke x. 24). It was not so, however, with Abraham, " the father of all them that believe " (Rom. iv. 11). To him, even before Christ's visit to Limbo, the work of Redemption on earth was made known. Unlike his degenerate children, the great patriarch rejoiced that he might see his Redeemer's day : " he saw it and was glad." The first joy, that of hope, was common to him and others : the latter, that of vision, was given to him alone. Christ's argument may be thus stated : " If the hope of my coming and the knowledge that I have come were necessary to complete the joy of Abraham, how justly may I not claim to have a dignity superior to that which he enjoyed."

Determined in their wickedness,

V. 57. The Jews therefore said to him : Thou art not yet fifty years old, and hast thou seen Abraham ?

Amongst the ancients the age of fifty was that at which one was supposed to be in the decline of life. According to some commentators, then, the meaning of the question is : " How can you, *who are still young*, have seen Abraham?" The jubilee, too, occurred every fifty years ; it formed an epoch in the history of the nation as well as of the individual ; and whereas long spaces of time are now reckoned by centuries, these spaces were divided by the Jews into the periods which intervened between one jubilee and another. The enemies of the truth whom our Lord addressed were well aware that the patriarchs and prophets had a knowledge of the future ; they could not deny that the father of their nation might have foreseen the wonderful events of Christ's life ; but still they wished to turn into ridicule the statement just now made. With this end in view, they falsely attributed to Christ the assertion that, though he had not yet lived the interval between one jubilee and another, he had known and conversed on earth with Abraham who had died so many centuries before.

Christ availed himself of the opportunity afforded by this question to assert most clearly his divine nature, and to show his audience that inadvertently they had spoken the truth. The evangelist records, therefore, that

V. 58. Jesus said to them : Amen amen I say to you, before Abraham was made I am.

Commentators rightly draw attention to the peculiar force of the two words placed in juxtaposition—γενέσθαι = *to come into existence, or to begin to be,* and ἐῖναι = *to be, or to be already in the possession of existence,* by which words Christ described respectively the condition of Abraham and of himself. The former condition is that of a creature who once had no existence : the latter is that of him who had existed from eternity, and who will continue to exist unchangeably when time has ceased. The Jews had said in effect : " Fifty years since, you had no being. How then can you have seen Abraham who lived so many ages ago?" Jesus replied : " Before Abraham was created, I was *from* eternity in the unchangeable state of being, which is the attribute of the Divinity." Thus did he declare himself to be the one God with him who in the same terms described himself to Moses. " Moses said to God : Lo, I shall go to the children of Israel and say to them : The God of your fathers hath sent me to you. If they will say to me : What is his name? what shall I say to them? God said to Moses : I am who am " (Exod. iii. 13, 14).

Having this text before their minds, and understanding Jesus to claim, as he did, one of the essential attributes of the eternal Creator,

V. 59. **They took up stones, therefore, to cast at him; but Jesus hid himself, and went out of the temple.**

It had been prescribed in the law of Moses that blasphemy should be punished by stoning (see Levit. xxiv. 16) ; and the Jews in their wilful blindness, thinking Jesus to be guilty of that crime, gathered the stones then being used in the completion of the Herodian temple, that they might put him to death upon the spot. His death, indeed, was near at hand, but was to take place neither on that occasion nor in that manner. Therefore, as he had formerly escaped from the hands of the Nazarenes who were bent on a similar murderous design, so now he " hid himself," that is, he rendered himself invisible to their eyes, and departed from the temple. St. Augustine remarks : " Cœlica potestate invisibilem insidiantibus se constituens, per medium illorum exivit, tanquam homo a lapidibus ; sed væ illis a quorum cordibus lapideis Deus fugit."

IV.—MORAL REFLECTIONS.

1. Christ urged the Jews to specify their charges against him, and challenged them to name a sin of which he had been guilty. They answered by vague denunciation and undeserved reproach. Their reproach, so unjustly and wickedly uttered against Christ, furnishes us with matter for reflection very important for ourselves. Walking in his footsteps we must expect to be treated as he was ; and we should be filled with consolation when our

attachment to religion draws down upon us vituperation from his enemies. We should consider that we thus become more like to our outraged Lord. According to the Sacred Scriptures, when we enter on the career of piety we must expect to be assailed ; for the Apostle says : " All that will live godly in Christ Jesus, shall suffer persecution " (2 Tim. iii. 12). The more our exemplary life becomes a reproach to sinners, the more that life becomes the object of their censure. But in these humiliations the follower of Christ finds his glory and his happiness : his glory, because of the motive which prompts these humiliations, and his happiness, because of the recompense which they secure for him. In the midst of detraction he hears the words of his Divine Master : " Blessed shall you be when men shall hate you, and when they shall separate you, and shall reproach you, and cast out your name as evil, for the Son of Man's sake. Be glad in that day and rejoice, for behold, your reward is great in heaven " (Luke vi. 22, 23).

2. The reply of our Lord to the charges of his enemies presents us with a model for our conduct when we are attacked by calumny. He did not deign to refute the imputation that he was a Samaritan ; but he repelled that of being possessed by the devil, because it would have interfered with the success of his ministry. Amongst the charges which wickedness makes against us, we should distinguish those which, because of their absurdity, are not likely to be believed, from such as will probably be credited ; and amongst the latter we should distinguish those which affect our person from such as regard our office. Those of the first-mentioned class merit only our contempt, and the most efficacious as well as the most noble manner of dealing with them is to give them no attention. As to the calumnies that regard our person, without doubt it is permitted us to justify ourselves, since it is lawful to repel the attacks of those who attempt to deprive us of any valuable possession. Against calumnies which, if unrefuted, would impede us in the fulfilment of our duties, there is an obligation to defend ourselves. We owe to the office with which we are charged, all that can gain respect ; because one of the most pernicious effects of vice in persons of high position, is that it degrades their dignity as well as their personal character. The necessity for having a care of his reputation was one of the instructions given by the great Apostle to his disciple Timothy. Speaking of a man who was to exercise the episcopal office, St. Paul says : " He must have a good testimony from them that are without ; lest he fall into reproach and the snare of the devil " (1 Tim. iii. 7).

3. This defence of our reputation, however, though legitimate in itself, ceases to be lawful when it exceeds just bounds ; and it is no longer a defence when it becomes an attack on others. In this matter, Jesus Christ gives us a noble example. When

violently assailed, he confined himself to a denial of the charge
made against him. He was content to complain that, whilst his
enemies pretended to give honour to his Father, they sought to
deprive himself of that honour which was his due. Formed on
this divine model, the Christian who is assailed by calumny acts
on the defensive, but makes no attack in return. Superior to
feelings of resentment, he not only pardons his enemies, but
also implores pardon for them from God. Truly salutary is the
admonition of the Apostle : " Be not wise in your own con-
ceits ; to no man rendering evil for evil ; providing good things
not only in the sight of God, but also in the sight of all men ; if
it be possible, as much as is in you, having peace with all men ;
not revenging yourselves, dearly beloved, but give place unto
wrath ; for it is written : Revenge to me : I will repay, saith
the Lord " (Rom. xii. 16-19).

4. There is another rule to be followed in our justification of
our conduct : it is that whilst defending our character, we should
not seek our own glory. In this too, Christ is our model when he
says : " If I glorify myself, my glory is nothing. It is my
Father that glorifieth me, of whom you say that he is your God."
(John viii. 54). In defending ourselves, our motive must be the
honour of God and the edification of our neighbour. We should
clearly distinguish between the care for our reputation, and
vanity : between the preservation of our honour, and the increase of our glory. Having stated the truth we should, after
the example of our Divine Master, put our case in the hands of
God, who alone is powerful to defend us against all aggressors,
and we should then await in religious confidence the day of
divine justice. Such was the practice of the Psalmist who said :
" In thee, O Lord, have I hoped. Let me not be put to confusion ; deliver me in thy justice, and rescue me. Incline thy ear
to me, and save me. Be thou unto me a God, a protector, and
a place of strength. . . . My enemies have spoken against
me ; and they that watched my soul have consulted together,
saying : God hath forsaken him : pursue and take him, for
there is no one to deliver him. . . . Let them be confounded
and come to nothing that detract my soul : let them be covered
with confusion and shame that seek my hurt " (Ps. lxx. 1, 2,
3, 10, 11, 13).

PALM·SUNDAY.

I.—TEXTS.

GREEK.

MATTHEW XXI. 1-9.

¹ Καὶ ὅτε ἤγγισαν εἰς Ἱεροσόλυμα, καὶ ἦλθον εἰς Βηθφαγῆ εἰς τὸ ὄρος τῶν ἐλαιῶν, τότε Ἰησοῦς ἀπέστειλεν δύο μαθητὰς, ² λέγων αὐτοῖς· πορεύεσθε εἰς τὴν κώμην τὴν κατέναντι ὑμῶν, καὶ εὐθέως εὑρήσετε ὄνον δεδεμένην, καὶ πῶλον μετ' αὐτῆς· λύσαντες ἀγετέ μοι. ³ Καὶ ἐάν τις ὑμῖν εἴπῃ τί, ἐρεῖτε, ὅτι ὁ κύριος αὐτῶν χρείαν ἔχει· εὐθὺς δὲ ἀποστελεῖ αὐτούς. ⁴ Τοῦτο δὲ ὅλον γέγονεν, ἵνα πληρωθῇ τὸ ῥηθὲν διὰ τοῦ προφήτου λέγοντος. ⁵ εἴπατε τῇ θυγατρὶ Σειών· ἰδοὺ ὁ βασιλεύς σου ἔρχεταί σοι πραΰς, καὶ ἐπιβεβηκὼς ἐπὶ ὄνον καὶ ἐπὶ πῶλον υἱὸν ὑποζυγίου. ⁶ Πορευθέντες δὲ οἱ μαθηταὶ καὶ ποιήσαντες καθὼς συνέταξεν αὐτοῖς ὁ Ἰησοῦς, ⁷ ἤγαγον τὴν ὄνον καὶ τὸν πῶλον, καὶ ἐπέθηκαν ἐπ' αὐτῶν τὰ ἱμάτια, καὶ ἐπεκάθισεν ἐπάνω αὐτῶν. ⁸ Ὁ δὲ πλεῖστος ὄχλος ἔστρωσαν ἑαυτῶν τὰ ἱμάτια ἐν τῇ ὁδῷ· ἄλλοι δὲ ἔκοπτον κλάδους ἀπὸ τῶν δένδρων, καὶ ἐστρώννυον ἐν τῇ ὁδῷ. ⁹ Οἱ δὲ ὄχλοι οἱ προάγοντες αὐτὸν καὶ οἱ ἀκολουθοῦντες ἔκραζον, λέγοντες· ὡσαννὰ τῷ υἱῷ Δαυείδ· εὐλογημένος ὁ ἐρχόμενος ἐν ὀνόματι κυρίου· ὡσαννὰ ἐν τοῖς ὑψίστοις·

VULGATE.

MATTHEW XXI. 1-9.

¹ Et cum appropinquassent Jerosolymis, et venissent Bethphage ad montem Oliveti, tunc Jesus misit duos discipulos, ² dicens eis : Ite in castellum quod contra vos est, et statim invenietis asinam alligatam, et pullum cum ea. Solvite, et adducite mihi. ³ Et si quis vobis aliquid dixerit, dicite quia Dominus his opus habet ; et confestim dimittet eos. ⁴ Hoc autem totum factum est ut adimpleretur quod dictum est per prophetam dicentem : ⁵ Dicite filiæ Sion : Ecce rex tuus venit tibi mansuetus, sedens super asinam, et pullum filium subjugalis. ⁶ Euntes autem discipuli fecerunt sicut præcepit illis Jesus. ⁷ Et adduxerunt asinam et pullum, et imposuerunt super eos vestimenta sua, et eum desuper sedere fecerunt. ⁸ Plurima autem turba straverunt vestimenta sua in via ; alii autem cædebant ramos de arboribus, et sternebant in via. ⁹ Turbæ autem quæ præcedebant et quæ sequebantur, clamabant, dicentes : Hosanna filio David. Benedictus qui venit in nomine Domini. Hosanna in altissimis.

II.—ENGLISH TRANSLATION, WITH PARALLEL PASSAGES FROM SS. MARK, LUKE, AND JOHN.

MATTHEW XXI. 1-9.

1 And when they drew nigh to Jerusalem, and were come to Bethphage, unto Mount Olivet, then Jesus sent two disciples, 2 saying to them : " Go ye into the village that is over against you, and immediately you shall find an ass tied and a colt with her. Loose them, and bring them to me. 3 And if any man shall say anything to you, say ye, that the Lord hath need of them ; and forthwith he will let them go." 4 Now all this was done that it might be fulfilled which was spoken by the prophet, saying : 5 " Tell ye the daughter of Sion : Behold thy king cometh to thee, meek, and sitting upon an ass and a colt the foal of her that is used to the yoke." 6 And the disciples going did as Jesus commanded them. 7 And they brought the ass and the colt, and laid their garments upon them, and made him sit thereon. 8 And a very great multitude spread their garments in the way ; and others cut boughs from the trees, and strewed them in the way. 9 And the multitudes that went before and that followed, cried, saying : " Hosanna to the son of David. Blessed is he that cometh in the name of the Lord. Hosanna in the highest."

MARK XI. 1-10.

1 And when they were drawing near to Jerusalem and to Bethany at the Mount of Olives, he sendeth two of his disciples, 2 and saith to them : " Go into the village that is over against you, and immediately at your coming in thither, you shall find a colt tied, upon which no man yet hath sat : loose him, and bring him. 3 And if any man shall say to you : What are you doing? say ye that the Lord hath need of him ; and immediately he will let him come hither." 4 And going their way, they found the colt tied before the gate without in the meeting of two ways ; and they loose him. 5 And some of those that stood there, said to them : " What do you loosing the colt?" 6 Who saith to them as Jesus had commanded them. And they let him go with them. 7 And they brought the colt to Jesus ; and they laid their garments on him ; and he sat upon him. 8 And many spread their garments in the way ; and others cut down boughs from the trees, and strewed them in the way. 9 And they that went before and they that followed, cried, saying : " Hosanna. Blessed is he that cometh in the name of the Lord. 10 Blessed be the kingdom of our father David that cometh. Hosanna in the highest."

LUKE XIX. 29-44.

29 And it came to pass, when he was come nigh to Bethphage and Bethany, unto the mount called Olivet, he sent two of his disciples, saying : 30 " Go into the town which is over against you, at your entering into which, you shall find the colt of an ass tied, on which no man ever hath sat : loose him, and bring him hither. 31 And if any man shall ask you : Why do you loose him? you shall say thus unto him : Because the Lord hath need of his service." 32 And they that were sent went their way, and found the colt standing, as he had said unto them. 33 And as they were loosing the colt, the owners thereof said to them : " Why loose you the colt?" 34 But they said : " Because the Lord hath need of him." 35 And they brought him to Jesus. And casting their garments on the colt, they set Jesus thereon. 36 And as he went, they spread their clothes underneath in the way. 37 And when he was now coming near the descent of Mount Olivet, the whole multitude of his disciples began with joy to praise God in a loud voice, for all the mighty works they had seen, saying : 38 " Blessed be the king who cometh in the name of the Lord. Peace in heaven, and glory on high." 39 And some of the pharisees from amongst the multitude said to him : " Master, rebuke thy disciples." 40 To whom he said : " I say to you, that if these shall hold their peace, the stones will cry out."

41 And when he drew near, seeing the city, he wept over it, saying : 42 " If thou also hadst known, and that in this thy day, the things that are to thy peace ; but now they are hidden from thy eyes. 43 For the days shall come upon thee ; and thy enemies shall cast a trench about thee, and compass thee round, and straiten thee on every side, and beat thee flat to the ground, and thy children who are in thee. 44 And they shall not leave in thee a stone upon a stone ; because thou hast not known the time of thy visitation."

JOHN XII. 12-19.

12 And on the next day a great multitude that was come to the festival day, when they had heard that Jesus was coming to Jerusalem, took branches of palm trees, and went forth to meet him, and cried : 13 " Hosanna. Blessed is he that cometh in the name of the Lord, the king of Israel." 14 And Jesus found a young ass, and sat upon it, as it is written : 15 " Fear not, daughter of Sion : behold, thy king cometh, sitting on an ass's colt." 16 These things his disciples did not know at the first ; but when Jesus was glorified, then they remembered that these things were written of him, and that they had done these things to him. 17 The multitude, therefore, which was with him when he called Lazarus out of the grave and raised him

from the dead, gave testimony. [18] For which reason also the people came to meet him, because they heard that he had done this miracle. [19] The pharisees therefore said among themselves : " Do you see that we prevail nothing? Behold, the whole world is gone after him."

III.—COMBINED NARRATIVE.

And it came to pass on the next day when **they were drawing** near to Jerusalem, and were come unto the mount called Olivet, to Bethphage and to Bethany, then Jesus sent two of his disciples, and said to them : " Go into the village that is over against you ; and immediately at your coming in thither, you shall find an ass and the colt of an ass tied, upon which no man yet hath sat. Loose them and bring them to me. And if any man shall say anything to you, and ask you : What are you doing? Why do you loose him? say ye, that the Lord hath need of them ; and forthwith he will let them come hither." And the disciples that were sent, went their way, and found, as he had said unto them, the colt standing [and] tied before the gate without in the meeting of two ways. And [they] did as Jesus commanded them ; and they loose him. And as they were loosing the colt, some of those that stood there, the owners thereof, said to them : " What do you, loosing the colt?" But they said as Jesus had commanded them : " Because the Lord hath need of him." And they let him go with them. And they brought the ass and the colt to Jesus ; and they laid their garments upon them. And casting their garments on the colt, [they] made him sit thereon. Now all this was done that it might be fulfilled which was spoken by the prophet, saying : " Tell ye the daughter of Sion : Fear not daughter of Sion. Behold, thy king cometh to thee, meek, and sitting upon an ass and an ass's colt, the foal of her that is used to the yoke." These things his disciples did not know at the first ; but when Jesus was glorified, then they remembered that these things were written of him, and that they had done these things to him. And as he went, a very great multitude spread their garments in the way ; and others cut boughs from the trees, and strewed them in the way. [And] a great multitude that was come to the festival day, when they heard that Jesus was coming to Jerusalem, took branches of palm trees, and went forth to meet him. And when he was now coming near the descent of Mount Olivet, the whole multitude of his disciples began with joy to praise God in a loud voice for all the mighty works they had seen. And the multitude that went before and they that followed cried, saying : " Hosanna to the Son of David. Blessed be the King, he that cometh in the name of the Lord, the King of Israel. Blessed be the kingdom of our father David that cometh. Peace in heaven, and glory on high. Hosanna in the highest." The multitude, therefore, which was with him when he called Lazarus out of the grave and raised him from the dead, gave testimony. For which reason also the people came to meet him ; because they heard that he had done this miracle. The pharisees, therefore, said among themselves : " Do you see that we prevail nothing? Behold, the whole world is gone after him." And some of the pharisees from amongst the multitude said to him : " Master, rebuke thy disciples." To whom he said : " I say to you, that if these shall hold their peace, the stones will cry out."

And when he drew near, seeing the city, he wept over it, saying : " If thou hadst known, and that in this thy day, the things that are to thy peace ; but now they are hidden from thy eyes. For the days shall come upon thee ; and thy enemies shall cast a trench about thee, and compass thee round, and straiten thee on every side, and beat thee flat to the ground, and thy children who are in thee. And they shall not leave in thee a stone upon a stone ; because thou hast not known the time of thy visitation."

V.—NOTES.

Introductory. As may be learned from John x., Jesus in the December of the last year of his public life, celebrated in Jerusalem the Feast of the Dedication of the temple, and then declared clearly that he was the Son of God. The Jews, on hearing this, wished to stone him as a blasphemer ; but he escaped out of their hands, and retired into Peræa beyond the Jordan. Having remained there for a considerable time he heard of the distress of his friends, Martha and Mary, in consequence of which he returned to the neighbourhood of Jerusalem to raise Lazarus their brother to life. Enraged at the effect of this miracle amongst the people, the pharisees again plotted against Christ's life, and he withdrew once more to Ephrem, near the desert of Judæa. Having passed northwards through Samaria and Galilee, in the month of April he crossed the Jordan (Introduction, p. l.) near its source, and commenced his journey through Peræa (Introduction, p. xxxvii.) to the Holy City. Leaving Jericho where he had cured two blind men and converted Zachæus, he arrived at Bethany six days before the Pasch. In Bethany (Introduction, p. lxiii.) on the sabbath day he was entertained at supper by Martha, Lazarus being present, Mary anointing his head and feet with the precious ointment, and many of the Jews coming to see him and Lazarus whom he had raised from the dead. He passed the sabbath there with his friends and disciples, and wished on the morrow to enter Jerusalem in triumph. In that city, more than once his enemies had attempted to kill him, and even now they were sitting in council to determine the manner in which his death might be brought about. He had come up to Jerusalem to die, and as the prophet Isaias had foretold, " he was offered because it was his own will." However, before his death, which was now resolved on, he wished to show himself in his royal dignity : he desired to be publicly acknowledged as the Messiah, and to receive the tribute of his people's homage. This triumph over the hearts of men had been predicted by the prophets, and in the present passage of the gospel it is shown that the prediction was fulfilled to the letter.

St. John's gospel describes the manner in which Christ spent the sabbath, and also states that on the following day he advanced with his disciples towards the Holy City. St. Matthew says : —

V. 1. And when they drew nigh to Jerusalem, and were come to Bethphage, unto Mount Olivet, then Jesus sent two disciples, etc.

Mount Olivet, or the Mount of Olives, as it is designated here in the Greek and usually throughout the New Testament, was so called because of the number of olive trees with which it was covered. This mountain, the scene of some of the most remarkable events in the history of the Passion, was situated to the east of Jerusalem, and between the two lay the deep and narrow valley of Cedron. Three places situated on it and taking their names from their respective products, are deserving of particular notice. The first, lowest down and nearest to the city, was called Gethsemani, or " the Oil-press," because here were placed the presses for the olives which gave its name to the mountain. It was to a garden in Gethsemani that Christ used to retire to pray during the evenings of these his last days ; it was here he suffered his agony and sweat of blood ; it was here, too, that he was betrayed by Judas and arrested by the soldiers. Another place, Bethany, or " the House of Palms " or" the House of Dates," was a village on the eastern slope of the mountain. It was less than two miles from Jerusalem ; and near it, or in it, was the residence of Lazarus, Martha, and Mary, friends of Jesus. This place, carefully to be distinguished from another of the same name where St. John baptised, was the hamlet where our Lord spent his last sabbath, and whence on the next day he set out for the city. Lastly, on the same eastern slope of the mountain and near Bethany, stood another village, Bethphage, or " the House of Figs." Although the site of Bethany has been handed down by tradition, and has been named el'Azarieh or Lazarieh, from its association with Lazarus, that of Bethphage is not exactly known, nor are there any remains near Bethany to assist in the identification. Coming,

then, from Bethany towards Bethphage, Jesus " sent two disciples " whose names are not mentioned,

**V. 2. Saying to them: Go ye into the village that is over
against you, and immediately you shall find an ass tied and
a colt with her. Loose them and bring them to me.**

This command indicated clearly that it was the intention of
Jesus to enter Jerusalem in triumph, and that he who had
hitherto performed all his journeys on foot, now prepared to
finish the present one in a different manner. The evangelist
appears to draw attention to the fact by stating that the orders
were given when Christ, his disciples, and the visitors to
Bethany were now near to Jerusalem. In the approach to the
city both regal pomp and profound humility were remarkably
combined. Knabenbauer (*in loco*) remarks that in ancient times
even nobles and most distinguished persons used the ass on
journeys of business and of pleasure. Examples are to be found
in the history of Abraham (Gen. xxii. 3), in that of Moses (Exod.
iv. 20), and in that of Balaam (Num. xxii. 21). In the canticle of
Deborah and Barac, the princes of Israel are thus addressed :
" My heart loveth the princes of Israel. O you that of your
own good-will offered yourselves to danger, bless the Lord.
Speak you that ride upon fair asses, and you that sit in judgment, and walk in the way " (Judges v. 9, 10). Afterwards in
the time of the kings, horses were used instead (see 3 Kings iv.
26, x. 28, and 2 Par. ix. 25, 28) ; but at no time was it considered vile or degrading in Palestine to ride upon an ass.
Indeed, the asses of that country are very much superior in
appearance to those of other regions. Although this is so, our
Lord's humility and the pacific character of his kingdom were
here shown, because in the prophecy in which this triumphal
entry was foretold, the prophet Zachary distinguishes between
the mildness and gentleness of the Messiah on the one hand, and
the warlike appearance of those whose chariots and horses were
not to avail against him. Our Lord provides his disciples with
an explanation to be given to the owner of the animals : —

**V. 3. And if any man shall say anything to you, say ye
that the Lord hath need of them ; and forthwith he will let
them go.**

By his minute directions, Christ showed here his wonderful
fore-knowledge of what was to occur ; by his statement regarding the permission to be given by the owner he showed his
power over the human heart ; and by the title which he assumed
he asserted his supreme dominion over all things created. He
did not direct his disciples to describe him as " our Lord " or
" our Lord, your Master "; but as " *the* Lord, *i.e.,* the Lord
by excellence, the Supreme Lord of creation,

St. Matthew, in accordance with the scope of his gospel, remarked that in this triumphal procession the Messianic prophecy of Zachary was fulfilled. He thus continues :—

Vv. 4, 5. Now all this was done that it might be fulfilled which was spoken by the prophet, saying : Tell ye the daughter of Sion : Behold thy King cometh to thee, meek, and sitting upon an ass and a colt the foal of her that is used to the yoke.

The latter part of the quotation is certainly from Zachary (ix. 9). Since, however, the words : " Tell ye the daughter of Sion " do occur in Isaias (lxii. 11), and do not in the passage from Zachary, it is thought by some that the evangelist joined the two predictions in this one citation, and spoke of *one* prophet, because all inspired writers were moved by the one Holy Spirit. On the other hand, according to McCarthy, Jansenius Ypr., etc., etc., it is not necessary to explain the matter thus, nor can it be explained thus, there being no instance of a similar reference given in this form. The whole passage in St. Matthew is *substantially* found in Zachary (ix. 9). Addressing " the daughter of Sion " (a Hebraism for the city or inhabitants of Jerusalem), Zachary exclaims : " Rejoice greatly, O daughter of Sion (that is : Tell joyful news to the daughter of Sion) ; shout for joy, O daughter of Jerusalem. Behold thy king will come to thee, the Just and Saviour. He is poor, and riding upon an ass and upon a colt the foal of an ass." The same quotation is substantially given by St. John, who adds : " These things his disciples did not know at the first ; but when Jesus was glorified, then they remembered that these things were written of him, and that they had done these things to him." The words : " the Just and Saviour " are omitted by St. Matthew ; and the word " poor " (Heb. עני) is changed into " meek " (Gr. πραΰς) after the Septuagint translators, who read perhaps עני = " meek." Without the vowel points, the one Hebrew word would have either meaning. (See McCarthy on this verse.) As already remarked, there is in the prophecy of Zachary a decided contrast between the proud conqueror with his chariots and war-horses, and the peaceful, meek, Messianic ruler, who, according to St. Chrysostom, is described as " not driving chariots, like the rest of kings, not demanding tributes, not thrusting men off and leading about guards, but displaying his great meekness even hereby (that he rides on an ass) " (Hom. lxii. 1, 2).

The command given may have appeared strange to the two disciples ; still, being the command of " *the* Lord," it should be obeyed,

V. 6. And the disciples going did as Jesus commanded them.

In the account by St. Mark, combined with that by St. Luke, the facts are thus more fully stated : " And the disciples that were sent, went their way, and found, as he had said unto them, the colt standing [and] tied before the gate without, in the meeting of two ways.   And [they] did as Jesus commanded them; and they loose him.   And as they were loosing the colt, some of those that stood there, the owners thereof, said to them : What do you, loosing the colt?   But they said as Jesus had commanded them : Because the Lord hath need of him.   And they let him go with them."

V. 7. And they brought the ass and the colt, and laid their garments upon them, and made him sit thereon.

Both in the original Greek text and in the Eng. translation there is an ambiguity about the meaning of the last words, in which it is said of the disciples that they " laid their garments upon them (the animals), and made him sit thereon."   Do the last words of the Greek text, ἐπάνω αὐτῶν=" thereon," refer to the animals, or to the garments?   Most probably they refer to the garments.   But as the garments were placed on both animals, must we suppose that Christ rode now on the one animal, now on the other?   This supposition is not necessary, and it even appears to be contrary to the statements of SS. Mark, Luke, and John, who throughout mention only one animal, i.e., the colt (Mark xi. 7 ; Luke xix. 35 ; John xii. 14).   If this be so, it may be asked, why the disciples spread their garments upon the two.   Apparently the disciples acted thus because, on the one hand, our Lord had ordered that the two animals be brought to him, and because on the other, he had not signified which of the two he wished to use.   He did actually use the colt " upon which no man yet hath sat " (Mark xi. 2, 7), because to God the first fruits of all things are to be consecrated, and because it was prescribed that animals, selected for the divine service, were to be taken from amongst those which had not hitherto borne the yoke (Numbers xix. 2 ; Deut. xxi. 3 ; 1 Kings vi. 7).   Lastly it is asked why our Lord commanded that both animals should be brought to him.   The colt, as may be learned from St. Mark (xi. 2), was still untrained, and it was therefore brought accompanied by the dam, in order that, without the intervention of the miraculous or the preternatural, it might be more easily led in her company.   The apostles, as already stated, were unaware of the selection which Christ might make, and prepared both animals for his use.

Not only in procuring the animals, but also during the triumphal procession itself, the divine power of Christ over the human heart was evidently shown ;

V. 8. And a very great multitude spread their garments in the way; and others cut boughs from the trees, and strewed them in the way.

Amongst both Gentiles and Jews, these were marks of the highest honour. When it was announced to the captains of the army that Jehu was anointed king of Israel, "then they made haste, and every man taking his garment, laid it under his (Jehu's) feet after the manner of a judgment-seat ; and they sounded the trumpet, and said : Jehu is king " (4 Kings ix. 13). Plutarch narrates the same of the soldiers of Cato surnamed Uticensis, when he resigned the government of his province. The custom, too, of strewing the ground with branches of palms and of other trees, was adopted in times of great national rejoicing. The reception given to Jesus by those who strewed the ground with palm branches, or who bore these branches in their hands during the procession to Jerusalem, was one of the ceremonies prescribed by Moses to be carried out during the Feast of Tabernacles (Lev. xxiii. 40). With similar rejoicings the people received Agrippa, and Alexander, king of Syria. When Judas Machabeus had regained possession of Jerusalem, and had purified the temple, the Jews celebrated a feast of eight days ; bore in procession branches of palms or of other trees ; and sang hymns in thanks to God, who had enabled their leaders to secure so great a victory (2 Mac. x. 6, 7). Such, too, was the reception given to Simon when, having made peace with his enemies, he entered Jerusalem in triumph (1 Mac. xiii. 51). In this manner did God will that Christ should be acknowledged as the Messiah, the Conqueror of the devil, and the true Liberator of the human race. St. Luke, completing this description, says that when he (Christ) was now coming near the descent of Mount Olivet, the whole multitude of his disciples began with joy to praise God in a loud voice, for all the mighty works they had seen, saying : " Blessed be the king who cometh in the name of the Lord. Peace in heaven and glory on high."

From the gospel of St. John (xii.) it would appear that whilst Jesus was still at Bethany, he was visited by a large number of people coming to the festival and attracted by the account of the resurrection of Lazarus. This seems to be the crowd described by SS. Luke and John. As Jesus advanced towards Jerusalem followed by this multitude, he was met by another crowd of people from the city itself, who, hearing of his approach, went out to receive him in triumph. Both these bodies are referred to by St. Mark, and in the following words by St. Matthew :

V. 9. And the multitudes that went before and that followed, cried, saying : Hosanna to the Son of David. Blessed is he that cometh in the name of the Lord. Hosanna in the highest.

" Hosanna," abbreviated from the Hebrew הוֹשִׁיעָה־נָּא, and rendered in the Greek version of Symmachus σῶσον δή, signifies : " Save, we pray." In the present case, it is a hymn of praise and of thanksgiving addressed to God who had sent Jesus, the Son of David, as the Messiah ; it is an address of welcome to the Son of David himself ; and it is a prayer that the Messianic office undertaken by him may be crowned with success. As Jansenius Gand. remarks, the Jews do not here pray to Jesus to save them. They rejoice that in him they have found the Messiah so long promised in the prophets ; taking him for their king, they pray that God may render his reign prosperous and happy ; and they express a hope that through him who comes in the name of the Lord, they themselves may be delivered from the slavery under which they groaned. The psalm from which this prayer was taken, is one of those called the Hallel or great Hallelujah (cxii.-cxvii. or in the Heb. cxiii.-cxviii.) which were sung by the Jews on the greatest feasts, and especially during the celebration of the Paschal Supper. It was, indeed, often on the lips of the people at this season of the Passover; but it was not without the special impulse of grace and the special ordinance of God that thus suddenly, and as it were by instinct, the crowd made use of these words when with regal pomp they conducted their Messiah to his city and to the temple—that house the chief glory of which was to receive him within its walls. Would that the religious fervour of this triumph had been more lasting, and that the inhabitants of Jerusalem had known the things that were " to their peace "! Such a happiness was not to be theirs. The murmurs of the pharisees during the popular outburst of joy on the journey, and the cold reception given to Jesus in Jerusalem itself foreboded but too plainly the tragedy of the Crucifixion with which the week was to close. With these words of sadness, therefore, St. Luke concludes his account of the day's proceedings : "When he (Christ) drew near, seeing the city, he wept over it, saying : If thou hadst known, and that in this thy day, the things that are to thy peace ; but now they are hidden from thy eyes. For the days shall come upon thee ; and thy enemies shall cast a trench about thee, and compass thee round, and straiten thee on every side, and beat thee flat to the ground, and thy children who are in thee. And they shall not leave in thee a stone upon a stone ; because thou hast not known the day of thy visitation " (Luke xix. 41-44). So complete was the fulfilment of this terrible prediction that not a trace of Jerusalem was left visible ; the very foundations were rooted up ; and on another site was built the city of to-day.

V.—MORAL REFLECTIONS.

1. The authority with which our Divine Saviour commanded his disciples to bring to him the animals to be used during his

triumphal entry into Jerusalem reminds us that he is absolutely Lord of all. Having created all things, he could truly say as he did in the Old Testament to Moses : " They are all mine " (Exod. xiii. 2). Under his dominion are all our gifts of fortune, of nature, and of grace. As God's stewards we hold all and even our life itself. This truth, of which we are persuaded in theory, leads in practice to three consequences. The first is that we are obliged to employ conformably to God's will all the goods received from him ; the second is that we should ever hold ourselves in readiness to render him an account of the use we make of all our possessions ; and the third is that we should be ever resolved without murmur and without hesitation to give all back to him when it may please him to deprive us of them.

2. This passage of the Gospel presents us with two examples of the submission with which we should receive and execute the commands of God. In the first place, the disciples might have looked on the order of Christ as one without motive ; they might have doubted his justice ; they might have feared that in obeying they should compromise themselves and meet with a harsh and humiliating refusal. None of these considerations entered into their mind. The Master had spoken, and they thought only of executing his commands. The other example of submission is that of the owners of the two animals. They did not know for what purpose these were required, nor for how long a time they were to be deprived of their possession. The owners were told merely that the Lord required the animals, and they could not refuse what was asked in that sacred name. If, after considering these two models of obedience, we reflect on our own conduct, how much reason shall we not have to condemn our shortcomings? How many Christians are there not who break the law of Christ, some publicly and without shame, others secretly : those with scandal to their neighbour, these with hypocrisy in the sight of God? Even amongst such as pride themselves on observing God's law, how is it ordinarily obeyed? How many difficulties are raised as to its meaning ; how many excuses are put forward to elude the obligation it imposes ; and if no excuse can be found to escape the precept, with what reluctance, and carelessness, and delay is it executed !

3. The evangelists tell us of the joy with which the people received Christ on this occasion ; but in the Parallel Passage St. Luke records that during the triumphal procession our Lord wept. Although at this moment Christ was saluted by the people with " Hosannas " as the Son of David, he knew that in five days they would demand his Crucifixion and by the crime of deicide bring about the ruin of themselves, of their city, and of their nation. This was the cause of the tears of Christ. From this narrative we learn the tenderness of Christ's Sacred Heart ; but we also learn the emptiness of popular applause, through

love of which so many are unfaithful in the performance of their duty to God.

4. Short-lived as was to be this triumph of Christ, it offended the leaders of the people, and embittered them more and more against him. A little further on in this chapter, St. Matthew writes : " The chief-priests and scribes, seeing the wonderful things that he did, and the children crying in the temple and saying : Hosanna to the Son of David, were moved with indignation " (Matth. xxi. 15). Here we have a warning against the passion of envy, the detestable effects of which are depicted for us most graphically in the history of our Lord's life. His extreme goodness did not guarantee him against the hatred of the heads of the Synagogue ; his infinite perfections did not shield him from their calumny ; his lessons of divine wisdom could not enlighten these men ; his virtues could not touch them ; his benefits could not soften them ; his miracles could not open their eyes. When our Divine Master, then, was so treated, which of us can be astonished at being the object of envy and of hatred? In such circumstances, instead of being afflicted or turned aside from our duty, we should imitate the example of our Divine Model. Disregarding the rage of those men who had sworn to bring about his death, he left them to continue their diabolical plots. Thus, after the example of the Just One by excellence, do those act who follow him in the way of justice. As far as in them lies, they avoid giving occasion to hatred and envy ; but if these passions be aroused against them, they, without irritation against their enemies, pursue their course in that peace which is above all that men can give.

EASTER SUNDAY.

I.—TEXTS.

GREEK.

MARK XVI. 1-7.

1 Καὶ διαγενομένου τοῦ σαββάτου, Μαρία ἡ Μαγδαληνὴ, καὶ Μαρία ἡ τοῦ Ἰακώβου, καὶ Σαλώμη, ἠγόρασαν ἀρώματα, ἵνα ἐλθοῦσαι ἀλείψωσιν αὐτόν. 2 Καὶ λίαν πρωὶ μιᾷ τῶν σαββάτων ἔρχονται ἐπὶ τὸ μνημεῖον, ἀνατείλαντος τοῦ ἡλίου. 3 Καὶ ἔλεγον πρὸς ἑαυτάς· τίς ἀποκυλίσει ἡμῖν τὸν λίθον ἐκ τῆς θύρας τοῦ μνημείου; 4 Καὶ ἀναβλέψασαι θεωροῦσιν ὅτι ἀνακεκύλισται ὁ λίθος· ἦν γὰρ μέγας σφόδρα. 5 Καὶ ἐλθοῦσαι εἰς τὸ μνημεῖον, εἶδον νεανίσκον καθήμενον ἐν τοῖς δεξιοῖς, περιβεβλημένον στολὴν λευκήν· καὶ ἐξεθαμβήθησαν. 6 Ὁ δὲ λέγει αὐταῖς· μὴ ἐκθαμβεῖσθε· Ἰησοῦν ζητεῖτε τὸν Ναζαρηνὸν τὸν ἐσταυρωμένον· ἠγέρθη, οὐκ ἔστιν ὧδε· ἴδε, ὁ τόπος ὅπου ἔθηκαν αὐτόν. 7 Ἀλλὰ ὑπάγετε, εἴπατε τοῖς μαθηταῖς αὐτοῦ, καὶ τῷ Πέτρῳ, ὅτι προάγει ὑμᾶς εἰς τὴν Γαλιλαίαν· ἐκεῖ αὐτὸν ὄψεσθε, καθὼς εἶπεν ὑμῖν.

VULGATE.

MARK XVI. 1-7.

1 Et cum transisset sabbatum, Maria Magdalene, et Maria Jacobi, et Salome emerunt aromata ut venientes ungerent Jesum. 2 Et valde mane una sabbatorum, veniunt ad monumentum, orto jam sole. Et dicebant ad invicem : Quis revolvet nobis lapidem ab ostio monumenti? 4 Et respicientes viderunt revolutum lapidem. Erat quippe magnus valde. 5 Et introeuntes in monumentum, viderunt juvenem sedentem in dextris, coopertum stola candida, et obstupuerunt. 6 Qui dicit illis : Nolite expavescere; Jesum quæritis Nazarenum, crucifixum ; surrexit, non est hic, ecce locus ubi posuerunt eum. 7 Sed ite, dicite discipulis ejus et Petro quia præcedit vos in Galilæam ; ibi eum videbitis, sicut dixit vobis.

II.—ENGLISH TRANSLATION, WITH PARALLEL PASSAGES FROM SS. MATTHEW, MARK, LUKE, AND JOHN.

MARK XVI. 1-7.

1 And when the sabbath was past, Mary Magdalen, and Mary the mother of James, and Salome bought sweet spices, that coming they might anoint Jesus. 2 And very early in the morning the first day of the week, they come to the sepulchre, the sun being now risen. 3 And they said one to another : " Who shall roll us back the stone from the door of the sepulchre?" (4 And looking, they saw the stone rolled back :) for it was very great. 5 And entering into the sepulchre, they saw a young man sitting on the right side, clothed with a white robe ; and they were as-

tonished. ⁶And he saith to them : Be not affrighted. You seek Jesus of Nazareth, who was crucified. He is risen ; he is not here. Behold the place where they laid him. ⁷But go, tell his disciples and Peter that he goeth before you into Galilee ; there you shall see him as he told you."

MATTHEW XXVII. 61-66 ; XXVIII. 1–15.

⁶¹ And Mary Magdalen was there, and the other Mary sitting over against the sepulchre. ⁶²And the next day which followeth the day of preparation, the chief-priests and the pharisees came together to Pilate, saying : ⁶³ " Sir, we have remembered that that seducer said, while he was yet alive : After three days I will rise again. ⁶⁴ Command therefore the sepulchre to be guarded until the third day ; lest perhaps his disciples come and steal him away, and say to the people : He is risen from the dead ; and the last error shall be worse than the first." ⁶⁵ Pilate said to them : " You have a guard. Go, guard it as you know." ⁶⁶ And they departing, made the sepulchre sure, sealing the stone and setting guards.

¹And in the end of the sabbath when it began to dawn towards the first day of the week, came Mary Magdalen and the other Mary to see the sepulchre. ² And behold, there was a great earthquake. For an angel of the Lord descended from heaven, and coming, rolled back the stone and sat upon it. ³ And his countenance was as lightning, and his raiment as snow. ⁴ And for fear of him, the guards were struck with terror, and became as dead men. ⁵ And the angel answering, said to the women : " Fear not you, for I know that you seek Jesus who was crucified. ⁶ He is not here, for he is risen, as he said. Come, and see the place where the Lord was laid. ⁷ And going quickly, tell ye his disciples that he is risen. And behold, he will go before you into Galilee : there you shall see him. Lo, I have foretold it to you." ⁸ And they went out quickly from the sepulchre with fear and great joy, running to tell his disciples. ⁹ And behold, Jesus met them, saying : " All hail." But they came up, and took hold of his feet, and adored him. ¹⁰Then Jesus saith to them : " Fear not. Go, tell my brethren that they go into Galilee : there they shall see me." ¹¹ Now when they were departed, behold, some of the guards came into the city, and told the chief-priests all the things that had been done. ¹² And they being assembled together with the ancients, taking counsel, gave a great sum of money to the soldiers, saying : ¹³ " Say ye : His disciples came by night, and stole him away when we were asleep. And if the governor shall hear of this, we will persuade him, and secure you." ¹⁵ So they, taking the money, did as they were taught ; and this word was spread abroad among the Jews even unto this day.

MARK XVI. 8-11.

8 But they going out, fled from the sepulchre ; for a trembling and fear had seized them.   And they said nothing to any man ; for they were afraid.   9 But he rising early the first day of the week, appeared first to Mary Magdalen, out of whom he had cast seven devils.   10 She went, and told them that had been with him, who were mourning and weeping.   11 And they hearing that he was alive and had been seen by her, did not believe.

LUKE XXIII. 54-56 ; XXIV. 1-12.

54 And it was the day of the parasceve, and the sabbath drew on.   55 And the women that were come with him from Galilee, following after, saw the sepulchre, and how his body was laid. 56 And returning, they prepared spices and ointments ; and on the sabbath-day they rested according to the commandment.

1 And on the first day of the week very early in the morning they came to the sepulchre, bringing the spices which they had prepared.   2 And they found the stone rolled back from the sepulchre.   3 And going in, they found not the body of the Lord Jesus.   4 And it came to pass, as they were astonished in their mind at this, behold, two men stood by them in shining apparel. 5 And as they were afraid and bowed down their countenance towards the ground, they said unto them : " Why seek you the living with the dead ?   6 He is not here, but is risen.   Remember how he spoke unto you, when he was yet in Galilee, saying : 7 The Son of Man must be delivered into the hands of sinful men, and be crucified, and the third day rise again."   8 And they remembered his words.   9 And going back from the sepulchre, they told all these things to the eleven, and to all the rest.   10 And it was Mary Magdalen, and Joanna, and Mary the mother of James, and the other women that were with them, who told these things to the apostles.   11 And these words seemed to them as idle tales ; and they did not believe them.   12 But Peter rising up, ran to the sepulchre ; and stooping down, he saw the linen cloths laid by themselves, and went away wondering in himself at that which was come to pass.

JOHN XX. 1-18.

1 And on the first day of the week, Mary Magdalen cometh early when it was yet dark unto the sepulchre ; and she seeth the stone taken away from the sepulchre.   2 She ran therefore, and came to Simon Peter and to the other disciple whom Jesus loved, and saith to them : " They have taken away the Lord out of the sepulchre, and we know not where they have laid him." 3 Peter therefore went out and that other disciple, and they came to the sepulchre.   4 And they both ran together ; and that other disciple did outrun Peter, and came first to the sepulchre. 5 And when he stooped down, he seeth the linen cloths lying ; but yet he went not in.   6 Then cometh Simon Peter following

him, and went into the sepulchre, and seeth the linen cloths lying, 7 and the napkin that had been about his head not lying with the linen cloths but apart wrapt up into one place. 8 Then went in that other disciple also who came first to the sepulchre ; and he saw and believed ; 9 for as yet they knew not the Scripture, that he must rise again from the dead. 10 The disciples therefore departed again to their home ; 11 but Mary stood at the sepulchre without, weeping. Now as she was weeping, she stooped down and looked into the sepulchre. 12And she saw two angels in white, sitting one at the head and one at the feet, where the body of Jesus had been laid. 13 They say to her : " Woman, why weepest thou?" She saith to them : " Because they have taken away my Lord, and I know not where they have laid him." 14 When she had thus said, she turned herself back and saw Jesus standing ; and she knew not that it was Jesus. 15 Jesus saith to her : " Woman, why weepest thou? Whom seekest thou?" She, thinking that it was the gardener, saith to him : " Sir, if thou hast taken him hence, tell me where thou hast laid him, and I will take him away." 16 Jesus saith to her : " Mary." She turning, saith to him : " Rabboni " (which is to say, " Master "). 17 Jesus saith to her : " Do not touch me, for I am not yet ascended to my Father ; but go to my brethren, and say to them : I ascend to my Father and your Father, to my God and your God." 18 Mary Magdalen cometh and telleth the disciples : " I have seen the Lord, and these things he said to me."

III.—COMBINED NARRATIVE.

It was the day of the parasceve, and the sabbath drew on. And Mary Magdalen was there and the other Mary sitting over against the sepulchre. And [another party of] the women that were come with him from Galilee, following after, saw the sepulchre, [and] beheld where and how his body was laid. And returning, they [i.e., the latter party of women from Galilee] prepared spices and ointments. And on the sabbath-day, the day which followeth the day of preparation, they rested, according to the commandment. [And] the chief-priests and the pharisees came together to Pilate, saying : " Sir, we have remembered that that seducer said while he was yet alive : After three days I will rise again. Command therefore the sepulchre to be guarded until the third day, lest perhaps his disciples come and steal him away, and say to the people : He is risen from the dead ; and the last error shall be worse than the first." Pilate said to them : " You have a guard. Go, guard it as you know." And they departing, made the sepulchre sure, sealing the stone and setting guards.

And in the end of the sabbath, when it began to dawn towards the first day of the week, came Mary Magdalen and the other

Mary to see the sepulchre. And when the sabbath was past, Mary Magdalen, and Mary the mother of James, and Salome bought sweet spices that coming, they might anoint Jesus. And behold, [during the night] there was a great earthquake. For an angel of the Lord descended from heaven, and coming, rolled back the stone and sat upon it. And his countenance was as lightning and his raiment as snow. And for fear of him the guards were struck with terror, and became as dead men.

And on the first day of the week, Mary Magdalen cometh early when it was yet dark unto the sepulchre ; and she seeth the stone taken away from the sepulchre. She ran therefore, and came to Simon Peter and to the other disciple whom Jesus loved, and saith to them : '' They have taken away the Lord out of the sepulchre, and we know not where they have laid him."

And . . . very early in the morning, they [*i.e.,* the women from Galilee, the party of Joanna] came to the sepulchre, bringing the spices which they had prepared ; and they found the stone rolled back from the sepulchre. And the angel [who had rolled back the stone] answering, said to the women : " Fear not you, for I know that you seek Jesus of Nazareth who was crucified. He is not here, for he is risen as he said. Come and see the place where the Lord was laid. And going quickly, tell ye his disciples that he is risen. And behold, he will go before you into Galilee : there you shall see him. Lo, I have foretold it to you." And going in, they found not the body of the Lord Jesus. And it came to pass, as they were astonished in their mind at this, behold, two men stood by them in shining apparel. And as they were afraid, and bowed down their countenance towards the ground, they [*i.e.,* the two men] said unto them : " Why seek you the living with the dead? He is not here, but is risen. Remember how he spoke unto you when he was yet in Galilee, saying : The Son of Man must be delivered into the hands of sinful men, and be crucified, and the third day rise again." And they remembered his words. And going back from the sepulchre, they told all these things to the eleven and to all the rest.

Peter, therefore, rising up, went out, and that other disciple. And they ran, [and] came to the sepulchre. And they both ran together ; and that other disciple did outrun Peter, and came first to the sepulchre. And when he stooped down, he seeth the linen cloths lying ; but yet he went not in. Then cometh Simon Peter following him, and stooping down, he went into the sepulchre ; and he seeth the linen cloths laid by themselves, and the napkin that had been about his [*i.e.,* Christ's] head not lying with the linen cloths but apart wrapt up into one place. Then went in that other disciple also, who came first to the sepulchre ; and he saw, and believed ; for as yet they knew not the Scripture, that he must rise again from the dead.

But he [*i.e.*, Christ] rising early the first day of the week, appeared first to Mary Magdalen out of whom he had cast seven devils. The disciples, therefore, departed again to their home ; and [Peter] went away, wondering in himself at that which was ccme to pass ; but Mary stood at the sepulchre without, weeping. Now as she was weeping, she stooped down, and looked into the sepulchre ; and she saw two angels in white, sitting one at the head, and one at the feet, where the body of Jesus had been laid.. They say to her : " Woman, why weepest thou?" She saith to them : " Because they have taken away my Lord, and I know not where they have laid him." When she had thus said, she turned herself back and saw Jesus standing ; and she knew not that it was Jesus. Jesus saith to her : " Woman, why weepest thou? Whom seekest thou?" She thinking that it was the gardener, saith to him : " Sir, if thou hast taken him hence, tell me where thou hast laid him, and I will take him away." Jesus saith to her : " Mary." She turning, saith to him : " Rabboni " (which is to say : " Master "). Jesus saith to her : " Do not touch me, for I am not yet ascended to my Father ; but go to my brethren, and say to them : I ascend to my Father and your Father, to my God and your God." Mary Magdalen cometh and telleth the disciples, them that had been with him, who were mourning and weeping : " I have seen the Lord, and these things he said to me." And they hearing that he was alive and had been seen by her, did not believe.

And very early in the morning, . . . they [*i.e.*, Salome and her party] come to the sepulchre, the sun being now risen. And they said one to another : " Who shall roll us back the stone from the door of the sepulchre ? " (And looking, they saw the stone rolled back) : for it was very great. And entering into the sepulchre, they saw a young man sitting on the right side, clothed with a white robe ; and they were astonished, And he saith to them : " Be not affrighted. You seek Jesus of Nazareth, who was crucified. He is risen : he is not here. Behold the place where they laid him. But go, tell his disciples and Peter that he goeth before you into Galilee : there you shall see him as he told you." But they going out quickly, fled from the sepulchre with fear and great joy ; for a trembling and fear had seized them. And running to tell his disciples, they said nothing to any man, for they were afraid. And behold Jesus met them, saying : " All hail." But they came up, and took hold of his feet, and adored him. Then Jesus saith to them : "Fear not. Go, tell my brethren that they go into Galilee : there they shall see me." And it was Mary Magdalen, and Joanna, and Mary the mother of James, and the other women that were with them, who told these things to the apostles. And these words seemed to them as idle tales ; and they did not believe them.

Now when they [*i.e.*, the women of Salome's party] were

departed [from the sepulchre], behold, some of the guards came
into the city, and told the chief-priests all the things that had
been done.   And they being assembled together with the
ancients, taking counsel, gave a great sum of money to the
soldiers, saying : " Say ye : His disciples came by night, and
stole him away when we were asleep.   And if the governor shall
hear of this, we will persuade him, and secure you." So they
taking the money did as they were taught ; and this word was
spread abroad among the Jews even unto this day.

IV.—NOTES.

Introductory. On the evening of Friday, the Jewish parasceve or day of preparation, Joseph of Arimathæa and Nicodemus
had with silent sadness consigned to the grave the dead body
of their Saviour (Matth. xxvii. 59, 60 ; Mark xv. 46 ; Luke xxiii.
53 ; John xix. 40-42), and had retired to their homes to weep
for the loss of their beloved Master.   As we may learn from the
Combined Narrative of the evangelists, Mary Magdalen, Mary
the mother of Joseph, and another party of women who had
come with Christ from Galilee, observed the position of the
sepulchre and how the body was laid.   This latter party on
returning to the city prepared spices and ointments for the subsequent embalming ; and on the sabbath-day they rested according to the commandment.   Not satisfied with what they had
already done, the chief-priests and the pharisees came in a body
to Pilate, and requested him to have the tomb guarded, lest the
disciples might steal away the body of Jesus, and spread amongst
the people the story of the Resurrection.   Pilate assented to
their wishes ; the tomb was secured ; and soldiers were put in
charge of the place.   Towards the end of this, the sabbath-day,
and before the guards had taken up their position, Mary Magdalen and a companion came to see the sepulchre.   What these
holy women did on their return to the city that evening, is told
us by St. Mark in the opening words of our present extract.
The evangelist says :

**V. 1. And when the sabbath was past, Mary Magdalen
and Mary the mother of James, and Salome bought sweet
spices, that coming, they might anoint Jesus.**

It has been asserted by some that St. Mark here contradicts
the statement of St. Luke (xxiii. 56), who says that the women
on returning from the burial of Jesus, prepared " spices and
ointments," and that " on the sabbath-day they rested according
to the commandment."   In answer to this objection it is sufficient to refer to the Combined Narrative prefixed to these notes.
In the construction of that Combined Narrative, without any violence to the text, it is supposed that there were three *parties*

of women, who lived perhaps in *different districts* of the city, or in different districts of the city and in Bethany, and that these three parties, *independently of each other*, visited the tomb at *different* times. One of these, which may be called the party of Joanna, is referred to by St. Luke ; another, that of Salome, by SS. Matthew and Mark ; and a third, that of Mary Magdalen, by St. John. As may be seen in the Combined Narrative, it was the party of Joanna composed of women from Galilee, that prepared the " spices and ointments " after the burial on Friday ; and they are not to be taken for the party of Salome with which Mary Magdalen was *sometimes* associated, and of which St. Mark here speaks.

Unlike the Egyptians, the Jews did not generally embalm the dead, but only wrapt them in linen cloths with aromatic herbs and ointments (see John xix. 40). On account of the approach of the sabbath, this had been hurriedly done with the body of Jesus (see John xix. 42). From St. Matthew, it is clear that when the sabbath was just coming to an end, " Mary Magdalen and the other Mary," of the party of Salome, paid a brief visit to the sepulchre in accordance with the custom of the Jews (Comp. John xi. 31). According to St. Mark in the present verse, these on their return to the city, " bought sweet spices, that coming, they might anoint Jesus."
St. Mark then continues :—

V. 2. And very early in the morning, the first day of the week, they come to the sepulchre, the sun being now risen.

The phrase μιᾷ τῶν σαββάτων (in the Vulgate = *unâ sabbatorum*, and in the English translation = " the first day of the week ") is a purely Hebrew expression—the cardinal number μιᾷ = *one* being used for the ordinal " first " (see Winer, xxxvii. 1, quoted by Gould in *loco*), שַׁבָּת in the Hebrew (see Leviticus xxiii. 15, xxv. 8) and in the Talmud, like τὰ σάββατα or even τὸ σάββατον in the Greek, signifies not only the day of rest, but also the week which terminates with that day. (See Knabenbauer, Winer, and Gould.)

St. John's statement (John xx. 1), that " Mary Magdalen cometh early, *when it was yet dark*, unto the sepulchre," appears to contradict the assertion of St. Mark that " very early in the morning . . . they (the party of women named in the preceding verse, and including Mary Magdalen) come to the sepulchre, *the sun being now risen.*"

In reply it is generally said that St. Mark's " very early in the morning," and St. John's " early, when it was yet dark," refer to the time when the journey *was begun* or *was being made*, whilst the concluding words of St. Mark, " the sun being now risen," refer to the time of arrival at the tomb. In support of this answer our attention is directed to the well-known fact that in Palestine, as in all southern countries, the transition from darkness to light of day is of much shorter duration than in these northern latitudes ; and it is assumed that during the journey from the city to the tomb this transition had taken place. Such a solution of the difficulty would be satisfactory if there were not against it a fatal objection founded on the following well-established facts : (*a*) The circuit of the city in the time of Christ was at the most 4,000 paces (*Comp*. Josephus Bell. Jud. L. V., c. xxxi. § 3) ; (*b*) the tomb of Christ was situated in Golgotha (John xix. 41, 42), and therefore near the city walls (*ib*. xix. 20) ; (*c*) from the Gate of Judgment which led to Golgotha, the distance to the tomb was less than 300 paces (Scholz. Commentat. de Golg. et Sanctissimi D. N. J. Ch. Sepulchri Situ. Bonæ, 1825) ; (*d*) in Jerusalem at the equinox—the time of Christ's Crucifixion—the duration of the twilight is half an hour. It is clear from these facts that the distance from any point in the city to the tomb was at most about 1,600 paces, and that those who accept the proposed solution of the difficulty must suppose the women to have spent half an hour in traversing this distance. (See Patrizi : De Evangeliis, Lib. iii., Diss. LIII.) This supposition is improbable, and some other explanation must be sought.

Again, it is suggested that Mary Magdalen with one or more companions forming an independent party, may have left the city and arrived at the tomb " when it was yet dark," and before the party of Salome had set out ; that she found the tomb opened ; that, with or without her companions, she at once returned ; and that, without having met the women of Salome's party of whom St Mark speaks, and who arrived at the tomb after sun-rise, she made known her discovery to St. Peter. This answer would be satisfactory if it were not that St. Mark so clearly couples Mary Magdalen's arrival at the tomb with that of the other women of whom he here speaks. The context requires that the clause : " They come to the sepulchre, the sun being now risen," be understood to refer to all the women of the party of Salome together with Mary Magdalen who had just been mentioned in connection with that party.

Lastly, and with most probability, it may be said that Mary Magdalen, whose visit is described by St. John (xx. 1), set out for the tomb " when it was yet dark," and not from Jerusalem, which was near at hand, but from her home in Bethany, which was at a considerable distance ; that she arrived at " the sepulchre, the sun being now risen " ; that by previous arrangement, or by accident, she there and then met the party of Salome ; and that on seeing the tomb opened, she ran to announce her discovery to the apostles. This answer appears to harmonise the statements of the different evangelists, and is the least open to serious difficulty.

The Combined Narrative of the evangelists prefixed to these notes, is based on the hypothesis here implied. As has been already said in the explanation of verse 1, the hypothesis is that there were three parties of women who visited the tomb of our Lord : the party of Mary Magdalen, the party of Joanna, and the party of Salome.   St. Mark is silent regarding the visit paid by Joanna and her companions (Luke xxiv. 10) ; he merely implies the two visits of Mary Magdalen (Mark xv. 47 ; xvi. 1, 2, 9), which were followed by that of SS. Peter and John (John xx. 3-10) ; but with St. Matth. (Matth. xxviii. 5-10), he gives in this and the following verses a detailed description of that of Salome, which took place last of all on Mary Magdalen's second departure from the sepulchre.

The disciples who had been resting during the sabbath " according to the commandment " (Luke xxiii. 56), had heard nothing about the interview between Pilate and the chief-priests and pharisees (Matth. xxvii. 62-66) ; nothing about the sealing of the tomb ; nothing about the soldiers placed there on guard. Hence after the return of Mary Magdalen on the preceding evening, only one difficulty appeared to impede their visit to the body of their Saviour.   This was the removal of the great stone which had been placed at the door of the monument by Joseph of Arimathæa (Matth. xxvii. 60).   On their way the holy women discussed the matter ;

V. 3. And they said one to another : Who shall roll us back the stone from the door of the sepulchre ?

The obstacle had been removed without their knowledge whilst they were on their journey ;

V. 4. (And looking they saw the stone rolled back :) for it was very great.

The explanation of this supernatural intervention is supplied by St. Matthew (xxviii. 2-4), who says : " Behold, there was a great earthquake.   For an angel of the Lord descended from heaven, and coming, rolled back the stone and sat upon it. And his countenance was as lightning, and his raiment as snow. And for fear of him the guards were struck with terror, and became as dead men."   When Mary Magdalen saw the tomb opened (John xx. 1), the soldiers placed on guard, and the angel who was perhaps accompanied by other angels in human shape, she concluded that the body of Christ had been removed, and she ran to communicate the news to SS. Peter and John.   On her departure, the rest of the party who remained, taking courage, moved forward ;

V. 5. And entering into the sepulchre, they saw a young man sitting on the right side, clothed with a white robe ; and they were astonished.

As McCarthy remarks, the Jewish tombs were either natural caves, or caverns artificially made in rocks. They consisted of two parts—a small outer court where there was room for the bier and bearers, and the inner cave which, according to the Rabbinical design, should be square or oblong, and with sides about nine feet in length. The passage from the outer court to the inner cave was closed by a large stone, which was rolled away before each burial. Into such a sepulchre three of four women could easily enter. (Introduction, p. c.) Passing then into the outer chamber of the tomb, the women saw the angel of whom St. Matthew speaks (Matth. xxviii. 2-4). Now as the Resurrection—one of the greatest truths of the Christian religion—was to be solemnly testified to by Heaven, an angel was sent to bear witness to it ; as this heavenly witness was to make himself visible to human beings, he assumed the form of " a young man " ; as he was to terrify the ministers of Christ's enemies, " his countenance was as lightning " ; and as he was to announce to Christ's friends the joyful news of the Resurrection, " his raiment was as snow."

It was natural that on beholding such a marvellous sight, the women " were astonished " (in the Greek ἐξεθαμβήθησαν = " were utterly or out and out amazed "). To reassure them, however, God had sent his angel,

V. 6. And he saith to them: Be not affrighted. You seek Jesus of Nazareth who was crucified. He is risen: he is not here. Behold the place where they laid him.

The message of the angel is recorded still more fully by St. Matthew in these words : " The angel answering, said to the women : Fear not you, for I know that you seek Jesus, who was crucified. He is not here, for he is risen as he said. Come, and see the place where the Lord was laid " (Matth. xxviii. 5, 6). By these first words the heavenly messenger distinguished between the guards who, as the ministers of the pharisees, were intent on proving that Christ was an impostor, and the holy women who had shown their love for their crucified Master. To these latter, therefore, the angel brings the joyful news that Christ has returned to life. Nay, more, he confirms this statement by showing the vacant tomb, and by thus appealing to the repeated prophecies of Christ himself : " He is not here, for he is risen *as he said*. Come, and see the place where the Lord was laid."

As the angel had been sent to announce this consoling truth to the holy women at the sepulchre, they were in their turn to convey the joyful news to the disciples in the city. Hence the command : —

V. 7. But go, tell his disciples and Peter that he goeth before you into Galilee : there you shall see him as he told you.

Although Christ was to manifest himself to his beloved disciples several times even on that very day, the subsequent appearance in Galilee is specially mentioned by the angel, because at the Last Supper it had been predicted by our Divine Lord himself in these terms : " But after I shall be risen again, I will go before you into Galilee " (Matth. xxvi. 32). In the message to the disciples the angel was commissioned to make particular mention of the Prince of the Apostles, St. Peter. In the very name " Peter " then used, the penitent apostle received an assurance that his sin was forgiven, and that his right to the primatial dignity in the future Church was confirmed. It is a remarkable fact that wherever all the apostles are *individually* named, as in the four catalogues, Matth. x. 2 ; Mark iii. 16 ; Luke vi. 14 ; Acts i. 13, or where some only are so named with Peter, as in Matth. xvii. 1 ; Mark ix. 1 ; Luke ix. 28 ; Acts iii. 1 ; iv. 19 ; v. 29, etc., he always takes the first place. The example before us belongs to another class, in which all the apostles are spoken of *collectively,* and Peter *specially.* Similar instances of this are found in Luke viii. 45 ; Acts ii. 14 ; v. 29.

Although the first to write, St. Matthew supplements the account of the Resurrection given by St. Mark and the other evangelists. Referring to the holy women he says : " They went out quickly from the sepulchre with fear and great joy, running to tell his disciples. And behold, Jesus met them, saying : All hail. But they came up, and took hold of his feet, and adored him. Then Jesus saith to them : Fear not. Go, tell my brethren that they go into Galilee : there they shall see me." The holy women departed on their mission. They were followed by the guards who " came into the city, and told the chief-priests all the things that had been done." Thus was evidence of the Resurrection offered from an unexpected and most unprejudiced source ; but avarice, which corrupted an apostle of Christ, corrupted the guards of Christ's tomb. The chief-priests " being assembled together with the ancients, taking counsel, gave a great sum of money to the soldiers, saying : Say you : His disciples came by night, and stole him away while we were asleep. And if the governor shall hear of this, we will persuade him and secure you. So they, taking the money, did as they were taught ; and this word was spread abroad among the Jews even unto this day " (Matth. xxviii. 8-15).

V.—MORAL REFLECTIONS.

1. The Resurrection is one of the greatest mysteries of our religion ; it is the miracle to which Christ pointed when asked by the Jews for a proof of his divine mission (John ii. 18-21) ; and it is the fact appealed to by the apostles in their preaching before both Jews and Gentiles alike. " If Christ be not risen

again," said St. Paul, "then is our preaching vain, and your faith also is vain. Yea, and we are found false witnesses of God " (1 Cor. xv. 14, 15). This being so, the first and most important elements in our commemoration of the Resurrection should be a profession of faith in Christ's teaching, which is rendered incontestable by this miracle, and a spirit of thankfulness that we are members of that Church for whose justification Christ rose again (Rom. iv. 25).

2. Still further, theologians teach that the glory which the Resurrection shed around the sacred humanity of Christ was his just reward as Man for his obedient and patient endurance of suffering and of sorrow. Jesus himself said to his disciples : " Ought not Christ to have suffered these things, and so to enter into his glory?" (Luke xxiv. 26). Now the Resurrection of Christ is the pledge and type of ours, because St. Paul says : " Christ is risen from the dead, the first fruits of them that sleep. For by a man came death, and by a man the resurrection of the dead ; and as in Adam all die, so also in Christ shall all be made alive " (1 Cor. xv. 20-22). Should not this festival, then, fill us with consolation and hope? When weighed down with affliction, when thinking of the departed friends whose look, and voice, and love were once our dearest earthly treasure, when beholding the gradual but sure decay of these bodies of ours tended with such care, we feel the full force of St. Paul's words : " If in this life only we have hope in Christ, we are of all men most miserable " (1 Cor. xv. 19). But no. Having the Resurrection of Christ as the pledge of our own, we can take courage and say with the same great Apostle : " [Our body] is sown in corruption, it shall rise in incorruption. It is sown in dishonour, it shall rise in glory. It is sown in weakness, it shall rise in power. . . . And when this mortal hath put on immortality, then shall come to pass the saying that is written : *Death is swallowed up in victory. O death, where is thy victory! O death, where is thy sting?* " (1 Cor. xv. 42, 43, 54, 55.)

3. This is not all ; for as in the Resurrection we have a mystery to honour by our faith, and a pledge of future blessedness to be contemplated with hope, so have we a model to be lovingly imitated in our daily life. St. Paul has written that the Resurrection of Christ from the dead ought to be the type of our resurrection from sin to the spiritual life of grace, or from tepidity to fervour in the service of God. " We are buried together with him by baptism unto death ; that as Christ is risen from the dead by the glory of the Father, so we also may walk in newness of life " (Rom. vi. 4). Now let us learn from the inspired writers the character of Christ's Resurrection.

In the first place, recording the words of the apostles to the disciples of Emmaus, St. Luke tells us that " the Lord is risen *indeed* " (Luke xxiv. 34). It was no appearance merely.

but a fact made evident to all ; for as our Redeemer had foretold the ignominy of his Passion, and as he died publicly for our sins, so did he foretell the glory of his Resurrection, and prove the reality of that Resurrection by his many and public apparitions.   Here is the type of our return to grace or to fervour.   If by our tepidity or by our negligence we have disedified our neighbour, if our fall into sin has been a scandal to those around us, let our conversion be as public ; let us give evidence by our good works that the Spirit of God is once more within us, and that where sin has abounded the grace of our Lord Jesus Christ still more abounds (Rom. v. 20).

Moreover, the Sacred Scriptures tell us that the Resurrection was but a prelude to the Ascension, and that the interval was employed by Christ in the instruction of his apostles regarding the kingdom of God (Acts i. 3).   St. Paul makes the application of this by exhorting his recent converts to forget the world which they had renounced, and in future to think of nothing but the heaven to which they aspired.   " If ye be risen with Christ, seek the things that are above, where Christ is sitting at the right hand of God.   Mind the things that are above, not the things that are upon the earth ; for you are dead (*i.e.*, to this world), and your life is hidden with Christ in God " (Coloss. iii. 1-3).   The Christian who by a true conversion has once risen from his sins, regards himself here below as a pilgrim ; he is ever engaged in promoting the interests of God's kingdom ; and like the Apostle of the Gentiles, he continually sighs for the hour of his deliverance when, loosed from the ties of earth, he may rest for ever in the possession of his Creator.

Lastly, in reviewing the features of the Resurrection, we are reminded " that Christ, rising again from the dead, dieth now no more ; death shall no more have dominion over him " (Rom. vi. 9).   These words are specially worthy of consideration. Many there are who, listening to the voice of the Church at this Paschal season, resolve on a change of life, confess their sins, are received again into the friendship of God, and give reason to hope that they will continue for the future in the state of grace to which they have been restored.   Sad experience teaches that all do not persevere.   Forgetting the warning of Christ : " Watch and pray that ye enter not into temptation," they confide in their own strength ; they are deprived of grace ; they go into the danger unarmed ; they fall again into sin ; and as Christ has said, their last state becomes worse than the first. Such must not be the history of our conversion.   Restored to God's friendship, we promise that we will fear for our weakness ; we will avoid the occasions, the places, the companions of our sins ; we will daily pray for perseverance ; and in the appointed channels of divine grace we will seek and secure the help by which alone we can persevere.

LOW SUNDAY

I.—TEXTS.

GREEK.

JOHN XX. 19-31.

¹⁹ Οὔσης οὖν ὀψίας τῇ ἡμέρᾳ ἐκείνῃ τῇ μιᾷ σαββάτων, καὶ τῶν θυρῶν κεκλεισμένων, ὅπου ἦσαν οἱ μαθηταὶ διὰ τὸν φόβον τῶν Ἰουδαίων, ἦλθεν ὁ Ἰησοῦς, καὶ ἔστη εἰς τὸ μέσον, καὶ λέγει αὐτοῖς· εἰρήνη ὑμῖν. ²⁰ Καὶ τοῦτο εἰπὼν, ἔδειξε καὶ τὰς χεῖρας καὶ τὴν πλευρὰν αὐτοῖς. Ἐχάρησαν οὖν οἱ μαθηταὶ ἰδόντες τὸν Κύριον. ²¹ Εἶπεν οὖν αὐτοῖς ὁ Ἰησοῦς πάλιν· εἰρήνη ὑμῖν· καθὼς ἀπέσταλκέν με ὁ πατήρ, κἀγὼ πέμπω ὑμᾶς. ²² Καὶ τοῦτο εἰπὼν, ἐνεφύσησε, καὶ λέγει αὐτοῖς· λάβετε πνεῦμα ἅγιον. ²³ Ἄν τινος ἀφῆτε τὰς ἁμαρτίας, ἀφίενται αὐτοῖς· ἄν τινος κρατῆτε, κεκράτηνται. ²⁴ Θωμᾶς δὲ, εἷς ἐκ τῶν δώδεκα, ὁ λεγόμενος Δίδυμος, οὐκ ἦν μετ᾽ αὐτῶν ὅτε ἦλθεν Ἰησοῦς. ²⁵ Ἔλεγον οὖν αὐτῷ οἱ ἄλλοι μαθηταί· ἑωράκαμεν τὸν Κύριον· ὁ δὲ εἶπεν αὐτοῖς· ἐὰν μὴ ἴδω ἐν ταῖς χερσὶν αὐτοῦ τὸν τύπον τῶν ἥλων, καὶ βάλω τόν δάκτυλόν μου εἰς τὸν τύπον τῶν ἥλων, καὶ βάλω μου τὴν χεῖρα εἰς τὴν πλευρὰν αὐτοῦ, οὐ μὴ πιστεύσω· ²⁶ Καὶ μεθ᾽ ἡμέρας ὀκτὼ πάλιν ἦσαν ἔσω οἱ μαθηταὶ αὐτοῦ· καὶ Θωμᾶς μετ᾽ αὐτῶν· ἔρχεται ὁ Ἰησοῦς τῶν θυρῶν κεκλεισμένων, καὶ ἔστη εἰς τὸ μέσον, καὶ εἶπεν· εἰρήνη ὑμῖν. ²⁷ Εἶτα λέγει τῷ Θωμᾷ· φέρε τὸν δάκτυλόν σου ὧδε, καὶ

VULGATE.

JOHN XX. 19-31.

¹⁹ Cum ergo sero esset die illo, una sabbatorum, et fores essent clausæ, ubi erant discipuli congregati propter metum Judæorum, venit Jesus, et stetit in medio, et dixit eis : Pax vobis. ²⁰ Et cum hoc dixisset, ostendit eis manus et latus. Gavisi sunt ergo discipuli, viso Domino. ²¹ Dixit ergo eis iterum : Pax vobis. Sicut misit me Pater, et ego mitto vos. ²² Hæc cum dixisset, insufflavit, et dixit eis : Accipite Spiritum sanctum. ²³ Quorum remiseritis peccata, remittuntur eis ; et quorum retinueritis, retenta sunt. ²⁴Thomas autem unus ex duodecim, qui dicitur Didymus, non erat cum eis quando venit Jesus. ²⁵ Dixerunt ergo ei alii discipuli : Vidimus Dominum. Ille autem dixit eis : Nisi videro in manibus ejus fixuram clavorum, et mittam digitum meum in locum clavorum, et mittam manum meam in latus ejus, non credam. ²⁶ Et post dies octo, iterum erant discipuli ejus intus, et Thomas cum eis. Venit Jesus januis clausis, et stetit in medio, et dixit : Pax vobis. ²⁷ Deinde dicit Thomæ : Infer digitum tuum huc, et vide manus meas ; et affer

ἴδε τὰς χεῖράς μου· καὶ φέρε τὴν χεῖρά
σου, καὶ βάλε εἰς τὴν πλευράν μου·
καὶ μὴ γίνου ἄπιστος, ἀλλὰ πιστός·
²⁸ Ἀπεκρίθη Θωμᾶς, καὶ εἶπεν αὐτῷ· ὁ
κύριός μου καὶ ὁ θεός μου. ²⁹ Λέγει αὐτῷ
Ἰησοῦς· ὅτι ἑώρακάς με, πεπίστευκας·
μακάριοι, οἱ μὴ ἰδόντες, καὶ πιστεύσαντες.
³⁰ Πολλὰ μὲν οὖν καὶ ἄλλα σημεῖα
ἐποίησεν ὁ Ἰησοῦς ἐνώπιον τῶν μαθη-
τῶν, ἃ οὐκ ἔστιν γεγραμμένα ἐν τῷ
βιβλίῳ τούτῳ. ³¹ Ταῦτα δὲ γέγραπται,
ἵνα πιστεύητε, ὅτι Ἰησοῦς ἐστιν ὁ
Χριστὸς ὁ υἱὸς τοῦ θεοῦ, καὶ ἵνα πιστεύ-
οντες ζωὴν ἔχητε ἐν τῷ ὀνόματι αὐτοῦ.

manum tuam, et mitte in latus meum ; et noli esse incredulus, sed fidelis. 28 Respondit Thomas, et dixit ei : Dominus meus, et Deus meus. 29 Dixit ei Jesus : Quia vidisti me, Thoma, credidisti. Beati qui non viderunt et crediderunt.

30 Multa quidem et alia signa fecit Jesus in conspectu discipulorum suorum, quæ non sunt scripta in libro hoc ; 31 hæc autem scripta sunt ut credatis quia Jesus est Christus, filius Dei, et ut credentes, vitam habeatis in nomine ejus.

II.—ENGLISH TRANSLATION, WITH PARALLEL PASSAGE FROM ST. LUKE.

JOHN XX. 19-31.

¹⁹ Now when it was late that same day, the first of the week, and the doors were shut where the disciples were gathered together for fear of the Jews, Jesus came and stood in the midst, and said to them : " Peace be to you." ²⁰ And when he had said this, he showed them his hands and his side. The disciples, therefore, were glad when they saw the Lord. ²¹ He said therefore to them again : " Peace be to you. As the Father hath sent me, I also send you." ²² When he had said this, he breathed on them, and he said to them : " Receive ye the Holy Ghost. ²³ Whose sins you shall forgive, they are forgiven them ; and whose sins you shall retain, they are retained." ²⁴ Now Thomas, one of the twelve, who is called Didymus, was not with them when Jesus came. ²⁵ The other disciples, therefore, said to him : " We have seen the Lord." But he said to them : " Except I shall see in his hands the print of the nails, and put my finger into the place of the nails, and put my hand into his side, I will not believe."

²⁶ And after eight days, again his disciples were within, and Thomas with them. Jesus cometh, the doors being shut, and stood in the midst, and said : " Peace be to you." ²⁷ Then he saith to Thomas : " Put in thy finger hither, and see my hands ; and bring hither thy hand, and put it into my side ; and be not faithless, but believing." ²⁸ Thomas answered, and said to him : " My Lord, and my God ! " ²⁹ Jesus saith to him : " Because

thou hast seen me, Thomas, thou hast believed. Blessed are they that have not seen, and have believed."

[30] Many other signs also did Jesus in the sight of his disciples, which are not written in this book ; [31] but these are written that you may believe that Jesus is the Christ, the Son of God, and that believing, you may have life in his name.

LUKE XXIV. 33-43.

[33] Rising up the same hour they went back to Jerusalem ; and they found the eleven gathered together, and those that were with them, [34] saying : " The Lord is risen indeed, and hath appeared to Simon." [35] And they told what things were done in the way, and how they knew him in the breaking of bread. [36] Now whilst they were speaking these things, Jesus stood in the midst of them, and saith to them : " Peace be to you. It is I. Fear not." [37] But they being troubled and affrighted, supposed that they saw a spirit. [38] And he said to them : " Why are you troubled, and why do thoughts arise in your hearts ? [39] See my hands and feet, that it is I myself. Handle, and see ; for a spirit hath not flesh and bones, as you see me to have." [40] And when he had said this, he showed them his hands and feet. [41] But while they yet believed not and wondered for joy, he said : " Have you here anything to eat ? " [42] And they offered him a piece of a broiled fish and a honeycomb. [43] And when he had eaten before them, taking the remains, he gave to them.

III.—COMBINED NARRATIVE.

Rising up the same hour, they [i.e., the disciples from Emmaus] went back to Jerusalem. Now when it was late that same day, the first of the week, and the doors were shut where the disciples were gathered together for fear of the Jews, [they] found the eleven gathered together, and those that were with them, saying : " The Lord is risen indeed, and hath appeared to Simon." And they [i.e., the disciples from Emmaus] told what things were done in the way, and how they knew him in the breaking of bread. Now whilst they were speaking these things, Jesus came and stood in the midst of them, and saith to them : " Peace be to you. It is I. Fear not." But they being troubled and affrighted, supposed that they saw a spirit. And he said to them : " Why are you troubled, and why do thoughts arise in your hearts ? See my hands and feet, that it is I myself. Handle, and see ; for a spirit hath not flesh and bones, as you see me to have." And when he had said this, he showed them his hands, and feet, and side. But while they yet believed not and wondered for joy, he said : " Have ye here anything to eat ? " And they offered him a piece of broiled fish and a honeycomb. And when he had eaten before them, taking the remains, he gave to them. The disciples therefore were glad when they saw the Lord. He said, therefore, to them again : " Peace be to you. As the Father hath sent me, I also send you." When he had said this, he breathed on them ; and he said to them : " Receive ye the Holy Ghost. Whose sins you shall forgive, they are forgiven them ; and whose sins you shall retain, they are retained." Now, Thomas, one of the twelve, who is called Didymus, was not with them when Jesus came. The other disciples, therefore, said to him : " We have seen the Lord." But he said to them : " Except I shall see in his hands the print of the nails, and put my finger into the place of the nails, and put my hand into his side, I will not believe."

And after eight days, again his disciples were within, and Thomas with them. Jesus cometh, the doors being shut, and stood in the midst, and said, " Peace be to you." Then he saith to Thomas : " Put in thy finger hither, and see my hands ; and bring hither thy hand, and put it into my side ; and be not faithless, but believing." Thomas answered, and said to him · " My Lord, and my God ! " Jesus saith to him : " Because thou hast seen me, Thomas, thou hast believed. Blessed are they that have not seen, and have believed."

Many other signs also did Jesus in the sight of his disciples, which are not written in this book ; but these things are written that you may believe that Jesus is the Christ, the Son of God, and that believing, you may have life in his name.

IV.—NOTES.

Introductory. We know that faith consists in the unwavering acceptance of all God has revealed to us, because he who has thus taught us is the infallible truth. But although our act of faith has for its motive the unerring word of God and not the dictates of human reason, reason has its place in preparing us for that act. Hence, besides the supernatural help which God gives us to accept the truths he has revealed and because he has revealed them, he disposes us for that acceptance by rendering credible the fact of this revelation. This was to be the economy of the Gospel (Mark xv. 15, 16, 20). In the miracles they worked by the power of their Master, the Apostles were to bear witness to Christ throughout the whole world (Acts i. 8). It was necessary, however, that these witnesses should first be confirmed in the faith they were to preach, and that they should especially be convinced of the reality of the Resurrection, the fundamental proof of Christian revelation. Hence St. Luke records that to these, and to others on their account, " He [*i.e.*, Christ] showed himselt after his Passion by many proofs, for forty days appearing to them, and speaking of the kingdom of God " (Acts i. 3). Of ten of these apparitions specially mentioned in the Sacred Scripture, three took place on the morning of the Resurrection. Christ had been then seen by Mary Magdalen (John xx. 14) ; again, by the other holy women (Matth. xxviii. 9) ; and subsequently by St. Peter (Luke xxiv. 34 ; 1 Cor. xv. 5). From the last named chapter of St. Luke we may learn that later in the day two disciples met our Lord as they were going to Emmaus (Introduction, p. lix.), a town sixty furlongs from Jerusalem ; and that, recognising him while at table in their house, they set out forthwith to bring the joyful news to the apostles. The evangelist adds that on the arrival of these men in Jerusalem, " they found the eleven gathered together, and those that were with them, saying : The Lord is risen indeed, and hath appeared to Simon. And they [*i.e.*, the disciples from Emmaus] told what things were done in the way, and how they knew him [*i.e.*, Christ] in the breaking of bread " (Luke xxiv. 33-35). Thomas, whose obstinate unbelief is afterwards noted, was not influenced by these witnesses to the Resurrection ; he appears at this point to have left the company for some reason ; and he was absent when, at a later hour in the evening, Jesus came.

On the departure of Thomas the disciples went on to discuss the marvellous events of the day, the history of which is continued by both St. Luke and St. John. The latter evangelist says :—

V. 19. **Now when it was late that same day, the first of the week, and the doors were shut where the disciples were gathered together for fear of the Jews, Jesus came and stood in the midst, and said to them : Peace be to you.**

To remove every shadow of doubt regarding this first manifestation of Christ to his apostles assembled in a body, each circumstance is minutely described. And first, what was the time ? The Jews were accustomed to indicate by the word " sabbath," not only the particular day which corresponded to our Saturday, but also the whole week which terminated with that day ; and in naming the days of the week, they used the cardinal instead of the ordinal numbers. Hence the expression in the Greek text : τῇ μιᾷ σαββάτων = " on the one of the sabbath," is a Hebrew idiom signifying " on the first day of the week." The evangelist says, therefore, that the apparition about to be described took place late on the first day of the week, our Sunday, the same day on which Christ rose from the dead and appeared to Magdalen as already recorded in this chapter. At that time the apostles and disciples with the exception of Thomas, who had just left (see introductory note), " were gathered together for fear of the Jews," who had slain their Divine Master. According to the Parallel Passage of St. Luke, they were speaking of that Master and of his apparition to some of their number at an earlier hour. Christ had foretold that his followers would be hated by all men for his name's sake ; and as they feared the worst consequences from the anger of the pharisees, now that the news of the Resurrection was noised abroad, the doors were *shut*, or according to the Greek text, were *shut and barred*, (τῶν θυρῶν κεκλεισμένων). Matter, however, was not at all an impediment to the glorified body of their Lord ; and to enable them to believe that he had passed out of the sealed sepulchre, that Lord now passed into the barricaded chamber of the apostles. What was the salutation of Christ ? As recorded in the Combined Narrative of SS. Luke and John, the words are : " Peace be to you. If is I. Fear not." As on the night of the Nativity the angel suddenly presented himself to the shepherds to announce the birth of their Saviour, so did that Saviour now suddenly appear in the midst of his disciples to make known his Resurrection ; and as the angel saluted his hearers with the glad tidings of " peace to men of good will," so did Christ now promise to his fear-stricken followers that same peace of God which " surpasseth all understanding " (Phil. iv. 7), and which he had purchased by his sufferings on the cross.

The salutation " Peace be to you," שלום לכם, is a well-known Hebrew form of greeting (Introduction, pp. lxxxix., xc.) On the lips of Christ, however, it had its highest spiritual signification, and was a prayer for, or rather a grant of, every gift conducive to the salvation of the apostles themselves and of those who were to be afterwards confided to their zealous care. In contrast to the peace promised by men, it was not to endure for a time only, but for ever : it was not in words only, but in truth. By this gift of the Redeemer we obtain peace with our own souls, into which his grace is infused ; we enjoy peace with God, who is reconciled to us by the sufferings on Calvary ; and we possess peace with our neighbour, to whom we are united by brotherhood with Jesus Christ. Well then might our Saviour say at his Last Supper: " Peace I leave with you ; my peace I give unto you. Not as the world giveth, do I give unto you. Let not your heart be troubled, nor let it be afraid " (John xiv. 27). The salutation of Christ on this occasion, though uttered in the well-known tone of voice, was not sufficient to confirm the faith and remove the fear of the apostles, who, on account of his unexpected entry through the barred doors, " being troubled and affrighted, supposed that they saw a spirit " (Luke xxiv. 37). Christ, then, adopted another means to calm their terror and to prove the fact of his Resurrection, by showing that he knew their inmost thoughts, and by exhibiting to them the wounds in his sacred flesh. " He said to them," adds the same St. Luke, " Why are you troubled ; and why do thoughts arise in your hearts ? " The meaning is : " Why do you doubt as to whether you see a material body, or a spirit ? Do you not hear the voice so well known to you ? " But this not being sufficient, he added : " See my hands and feet, that it is myself : nay even, handle my wounded members and see ; for, as you know, a spirit hath not flesh and bones, as you see me to have."

The disciples were somewhat calmed by the reassuring words of Christ ;

V. 20. **And when he had said this, he showed them his hands and his side. The disciples, therefore, were glad when they saw the Lord.**

St. Luke says : " He showed them . . . his feet " as well ; and this he did, that on seeing all the sacred wounds the apostles might recognise their crucified Master. Christ retained these relics of the Passion in his now glorified body, both that they might be a proof of the identity of that body with the one which had hung upon the cross, and that afterwards in heaven he might present these marks of his meritorious sufferings to his Father, with whom, according to the Apostle, he is " always living to make intercession for us " (Hebrews vii. 25). On the night before he suffered, Christ, in his farewell address, consoled his apostles with the promise : " I will see you again, and your heart shall rejoice " (John xvi. 22). The evangelist seems to have had this prophetic announcement before his mind when he thus recorded its fulfilment : " The disciples, therefore, were glad when they saw the Lord."

Notwithstanding the evidence of our senses, we sometimes doubt when we see realised what we ardently wish to take place. Thus was it now with some of the disciples ; and we learn from St. Luke that Jesus deigned to give them a third and most convincing proof of his Resurrection. " While they yet believed not and wondered for joy, he said : Have ye here anything to eat ? And they offered him a piece of a broiled fish and a honeycomb. And when he had eaten before them, taking the remains, he gave to them " (Luke xxiv. 41-43).

The use of food affords the strongest evidence to demonstrate the fact that one lives ; and hence Christ availed himself of this evidence in the case of the daughter of Jairus (Mark v. 43). On the present occasion our Redeemer asked for food, not that in his glorified state he needed material nourishment, but that he might prove to his still doubting disciples and to us the reality of the vivified body in which he had returned from the tomb. The angel Raphael once said to Tobias (Tob. xii. 18, 19) : " When I was with you . . . I seemed indeed to eat and to drink with you ; but I used an invisible meat and drink, which cannot be seen by men." It was different with Christ. Unlike the apparent body assumed for a time by the angel, the body of the risen Saviour was real and animated. As then, according to St. Augustine, such immortal bodies are freed from the *necessity* but are not deprived of the *power*, of eating, the evangelist takes care to add that " when he had eaten before them, taking the remains, he gave to them " (Luke xxiv. 43).

When Christ had thus proved in various ways the reality of his Resurrection, he proceeded to point out to the apostles the nature of their future mission, and to confer upon them some of the powers they were to exercise after his Ascension into heaven.

V. 21. He said, therefore, to them again: Peace be to you. As the Father hath sent me, I also send you.

Whilst renewing his assurance of heavenly peace, our Redeemer in these words indicates his equality with the Father as God, and the sublime dignity of his apostles whom he sends to carry on the same mission delegated to himself as Man. The mission of the apostles, who were mere men, could not have been in all things co-extensive with that of the Word Incarnate ; but as far as it did extend, it was identical with his. These ambassadors were sent with the same power, which was to forgive sins ; with the same purpose, which was the salvation of fallen men ; with the same means of conversion, which were the preaching of the gospel and the working of miracles ; and in the same spirit of love with which God " so loved the world as to give his Only-begotten Son " (John iii. 16).

To carry out such a mission was beyond the strength of creatures, human or angelic. Hence,

V. 22. When he had said this, he breathed on them ; and he said to them: Receive ye the Holy Ghost.

It is remarked that ἐνεφύσησε, a Greek verb unusual in this connection and adopted here to describe the action of Christ, is precisely the same which occurs in the LXX version when describing the infusion of the human soul into the newly-created body of Adam (Gen. ii. 7). As, therefore, God in the beginning breathed on the face of our first parent and thus bestowed upon him a living soul in the order of nature, so, before confiding to the apostles the duty of bringing back to supernatural life a world dead in sin, Christ on this occasion by a similar and fitting sign bestowed upon these apostles the Holy Ghost, the very source of all supernatural life. St. John had said : " As yet the Spirit was not given, because Jesus was not yet glorified " (John vii. 39). Our Redeemer having suffered and having thus entered into his glory, began at once after his Resurrection to give his Spirit to his disciples, although he intended to confer on them that same Spirit more abundantly, more efficaciously, and more visibly, after the Ascension.

It will be said that Christ had already declared the apostles to be just (John xiii. 10), and that therefore they had already the gifts of the Holy Ghost, who is the source of justification. Why then was it needed that they should receive the Holy Ghost on the present occasion ? It is answered that the gifts of the Holy Ghost are of two kinds—that which conduces directly to the personal sanctity of the individual (gratia gratum faciens), and those which conduce directly to the sanctification of others (gratiæ gratis datæ). The first mentioned is that which the apostles had already, the others were those which it was neces-sary to confer upon them now when they received their mission from our Divine Lord. But it will be asked : If this be so, and if the Holy Ghost was now given to the apostles to fulfil their mission for the sanctification of others, how could Jesus have said at his Last Supper (John xvi. 7) : " If I go not, the Para-clete will not come to you ; but if I go, I will send him to you " ? Some with Theophylactus have endeavoured to solve this diffi-culty by supposing that Christ did not now give the Holy Ghost to the apostles, but prepared them for the future reception of that grace. This explanation is inadmissible ; for the word in the text λάβετε =" receive ye," being in the aorist, necessarily indicates what then and there took place. Therefore, with reason, St. Cyril of Alexandria says : " They are made partici-pators (δέχονται μὲν τὴν . . . μέθεξιι) of the Holy Ghost ; for Christ could not speak an untruth : he would not say : ' Re-ceive ye,' unless he bestowed that gift." Whilst approving of this statement, Maldonatus points out that the present action of Christ is not opposed to what he had previously foretold regard-ing the descent of the Holy Ghost after the Ascension. The apostles, being just men, had already *invisibly* received the Holy Ghost and his gifts as far as was required for their *personal sanctification ;* they now *invisibly* received him and such a partial outpouring of his graces as was required for the *sanctification of others* in the exercise of the office conferred on this occasion ; and after the Ascension these same apostles received in a *visible and solemn manner* the same Holy Ghost with the plenitude of grace required for the exercise of *all their functions* as pastors of the Church.

But what was the office committed to the apostles on this day of the Resurrection ? It is made known in the words of Christ :—

V. 23. **Whose sins you shall forgive, they are forgiven them ; and whose sins you shall retain, they are retained.**

The dignity of the priesthood supposes the possession of a

power over Christ's *real* body offered in the sacrifice of the Mass, together with the power of ruling Christ's *mystic* body by inflicting or removing censures in the public tribunal of the Church, and by absolving or retaining sins in the tribunal of penance. At their ordination during the Last Supper, the apostles had received the power of offering the Mass or sacrifice of the New Law. Long before his Passion Christ had given these chosen twelve the external jurisdiction required in the public administration of the Church's laws. " Whatsoever you shall bind upon earth, shall be bound also in heaven ; and whatsoever you shall loose upon earth, shall be loosed also in heaven " (Matth. xviii. 18). On the present occasion, however, the apostles receive jurisdiction over the consciences of their subjects in the tribunal of penance ; and by the words with which that jurisdiction was conferred the sacrament of penance itself was instituted. The same authority of forgiving sins is *radically* given in a similar form of words to every priest at his ordination ; but to *exercise* this authority even validly, the priest requires subjects to be assigned to him in the collation of jurisdiction by the chief pastor of the church in which he is to minister.

From the words of the text, from the unanimous testimony of the Fathers, from the teaching of theologians, and from the express declaration of the Council of Trent, it is certain that the authority here conferred by Christ is not the power to admit into the Church by baptism, nor to preach the Gospel, nor to heal diseases, nor to inflict and to absolve from excommunication, nor merely to remit the penalty of sin, but to forgive and to retain sin itself. This being so, the apostles and their successors are hereby appointed judges, on whom it is incumbent to exercise a judicial office with regard to sins committed. As, however, no one can exercise a judicial office without a knowledge of the cause to be tried, it follows that the sins to be judged must be made known. Hence the Catholic Church has always understood that these words of our Lord imply the precept of auricular confession ; and the faithful have ever looked on the fulfilment of this precept, when possible, as an essential condition of pardon for mortal sin committed after baptism. (See Council of Trent ; Sess. xiv., chap. 1, 5, 6 ; Can. 2, 3, 6, 7, 9.)

St. John records another apparition of Christ to the apostles assembled together—an apparition which contributes much to strengthen our faith in the Resurrection, and to confirm our hope in the infinite mercy of God. The evangelist details the circumstances thus :—

Vv. 24, 25. **Now Thomas, one of the twelve, who is called Didymus, was not with them when Jesus came. The other disciples, therefore, said to him : We have seen the Lord. But he said to them : Except I shall see in his hands the print of**

the nails, and put my finger into the place of the nails, and put my hand into his side, I will not believe.

The word Thomas (in Aramaic תּוֹמָא) is the same as Didymus (in Greek Δίδυμος), and signifies *a twin ;* but we have no means of knowing why the apostle received this name. As has been already said, and as may be learned from the Combined Narrative, Thomas was present when the two disciples returned from Emmaus ; but it is probable that he left the place immediately on hearing the account of the Resurrection of Christ, and therefore he was not present when soon afterwards Jesus came. He had disbelieved the statement of Mary Magdalen ; that of the other holy women ; that of St. Peter ; that of the two disciples from Emmaus ; and now he refused to credit the united testimony of all, that they had " seen the Lord." According to St. Augustine indeed, St. Thomas was merely seeking for further proof of the Resurrection ; and St. Ambrose thought that the doubt on the part of the apostle regarded only the attributes of our Lord's risen body. The words of Christ (verse 27), " Be not faithless, but believing," exclude any such explanation. He did not doubt the *veracity* of the other disciples, but he supposed that they, depending on the evidence of sight, were *deceived* by a spirit. He therefore declared that, before believing, he must have the evidence afforded to the others, and must also test this evidence of sight by that of touch. He presumed to lay down these conditions, and said, unless these be fulfilled, " I will not believe," or, as in the original Greek, " I will in no wise believe." We must admit the fact then that, although supplied with a sufficient proof, Thomas remained for eight days in determined and reprehensible unbelief. But " the Son of Man is come to seek and to save that which was lost " (Luke xix. 10) ; and at his last Supper our Lord had declared that of those given him by his Father, no one was to be finally lost but " the son of perdition." Taking pity, then, on an apostle whose incredulity arose not from malice, like the incredulity of the pharisees, but from human weakness, Christ condescended to assist that weakness ;

V. 26. And after eight days, again his disciples were within, and Thomas with them, Jesus cometh, the doors being shut, and stood in the midst, and said : Peace be to you.

This occurred on the Sunday following the day of the Resurrection, the evangelist including both extreme points of time according to the Jewish mode of reckoning. By his profession of faith, Thomas was to make reparation for his fault before all those whom he had disedified by his unbelief ; but, although probably the disciples were assembled each day in the interval, it was only after a week that the opportunity was given. Matters

were so ordained that in the meantime the influence of the other
disciples might predispose Thomas to make his submission ;
that men might have a great idea of the divine mercy which so
long bore with the unbelieving apostle ; and that the sudden and
complete admission of the truth after such an obstinate resistance, might be a strong confirmation of the truth itself.   At
length, in probably the same place and at the same hour of the
evening meal, the doors being shut (in the Greek, τῶν θυρῶν
κεκλεισμένων = " having been, and continuing to be, closed and
barred "), Christ miraculously passed into the room, and addressed to all the well-known salutation : " Peace be to you."

Christ's visit was paid to all, but had for its direct object the
conversion of one.

V. 27. Then he saith to Thomas: Put in thy finger hither, and see my hands; and bring hither thy hand, and put it into my side; and be not faithless, but believing.

Anticipating Thomas, and using the same form of words in
which the unbelieving apostle had laid down the conditions of
submission, Christ showed that the events of the past week were
known to him, and that he had been an invisible witness of
each thing said and done.   Thomas had demanded to see in the
Redeemer's hands the print of the nails, and to put his finger
into the place of the nails, and to put his hand into the sacred side.
To this the apostle is now invited, in order that, applying the
test he had himself selected, he might no longer remain " faithless, but [become] believing."   Though the matter is not certain,
still from the subsequent words of Christ to Thomas (verse 29),
it is probable that the apostle was satisfied with the sight and
voice of his Divine Master, and that out of reverence, he did
not dare to touch the sacred wounds.   In his grief, it is likely
that he had overrated the possibility of being convinced regarding the Resurrection ; but whether the one proof sufficed or both
were required, the conviction produced was instantaneous and
truly marvellous.

The evangelist records that

V. 28. Thomas answered, and said to him: My Lord and my God!

As Thomas had hitherto been the slowest of all to believe,
so did he now exceed all in the fullness of his profession of faith.
Although St. Peter (Matth. xvi. 16), in response to the question
of Christ, had answered and said : " Thou art Christ, the Son
of the living God," we have here a fuller and more explicit declaration of the doctrine of the Incarnation.

According to Theophylactus the penitent apostle proclaimed
that in the Being before him, there were two natures united in
the one person.   By the designation " My Lord," he indicated

the human nature of him whom he had hitherto followed as his Master, and whose sacred body he had just been invited to see and to touch ; by the words " My God " he confessed the divine nature of him whose uncreated wisdom in discerning the hidden thoughts of man, and whose miraculous power in rising from the dead, had just been so conclusively proved ; by addressing both these statements to one and the same Christ, he professed his belief in the hypostatic union of these two natures in the one person of the God made Man. That we have here a clear testimony to the divinity of Christ, is denied by those only who deny the doctrine itself. It is in vain, however, to seek to evade the force of this testimony by supposing that the expression ὁ θεός μου = " My God," may be taken in a *figurative* or *lower* sense ; for, as St. Cyril of Alexandria remarks, the use of the prefixed article in the Greek excludes all but the *proper* and *highest* signification of the word θεός = " God." Still more untenable is the opinion of the Socinians, who teach that the expression used by Thomas is equivalent to the exclamation, " O Lord God, what is it I see ! " and that this exclamation is addressed not to Christ, but to God the Father. Such an interpretation was proposed by Theodore of Mopsuestia, the teacher of Nestorius, and was condemned at Constantinople in the 12th canon of the Fifth General Council, A.D. 553. That it was justly condemned is clear, 1°, from the fact that an exclamation of this nature, though usual among the heathens, was unknown to the Jews, whose reverence for the name of the Deity was extreme ; 2°, from this statement of St. John : " Thomas . . . said to him " (Christ), for if the words of Thomas were a mere cry of surprise addressed to God the Father, this statement of the evangelist would be untrue ; 3°, from the usage of expressing the vocative by the nominative with the article as here ; 4°, from the design of the writer, manifested in verse 31, viz., to prove the divinity of Christ, because, with such a design in view throughout his gospel, St. John would not have recorded a mere exclamation so very much beside his purpose, and therefore so very much out of place ; 5°, from the approval given by Christ to these words as a *profession of faith*, because a mere expression of wonder could not be regarded as such a profession. With Patrizi, then, we should reject this interpretation of the Socinians as one meriting our laughter rather than calling for a refutation ; and we find in the testimony of St. Thomas the most explicit confession of faith in the divinity of Christ, which had yet been made.

Not only is the testimony unmistakably clear : the authority which stamped that testimony as true is irrefragable. By *not refusing* the name of God now first applied to him by the apostle, our Lord *virtually takes it to himself* as thinking it (to use the words of the Apostle) " not robbery to be equal with

God." (See Bloomfield, *in loco*.) This gospel begins and ends with a declaration of the divinity of Christ. Thus, in the first verse, we read : " In the beginning was the Word, and the Word was with God, and the Word was God. . . . And the Word was made flesh, and dwelt amongst us. And we saw his glory." Throughout the gospel we have a record of instances in which that glory of the Incarnate Word was manifested. Now, as it were concluding his work, the evangelist says that an apostle who was at first determined not to believe, was at length over-come by one of these manifestations ; made his submission ; and exclaimed with all the energy of his soul, " My Lord and my God ! "

Thomas's profession of faith was received and approved ; but the delay in making this profession called for a gentle reproach. Therefore

V. 29. **Jesus saith to him : Because thou hast seen me, Thomas, thou hast believed. Blessed are they that have not seen, and have believed.**

According to St. Paul (Hebr. xi. 1), " Faith is the substance of things to be hoped for, the evidence of things that appear not." Although this is so, it is certain that Thomas made a true and supernatural act of faith on this occasion ; for Christ said to him : " Thou hast believed." That indeed which the apostle saw was different from that in which he professed his faith. He saw the wounds of the risen body of his Master ; he believed in the divinity of his risen Saviour. The conviction that Christ had returned to life came from reason : the assent to this truth as revealed by God came from the gift of divine faith. To be convinced of the truth it is useful, nay even, in the case of adults who have not yet received the habit of faith, it is generally necessary to examine *the motives of credibility*, that is, the grounds on which the matter to be believed commends itself to our acceptance (see Perrone : *De Subjecto Baptismi*, Vol. iii., p. 39, note) ; but to withhold assent when these motives are already sufficient in themselves and sufficiently examined, implies a want of correspondence with divine grace. This was the defect of the " ruler " to whom Christ said reproachfully : " Unless you see signs and wonders, you believe not " (John iv. 48). Such was the fault of Thomas whose act of faith was a true one, but whose mode of arriving at faith was imperfect. The apostle had heard sufficient arguments to prove the reality of the Resur-rection ; but through obstinacy of will and a spirit of curiosity, he presumptuously demanded further and stronger evidence. Hence, notwithstanding the more explicit nature of his con-fession, he did not receive the praise given to St. Peter on a former occasion (Matth. xvi. 17) : " Blessed art thou, Simon Bar-Jona ; because flesh and blood hath not revealed it to thee, but my Father who is in heaven."

Nor was St. Thomas the only one reproved for the tardiness of an act of faith. The angel had been commissioned to announce the Resurrection to the holy women, and they to all the apostles ; but " these words seemed to them (the apostles) as idle tales ; and they did not believe them " (Luke xxiv. 11). Like Thomas, they admitted the truth only " when they saw the Lord " (John xx. 20). On the day of the Ascension, therefore, that Lord appearing to *all* the eleven as they were at table, " upbraided them with their incredulity and hardness of heart, because they did not believe them that had seen him after he was risen again " (Mark xvi. 14). Christ, then, did not regard as worthless the faith of Thomas and of the rest who, on seeing, believed ; but, using a Hebrew idiom, he declares that *blessed in comparison with them*, or *more blessed than they*, are all who " have not seen, and have believed." It might be objected that Christ himself (Matth. xiii. 16, 17 ; Luke x. 23, 24) pronounced the apostles, who had seen and heard him, more blessed thereby than the prophets, kings, and just men who had lived before his time. To this objection Jansenius Gand. (*in loco*) answers that, in some respects the apostles were more blessed than these others : in some respects these others were more blessed than the apostles. Because to see and to hear Christ during his life on earth was a great gift, the apostles to whom that gift was given, were in this point of view more blessed than all to whom it was denied. Those, however, who did not see Christ in this life and still believed in him, were more blessed than the apostles in their act of faith, which in such circumstances, was more difficult and more meritorious before God. Of such blessedness, arising as it did from a more meritorious faith, Christ spoke in his address to Thomas. Of more merit than he and more blessed than he were the disciples who believed in the Resurrection before they saw the risen Saviour, and who said to the travellers from Emmaus : " The Lord is risen indeed, and *hath appeared to Simon* " (Luke xxiv. 34). Such, too, is the condition of ourselves who live after Christ ; such finally was the lot and the graces of the patriarchs, prophets and just men of the Old Testament, regarding whom St. Paul writes : " All these died according to faith, not having received the promises, but beholding them afar off, and saluting them, and confessing that they are pilgrims and strangers on the earth . . . of whom the world was not worthy " (Hebrews xi. 13 and 38).

Having narrated in this chapter some of the apparitions by which Christ proved his Resurrection and manifested to his followers the glory of his risen humanity, the evangelist remarks that

V. 30. **Many other signs also did Jesus in the sight of his disciples which are not written in this book.**

Knowing the additional matter contained in the other gospels and providing against any doubt as to the truthfulness of these other records, St. John concluded his account by stating that, besides what are here mentioned, Christ worked "many other signs," or, as in the Greek text, "many *and* other signs" or miracles. Some have thought with St. Chrysostom, Maldonatus, and Toletus, that the evangelist speaks of the miracles subsequent to the Resurrection, and of these only. More generally and with more probability he is understood to refer to all the miracles of Christ's previous life on earth. St. John, then, in this epilogue to the gospel is glancing back at the proposition laid down in the beginning (John i. 14): "We saw his glory, the glory as it were of the Only-begotten of the Father." Throughout his work the evangelist aims at the proof of this proposition; and now he briefly refers to the miraculous works of Christ which had been, or which might have been, recorded by others, and which, if recorded, would have served as a part of his own demonstration of Christ's divinity.

Having stated, then, that besides these miracles which he was inspired to enumerate, those not enumerated by him were "many and other," *i.e.*, many in number and different in kind (πολλὰ . . . καὶ ἄλλα), St. John declares that it is not necessary for the purpose in hand to specify any more;

V. 31. But these are written that you may believe that Jesus is the Christ, the Son of God, and that believing, you may have life in his name.

We have here the purpose for which *any* miracles were recorded, and the end for which the gospel was written. It was not intended as a biography of our Lord, but as a proof that in Christ were fulfilled the legitimate expectations of both Jews and Gentiles. Written for the mixed communities of Asia Minor, the gospel of St. John showed that in Jesus the Jews had their Messiah or "the Christ" foretold by the prophets, and the Gentiles that Divine Saviour, "the Son of God," who was spoken of by their poets, and who alone through "his name" and merits could raise them up from their moral degradation to the possession of eternal "life." How truly did St. Paul say (1 Cor. i. 22-24): "Both the Jews require signs, and the Greeks seek after wisdom; but we preach Christ crucified, unto the Jews indeed, a stumbling-block, and unto the Gentiles, foolishness, but unto them that are called, both Jews and Greeks, Christ, the power of God and the wisdom of God."

V.—MORAL REFLECTIONS.

1. It is remarked that the first salutation addressed by the risen Saviour to his apostles was a prayer for their peace, and

that this salutation was repeated more than once during the interview. It was not without motive that Christ acted thus; and the motive was to direct their attention and ours to the importance of this heavenly gift. In the world peace is often on the lips of men; it is ever desired; but it is seldom found. Nations are continually at war; societies are ceaselessly disturbed; and the hearts of men are violently agitated. The explanation of this is given to us by the Holy Ghost when he says: " The work of justice shall be peace " (Isaias xxxii. 17); and again : " The fruit of justice is sown in peace " (James iii. 18). Virtue alone can produce peace, which, in its turn, maintains virtue ; whilst vice foments divisions, which are a fruitful source of crime. God wills that we owe to religion not only that everlasting rest in heaven to which we aspire, but also the measure of rest we may enjoy in this life : he wishes that here below the just shall find in their interior calm a foretaste of that which awaits them in eternity.

2. The peace which Christ wished for his apostles and for us, is threefold—peace with God, peace with our neighbour, and peace with ourselves. Of these the first is the most important, and the source of the two others. Into what a dreadful war does sin plunge us, and what a fearful enemy it arouses against us ! This enemy is an angry God who pursues his disobedient creatures with his vengeance, and prepares for them an unending punishment. On the contrary, the virtuous man has in God a friend—the most tender, faithful, and generous of all. " You are my friends," says Jesus Christ, " if you do the things that I command you. I will not now call you servants ; for the servant knoweth not what his lord doth. But I have called you friends ; because all things whatsoever I have heard from my Father I have made known to you " (John xv. 14, 15). Who or what can interrupt this union with God ? In it the soul has but one will with its Creator ; from his hand it receives prosperity with gratitude, and adversity with patience ; it honours him with its goods, and parts from them for him without murmur ; it attributes to him all its glory, and endures humiliation for his sake. In the midst of joy it finds its delight in him ; and under the weight of sorrow it is consoled with the thought of resembling him so closely. The friendship of God and the peace that springs from this friendship are the most precious of all possessions. All others must pass away, whilst these will remain. These will survive our present state ; and after having given on earth a support, a consolation, and a pleasure, they will become in heaven our eternal recompense.

3. The blessing of Jesus Christ includes the gift of peace with our neighbour. " Whence are wars and contentions among you ? Are they not hence, from your concupiscences, which war in your members ? You covet, and have not ; you kill and

envy, and cannot obtain " (James iv. 1, 2). The source of
division is to be found in sin, and in the pursuit of what may
minister to the indulgence of sinful passions. The goods of this
world are too limited to be owned by all ; and still, most men
desire them, dispute the possession of them, and often unjustly
seize upon them. On the other hand, what can interrupt the
peace with his brethren in which the true Christian lives ? He
does not ambition anything for himself which he does not desire
for them ; he gives much, but exacts nothing ; he does not malign
others, nor is he embittered when undeservedly attacked ; and
whilst he is unjust to none, he pardons the unjust acts of all.
In such a soul there is no room for discord. Happy, therefore,
were the early days of Christianity when men gave such a spectacle as this to the world, and when, according to St. Luke,
" the multitude of believers had but one heart and one soul "
(Acts iv. 32).

4. The last effect of Christ's blessing is that of peace with
ourselves ; and this consists in the two-fold subjection of our
passion to reason, and of reason to God's law. Can peace
exist in a soul which is carried away by anger, or tormented
by avarice, or puffed up with pride, or agitated by evil desires ?
It is written : " The wicked are like the raging sea, which cannot
rest, and the waves thereof cast up dirt and mire. There is no
peace to the wicked " (Isaias lvii. 20, 21). Nor are the passions
ever quieted by indulgence : it is folly to think that any one of
them on being gratified, will say : " It is enough." Reason has
not sufficient strength to control them when they are once let
loose ; and therefore peace of the soul can be secured only on
the condition of self-denial from the beginning. Where can we
find arms against enemies which, whilst fighting against us,
minister to our corrupt inclinations, and which attack us at once
by their open violence and by their treacherous seductions ?
Religion alone can afford us help, when by her precepts she
points out the manner in which the passions are to be subdued,
and by her graces puts in our hands the means of securing that
victory. If by the use of grace, our reason be subjected to the
divine law, it will hold our passions in subjection. If we constantly do the will of God our passions will do ours, and in
serving our Supreme Master, we shall become masters of ourselves. Thus shall we secure that peace with ourselves which,
on the day of his Resurrection, Christ wished to the apostles
and to us.

SECOND SUNDAY AFTER EASTER.

I.—TEXTS.

GREEK.

JOHN X. 11-16.

¹¹ Ἐγώ εἰμι ὁ ποιμὴν ὁ καλός· ὁ ποιμὴν ὁ καλὸς τὴν ψυχὴν αὐτοῦ τίθησιν ὑπὲρ τῶν προβάτων. ¹² Ὁ μισθωτὸς καὶ οὐκ ὢν ποιμήν, οὗ οὐκ ἔστιν τὰ πρόβατα ἴδια, θεωρεῖ τὸν λύκον ἐρχόμενον, καὶ ἀφίησι τὰ πρόβατα, καὶ φεύγει· καὶ ὁ λύκος ἁρπάζει αὐτά, καὶ σκορπίζει. ¹³ †Ὁ δὲ μισθωτὸς φεύγει,† ὅτι μισθωτός ἐστιν, καὶ οὐ μέλει αὐτῷ περὶ τῶν προβάτων. ¹⁴ Ἐγώ εἰμι ὁ ποιμὴν ὁ καλός, καὶ γινώσκω τὰ ἐμά, καὶ γινώσκουσί με τὰ ἐμά. ¹⁵ Καθὼς γινώσκει με ὁ πατήρ, κἀγὼ γινώσκω τὸν πατέρα· καὶ τὴν ψυχήν μου τίθημι ὑπὲρ τῶν προβάτων. ¹⁶ Καὶ ἄλλα πρόβατα ἔχω ἃ οὐκ ἔστιν ἐκ τῆς αὐλῆς ταύτης· κἀκεῖνα δεῖ με ἀγαγεῖν, καὶ τῆς φωνῆς μου ἀκούσουσιν, καὶ γενήσονται μία ποίμνη, εἷς ποιμήν.

VULGATE.

JOHN X. 11-16.

¹¹ Ego sum pastor bonus. Bonus pastor animam suam dat pro ovibus suis ; ¹² mercenarius autem, et qui non est pastor, cujus non sunt oves propriæ, videt lupum venientem, et dimittit oves, et fugit ; et lupus rapit, et dispergit oves. ¹³ Mercenarius autem fugit, quia mercenarius est, et non pertinet ad eum de ovibus. ¹⁴ Ego sum pastor bonus ; et cognosco meas, et cognoscunt me meæ. ¹⁵ Sicut novit me Pater, et ego agnosco Patrem; et animam meam pono pro ovibus meis. ¹⁶ Et alias oves habeo quæ non sunt ex hoc ovili : et illas oportet me adducere, et vocem meam audient, et fiet unum ovile et unus pastor.

II.—ENGLISH TRANSLATION.

JOHN X. 11-16.

¹¹ " I am the good shepherd. The good shepherd giveth his life for his sheep ; ¹² but the hireling, and he that is not the shepherd, whose own the sheep are not, seeth the wolf coming, and leaveth the sheep, and fleeth ; and the wolf catcheth, and scattereth the sheep. ¹³ And the hireling fleeth, because he is a hireling, and he hath no care for the sheep. ¹⁴ I am the good shepherd ; and I know mine, and mine know me. ¹⁵ As the Father knoweth me, and I know the Father ; and I lay down

my life for my sheep. [16] And other sheep I have, that are not of this fold : them also I must bring, and they shall hear my voice, and there shall be made one fold and one shepherd."

III. —NOTES.

Introductory. During the third and last year of his public life, our Lord had preached in Galilee from the Pasch in April until the Feast of Tabernacles in October. He then attended this latter feast in Jerusalem, and on the following sabbath restored sight to a man born blind. Although the reality of the miracle could not be denied, the pharisees refused to credit it ; and in their rage excommunicated the poor sufferer, who had just been the recipient of the divine bounty. This man, afterwards meeting Jesus, declared him to be the Son of God, and falling down, adored him. Reflecting, then, on the readiness with which the poor received the light of faith, whilst the scribes and pharisees, leaders of the people hardened their own hearts against grace, and endeavoured to seduce his disciples from him, Christ put before his hearers a clear exposition of his relation to mankind. In the first verses of the present chapter, he drew a sharp distinction between the lawful pastors, who gain admittance to the sheep through him the gate of the sheepfold, and those who, unlawfully assuming or exercising the pastoral office, climb up another way to steal by cunning deceit or to carry off and destroy by open violence.

Having thus pointed out the distinction between himself the shepherd, and the thief or robber, he, in the present passage, distinguishes between the true shepherd and the hireling. He says :

V. 11. I am the good shepherd. The good shepherd giveth his life for his sheep.

It is to be remarked in the first place, that the Greek adjective καλός by which Christ describes himself, has no exact equivalent in our language. It signifies *beautiful, noble, eminently good ;* and it includes in itself at once all the elements of ideal perfection. Again it is to be observed that the expression τὴν ψυχὴν τιθέναι is the same as the Hebrew נפש שׂוּם, שׂוּם נפש, which means not only to *hazard one's life,* but literally *to expend one's life lavishly* and without stint, or *to pay down one's life as a price.* (See Bloomfield, *in loco.*) To say that a shepherd would lay down his life to save his flock, or would even risk his life in the pursuit of his calling, may appear extravagant to persons in these countries ; but it was not so where our Lord was speaking. David thus describes to Saul the risk he ran when in charge of his father's flock : " Thy servant kept his father's sheep ; and there came a lion or a bear, and took a ram out of the midst of the flock. And I followed after them, and struck them, and delivered it out of their mouth ; and they rose up against me ; and I caught them by the throat ; and I strangled and killed them " (1 Kings xvii. 34, 35). Christ says, then, that it is the characteristic of the true shepherd who really owns the sheep, to risk his life, or even to sacrifice his life, if necessary for the safety of his flock. At the same time, saying that he himself is the good shepherd by excellence, he here implies what he afterwards explicitly states, that he will not only run that risk, but that he will actually make this sacrifice. In the Psalms, the people of God were frequently called the flock of the Lord (Jehovah). " He is the Lord our God ; and we are the people of his pasture, and the sheep of his hand " (Ps. xciv. 7 and xcix. 3). At the same time, it had been foretold that the Messiah was to be sent as the supreme shepherd of this flock. " I will set up one shepherd over them ; and he shall feed them, even my servant David. He shall feed them, and he shall be their shepherd " (Ezech. xxxiv. 23). Because, then, Christ here calls himself emphatically *the* " Good Shepherd," it follows that he claims to be the Messiah ; and because he speaks of the flock as his own, it follows that he attributes to himself the divine nature of Jehovah. The words of the text are, in a certain sense and in a certain measure, applicable to every pastor charged with the care of souls ; but literally and in their fullness, they refer to Christ alone. Others risk or sacrifice their lives to *defend* the flock, which *belongs to another*, their master. Christ laid down his life *as a price to redeem* a flock which *is his own*.

To give a higher idea of his pastoral care for his flock, our Lord now contrasts with that care the conduct of a hireling. He says :—

Vv. 12, 13. **But the hireling, and he that is not the shepherd, whose own the sheep are not, seeth the wolf coming, and leaveth the sheep, and fleeth ; and the wolf catcheth, and scattereth the sheep. And the hireling fleeth, because he is a hireling, and he hath no care for the sheep.**

Except in Mark i. 20, with reference to the hired men of Zebedee, and in the present passage, the Greek word μισθωτὸs = *a hireling*, occurs nowhere else in the New Testament. Generally it signifies one who, for fixed wages, agrees to do work for another ; but here it means one who, in engaging to serve another, has no higher object at heart than his own benefit and the remuneration promised. The service of Jacob to Laban was hired, but it was accompanied by a care, and love, and self-sacrifice, which could not be purchased (Gen. xxxi. 36-41). Very different are the feelings of him who is *merely* a hireling. In the fact that he does not own the sheep, he seeks to justify his unconcern both for them and for their master. Hence in quiet times he does what is exacted, that he may secure his reward ; but in the presence of danger, or even at the supposed approach of danger, he provides for his own safety in flight. He differs, indeed, from the thief and from the robber already referred to (John x. 1, 8, 10). These have no authority over the fold, and enter therein for the express purpose of destroying the flock ; whilst the hireling is invested with authority, but in times of difficulty deserts his post and proves false to his engagements. In this latter case, the loss is not less than in the former ; for, on the flight of the hireling, " the wolf catcheth, and scattereth," that is, he seizes on some of the sheep, and disperses far and wide such others as for the moment may have escaped his jaws.

In this figurative language, Christ gave a striking picture of the scribes (Introduction, p. cxxviii.) and pharisees (Introduction, p. clxxiii), who being slaves of avarice, vain glory, and love of ease, had no love for the people of the Lord whom they were commissioned to teach and to reform. Hence it is written of our Lord that at an early stage of his ministry, " seeing the multitudes, he had compassion on them, because they were distressed, and lying like sheep that have no shepherd " (Matth. ix. 36). To such pastors as the scribes and pharisees the Lord addressed these words of Ezechiel : " Wo to the shepherds of Israel, that fed themselves. Should not the flocks be fed by the shepherds ? You ate the milk, and you clothed yourselves with the wool, and you killed that which was fat ; but my flock you did not feed, . . . and my sheep were scattered because there was no shepherd " (Ezech. xxxiv. 2, 3, 5).

Though the scribes and pharisees were indeed the direct object of our Lord's denunciation, his words are applicable to those who, in the Christian Church, abandon a post or neglect a duty in which sacrifice of ease, danger to health, or loss of life is the price to be paid for the salvation of souls. Of such, even in apostolic times, St. Paul complained when, singling out Timothy for a mission to the Philippians, he wrote : " I have no man so of the same mind, who with sincere affection, is solicitous for you ; for all seek the things that are their own, not the things that are Jesus Christ's " (Phil. ii. 20, 21). Under such pastors in times of difficulty or danger, the sheep, that is, the members of the Church, do not meet with a better fate than that which threatens when the fold is stealthily entered by the thief, or violently broken into by the robber. Christ says that when the hireling betrays his trust by flight or by a timorous silence, the wolf " catcheth and scattereth," or, in other words, seizes on some of the sheep and disperses the rest. " The wolf " represents all such as in matters of faith or morals, attack the precious and life-giving treasure of divine teaching. These

are persecutors of the faithful, scandalous livers, disseminators
of heresy—all instruments or ministers of the devil, who " was
a murderer from the beginning " (John viii. 44), and who, " as
a roaring lion, goeth about, seeking whom he may devour "
(1 Peter v. 8). Against this adversary and against his instruments there is little help to be expected from the hireling, who
" fleeth because he is a hireling, and he hath no care for the
sheep." To inspire *true* pastors, then, with the spirit of their
vocation, and to encourage them in their work, St. Peter has
written : " Feed the flock of God which is among you, taking
care of it not by constraint, but willingly, according to God ;
not for filthy lucre's sake, but voluntarily. . . . And when the
Prince of Pastors shall appear, you shall receive a never-fading
crown of glory " (1 Peter v. 2-4).

The Prince of Pastors himself describes in the following words
his relation with his flock :—

**Vv. 14, 15. I am the good shepherd; and I know mine,
and mine know me.   As the Father knoweth me, and I know
the Father ; and I lay down my life for my sheep.**

It is to be observed that in the Vulgate and in the English
Translation, the separation of these two verses obscures the
sense. The last clause of verse 14 and the first of verse 15
are the two terms of a comparison which might be thus expressed : " In the same manner I know my sheep and my sheep
know me, even as the Father knoweth me and I know the
Father." Again it is noticed that the use of the word " know "
is here a Hebrew idiom. The reference is to a knowledge which
has its source in love, and is accompanied by an exercise of
love. In this sense the expression occurs in Psalm i. 5 and 6 :
" The wicked shall not rise again in judgment ; nor sinners in
the counsel of the just. For the Lord *knoweth* the way of the
just ; and the way of the wicked shall perish." The absence
of reciprocal knowledge and love is thus described in Isaias
i. 3 : " The ox knoweth its owner, and the ass his master's
crib ; but Israel hath not known me, and my people hath not
understood." The sense being thus made clear, it is to be
remarked that in a former portion of this chapter, Christ had
laid down the contrast between the *thief* or *robber* on the one
hand, whose voice as that of a stranger, the flock knew not, and
on the other the *shepherd* whom the sheep recognise. Afterwards our Lord distinguished between a *hireling shepherd* who
flees in the presence of difficulty or danger, and a *good shepherd*
who risks and even sacrifices his life for his sheep. In the present
verse Christ declares himself to be a good shepherd, nay more,
the good shepherd by excellence, and proves this assertion by
applying to himself the tests he had already referred to. He

shows in the first place, that he is the shepherd by the existence of a mutual knowledge between himself and his sheep—a knowledge which he compares with the mutual knowledge between himself and the Eternal Father. Here, on the one hand, we are not to understand that there is an equality, but only a partial likeness, between the things compared ; because it is impossible for us to know Christ in the infinite degree in which he knows the Eternal Father. Between the Father and the Son there is a communication of the same divine nature ; so that Christ could say : " I and the Father are one " (John x. 30). Hence springs the mutual union, knowledge, and love of these two Divine Persons. On the other hand, by sanctifying grace, the soul of the faithful Christian is ingrafted on Christ. Christ, indeed, lives in the Christian soul, and the Christian soul in Christ ; so that St. Paul could say : " With Christ I am nailed to the cross ; and I live, now not I, but Christ liveth in me." (Gal. ii. 19, 20). Hence springs the reciprocal knowledge of the Divine Shepherd and his flock. What is the character of this knowledge in each case, between the Father and the Son on the one hand, and the Divine Shepherd and his flock on the other ? It is a knowledge which has its source in love, and is accompanied by the exercise of love. The Father knows the Son as God, because, in contemplating himself, he communicated to that Son the divine substance and life ; he knows Christ as Man, because he bestowed on the sacred humanity its unspeakable gifts and perfections. Christ, as God, recognises what was communicated to him by the Father, and loves that Father with an infinite love : Christ, as Man, knows and loves the Father by fulfilling the divine will in all things, and by manifesting the divine perfections to the world. This reciprocal knowledge and love between the Father and the Son is, then, the type of the mutual knowledge and love between Christ as the Divine Shepherd and his flock. He knows his sheep, not merely with that knowledge by which " all things are naked and open to his eyes," but with that knowledge which, joined with, or including love, pours out on the beloved object all the gifts of nature and of grace. In return for this, the faithful sheep know and acknowledge him to be the true Shepherd from whom they have received all things ; and they are filled with love for him through whose ministry there is opened for them the way to eternal life. (See Knabenbauer, who quotes Cajetan and Toletus.)

Having thus shown that he is the *shepherd* as contrasted with the *stranger* who came to steal or rob, he now proves that he is the *good shepherd* as distinguished from the *hireling*, who deserted the sheep. The mark of every good shepherd is at least to *give* his life for his sheep. Christ had already stated this in verse 11. He says now that he does more. " I *lay down* my life for my sheep." As has been already remarked in the explanation of verse 11, the Greek expression τὴν ψυχήν μου τίθημι recorded by the evangelist signifies more than is implied in risking, or even in giving one's life for another. Considered in itself, and apart from the context, the clause includes the idea of perfect dominion over the life which is freely paid down as a price for another's sake, and to secure that other's safety. That this meaning is here intended is put beyond all doubt by the context in verses 17 and 18, where Christ says : " Therefore doth the Father love me, because I lay down my life that I may take it again. No man taketh it away from me ; but I lay it down of myself ; and I have power to lay it down, and I have power to take it up again." Other pastors may even voluntarily suffer death for their flocks, and may even offer themselves to the persecutors ; but to no one, except to Christ, are these words applicable in their full extent. He alone had perfect dominion over his life ; and he alone could by his death purchase eternal life for those for whom he died. Of him alone could it be written by the prophet : " By his knowledge shall this my just servant justify many ; and he shall bear their iniquities. Therefore will I distribute to him very many ; and he shall divide the spoils of the strong, because he hath delivered his soul unto death, and was reputed with the wicked, and he hath borne the sins of many, and hath prayed for the transgressors " (Isaias liii. 11, 12).

Such is the shepherd as contrasted with the thief and the robber ; such is the good shepherd as compared with the hireling ; such is Christ, the good shepherd by excellence as distinguished from the delegated shepherds who faithfully carry on his work. But what is the extent of the fold, over which Christ is to exercise his pastoral care ? Our Divine Lord thus answers our question in the concluding words of the gospel passage :—

V. 16. And other sheep I have that are not of this fold : those also I must bring, and they shall hear my voice, and there shall be made one fold [more exactly, *one flock*] **and one shepherd.**

There are few Gospel passages that have of late so much attracted the attention of non-Catholic interpreters as has the one just now under review. This special interest is aroused at the supposed change of meaning produced through the rendering of ποίμνη by " ovile " or " fold," as if it were the same as αὐλή which occurs in the first part of the verse. It is asserted that in this way the translation of the passage has been falsified, and that the falsified translation has brought about the most baneful effects on popular ecclesiastical ideas. A dispassionate examination of the matter will lead us to the conclusion that these statements are without foundation.

It must be admitted, and it is admitted, that the more exact and literal rendering of ποίμνη is " flock," but it does not follow that the rendering " fold " is inexact or false. As in the use of the word " grex " or " flock," if it had been used, we should have an instance of the figure of speech called metaphor, so, in the use of the word " ovile " or " fold," the translators employed the figure metonymy, whereby the container is taken to signify that which is contained. By this the sense was by no means lost nor even obscured. Indeed, inasmuch as this Scriptural passage, taken with others of a kindred nature, represents the future disciples not as individuals acting apart and independently of each other, but rather as members of a body brought together, bound together, and fenced around, in the profession of the same faith, in the reception of the same sacraments, and in obedience to the same divine authority, inasmuch as this is so, Christ's saving work here predicted (" those also I must bring," etc.) will be described with equal clearness whether in the original text we read of the " flock," which is called together in unity, or in the version we have mention of the " fold " wherein that flock and this unity are to be preserved.

With such considerations in mind we shall be in a position to estimate at their true value the statements of those who say that the substitution of " fold " for " flock " in the translation of ποίμνη is an error that " has done grievous injury " (Pulpit Comm.), or that it is " all loss ; and leading to calamitous misunderstanding " (Cambridge Bible for Schools and Cambridge Gr. Testament), or that it is " disastrous in idea and in influence " (Westcott). If, indeed, so far as the sense is concerned, it were not a matter of indifference, it would be difficult to understand how, from the fourth century till the publication of the Revised Version in our own times, the rendering " ovile " or " fold " was received by all, Catholics and non-Catholics if we except Tyndale, Luther, and Coverdale. But such appears to have been the case, for we learn that the translation in question was sometimes followed by St. Augustine (Cambridge Gr. Testament) ; that it was introduced into the Vulgate by St. Jerome, and through the Vulgate into Wyclif's and other European versions (Pulpit Comm.) ; that it became practically universal among Latin mediæval writers, and was left unchanged by Erasmus and Beza until 1582 (Westcott, *Add. Note*) ; in fine, that it was found in the Great Bible of 1539 as well as in the Authorised version of 1611 (Cambridge Gr. Testament).

Having examined the validity of the statement that the

ordinary rendering of the present passage is erroneous or misleading, we may now ask the purpose which Christ had in view when adding these words to what he had already said.

These words were added by Christ, lest it should be thought that what he had said regarding his sheep, referred to those only who then heard his words and became his disciples. It had been foretold by the prophets, especially by the Psalmist and by Isaias, that the Gentiles were to be admitted to the kingdom of the Messiah. These Gentiles are the sheep now alluded to by our Lord. Although not yet admitted to the fold, they are called his " sheep," because they were predestined to this grace in the eternal designs of God with whom there is no succession of time, and before whom the past and the future are one unchanging present. " He chose us in 'him," says the Apostle, " before the foundation of the world, that we should be holy and unspotted in his sight in charity, who hath predestined us unto the adoption of children through Jesus Christ, unto himself " (Ephes. i. 4, 5). Hitherto, the Gentiles had wandered abroad without a shepherd ; but, as Caiphas prophesied, " Jesus should die for the nation, and not only for the nation, but to gather together in one the children of God that were dispersed " (John xi. 51, 52). By the command of his Eternal Father, Jesus as the Messiah must perform this work. In the preaching of the apostles from without, and in the movements of grace from within, men were, and are, to hear the voice of their Saviour ; and so, from Jews and Gentiles there shall be formed " one flock " under the care of one shepherd. Thus were to be fulfilled the words of the prophet addressed to the Messiah : " It is a small thing that thou shouldst be my servant to raise up the tribes of Jacob and to convert the dregs of Israel. Behold, I have given thee to be the light of the Gentiles, that thou mayest be my salvation even to the farthest part of the earth " (Isaias xlix. 6).

IV.—MORAL REFLECTIONS.

1. How fully did Jesus merit our love by becoming the Shepherd of our souls, and by realising in himself all that is indicated by that tender name ! Not content with giving his life to save us from death, he merited and bestowed on us all the helps necessary to preserve us in spiritual vigour. As the shepherd leads his sheep to good pastures which nourish them, Jesus Christ instructs us by his doctrine, sanctifies us by his sacraments, strengthens us by his grace, removes from our path obstacles to our eternal salvation, defends us against the devil by the power of his cross, and supports us in affliction by his sweet consolations. Well, then, may we say with the Psalmist :

"The Lord ruleth me, and I shall want nothing. He hath set me in a place of pasture ; he hath brought me up on the water of refreshment ; he hath converted my soul ; he hath led me on the paths of justice for his own name's sake ; for though I should walk in the midst of the shadow of death, I will fear no evils, since thou art with me " (Psalm xxii. 1-4). Nor does his care end here. When he has watched over us during our journey through life, and has fortified us in our last moments, he crowns his other gifts by introducing us to the joys of heaven. "Thy mercy," says the Psalmist, "will follow me all the days of my life, and that I may dwell in the house of the Lord unto length of days " (Psalm xxii. 6).

2. The love of the Good Shepherd demands a return from his faithful sheep ; and the character of this return is indicated by himself in the present gospel passage. In the first place, we should strive to know him ; for he says : " I know mine, and mine know me " (verse 14). In this knowledge consists eternal life, as he assures us when saying : " This is eternal life, that they may know thee the only true God, and Jesus Christ whom thou hast sent " (John xvii. 3). Without the knowledge of God and of Christ no other knowledge can avail for salvation. Of what use to the philosophers of antiquity or to the sages of other times are the discoveries they have made, and the science they have acquired, when they did not know Jesus Christ ? All their light is darkness ; all their science is no better than vanity and error. The author of the *Imitation* has well said : " All men desire to know ; but what doth knowledge avail without the fear of God ? Indeed a humble husbandman who serveth God, is better than a proud philosopher who, neglecting himself, considereth the course of the heavens " (B. i., c. 2). Before all things else we should apply ourselves to the knowledge of Christ the Good Shepherd, and of his gospel, after the example of the great Apostle who said : " I judged not myself to know anything among you, but Jesus Christ, and him crucified " (1 Cor. ii. 2). It is not, however, a mere speculative or barren knowledge that is expected of us by Jesus Christ ; for it is written : " The devils also believe and tremble " (James ii. 19). As the " Good Shepherd " knows his sheep with that practical knowledge which promotes their welfare, so our knowledge of him, to be of any value, should be accompanied by that love which seeks in all things to promote his glory. Having once known him and his claims upon us, we should prove our love by submitting our will to the performance of his law, and by renouncing every attachment that might withdraw us from his service. Such was the effect of the knowledge and love of Christ on the Apostle when he wrote : " Who then shall separate us from the love of Christ ? . . . I am sure that neither death, nor life, . . . nor any other creature shall be able to

separate us from the love of God which is in Christ Jesus, our Lord " (Rom. viii. 35, 38, 39).

3. If we have these dispositions, we shall be docile to the Divine Shepherd, who points out the second characteristic of his sheep in the words : " They shall hear my voice " (John x. 16). Jesus Christ speaks to us in different ways. Sometimes it is in interior graces by which he calls us to his service ; sometimes, in the voice of our pastors, who are his ministers ; now in good books which he puts into our hands ; then in the good example which he puts before our eyes ; at one period of our life in the happiness which he sends as an answer to our prayers ; at another in the afflictions which he uses to wean us from the world. Have we not often closed our ears to this loving voice ? And still, if we continue to resist its calls, what will be our lot ? Let us, then, give ourselves up with docility to this Good Shepherd who has deigned to follow us when, like the lost sheep, we were wandering from him in tepidity or in sin. Let us listen to the invitation he continues to address to us : " Come to me all you that labour and are burdened, and I will refresh you. Take up my yoke upon you, . . . and you shall find rest to your souls ; for my yoke is sweet and my burden light " (Matth. xi. 28-30).

4. Besides knowing the Good Shepherd with love and hearing his voice with docility, we should follow in his steps by an imitation of his life. " He that entereth in by the door, is the shepherd of the sheep. . . . When he hath led out his own sheep, he goeth before them ; and the sheep follow him " (John x. 2-4). Since the sheep that wanders away from the shepherd is exposed to a thousand dangers, if we wish to be secure we shall not quit the presence of Jesus Christ, but shall keep close to him and walk constantly in his footsteps. He is " the way " which we should follow ; he is " the life " which we should seek ; and we cannot arrive at this life except by the imitation of his virtues. The road he points out is that of a spirit of poverty, of self-denial, of mortification of the senses, of detachment from pleasures, and of patience in suffering. Though this may appear to his followers a rugged road, they should be encouraged by the thought that, like the shepherd with his sheep, " he goes before them ; " that he demands nothing of them which he has not first practised and rendered easy by his grace ; and that he has inspired the Apostle to tell them : " The sufferings of this time are not worthy to be compared with the glory to come, that shall be revealed in us " (Rom. viii. 18).

THIRD SUNDAY AFTER EASTER.

I.—TEXTS.

GREEK.

JOHN XVI. 16-22.

¹⁶ Μικρὸν, καὶ οὐκέτι θεωρεῖτέ με· καὶ πάλιν μικρὸν, καὶ ὄψεσθέ με. . . . ¹⁷ Εἶπαν οὖν ἐκ τῶν μαθητῶν αὐτοῦ πρὸς ἀλλήλους· τί ἐστι τοῦτο ὃ λέγει ἡμῖν· μικρὸν, καὶ οὐ θεωρεῖτέ με· καὶ πάλιν μικρὸν, καὶ ὄψεσθέ με· καὶ ὅτι ὑπάγω πρὸς τὸν πατέρα; ¹⁸ Ἔλεγον οὖν· τί ἐστι τοῦτο ὃ λέγει, μικρὸν, οὐκ οἴδαμεν· ¹⁹ Ἔγνω Ἰησοῦς ὅτι ἤθελον αὐτὸν ἐρωτᾶν, καὶ εἶπεν αὐτοῖς· περὶ τούτου ζητεῖτε μετ' ἀλλήλων, ὅτι εἶπον· μικρὸν καὶ οὐ θεωρεῖτέ με· καὶ πάλιν μικρὸν, καὶ ὄψεσθέ με; ²⁰ Ἀμὴν ἀμὴν λέγω ὑμῖν, ὅτι κλαύσετε καὶ θρηνήσετε ὑμεῖς, ὁ δὲ κόσμος χαρήσεται· ὑμεῖς λυπηθήσεσθε, ἀλλ' ἡ λύπη ὑμῶν εἰς χαρὰν γενήσεται. ²¹ Ἡ γυνὴ ὅταν τίκτῃ, λύπην ἔχει, ὅτι ἦλθεν ἡ ὥρα αὐτῆς· ὅταν δὲ γεννήσῃ τὸ παιδίον, οὐκέτι μνημονεύει τῆς θλίψεως, διὰ τὴν χαρὰν, ὅτι ἐγεννήθη ἄνθρωπος εἰς τὸν κόσμον. ²² Καὶ ὑμεῖς οὖν νῦν μὲν λύπην ἔχετε· πάλιν δὲ ὄψομαι ὑμᾶς, καὶ χαρήσεται ὑμῶν ἡ καρδία, καὶ τὴν χαρὰν ὑμῶν οὐδεὶς ἀρεῖ ἀφ' ὑμῶν.

VULGATE.

JOHN XVI. 16-22.

¹⁶ Modicum, et jam non videbitis me ; et iterum modicum, et videbitis me ; quia vado ad Patrem.

¹⁷ Dixerunt ergo ex discipulis ejus ad invicem : Quid est hoc quod dicit nobis : Modicum, et non videbitis me ; et iterum modicum, et videbitis me, et : Quia vado ad Patrem?

¹⁸ Dicebant ergo : Quid est hoc quod dicit : Modicum? Nescimus quid loquitur. ¹⁹ Cognovit autem Jesus quia volebant eum interrogare, et dixit eis : De hoc quæritis inter vos quia dixi : Modicum, et non videbitis me ; et iterum modicum, et videbitis me. ²⁰ Amen amen dico vobis, quia plorabitis et flebitis vos, mundus autem gaudebit ; vos autem contristabimini, sed tristitia vestra vertetur in gaudium. ²¹ Mulier quum parit, tristitiam habet, quia venit hora ejus ; cum autem pepererit puerum, jam non meminit pressuræ propter gaudium, quia natus est homo in mundum. ²² Et vos igitur nunc quidem tristitiam habetis ; iterum autem videbo vos ; et gaudebit cor vestrum ; et gaudium vestrum nemo tollet a vobis.

II.—ENGLISH TRANSLATION.

JOHN XVI. 16-22.

16 " A little while, and now you shall not see me ; and again a little while, and you shall see me ; because I go to the Father."
17 Then some of his disciples said one to another : " What is this that he saith to us : A little while, and you shall not see me ; and again a little while, and you shall see me ; and : Because I go to the Father ? " 18 They said therefore : " What is this that he saith : A little while ? We know not what he speaketh."
19 And Jesus knew that they had a mind to ask him ; and he said to them : " Of this do you inquire among yourselves, because I said : A little while, and you shall not see me ; and again a little while, and you shall see me. 20 Amen amen I say to you, that you shall lament and weep, but the world shall rejoice ; and you shall be made sorrowful, but your sorrow shall be turned into joy. 21 A woman, when she is in labour, hath sorrow, because her hour is come ; but when she hath brought forth the child, she remembereth no more the anguish, for joy that a man is born into the world. 22 So also, you now indeed have sorrow ; but I will see you again, and your heart shall rejoice, and your joy no man shall take from you."

III.—NOTES.

Introductory. The passages of the gospel read in the Mass on this and the succeeding Sundays until Pentecost, are taken from the discourse delivered by our Lord at his Last Supper. Having on that occasion given to his apostles a wonderful lesson in humility by washing their feet, Christ instituted the Holy Eucharist for their spiritual nourishment, and at the same time raised them to the high dignity of priests of the New Law. To prepare them for the future, he then addressed them in words which manifested more than ever before, the depth and tenderness of his love. Commencing with the prediction of his approaching death, he exhorted them to union with himself and with each other ; he spoke of the trials they might expect to meet ; he comforted them with the promise of the Holy Ghost ; and he concluded with a solemn prayer which is recorded by St. John in the 16th chapter of this gospel. In his prayer, Christ as Man besought his Eternal Father to give to him the glory which was his from eternity, to sanctify and preserve his apostles, and to grant to all future believers in his name the gifts of perfect charity here, and of perfect bliss hereafter. Such was the farewell of our Divine Redeemer to those who had been committed to his care on earth.

The present extract is taken from that portion of the discourse which aims at consoling the apostles in the sorrow they feel on hearing that they are now to be separated from their beloved Master. Having learned in the preceding sentences that the Holy Ghost would convince the world of sin, of justice, and of judgment (John xvi. 8), that he would communicate all knowledge to themselves (verse 13), and that he would glorify Christ before all mankind (verse 14), the apostles are now told of a new source of consolation—that their separation from Jesus will be but for a short time. It was said :—

V. 16. A little while, and now you shall not see me ; and again a little while, and you shall see me ; because I go to the Father.

It is to be remarked in the first place, that the word " now ' has no corresponding expression in the Greek text. Again, the clause " because I go to the Father " is wanting in the best manuscripts (ℵ, B, D, L) and critical editions (Introduction, pp. xxiv., xxv.), but was certainly used by our Divine Lord, since it appears in the undoubtedly authentic repetition of his words by the apostles in the next verse. Lastly, the phrase " a little while, and " is a Hebraism, as is seen in the Parallel Passages (Isaias x. 25 ; Osee i. 4 ; Aggeus ii. 7 ; John xiv. 19 ; Hebr. x. 37). It signifies " *after* a little while," and not " *for* a little while." Consequently the whole verse means that after the lapse of " a little while " the apostles were to behold their Lord no longer ; and after another " little while " they were to see him again. But what does Christ mean by the words " little while " in each clause ? The intentional obscurity of these words constitutes a great difficulty ; and still, on the solution of this difficulty depends the interpretation of the entire passage.

Some interpreters (as Fillion, St. Cyril, St. Chrysost., Beelen) understand by the first " little while," the short time up to the Ascension, after which the apostles were not to see Christ ; and by the second " little while " the space between the Ascension of Christ and the Descent of the Holy Ghost, in whom, as in another Comforter, the apostles were again to enjoy the sight of their Divine Master. This is improbable, for the parallelism between the clauses seems to require on the part of the apostles a similar and true vision of Christ himself in each case.

Others with Patrizi, take the first " little while " to refer to the interval up to the death of Christ, and the second to signify the space between the Resurrection and the Ascension, at which the apostles were to see Christ going up to the Father. Such a solution of the difficulty appears to be unsatisfactory. In the first place, according to this explanation, the two intervals of time spoken of by our Lord differed from each other as do a few hours and forty days ; but this difference appears to be too great to allow of their being compared as " a little while," and

" again, a little while." Moreover, in this explanation the words, " because I go to the Father," are supposed to be given as a reason for a statement in the second clause only ; whereas in the parallel places (John xiv. 28 ; xvi. 10), they are put forward as a reason for what is here contained in the first. Still further, in this explanation the " going to the Father " at the Ascension is taken to be the fulfilment of the prophecy : " You shall see me ; " whereas this " going to the Father " is elsewhere proposed solely as a reason for an antecedent statement, and never as a thing to be seen. (*Cfr.* John, *ibid.*) Lastly, in opposition to what is supposed in this explanation, parallelism requires that as the first clause ends with the words : " You shall not see me," so the second clause should end with : " You shall see me," and not with : " Because I go to the Father."

Other commentators (*e.g.*, St. Augustine, St. Bede, M'Carthy, MacRory, Maldonatus) think the " first little while " ended with the Ascension, after which the apostles no longer saw Christ on earth ; and the second with the Last Judgment or with the admission of the apostles into heaven after death. After this second interval, all sorrow being past (verse 20), and all knowledge and happiness being given to the apostles in the beatific vision, they would now no longer need to ask anything of Christ (verse 23). This exposition is recommended both by the learning of the interpreters who adopt it, and by the reasons put forward in its defence.

In the absence of certainty, the most probable opinion appears to be that which is elsewhere viewed with favour by St. Augustine, and is fully adopted by the Greek FF. generally and by the interpreters St. Thomas, Toletus, Lucas Brugensis, Knabenbauer, Corluy, and MacEvilly. These understand by the first " little while " the few hours up to Christ's death, and by the second " little while " the interval between that and the Resurrection, after which Christ appeared many times to his disciples. The reasons are very strong :—1°. The " little while " in the two members of the sentence must refer to pretty nearly equal spaces of time, and these very brief. But the only spaces of time that have these two conditions are the interval from the Last Supper to the Crucifixion, and that from the Crucifixion to the Resurrection. 2°. In defence of the previous interpretation it is said that the space of time during which the apostles were no longer to see Christ, *i.e.*, from the Ascension until their admission into heaven or until the Last Judgment, might appear long to men, but not to God, with whom a thousand years are as one day (2 Peter iii. 8). It is to be remembered, however, that intending to console the apostles, Christ must have been speaking of an absence which would be brief even *in their eyes*. 3°. Again, in defence of the previous interpretation, it is said that Christ, in here referring to his reappearance, cannot have referred to the time after his Resurrection, because, contrary to the promise of verse 23, the apostles then asked him many things. To this argument it is answered that the "asking" of which Christ spoke in verse 23, referred to the meaning of his departure to the Father, and to the meaning of the "little whiles" which now presented such difficulty to the apostles, but which would afterwards be made clear by the event. Our Lord wished that the apostles might have their sorrow cheered by the present intentionally obscure announcement, and that they might be strengthened in their faith by the future fulfilment of his words. The whole passage may be thus paraphrased in accordance with the explanation just given: "Only 'a little while'—the space of a few hours—now remains before my death, and then you shall no longer see me living amongst you as at present. In this condition of loneliness you shall pass another 'little while'—the space of a few days—ending with my Resurrection, and then until my Ascension you shall frequently behold me in the new life to which I shall have risen from the dead. My Death, Resurrection, and Ascension being the stages by which I must return to my Father, I make known to you the alternations which are about to take place in your state and mine, and this with a view to your present comfort and the future confirmation of your faith."

As has been remarked, these words of Christ were intentionally obscure ; and

Vv. 17, 18. Then some of his disciples said one to another: What is this that he saith to us: A little while, and you shall not see me ; and again a little while, and you shall see me ; and: Because I go to the Father? They said therefore: What is this that he saith: A little while? We know not what he speaketh.

If the words "because I go to the Father" were not spoken by Christ with the words found in verse 16, they are a repetition on the part of the apostles of what is recorded in verse 10. Alford says: "The disciples are perplexed by this μικρόν *a little while* as connected with what our Lord had asserted (verse 10), ὑπάγω πρὸς τὸν πατέρα = *I go to the Father*. That seemed to them a long and hopeless withdrawal ; how was it then to be reconciled with what he now says of a short absence ? What was this τὸ μικρόν ? " As has been already explained, our Lord's words referred to his approaching Death and Resurrection—events frequently foretold. (See Mark ix. 30 ; Luke ix. 22 ; Matth. xvii. 22 ; xx. 18, 19 ; Mark x. 32-34 ; Matth. xxvi. 1, 2 ; Mark x. 34 ; Matth. xii. 39, 40 ; John ii. 18-22 ; xii. 32, 33.) At first sight then, it seems strange that the meaning of these words should be hidden from the apostles ;

but before the Descent of the Holy Ghost, the incapacity of these apostles to understand heavenly things was frequently commented on by Christ himself. (See Matth. xv. 16, 17; Mark vii. 17, 18; Matth. xvi. 8-12; xvi. 23.) Moreover, there were special causes for a misunderstanding on the present occasion. " The thing is easily accounted for, when we consider the conciseness of his (Christ's) words, and remember that they were *predictive*, perhaps intentionally obscure, and only to be understood after their fulfilment. Besides, the apostles' perceptions were clouded by deep-rooted prejudices as to the nature of Christ's temporal kingdom, and dulled by their excess of sorrow on learning that, whatever might be the meaning of the words, they were at least to be deprived of their Lord. Their greatest perplexity, no doubt, was with the words ὅτι ὑπάγω πρὸς τὸν πατέρα ('because I go to the Father'). They might, indeed, comprehend that they were first to be deprived of, and then to receive back, their Lord; but as they firmly believed that the Messiah was to come and establish an *earthly* kingdom, they could make nothing out of the last words " (Bloomfield, *in loco*).

During a pause in our Lord's discourse, " some of his disciples said to one another " these things. As they themselves confessed, their utter perplexity remained;

V. 19. And Jesus knew that they had a mind to ask him; and he said to them: Of this do you inquire among yourselves, because I said: A little while, and you shall not see me: and again a little while, and you shall see me.

Earlier in the evening (John xiv. 5, 6, 7, 9, 22, 23) Thomas, Philip, and Judas or Thaddaeus appeared to have been reproved for questions which they put. The apostles, therefore, whose words are given in the preceding verse, discussed Christ's predictions in secret, and did not venture to express their wish for further explanation. The thoughts, however, and wishes of all were known to him who, as God, knew all things possible, and who, as Man, knew all things past, present, and to come that appertained to his office. Responding, therefore, to their desires as far as was at present useful for them, Christ continued:—

V. 20. Amen amen I say to you, that you shall lament and weep, but the world shall rejoice; and you shall be made sorrowful, but your sorrow shall be turned into joy.

Christ here speaks with great emphasis indicated by the repeated " amen." Deferring a full explanation until the accomplishment of the prophecy, he declares his previous words to signify that whilst the world will exult, some great sorrow is in store for the apostles; but that afterwards this sorrow of theirs is to be turned into joy. The original Greek text is still stronger. The sentence ἡ λύπη ὑμῶν εἰς χαρὰν γενήσεται means

literally : " Your sorrow *shall be unto joy."* As Alford *in loco*
well remarks, these words do not signify that the approaching
sorrow of the apostles shall be afterwards *exchanged for joy ;*
but that the very matter of grief shall *become the matter of joy,*
as Christ's cross of shame has become the glory of the Christian
(Gal. vi. 14). The same Greek construction and the same meaning will be found in the history of the corner-stone (Matth. xxi.
42 ; Acts iv. 11) and in that of the mustard-seed (Luke xiii. 19)

The first part of this prophecy was fulfilled at the Crucifixion.
Then, amidst the joy of Christ's enemies who were seemingly
victorious, his apostles were overwhelmed with grief at the
death of their Master, at the apparent wreck of their hopes, and
at the dangers that beset themselves. The second part came to
pass after the Resurrection. At that time the apostles saw
Christ return victorious over death and hell, and bearing in his
now immortal body the marks of that conflict by which he had
gloriously won the spiritual freedom of the human race.

Thus did Christ forewarn, and therefore prepare, his apostles
by a prediction of their approaching sorrow, whilst with equal
emphasis he supported them in that sorrow by foretelling the
joy that was quickly to succeed. He did more when he said :—

**V. 21. A woman, when she is in labour, hath sorrow,
because her hour is come ; but when she hath brought forth
the child, she remembereth no more the anguish, for joy
that a man is born into the world.**

In the Sacred Scripture the pangs of childbirth are mentioned as an example of the most intense pain or suffering.
(See Jeremias xxii. 23 ; Psalm xlvii. 7 ; Ecclus. xlviii. 21 ; Osee
xiii. 13 ; Micheas iv. 9, 10 ; Isaias xiii. 6, 7, 8 ; xxi. 3.) The
illustration is most suitable for our Lord's purpose. By it he
shows in the first place that, as the sorrows of childbirth are
surely followed by the contentment peculiar to the mother's
heart, and especially to the Jewish mother's heart, so shall the
bitterness of the apostles' parting from Christ be *surely* the
prelude of a future joyous meeting. Again, as the pains of
childbirth are sharp indeed, but of very brief duration, and as
they are succeeded by a joy so great and so lasting as to oblite.-
ate the mother's memory of previous suffering (" she remembereth no more the anguish "), so shall it be with the apostles.
More than once in this discourse Christ testified to the bitterness
of the apostles' grief ; but this grief was to be short-lived, and
to be followed by a happiness intense in its force and unceasing
in its duration. Lastly, as in the case of the mother, the cause
of pain, namely, the birth of her child, becomes in itself the
material of subsequent joy, so in the case of the apostles, the
Passion and Crucifixion, which at first plunged them into grief,

were the source of their consolation at the Resurrection when
Christ entered as Man on that new and immortal life in which
he is, according to St. Paul, "the first born from the dead."

Such was clearly the force of this illustration; but Christ
wished himself to make the application in the following words:

**V. 22. So also, you now indeed have sorrow; but I will
see you again, and your heart shall rejoice, and your joy no
man shall take from you.**

According to the explanation of verse 20, the time of sorrow
for the apostles was to be the " little while " of Christ's absence; and according to the opinion adopted in these notes,
the " little while " of Christ's absence was to be the space
between the Crucifixion and the Resurrection. This time of
distress for them was now so near at hand that it was referred
to by Christ as already present. " So also you now indeed have
sorrow." Their sorrow, however, was to be little more than
momentary; for at the Resurrection, as the same evangelist
records, " the disciples . . . were glad when they saw the
Lord " (John xx. 20). Nor was this joy to last merely for
the forty days before the Ascension: it was to remain for ever.
" Your joy no man shall take from you." It is true that after
forty days the apostles were again, and for life, to lose the consolation of Christ's visible presence, and were destined to suffer
much at the hands of the enemies of the Gospel. Still the
abundant graces of the Holy Spirit, the knowledge that their
Redeemer was living in the glory of the Father, and the consciousness that, according to his promise, he was ever invisibly
present and working with them, all this filled their souls with
an interior joy quite proof against every assault of persecution
from without. Nor is a record of this joy wanting in the Sacred
Scriptures. It is of this unfailing happiness that St. Luke writes
when describing the return of the disciples from Mount Olivet
after the Ascension (Luke xxiv. 52, 53). It is this state of
mind the same evangelist refers to when narrating the scourging
of the apostles by the Jewish Council (Acts v. 41). It was a
large share in this feeling that enabled St. Paul to write to the
Corinthians : " I am filled with comfort : I exceedingly abound
with joy in all our tribulations " (2 Cor. vii. 4). Whilst
awaiting the eternal rest of heaven, each one of the apostles
could truly say with Christ himself in the Messianic Psalm :
" I set the Lord always in my sight, for he is at my right
hand that I be not moved. Therefore my heart hath been
glad, and my tongue hath rejoiced, moreover my flesh shall rest
in hope. . . . Thou hast made known to me the ways of life.
Thou shalt fill me with joy with thy countenance. At thy
right hand are delights even to the end " (Ps. xv. 8-11).

IV.—MORAL REFLECTIONS.

Interpreters have seen in the departure and return of Jesus predicted in this passage, a figure of the manner in which he is pleased to deal with Christian souls ; for the whole course of the spiritual life is an alternation of joys and sorrows. At one time he refreshes us by his sensible presence, and again he afflicts us by withdrawing that consolation ; but it is his fatherly love that causes him to act both in the one manner and in the other. Desiring in all things our greater benefit, he makes use of these different states to prove our virtue and to bring us to perfection.

1. In the first place, by this alternation of joy and sorrow he intends to prove or try us as he did holy Job. That patriarch, in a greater measure than other men, was made acquainted with the extremes of prosperity and adversity ; and it was so, as we learn from the Sacred Scriptures, that his already shining virtues might be made manifest to all. He himself speaks of all God's visitations as instances of divine goodness designed to try him. "What," said he, "is a man that thou shouldst magnify him, or why dost thou set thy heart upon him ? Thou visitest him early in the morning, and thou provest him suddenly" (Job vii. 17, 18). Whilst a soul is ever supported by the visible assistance of grace and continually refreshed by interior consolations, its fidelity is not yet tested ; and to such a soul might be applied the words : "Doth Job fear God in vain ? Hast thou not made a fence for him, and his house, and all his substance round about ; blessed the work of his hands ; and his possession hath increased on the earth ? But stretch forth thy hand a little, and touch all that he hath, and see if he blesseth thee not to thy face" (Job i. 9-11). Jesus Christ, then, sometimes hides himself from us, and withdraws the sweetness of his consolations, that we may prove our constancy, show our love, and give an instance of what we are prepared to do and to suffer for him. This absence of our Lord must indeed be painful to us as it was to the apostles ; but instead of casting us down, it should cause us to redouble our efforts in his service. From us as from the apostles, Christ departs only for "a little while" ; and then returning, he will bestow upon us more abundant joy and blessings than before. It is written : "The souls of the just are in the hand of God, and the torment of death shall not touch them. . . . Afflicted in a few things, in many things they shall be well rewarded ; because God hath tried them, and found them worthy of himself" (Wisdom iii. 1-5).

2. Again, in the spiritual life, the alternations of joy and sorrow not only try the virtues of the just, but also bring these

virtues to perfection. " As gold in the furnace, he hath proved them ; and as a victim of a holocaust, he hath received them ; and in time there shall be respect had to them. The just shall shine, and shall run to and fro as sparks among the reeds " (Wisdom iii. 6, 7). It is in the crucible of tribulation that we may purify ourselves from the taint of earthly affections, and become worthy of being offered to God as a victim without spot. In sorrow and desolation we may practice many virtues which uninterrupted happiness might, perhaps, cause us to neglect. The Holy Ghost has said : " What doth he know that hath not been tried ? . . . He that hath no experience, knoweth little ; and he that hath been experienced in many things, multiplieth prudence " (Ecclus. xxxiv. 9, 10). Our resignation in meeting afflictions, our patience in bearing them, the humility with which they inspire us, the mortification to which they accustom us, the diffidence in self which they teach us, are so many steps by which Jesus wishes to raise us in the scale of sanctity and perfection. " Many," says Thomas à Kempis, " love Jesus as long as they meet with no adversity ; many praise him as long as they receive consolations from him ; but if Jesus hide himself and leave them for a little while, they either fall into complaints or excessive dejection. But they that love Jesus for Jesus' sake, and not for any comfort of their own, bless him no less in tribulation and anguish of heart, than in the greatest consolation ; and if he should never give them his comfort, yet would they always praise him and give him thanks. Oh ! how much is the pure love of Jesus able to do, when it is not mixed with any self-interest or self-love ! " (*Imitation of Christ*, B. ii., c. 11). Very opportune, therefore, for all of us is the admonition of St. Peter : " Dearly beloved, think not strange the burning heat which is to try you, as if some new thing happened to you. But if you partake of the suffering of Christ, rejoice that also when his glory shall be revealed, you may be glad with exceeding joy " (1 Peter iv. 12, 13).

FOURTH SUNDAY AFTER EASTER.

I.—TEXTS.

GREEK.

JOHN XVI. 5-14.

⁵ Νῦν δὲ ὑπάγω πρὸς τὸν πέμψαντά με, καὶ οὐδεὶς ἐξ ὑμῶν ἐρωτᾷ με· ποῦ ὑπάγεις; ⁶ Ἀλλ᾽ ὅτι ταῦτα λελάληκα ὑμῖν, ἡ λύπη πεπλήρωκεν ὑμῶν τὴν καρδίαν. ⁷ Ἀλλ᾽ ἐγὼ τὴν ἀλήθειαν λέγω ὑμῖν, συμφέρει ὑμῖν ἵνα ἐγὼ ἀπέλθω· ἐὰν γὰρ μὴ ἀπέλθω, ὁ παράκλητος οὐ μὴ ἔλθῃ πρὸς ὑμᾶς· ἐὰν δὲ πορευθῶ, πέμψω αὐτὸν πρὸς ὑμᾶς. ⁸ Καὶ ἐλθὼν ἐκεῖνος, ἐλέγξει τὸν κόσμον περὶ ἁμαρτίας καὶ περὶ δικαιοσύνης, καὶ περὶ κρίσεως. ⁹ Περὶ ἁμαρτίας μέν, ὅτι οὐ πιστεύουσιν εἰς ἐμέ. ¹⁰ Περὶ δικαιοσύνης δέ, ὅτι πρὸς τὸν πατέρα ὑπάγω, καὶ οὐκέτι θεωρεῖτέ με. ¹¹ Περὶ δὲ κρίσεως, ὅτι ὁ ἄρχων τοῦ κόσμου τούτου κέκριται. ¹² Ἔτι πολλὰ ἔχω ὑμῖν λέγειν, ἀλλ᾽ οὐ δύνασθε βαστάζειν ἄρτι. ¹³ Ὅταν δὲ ἔλθῃ ἐκεῖνος, τὸ πνεῦμα τῆς ἀληθείας, ὁδηγήσει ὑμᾶς εἰς τὴν ἀλήθειαν πᾶσαν· οὐ γὰρ λαλήσει ἀφ᾽ ἑαυτοῦ, ἀλλ᾽ ὅσα ἀκούσει, λαλήσει, καὶ τὰ ἐρχόμενα ἀναγγελεῖ ὑμῖν. ¹⁴ Ἐκεῖνος ἐμὲ δοξάσει, ὅτι ἐκ τοῦ ἐμοῦ λήμψεται καὶ ἀναγγελεῖ ὑμῖν.

VULGATE.

JOHN XVI. 5-14.

. . . . . .

⁵ Et nunc vado ad eum qui misit me ; et nemo ex vobis interrogat me : Quo vadis? ⁶ Sed quia hæc locutus sum vobis, tristitia implevit cor vestrum. ⁷ Sed ego veritatem dico vobis : expedit vobis ut ego vadam ; si enim non abiero, Paraclitus non veniet ad vos ; si autem abiero, mittam eum ad vos. ⁸ Et cum venerit ille, arguet mundum de peccato, et de justitia, et de judicio : ⁹ de peccato quidem, quia non crediderunt in me ; ¹⁰ de justitia vero, quia ad Patrem vado, et jam non videbitis me ; ¹¹ de judicio autem, quia princeps hujus mundi jam judicatus est. ¹² Adhuc multa habeo vobis dicere ; sed non potestis portare modo. ¹³ Cum autem venerit ille Spiritus veritatis, docebit vos omnem veritatem. Non enim loquetur a semetipso ; sed quæcumque audiet loquetur, et quæ ventura sunt annuntiabit vobis. ¹⁴ Ille me clarificabit, quia de meo accipiet et annuntiabit vobis.

II.—ENGLISH TRANSLATION.

JOHN XVI. 5-14.

"   .   .   5 And now I go to him that sent me, and none of you asketh me : Whither goest thou ?   6 But because I have spoken these things to you, sorrow hath filled your heart.   7 But I tell you the truth : It is expedient for you that I go ; for if I go not, the Paraclete will not come to you ; but if I go, I will send him to you.   8 And when he is come, he will convince the world of sin, and of justice, and of judgment :   9 of sin, because they believed not in me ;   10 and of justice, because I go to the Father, and you shall see me no longer ;   11 and of judgment, because the prince of this world is already judged.

12 " I have yet many things to say to you ; but you cannot bear them now.   13 But when he, the Spirit of truth, is come, he will teach you all truth.   For he shall not speak of himself ; but what things soever he shall hear, he shall speak.   And the things that are to come, he shall show you.   14 He shall glorify me ; because he shall receive of mine, and shall show it to you."

III.—NOTES.

Introductory. The present gospel passage which is taken from Christ's discourse after the Last Supper, and which makes known the reasons for sending the Holy Ghost, is intended by the Church to serve as a preparation for the approaching feast of Pentecost.   As may be learned from the preceding verses, our Lord complained of the hatred he had met with amongst men ; he foretold the testimony that would be rendered to him by the Holy Spirit and by the apostles ; he described the persecutions which these apostles were to endure for his sake ; and he then added : " I told you not these things from the beginning, because I was with you."   This was not absolutely the first time that Christ referred to the dangerous character of the apostolic office.   More than once the Divine Master had revealed to his disciples that their road to glory like his own was to be the way of the cross, but he had never given them so detailed a statement about the matter as on the present occasion.   Hitherto his presence had rendered superfluous all other safeguards, but now he was about to disappear from their sight.   Hence to the announcement of his approaching departure, he added a minutely circumstantial prediction of their future difficulties and dangers, in order that being forewarned, they might prepare their souls to look forward to these trials with courage, and to endure them with success.   At this prophecy the apostles were overwhelmed with distress, and much needed the consolation conveyed in the words which they next heard from their beloved Master.

At an earlier stage in this address (see John xiv. 28), Christ said to them : " If you loved me, you would indeed be glad because I go to the Father ; for the Father is greater than I." Gently reproving their excessive sorrow, he reverts to this thought when saying :

V. 5. And now I go to him that sent me, and none of you asketh me : Whither goest thou ?

Before now (John xiii. 36), St. Peter had asked the question ; but at this time when an inquiry as to the object and effects of Christ's departure would have been opportune, he and the other apostles were silent. They had already heard Christ say : " If you loved me, you would indeed be glad, because I go to the Father, for the Father is greater than I " (John xiv. 28) ; but their minds were fixed on the loss they were about to sustain, and they could not give a thought to the glory which was to accrue to the sacred humanity of their Lord on his departure from this world. In the designs of God it was decreed that Christ as Man should be in the highest place in heaven, next to God in power and glory ; that he should be the Mediator between God and man ; that he should dispense to men the graces he had merited ; that he should be the Judge of the living and of the dead.

All this glory he was to merit for himself as Man by the suffering of his Passion, and he was to acquire it in its fulness on going to the Father at his Ascension. St. Paul says : " He humbled himself, becoming obedient unto death, even to the death of the cross. For which cause God also hath exalted him, and hath given him a name which is above every name, that in the name of Jesus every knee should bow, of those that are in heaven, on earth, and under the earth, and that every tongue should confess that the Lord Jesus Christ is in the glory of God the Father " (Phil. ii. 8-11). The disciples, as was said to two of them on the day of the Resurrection, were still " foolish and slow of heart to believe in all things which the prophets have spoken. Ought not Christ to have suffered these things, and so to enter into his glory ? " (Luke xxiv. 25, 26.)

The only effect of the observation just made, was to increase the grief of the apostles, and therefore their Divine Master thus continued :—

V. 6. But because I have spoken these things to you, sorrow hath filled your heart.

Whilst Christ gently reproved his disciples for their silence, he found an excuse for it in the affliction which had settled down upon them, and which was common to all as if they had but one heart ($\dot{\eta}$ $\lambda\dot{\upsilon}\pi\eta$ $\pi\epsilon\pi\lambda\dot{\eta}\rho\omega\kappa\epsilon\nu$ $\dot{\upsilon}\mu\hat{\omega}\nu$ $\tau\dot{\eta}\nu$ $\kappa\alpha\rho\delta\dot{\iota}\alpha\nu$). How unlike to this were their feelings when the actual separation took place on the day of the Ascension! St. Luke tells us that the angel having then assured them of Christ's second coming, " they, adoring, went back to Jerusalem with great joy " (Luke xxiv. 52).

Notwithstanding the distress which Christ knew his words had caused them, he did not cease to refer to this painful subject of his departure. However, he wished to present it to them from another point of view, and said:—

V. 7. But I tell you the truth: It is expedient for you that I go; for if I go not, the Paraclete will not come to you; but if I go, I will send him to you.

Emphasising the certainty of this statement as coming from himself, the infallible source of knowledge (ἐγὼ τὴν ἀλήθειαν λέγω ὑμῖν), Christ here says in effect that if the apostles will not, or cannot be reconciled to his departure by reflecting on the glory which will then be his, they should be consoled by the benefits which will thence accrue to themselves, and which cannot be conferred in other circumstances. These blessings are the gifts of the Holy Ghost. When it was said: " If I go not, the Paraclete will not come to you," the contrast in the second part of the sentence would seem to require: " But if I go, he will come to you." The words actually used, however, foretell the coming of the Holy Ghost, and at the same time imply the eternal procession of this Holy Spirit from the Son, by whom he is to be sent.

The apostles themselves might have asked, and many commentators inquire as to why Christ's departure was a condition necessary to the coming of the Holy Ghost. The only satisfactory answer is that such was the will of God. Although there was no *a priori* necessity for this order of things, and although, *absolutely* speaking, the work of redemption and sanctification might have been otherwise accomplished, still in the divine economy, each of the three Divine Persons was to take a special part in the regeneration of fallen man. The Father was to send the Son into the world, and to draw to him the predestined members of the Church. " No man can come to me, except the Father, who hath sent me, draw him " (John vi. 44). The Son was to teach mankind the truths of faith; for according to St. Paul: " God, who at sundry times and in divers manners spoke in times past to the fathers by the prophets, last of all, in these days hath spoken to us by his Son, whom he hath appointed heir of all things, by whom also he made the world " (Heb. i. 1, 2). Again, this Son of God was to redeem us and to free us from the slavery of the devil; for " there is . . . one Mediator of God and men, the Man Christ Jesus, who gave himself a redemption for all " (1 Tim. ii. 5, 6). Lastly, this Son of God was to distribute to all the rewards or the punishment merited in this life, for " it is he who was appointed by God to be Judge of the living and of the dead " (Acts x. 42). The Holy Ghost was to finish the work of Christ on earth and to unite the members of Christ's mystical body in the bonds of perfection. Hence the Apostle says : " There are diversities of graces, but the same Spirit ; and there are diversities of ministries, but the same Lord; and there are diversities of operations, but the same God, who worketh all in all. But the manifestation of the Spirit is given to every man unto profit. . . . All these things one and the same Spirit worketh, dividing to every one according as he will. For as the body is one, and hath many members, and all· the members of the body, whilst they are many, yet are one body, so also is Christ. For in one Spirit were we all baptised into one body, whether Jews or Gentiles, whether bond or free " (1 Cor. xii. 4-7, 11-13). In our regeneration, then, each Divine Person took his part ; each had the time of his manifestation ; and in these special works and distinct manifestations, the distinction of persons and the processions in the Trinity were clearly revealed. It was the will of the Father, therefore, that the Son, sent into the world by him, should redeem us by his sufferings ; that he should afterwards ascend into heaven ; and that there, seated in glory, he should send from the Father and from himself the Holy Spirit, the Sanctifier, to complete the work of our restoration.

Having thus stated that his departure was expedient for the apostles since it was a necessary condition of the coming of the Holy Ghost, Christ in the remaining verses of this passage, indicated the result of that coming. This result is three-fold : first, on the part of the world (verse 8-11) ; secondly, on the part of the disciples (verse 12, 13) ; and thirdly, on the part of Christ himself (verse 14). As to the first Christ says : —

V. 8. And when he is come, he will convince the world of sin, and of justice, and of judgment.

Frequently in the New Testament (see Matth. xviii. 15 ; Luke iii. 19 ; John iii. 20), the verb ἐλέγχειν in its primary sense signifies *to reprove* ; but as it cannot be so understood in all the clauses of this sentence, it is here taken in its secondary sense, *i.e.*, *to convince* or *to convict*. According to the best commentators, ὁ κόσμος=*the world* signifies not only the Jews who heard and rejected Christ's words, but all those, whether Jews or Gentiles, who until the end of time resist the preaching of the gospel. Ἁμαρτία=*sin* here means not merely the sin of unbelief, but all offences, original and actual which, in the case of unbelievers, will remain unremitted. " Without faith it is impossible to please God ; for he that cometh to God must believe that he is, and is a rewarder to them that seek him " (Hebr.

xi. 6). Δικαιοσύνη = *justice*, as appears from verse 10, can mean nothing else than the holiness of Christ himself. The passage, therefore, may be thus paraphrased : " When the Holy Ghost cometh, he will give convincing proofs that the unbelieving world has committed sin and remains in its sinful state ; he will manifest to this sinful world my justice and holiness of life ; and he will show it how well deserved is the sentence of condemnation passed upon it." This three-fold conviction, which is the work of the Holy Ghost and the object of the apostles' mission, is intended indeed for the good of mankind ; but it may result in either conversion or reprobation. As was the case in Jerusalem at St. Peter's sermon (Acts iv. 1-4), and at Antioch in Pisidia on the preaching of St. Paul, the same testimony brought repentance to some, whilst others became more hardened in heart. " Almost the whole city came together to hear the word of God. And the Jews, seeing the multitude, were filled with envy, and blaspheming contradicted those things which were said by Paul. Then Paul and Barnabas said boldly : To you it behoved us first to speak the word of God ; but because you reject it, and judge yourselves unworthy of eternal life, behold, we turn to the Gentiles. . . . And the Gentiles, hearing this, were glad, and glorified the word of the Lord ; and as many as were ordained to life everlasting, believed " (Acts xiii. 44-48).

Christ continues and says :—

V. 9. [He will convince the world] of sin, because they believed not in me.

It is to be remarked that in the second clause of this verse, Christ does not limit or define the nature of the sin committed, but gives the reason why the world is to be convinced of its guilt. As already stated, the sin to which he refers is not merely the sin of unbelief, but all sin committed by unbelievers, the first step to whose justification should have been faith in Christ. The meaning is then : " Because they (the unbelieving hearers of my words, whether Jews or Gentiles) have not believed in me (or better, " do not believe in me," ὸυ πιστεύουσιν ἐις ἐμέ), the Holy Spirit will convince them of being still in their sins." This conviction was brought home to the world when, in the preaching of the apostles and in the epistles of St. Paul the Holy Ghost declared that whilst on the one hand " all have sinned, and do need the glory of God " (Rom. iii. 23) ; on the other, " without faith it is impossible to please God " (Hebr. xi. 6), and again, " man is not justified by the works of the law, but by the faith of Jesus Christ " (Gal. ii. 16). " The want of belief in Christ when he is made known, lies at the root of all sin, and reveals its nature. Sin is essentially the selfishness which sets itself up apart from, and so, against God. It is not defined by any limited rules, but expresses a general spirit. Christ is thus the touchstone of character. To believe in him, is to adopt the principle of self-surrender to God. Not to believe in him, is to cleave to legal views of duty and service which involve a complete misunderstanding of the essence of sin. The Spirit, therefore, working through the written and spoken word, starts from the fact of unbelief in the Son of Man, and through that lays open what sin is. In this way the condition of man standing alone is revealed, and he is left without excuse. Comp. viii. 21, ix. 41 " (Westcott, *in loco*).

To prove that these are in sin and remain in sin who refuse obedience to Christ, it was necessary to put beyond doubt Christ's righteousness and holiness. This being the second office of the Holy Ghost in the world, our Lord continues :—

V. 10. And [he will convince the world] of justice, because I go to the Father, and you shall see me no longer.

As appears from the second clause of this verse, the " justice " spoken of is no other than the holiness of Christ and his faithful fulfilment of his mission to mankind. Whilst living, he had been looked upon as a false prophet ; and when dead, he was denounced as a deceiver by the scribes and pharisees in their petition to Pilate (Matth. xxvii. 63). He foretells in these words, however, that his sanctity will be proved to all by the miracles of his Resurrection and Ascension, and by his permanent abode in the glory of the Father into which there shall not enter " anything defiled, or that worketh abomination and maketh a lie, but they that are written in the book of life " (Apocal. xxi. 27). This prophecy, as far as Christ is concerned, was fulfilled by the Holy Ghost speaking by the lips of Peter, who in his first discourse to the people, adduced the miracles of the Resurrection and Ascension, and the wonders performed at the invocation of the Sacred Name, as a proof of the righteousness and holiness of our Lord's life. The Prince of the Apostles said : " Ye men of Israel, hear these words : Jesus of Nazareth, a man approved of God among you by miracles and wonders and signs which God d.l by him in the midst of you, as you also know, this same being delivered up, . . . you by the hands of wicked men have crucified and slain. . . . This Jesus hath God raised again, whereof all we are witnesses. Being exalted therefore by the right hand of God, and having received of the Father the promise of the Holy Ghost, he hath poured forth this which you see and hear. . . . Therefore let all the house of Israel know most certainly that God hath made both Lord and Christ this same Jesus whom you have crucified " (Acts ii. 22, 23, 32, 33, 36).

The distinguished commentator last quoted has well said :—
" The Person of Christ, offered as the object of man's faith,
serves as a test of the true appreciation of sin. The historical
work of Christ, completed at his Ascension, serves as a test of
the true appreciation of righteousness. The Life and Death
and Resurrection of the Son of God placed righteousness in a
new light. By these the majesty of the law, and the power of
obedience, and the reality of a divine fellowship, stronger than
death, were made known once for all. For a time the Lord
had shown in an outward form the perfect fulfilment of the
Law, and the absolute conformity of a human life to the divine
ideal. He had shown also how sin carries with it consequences
which must be borne ; and how they had been borne in such
a way that they were potentially abolished. In that life, closed
by the return to the Father, there was a complete exhibition of
righteousness in relation to God and man. The Son had received a work to do, and having accomplished it, he returned
not simply to heaven but to the Father who sent him, in token
of its absolute fulfilment. This revelation once given was
final. *Because* nothing could be added to it (*I go to the Father*) ;
because after that Christ was withdrawn from human eyes he
had passed into a new sphere (*ye see me no more*), there was fixed
for all time that by which men's estimate of righteousness
might be tried. On the other hand till Christ had been raised
to glory, " righteousness " had not been vindicated. The condemnation of Christ by the representatives of Israel showed in
the extremest form how men had failed to apprehend the nature
of righteousness. The spirit, therefore, starting from the fact
of Christ's life, his suffering, and his glory, regarded as a whole,
lays open the divine aspects of human action as concentrated
in the Son of Man. In this way the possibilities of life are revealed in fellowship with him who has raised humanity to
heaven " (Westcott, *in loco*).

Nor is this all. The Holy Ghost will convince the world of its
own sinfulness ; of the righteousness of its crucified Redeemer ;

V. 11. And of judgment ; because the prince of this world is already judged.

The judgment to which Christ refers, is the condemnation
of the unbelieving world—a condemnation made certain beforehand to that world in the condemnation of its prince the devil,
who will be seen to be deprived of his power over the souls and
bodies of men. Before the Descent of the Holy Ghost the power
of the prince of darkness was visible everywhere in the worship
of false gods, in the immoral lives of men especially among the
pagans, and in frequent diabolical possession. This power was
much restricted on the propagation of the faith ; and the devil

was put to flight by the sign of the cross or by the invocation of the name of Jesus.

Such was our Redeemer's prophecy regarding the office of the Holy Ghost, who on his coming was to perfect and continue Christ's work by convincing the unbelieving world that (a) without faith in its Saviour it remains and will remain in its sins ; that (b) this Saviour, so falsely accused and condemned, was justice and innocence itself ; and (c) that the judgment and condemnation of the wicked are already foreshadowed in the condemnation and spoliation of their chief the prince of darkness. Although many might, and did close their eyes to the proofs which were given, the Holy Ghost clearly demonstrated all this when after the Ascension, he was sent by Christ ; when he gave himself so wonderfully and efficaciously to the first disciples ; when he bestowed upon these the gifts of miracles and of tongues ; and when he enabled the apostles to draw whole nations from the errors and corruption of paganism into the light of faith and into the practice of Christian perfection. " The world hitherto had passed sentence on success and failure according to its own standard. At length this standard had been overthrown. He in whom the spirit of the world was concentrated had been judged at the very moment and in the very act by which he appeared to common eyes to have triumphed. The Lord therefore looks forward to the consummation of his own Passion as the final sentence in which men could read the issues of life and death. And the Spirit, starting from this, lays open the last results of human action in the sight of the Supreme Judge. In this way the final victory of right is revealed in the realisation of that which has been indeed already done " (Westcott, *in loco*).

Thus did Christ console the sorrow of his apostles at his departure by showing the effects which the Holy Ghost would then, and not till then, produce on mankind. He now proceeds to point out another source of comfort in the fullness of knowledge which the same Holy Spirit would then impart to the apostles themselves. Not to distress them, but to excite in them an ardent desire of the Spirit of Wisdom and of Knowledge, he continues :—

V. 12. I have yet many things to say to you ; but you cannot bear them now.

In this discourse, at the Last Supper, Christ had revealed to his apostles some of the most sublime mysteries of faith ; but in the words just cited he told them that they were still in need of much instruction before they could enter on their office as teachers of the world. Amongst the truths still to be revealed were probably the merely typical relations of the Old Law to the New ; the spiritual nature of the Messianic Kingdom to be established; the constitution and government of the Church; the vocation of the Gentiles; and the clear and distinct exposition of the Trinity. The apostles, still weak, imperfect, and overwhelmed with grief, were unable now to understand, or even to hear with profit, these important points of Christian doctrine; but it was promised that the time was to come when such knowledge would be conveyed to them by another Divine Teacher.

Having completed his instruction as far as the present condition of his hearers would permit, Christ added:—

V. 13. **But when he, the Spirit of Truth, is come, he will teach you all truth, etc.**

It is to be remarked, in the first place, that the Holy Ghost is called the "Spirit of Truth." He is this because he is essentially true, or truth itself, and therefore incapable of leading into error. Again, as the object of the Holy Ghost's coming was to fit the apostles and their successors to continue Christ's mission on earth, the matter of his instruction was to be "all truth" which God the Father wished to reveal to man through his Divine Son. Lastly, since the expression "will teach," "docebit," is represented in the Greek text by ὁδηγήσει = *will lead the way* or *will conduct*, it was here intimated that, though the Christian revelation was to be complete before the death of the apostles, this fullness of religious knowledge was not to be communicated to them suddenly or at once, but was to be gradually more and more clearly unfolded to them when necessity arose. Franzelin says well: "Non utique ipso die Pentecostes, sed tempore adventus Spiritus Sancti paullatim et per gradus inducti sunt in omnem veritatem, ut ex manifestis factis et ex ipsis verbis constat: 'inducet,' 'inducet in omnem veritatem,' 'ὁδηγήσει ὑμᾶς.'" (De Div. Trad. p. 267, n. 1.)

The communication of divine truth made by Christ himself while on earth, and afterwards through the Holy Ghost, would be unreasonably limited to what is contained in the inspired writers. The inspiration to *write* does not supersede the command to *teach all nations orally until the end of time*. Not in the former work, but in the latter, the Holy Ghost was to *abide* with the Church *for ever* (John xiv. 16).

Christ promised immediately to the apostles, and in them to the whole teaching Church in every age, that the Holy Ghost would gradually "lead the way" to the possession of "all truth" for which the apostles were now unprepared, but which would be necessary for the exercise of their office. Our Divine Master next commends the authority of this Witness, and says:

For he shall not speak of himself; but what things soever he shall hear, he shall speak. And the things that are to come he shall show you.

Speaking to men, Christ made use of a mode of expression usual amongst men, to signify that the revelation of the Holy Spirit would not be contrary to anything he himself had already said, and that it would embrace all he had still to communicate. The reason given is that the Holy Ghost will neither speak nor act independently of the Father and the Son, from whom, as from one principle, he proceeds. This is the exposition of St. Augustine, who says (Tract. 99 in Joann.) : " Ab illo audiet, a quo procedit. Audire illi scire est, scire vero esse. Ab illo a quo procedit, illi est essentia et audientia. Semper audit Spiritus Sanctus quia semper scit." As Knabenbauer remarks, these words of Christ reveal the relation which subsists between the Holy Spirit and the Son. Just as the Son is said not to do anything unless what he sees the Father doing, and again as the Son is said to speak what he hears from the Father (John v. 19 ; viii. 26-40 ; xv. 15), for this reason only, that he has the divine nature from the Father and acts with him, so the Holy Spirit is said to speak nothing of himself, but what he hears, for this reason that he has his divine knowledge, and therefore his divine nature, from the Father and the Son who sent him. The future tense (" he shall hear ") is used not to signify that this knowledge was to be *communicated to the Holy Ghost* at a subsequent time, but to signify that the divine knowledge and nature which were communicated to the Holy Ghost from all eternity, were to be *manifested to man* at a time subsequent to that at which Christ was speaking.

Christ promises a revelation of all truths, and the knowledge of all that is necessary in the exercise of the apostolic ministry ; but for the greater consolation of the apostles, one class of truths is singled out for special mention in the following words :

And the things that are to come he shall show you.

Corluy remarks that in the Old Testament the foreknowledge and the prediction of the future are always referred to as attributes of the Divinity. " Show the things that are to come hereafter, and we shall know that ye are gods. . . . I am the first, and I am the last, and besides me there is no God. Who is like to me ? Let him call and declare, and let him set before me the order, since I appointed the ancient people. And the things to come, and that shall be hereafter, let them show unto them " (Isaias xli. 23 ; xliv. 6, 7). " The king spoke to Daniel, and said : Verily, your God is the God of gods, and Lord of kings, and a revealer of hidden things, seeing thou couldst discover this secret " (Dan. ii. 47). Because, therefore, God alone has the knowledge of " all truth " and especially the knowledge of the " things that are to come," Christ, in attributing such knowledge to the Holy Ghost, attributes to him by implication the divine nature itself. He thus most forcibly indicated the dignity of the Teacher whom the apostles were to receive.

Another effect of the coming of the Holy Ghost regarded Christ himself, and it is announced in the following words :—

V. 14. He shall glorify me ; because he shall receive of mine, and shall show it to you.

According to Maldonatus, Lucas Brugensis, and others, Christ's words may be thus paraphrased : " He shall glorify me, since he shall not teach otherwise than as I have taught ; and this because he shall receive of my doctrine, and shall make it known to you." Such an interpretation does not appear to convey Christ's meaning in its fullness. According to St. Thomas, Toletus, and others, the meaning is : " He shall glorify me, because he shall receive of my divinity ($\dot{\epsilon}\kappa$ $\tau o\hat{v}$ $\dot{\epsilon}\mu o\hat{\iota}$) and shall declare it to you." This exposition seems more probable, but still it is not quite satisfactory. It appears from the context, where the fullness of divine knowledge is attributed to the Holy Ghost, that Christ is here speaking of the source from which this knowledge comes. Therefore the words " of mine " ($\dot{\epsilon}\kappa$ $\tau o\hat{v}$ $\dot{\epsilon}\mu o\hat{v}$) mean here " of my knowledge " ; and the verse may be paraphrased in this manner : " He shall glorify me by manifesting my divine nature, because from the treasure of my divine knowledge, which is identical with my nature, he shall receive the knowledge of things to come, and as thus received from me he shall communicate it to you." In other words the Holy Ghost receives from the Son the fullness of divine knowledge, which is identical with the divine nature ; and manifesting this to the apostles as having been received from the Son, the Holy Ghost was to show that the Son possessed them as his own, and that thus the Son was God.

But if the Holy Ghost has the divine knowledge with the divine nature, how can he be said to have *received it ?* Does not this expression seem to imply an inferiority, which is impossible in a Divine Person ? St. Cyprian answers : " Nemo turbetur, cum hic audiat verbum *accipiendi ;* sed illud in animum inducat, nostro modo enuntiari res divinas, non sic tamen intelligi, sed modo nostrum captum excedente, atque ita nos dicere Spiritum a Patre et Filio accipere quae eorum sunt, non quod cognitionem et virtutem eorum aliquando non haberet ; sapiens enim semper est et potens, imo ipsa sapientia et potentia." (See Knabenbauer, *in loco.*)

How did the Holy Ghost receive this divine knowledge ? Not as did the prophets, by inspiration, nor by infusion, nor by any other way than by a communication of the divine nature in an eternal procession from the Father and the Son. " A divine person (who is not possessed of two natures like Jesus Christ) cannot be conceived to acquire anything except in his procession; for once he is a divine person he is infinite, and can receive nothing which he does not already possess.   Hence, whatever the Holy Ghost *heard*, he heard from eternity in proceeding from the Father and the Son" (MacRory).   St. Augustine makes the profound observation: "Semper itaque audit Spiritus Sanctus quia semper scit: ergo et scivit, et scit, et sciet; ac per hoc et audivit, et audit, et audiet: quia sicut jam diximus, hoc est illi audire quod scire; et scire illi hoc est quod esse.   Ab illo igitur audivit, audit, et audiet, a quo est; ab illo est, a quo procedit" (St. Aug., Tract. 99 in Joann.).

But if the Holy Ghost in eternity *received* from the Father and the Son his divine knowledge with the divine nature, why does our Divine Lord speak of this communication as of a thing still to come?   St. Augustine again answers in the same treatise: " Non moveat quod verbum futuri temporis positum est; est enim illa sempiterna audientia quia sempiterna scientia. In sempiterno autem sine initio et sine fine, cujuslibet verbum temporis ponitur, nec mendaciter dicimus: Fuit, et Est, et Erit.   Fuit, quia nunquam defecit; erit quia nunquam deerit; est, quia semper est."   In the eternal instant in which without succession of time the Holy Ghost exists, past, present, and future are one.   Here, however, as in the preceding verse, the future tense is employed to adapt the revelation of divine things to our understanding, and to signify that the *external communication* of the Holy Ghost's eternal knowledge had not yet been made at the time when Christ was speaking.

IV.—MORAL REFLECTIONS.

1. In the first part of this gospel passage we learn the kind of love which Jesus expects from us.   Before the descent of the Holy Ghost the love of the apostles for their Divine Master was in a great measure a merely natural feeling due to the sweetness of his presence, to the words of wisdom which they daily heard from his sacred lips, to the marvellous example of every virtue which they beheld in him, to all those attractions with which his sacred humanity was adorned, and to the prospect they saw of occupying a distinguished place around him in the kingdom of the Messiah.   This love was too selfish and imperfect.   To correct its defects in his apostles and in us, Christ on this occasion announced his approaching death and return to the Father; he taught us to raise our thoughts above mortal and transitory things around us; he demanded of us a love worthy of that new and eternal life into which he was about to enter; he required that we prefer his glory to our own

temporal consolation or advantage ; and as it was decreed that he was not to enter into this glory until he had left the world, he pointed out to us this departure as a subject of joy rather than of sorrow. In a previous part of his discourse he had said : " If you loved me, you would indeed be glad because I go to the Father ; for the Father is greater than I " (John xiv. 28). Here he says : " Sorrow hath filled your heart. But I tell you the truth : It is expedient for you that I go ; for if I go not, the Paraclete will not come to you, but if I go I will send him to you " (John xvi. 6, 7). On hearing these words, we Christians should examine the character of our love for Jesus. If our love for him arises from a feeling of personal interest only, if we love him merely because of temporal favours received or expected, and not for the spiritual gifts of grace conferred upon us, our devotion is neither true nor pleasing to him. Indeed if these be our dispositions it is not surprising that in affliction we lose heart, become negligent in prayer, and even abandon our spiritual exercises altogether. How different is the conduct of those who love Jesus for Jesus' sake ! Nothing that happens in this world can diminish their piety ; in the midst of contradictions and sorrows they are ever steadfast ; and rejoicing in the opportunity of sacrificing their will for God, they bless the fatherly hand that tries them. Such is the true and disinterested love which Jesus asked from the apostles, and which he asks from us.

If this pure love of God reigns in our hearts, the Paraclete or Consoler will descend on us, and will fill us with his gifts. In trouble of mind or of body it is not wrong, nor even imperfect, to seek comfort from our fellow-men ; for Jesus himself, to whom in his agony angels ministered, has sanctioned this by his example. It is in the Holy Spirit, however, we shall find our principal and unfailing support. When human lips are silent, or human words are powerless to comfort us, he will speak to our heart ; he will shed his light upon our minds ; he will enable us to see that all things happen by the providence of God who ever ordains what is best for us ; he will make us realise that our true goods are not the pleasures, the riches, or the honours of this world, but grace, and virtue, and peace in the Lord. Such was the feeling of the Psalmist who said : " Thou hast held me by my right hand ; and by thy will thou hast conducted me ; and with glory thou hast received me. For what have I in heaven, and besides thee what do I desire upon earth ? For thee my flesh and my heart hath fainted away. Thou art the God of my heart, and the God that is my portion for ever " (Ps. lxxii. 23-25).

2. The Holy Ghost was sent not merely to comfort and to perfect the apostles, but also to disabuse the world of its fatal prejudices, and to convince it of all that is necessary to be believed. Jesus Christ refers especially to three things regarding

which the world was to be convinced—sin, justice, and judgment.

In the first place, the world was to be convinced of its *sinful condition*, a condition which our Lord expressly declared to be due to unbelief. The Holy Ghost brought this conviction home to the minds of men when by the ministry of the apostles, he spread abroad the light of faith, and brought all nations to the knowledge of the true God. The world recognised and acknowledged its sin of unbelief, when renouncing its idolatry it embraced the religion which for three centuries it had persecuted, and adored the God whom it had so long blasphemed. Looking with admiration at this miracle of conversion, and beholding with sorrow the present want of faith, we are tempted to ask is it necessary that the Holy Ghost should again descend visibly upon the earth to convince the world once more of its sin of incredulity? It is no longer to the idols that men turn when rejecting the teaching of the Church : modern unbelievers wish to banish from the earth all divine worship, all religion, all ideas of God. We seem to have been reserved for the times predicted by our Lord when he said : " There shall arise false Christs and false prophets, and they shall show great signs and wonders, insomuch as to deceive (if possible) even the elect " (Matth. xxiv. 24). Let us fear lest we become victims of this unbelief which has already seized on so many of our fellow-men. Let us attach ourselves firmly to the teaching which the Church has handed down from the beginning. Let us pray that the Holy Spirit who lives in the Church may bring about her speedy triumph over the powers of hell ever leagued against her existence and our salvation. " Let God arise, and let his enemies be scattered ; and let them that hate him flee before his face " (Psalm lxvii. 2).

A second effect of the coming of the Holy Ghost was to convince the world of *justice*, by which we are to understand the sum total of all virtues. He who was to enlighten men by the gift of faith, was to give them a more perfect knowledge of justification by putting before them for imitation the sinless example of Jesus Christ. Without doubt the ideas of right and of wrong had never been entirely obliterated from the human mind ; but as the Psalmist had foretold, God sent his Holy Spirit, and the moral world was, as it were, again created. " Thou shalt send forth thy Spirit, and they shall be created ; and thou shalt renew the face of the earth " (Ps. ciii. 30). For the imperfect moral teaching of the pagan philosophers, there was substituted a universal code of precepts extending to all duties, embracing all virtues, and leading to the highest perfection. Instead of a moral teaching ever changing and without authority to bind the conscience, there was given to us a legislation which is immutable as the word of God, and which is enforced by the prospect of eternal happiness or misery. How do we stand with regard to the practice of this justice or righteousness illustrated in the life of Christ, and taught us by his Holy Spirit? If we have been unfaithful to this practice, we may well tremble at these words of the Sacred Scripture: " It had been better for them not to have known the way of justice, than after they have known it, to turn back from that holy commandment which was delivered to them " (2 Peter ii. 21).

A third point on which the Holy Ghost was to instruct and to convince the world was *judgment*. Men, it is true, had never entirely forgotten the primitive revelation that their acts are to be subjected to examination after death, and to be rewarded or punished according as they are good or bad. Though such was the case, however, the fables of paganism had obscured this salutary truth ; it was denied by some philosophers ; and it was doubted by almost all the others. The Holy Spirit came to teach it in all its purity, and to make it felt in all its force. By the voice of the Apostle he caused this maxim to resound throughout the world : " It is appointed unto men once to die, and after this, the judgment " (Hebr. ix. 27). And what must be the sentence of the wicked at this judgment ? Jesus Christ supplies us with an answer in the present passage of the gospel, and still more clearly in Matth. xxv. 41. The sentence to be passed on the wicked is that which has been passed, which has been executed, and which must be eternally executed on the devil, the prince of this world. The thought is terrifying, but at the same time most salutary to us all. What more efficacious preservative against sin, than to contemplate the fearful consequences of sin ? What more powerful help in temptation, than to compare the momentary satisfaction which temptation suggests, with the unending torments which sin brings in its train ?

FIFTH SUNDAY AFTER EASTER.

I.—TEXTS.

GREEK.

JOHN XVI. 23-30

²³ Καὶ ἐν ἐκείνῃ τῇ ἡμέρᾳ ἐμὲ οὐκ ἐρωτήσετε οὐδέν. Ἀμὴν ἀμὴν λέγω ὑμῖν, ἄν τι αἰτήσητε τὸν πατέρα δώσει ὑμῖν ἐν τῷ ὀνόματί μου. ²⁴ Ἕως ἄρτι οὐκ ᾐτήσατε οὐδὲν ἐν τῷ ὀνόματί μου· αἰτεῖτε, καὶ λήμψεσθε, ἵνα ἡ χαρὰ ὑμῶν ᾖ πεπληρωμένη.

²⁵ Ταῦτα ἐν παροιμίαις λελάληκα ὑμῖν· ἔρχεται ὥρα ὅτε οὐκέτι ἐν παροιμίαις λαλήσω ὑμῖν, ἀλλὰ παρρησίᾳ περὶ τοῦ πατρὸς ἀπαγγελῶ ὑμῖν. ²⁶ Ἐν ἐκείνῃ τῇ ἡμέρᾳ ἐν τῷ ὀνόματί μου αἰτήσεσθε· καὶ οὐ λέγω ὑμῖν ὅτι ἐγὼ ἐρωτήσω τὸν πατέρα περὶ ὑμῶν· ²⁷ Αὐτὸς γὰρ ὁ πατὴρ φιλεῖ ὑμᾶς, ὅτι ὑμεῖς ἐμὲ πεφιλήκατε, καὶ πεπιστεύκατε ὅτι ἐγὼ παρὰ τοῦ πατρὸς ἐξῆλθον. ²⁸ Ἐξῆλθον ἐκ τοῦ πατρὸς, καὶ ἐλήλυθα εἰς τὸν κόσμον· πάλιν ἀφίημι τὸν κόσμον, καὶ πορεύομαι πρὸς τὸν πατέρα. ²⁹ Λέγουσιν οἱ μαθηταὶ αὐτοῦ· ἴδε, νῦν ἐν παρρησίᾳ λαλεῖς, καὶ παροιμίαν οὐδεμίαν λέγεις. ³⁰ Νῦν οἴδαμεν ὅτι οἶδας πάντα, καὶ οὐ χρείαν ἔχεις ἵνα τίς σε ἐρωτᾷ· ἐν τούτῳ πιστεύομεν ὅτι ἀπὸ θεοῦ ἐξῆλθες.

VULGATE.

JOHN XVI. 23-30

23 Et in illo die me non rogabitis quidquam. Amen, amen dico vobis, si quid petieritis Patrem in nomine meo, dabit vobis. 24 Usque modo non petistis quidquam in nomine meo. Petite, et accipietis, ut gaudium vestrum sit plenum. 25 Hæc in proverbiis locutus sum vobis. Venit hora cum jam non in proverbiis loquar vobis, sed palam de Patre annuntiabo vobis. 26 In illo die in nomine meo petetis ; et non dico vobis quia ego rogabo Patrem de vobis. 27 Ipse enim Pater amat vos, quia vos me amastis, et credidistis quia ego a Deo exivi. 28 Exivi a Patre, et veni in mundum ; iterum relinquo mundum, et vado ad Patrem. 29 Dicunt ei discipuli ejus : Ecce nunc palam loqueris, et proverbium nullum dicis. 30 Nunc scimus quia scis omnia, et non opus est tibi ut quis te interroget ; in hoc credimus quia a Deo existi.

II.—ENGLISH TRANSLATION.

JOHN XVI. 23-30.

23 " And in that day you shall not ask me any thing. Amen amen I say to you : If you ask the Father any thing in my name, he will give it you. 24 Hitherto you have not asked any thing in my name. Ask, and you shall receive, that your joy may be full.

²⁵ These things I have spoken to you in proverbs : the hour cometh when I will no more speak to you in proverbs, but will show you plainly of the Father. ²⁶ In that day you shall ask in my name ; and I say not to you, that I will ask the Father for you ; ²⁷ for the Father himself loveth you, because you have loved me, and have believed that I came out from God. ²⁸ I came forth from the Father, and am come into the world : again I leave the world, and I go to the Father." ²⁹ His disciples say to him : " Behold, now thou speakest plainly, and speakest no proverb." ³⁰ Now we know that thou knowest all things, and thou needest not that any man should ask thee. By this we know that thou comest forth from God.

III.—NOTES.

Introductory. The present gospel passage is taken from the concluding portion of Christ's discourse at the Last Supper, and is followed by the solemn prayer which our Divine Lord, now terminating his public ministry, addressed to his Father for himself as Man, for his apostles, and for those who by their preaching were one day to be brought to the faith. In their grief at his approaching departure, the apostles had been consoled by the promise of many gifts, the bestowal of which could not take place until after Christ's death. Thus they were told that they would then receive the Holy Spirit who, convincing the world of " sin, of justice, and of judgment," would put them in possession of " all truth " (John xvi. 7, 8, 13). (See the Gospel of the Fourth Sunday after Easter.) Then it was announced to them that after a short absence which would plunge them into mourning, Christ would visit them again to fill them with abiding joy ; and it was added that from the joyful day of his return, they should no longer have need to question their Divine Master as to the meaning of this prophecy, the fulfilment of which would then have rendered unnecessary any further explanation. That Divine Master said : " You now indeed have sorrow, but I will see you again, and your heart shall rejoice ; and your joy no man shall take from you " (John xvi. 22, in the Gospel of Third Sunday after Easter). In the present passage, Christ put before the apostles another motive for consolation, viz., the full efficacy of their prayers when he who was here their Redeemer, would have merited by his Passion to become their Mediator and Intercessor with the Father.

Entering then on this last point of his address, Christ declared to them :—

V. 23. **Amen amen I say to you : If you ask the Father any thing in my name, he will give it you.**

It is to be remarked that according to many of the Greek codices, including B, the verse is thus read : " Amen amen I say to you : If you ask the Father any thing, he will give it you in my name." The Vulgate reading, which has the words " in my name " in the conditional clause, seems to be preferable, for this is the order in the following verse.

To ask in the name of Christ is something more than to ask " on account of," or " for the sake of Christ." Indeed, Knabenbauer observes that by the *name* the *person* is designated. The name of God is often used for those things which God has revealed regarding himself and which are known by men concerning him. Therefore the name of God stands for God himself ; and consequently, the name of Christ signifies Christ himself as far as his dignity, his will, and the nature of his office are revealed to us. Thus to ask in the name of Christ is to ask in Christ, in union with Christ by grace, and with a view to promote the work for which Christ was sent. This is the meaning attached to the words by the Church, the authentic interpreter of the Scripture, when, in obedience to the injunction of her Divine Spouse, she terminates all her petitions to the Father with the clause : " Through Jesus Christ our Lord." The Church does not cease to pray in the name of Christ when she prays to be heard through the merits of the saints, because the merits of the saints are not different from those of Christ ; nay even, they are the very merits of the Redeemer himself, which are crowned and rewarded in the saints. Hence the Church and her children, praying to be heard through the merits of the saints, pray through the merits of Christ, or pray " in the name " of Christ, because it is through a union with him, and through his grace that the works of man have any supernatural value.

On the words, " He will give it you," St. Augustine says : " Exaudiuntur quippe omnes sancti pro se ipsis, non autem pro omnibus exaudiuntur, vel amicis vel inimicis vel quibuslibet aliis ; quia non utcumque dictum est *dabit*, sed *dcbit vobis*." This interpretation appears improbable. Would not that in a certain sense be given to us which God at our intercession might confer on others ; and are we not commanded to pray for others, and this with a hope that our prayers, offered under certain conditions, will be heard ? But all doubt on the matter is removed by the statement of St. John in his first epistle (c. v. verses 14-16). Commenting, as it were, on the words of Christ, the evangelist says : " This is the confidence which we have towards him : That whatsoever we shall ask according to his will, he heareth us. And we know that he heareth us whatsoever we ask : we know that we have the petitions which we request of him. He that knoweth his brother to sin a sin which is not unto death, let him ask, and life shall be given to him." Christ's meaning is then : " Amen amen most truly and most faithfully do I promise you, that when you are united with me by grace, when you seek to promote the work for which I have been sent on earth, and when you ask through my merits, all your petitions, whether for yourselves or for others, will. be granted to you by my Heavenly Father."

Having thus promised all things to prayer, Christ remarks :

V. 24. Hitherto you have not asked any thing in my name.

This is not a reprehension for the past, but an instruction that in future the prayer of the apostles is to take a new form. Like other Jews, they had hitherto begged the Father to grant their requests through his goodness, his mercy, his providence, his remembrance of the patriarchs Abraham, Isaac, and Jacob. They had petitioned Christ himself to give them an increase of faith (Luke xvii. 5), to teach them to pray (Luke xi. 1), and to show them the Father (John xiv. 8) ; but they had not in the full sense of the words *asked any thing of the Father in Christ's name.* Up to this, Christ had been their Friend and Master only. They had not recognised him in his other offices as Redeemer, as Mediator, and as Head of the Church, who himself asks for the blessings to be conferred on his mystical body. For the future, they are to pray *in his name,* that is, being united with him by grace, and trusting in his merits and in his power, they are to seek for all things which in them and in others, may bring about the accomplishment of his will, and the perfecting of the work for which he was sent on earth.

To adopt this new mode of prayer they are encouraged by the following words :—

Ask, and you shall receive, that your joy may be full.

In the first place, we should observe with Plummer (Cambridge Bible) that the meaning of the Greek $αἰτεῖτε$ is : " Go on asking." The tense is the present, not the aorist, imperative. Compare Mark vi. 22 : $αἴτησόν με ὃ ἐὰν θέλῃς$ = " Ask of me what thou wilt." Again, it is remarked that the phrase " that your joy may be full," implies not only the fact $(ἵνα$ . . . . $πληρωθῇ,$ xv. 11), but the abiding state which follows $ἵνα$ . . . $ᾖ$ $πεπληρωμένη$ (comp. xvii. 13 ; 1 John i. 4 ; 2 John 12). (Westcott, *in loco.*) Still further, we should not, with St. Augustine, take the command of Christ to signify : " Ask that your joy may be full, and you shall receive." There is no reason for the inversion. Therefore the meaning is : " Henceforth persistently ask the Father in my name, and he will grant your requests, in order that the joy you have begun to feel in my company, may be complete. This joy of yours will be complete when. receiving your petitions through me, you will recognise the omnipotence of my name, and will learn that your faith and hope in me are not vain." The fulfilment of the promise here

made by Christ is not deferred until the next life when the joy
of the blessed cannot receive any addition ; it has its fulfilment
on earth in the hearts of the just, whose prayers in the name
of Christ secure the bestowal of all the gifts of the Holy Ghost,
with that spiritual joy, which is one of the fruits of the Holy
Ghost, dwelling within us.

It might be objected against this statement regarding the
power of prayer that not all who ask receive all they ask. The
answer is supplied in the words of St. James (James iv. 3) :
" You ask, and receive not ; because you ask amiss." The
fault is to be found in the person who prays, or in the object
of the prayer, or in the person for whom the prayer is offered.
In the first place, when one prays without the proper dispositions of devout attention, perseverance, humility, and hope, he
cannot be said to pray in union with Christ, nor in the name
of that " Mediator of God and man." Again, if one seeks for
what is unnecessary, or useless, or detrimental to that eternal
salvation to secure which the Redeemer came upon earth and
died, such a man cannot be said to pray in the sacred name
of Christ, whatever may be the form of words used. Lastly,
though the prayer may be offered with the proper dispositions,
and though the object of the prayer may be pleasing to God, still
the intended recipient of the divine bounty may be incapable of
receiving, or unworthy to receive the blessing sought for. In
this case the petition is salutary and efficacious, if not for others,
at least for the petitioner. He fulfils the commandment and
receives the reward promised by Christ when it was said to the
apostles as they set out on their first mission : " Into whatsoever house you enter, first say : Peace be to this house. And if
the son of peace be there, your peace shall rest upon him ; but
if not, it shall return to you " (Luke x. 5, 6 ; cf. Matth. x. 11-13).

Having cheered his apostles with the hope of obtaining all
things from the Father by prayer when they could no longer
enjoy his own visible presence, Christ now removes a cause of
anxiety arising from the character of much of his previous
address. He says :—

**V. 25. These things I have spoken to you in proverbs :
the hour cometh when I will no more speak to you in proverbs, but will show you plainly of the Father.**

The word " proverb " ($\pi\alpha\rho o\iota\mu\iota\alpha$) is not taken here in the sense
of *a trite popular saying,* as is the case when used by others
than the inspired writers. In the Sacred Scripture the word
has the wider signification of figurative and somewhat obscure
language, partly conveying and partly concealing important
truths. This is its meaning in John x. 6 and in the present
passage. Recalling to the minds of his apostles his references
to the " little while " preceding his departure, and the subse-

quent "little while" during which they were no longer to see
him, together with the prophecy regarding his departure to the
Father and the Descent of the Holy Ghost, our Lord speaks of
those references and of this prophecy as intentionally obscure
announcements. His meaning is as if he had said: "Considering your power of comprehension and the requirements of
the occasion, I have at present spoken these things to you in
an obscure manner. Let not the obscurity of my language per-
plex or sadden you. The hour, that is, the time is at hand
when I will not any longer speak thus to you, but will openly
and clearly manifest to you the attributes of the Father which
you now so ardently desire to know." This promise was fulfilled not only in heaven, where God is seen face to face, but
in a large measure even here on earth. After the Resurrection Christ made known to his apostles the meaning of the
Scriptures; during the forty days he was appearing to them, and
speaking to them regarding the kingdom of God; and after
his Ascension he imparted to them as far as necessary the knowledge of all truth through the Holy Ghost, the Spirit of Truth.

Besides the full knowledge of divine things, another blessing
—the greatest of all—was to be conferred on the apostles in the
love of God the Father. Introducing this subject, Christ says :—

V. 26. In that day you shall ask in my name.

Our Divine Lord here foretells that the apostles, on being
fully instructed by himself in person after the Resurrection, and
by the Holy Ghost after the Ascension, will carry out his commandment to present their petitions in his name. That they
did so, is shown by the practice of the Church which, as
already stated, ever terminates her prayers to the Father with
these words: "Through our Lord Jesus Christ."

Lest it might be thought that they were thus to pray because
they themselves were not in favour with God, Christ adds :—

And I say not to you, that I will ask the Father for you.

The sense is: "Although I can say, and I have said, that I
will intercede for you with the Father (John xiv. 16), I do not
say this now, lest you conclude that you are not acceptable to
the Father." By a divine decree the merits of Christ are necessary for man's salvation; and without the application of these
merits no one is heard, no one is loved by God. Before the
Jewish Council St. Peter said of our Redeemer: "This is the
stone which was rejected by you the builders, which is become
the head of the corner; neither is there salvation in any other.
For there is no other name under heaven given to men, whereby
we must be saved" (Acts iv. 11, 12). Having whilst on earth
redeemed us by his merits, Christ now presents these merits to
his Father for us; he continues thereby to manifest his desire of

our salvation ; he is our Mediator with God ; and by this his eternal priesthood, " he is able also to save for ever them that come to God by him, always living to make intercession for us " (Hebr. vii. 25). Taken in connection with these truths, the present statement of Christ makes known to the apostles the consoling fact that, prescinding from the power of his own intercession at the time of their prayer, their petitions will be ever pleasing to the Father and will ever obtain a favourable answer.

The reason was given when our Lord added :—

V. 27. **For the Father himself loveth you, because you have loved me, and have believed that I came out from God.**

According to Westcott the sense of the first clause is : " The Father himself, without any pleading on my part, loveth you with the love which springs from a natural relationship " ($\phi\iota\lambda\epsilon\hat{\iota}$.) The disciples are also sons (Rom. viii. 15) ; and the assurance here given to them, carries out still further the promise in John xiv. 21, 23. The word $\pi\epsilon\phi\iota\lambda\dot{\eta}\kappa\alpha\tau\epsilon = you\ have\ loved$, is used only here in the gospels to express the affection of the disciples for their Lord ; and the juxtaposition of the pronouns ($\dot{\upsilon}\mu\epsilon\hat{\iota}s\ \dot{\epsilon}\mu\dot{\epsilon}\ \pi\epsilon\phi\iota\lambda\dot{\eta}\kappa\alpha\tau\epsilon$) gives force to the personal relationship. Comp. Matth. x. 37. (See Westcott, *in loco*.) It is said that the Father loves the disciples, because by faith and charity they are united with him who for his own sake is the only object of the Father's love. It is to be carefully observed that these words of Christ do not signify that faith and charity on our part absolutely forestall and merit all love on the part of God. This would be the heresy of Pelagius. The first grace cannot be merited. " When the goodness and kindness of God our Saviour appeared, not by the works of justice which we have done, but according to his mercy he saved us by the laver of regeneration and renovation of the Holy Ghost, whom he hath poured forth upon us abundantly through Jesus Christ our Saviour, that being justified by his grace, we may be heirs according to hope of life everlasting " (Titus iii. 5-7). Christ means, therefore, that the apostles' faith and charity, which *were themselves* the effect of divine grace, were followed and rewarded by fresh indications and proofs of divine love— amongst these being a free access to the Father and a favourable response to their prayer. It is well said : " The love of the disciples is to be regarded no less as the sign than as the cause of the Father's love (xiv. 21-23). His love made their love possible, and then again responded to it (1 John v. 10 ; Donum Dei est diligere Deum. Aug. *ad locum*). Their love is regarded both in its origin, and in its continuance (*have loved*, $\pi\epsilon\phi\iota\lambda\dot{\eta}\kappa\alpha\tau\epsilon$), his love in its present operation (*loveth*, $\phi\iota\lambda\epsilon\hat{\iota}$)." (See Westcott, *in loco*.)

In reference to the apostles' faith which made them so acceptable to the Father, Christ had just said: "You . . . have believed that I came out from God." He now confirms their profession of faith with the words :—

V. 28. **I came forth from the Father, and am come into the world : again I leave the world, and I go to the Father.**

According to many commentators, *e.g.*, Toletus, A Lapide, McCarthy, SS. Bede, Augustine, Thomas, etc., the words : " I came forth from the Father," describe Christ's eternal generation, whilst the clause " and am come into the world " refers to his temporal birth. According to others (Jansenius Gand., MacRory, etc.), it seems more probable that both clauses refer to the Incarnation and coming of our Lord. The following is the reason. The word " again " indicates another journey, not another " leaving of the world. The first journey was from the Father into the world ; the second was, in inverse order, from the world to the Father. Hence, as there is a relation between the clauses, " I . . . am come into the world," and " I leave the world," there is the same relation between " I came forth from the Father," and " I go to the Father." As, then, the going to the Father happened in time, so we are to understand the contrasted idea of coming forth from the Father to be nothing else than Christ's temporal mission when, at his Incarnation, he was sent into the world for our redemption. Still, though not *expressed*, the eternal generation of the Word, is here *implied*. Inasmuch as the Word is said to have come forth from the Father when at his Incarnation he assumed human nature, it is implied that till then he was remaining with the Father. Now this being so, and it being elsewhere stated that the Word is not inferior to the Father, his temporal mission from the Father cannot be admitted without presupposing his eternal generation. As theologians teach, the mission of one Divine Person by another implies the procession of the Person sent from the Person who sends. " Thus the Lord, while he recognises the faith of the disciples, lays before them a revelation of deeper mysteries. The verse is indeed a brief summary of the whole historic work of Christ : clause answers to clause : the Mission, the Nativity, the Passion, the Ascension " (Westcott, *in loco*).

The discourse of Christ had been listened to in sorrowful silence, broken only by anxious discussions apart as to the hidden meaning of his words. Taking courage now from the praise bestowed on them, and from the promises made to them by their divine Master,

Vv. 29, 30. **His disciples say to him : Behold now thou speakest plainly, and speakest no proverb. Now we know that thou knowest all things, and thou needest not that any man should ask thee. By this we believe that thou comest forth from God.**

Allusion seems to be here made to the two modes of instruction which, according to Schoettgen, were in use amongst the Jews—that which consisted of " similitudes " or figures, and that which was without " enigma." According to the dispositions and requirements of his audience, Christ adopted, now one mode of teaching, now another. The time was not yet come when, first by himself, and afterwards by the Holy Spirit, Christ was to communicate to the apostles a clear knowledge of what was now obscurely hinted (v. 25) regarding the " little while," the other " little while," his departure from this world, and his relations with the Father. These apostles, however, were now carried away with joy on learning the favour in which they stood with God, and they imagined that they already fully comprehended the sayings which had hitherto perplexed them. Under the influence of this excitement, they addressed their Divine Master in words which may be thus paraphrased : " Behold, thou now doest what thou didst promise to do at a future time. Whereas thou hast been hitherto speaking obscurely and enigmatically, thou now speakest plainly and hidest nothing. Taught by experience we are now aware that thou knowest all things, even our secret thoughts, and the difficulties about which we wished for light. Thou hast not need that we should interrogate thee ; for, anticipating our question, thou dost give the answer. As, therefore, it belongs to God alone to know the secrets of the heart, we more and more firmly believe that thou art come forth from God."

Because in the apostles' profession of faith there was something of self-complacency, that feeling was at once firmly, but gently repressed by the warning with which the discourse terminates. " Jesus answered them : Do you now believe ? Behold the hour cometh, and it is now come, that you shall be scattered every man to his own, and shall leave me alone. And yet I am not alone, because the Father is with me " (John xvi. 31, 32). Christ does not here deny the apostles' faith in him— a faith to which he had just borne testimony (v. 27) ; but he declares that their faith is still weak and imperfect. The truth of this declaration is shown in the history of the Passion, when all abandoned their Divine Master (Matth. xxvi. 56 ; Mark xiv. 50), and in the history of the Resurrection, when they refused to believe those who had seen him risen from the dead (Mark xvi. 11, 13, 14).

IV.—MORAL REFLECTIONS.

1. The exhortation to pray was addressed to us as well as to the apostles, and the promise which accompanied that exhortation is no less our inheritance than theirs. To all man-

kind Christ said : " Ask and you shall receive, that your joy may be full." Everything, then, without exception is promised to prayer, and the divine munificence is limited only by our desires.   The Fathers of the Church have not feared to liken the irresistible force of prayer to the divine omnipotence ; they have found here a power which can be exercised over God himself ; and they have justified the expression by the words of the Holy Ghost, who says that in granting the petition of Josue the Lord obeyed the voice of man (Josue x. 14).

2. But if this holy exercise be so powerful, how is it that in the case of many it seems to be without effect ?   St. James answers this question when he says : " You ask, and receive not, because you ask amiss " (James iv. 3).   Jesus Christ has promised to hear our prayer, but not every kind of prayer : he has pledged himself to grant all things to prayer, but it is to prayer well made.   It is important then to know the conditions necessary to secure an answer to our petitions.

(a) The first condition of efficacious prayer—a condition to which the Holy Fathers refer all others—is that we ask in the name of Jesus Christ, through his mediation, and in virtue of his merits.   Of ourselves we are but sinners, meriting only God's anger ; and when God hears us, it is in consideration of the Mediator between God and man who continually offers to his Eternal Father our poor petitions.   Nothing is pleasing to this Eternal Father except what passes through the hands of his Son.   Presented by the Son, however, and incorporated as it were with his, our prayers become in some sort divine and infallible in their efficacy with the Father.

(b) The second condition of efficacious prayer is that it be a request for what is really beneficial to us.   This condition is intimately connected with the first, for we cannot ask in the name of Christ what is useless to us or opposed to our welfare. As there are two classes of goods—temporal and spiritual— there are two objects of our prayer ; but the form of prayer is not the same for both.   To pray for temporal things is not forbidden, since it is taught by Jesus Christ (Luke xi. 3), prescribed by the Apostle (1 Tim. ii. 1, 2), and daily practised by the Church.   But when we ask these temporal blessings with the Church, we should ask them as she does.   Now, following the order laid down by her Founder, she asks first for the kingdom of God and his justice (Matth. vi. 33), and in the second place she seeks for all things else under the condition that they be helpful to her children's eternal salvation, and as far as they may be helpful thereto.   If in our prayers we imitate the Church, we shall either obtain the precise blessing for which we ask, or when this would be detrimental to us and in consequence is mercifully denied us, the promise of God will be fulfilled by the bestowal of some other favour of greater value. In our petitions for spiritual blessings, it may happen that we pray in general for eternal salvation and the means to attain it, or it may be that we ask for some special grace that seems helpful to us. We can offer the first kind of prayer unconditionally, at all times, and in all circumstances ; and it is ever certain to be granted, because God desires our salvation more than we do ourselves. Sometimes, however, the bestowal of a special grace asked by us would interfere with our reception of one greater, or would be unsuited to our circumstances. It was thus with the great Apostle whose thrice-repeated petition was not acceded to, lest he should be deprived of the merit he was to gain by humility and resistance to temptation (2 Cor. xii. 7, 8, 9). Our prayer, then, for special favours even of a purely spiritual kind, must be ever accompanied by the condition that what we ask be pleasing to God and useful for us.

(c) Another condition of efficacious prayer is a pious attention to what we say. With voluntary distraction there is no prayer, for the most necessary act of religion cannot be one purely external. Prayer does not consist merely in the words spoken by the lips, but principally in the feelings of the heart which is raised up to God. Hence attention in this holy exercise is as much prescribed as the exercise itself ; and the moment we divert our mind to other things, we cease to pray. But in this matter we should beware of exaggeration, and should remember that what is culpable in distraction is not the wandering of the mind, but the will that lends itself thereto. The Author of our nature knows our feebleness, and is not offended at what is involuntary on our part. It is the moment of advertence to distraction that decides whether we be blameworthy or free from fault. We are blameworthy if we continue to entertain the distraction ; we are free from fault if with renewed fervour we again fix our mind on God.

(d) It is scarcely necessary to say that our prayer should be humble, for it is written : " The prayer of him that humbleth himself shall pierce the clouds " (Ecclesiasticus xxxv. 21). We cannot be ignorant of this, because arrogance in a suppliant is a contradiction ; and the need we have of prayer should make us sensible of our utter dependence on the divine bounty.

(e) The humility of our petition should not lessen our confidence—another requisite essential to our success. The one quality springs from the conviction of our nothingness ; the other is based on our knowledge of the divine promises. Inasmuch as nothing is due to us, we should be humble ; but inasmuch as all things are promised to us, we should be hopeful. Whereas we of ourselves cannot merit, we have no reason for pride ; but since Christ has merited for us, we have no reason to despair.

(*f*) Lastly, to be efficacious our prayers should be persevering. Although God has promised that our petitions will be granted, he has not promised that they will be granted at the moment when we present them. If, then, he sometimes appears to be indifferent to our needs and deaf to our supplications, we should not be discouraged. This is a refinement of goodness in which, while preparing to satisfy our desires, he wishes to give us an occasion for greater merit by exercising our patience, faith, humility, and fervour. By failing in perseverance we lose all at the moment we are on the point of receiving the reward ; and we abandon the race when the prize is within our reach. " If," said St. James, " any of you want wisdom, let him ask of God, who giveth to all men abundantly, and upbraideth not ; and it shall be given him. But let him ask in faith, nothing wavering. For he that wavereth is like a wave of the sea, which is moved and carried about by the wind. Therefore, let not that man think that he shall receive anything of the Lord " (James i. 5-7).

FEAST OF THE ASCENSION.

I.—TEXTS.

GREEK.

MARK XVI. 14-20.

¹⁴ Ὕστερον ἀνακειμένοις αὐτοῖς τοῖς ἕνδεκα ἐφανερώθη, καὶ ὠνείδισεν τὴν ἀπιστίαν αὐτῶν καὶ σκληροκαρδίαν, ὅτι τοῖς θεασαμένοις αὐτὸν ἐγηγερμένον οὐκ ἐπίστευσαν. ¹⁵ Καὶ εἶπεν αὐτοῖς· πορεύθέντες εἰς τὸν κόσμον ἅπαντα, κηρύξατε τὸ εὐαγγέλιον πάσῃ τῇ κτίσει. ¹⁶ Ὁ πιστεύσας καὶ βαπτισθεὶς, σωθήσεται· ὁ δὲ ἀπιστήσας, κατακριθήσεται. ¹⁷ Σημεῖα δὲ τοῖς πιστεύσασιν ταῦτα παρακολουθήσει· ἐν τῷ ὀνόματί μου δαιμόνια ἐκβαλοῦσιν· γλώσσαις λαλήσουσιν καιναῖς· ¹⁸ ὄφεις ἀροῦσιν· κἂν θανάσιμόν τι πίωσιν, οὐ μὴ αὐτοὺς βλάψει· ἐπὶ ἀρρώστους χεῖρας ἐπιθήσουσιν, καὶ καλῶς ἕξουσιν. ¹⁹ Ὁ μὲν οὖν κύριος, μετὰ τὸ λαλῆσαι αὐτοῖς, ἀνελήφθη εἰς τὸν οὐρανόν, καὶ ἐκάθισεν ἐκ δεξιῶν τοῦ θεοῦ. ²⁰ Ἐκεῖνοι δὲ ἐξελθόντες ἐκήρυξαν πανταχοῦ, τοῦ κυρίου συνεργοῦντος, καὶ τὸν λόγον βεβαιοῦντος διὰ τῶν ἐπακολουθούντων σημείων. Ἀμήν.

VULGATE.

MARK XVI. 14-20.

¹⁴ Novissime recumbentibus illis undecim apparuit ; et exprobravit incredulitatem eorum et duritiam cordis ; quia iis qui viderant eum resurrexisse, non crediderunt. ¹⁵ Et dixit eis : Euntes in mundum universum prædicate evangelium omni creaturæ. ¹⁶ Qui crediderit, et baptizatus fuerit, salvus erit ; qui vero non crediderit, condemnabitur. ¹⁷ Signa autem eos qui crediderint, hæc sequentur : In nomine meo dæmonia ejicient ; linguis loquentur novis ; ¹⁸ serpentes tollent ; et si mortiferum quid biberint, non eis nocebit; super ægros manus imponent, et bene habebunt. ¹⁹ Et Dominus quidem Jesus postquam locutus est eis, assumptus est in cœlum, et sedet a dextris Dei. ²⁰ Illi autem profecti prædicaverunt ubique, Domino cooperante, et sermonem confirmante, sequentibus signis.

II.—ENGLISH TRANSLATION, WITH PARALLEL PASSAGES FROM ST. LUKE.

MARK XVI. 14-20.

¹⁴ At length he appeared to the eleven as they were at table ; and he upbraided them with their incredulity and hardness of heart, because they did not believe them who

had seen him after he was risen again. ¹⁵ And he said to them : " Go ye into the whole world, and preach the gospel to every creature. ¹⁶ He that believeth and is baptised, shall be saved ; but he that believeth not, shall be condemned. ¹⁷ And these signs shall follow them that believe : In my name they shall cast out devils ; they shall speak with new tongues ; ¹⁸ they shall take up serpents ; and if they shall drink any deadly thing, it shall not hurt them ; they shall lay their hands upon the sick, and they shall recover."

¹⁹ And the Lord Jesus, after he had spoken to them, was taken up into heaven, and sitteth on the right hand of God. ²⁰ But they going forth, preached everywhere, the Lord working with them, and confirming the word with the signs that followed.

LUKE (GOSPEL) XXIV. 44-53.

⁴⁴ And he said to them : " These are the words which I spoke to you while I was yet with you, that all things must needs be fulfilled which are written in the law of Moses, and in the prophets, and in the psalms, concerning me." ⁴⁵ Then he opened their understanding, that they might understand the Scriptures ; ⁴⁶ and he said to them : " Thus it is written, and thus it behoves that Christ should suffer and rise again from the dead the third day, ⁴⁷ and that penance and remission of sins should be preached in his name unto all nations, beginning at Jerusalem. ⁴⁸ And you are witnesses of these things. ⁴⁹ And I send the promise of my Father upon you ; but stay you in the city till you be indued with power from on high."

⁵⁰ And he led them out as far as Bethany ; and lifting up his hands, he blessed them. ⁵¹ And it came to pass, whilst he blessed them, he departed from them and was carried up to heaven. ⁵² And they adoring, went back into Jerusalem with great joy. ⁵³ And they were always in the temple, praising and blessing God. Amen

LUKE (ACTS) I. 4-12.

⁴ And eating together with them, he commanded them that they should not depart from Jerusalem, but should wait for the promise of the Father, " which you have heard (saith he) by my mouth ; ⁵ for John indeed baptised with water, but you shall be baptised with the Holy Ghost not many days hence." ⁶ They therefore who were come together, asked him, saying : " Lord wilt thou at this time restore again the kingdom to Israel ? " ⁷ But he said to them : " It is not for you to know the times or moments which the Father hath put in his own power. ⁸ But you shall receive the power of the Holy Ghost coming upon you ; and you shall be witnesses unto me in Jerusalem, and in all Judæa, and Samaria, and even to the uttermost part of the earth."

[9] And when he had said these things, while they looked on, he was raised up ; and a cloud received him out of their sight. [10] And while they were looking at him going up to heaven, behold, two men stood by them in white garments, [11] who also said : " Ye men of Galilee, why stand you looking up to heaven ? This Jesus who is taken up from you into heaven, shall so come as you have seen him going into heaven."

[12] Then they returned to Jerusalem from the mount that is called Olivet, which is nigh Jerusalem, within a sabbath day's journey.

III.—COMBINED NARRATIVE.

At length he appeared to the eleven as they were at table, and he upbraided them with their incredulity and hardness of heart, because they did not believe them who had seen him after he was risen again. And he said to them : " These are the words which I spoke to you while I was yet with you, that all things must needs be fulfilled which are written in the law of Moses, and in the prophets, and in the psalms, concerning me." Then he opened their understanding that they might understand the Scriptures ; and he said to them : " Thus it is written and thus it behoved that Christ should suffer, and rise again from the dead the third day, and that penance and remission of sins should be preached in his name unto all nations, beginning at Jerusalem. And you are witnesses of these things." And he said to them : " Go ye into the whole world, and preach the gospel to every creature. He that believeth and is baptised, shall be saved ; but he that believeth not, shall be condemned. And these signs shall follow them that believe : In my name they shall cast out devils ; they shall speak with new tongues ; they shall take up serpents ; and if they shall drink any deadly thing, it shall not hurt them ; they shall lay their hands upon the sick, and they shall recover. And I send the promise of my Father upon you."

And eating together with them, he commanded them that they should not depart from Jerusalem, but should wait for the promise of the Father, " which you have heard (saith he) by my mouth ; for John indeed baptised with water, but you shall be baptised with the Holy Ghost not many days hence." They therefore who were come together, asked him, saying : " Lord, wilt thou at this time restore again the kingdom to Israel ? " But he said to them : " It is not for you to know the times or moments which the Father hath put in his own power. But you shall receive the power of the Holy Ghost coming upon you ; and you shall be witnesses unto me in Jerusalem, and in all Judæa, and Samaria, and even to the uttermost part of the earth."

And the Lord Jesus, after he had spoken these things to them, led them out as far as Bethany; and lifting up his hands he blessed them. And it came to pass, whilst he blessed them, he departed from them; and while they looked on, he was raised up; and a cloud received him out of their sight; and [he] was carried up into heaven, and sitteth on the right hand of God. And while they were looking at him going up to heaven, behold two men stood by them in white garments, who also said: "Ye men of Galilee, why stand you looking up to heaven? This Jesus who is taken up from you into heaven, shall so come as you have seen him going into heaven."

And then they adoring, returned with great joy to Jerusalem from the mount that is called Olivet, which is nigh Jerusalem, within a sabbath day's journey. And they were always in the temple, praising and blessing God. Amen. But [having received the Holy Ghost], they going forth, preached everywhere, the Lord working with them, and confirming the word with the signs that followed.

IV.—NOTES.

Introductory. The Ascension of Christ, honoured by the Church to-day, is recorded by SS. Mark and Luke, whose accounts of this event are supplementary, one of the other. It is to be noticed that many commentators (*e.g.*, Jans. Gand., Jans. Ypr., A Lap., Lamy, Bisp., Schegg, Fillion, Knabenbauer) think the apparition spoken of by St. Mark in the first verse of this extract did not occur on the day of the Ascension, but on the evening of the Resurrection. To defend their position they point out (1) that the Greek word ὕστερον is not properly rendered by " novissime " = " last of all," but by " tandem " or " postea " = " afterwards "; and they remark (2°) that our Lord could not be supposed to reproach the apostles on the day of the Ascension for a state of unbelief which must have entirely ceased during the repeated apparitions of the past forty days (Acts i. 3). An opinion held by such distinguished writers is not without a certain degree of probability. In the absence of certainty, however, it appears preferable to accept the view of St. Gregory the Great (Hom. 29 in Ev.), of St. Augustine (Lib. iii. De Consensu, cap. 25), and of Patrizi (Com. in Marcum), who think that St. Mark here describes the apparition of Christ to his apostles on the day of the Ascension. In the first place, it is true that the Greek word ὕστερον signifies " afterwards," and not " last of all "; but still, is not such an expression applicable to the day of the Ascension as well as to that of the Resurrection? Again, the fact that Christ upbraided his apostles with their incredulity and hardness of heart (Mark xvi. 14) does not militate against the opinion of SS. Augustine and Gregory.

Christ's reproof on this occasion had reference not to the present but to past dispositions, and could have been addressed to the apostles on the day of the Ascension for sufficient reasons which will be indicated in a subsequent note. Lastly, we should remember that on the day of the Resurrection Christ did not appear " to *the eleven* as they were at table " (Mark xvi. 14) ; for it is expressly said that during the apparition to the apostles on that occasion, " Thomas, one of the twelve (then reduced to eleven by the death of Judas), was not with them when Jesus came " (John xx. 24). The attempt to explain away this statement of St. John does not appear satisfactory.

SS. Augustine and Gregory's opinion being adopted, it is clear from a review of the gospel history subsequent to the Resurrection, that Christ appeared to his disciples first in Jerusalem ; that they were commanded to meet him afterwards in Galilee, where " he showed himself alive after his Passion by many proofs, for forty days appearing to them, and speaking of the kingdom of God " (Acts i. 3) ; and that, in obedience to another order, not recorded in the gospels, they assembled in the Holy City to receive his last instructions and to witness his Ascension into heaven. These journeys of the apostles from Jerusalem to Galilee, and from Galilee to Jerusalem, corresponding as they did to the order followed by Christ himself in his public ministry, prefigured the course of the gospel preaching, which was to be announced first to the Jews, afterwards to the Gentiles, and finally to that remnant of the Jews who are to be converted at the end of the world (Rom. ix. 27).

The apostles, then, were assembled in Jerusalem to see their Divine Master for the last time on earth, and the circumstances are thus described by the evangelist St. Mark :—

V. 14. At length he appeared to the eleven as they were at table ; and he upbraided them with their incredulity and hardness of heart, because they did not believe them who had seen him after he was risen again.

As our Lord just risen from the tomb, made his first appearance to the apostles in a body whilst they were at table, so did he make his last. But why did he now reproach them with a slowness to believe, which cannot be supposed to have still continued after the instructions and miracles of the preceding forty days ? He did so to remind them that the grace of faith which they now possessed, and the knowledge of heavenly things which they were to communicate to others, were gratuitous gifts from God, and entirely beyond the reach of their natural powers unassisted by him. To prepare them to enter on their sublime office of teachers of the world, he recalled to their memory the obstinate unbelief with which some of their number had received the news of the Resurrection, attested as that fact was by Mary Magdalen (John xx. 18), by the other holy women (Matth. xxviii. 8, 10), by Peter (Luke xxiv. 34), and by the two disciples from Emmaus (Mark xvi. 12, 13 ; Luke xxiv. 35). To render this lesson the more effective, Christ, according to St. Luke (xxiv. 44) (see Combined Narrative), reminded them that the events of his Passion, Death, and Resurrection had frequently been the subject of his conversation during his mortal life. " These are the words which I spoke to you while I was yet with you, that all things must needs be fulfilled which are written in the law of Moses, and in the prophets, and in the psalms, concerning me " (Luke xxiv. 44). Nay more, since none of them, even after the fulfilment,could fully comprehend the prophecies regarding Christ, he then " opened their understanding that they might understand the Scriptures " (Luke xxiv. 45). In conclusion, " he said to them : Thus it is written, and thus it behoved that Christ should suffer, and rise again from the dead the third day, and that penance and remission of sins should be preached in his name unto all nations, beginning at Jerusalem " (Luke xxiv. 46, 47).

In this manner Christ confirmed the apostles themselves in their faith, and supplied them with the chief matter of their instructions to their future disciples. It remained to give them their solemn commission as his ambassadors ;

V. 15. And he said to them: Go ye into the whole world, and preach the gospel to every creature.

In the apparition on the mountain in Galilee, Christ had given a similar command in these words : " Going therefore, teach ye all nations, baptising them in the name of the Father, and of the Son, and of the Holy Ghost " (Matth. xxviii. 19). On both occasions, indeed, the terms used are quite general, and have as wide a signification as is permitted by the *subject matter*, which is one of the criterions of interpretation. The subject matter—the preaching of the gospel—limits the meaning of the phrase " every creature," and shows that by this phrase is meant every creature capable of instruction, every rational being on earth, every man of every nation, whether Jew or Gentile (*Cf.* Col. i. 23). The phrase is a Hebraism having this signification, as Lightfoot (*in loco*) proves by many examples from the Talmudists. It is true that St. Paul, referring to the inanimate creation, says : " The expectation of the creature waiteth for the revelation of the sons of God. . . . Because the creature also itself shall be delivered from the servitude of corruption, unto the liberty of the glory of the children of God " (Rom. viii. 19-21). This is true ; but it does not follow that the command : " Preach . . . to every creature," has in view the inanimate world which is incapable of receiving the gospel message

The necessity for this apostolic office is made clear in the following words of Christ :—

V. 16. He that believeth and is baptised shall be saved; but he that believeth not shall be condemned.

As was customary with the Hebrews in matters of great importance, our Lord here uses both the affirmative and the negative form of expression to enforce the necessity of the faith which must accompany baptism. On the one hand this belief in the gospel is essential for salvation, because Christ had said : " He that doth not believe is already judged " (John iii. 18), and because the Apostle afterwards declared that " without faith it is impossible to please God " (Hebr. xi. 6). On the other hand, true faith brings in its train the observance of the commandments ; for St. John has written : " By this we know that we have known him, if we keep his commandments. He who saith that he knoweth him, and keepeth not his commandments, is a liar, and the truth is not in him " (1 John ii. 3, 4). The present passage of St. Mark, taken in connection with its parallels, affords no support for the doctrine of justification by faith only without good works. St. Gregory has well said : " Fortasse unusquisque apud semetipsum dicat : Ego jam credidi, salvus ero. Verum dicit si fidem operibus tenet ; vera etenim fides est quae in hoc quod verbis dicit, moribus non contradicit. Hinc de quibusdam falsis fidelibus Paulus dicit : Qui confitentur se nosse Deum, factis autem negant " (Titus i. 16). (See Knabenbauer.) It does not follow, then, from this passage, that faith and baptism are sufficient for salvation. Neither can it be said that the order of the words, " He that believeth and is baptised shall be saved," is conclusive against the rite of infant baptism. That infant baptism is useful and necessary cannot indeed be proved from *explicit* statements in the Holy Scriptures, but this truth *is easily deducible* from principles laid down in the inspired writings, and from the theoretical and practical teaching of the Church. The subject of infant baptism is not at all alluded to here. This passage refers to the baptism of those only who, having come to the use of reason, are capable of receiving instruction in the Christian doctrine.

The dangers that attended the mission to teach the gospel to a hostile world were foretold at the Last Supper (John xv. 19 ; xvi. 2). Lest such dangers might turn the apostles aside from their vocation, or even discourage them in their work, Christ now makes known the powers which they and their disciples are about to receive. He said :—

Vv. 17, 18. And these signs shall follow them that believe : In my name they shall cast out devils ; they shall speak with new tongues ; they shall take up serpents ; and if they shall

drink any deadly thing, it shall not hurt them ; they shall lay their hands upon the sick, and they shall recover.

After having promised that faith in his word is to be recompensed by salvation in the future life, Christ here declares that it will be accompanied by the gift of " signs " or miracles in the present. It is to be observed (1°) that this promise was made, not so much to excite faith in those who would hear the apostles, as to encourage the apostles themselves to prosecute with vigour and without fear a work which God was to mark with the astounding miracles here enumerated. (2°) Christ did not mean that this power over demons, this faculty of speaking unknown tongues, this preservation from danger, and this gift of healing, were to be marks to distinguish the believer from the unbeliever. He meant that these " signs," *i.e.*, miracles and prodigies, on being worked by the apostles and by their disciples, would be evidence of the credibility of the Christian revelation. (3°) As interpreters teach, the phrase " in my name " signifies not merely " at the invocation of my name," but also " by my authority and for the promotion of my work on earth."

From all this it follows that miracles were to be more frequent in the early ages of the Church when Christ's work was for the first time taken up by men, and when the truth of Christ's mission was to be proved to the benighted Gentile and to the unbelieving Jew. On the other hand, it does not follow that the power of working miracles was then to cease. Being conferred on the apostles not as a personal gift, but as a help to fulfil their office, it should, and shall, descend to their successors : it could, and can, be exercised in the Church as often as may be required in the promotion of the work for which the Church is instituted. " The Spirit breatheth where he will " (John iii. 8). On each age in the Church's history, and on each person in the Church's service, there is bestowed all that is necessary to secure the purposes of that supernatural providence by which our destiny is governed, and for which we live.

When Christ had thus given to the apostles their mission to preach, when he had announced the rewards and punishments respectively of those who receive, and of those who reject his gospel, and when he had encouraged his followers to enter on a work to be blessed by many and manifest miracles, he put before them the source from which their power was to be derived. According to St. Luke, he said : " You are witnesses of these things. And I send the promise of my Father (the Holy Spirit foretold in the prophets, Isaias xliv. 3 ; Joel ii. 28) upon you ; but stay you in the city till you be indued with power from on high " (Luke xxiv. 48, 49). Christ had already promised that he would not leave them orphans (John xiv. 18) ; that he would ask the Father to send them another Paraclete the Spirit of Truth, who would abide with them for ever (John xiv. 16, 17) ; and that this Spirit of Truth, on coming, would teach them all truth (John xvi. 13).   He now recalls these words to their memory, and tells them that in the Holy Ghost they will " be indued with power from on high " (ἕως δυ ἐνδύσησθε ἐξ ὕψους δύναμιν) = " until as with a coat of mail you be clothed with power from on high " (Luke xxiv. 49).   Secure in this strength as in invulnerable armour, they would no longer have cause to fear or to falter in their mission.

Such were the last recorded words of Christ on earth.   St. Mark giving to our Redeemer the title becoming his glorified state thus continues :—

V. 19. And the Lord Jesus, after he had spoken to them, was taken up into heaven, and sitteth on the right hand of God.

St. Luke gives some further particulars, and remarks that " when he (Christ) had said these things (Acts i. 9), he led them out as far as Bethany " (Gospel xxiv. 50).   The original Greek text is more correctly rendered : " He led them out *in the direction* of Bethany " (ἕως πρὸς Βηθανίαν), that is not to the village itself, but to the part of Mount Olivet where the road branches off towards Bethany.   This evangelist, with his love for details, states that " lifting up his hands he (Christ) blessed them.   And it came to pass, whilst he blessed them, he departed from them " (Luke xxiv. 50, 51) ; " and a cloud received him out of their sight " (Acts i. 9).   From the combined accounts of the evangelists we learn that Christ selected as the scene of his triumphant Ascension, the place from which he set out to undergo the ignominy of his Passion, and to which he will return to judge the world.   " This Jesus who is taken up from you into heaven, shall so come as you have seen him going into heaven " (Acts i. 11).   After the manner of the patriarchs leaving their children for ever, Christ being come to this spot, raised his hands to his Father and asked every blessing for his apostles.   Whilst these apostles were beholding him, " he departed from them, and was carried up to heaven," not in a fiery chariot like Elias, nor by the ministry of angels like Habacuc, nor by the power of his divinity only, but also by his power as Man.   Although the Ascension could not have taken place by natural means, still the virtue by which the blessed soul of Christ has been endowed, was capable of moving the body as it pleased (Catechism of the Council of Trent ; 6th Article of the Creed).   According to St. Paul (Eph. iv. 10) " he that descended, is the same also that ascended above all the heavens, that he might fill all things."   There, according to St. Mark, " he sitteth on the right hand of God."   As the Catechism of the Council of Trent notices, this expression of the evangelist does not imply position or posture of body; but it declares the fixed and permanent possession of even royal and supreme power and glory, which Christ has received from his Father. The evangelist signifies that whilst Christ as God is equal to the Father in all things, he as Man has a dignity and authority special, exclusive, and not to be conferred on any other created nature.

As the apostles behold with wonder this marvellous triumph of their Divine Master, they hear from the angels present that he will in the same manner appear at his second coming to judge the world. They then fully realised what St. Paul afterwards wrote, viz., that " God also hath exalted him and hath given him a name which is above all names ; that in the name of Jesus every knee should bow, of those that are in heaven, on earth, and under the earth " (Phil. ii. 9, 10). Filled with veneration for him who, in the unity of one person, is both God and Man, and being assured of the gifts of the Holy Ghost to be conferred on them " not many days hence " (Acts i. 5), " they adoring, went back into Jerusalem with great joy " (Luke xxiv. 52) to prepare for the reception of the " Comforter." To await the coming of this " other Paraclete " they entered into the " upper room," now hallowed by so many sacred memories ; and there and in the temple they were always praising and blessing God (Acts i. 13 ; Luke xxiv. 53).

Thus does St. Luke terminate his account of Christ's Ascension. St. Mark, passing over the events of Pentecost, sketches in the following words the early history of the apostles' labours :—

V. 20. **But they going forth, preached everywhere, the Lord working with them, and confirming the word with the signs that followed.**

It is noticed that whilst St. Mark omits the early history of our Redeemer's life on earth, his narrative includes the early history of the Church founded by that Redeemer, and just as his opening words describe the first announcement of the " good news " (" the beginning of the gospel of Jesus Christ the Son of God ") made by John the Baptist to the Jews, so does his concluding sentence give us a description of the apostles' successful labours to make known that same " good news " to all the world. Christ had commanded his apostles and their successors to " preach the gospel to every creature " ; and here we are told how the command had been fulfilled up to the time when St. Mark wrote. The meaning of Christ's injunction was not that the apostles were personally to visit every country and to preach to every tribe, but that, unlike the ministry of Christ and their early missions, their message was now to Jews, to Samaritans, and to Gentiles alike. Taken in this sense, the injunction was fulfilled even before the death of the apostles.

Before the gospel of St. Mark was written the messengers of Christ had preached in the principal places of the then known world; had baptised representatives of every race, both Jew and Gentile; and had proved the divine character of the Christian revelation, not by the "persuasive words of human wisdom," but by an appeal to the "signs that followed."

V.—MORAL REFLECTIONS.

It was decreed that after having accomplished the work of our Redemption, the Saviour of the World should on this day return to the bosom of his Father, and should enter into the glory which as Man he had merited for himself by his sufferings and death. It was not, however, for this alone that the Ascension came to pass. Since the fall of our first parents heaven had been shut against mankind; and Christ, who had purchased our salvation by his death, went to-day to open the gates of his eternal kingdom, and in it to prepare a place for us beside his throne. Such was the revelation made to the apostles, and with them to us, when, at the Last Supper, our Divine Lord uttered these loving words: "Let not your heart be troubled. . . . In my Father's house there are many mansions. If not I would have told you; because I go to prepare a place for you. And if I shall go, and prepare a place for you, I will come again, and will take you to myself, that where I am, you also may be" (John xiv. 1-3).

How helpful is this thought, and how sweet this consoling promise! We know full well that "we have not here a lasting city" (Hebr. xiii. 14), but an exile embittered by many woes. To-day we are consumed with grief; to-morrow we are struck down by sickness; and we are ever awaiting death. Even if for a time we possess the honours, pleasures, and goods of this world, are they not quite insufficient to content the heart? Surely our experience teaches us the truth of Solomon's conclusion: "All is vanity and vexation of spirit" (Eccles. i. 14). "Thou hast made us for thyself, O Lord," said St. Augustine truly, "and our hearts are ill at ease until they repose in thee." It is this repose in the possession of God that Christ has gone to prepare for us. In possessing God we shall possess the Supreme Good which includes all goods; and we shall possess it for ever. Thus our happiness will be complete and eternal, and in this complete and eternal happiness we shall experience the truth of the prophet's words: "The children of men shall put their trust under the covert of thy wings; they shall be inebriated with the plenty of thy house; and thou shalt make them drink of the torrent of thy pleasure. For with thee is the fountain of life; and in thy light we shall see light" (Ps. xxxv. 8-10).

As, therefore, he who is our "Fore-runner" (Hebr. vi. 20) this day entered into heaven hitherto closed but now open to all mankind, and as very many once like ourselves, have walked in his footsteps and already enjoy his eternal rest, may we not hope to share their bliss? Will not this hope bring consolation in our sorrows? With such hope and consolation laid up in our bosom, we must surely confess with the Apostle : " We are the sons of God, and if sons, heirs also : heirs indeed of God, and joint heirs with Christ ; yet so, if we suffer with him, that we may be also glorified with him. For I reckon that the sufferings of this time are not worthy to be compared with the glory to come, that shall be revealed in us" (Rom. viii. 16-18).

SUNDAY WITHIN OCTAVE OF ASCENSION.

I. —TEXTS.

GREEK.

JOHN XV. 26 ; XVI. 4.

²⁶Ὅταν ἔλθῃ ὁ παράκλητος, ὃν ἐγὼ
πέμψω ὑμῖν παρὰ τοῦ πατρός, τὸ πνεῦμα
τῆς ἀληθείας, ὃ παρὰ τοῦ πατρὸς ἐκπο-
ρεύεται, ἐκεῖνος μαρτυρήσει περὶ ἐμοῦ.
²⁷ Καὶ ὑμεῖς δὲ μαρτυρεῖτε, ὅτι ἀπ᾽
ἀρχῆς μετ᾽ ἐμοῦ ἐστέ.

Κεφ. Ις. (XVI.)

¹ Ταῦτα λελάληκα ὑμῖν, ἵνα μὴ σκαν-
δαλισθῆτε. ²Ἀποσυναγώγους ποιήσουσιν ὑμᾶς, ἀλλ᾽ ἔρχεται ὥρα, ἵνα πᾶς ὁ
ἀποκτείνας, δόξῃ λατρείαν προσφέρειν
τῷ θεῷ. ³ Καὶ ταῦτα ποιήσουσιν, ὅτι
οὐκ ἔγνωσ ιν τὸν πατέρα οὐδὲ ἐμέ.
⁴ Ἀλλὰ ταῦτα λελάληκα ὑμῖν, ἵνα ὅταν
ἔλθῃ ἡ ὥρα αὐτῶν, μνημονεύητε αὐτῶν,
ὅτι ἐγὼ εἶπον ὑμῖν.

VULGATE.

JOHN XV. 26 ; XVI. 4.

26 Cum autem venerit Paraclitus, quem ego mittam vobis
a Patre, Spiritum veritatis qui
a Patre procedit, ille testimonium perhibebit de me. 27 Et
vos testimonium perhibebitis,
quia ab initio mecum estis.

XVI.

1 Hæc locutus sum vobis, ut
non scandalizemini. 2 Absque
synagogis facient vos, sed
venit hora, ut omnis qui in-
terficit vos, arbitretur obse-
quium se præstare Deo. 3 Et
hæc facient vobis, quia non
noverunt Patrem neque me.
4 Sed hæc locutus sum vobis, ut
cum venerit hora eorum, remi-
niscamini quia ego dixi vobis.

II.—ENGLISH TRANSLATION.

JOHN XV. 26; XVI. 4.

²⁶ But when the Paraclete cometh, whom I will send you from
the Father, the Spirit of truth, who proceedeth from the Father,
he shall give testimony of me ; ²⁷ and you shall give testimony,
because you are with me from the beginning.

XVI. ¹ These things have I spoken to you, that you may not
be scandalised. ² They will put you out of the synagogues : yea,
the hour cometh, that whosoever killeth you, will think that he
doth a service to God. ³ And these things will they do to you,
because they have not known the Father nor me. ⁴ But these
things I have told you, that when the hour shall come, you may
remember that I told you of them.

III.—NOTES.

Introductory. In writing his gospel against the heretics of his age, St. John proposed to himself to prove that Christ at all times during his life gave evidence of the glory of the divinity that dwelt within him. " We saw his glory, the glory as it were of the Only-Begotten of the Father " (John i. 14). Notwithstanding the proofs of this divine glory given in the miracles and marvellous discourses recorded especially by this evangelist, the scribes and pharisees, leaders of the people had ever scornfully rejected the teaching of the Son of God, and had pursued him with a hatred which was to be satisfied only with his death. On the eve of his death, in the address to the apostles, from which the present extract is taken, our Lord complained of this hatred on the part of his enemies who regarded him as a false prophet and seducer of the people, and he declared that a similar lot was in store for his faithful followers. The designs of God, however, were not to be frustrated. Christ predicted at the same time that he was yet to be justified before men by the divine witness of the Holy Ghost and by the human testimony of those who had been his companions from the beginning of his public life. The subject matter of the present gospel passage is the descent of the Holy Ghost, the witness borne by the Holy Ghost and by the apostles to the divine character of Christ's mission, and lastly, the persecutions to be endured by the apostles in their heroic defence of the truth.

Having told his hearers that the hatred of the scribes and pharisees had been foretold by the Psalmist (Ps. xxiv. 19), our Redeemer added these consoling words :—

V. 26. But when the Paraclete cometh, whom I will send you from the Father, the Spirit of Truth, &c.

The word " Paraclete " (Gr. Παράκλητος), found only in St. John, signifies properly *one called upon to assist* especially in a court of justice, or in other words, *an advocate.* In this sense it is applied to Christ himself who, as Man, is our advocate with the Father (1 John ii. 1), and to the Holy Ghost, who " asketh for us with unspeakable groanings " (Rom. viii. 26). In a secondary sense, it signifies a *helper* or *comforter.* With this meaning Christ applied the name to himself and to the Holy Ghost when, bidding adieu to his apostles, he said (John xiv. 16) : " I will ask the Father and he shall give you another Paraclete that he may abide with you for ever." This is the meaning of the word on the present occasion, when the apostles are told of the trials that await them as witnesses of the truth, and are promised the heavenly aid that will be necessary in the difficulties of their mission. Christ thus declares that his followers will find their help and comfort in the " Paraclete," the circumstances of whose coming are now to be enumerated as an assurance that the hopes of those followers are not to be disappointed. In the first place, as Christ once said (John viii. 42) in commendation of his own mission, " From God I proceeded and came ; for I came not of myself, but he sent me," so now does he promise to send from the same source, that is, from the bosom of the Father (παρὰ τοῦ Πατρὸς), the Holy Spirit who is to continue and perfect the work of the Redemption amongst men. How convincing is the testimony of a witness who comes from the bosom of the Father, and who as such, knows all the mysteries of God ! With this thought before him, St. Paul some years afterwards, could write to the Corinthians concerning these mysteries : " To us God hath revealed them by his Spirit. For the Spirit searcheth all things, yea, the deep things of God. For what man knoweth the things of a man, but the spirit of a man that is in him ? So the things also that are of God no man knoweth but the Spirit of God. Now, we have received not the spirit of this world, but the Spirit that is of God, that we may know the things that are given us from God " (1 Cor. ii. 10-12).

This is not all. Whereas, in the previous part of this discourse (John xiv. 16), Christ promised to ask the Father to send the Paraclete, by speaking now of that Paraclete as one whom *he himself* would send, he implies his own divinity and equality with the Father. By thus implying his own divinity and equality with the Father, he leaves the apostles no room to doubt the fulfilment of his promise, or the efficacy of the means he is selecting to secure his glory amongst men.

Still further, the Paraclete is called " the Spirit of Truth." The Holy Ghost is so named, not because he will put aside the empty figures of the law, and replace them by the reality ; not because his teaching is opposed to the vanity of the world ; not because he is the Spirit of Christ, who is the Way, the Truth, and the Life ; but because he is essentially true and can teach only the truth, inasmuch as he too is the Truth itself.

Lastly, the dignity of the Paraclete is made known by the statement that he " proceedeth from the Father." As Christ, in this same sentence, had already mentioned the *temporal* mission or procession of the Holy Ghost from the Father, these last words can refer only to the Holy Spirit's *eternal* procession, by which he has the same divine nature as the Father.

Having thus gradually unfolded the dignity and trustworthiness of " the Paraclete," who is at last implicitly declared to be God, Christ says that this divine Witness will bear testimony to him. Such testimony was borne, and will ever be borne, exteriorly by the miracles worked and the prophecies spoken in confirmation of the gospel. and interiorly by that light and grace which, being infused into the human heart, lead mankind to Christian faith and Christian perfection from the darkness of unbelief and the degrading slavery of sin.

To this witness of the Paraclete was to be joined the personal testimony of the apostles themselves. Hence Christ adds :—

V. 27. And you shall give testimony, because you are with me from the beginning.

To bring the world to believe in the coming of its Redeemer, it was necessary that testimony should be borne to him by the Holy Ghost, who, by the grace of faith, causes us to submit to the teachings of revelation ; but that this revelation might be made known to us as *credible* and *evidently credible*, it was necessary that the apostles should bear witness to the life and acts of Christ by whom revelation was brought to us from heaven. It was required that the mind should be convinced of the truth through the preaching of the apostles supported by miracles, before we could yield the obedience of faith which was secured by the interior voice and grace of the Holy Ghost. That the apostles might be able to fulfil this command of giving testimony to their Divine Master, St. Peter, on the fall of Judas, thus commands the election of one who may take the place of the traitor : " Of these men who have companied with us all the time that the Lord Jesus came in and went out among us, . . . one of these must be made a witness with us of his Resurrection " (Acts i. 21, 22). From St. John we learn that the apostles obeyed the command of Christ. He says : " That which was from the beginning, which we have heard, which we have seen with our eyes, which we have looked upon, and our hands have handled, of the word of life, . . . we declare unto you, that you also may have fellowship with us, and our fellowship may be with the Father, and with his Son Jesus Christ " (1 John i. 1-3. Compare 2 Peter i. 16, 17). This two-fold testimony, human and divine, or rather these two aspects of the same divine testimony, men have still in the Catholic Church. From the historical documents left by the apostles the world may be *convinced of the fact* of divine revelation ; and then the grace of the Holy Ghost working within the soul, enables the will to *subject itself* to the teachings of Jesus Christ.

When Christ had thus revealed to the apostles their glorious mission as preachers of the gospel, and the help they were to receive in this work from the presence of " the Paraclete, the Spirit of Truth," he pointed out the obstacles for which they were to be prepared. He said :—

Chap. xvi. verse 1. These things have I spoken to you, that you may not be scandalised.

In the preceding part of his discourse (John xv. 20), Christ had foretold in general the persecutions that awaited his followers. " The servant is not greater than his master. If they have persecuted me, they will also persecute you." In these next verses he returns to that sad subject ; he treats it in greater detail ; and he gives his reason for his repeated reference thereto. The expression *to be scandalised* (from the Greek σκάνδαλον = an *obstacle* or *stumbling block*), signifies literally *to be impeded* or *to be made to fall* in our journey ; and here it means *to be turned away* from the faith or from the fulfilment of the commands of Christ. One of the greatest obstacles to Christian faith and obedience was to be the hatred of the world against the kingdom of the Messiah. Nor was persecution to come from the Gentiles only : the Jews to whom the kingdom of the Messiah was first promised, and whose office was to prepare mankind to receive that kingdom, would, as a nation, reject it and seek to destroy it. Our Lord, then, tells the apostles that he has predicted their future trials lest, when these trials come, anyone may be taken by surprise.

The opposition to be offered by the Jews to the preaching of the gospel is thus described by Jesus Christ :—

V. 2. They will put you out of the synagogues, &c.

This was an excommunication (Introduction, p. cx.) of which, according to Calmet, there were three kinds in use amongst the Jews. The first called by them *Niddui*, *i.e.*, *separation*, consisted in a simple exclusion from the sacred assembly and from the functions of public worship. The second, called *Hherem*, *i.e.*, *extermination*, was once solemnly pronounced against a relapsing sinner. With lighted candles, and in presence of the whole synagogue, the officiating ministers recited the fearful imprecations of the formula, and then extinguished the lights, to signify that the delinquent was unworthy of enjoying the brightness of eternal life. The third kind of excommunication was called *Schiammata*, *i.e.*, *God cometh*. By its very name it indicated that all human efforts at conversion having been tried in vain, the sinner was now abandoned to the fearful judgment of a God who would soon avenge the crimes committed, and who, in the meantime, gave permission to anyone to take away a life so hopelessly wicked and ill-spent. It was the fear of this punishment of excommunication that withheld " many of the chief men " amongst the Jews from professing their belief in Christ (John xii. 42), and this was the penalty actually inflicted on the blind man for his courageous defence of his Divine Benefactor (John ix. 22-34).

Christ next warned his disciples that the hatred excited against them was not to be satisfied with their exclusion from the synagogues, as though they were atheists whose presence would defile the holy place. He says :—

Yea, the hour cometh, that whosoever killeth you, will think that he doth a service to God.

The words in the Greek text are sacrificial terms, for λατρεία = *service*, was the supreme worship due to God alone, and προσφέρειν signified the offering of the victim. It was foretold, therefore, that the enemies of the gospel would consider they were " doing a service " (better, " offering an agreeable sacrifice ") in killing the apostles. These ambassadors of Christ would be regarded as false prophets and seducers of the people —a class whose sentence in the law was death (Deut. xviii. 20 ; and xiii. 8, 9), and the killing of whom had been commended as a holy deed (Exod. xxxii. 29). St. Paul confesses that before his conversion he was filled with this spirit, and he describes himself as " being . . . according to the law, a pharisee ; according to zeal, persecuting the Church of God ; according to the justice that is in the law, conversing without blame " (Phil. iii. 5, 6). St. Luke tells us that the Apostle, after his conversion, was persecuted by his countrymen, and that his persecution was regarded by them as a religious duty. " When day was come, some of the Jews gathered together, and bound themselves under a curse, saying that they would neither eat nor drink till they killed Paul. And they were more than forty men that had made this conspiracy " (Acts xxiii. 12, 13). On a former occasion, as we read, St. Paul announced to the Jews that he was to preach the Gospel to the Gentiles. " They heard him until this word, and then lifted up their voice, saying : Away with such a one from the earth ; for it is not fit that he should live. And as they cried out, and threw off their garments, and cast dust into the air, the tribune commanded that he should be brought into the castle, and that he should be scourged and tortured, to know for what cause they so cried out against him " (Acts xxii. 22-24).

Christ next ·nentions the cause of this extraordinary perversity :

V. 3. And these things will they do to you, because they have not known the Father nor me.

There is here an extenuating circumstance, but not a justification. In the presence of the clearest evidence regarding the character and mission of Christ, the blind unbelief of the Jews was inexcusable, and was their greatest sin. Christ says of them : " If I had not come and spoken to them, they would not have sin ; but now they have no excuse for their sin. . . . If I had not done among them the works that no other man hath done, they would not have sin ; but now they have both seen and hated both me and my Father " (John xv. 22-24. Comp.

John viii. 24). St. Paul states (1 Tim. i. 13) that in his persecution of the Church he too acted through ignorance, and that,
for this reason, he was mercifully dealt with by God ; but whilst
saying this he does not deny his culpability. On the contrary
he declares (1 Cor. xv. 9) that, having been a persecutor, he
was unworthy to be called an apostle, and (1 Tim. i. 15) that of
all sinners, redeemed by Jesus Christ, he was the chief.

Finally, Christ makes known to the apostles the benefit he
wishes them to derive from this prediction of their future trials.
He says :—

**V. 4. But these things I have told you, that when the hour
shall come, you may remember that I told you of them.**

He does not counsel them to avoid this persecution ; for the
patient endurance of opposition, of danger, and of death was
to be a part of their mission. " Behold, I send you as sheep in
the midst of wolves " (Matth. x. 16). He wishes them to remember his prediction when the things predicted will have come
to pass. The effect of such a remembrance would be two-fold.
In the fulfilment of the prophecy itself they would see a proof
of his foreknowledge and therefore of his divinity ; whilst the
advent of the trials which were predestined for them would
encourage them with the hope of the blessedness which was
foretold together with these trials.

IV.—MORAL REFLECTIONS.

When predicting the persecution which was to be the lot of
his followers, Christ consoled the apostles with the promise of
the Holy Ghost, and gave to this third Person of the Blessed
Trinity two names—the Comforter and the Spirit of Truth.
These two names indicate the effects which the Holy Ghost
was to produce, first in the apostles themselves after a few
weeks, and subsequently in the souls of the faithful during the
course of ages.

1. In the first place, the Holy Ghost was to be the Comforter
of the apostles. In the midst of the contradictions, labours,
fatigues, humiliations, and sufferings of their ministry, he was
to be ever with them, sustaining them by his grace, supporting
them by his strength, and enriching them with his admirable
gifts. Such are still the functions which he exercises in the
souls of the just, with whom he dwells. In all the tribulations
which we endure, and which since the first sin, are the inheritance of fallen man, he is our comfort and support. He does
not take away the sense of our sufferings, for that would be
to change our nature, but he sweetens their bitterness ; and
though he permits us to shed tears, he wipes these tears away.

When, therefore, we are overwhelmed by disappointment, by sorrow, by pain of body or of mind, we should turn to this unfailing source of consolation.   Other remedies often bring but an aggravation of our ills ; for men can only exhort us to patience, and give as a reason, the necessity of suffering.   That we must suffer is an incontestable truth ; but apart from the teaching of religion, it is one that leads to dejection and despair. Apart from what is promised by religion, suffering has neither motive nor reward ; and for the unbeliever the prospect of the future increases the painful feeling of the present.   It is different, however, when our earthly condition is viewed in the light of the consoling truths which the Holy Ghost has revealed. We acknowledge the justice of our sufferings when we are reminded that the evils of this life are the punishment of our sins (Jeremias xliv. 23).   We return thanks for our afflictions when we learn that, by patiently enduring these, we may expiate our offences here below (Judith viii. 27).   With the Apostle we shall exult in our infirmities, that the power of Christ may dwell in us (2 Cor. xii. 9).   Our tribulations will be a source of joy when we feel that through these our piety is enkindled, our strength increased, and our virtues purified like gold in the furnace (1. Peter i. 6, 7).

2. Again, the Holy Ghost to be sent on the apostles and on us, is called the Spirit of Truth.   He is so named because he is the author and fountain of truth, because he diffuses it through the world, and because he alone can, by his grace, cause it to be accepted.   As in the time of St. Paul, so in ours, there is in the world another spirit, the spirit of error, in deadly opposition to the Spirit of God.   To lead us astray, this spirit of error presents to us, sometimes one by one, sometimes all at once, the sophisms of unbelief, the subtleties of heresy, the illusions of the world, the seductions of temptation, the charm of pleasure.   In a word, according to the Apostle, to secure our destruction, Satan " transformeth himself into an angel of light " (2 Cor. xi. 14).   In dealing with such an enemy, we need the divine help promised by Jesus Christ.   If, then, we wish to be saved, we shall confide the direction of our conduct not to our own ideas and tastes, which are blind guides, but to the infallible guide which is enlightened by the Spirit of Truth. We shall follow in faith and morals the sacred teaching of the Catholic Church ; and as " wisdom will not enter into a malicious soul, nor dwell in a body subject to sins " (Wisdom i. 4), we shall remove from our hearts all that may give offence to him whose temples we are (1 Cor. vi. 19).   Thus walking in the clear light which the Holy Ghost sheds upon our path, we shall not wander after that by which the spirit of evil would lure us to the abyss.

WHIT SUNDAY.

I.—TEXTS.

GREEK.

JOHN XIV. 23-31.

²³'Απεκρίθη 'Ιησοῦς καὶ εἶπεν αὐτῷ·
'Εάν τις ἀγαπᾷ με, τὸν λόγον μου τηρή-
σει· καὶ ὁ πατήρ μου ἀγαπήσει αὐτόν,
καὶ πρὸς αὐτὸν ἐλευσόμεθα, καὶ μονὴν
παρ' αὐτῷ ποιησόμεθα. ²⁴'Ο μὴ ἀγα-
πῶν με, τοὺς λόγους μου οὐ τηρεῖ· καὶ
ὁ λόγος ὃν ἀκούετε, οὐκ ἔστιν ἐμὸς,
ἀλλὰ τοῦ πέμψαντός με πατρός.
²⁵Ταῦτα λελάληκα ὑμῖν παρ' ὑμῖν
μένων. ²⁶'Ο δὲ παράκλητος, τὸ πνεῦμα τὸ ἅγιον, ὃ πέμψει ὁ πατὴρ ἐν
τῷ ὀνόματί μου, ἐκεῖνος ὑμᾶς διδάξει
πάντα, καὶ ὑπομνήσει ὑμᾶς πάντα ἃ
εἶπον ὑμῖν. ²⁷'Εγὼ εἰρήνην ἀφίημι ὑμῖν,
εἰρήνην τὴν ἐμὴν δίδωμι ὑμῖν, οὐ
καθὼς ὁ κόσμος δίδωσιν, ἐγὼ δίδωμι
ὑμῖν· μὴ ταρασσέσθω ὑμῶν ἡ καρδία,
μηδὲ δειλιάτω. ²⁸'Ηκούσατε ὅτι ἐγὼ
εἶπον ὑμῖν· ὑπάγω καὶ ἔρχομαι πρὸς
ὑμᾶς· εἰ ἠγαπᾶτέ με, ἐχάρητε ἂν, ὅτι
πορεύομαι πρὸς τὸν πατέρα· ὅτι ὁ πατὴρ
μείζων μου ἐστίν. ²⁹Καὶ νῦν εἴρηκα
ὑμῖν πρὶν γενέσθαι, ἵνα ὅταν γένηται,
πιστεύσητε. ³⁰Οὐκέτι πολλὰ λαλήσω
μεθ' ὑμῶν· ἔρχεται γὰρ ὁ τοῦ κόσμου
ἄρχων, καὶ ἐν ἐμοὶ οὐκ ἔχει οὐδέν.
³¹'Αλλ' ἵνα γνῷ ὁ κόσμος ὅτι ἀγαπῶ
τὸν πατέρα, καὶ καθὼς ἐντολὴν ἔδωκέν
μοι ὁ πατήρ, οὕτως ποιῶ. 'Εγείρεσθε,
ἄγωμεν ἐντεῦθεν.

VULGATE.

JOHN XIV. 23-31.

²³ Respondit Jesus et dixit
ei : Si quis diligit me, sermonem meum servabit, et Pater
meus diliget eum, et ad eum
veniemus, et mansionem apud
eum faciemus. ²⁴ Qui non diligit me, sermones meos non
servat. Et sermonem quem
audistis, non est meus, sed
ejus qui misit me Patris.
²⁵ Hæc locutus sum vobis,
apud vos manens. ²⁶ Paraclitus autem Spiritus sanctus,
quem mittet Pater in nomine
meo, ille vos docebit omnia, et
suggeret vobis omnia, quæcumque dixero vobis. ²⁷ Pacem
relinquo vobis, pacem meam
do vobis. Non quomodo mundus dat, ego do vobis. Non
turbetur cor vestrum, neque
formidet. ²⁸ Audistis quia ego
dixi vobis : Vado, et venio ad
vos. Si diligeretis me, gaude-
retis utique quia vado ad Patrem, quia Pater major me est.
²⁹ Et nunc dixi vobis priusquam fiat, ut quum factum
fuerit, credatis. ³⁰ Jam non
multa loquar vobiscum ; venit
enim princeps mundi hujus, et
in me non habet quidquam ;
³¹ sed ut cognoscat mundus
quia diligo Patrem, et sicut
mandatum dedit mihi Pater, sic
facio. Surgite, eamus hinc.

II.—ENGLISH TRANSLATION.

JOHN XIV. 23-31.

23 Jesus answered and said to him: " If any one love me, he will keep my word ; and my Father will love him, and we will come to him, and will make our abode with him. **24** He that loveth me not, keepeth not my words. And the word which you have heard is not mine, but the Father's who sent me.

25 These things have I spoken to you, abiding with you. **26** But the Paraclete, the Holy Ghost, whom the Father will send in my name, he will teach you all things, and bring all things to your mind, whatsoever I shall have said to you. **27** Peace I leave with you, my peace I give unto you. Not as the world giveth, do I give unto you. Let not your heart be troubled, nor let it be afraid. **28** You have heard that I said to you : I go away and I come unto you. If you loved me, you would indeed be glad because I go to the Father ; for the Father is greater than I. **29** And now I have told you before it come to pass, that when it shall come to pass, you may believe. **30** I will not now speak many things with you ; for the prince of this world cometh, and in me he hath not anything ; **31** but that the world may know that I love the Father, and as the Father hath given me commandment, so do I. Arise, let us go hence."

III.—NOTES.

Introductory. This passage is another extract from the long discourse delivered by our Divine Lord after the Last Supper and recorded by St. John from the 13th to the 16th chapter of his gospel. As already stated, the matter of this address is comprised under four heads. First, Christ foretold his approaching death ; next, he laid down for his apostles the rules of brotherly love and humble deference which they were to observe towards each other when he would no longer be visibly present in their midst ; then, he put before them many motives of consolation in their sorrow at their separation from him ; last of all, he made known to them the persecutions that awaited them in the world, and exhorted them to a patient and courageous endurance of these trials after his example. In the particular part of his discourse from which this extract is taken, Christ had comforted his apostles by the promise of many benefits, the bestowal of which depended on his departure. Thus he said that in going, he was about to prepare a place for them with the Father ; that they would have the power of working miracles even greater than those which he himself had wrought ; that with certainty all their petitions presented in his name to

the Father would be granted ; that he would send the Holy Ghost
with all his gifts ; and finally, that whilst the world was to see
nim no more, he would come and manifest himself to them.
At this point Judas or Thaddæus, the brother of James the
Less, interposed and said : " Lord, how is it that thou wilt
manifest thyself to us and not to the world ? "   Sharing in the
ideas then so common amongst the Jews, this apostle believed
that the reign of Christ was to be that of a great temporal
sovereign, to whom all kingdoms were to be subjected. The
meaning, therefore, of his question is : " Whereas we have
hitherto believed that thou wouldst rule over the whole earth
and wouldst restore the kingdom of Israel, how does it now
come to pass that thou wilt manifest thyself to us only, and
not to the world ? "

According to the evangelist,

V. 23. **Jesus answered and said to him : If any one love
me, he will keep my word ; and my Father will love him, and
we will come to him, and will make our abode with him.**

At first sight it would appear as if Christ did not reply to the
question of his apostle, and that he merely continued the discourse which had been interrupted ; but it was customary with
our Divine Lord to reply indirectly by repeating and developing
the statement which had given rise to the question.   He does
so on the present occasion in the words of this and the following
verses.   Rejecting all idea of temporal sovereignty, he shows
that his manifestation is to be of a spiritual character ; he asserts
that this spiritual manifestation is for those who are united to
him by love in the practice of good works ; and he leaves it to
be inferred that this is why the world is to be excluded from
such a blessing.   It must be remarked that Christ is not here
speaking of the everlasting " abode " of the saints with God
in heaven.   Against Maldonatus, the common opinion of interpreters is that Christ speaks of the special in-dwelling of the
Holy Trinity in the souls of the just on earth—an in-dwelling
which causes these souls to become the temples of the living
God.   " Know you not," says the Apostle, " that you are the
temple of God, and that the Spirit of God dwelleth in you ? "
(1 Cor. iii. 16 ; Cf. Rom. viii. 9 ; Gal. iv. 6 ; 2 Tim. i. 14).

In the promise made by Christ, three things are mentioned in
such an order that each subsequent blessing is greater than the
preceding, and is a more signal manifestation of God's goodness
to man.   The first reward of the practical lovers of Christ is
the love of the Father.   " If any one love me, he will keep my
word ; and my Father will love him."   As a subject values much
the friendship of his sovereign even if no further benefit than
the honour accruing is to follow from such friendship, so should
it be with those who are marked out as the beloved of God.   Of

still greater worth is the blessing to which Christ next refers when he says : " And we will come to him." In the present life we cannot go to God ; but we are here told that God the Father, God the Son, and, by the nature of the case, God the Holy Ghost will come and visit us as a friend visits his friend. The extent of this condescension is to be estimated by him only who can fully comprehend the distance between the infinite dignity of the Creator and the nothingness of the creature. Last and greatest of all is the gift promised to the just man when Christ said : " We . . . will . . . make our abode with him." A friend to show his love, often visits his friend ; but after a brief space of time he is obliged to leave, and causes more pain at his departure than joy at his coming. It is not so with the visit of the Holy Trinity to the human soul. This visit is to be a permanent in-dwelling, bringing with it such a security against all evil and such a possession of every good, that the Psalmist, speaking from experience, could say : " Though I should walk in the midst of the shadow of death I will fear no evils, for thou art with me. . . . Thou hast anointed my head with oil ; and how goodly is my chalice which cheereth me ! And thy mercy will follow me all the days of my life ; and that I may dwell in the house of the Lord unto length of days " (Psalm xxii. 4, 5, 6). It is true, as St. Gregory says, that God comes to some and does not remain. This is so because they expel him by the commission of mortal sin ; but as far as in him lies, he enters the soul to dwell there until death in this world and throughout eternity in the next.

Having thus indicated the nature of his manifestation and why it is made to the disciples, Christ says :—

V. 24. **He that loveth me not, keepeth not my words. And the word which you have heard is not mine, but the Father's who sent me.**

He does not say : " He that keepeth not my words (*i.e.*, my commandments or laws), loveth me not." The present form of expression is adopted because Christ does not here point out a sign of our love for him, but rather continues to give the reason why he will not manifest himself unto the world, viz., because those who love him not, reject his law and are in turn rejected by him and by the Father.

From this and the preceding verses we learn that, as there cannot be a true love of Christ without the observance of the commandments, so neither can there be a true observance of the commandments without the love of Christ. That the neglect of his law will be justly punished, is shown in the following sentence where Christ declares that the doctrine which he reveals to man, is not invented by him, nor promulgated by him exclusively, but comes also from the Father, from whom he himself, true God and true Man, has all he has, both divine and human.

Having answered the question of Judas or Thaddæus, our Lord continued his discourse and said :—

Vv. 25, 26. These things have I spoken to you, abiding with you. But the Paraclete, the Holy Ghost, whom the Father will send in my name, he will teach you all things, and bring all things to your mind, whatsoever I shall have said to you.

Four of the apostles, Peter, Thomas, Philip, and Thaddæus, had shown by their remarks that they did not understand the words of their Divine Master. To anticipate, therefore, any discouragement arising from this cause, and to repress the desire of further inquiry into matters which were at that time beyond their power of comprehension, Christ made the statements contained in these verses. As to the present, he told them that it was unprofitable to ask the meaning of what they were unprepared to grasp ; as to the future, he assured them that the Holy Ghost, already promised (xiv. 16), would be a Teacher who would enable them both to remember and to understand (Greek ὑπομνήσει) all that he himself " shall have said " to them, or, more correctly, " had said " to them (Greek εἶπον). The words, " whom the Father will send in my name," indicate 1°, that the Holy Ghost is to be sent from the Father and the Son, from both of whom as from one principle he eternally proceeds ; and 2°, that the mission of the Holy Ghost is not only for the personal benefit of the apostles, but also for the continuation and the perfecting of the work which Christ had begun. It follows, therefore, that this promise is to be fulfilled in the Church till the end of time.

" As compared with Christ the Paraclete fulfils a double office : he teaches and he recalls Christ's teachings. His work indeed is to teach by bringing home to men the whole of Christ's teaching. The revelation of Christ in his person and work was absolute and complete, but without the gradual illumination of the Spirit it is partly unintelligible and partly unobserved. (Comp. xvi. 13 ; 1 John ii. 20, 27.) As Christ came ' in his Father's name ' (v. 43, x. 25), so the Spirit is sent ' in his name.' The purpose of Christ's mission was to reveal God as his Father, and through this to make known his relation to men, and to humanity, and to the world. The purpose of the mission of the Holy Spirit is to reveal Christ, to make clear to the consciousness of the Church the full significance of the Incarnation. Christ's ' name,' all, that is, which can be defined as to his nature and his work, is the sphere in which the Spirit acts ; and so, little by little, through the long life of the Church, the meaning of the primitive confession ' Jesus is Lord ' (Rom. x. 9 ; 1 Cor. xii. 3) is made more fully known " (Westcott, *in loco*).

Having precluded any further interrogation by reminding the apostles that the Holy Ghost was to complete their instruction, Christ returned to his purpose of consoling these apostles ; and he anticipated all cause for anxiety by saying :—

V. 27. Peace I leave with you, my peace I give unto you. Not as the world giveth, do I give unto you. Let not your heart be troubled, nor let it be afraid.

שָׁלוֹם לְךָ or שָׁלוֹם לָכֶם = " Peace be to thee " or " Peace be to you," was the common form of greeting and of leave-taking among the Jews ; and by it they wished every blessing to the person addressed. In these words Christ spoke as the Messiah whom the prophets represent as the " Prince of Peace " (Psalm lxxi. 3, 7 ; Isaias ix. 6, 7 ; xi. 6 ; xxvi. 3 ; xxvii. 5 ; liv. 10-13 ; lxvi. 12 ; Micheas v. 5), and whose birth the angels celebrated, as an assurance of peace to the world. It is as if he said : " I the author of peace (the ' I ' is emphatic : ἐγὼ εἰρήνην ἀφίημι ὑμῖν) do not merely *wish* you peace, but *give* it ; and with it on my departure I give and leave to you that love of God, that calm of soul, that mutual concord which are the unfailing source of peace." Well might he add : " Not as the world giveth, do I give unto you." The happiness of the world is short-lived and false : that which Christ confers is lasting and real. The world promises a peace which it has not, and therefore could not bestow even if it would : Christ promises and bestows a peace " which surpasseth all understanding " (Phil. iv. 7).

Having here and in the preceding portion of this discourse put before the apostles many motives of consolation, Christ next pointed out the conclusion at which he wished them to arrive. He said : " Let not your heart be troubled, nor let it be afraid," and he added :—

V. 28. You have heard that I said to you : I go away, and I come unto you. If you love me, you would indeed be glad because I go to the Father ; for the Father is greater than I.

The " trouble " of the apostles and their " fear " arose respectively from their love of the Master now about to leave them, and from the dangers they should have to face in the midst of a hostile world. Christ reminds them that there is no cause for fear of danger to themselves at his departure, because, as they had already heard, although he was now taking leave of them, he would soon return (John xiv. 18). Neither was there any reason that through love of him they should be troubled, but rather that they should rejoice, inasmuch as his departure to the Father who " is greater," was to be a source of glory to Christ himself

But how could it be said that the Father is greater than Christ who is the same God as the Father ?   In various ways commentators have explained this text, which was eagerly seized on by the Arians as a proof that the Second Person of the Trinity is a mere creature.

In the first place there is the exposition mentioned by St. Augustine and adopted by St. Chrysostom.   According to the latter holy Doctor, Christ says the Father is greater than he, not because this is really so, but because it was so in the opinion of the apostles.   Thus on another occasion our Lord said : " If I bear witness of myself, my witness is not true " (John v. 31. Comp. John vii. 16-18).   According to this exposition, Christ wished to say : " If you believe the Father to be greater in dignity than I, then, in accordance with your own principles, you ought not to be troubled, but rather to rejoice that I go to the Father."   This answer is not received with favour, nor does it appear admissible.   Such an error is never even tolerated by Christ, who claimed to be equal in perfection and identical in nature with the Father when he said : " Philip, he that seeth me, seeth the Father also " (John xiv. 9), and again : " I and the Father are one " (John x. 30).

Another explanation was offered by SS. Athanasius, Cyril of Alexandria, Basil, Gregory Naz., Epiphanius, John Damascene, and the Greek Fathers generally.   Many extracts from their works have been collected by Westcott (in loco), but the following taken from him may suffice as illustrations.   In the first place, these writers thought that the Father was here said to be greater than Christ considered not merely as the Son *Incarnate*, but as the Son *simply ;* and St. Gregory Naz. thus sets aside as inadequate the interpretation which would refer our Lord's words to the sacred humanity alone : " To say that the Father is greater than the Son considered as Man (τὸν κατὰ τὸν ἄνθρωπον ιοουμένου) is certainly true, but no great thing to say.   For what marvel is it if God is greater than man ? " (*Orat.* 30, § 7). In the second place, these writers did not mean that the Father is here said to be greater than the Son as to duration of existence, or as to perfection, or as to essence.   The contrary is maintained by St. John Damascene, who thus reproduces and adopts the teaching of the earlier Greek Doctors : " If we say that the Father is the origin of the Son, and greater, we do not indicate that he is before the Son (προτερεύειν) in time, or in nature, or in any other point, except in being the cause (κατὰ τὸ αἴτιον) ; that is, that the Son was begotten of the Father, and not the Father of the Son, and that the Father is the cause of the Son naturally (αἴτιος φυσικῶς), as we say that the fire does not come from the light, but rather the light from the fire " (*De Fide*, i. 8).   In the Athanasian creed too, the contrary is

professed when we say : " In hac Trinitate nihil prius aut pos-
terius, nihil majus aut minus ; sed totæ tres personæ coæternæ
sibi sunt et coæquales " ; and in the 4th Council of Lateran where
the Greeks were represented, it was defined : " Una quædam
summa res est, incomprehensibilis quidem et ineffabilis, quæ
veraciter est Pater, et Filius, et Spiritus Sanctus." Nor should
any difficulty arise from the use of the word ἀιτια applied to
the Father in the Greek theological treatises ; for we should remember that the Greek writers did not there give to the word
ἀιτια the restricted meaning which the word " causa " had
with the Latins, and which the word " cause " has generally with
ourselves. This is rendered very clear by the illustration just
quoted in the passage from St. John Damascene, where the word
ἀιτια applied to the Father was taken in the wider signification
of the Latin " principium " and of the English " source," or
" origin," or that from which anything derives its being. Taken
in this wider signification in treatises on the Trinity, the word
did not imply any later existence, or difference of essence, or inferiority of perfection in the Person who proceeds from another.
Hence, as the ἀιτια of the Greek had both a more extended and
a more restricted signification represented respectively by the
Latin " principium " and " causa," and as it is in the former
signification only that it could be used in speaking of the Trinity,
the Latin writers on this subject never employed the word
" causa " in reference to the Father and the Son. This is the
remark of St. Thomas, who says : " Græci utuntur in divinis
indifferenter nomine *causæ* sicut et nomine *principii*. Sed Latini
doctores non utuntur nomine *causæ* sed solum nomine *principii*.
. . . In omnibus enim causæ generibus semper invenitur dis-
tantia inter causam et id cujus est causa, secundum aliquam per-
fectionem aut virtutem. Sed nomine principii utimur etiam in
his quae nullam hujusmodi differentiam habent, sed solum secundum ordinem " (*Summa*, 1 Pars, q. xxxiii. art. 1, ad 1). But in
the third place, if the Greek Doctors teach that the Father is here
said to be greater than the Son considered as the Son *simply*,
and if this superior greatness is not one implying priority of
existence, or difference of nature, or greater perfection, in what do
they say that it consists ? They say that it consists in a certain
pre-eminence arising from the different manner in which the
Father has the Divine Essence and perfections as compared
with the Son, inasmuch as the Father is the principle (principium sine principio) from whom the Son (principium a principio)
derives his origin by an eternal generation. This we learn from
St. John Damascene in the passage quoted, as well as from
St. Basil (*c. Eunom.*, i. 25 ; iii. 1), and their teaching is illustrated
in the words of St. Augustine (*De Fid. et Symb.*, c. ix, 1-8) :
" The Son owes to the Father that he is ; as he even owes to

the Father that he is equal (equalis aut par) to the Father, while to no one does the Father owe whatever he is " (Westcott). It has been well said : " The doctrine of the Fathers holds the right mean between the errors of the Jews and the Sabellians on the one hand, and those of the Arians and pagans on the other. For with the former it denies the multiplication of the Divine Nature, yet without denying the distinction of Persons ; with the latter it admits the distinction of Persons, yet without limiting their unity to a similarity or likeness of Essence (St. Greg. of Nyssa, *Or. Cat.*, n. 3). The Fathers represent the unity of Essence as admitting of no other distinction than that based upon the divers relations of origin ; so that there would be no difference whatsoever, except for this relation of origin and the consequent manner of possessing the Divine Essence " (St. Greg. Naz., *Or.*, 31 (al. 37), n. 3), (*Manual of Catholic Theology*, based on Scheeben's " Dogmatik." Wilhelm and Scannell, vol. i., p. 292).

It was, then, the opinion of the Greek Doctors that in the passage under review the Father was said 1°, to be greater than Christ considered not only as the Son *Incarnate*, but also as the Son *simply ;* 2°, that this superior greatness was not one of *duration in existence*, or of *perfection*, or of *essence ;* but 3°, a certain pre-eminence based on the relation of origin and the consequent *different manner of possessing the divine essence*, inasmuch as the Father is the principle (principium sine principio) of whom the Son (principium a principio) is begotten, and from whom the Son has all that he has.

What are we to think of this opinion ? Even if the words : " The Father is greater than I " were to be considered apart from the context, the foregoing exposition would not commend itself to us : still less are we disposed to receive it when we find that in these words Christ was laying down a reason for his return to the Father, from whom he was never absent as God. As Billuart, quoting St. Augustine (4 *de Trinit.* c. 20), observes : " Hæ itaque locutiones Patrum, quos certum est totis viribus dimicasse contra Arianos, benigne sunt interpretandae, non tamen frequentandae." The explanation, then, given by St. Augustine (*de Trin.* lib. i. cap. 7) and followed now by nearly all Catholic commentators, seems to be the best. These writers understand that Christ was here speaking of himself not as God, but as Man : not as the Son *simply*, but as the Son *Incarnate*. The Father was certainly greater than he considered as Man, and it was only as Man that the Son could return to the Father. Speaking, therefore, of himself in his human nature, Christ tells the apostles that, so far from being troubled at his departure to the Father, they in their love for him should rejoice, because at his departure from them he was

as Man to enter into his heavenly home, and to take possession
of the glory which he had merited for himself whilst redeeming us.
" He humbled himself," said the apostle, " becoming obedient
unto death, even to the death of the cross ; for which cause
God also hath exalted him,   .   .   .   that in the name of Jesus
every knee should bow,   .   .   .   and that every tongue should
confess that the Lord Jesus Christ is in the glory of God the
Father " (Phil. ii. 8-11).

Christ had told his apostles of their approaching separation
from him.   Lest any one might think that by so speaking he had
shown less kindness than he would have shown by keeping
silence on so painful a subject, he justified his mode of action
when saying :—

V. 29. **And now I have told you before it come to pass, that
when it shall come to pass, you may believe.**

It is not necessary to restrict Christ's meaning to the prediction of his departure and return (verse 28).   It is probable that
he here referred to all that he had foretold in this discourse.
Neither is it here indicated that the apostles would be without
faith until the fulfilment of these prophecies.   Christ merely
stated that their faith in him, and their consolation, and their
courage would receive a continual increase on seeing the gradual
accomplishment of what they were now told to expect, and that
they would then know *by experience* that nothing happening to
them was ever hidden from their Master.

The discourse in the supper room was now coming to a close,
and Christ said :—

V. 30. **I will not now speak many things with you ; for the
prince of this world cometh, and in me he hath not anything.**

That Christ had still much information to give to his apostles
is clear from the continuation of the discourse recorded in the
following chapter.   Compared, however, with the many revelations made during his public life now drawing to an end, and
even with the revelations made during the present evening, those
which remained were " not many."   He was now about to enter
on his last conflict with " the prince of this world."   By " the
prince of this world," was signified Satan, who is thus named
elsewhere in this Gospel and equivalently in the epistles of St.
Paul (John xii. 31 ; xvi. 11 ; 2 Cor. iv. 4 ; Eph. ii. 2 ; vi. 12),
he having dominion over all that become his subjects by sin.
The evil spirit was now coming in the persons of the Jews his
ministers, to bring about the death of Christ.   Lest, then, the
sufferings and death about to be endured might be attributed
to the superior power of the devil, our Lord stated that Satan
has no power over him as he has over others : that there could

be found in him no sin, and therefore, no cause of death which is the punishment of sin.

Christ thus continued :—

V. 31. But that the world may know that I love the Father, and as the Father hath given me commandment, so do I.

Some interpreters think that all the words in this verse form but one sentence, and they separate the whole from what precedes. According to these writers, the sentence would thus stand : " But arise, let us go hence, that the world may know that I love the Father ; and as the Father hath given me commandment, so do I." The greater number, with apparently more reason, follow St. Augustine in separating the last words : " Arise, let us go hence," from the first words of the verse, and they regard the first words as a continuation of the preceding sentence. In the clause : " But that the world may know," Christ is anticipating a difficulty suggested by what he had just stated. It might be asked : " Why does the ' prince of this world,' Satan, come to wreak his vengeance on thee, if he has no dominion or right over thee ? Why dost thou die, if thou hast no sin which is punished by death ? " Christ answered that his death was to be attributed not to weakness on his part, nor to any dominion of the devil over him, but to a free and loving spirit of obedience to the commandment of his Father. In verses 15, 21, and 23 he had proposed obedience to God's will as the test of love : he now applies this test to himself ; and by his fulfilment of the precept laid upon him he wishes to prove to the world his love for his Father.

To show his readiness to obey the divine ordinance, he called on his apostles to prepare to leave the supper room, and said :—

Arise, let us go hence.

There is no reason to doubt that Christ and his apostles now arose from table ; but interpreters are not agreed as to what afterwards occurred. Some think that Christ immediately left the supper room (Cajetan, Patrizi, Corluy, Fill.) ; went with his apostles to some other place (St. Chrysostom) more secure from attack (St. Chrysostom, Euthym.) ; and there delivered the discourse and offered the prayer next recorded by St. John. " Quoniam, inquit, ecce appropinquat qui me tradet et turba cum eo, ne in angusto intra parietes cœnaculi hujus nos comprehendat, vobisque non sit libera effugiendi facultas, surgite, eamus, ne vel iste cujus diversorio fruiti sumus ullam propter nos inquietudinem patiatur " (Rup.). This does not appear probable, for after recording what Christ had still to say, St. John remarks : " When Jesus had said these things, he went forth with his disciples over the brook of Cedron " (John xviii. 1). Whence did he go forth ? Apparently from no other place than the supper-room, for the evangelist mentions no other house from which he departed. But it may be said that Christ went forth immediately from the supper-room to Gethsemani, and that on the way he delivered the address and offered the prayer contained in the following three chapters. This view, which is adopted by Cajetan, seems improbable. It appears even impossible that the matter contained in this portion of the gospel could have been spoken in the short distance from the walls of the city to the brook of Cedron; and it is very unlikely that in the streets of Jerusalem itself and in the midst of the crowds attending the Paschal Solemnity Christ could have addressed the apostles at such length with any prospect of being understood or even heard. In the absence, then, of any intimation to the contrary from St. John, it may be assumed that the discourse was continued and terminated in the place in which it was commenced, and that the words, " Let us go hence," did not signify a command to leave at once, but to prepare to leave. " Why, therefore," it may be asked, " did Christ delay so long after this announcement of his intention to depart?" The answer is supplied by A Lapide. As friends bidding adieu to each other are accustomed to resume and protract a farewell conversation, so was it on this occasion with Christ who, in assuming our human nature, took to himself with it its feelings, affections, and all that appertained to it, excepting sin and whatever was the consequence of sin.

IV.—MORAL REFLECTIONS.

In the words before us, Christ promised to send the Holy Ghost upon the apostles, and described some of the effects which would then be produced in their souls. But it is not upon the apostles only that Christ wished to send the Holy Ghost: the mystery we now commemorate is renewed invisibly, but not less really, in the soul of each Christian who prepares himself to receive this gift of God. For each of us, therefore, the promise of Christ has a personal interest; and it behoves each of us to consider well the nature of the grace which was this day bestowed.

1. The first effect produced in the apostles and here specially mentioned, was the infusion of knowledge. Finding the apostles unable to understand the simplest truths, the Holy Ghost gave them a capacity far surpassing that of the best trained intellects; he laid open to their minds every revealed truth; and he did this not by means of lengthened instructions, but by the instantaneous operation of his infinite power. " Nescit tarda molimina Sancti Spiritus gratia " (St. Ambrose). When the Holy Ghost descends upon us, he prepares our minds for the reception of his truth; he infuses into our souls the habit of faith;

he induces us to accept the incomprehensible mysteries which
he has made known ; and he does this not by the slow process of
human reasoning but by the instantly effective working of his
grace.   How true is it that the knowledge of divine things is
to be found much less in books than in the secret communication
of the Spirit of God !   " They that approach to his feet, shall
receive of his doctrine " (Deut. xxxiii. 3).   All t⸢ ⸍ saints and
all the masters of the spiritual life have decla⸜ ⸝ that they
learned more in prayerful union with God, than by their labours
and research.   We are not indeed to suppose that pious reading,
meditation, and the preaching of the Church are needless for
us.   On the contrary, these are the ordinary means which the
Holy Ghost makes use of to give us a knowledge of divine truth,
and in connection with which he gives the grace of faith.   Still,
in employing such means, we should keep two things in mind.
The first is that these natural means must derive their efficacy
from the supernatural influence of the divine grace ; and the
second—a consequence of the first—is that, in applying ourselves to learn the truths of faith, we should, after the example
of the apostles, seek the light of the Holy Spirit by fervent and
persevering prayer.   " Blessed is the man whom thou shalt
instruct, O Lord, and shalt teach him out of thy law " (Ps.
xciii. 12).

2. Whilst enlightening the minds of the apostles, the Holy
Ghost sanctified their hearts ; and this second effect of his coming was signified by the tongues of fire in which he appeared.
The fire was the emblem of charity with which he wished to inflame their souls.   Hitherto they had been in the state of grace
indeed, but were subject to many imperfections and faults.   They
were ambitious of worldly honours, jealous of each other, given
to frequent disputes, weak and halting in the practice of virtue—
a condition of things not incompatible with the state of justification, but far removed from that of the exalted sanctity which
became their calling.   After the Holy Ghost had descended upon
them, they became other men ; their spiritual feebleness ceased ;
their defects disappeared ; they became not only holy, but models
of the highest holiness ; and thenceforth they were estranged
from the world, dead to every passion, superior to all interests
except to those of their Divine Master.   Now, although we also
may be in the friendship of God, we have many imperfections ;
for St. James says : " In many things we all offend " (James iii. 2).
The Holy Ghost is ready to produce in us the holiness that
becomes our state if, like the apostles, we prepare to admit
him.   The same sacred fire descending into our hearts will rectify
our irregular inclinations ; it will free us from our worldly attachments ; and purifying us from every sin, it will make of us a
holocaust pleasing to the Lord.   The Apostle has said : " The

charity of God is poured forth in our hearts by the Holy Ghost who is given to us " (Rom. v. 5).

3. A third effect of the coming of the Holy Ghost was to give the apostles courage and strength to fulfil their high destiny. These men who before had abandoned their Master through fear, now boldly proclaimed his divinity ; they who had trembled at the fate of Jesus, now desired to share it ; they who in the upper room had hidden themselves from the Jews, now went forth to brave their enemies ; they who had feared to follow Christ in his last journey to Jerusalem, now preached in every country, and succeeded in effecting the conversion of the world. That all this was brought about not by human means, but by the Holy Ghost working in the apostles, is clearly proved from the words of St. Paul : " Christ sent me . . . to preach the gospel, not in wisdom of speech, lest the cross of Christ should be made void. For the word of the cross, to them indeed that perish, is foolishness ; but to them that are saved, that is to us, it is the power of God. . . . Seeing that in the wisdom of God the world by wisdom knew not God, it pleased God by the foolishness of our preaching to save them that believe " (1 Cor. i. 17, 18, 21). To be faithful to our religious duties amidst the sarcasm and raillery of an unbelieving and wicked age, have we not need of the courage which the Holy Ghost communicated to these first recipients of his gifts ? We shall call then on this Spirit of strength, without whom we can do nothing, but with whom we can do all things. " The Lord," said Jeremias, " is with me as a strong warrior : therefore they that persecute me shall fall " (Jeremias xx. 11). The same divine power that fortified the apostles and enabled them to triumph over the world, the devil, and themselves, will fortify us and secure our victory if it find in us the same dispositions which it found in them.

TRINITY SUNDAY.

I.—TEXTS.

GREEK.

MATTH. XXVIII. 18-20.

¹⁸ Καὶ προσελθὼν ὁ Ἰησοῦς, ἐλάλη-
σεν αὐτοῖς, λέγων· ἐδόθη μοι πᾶσα
ἐξουσία ἐν οὐρανῷ καὶ ἐπὶ τῆς γῆς.
¹⁹ Πορευθέντες οὖν μαθητεύσατε πάντα
τὰ ἔθνη, βαπτίσαντες αὐτοὺς εἰς τὸ
ὄνομα τοῦ πατρὸς καὶ τοῦ υἱοῦ καὶ τοῦ
ἁγίου πνεύματος· ²⁰ διδάσκοντες αὐτοὺς
τηρεῖν πάντα ὅσα ἐνετειλάμην ὑμῖν.
καὶ ἰδοὺ ἐγὼ μεθ᾽ ὑμῶν εἰμὶ πάσας τὰς
ἡμέρας, ἕως τῆς συντελείας τοῦ αἰῶνος

VULGATE.

MATTH. XXVIII. 18-20.

¹⁸ Et accedens Jesus, locutus
est eis, dicens : Data est mihi
omnis potestas in cœlo et in
terra. ¹⁹ Euntes ergo docete
omnes gentes, baptizantes
eos in nomine Patris et Filii et
Spiritus sancti ; ²⁰ docentes
eos servare omnia quæcumque
mandavi vobis. Et ecce ego
vobiscum sum omnibus die-
bus, usque ad consumma-
tionem sæculi.

II.—ENGLISH TRANSLATION.

MATTHEW XXVIII. 18-20.

¹⁸ And Jesus coming, spoke to them, saying : " All power is
given to me in heaven and in earth. ¹⁹ Going, therefore, teach
ye all nations, baptising them in the name of the Father, and
of the Son, and of the Holy Ghost ; ²⁰ teaching them to observe
all things whatsoever I have commanded you. And behold, I
am with you all days, even to the consummation of the world."

III.—NOTES.

Introductory. At his Last Supper Christ had told his apostles
that the time was about to come when they were no longer to
enjoy the comfort and support of his visible presence. Between
the Resurrection and the Ascension the prediction began to be
fulfilled, for in that interval, as we learn from St. Luke, our
Divine Lord showed himself to his disciples in apparitions
which were numerous indeed, but brief in duration. Christ
acted thus to convince his followers of the reality of his return

to life, to complete their instruction, to fit them for their future mission, and gradually to prepare them for his final departure. Of all these apparitions twelve are mentioned in the gospels and St. Paul's epistles. The most remarkable is the one which the present passage of St. Matthew records. It was memorable above all others because the time and place had been previously arranged, and because it was then that Christ gave to the apostles their commission to preach the faith to the entire world. We know, both from the present extract and from the words of the angel to the holy women at the sepulchre, that this arrangement of time and place had been previously made, but we do not know the date of the arrangement, nor have we any information as to the particular mountain on which our Lord was seen. We are merely told by St. Matthew that the apostles, whose number through the death of Judas was now reduced to eleven, "went into Galilee unto the mountain where Jesus had appointed them; and seeing him, they adored, but some doubted" (Matth. xxviii. 16, 17). These doubted not the fact of the Resurrection of which they had already received abundant evidence, but rather the identity of the figure before them with that of their risen Lord. When Christ, therefore, had approached them more closely, so that his dress and person might be more clearly recognised, according to St. Matthew he said:—

V. 18. All power is given to me in heaven and in earth.

Christ, having paid the price of our redemption, was now about to establish his kingdom upon earth, and to send forth his apostles to conquer that kingdom in his name. That, then, they might know the authority by which he acted, he, according to the expression of Maldonatus, showed them his *letters patent*. Inasmuch as all power was conferred upon him, he could delegate to them the authority requisite for the wonderful task in which they were to be engaged. Christ, as God, had the infinite power to create, to preserve in existence, and to rule the creatures to which he had given being; but it is not of this infinite power that he here speaks. He here speaks as Man, as the Redeemer of the human race, as the Conqueror of the devil, as the Ruler of the world. With these titles there was given to him authority over angels, men, and all created things in heaven and on earth; and he was to exercise his authority in making all mankind citizens and subjects of his kingdom (See Knabenbauer, *in loco*). This authority was *given* to Christ when, in his human nature, he became at his Incarnation Lord of creation and Head of angels and of men; but it was not *exercised* fully by him until after his Resurrection, when, by right of purchase, he was entitled to our service; and it is to *have its full effect* only after the General Judgment, when his blessed will must be accomplished absolutely and without opposition on the part of any free agent. The power of Christ extends to heaven, where angels and saints ever adore him, and it is to be felt throughout the entire earth, where his apostles and their successors are to preach his name as the only one given to men by which they may be saved (Acts iv. 12).

The solemn commission to the apostles was conferred in the following words :—

V. 19. Going, therefore, teach ye all nations, baptising them in the name of the Father, and of the Son, and of the Holy Ghost.

The Greek verb $\mu\alpha\theta\eta\tau\epsilon\acute{u}\omega$ when followed by the dative, means : " I am a disciple to," and in connection with the accusative, as here, it means . " I make a disciple of." Christ confined his preaching to the Jews, and during his lifetime limited the mission of his followers to the same nation. He said · " Go ye not into the way of the Gentiles, and into the cities of the Samaritans enter ye not ; but go ye rather to the lost sheep of the house of Israel " (Matth. x. 5, 6). The Jews were the chosen people, and Christ was their king by inheritance. Now, however, when by his death he has purchased all mankind and has " made both [Jews and Gentiles] one, . . . breaking down the middle wall of partition, . . . in his flesh " (Eph. ii. 14), he sends his apostles to make " disciples of all nations " (Maldonatus).

How were the apostles to " make disciples of all nations " ? By " baptising them in the name of the Father, and of the Son, and of the Holy Ghost." The verb $\beta\alpha\pi\tau\acute{\iota}\zeta\omega$ signifies in classical Greek, to dip repeatedly in water, and in New Testament Greek, to immerse in water or to sprinkle with water. Though sometimes taken in the metaphorical sense of richly endowing with the gifts of the Holy Ghost (Matth. iii. 11 ; Mark i. 8 ; Luke iii. 16 ; John i. 33 ; Acts i. 5 ; xi. 16), and again in the metaphorical sense of overwhelming with calamities (Mark x. 38, 39 ; Luke xii. 50), the word has here its literal signification. The reasons for this assertion are that (1°) we have nothing in the context nor in the parallel passages to indicate the use of a metaphor in the word before us ; (2°) the apostles understood the word in its literal sense, as is shown by their subsequent practice (Acts ii. 38 ; viii. 38 ; x. 47, 48) ; (3°) the Fathers of the Church from the earliest times adopted this interpretation ; (4°) the perpetual teaching of the Church on this subject was defined and confirmed by the Council of Trent when it declared : " Si quis dixerit aquam veram et naturalem non esse de necessitate baptismi. . . . Anathema sit." The *matter*, therefore, which Christ prescribed for the rite of initiation into membership of his Church is an ablution with water.

Immediately after the words βαπτίσαντες αὐτοὺς, we have in the Greek text εἰς τὸ ὄνομα κ.τ.λ ="*into* or *unto the name*," etc. What is the meaning of this whole clause? Since names serve to indicate the nature of things as far as that nature is known to us, the names of the three Divine Persons indicate what God has revealed to us regarding these Divine Persons. To be baptised, then, " in (or rather, *into* or *unto*) the name of the Father, and of the Son, and of the Holy Ghost " signifies to be initiated by faith into an acceptance of the truths which have been revealed to us regarding the Father, the Son, and the Holy Ghost ; to be subjected by obedience to an observance of what the Father, the Son, and the Holy Ghost have enjoined on us when revealing themselves to us ; to be admitted to a participation of the divine life of the Father, and of the Son, and of the Holy Ghost, as far as they have deigned to reveal and to communicate that divine life to men. St. Paul's epistles clearly refer to these purposes of Christian baptism, and (Rom. vi. 3-11 ; Gal. iii. 27) make special mention of the participation in the divine life enjoyed by those " who are baptised in Christ Jesus " (Gr. εἰς Χριστὸν =*unto Christ*). Being so closely united to Christ as to have him dwelling within us (Rom. viii. 9, 10), being planted together with Christ unto the likeness of his death (Rom. vi. 5), living unto God in the life communicated by Christ (Rom. vi. 11), we are at the same time intimately united with the Father and the Holy Ghost (Rom. vi. 11 ; viii. 9-11 ; 1 Cor. ii. 12-16 ; Gal. iv. 6), and we have fulfilled in us the prophecy spoken at the Last Supper : " We will come to him, and will make our abode with him " (John xiv. 23). This exposition of our Lord's words is in accordance with the Greek text εἰς τὸ ὄνομα κ.τ.λ.=*unto the name*, etc. We are to understand in the same way the text of the Vulgate, where we have *in nomine*, etc.=*in the name*, etc. ; for it is well known that the Vulgate has *in* with the ablative case for the Greek εἰς τὸ ὄνομα (Acts viii. 16 ; xix. 5 ; 1 Cor. i. 13, 15), for ἐν τῷ ὀνόματι (Acts x. 48), and for ἐπὶ τῷ ὀνόματι (Acts ii. 38). Indeed in the popular Latin the preposition *in* was used indifferently with the ablative and with the accusative, just as in the later Greek the difference between εἰς and ἐν was scarcely observed. From what has been said, therefore, we clearly see the inaccuracy of those interpreters who think that the being baptised in the name of the Father, and of the Son, and of the Holy Ghost is equivalent to being baptised in the power of that name (St. Thomas, A Lapide, Patrizi), or by the authority and in the efficacy of that name (Jansenius Gand.). Salmeron (Tom x. Tract. 32) falls very much short of the full meaning when he says the name of the Blessed Trinity is mentioned in the administration of baptism that those baptised may henceforth be called the sons of God the Father, the brothers of God the Son, and the temples of God the Holy Ghost.   In baptism we receive a *new name* indeed, and enter into a *new relation* with the three Divine Persons ; but the baptismal rite effects much more, and the invocation of the Persons of the Blessed Trinity is intended to signify much more than this.

Does our Lord here give the *essential form* of baptism, so that this sacrament is null and void unless the three Divine Persons are expressly named whilst it is being administered ?   He does ; and this can be proved with certainty, if not from the passage itself, at least from the constant teaching and practice of the Church.   It is said, " if not from the passage itself," for Jansenius Gand., *in loco*, remarks that a command to perform an action in the name of this person or of that, does not necessarily imply that the action is to be accompanied by the mention of any name or by the use of any form of words.   In the same way Maldonatus states that the necessity of the form we use in baptism, cannot be proved from the words here spoken by Christ, but from the tradition of the Church interpreting these words.   That the Church enlightened by the Holy Ghost has always understood these words of Christ to prescribe the essential form of baptism is clear from the writings of the early Fathers.   Thus St. Bede (Lib. Var. Quæst. 14) says : " Notandum, si quis baptizans dicat : Baptizo te in Christo Jesu, et non dicat : In nomine Patris, et Filii, et Spiritus Sancti, sicut Dominus instituit, non est verus baptismus."   St. Ambrose (De Myst., cap. iv) lays down : " Nisi baptizatus fuerit (catechumenus in nomine Patris, et Filii, et Spiritus Sancti, remissionem non potest accipere peccatorum."   St. Basil (Lib. de Spiritu S.) writes : " For just as we believe in the Father, and the Son, and the Holy Ghost, so we are also baptised in the name of the Father, etc."   Still more important for our purpose is the testimony of St. Cyprian (Ep. lxxiii., Ad. Jubaian) who says : " Quando ipse Christus baptizari jubeat in plena et adunata Trinitate," etc. Most important is the statement of Tertullian who says : " Lex tingendi imposita est et forma praescripta.   Ite, inquit, docete nationes, tingentes eas in nomen Patris, et Filii, et Spiritus Sancti."   In a work which many look upon as having come down from the apostolic age, and which is entitled " The Doctrine of the Apostles," we read (chap. 7) the words : Βαπτίσατε εἰς τὸ ὄνομα τοῦ Πατρὸς, etc., ἐν ὕδατι ζῶντι = " Baptise in living water unto the name of the Father, and of the Son, and of the Holy Ghost."   In chapter 9 of the same work, baptism thus described is called a baptism εἰς ὄνομα Κυρίου = " unto the name of the Lord."   In the first place, collating these two statements, we learn the sense in which we are to understand such passages as Acts ii. 38, Acts viii. 16, Acts xix. 5, where we read of a baptism conferred " in the name of Jesus Christ," or " in the name of the Lord Jesus." These expressions merely signify that baptism was instituted by Christ ; that in it we are consecrated to Christ ; and that it is a rite quite distinct from the baptism of John, which still continued to be administered in certain parts of the East (Acts xix. 3). In the second place, we see how justly all theologians now reject the opinion of those writers who held that the apostles were *by special dispensation* permitted to baptise in the name of Christ alone.

Inasmuch as Christ says : " Going, therefore, teach ye (Gr. μαθητεύσατε = *make disciples of*) all nations, baptising them," etc., does it not appear that all must be instructed in the Christian doctrine before being baptised ; and if so, what are we to think of the validity of infant baptism ? Grounding their teaching on the interpretation of the Church, the authentic exponent of our Lord's words, theologians reply that this passage refers not to infants, but to adults : that Christ does not here exclude from baptism those who are incapable of instruction, but directs that such as are instructed shall be baptised. That infant baptism is valid follows as a conclusion from other truths clearly laid down in the Sacred Scriptures. We there learn that all men, and therefore infants, are called to salvation, for the Apostle writes : " God will have all men to be saved " (I Tim. ii. 4). But if this be so, all men, and therefore infants, must be capable of receiving baptism, which is a necessary condition of salvation, Christ having said : " Unless a man be born again of water and the Holy Ghost, he cannot enter into the kingdom of God " (John iii. 5).

Having commanded his apostles to make disciples of all mankind by bringing all to the profession of the faith and to the reception of baptism, Christ completes his instructions in these words :—

V. 20. Teaching them to observe all things whatsoever I have commanded you.

It was not sufficient to found the Church and to add to its membership from age to age : the ministers of Christ must be the ever living witnesses of his teaching, and all must hear and obey these teachers as the authorised exponents of his will. Thus did our Divine Lord, shortly before his departure, give a solemn confirmation to what he had already said : " If he will not hear the Church, let him be to thee as the heathen and the publican. Amen I say to you, whatsoever you shall bind upon earth, shall be bound also in heaven ; and whatsoever you shall loose upon earth, shall be loosed also in heaven " (Matth. xviii. 17, 18).

What assurance had the apostles that they could carry out this mission of instructing the world, and what guarantee had their disciples that this teaching would be without admixture of error ? The answer is found in the concluding words of the passage :—

And behold, I am with you all days even to the consummation of the world.

Calling attention not so much to the nearness of the aid as to its greatness by the word $ἰδοὺ = behold$, Christ tells his apostles that he himself to whom all power has been given in heaven and on earth, will be with them, not bodily as heretofore, but invisibly, effectively, and at all times. These words contain a divine promise that our Lord will watch over them and assist them, not merely by that general providence with which he directs all creatures to their end, not merely by that special providence which he exercises towards his rational creatures, but by a higher kind of help. The help promised is a supernatural and absolutely efficacious aid which ($1°$) no obstacle or set of circumstances can withstand, and which ($2°$) will be given to their successors with the same certainty of result and in the same measure as to themselves. That this aid is to be absolutely efficacious is made clear, in the first place, by the circumstances of the speaker and his audience, and in the second place, by the terms in which the promise was given. When a master commands his servant to do a certain work and promises his constant assistance in the execution of the order, it is a sign that he wishes the work to be done, and that he will certainly have it done unless he be wanting in the power to overcome the obstacles that may present themselves. Now this is precisely what Christ did. In his address to the apostles, he, on the one hand, commanded them to establish his Church and to direct it aright in accordance with the full revelation he had communicated to them ; and on the other hand, to remove all hesitation on their part and all fear of difficulty, he declared that he was to be ever with them in bringing about the end for which they laboured. We must conclude, therefore, that Christ wished to have his Church established, infallibly taught, and securely governed by the apostles ; and that, unless he who has all power in heaven and on earth, becomes unable to carry out his will, the Church must be established, infallibly taught, and securely governed. Again, we are led to the same conclusion by a consideration of the form in which Christ promised his aid to the apostles. According to Scriptural usage the expression : " I am with you," implies the absolutely certain successful issue of the work in which God promises to be with his servants ; and in the Sacred Scripture there is no instance in which, under any circumstances or from any cause, a work undertaken with such a promise has failed to be accomplished. In proof of this statement theologians appeal to the case of Moses when sent to liberate the Israelites from the bondage of Egypt (Exod. iii. 12) ; to that of Josue when appointed leader of the people in their invasion of the Promised Land (Josue i. 5) ; to the case of Gideon when raised up for the extermination of the Madianites (Judges vi. 16) ; and to that of the Blessed Virgin when it was announced that, preserving her virginity, she was to become the Mother of God (Luke i. 28). Nor was it to the apostles alone that this promise was made, but also to their successors in the government of the Church ; for whereas the apostles were but mortal men, the Church was to last till the end of time. It is with reason, therefore, that the Church has ever appealed to these words of her Divine Founder in justification of her claim to teach infallibly the truths of faith, and to prescribe without error the rules of a Christian life.

IV. —MORAL REFLECTIONS.

From Advent until now, the Church has been commemorating the works accomplished for our Redemption. To-day in the Blessed Trinity she proposes for our veneration the source from which these works have proceeded and the end to which the glory of these works must be referred. It is becoming, then, that we learn from her what we are bound to know regarding this ineffable mystery of our faith, and what we are bound to do in order to honour this mystery as we ought.

1. We must know and believe that in the Trinity there is one God in three Persons : the Father, the Son, and the Holy Ghost. There is one God, *i.e.*, a Being on whom all things else depend, a Being infinitely holy, infinitely good, infinitely just, infinitely powerful, infinitely perfect ; and in this one God there are three Persons who, although really distinct one from the other, have identically the same nature, the same essence, the same perfection. Thus the Father is not the Son, nor is the Son the Holy Ghost ; nevertheless the Father, and the Son, and the Holy Ghost are but one God, one Lord, one Creator of all things. The Son was begotten of the Father, and the Holy Ghost proceeded from the Father and the Son ; but the Father was not in existence before the Son, nor were the Father and the Son before the Holy Ghost. The Father is eternal, the Son is eternal, the Holy Ghost is eternal ; and still, they are not three eternal beings, but one. The Father is almighty, the Son is almighty, the Holy Ghost is almighty ; and still, there are not three almighty beings, but one. The Father was neither created nor begotten ; the Son was not created, but he was begotten of the Father ; the Holy Ghost was neither created nor begotten, but he proceeded from the Father and the Son. Any one of these

three Divine Persons is as perfect as the other two, and any two are not more perfect than one ; because each. possesses fully every perfection of that divine nature which is identical in all. In a word, the Father and the Son and the Holy Ghost are equal in all things ; and in God we adore a Unity of nature in a Trinity of Persons, and a Trinity of Persons in a Unity of nature.   Such is the object which the Church this day proposes for our homage —an object the contemplation of which constitutes the happiness of the blessed, and which the seraphim perpetually honour in the canticle recorded by Isaias : " Holy, Holy, Holy, the Lord God of hosts.   All the earth is full of his glory " (Isaias vi. 3).

2. As it is not sufficient to believe in the Trinity, let us next inquire as to the manner in which we may give a practical ex‹ pression of our devotion to this mystery. We have in our souls three faculties—understanding, will, and memory—which are a faint representation of the three Divine Persons, and we cannot offer a more agreeable sacrifice to the Blessed Trinity than by consecrating to it the exercise of these three faculties in the acts of virtue proper to each.

In the first place, then, we should offer to the Blessed Trinity the homage of our understanding by a humble and unquestioning belief in this and all other mysteries of our faith.   However incomprehensible these mysteries may be to our reason, they have been revealed by God, and this should suffice to secure our assent. We should not regulate our ideas of God according to those which we have of creatures.   In God all is infinite, all is incomprehensible ; and if we could comprehend him, he would no longer be God.   As St. Augustine says : " It is this incomprehensibility that gives us a more noble idea of his greatness, and in this incomprehensible greatness we have the motive of our faith." We shall then submit our intelligence to God who wishes to hide himself from us in order to make us recognise our ignorance, and in order to humble our minds to his Supreme authority.   By this submission we shall offer him a sacrifice most pleasing to him and most meritorious for us, since we shall thereby renounce ourselves, and, on his word, believe mysteries which are not only beyond our understanding, but appear to be contrary to reason.

We should also offer to the Blessed Trinity the homage of our will in the most perfect love of God and inviolable attachment to the divine law.   What is more just than to love that which is infinitely lovable, which contains all perfections and every attraction to gain the heart ?   What is more advantageous than to devote ourselves to that which alone can make us happy, and outside of which we can find but vanity and affliction of spirit ?   Our hearts were made for God, and they cannot rest until they repose in him.   And how shall we prove our love of

God? By keeping the commandments. "He," says Christ, "that hath my commandments and keepeth them, he it is that loveth me. And he that loveth me shall be loved of my Father; and I will love him, and will manifest myself to him" (John xiv. 21). Thus shall we secure our happiness on earth, and commence here below that union with the Persons of the Blessed Trinity which is the essential happiness of the elect.

Lastly, to acquit ourselves of our duty to the Blessed Trinity, we should often exercise our memory by the recollection of God's goodness; and recollecting this, we should be filled with gratitude for the favours conferred on us by each of the three Divine Persons. What are these favours? It was the Father who created us; it was the Son who redeemed us; and it was the Holy Ghost who sanctified us. But that which should particularly excite our gratitude is the thought of our unmerited call to the faith, the thought of the grace of baptism which we have received, and the thought of the august character of a Christian with which we are honoured. By these blessings we entered into a special relation with the Blessed Trinity; and in virtue of this relation we are the children of God the Father, the brethren of Jesus Christ, the temples of the Holy Ghost. We will then a thousand times bless the three Divine Persons who have chosen us for these privileges before so many that would have been more worthy, and we will show our gratitude in supporting by a holy life the glorious titles by which we have been ennobled. "To the King of Ages immortal and invisible, the only God, be honour and glory for ever and ever. Amen" (1 Tim. i. 17).

FIRST SUNDAY AFTER PENTECOST.

I.—TEXTS.

GREEK.

LUKE VI. 36-42.

³⁶ Γίνεσθε οἰκτίρμονες, καθὼς ὁ πατὴρ ὑμῶν οἰκτίρμων ἐστίν. ³⁷ Καὶ μὴ κρίνετε, καὶ οὐ μὴ κριθῆτε· καὶ μὴ δικάζετε, καὶ οὐ μὴ δικασθῆτε. Ἀπολύετε, καὶ ἀπολυθήσεσθε. ³⁸ Δίδοτε, καὶ δοθήσεται ὑμῖν· μέτρον καλὸν, πεπιεσμένον, σεσαλευμένον, ὑπερεκχυνόμενον, δώσουσιν εἰς τὸν κόλπον ὑμῶν· ᾧ γὰρ μέτρῳ μετρεῖτε, ἀντιμετρηθήσεται ὑμῖν. ³⁹ Εἶπεν δὲ καὶ παραβολὴν αὐτοῖς· μήτι δύναται τυφλὸς τυφλὸν ὁδηγεῖν; οὐχὶ ἀμφότεροι εἰς βόθυνον ἐμπεσοῦνται; ⁴⁰ Οὐκ ἔστιν μαθητὴς ὑπὲρ τὸν διδάσκαλον· κατηρτισμένος δὲ πᾶς ἔσται ὡς ὁ διδάσκαλος αὐτοῦ. ⁴¹ Τί δὲ βλέπεις τὸ κάρφος τὸ ἐν τῷ ὀφθαλμῷ τοῦ ἀδελφοῦ σου, τὴν δὲ δοκὸν τὴν ἐν τῷ ἰδίῳ ὀφθαλμῷ οὐ κατανοεῖς; ⁴² Πῶς δύνασαι λέγειν τῷ ἀδελφῷ σου· ἀδελφέ, ἄφες, ἐκβάλω τὸ κάρφος τὸ ἐν τῷ ὀφθαλμῷ σου· αὐτὸς τὴν ἐν τῷ ὀφθαλμῷ σου δοκὸν οὐ βλέπων; ὑποκριτὰ· ἔκβαλε πρῶτον τὴν δοκὸν ἐκ τοῦ ὀφθαλμοῦ σου, καὶ τότε διαβλέψεις τὸ κάρφος τό ἐν τῷ ὀφθαλμῷ τοῦ ἀδελφοῦ σου ἐκβαλεῖν.

VULGATE.

LUKE VI. 36-42.

36 Estote ergo misericordes sicut et Pater vester misericors est. 37 Nolite judicare, et non judicabimini ; nolite condemnare, et non condemnabimini ; dimittite, et dimittemini. 38 Date, et dabitur vobis : mensuram bonam, et confertam, et coagitatam, et supereffluentem dabunt in sinum vestrum. Eadem quippe mensura, qua mensi fueritis, remetietur vobis. 39 Dicebat autem illis et similitudinem : Numquid potest cæcus cæcum ducere? Nonne ambo in foveam cadunt? 40 Non est discipulus super magistrum ; perfectus autem omnis erit, si sit sicut magister ejus. 41 Quid autem vides festucam in oculo fratris tui, trabem autem quæ in oculo tuo est non consideras? 42 Aut quomodo potes dicere fratri tuo : Frater, sine ejiciam festucam de oculo tuo, ipse in oculo tuo trabem non videns? Hypocrita, ejice primum trabem de oculo tuo, et tunc perspicies ut educas festucam de oculo fratris tui.

II.—ENGLISH TRANSLATION.

LUKE VI. 36-42.

36 " Be ye therefore merciful, as your Father also is merciful.
37 Judge not, and you shall not be judged. Condemn not, and
you shall not be condemned. Forgive, and you shall be forgiven. 38 Give, and it shall be given to you : good measure, and
pressed down, and shaken together, and running over, shall they
give into your bosom. For with the same measure that you
shall mete withal, it shall be measured to you again." 39 And
he spoke also a similitude to them : " Can the blind lead the
blind ? Do they not both fall into the ditch ? 40 The disciple
is not above his master ; but every one shall be perfect, if he be
as his master. 41 And why seest thou the mote in thy brother's
eye ; but the beam that is in thy own eye thou considerest not ?
42 Or how canst thou say to thy brother : Brother, let me pull
the mote out of thy eye, when thou thyself seest not the beam
in thy own eye ? Hypocrite, first cast the beam out of thy own
eye : and then shalt thou see clearly to take out the mote from
thy brother's eye."

III.—NOTES.

Introductory. This gospel passage is taken from a discourse
which was delivered by our Divine Lord in the second year of
his public life, and which by most commentators is identified
with that recorded in the gospel of St. Matthew from the 5th to
the 7th chapter. The place where the discourse was delivered
is a hill in the neighbourhood of Capharnaum, and is about
three miles distant from Mount Thabor. This hill was called
by pilgrims the " Mount of the Beatitudes " ; but it is locally
known as " Kurin Hattin," *i.e.*, " The Horns of Hattin," from
the horn-like shape of its double summit, and from the name of the
village at its foot. Here after a night spent in prayer, Christ
had just selected his apostles (Luke vi. 12-16), and in their presence and in that of a " great multitude of people from all Judæa
and Jerusalem, and the sea-coast both of Tyre and Sidon (Introduction, p. lii.), who were come to hear him and to be healed of
their diseases " (verses 17, 18), he gave his compendium of
gospel morality called the " Sermon on the Mount." By selecting his apostles as princes and rulers of his Messianic kingdom,
he showed that the ministers of the Synagogue were to be rejected ; and by his authentic exposition of revealed truth, he
put aside for ever the false interpretations with which the Sacred
Scriptures had been overlaid.

Having, then, commenced his address by making known in the "Beatitudes" the true nature of that happiness for which all men are ever consciously or unconsciously seeking and the means by which that happiness may be obtained, having afterwards insisted on that love of our neighbour which embraces even our enemies, our Redeemer gathers up as it were the substance of what he had said, in the following practical conclusion recorded by St. Luke :—

V. 36. Be ye therefore merciful, as your Father also is merciful.

Although the equivalent of the connecting particle "therefore" is not found in Codex B, and probably does not belong to the Greek text, the present statement is clearly linked in sense with the preceding verse. Christ had just said that the great God, "the Highest," whose sons we are, "is kind to the unthankful and to the evil"; and he now draws the conclusion that, as children should resemble their parents, we should aim at imitating our Heavenly Father in the attribute of mercy which is above all his works. But what is this "mercy" of which Christ speaks? Our Lord does not here refer to that special moral virtue in the exercise of which we have a fellow-feeling for the miseries of others, and are accustomed to relieve these miseries when relief is possible. Here and in many other parts of the Sacred Scriptures the word "merciful" is the same as the Hebrew חָסִיד=*benign, kind, beneficent;* and the word "mercy," representing the Hebrew חֶסֶד frequently means any great kindness or benefit. Thus it was that, on receiving a great favour from God or man, people were accustomed to say : "He hath done me a mercy." An instance of this is found when Abraham, by no means an object of mercy in the strict sense, said to Sara : "Thou shalt do me this kindness (misericordiam) : In every place to which we shall come, thou shalt say that I am thy brother" (Gen. xx. 13). Abimelech, king of Gerara, said to Abraham : "According to the kindness (juxta misericordiam) that I have done to thee, thou shalt do to me" (Gen. xxi. 23). This beneficence rather than justice is the chief attribute shown in his dealings with his creatures by that God whose mercies are above all his works. When, therefore, in the preceding verse he exhorted us to be the "sons of the Highest," and when in the parallel passage of St. Matthew he counselled us to be perfect as our Heavenly Father is perfect, Jesus presented to us as a model One whose goodness to ourselves is not measured entirely by the moral worth of the recipients nor arrested by the fore-knowledge of their ingratitude.

Giving only a compendium of our Lord's discourse, and passing over much that is narrated by St. Matthew, St. Luke next proceeds to record Christ's instructions as to the manner in which kindness to our neighbour should be shown in thought, and word. Our Lord said :—

V. 37. Judge not, and you shall not be judged. Condemn not, and you shall not be condemned. Forgive, and you shall be forgiven.

After the Divine Master had exhorted his disciples to the practice of kindliness and charity towards all, he now warned us against the opposite vice of censoriousness—a besetting sin of the pharisees, and one from which few men are altogether exempt. He told his audience (a) that we should not enter on a curious examination of another's acts ; (b) that if these acts considered in themselves clearly deserve reproof we should not hastily pass sentence on the intention of the doer ; and (c) that if not only the act but also the intention of the doer be evidently evil, we should, as far as in us lies, extend to our erring neighbour a full measure of pardon for the offence committed. According to St. Jerome, Christ does not forbid all judgment, but teaches Christians how to judge. He does not deprive rulers, ecclesiastical or civil, of their right to take cognisance of the acts of their subjects and to punish the convicted transgressors of the law. Writing to those who governed the Church of Corinth, St. Paul thus asserted the authority of ecclesiastical rulers : " What have I to do to judge them that are without ? Do not you judge them that are within ? " (1 Cor. v. 12). With respect to the power of a secular magistrate, the same Apostle wrote to the Romans : " He is God's minister to thee for good. But if thou do that which is evil, fear ; for he beareth not the sword in vain. For he is God's minister, an avenger to execute wrath upon him that doth evil " (Rom. xiii. 4). So much for those in authority when acting in their *official* capacity.

But is it not forbidden to private persons, or to others acting in a *private* capacity, to judge and to condemn the evil which they see ? By no means in every circumstance. Warning us to beware of false prophets, Christ said : " By their fruits you shall know them " (Matt. vii. 16) ; and in similar circumstances St. John wrote : " Dearly beloved, believe not every spirit, but try the spirits if they be of God ; because many false prophets are gone out into the world " (1 John iv. 1). As the circumspection which is thus prescribed cannot be exercised without passing sentence on others, it follows that in the present passage our Lord does not prohibit all judgment on the part of even private individuals. Three things are prohibited. First, it is forbidden to pass judgment on the words or acts of our neighbour when our neighbour's intention or the nature of his word or act is not manifest. When we are not certain as to

the intention of another, the words of St. Paul are applicable :
" Let not him that eateth, despise him that eateth not ; and
let not him that eateth not, judge him that eateth " (Rom. xiv.
3).   The same Apostle had both cases of uncertainty before his
mind when he wrote : " He that judgeth me is the Lord.
Therefore judge not before the time until the Lord come, who
both will bring to light the hidden things of darkness, and will
make manifest the counsels of the hearts, and then shall every
man have praise from God " (1 Cor. iv. 4, 5).   The first kind of
judgment forbidden, therefore, is that which is rash because
the nature of the deed or the intention of the doer is not fully
known to him who criticises.   The second kind of judgment forbidden is one which deals with words or acts that are manifestly bad, but in which the critic seeks not so much the correction
or prevention of another's fault as the exhibition of his own
excellence when compared with the blackened reputation of his
neighbour.   This is the judgment of the detractor, which is so
severely condemned by St. James in the following words :—
" Detract not one another, my brethren.   He that detracteth his
brother, or he that judgeth his brother, detracteth the law and
judgeth the law.   But if thou judge the law, thou art not a
doer of the law, but a judge.   There is one Lawgiver and Judge
that is able to destroy and to deliver.   But who art thou that
judgest thy neighbour ? " (St. James iv. 11-13).   Lastly, there
is the judgment of those who, at the sight of an evidently evil
act done with an evidently evil intention, condemn the sinner
as incapable of repentance and without hope of pardon.   To
such persons St. Paul wrote : " Who art thou that judgest
another man's servant ?   To his own lord he standeth or falleth.
And he shall stand ; for God is able to make him stand.   .   .   .
But thou, why judgest thou thy brother ?   Or thou, why dost
thou despise thy brother ?   For we shall all stand before the
judgment-seat of Christ.   .   .   .   Therefore everyone of us
shall render account to God for himself " (Rom. xiv. 4, 10,
12).

From speaking of the necessity of kindness in general, and
of charitable thoughts and works in particular, Christ naturally
passes on to recommend generosity in act towards even those
who have offended us.   He says :—

**V. 38. Give, and it shall be given to you : good measure
and pressed down, and shaken together, and running over,
shall they give into your bosom.**

In the preceding sentence Christ had commanded us his followers to lay aside especially all revengeful feelings towards
those whose evil deeds are injurious to us.   " Forgive," said
he, " and it shall be forgiven you."   With that precept he

ɴow joins the command to render assistance, as far as possible, to all who are in need.   For the fulfilment of each of these injunctions he promises the same reward, which is that " they (the angels of God as ministers of the divine justice) shall give into your bosom good measure, and pressed down, and shaken together, and running over."   It is to be remembered in the first place, that the word here translated " bosom," is the fold of the robe gathered up by the girdle and allowed to hang over in front of the breast.   Pockets being unknown at the time, it was in this fold of the garment that both Jews and Gentiles carried whatever was necessary even for a journey.   In the second place, it is to be observed that the figurative epithets here employed are borrowed from the practice of those who measured out corn or other materials of that nature.   Such men, when wishing to deal generously with their customers, first fill up the vessel ; then by shaking and by pressing down with the hand, they cause the contents to subside ; and lastly, on the addition of more, they cause the vessel to flow over.   Christ, therefore, in this climax promises that God will dispense his rewards in a most generous manner.   The same thought is expressed by the Apostle, who writes : " He who soweth sparingly, shall also reap sparingly ; and he who soweth in blessings, shall also reap of blessings.   Everyone as he hath determined in his heart, not with sadness, or of necessity ; for God loveth the cheerful giver " (2 Cor. ix. 6, 7).   But, as is stated in the text, this reward will be according to " measure " ; for although generous and immense when compared with the work done, and although infinite in itself, the enjoyment of it is to be in proportion to each one's deeds.   It is written : " Star differeth from star in glory : so also is the resurrection of the dead " (1 Cor. xv. 41, 42).

Having thus specially encouraged an open-handed spirit of beneficence, Christ next mentions the rewards to be given for the practice of any of these precepts of kindness in thought, word, or deed, and the punishment in store for all who transgress them.   He does so in this proverbial saying, then so well known to the Jews, and afterwards inserted in the Talmud :—

For with the same measure that you shall mete withal, it shall be measured to you again.

To what judgment or retribution does our Lord refer ?   Is it the judgment that follows after death ?   Are we to understand that the charitable who die in mortal sin, are to have their sins remitted or overlooked before the judgment-seat of Christ, and that the uncharitable alone are to have their transgressions remembered and punished ?   The retribution to which reference is here made is not that which follows after death.   With our term of probation in this life, the time of mercy ceases, and we at once enter into the state where unmixed justice is to be meted out to the charitable and to the uncharitable alike. Our Lord's meaning, then, is that whilst we are still here on earth, God will secure the conversion or sanctification of the kindly-disposed and charitable by abundant efficacious graces which he does not owe to anyone, and which he will deny to the severe critic of an erring brother and to the heartless spectator of a neighbour's wants. It follows that God has placed our fate in our own hands. "Before man is life and death, good and evil: that which he shall choose, shall be given him" (Ecclus. xv. 18). Our judgment will be such as we have passed on others; and our dealings with others will find a counterpart in God's dealings with ourselves. If we be kind and charitable in our thoughts and words, if we be generous in our acts of charity, God will remove our faults from his sight; and by his grace he will prepare us for a reward exceeding the works which we have accomplished for him. If on the other hand, we give way to uncharitable severity in thought, or word, or act, God who owes us nothing, will deal severely with us, and we shall experience the truth of the inspired words: "Judgment without mercy to him that hath not done mercy" (James ii. 13).

Our Lord had forbidden to his disciples, especially in their private capacity, all unkindly criticism and harsh judgment of their neighbour. He now proceeded to anticipate an objection to this precept;

V. 39. And he spoke also a similitude to them: Can the blind lead the blind? Do they not both fall into the ditch?

The word "similitude" (in the Greek παραβολή) has sometimes a wider, sometimes a more restricted signification. Here it has its wider signification, and stands for a simple *comparison* or *simile*. With four of these Christ terminated his discourse. In the first—that recorded in the present passage—βόθυνος signified not so exactly a ditch as a pit or well. In Palestine such excavations are very frequently to be met with; they are left quite unprotected by fence or parapet; and they are a source of danger to the unwary traveller. This simile occurs elsewhere in the discourses of our Lord, but in a different connection and with a different meaning. Lest in the present instance his hearers might reply that they judged and condemned their brother with a view to that brother's good, Christ describes the character of him who as a private individual, may without danger practise this fraternal correction. It is as if he had said: "The person who wishes to reprehend another's error, or to point out to him the way of virtue and to be a guide therein, should first examine if his own mind be in possession of the truth, and if his own heart be free from inclination to evil. What will be the consequence of a neglect of this precaution? As happens to the blind wayfarer in the hands of the blind guide, both must fall into the pit of eternal death."

To enforce this truth still further in another simile, Christ adds:

V. 40. The disciple is not above his master; but everyone shall be perfect if he be as his master.

St. Luke was a physician; and Plummer remarks that the verb καταρτίζω here used by the evangelist is a surgical term employed with reference to the setting of a bone or joint. The Greek word κατηρτισμένος, therefore, signifies one whose defects of mind are set right by instruction, as a dislocated joint or broken bone is set right by surgical appliances. On this passage in the Greek text κατηρτισμένος δὲ πᾶς ἔσται ὡς ὁ διδάσκαλος αὐτοῦ, Plummer again says: "The sentence may be taken in different ways:—1. 'Every well-instructed disciple shall be as his master' (A.V.) 2. 'Every disciple when he has been well-instructed shall be as his master.' 3. 'Every disciple shall be as well-instructed as his master' (Tyn. Cran.). But 'Perfectus autem omnis erit, si sit sicut magister ejus' (Vulgate), 'everyone shall be perfect, if he be as his master' (Rhem.) . . . . is impossible. The meaning is that the disciple will not excel his master; at the best he will only equal him. And if the master has faults, the disciple will be likely to copy them." The conclusion which was to be drawn by the audience is that no one can usefully undertake the office of instructing or of reproving others if his own mind be clouded by error or his own heart be a slave to vice.

The importance of the lesson to be conveyed was so great, that Christ wished to enforce it by this third simile:—

V. 41. And why seest thou the mote in thy brother's eye; but the beam that is in thy own eye thou considerest not?

The mote (κάρφος) is a particle or splinter of wood almost imperceptible, but very painful and injurious when inserted in the flesh or in the eye; the beam (δοκός) is a piece of timber which receives (δέχομαι) into itself and supports the other timbers of the roof; and the two which differ so much in size, are the symbols respectively of slight faults and of great sins. Our Lord's meaning is, then, that before observing even in a passing way (βλέπεις) the small deficiencies of others, we should give prolonged and careful attention (κατανοεῖς) to our own great transgressions. The self-constituted censors of their neighbour who neglect this preparation are called hypocrites, and are declared to be quite unfit to engage in the work of fraternal correction. They are said to be hypocrites, either because they seek the reputation of being just and without defect, when under the mask of a holy zeal they studiously hide much greater vices than those they condemn in others, or because under the pretence of a charitable concern for their neighbour's well-being, they indulge the passion of self-esteem and give themselves pleasure in inflicting humiliation. If the motive of their actions were a sincere desire to benefit their brother, they would first seek to benefit themselves by a correction of their own disorders. Christ having pointed out the love we bear ourselves as the type of love we should have for others, no one can be supposed to love his brother, who does not first love himself. The man, therefore, who, shutting his eyes to glaring sins in himself, pretends to be troubled at the smaller faults of a neighbour, does harm to himself by meriting the name of hypocrite, and he does harm to the person admonished by exciting contempt and hatred of the truth.

The golden rule proposed by Christ is found in the following words :—

Hypocrite, first cast the beam out of thy own eye; and then shalt thou see clearly to take the mote from thy brother's eye.

Our Lord has for his audience on the present occasion not the apostles only—the rulers of the Church—but also the general body of disciples. Hence he does not here impose on all the duty of fraternal correction ; but, using the simple future, ($\delta\iota\alpha\beta\lambda\acute{\epsilon}\psi\epsilon\iota\varsigma = thou\ shalt\ see\ clearly$), he points out the first requisite qualification of those who *may* have to fulfil that duty. To censure others safely and effectually when censure is not demanded by our office, presupposes such a rare combination of qualities and is a work in which we may be so easily deluded by self-love, vanity, or other passions, that a grave obligation in this matter rarely exists in the case of private individuals towards each other, and still more rarely in the case of subjects towards their superiors. (See Gury : *Theol. Mor. De Correct. Frat.*) If we seek to withdraw others from evil, whether we be bound to this by reason of our office or be moved to undertake it by zeal, we must ourselves have been ever free from the sin which we denounce, or we must be known to have repented of the crimes which we forbid. Then, and not till then ($\tau\acute{o}\tau\epsilon$), will admonition take effect. It is written : " Wherein thou judgest another thou condemnest thyself; because thou dost the same things which thou judgest. For we know that the judgment of God is according to truth against them that do such things. And thinkest thou this, O man, that judgest them who do such things, and dost the same, that thou shalt escape the judgment of God ? " (Rom. ii. 1-3).

IV.—MORAL REFLECTIONS.

In the instruction delivered on this occasion, our Lord proposed the love of his Heavenly Father for his creatures as the model of our love for our neighbour, and he indicated the several ways in which this most important duty is violated by us.

1. To be like the love of our Heavenly Father, our charity should embrace all men without exception whether they be noble or of low degree, whether they be known or unknown, whether they be friends or enemies. The author of the book of Wisdom says: " Thou lovest all things that are, and hatest none of the things which thou hast made ; . . . but thou sparest all because they are thine, O Lord, who lovest souls " (Wisdom xi. 25-27). The law of Christian charity does not forbid that in our love and in our services we make a distinction between the members of the human race : it does not forbid us to give a preference to those to whom we are bound by special ties of kinship, of acquaintance, or of country. What it does forbid is to exclude any from our good wishes or beneficence. All our brethren have claims upon us, though the claims of some are stronger than those of others : we do not sin by loving one more than another, but we do sin if there be even one whom we do not love, or one whom we are not disposed to serve. To resemble our Heavenly Father, then, our heart should be open to all mankind, and to each one we should wish every kind of blessing. Still further, as God has given us all we have in the temporal and in the spiritual order, to be like him in his paternal goodness, we should wish for our brethren every benefit that can be conferred in the one order and in the other. Our obligations to our neighbour are measured by his necessity ; and our discharge of these obligations should be limited only by our opportunity for doing good.

2. The first violation of charity pointed out by Christ in the present passage is rash judgment. This consists in two things —the believing too readily in the existence of what is defamatory of our neighbour's character, and the giving without sufficient reason a bad interpretation to his words or acts. Rash judgment is sinful in itself, and it springs from a sinful source. In some of us it arises from envy at a reputation which excels our own, and which we would lower when it cannot be reached. Again, this rash judgment is often due to pride, which urges us to censure all who come within the circle of our acquaintance, and to glory in our fancied superiority to all. Another cause of this vice is our desire to excuse our evident faults and to minimise their gravity in our own eyes by representing to ourselves that others are subject to the same defects. Thus on the one hand, rash judgments are very common, because the vices that

give rise to them are found in most men ; and on the other, they are very reprehensible, inasmuch as they partake of the vicious nature of the causes from which they spring.

3. Christ warns us against a second form of uncharitableness which is found in the unforgiving spirit that refuses pardon for an offence committed against us. The gospel does not forbid us to seek reparation for injuries inflicted on us in our persons, in our honour, or in our goods. What it does forbid is to take matters into our own hands, or to substitute our will for the law ; it prohibits that even before the tribunal of justice, we pursue our enemy in a spirit of revenge ; and it counsels us to condone, when possible, the act of an offending but repentant brother. We have received pardon of many sins from God, and we are still in need of his divine mercy ; for " if we say that we have no sin, we deceive ourselves, and the truth is not in us " (1 John i. 8). We should remember, then, that our fate is placed in our own hands ; that God will act towards us as we act towards our brethren ; and that, in giving the history of the unmerciful debtor, Christ said : " His lord being angry, delivered him to the torturers until he paid all the debt. So also shall my Heavenly Father do to you, if you forgive not every one, his brother, from your hearts " (Matth. xviii. 34, 35).

4. The third manner in which we offend against charity is by hard-heartedness towards the poor. The unequal distribution of the goods of fortune is intended by Providence to give to the poor an opportunity for merit by humility and patience, and to afford to the rich a means of laying up treasures in heaven by their benefactions to the needy. Thus religion, by the wisdom of its precepts, balances the different orders of society. It gives to all men the equality of which they are capable ; it smoothes over the difficulties which spring from the nature of things : and it cures the evils which are incidental to social institutions. The Holy Ghost has said : " The rich man and the poor man have met one another : the Lord is the maker of them both " (Prov. xxii. 2). This Lord of all commands the poor to labour for the rich, and the rich, as his stewards, to dispense their treasures to the poor. The observance of these two precepts banishes jealousy from the hearts of the indigent, whilst it suppresses vanity in the minds of the affluent ; and thus promoting the contentment of both classes on earth, it secures for them eternal happiness in heaven.

CORPUS CHRISTI.

I.—TEXTS.

GREEK.

JOHN VI. 55-58.

⁵⁵ Ἡ γὰρ σάρξ μου ἀληθής ἐστιν βρῶσις, καὶ τὸ αἷμά μου ἀληθής ἐστιν πόσις. ⁵⁶ Ὁ τρώγων μου τὴν σάρκα, καὶ πίνων μου τὸ αἷμα, ἐν ἐμοὶ μένει, κἀγὼ ἐν αὐτῷ. ⁵⁷ Καθὼς ἀπέστειλέν με ὁ ζῶν πατὴρ, κἀγὼ ζῶ διὰ τὸν πατέρα, καὶ ὁ τρώγων με, κἀκεῖνος ζήσει δι' ἐμέ. ⁵⁸ Οὗτός ἐστιν ὁ ἄρτος ὁ ἐξ οὐρανοῦ καταβὰς· οὐ καθὼς ἔφαγον οἱ πατέρες, καὶ ἀπέθανον· ὁ τρώγων τοῦτον τὸν ἄρτον, ζήσει εἰς τὸν αἰῶνα.

VULGATE.

JOHN VI. 56-59.

⁵⁶ Caro enim mea vere est cibus ; et sanguis meus vere est potus. ⁵⁷ Qui manducat meam carnem, et bibit meum sanguinem, in me manet, et ego in illo. ⁵⁸ Sicut misit me vivens Pater, et ego vivo propter Patrem, et qui manducat me, et ipse vivet propter me. ⁵⁹ Hic est panis qui de cœlo descendit. Non sicut manducaverunt patres vestri manna, et mortui sunt : qui manducat hunc panem, vivet in æternum.

II.—ENGLISH TRANSLATION.

JOHN VI. 56-59.

⁵⁶ "For my flesh is meat indeed, and my blood is drink indeed. ⁵⁷ He that eateth my flesh and drinketh my blood, abideth in me, and I in him. ⁵⁸ As the living Father hath sent me and I live by the Father, so he that eateth me, the same also shall live by me. ⁵⁹ This is the bread that came down from heaven. Not as your fathers did eat manna, and are dead : he that eateth this bread, shall live for ever."

III.—NOTES.

Introductory. This brief extract is taken from a discourse delivered by our Lord in the synagogue at Capharnaum (Introduction, p. liii.) just before the third Pasch of his public life (John vi. 4). As Knabenbauer remarks, Christ had prepared the way for this

discourse by two miracles.   By the multiplication of the loaves
(Matth. xiv. 13-21 ; Mark vi. 30-44 ; Luke ix. 10-17 ; John vi.
1-15), and by his walking on the waters of Lake Genesareth
(Matth. xiv. 22-34 ; Mark vi. 45-51 ; John vi. 15-21), he had so
manifested his power that his hearers on this occasion might
reasonably give credence to his promises however incomprehensible the mode of fulfilment.   Nor is this all.   The miracles
just referred to, which were worked, one during the evening,
and one during the night before, were singularly suited as an
introduction to this address regarding the Blessed Eucharist.
By the multiplication of the loaves he proved to the people
and to his disciples his boundless power of supplying their corporal wants, and he left them to conclude that it was equally
possible for him to supply them with the spiritual food of which
he was about to speak : by walking on the water he demonstrated
to his disciples, and through them to the people, that his body
was not necessarily subject to the laws of material nature, and
that these laws of nature would be no impediment to the presence of his body in the sacrament of the Eucharist.   Having
thus prepared his audience, he told them to seek not a perishable nourishment, but the nourishment which would endure
to life everlasting ; that he himself would give them the Bread
of Life ; and that the bread which he would give was his flesh
for the life of the world.   The announcement was received with
the incredulous remark : " How can this man give us his flesh
to eat ? "   Jesus who had already proved his omnipotence, could
with every right require the submission of their understanding.
Without entering, therefore, into the explanation they asked,
he declared that this reception of his body and blood not only
was possible, but also was a condition necessary to their salvation
and at the same time an act which would secure their salvation.
" Amen amen I say to you : Except you eat the flesh of the
Son of Man and drink his blood, you shall not have life in you.
He that eateth my flesh and drinketh my blood, hath everlasting
life ; and I will raise him up at the Last Day " (John vi. 54, 55).

Our Divine Lord now proceeds to prove this in the following
words of our passage :—

V. 56. **For my flesh is meat indeed, and my blood is drink indeed.**

In the opening portion of his address to the people, Christ
had compared the food which he was to give them with that
which he had given them on the preceding day, and with the
manna which their fathers had received through Moses in the
desert.   Both of these latter kinds of food were earthly ; and
neither could secure perpetually the end for which food is taken.
Different from these, he said, is to be " the true bread from

heaven ; for the bread of God is that which cometh down from heaven and giveth life to the world " (verses 32, 33). He now shows that this " bread of God," which is his flesh and blood, must confer everlasting life on the soul and secure a glorious and immortal resurrection for the body of the recipient. The reason assigned is that his body and blood are " true meat and true drink." He calls his body " true meat " and his blood " true drink " (*a*) because they are to be received not figuratively, symbolically, or virtually, but truly, really, and substantially in the Holy Eucharist ; (*b*) because on being received thus truly, really, and substantially, they confer immortality on the soul and communicate that immortality to the body ; and (*c*) because without the worthy reception of the Holy Eucharist, which is the fountain of grace, the other means of salvation lose their efficacy. With reason did Tertullian say of the worthy communicant : " Truly he is nourished with the Divinity."

Having stated that his body and blood are the true meat and the true drink by which man may secure perseverance in the life of grace here and the possession of the life of glory hereafter, Christ in the next two verses justifies this assertion. In the first he says :—

V. 57. He that eateth my flesh and drinketh my blood, abideth in me, and I in him.

It is to be observed that communion under both kinds is not here prescribed for all. The precept to communicate under both kinds was always regarded by the Church as one obligatory on the priest when actually offering the Holy Sacrifice, but not obligatory on the rest of the faithful. To these it was formerly permitted to communicate either under one kind or under both kinds ; but at the beginning of the fifteenth century, in order to remove abuses, to repress the disturbances of the Hussites, and to correct the false teaching of these heretics, the Council of Constance prescribed that the faithful should communicate under the form of bread only. This decree was confirmed in the 22nd session of the Council of Trent, although it was there expressly stated that it was left to the discretion of the Pope to grant the use of the chalice when in any extraordinary circumstances the good of the Church might demand this concession. Again, it is to be noticed that what is here mentioned as an effect of the reception of Christ's body and blood, is mentioned in St. John's first epistle as the effect of charity, of faith, and of the observance of the commandments. (See 1 John iii. 22-24 ; iv. 16.) It follows, therefore, that the reception of the Holy Eucharist which will secure our union with Christ and the consequent blessing of eternal life, is that which is accompanied by faith, charity, and a spirit of obedience to God's law. Lastly, from the same St. John we learn the nature of the union with Christ which takes place in the Holy Eucharist. It is not merely such a union as exists between friends, who think often of each other, wish well to each other, and take pleasure in mutual intercourse. It is far more. Describing this union and, as it were, commenting on the words of his Divine Master, St John says (1 John iv. 13) : " In this we know that we abide in him, and he in us : because he hath given us of his Spirit." When, therefore, in the gospel of the same evangelist it is said that the recipient of the Holy Eucharist abideth in Christ and Christ in him, this mutual in-dwelling can be no other than a true union of our human nature with the Divinity through the Spirit of Christ—a union by which we become in a mysterious manner participators of the divine nature. Developing this idea St. Cyril of Jerusalem thus addressed the catechumens under his charge : " Wherefore with full assurance let us partake as of the body and blood of Christ : for in the figure of bread is given to thee his body, and in the figure of wine his blood, that thou by partaking of the body and blood of Christ, mayest be made of the same body and the same blood with him " ($\H{\iota}\nu\alpha\ \gamma\acute{\epsilon}\nu\eta\ \mu\epsilon\tau\alpha$- $\lambda\alpha\beta\grave{\omega}\nu\ \sigma\acute{\omega}\mu\alpha\tau\text{os}\ \kappa\alpha\grave{\iota}\ \alpha\H{\iota}\mu\alpha\tau\text{os}\ X\rho\iota\sigma\tau\text{o}\hat{\text{u}},\ \sigma\acute{\iota}\sigma\sigma\omega\mu\text{os},\ \kappa\alpha\grave{\iota}\ \sigma\acute{\upsilon}\nu\alpha\iota\mu\text{os}\ \alpha\grave{\upsilon}\tau\text{o}\hat{\upsilon}$). St. Cyril of Alexandria gives a striking illustration of what takes place in this union when he says : " As two pieces of melted wax on being brought together are necessarily commingled the one with the other, in the same manner the recipient of the body and blood of the Lord is so united to him that he has Christ dwelling within him, and he dwells in Christ." The communicant being thus intimately united with Christ's body, shares in the privileges of that body ; and as one of these privileges is immortality, he receives a right to immortality.

Such was the first argument by which Christ proved that the reception of his body would confer eternal life. The second was contained in the following words :—

V. 58. As the living Father hath sent me and I live by the Father, so he that eateth me, the same also shall live by me.

Knabenbauer remarks that the words $\delta\iota\grave{\alpha}\ \tau\grave{o}\nu\ \pi\alpha\tau\acute{\epsilon}\rho\alpha$ (Vulgate : *propter patrem,* and English : *by the father*) do not indicate a *final* cause or signify " for the glory of the Father." They indicate an *efficient* cause and point out the source from which Christ receives his life. Such is the force of the preposition $\delta\iota\grave{\alpha}$ followed by the accusative case. But it is asked : To what do the words, " I live by the Father," refer ? Is it in regard to the divine nature and life of Christ, or is it in reference to his human nature and life that we are to understand this expression ? Interpreters do not agree in their answers to this question. Some think that Christ speaks of his divine life and nature only ;

Mens" Blessed Sac. Confrat.

The Four Churches
Jubilee Pilgrimage.

Sun. Oct. 14th 1951.

Assemble 4·55   Leave 5p.m.

others that he refers to his human life and nature only ; and not a few say we are to understand that Christ was here speaking of himself both as God and Man. Although there are reasons for each opinion, it is most probable that the clause regards only the human nature of Christ, which being united to the Word in the unity of one person, has a divine life derived from its union with the Divinity in addition to its corporal life derived from its human soul. This seems to be the only interpretation that fits in with the scope of our Lord's discourse. There is, then, a parallel drawn between the life of Christ as man and the spiritual life of him who is united to Christ by the reception of Christ's body and blood. It is as if Christ said : "The Father who has in himself a life and being not communicated to him by any other, has begotten me and communicated his life to me. As, then, I live by the life communicated to me by the Father, so he that eateth me shall live because I live, shall live by me, shall live by the life communicated to him by me." The Jews were unable to understand how the reception of Christ's body and blood and this union with him who was Man, could bring with it the possession of eternal life. He here gives a solution of their difficulty. He admits and asserts that he is made Man, but at the same time he tells his hearers that this is the very reason why he can give eternal life to those who become one with him by eating his flesh and drinking his blood. He says, as it were, that his body and blood have indeed a human life derived from his human soul with which these are united in the unity of one nature, but that they at the same time have a divine life derived from the Word with which they are united in the unity of one person, and that the very purpose of his Incarnation and mission from the Father was that his sacred humanity might be the medium of communicating to those who received him, that divine life which he himself had received from the Father.

Thus did Christ give a second proof of what he had previously asserted, namely, that his flesh is meat indeed, and his blood drink indeed ; that he who eats this flesh and drinks this blood, will have, or rather already has, eternal life ; and that the possession of eternal life is the effect of the union which takes place in the reception of the Holy Eucharist. The discourse concludes with the following words :—

V. 59. This is the bread that came down from heaven. Not as your fathers did eat manna, and are dead : he that eateth this bread, shall live for ever.

Having shown how he is the living and life-giving food of man, and being about to dismiss his audience, our Lord for the third time points out the difference between the heavenly nourishment he is to give, and the manna obtained through Moses. The mention of the manna had given occasion to the discourse, and Christ now returns to the point from which he had set out. The Jews, denying or extenuating the greatness of the miracle worked on the previous day, had been asking for a fresh sign or miracle which might be equal to that of Moses, and which might enable them to believe in this new Legislator as their fathers believed in the first Legislator of their nation. In answer, Christ here declares that the gift which he is prepared to bestow is greater than that of Moses ; that the bread which he will give is truly from heaven ; and that this bread as far surpasses the manna in excellence as the spiritual life surpasses the corporal, and life eternal the brief span of our existence here below. The manna was eaten to preserve the life of the body, but it was powerless to ward off death for ever : the bread which he will give is to be the nourishment of the soul, and is capable of communicating to soul and body an existence as unending as that which Christ himself had received from the Father.

A difficulty here presents itself. It has been asked : " How can it be truly said that all have died who ate of the manna, whilst all are to live who eat of this food promised by Christ ? If there is question of the life of the body, must it not be admitted that death is the lot of such as receive the Holy Eucharist as well as of those who ate of the manna ; and if there is question of the life of the soul, may it not be urged that not all reach eternal life who eat of the body of Christ, whilst it is impossible to admit that all were lost who ate of the manna ? To solve this difficulty and to understand the meaning of the words, it is necessary to keep before us the object which Christ had in view. The purpose of our Divine Lord was to prove the difference of nature and of efficacy in the two kinds of food mentioned ; for this purpose he showed that, whilst the manna taken to preserve the life of the body could not secure that end for ever, the bread which he would give for the life of the soul, if received with proper dispositions, would be an efficacious means, and at the same time a necessary means, of warding off eternal death.

Having recorded this discourse which contains the promise of God's greatest gift to men, the evangelist mentions the place where the discourse was delivered, and the effect produced on the hearers. Christ spoke in the synagogue of Capharnaum, and the effect produced by his words is one of the saddest circumstances mentioned in the gospels. St. John says that on hearing Christ's bountiful promises, many replied : " This saying is hard, and who can hear it ? " Jesus answered : " It is the spirit that quickeneth : the flesh profiteth nothing. The words that I have spoken to you, are spirit and life ; but there are some of you that believe not." "After this," says the evangelist, "many of his disciples went back, and walked no more with him." All were not so ungrateful; for "then Jesus said to the twelve: Will you also go away? And Simon Peter answered him: Lord, to whom shall we go? Thou hast the words of eternal life; and we have believed; and have known that thou art the Christ, the Son of God" (John vi. 60-70).

IV.—MORAL REFLECTIONS.

On the Feast of Corpus Christi, the children of the Church throughout the world are gathered round the altar to profess their faith in their hidden Lord, to be filled with the hope which the mystery of the Holy Eucharist inspires, and to enkindle their charity at this furnace of divine love. That we may share in this feeling it is enough to reflect on what we here receive.

1. What did Christ here bestow on man? The Council of Trent answers our question when, summing up the teaching of faith, it declares that in the Holy Eucharist our Lord poured out for us all the treasures of divine love. Christ gave to his apostles, and by their ministry to us, the same sacred body which he received from Mary, the same precious blood with which he redeemed the world, the same blessed soul which he commended to his Father on the cross—in a word the same adorable humanity which he assumed at his Incarnation, and which is now enthroned in glory at the right hand of God. Nor is this all. Being God as well as Man, and being infinite in generosity as he is infinite in love, he gave us in this sacrament his divinity itself, which from the time of the Incarnation never was, and never shall be separated from his body or from his soul. Such a gift deserves a return. Since, then, in his liberality he has given us all that he is, let us show our gratitude by giving him all that we have. Let us consecrate to him our body that it may be his living temple and the unsullied dwelling-place of his Holy Spirit, our blood to be poured out in his service if such a sacrifice be demanded, our soul with all its faculties, our memory to recall unceasingly his benefits and his precepts, our understanding to meditate continually on his law, our will to be entirely conformable to his, our heart to love only him and creatures in him. In this entire offering of ourselves, we fall very far short of what we receive. Is it not, then, another proof of his infinite goodness and condescension to be contented with so little from us to whom he has given so much?

2. And what is the effect of this heavenly gift upon our souls? Christ describes this effect when he says in the present passage: "As the living Father hath sent me and I live by the Father, so

he that eateth me, the same also shall live by me " (John vi. 58). The meaning is that as the Father by reason of the identity of the divine nature communicates eternally his divine life to the Son, and as the Son on becoming Man, by reason of his personal union with the sacred humanity communicates to that sacred humanity the divine life he has from the Father, so does that sacred humanity infuse its heavenly life into the souls of those who are sacramentally united to it in the Holy Communion. Such being the intended effect of the Holy Eucharist, should we not here seek for a daily increasing store of sanctifying grace—a gift which raises us above ourselves, adorns us with a heavenly beauty, renders us like to God, and makes us worthy objects of God's love, the adopted children of God, the heirs of God, and co-heirs with Jesus Christ ? Should we not in the frequent reception of this sacrament, gradually but surely light up within us the fire of divine charity—a fire in which our corrupt inclinations and our imperfections are consumed, our venial offences are effaced, and our weakness is rendered proof against temptation to mortal sin ?

3. If this were all, it would be much ; but the divine bounty is not yet exhausted. Our Redeemer was sent to restore to us, partly here, and wholly hereafter, the blessings of body and of soul which we had forfeited by our first parents' fall. One of the blessings thus forfeited was immortality, for " by one man sin entered into this world, and by sin death ; and so death passed upon all men, in whom all have sinned " (Rom. v. 12). For this poison which infects the whole human race, Christ promised an antidote when he said : " He that eateth my flesh and drinketh my blood hath everlasting life, and I will raise him up at the last day " (John vi. 55). As, then, Christ's sacred body, by reason of its personal union with the divinity, had a right to a glorious resurrection from the tomb, so by reason of our sacramental union with Christ as members with our head, we receive in the Holy Eucharist a right and a pledge of a glorious triumph over death. With this promise sounding in our ears, must we not exclaim as did the Apostle, " Death is swallowed up in victory. O Death, where is thy victory ? O Death, where is thy sting ? " (1 Cor. xv. 54, 55). Hence it is that, in presence of the nameless and forgotten grave of the mendicant whose body during life was so often consecrated by contact with the flesh of the Incarnate Word, if we be men of faith, we may hear the angel that is deputed to guard the spot say to us as was said to Moses from the burning bush : " Come not nigh hither. Put off the shoes from thy feet ; for the place whereon thou standest is holy ground " (Exod. iii. 5). This thought should moderate our grief at the loss of friends who are one day to be united with us in the heavenly home ; it should

support us in trials and reverses of fortune which are to be succeeded by the possession of God ; it should inspire us with resignation and fortitude in sickness and at the approach of death which are the prelude to eternal life. " Christ," says the Apostle, " is risen from the dead, the first-fruits of them that sleep. For by a man came death, and by a man the resurrection of the dead ; and as in Adam all die, so in Christ shall all be made alive " (1 Cor. xv. 20-22).

4. Such being the character of Christ's gift to us in the Holy Eucharist, and such being the marvellous effects it is intended to produce, we must confess in St. Peter's words that our Redeemer has here " given us most great and precious promises, that by these you may be made partakers of the divine nature, flying the corruption of that concupiscence which is in the world " (2 Peter i. 4). Here the young may find strength against the violence of their passions ; the aged their consolation in the face of death ; the sinner a reconciliation with his Saviour ; the just man the means of perseverance ; and all of us an estimate of the glory that is shed around us when the King of Heaven becomes our guest. " What," says the Psalmist, " shall I render to the Lord for all the things that he hath rendered to me ? " Each of us will surely answer with that inspired writer : " I will take the chalice of salvation ; and I will call upon the name of the Lord. I will pay my vows to the Lord, before all his people " (Ps. cxv. 12-14). In this spirit of faith, and hope, and love, preparing ourselves for the bread of angels, frequently receiving this Sacred Body, nourished often by this Precious Blood, we resolve that our mind shall ever dwell in the grateful contemplation of the bounty of Jesus Christ, that our eyes shall not cease their longing until they behold the unveiled beauty of his countenance, and that our heart shall not seek for rest or resting-place until it repose in him.

SECOND SUNDAY AFTER PENTECOST.

I.—TEXTS.

GREEK.

LUKE XIV. 16-24.

¹⁶ Ὁ δὲ εἶπεν αὐτῷ· ἄνθρωπός τις ἐποίει δεῖπνον μέγα, καὶ ἐκάλεσεν πολλούς· ¹⁷ Καὶ ἀπέστειλεν τὸν δοῦλον αὐτοῦ τῇ ὥρᾳ τοῦ δείπνου εἰπεῖν τοῖς κεκλημένοις· ἔρχεσθε, ὅτι ἤδη ἕτοιμά ἐστιν. ¹⁸ Καὶ ἤρξαντο ἀπὸ μιᾶς πάντες παραιτεῖσθαι· ὁ πρῶτος εἶπεν αὐτῷ· Ἀγρὸν ἠγόρασα, καὶ ἔχω ἀνάγκην ἐξελθὼν ἰδεῖν αὐτόν· ἐρωτῶ σε, ἔχε με παρῃτημένον. ¹⁹ Καὶ ἕτερος εἶπεν· Ζεύγη βοῶν ἠγόρασα πέντε, καὶ πορεύομαι δοκιμάσαι αὐτά· ἐρωτῶ σε, ἔχε με παρῃτημένον. ²⁰ Καὶ ἕτερος εἶπεν· Γυναῖκα ἔγημα, καὶ διὰ τοῦτο οὐ δύναμαι ἐλθεῖν. ²¹ Καὶ παραγενόμενος ὁ δοῦλος ἀπήγγειλεν τῷ κυρίῳ αὐτοῦ ταῦτα· τότε ὀργισθεὶς ὁ οἰκοδεσπότης εἶπε τῷ δούλῳ αὐτοῦ· Ἔξελθε ταχέως εἰς τὰς πλατείας καὶ ῥύμας τῆς πόλεως, καὶ τοὺς πτωχοὺς καὶ ἀναπήρους καὶ τυφλοὺς καὶ χωλοὺς εἰσάγαγε ὧδε. ²² Καὶ εἶπεν ὁ δοῦλος· κύριε, γέγονεν ὃ ἐπέταξας, καὶ ἔτι τόπος ἐστίν. ²³ Καὶ εἶπεν ὁ κύριος πρὸς τὸν δοῦλον· Ἔξελθε εἰς τὰς ὁδοὺς καὶ φραγμούς, καὶ ἀνάγκασον εἰσελθεῖν, ἵνα γεμισθῇ μου ὁ οἶκος· ²⁴ Λέγω γὰρ ὑμῖν ὅτι οὐδεὶς τῶν ἀνδρῶν ἐκείνων τῶν κεκλημένων γεύσεταί μου τοῦ δείπνου.

VULGATE.

LUKE XIV. 16-24.

16 At ipse dixit ei : Homo quidam fecit coenam magnam, et vocavit multos. 17 Et misit servum suum hora coenæ dicere invitatis ut venirent, quia jam parata sunt omnia. 18 Et cœperunt simul omnes excusare. Primus dixit ei : Villam emi, et necesse habeo exire, et videre illam ; rogo te, habe me excusatum. 19 Et alter dixit : Juga boum emi quinque, et eo probare illa ; rogo te, habe me excusatum. 20 Et alius dixit : Uxorem duxi, et ideo non possum venire. 21 Et reversus servus nuntiavit hæc domino suo. Tunc iratus pater familias dixit servo suo : Exi cito in plateas et vicos civitatis ; et pauperes, ac debiles et cæcos, et claudos introduc huc. 22 Et ait servus : Domine, factum est ut imperasti et adhuc locus est. 23 Et ait dominus servo : Exi in vias et sepes, et compelle intrare, u impleatur domus mea. 24 Dico autem vobis quod nemo virorum illorum qui vocati sunt gustabit coenam meam.

II.—ENGLISH TRANSLATION.

LUKE XIV. 16-24.

[16] But he said to him : " A certain man made a great supper, and invited many. [17] And he sent his servant at the hour of supper to say to them that were invited, that they should come, for now all things are ready. [18] And they began all at once to make excuse. The first said to him : ' I have bought a farm, and I must needs go out and see it ; I pray thee, hold me excused.' [19] And another said : ' I have bought five yoke of oxen, and I go to try them ; I pray thee, hold me excused.' [20] And another said : ' I have married a wife, and therefore I cannot come.' [21] And the servant returning told these things to his lord. Then the master of the house being angry, said to his servant : ' Go out quickly into the streets and lanes of the city, and bring in hither the poor, and the feeble, and the blind, and the lame.' [22] And the servant said : ' Lord, it is done as thou hast commanded, and yet there is room.' [23] And the lord said to the servant : ' Go out into the highways and hedges, and compel them to come in, that my house may be filled. [24] But I say unto you, that none of those men that were invited shall taste of my supper.' "

III.—NOTES.

Introductory. We learn from St. John that Christ attended the Feast of the Dedication of the temple (Introduction, p. clxx.) towards the end of the December before his death, and that to avoid the murderous designs of the Jews, he then retired to Peræa, (Introduction, p. xxxvii.), a district on the east of Judæa and Samaria, beyond the Jordan, and within the dominions of Herod Antipas. Here, notwithstanding the ill-will of Herod, he remained with his disciples for some months until recalled to Judæa, on the death of Lazarus. St. Luke alone narrates the events of this interval, and amongst these events, the feast at the pharisee's house, where Jesus spoke the parable recorded in the present gospel passage. The following were the circumstances that called for the instruction. On entering the house, our Divine Lord had healed a dropsical man, and had corrected the false notions of all present regarding the sabbath observance ; afterwards, on sitting down to eat, he reproved the pride of the guests who sought the first places at the entertainment ; and then he gently indicated to his host the manner in which an eternal reward might be secured for the hospitality dispensed. Sharing probably in the persuasion that these eternal rewards belonged by right to the chosen people and especially to the pharisees, one of the guests remarked : " Blessed is he that shall eat bread in the kingdom of God." In order to remove a false sense of security, and to show that the kingdom of God is the inheritance not of the Jews only who were first called to the faith, but of all those who will obey that call whether they be Jews or Gentiles, Christ replied in the following parable :—

V. 16. **A certain man made a great supper, and invited many.**

The supper ($\delta\hat{\epsilon}\iota\pi\nu o\nu$=*coena*), the last meal taken at the conclusion of the day's work, is a figure neither of the Blessed Eucharist nor of the other blessings which are dispensed in the Church Militant, and which are described in a different parable recorded by St. Matthew (xxii. 1-14). The supper here spoken of represents the eternal joys of the Church Triumphant which are the lot of the blessed when the labour of life is over. The " certain man," or as he is called in verse 21, the " master of the house " represents the Great Creator who has provided in his heavenly dwelling-place a great feast for his friends. To this feast St. Paul referred in part when, quoting from Isaias, he said: " Eye hath not seen, nor ear heard, neither hath it entered into the heart of man, what things God hath prepared for them that love him " (1 Cor. ii. 9). To the supper many were invited. God would have no one excluded from this feast· for we read that he " will have all men to be saved, and to come to the knowledge of the truth " (1 Tim. ii. 4). Thus by the light of reason even the Gentiles were called to his knowledge and love ; " because that which is known of God is manifest in them ; since God hath manifested it unto them. For the invisible things of him, from the creation of the world are clearly seen, being understood by the things that are made, his eternal power also and divinity " (Rom. i. 19, 20). Nay more, this natural knowledge, in itself a grace, would have been supplemented by a higher and supernatural knowledge if it had been used aright ; and it was so supplemented in the case of those Gentiles who, like Job, did use it aright. Still, inasmuch as the Jews, and especially the leaders and teachers of that chosen people, were not left dependent on the light of reason, but had also the light of revelation, they might be said to have been specially invited to the heavenly feast through faith in Christ who was so clearly foretold in the prophetical books entrusted to their keeping. " What advantage then hath the Jew," says St. Paul, " or what is the profit of circumcision ? Much every way. First indeed, because the words of God were committed to them " (Rom. iii. 1, 2). It is of these, therefore, that our Lord speaks when he says that " many were invited " ; and it is to these that he again refers in the following words :—

V. 17. **And he sent his servant at the hour of supper to**

say to them that were invited, that they should come, for now all things are ready.

After t fall of Adam heaven was closed against the human race ; and though the Redeemer was immediately promised, and though men by faith in him and in his anticipated merits, could and did become saints, still the beatific vision and the joys prefigured by the " great supper " were not to be theirs until Christ, the First-born of the elect, had entered into that kingdom purchased by his blood.   It is customary in the East (*Cf.* Esther v. 8 ; vi. 14 ; and the classics) to send notice to the previously invited guests when the appointed hour for the feast approaches. (Introduction, p. lxxxviii.)   We learn from the parable that the master of the house did this on the occasion of which the gospel now speaks.   " He sent his servant at the hour of supper to say to them that were invited, that they should come, for now all things are ready."   The " servant " here mentioned is none other than our Lord, who in his human nature and in his office of preacher, is designated by this name in the prophecy of Isaias (xlii. 1 ; lii. 13).   Associated with our Lord were to be his apostles and their successors who as his ambassadors (2 Cor. v. 20) would by their labours " fill up those things that are wanting of the sufferings of Christ . . . for his body, which is the Church " (Coloss. i. 24).   In obedience to his Father's will, Christ came to the pharisees, to the doctors of the law, to the leaders of the Jewish people, all typified by those who received the first set of invitations.   To these their Redeemer made known " that they should come, for now all things are ready " if they will but prepare themselves by faith and good works for the joys of heaven.   The response to this invitation is given in the following verse :—

V. 18. And they began all at once to make excuse. The first said to him : I have bought a farm, and I must needs go out and see it ; I pray thee hold me excused.

As in many other passages of the Sacred Scriptures and of the classics, the clause ἀπὸ μιᾶς is elliptical, and requires that we supply the word γνώμης, or ψυχῆς, or βουλῆς.   Thus the sense is not that they excused themselves " all at once," but that they gave excuses " with one accord," in the same spirit, and actuated by equally unworthy principles.   These men are grouped in classes, and a representative of each class is introduced.   The first person referred to is one who, intent on surpassing others in power and dignity, has lately increased his possessions.   He says that he *must* go and see these—a manifest untruth—for the farm was already inspected and bought.   On this pretence he prays to be excused from attending the feast.

His earnestness is shown in the form of his petition, for the Greek word employed is ἐρωτῶ=*I beg off, deprecor.*

What was the answer of the second intended guest ? It was still more uncourteous than that of the first, and our Lord gives it in the following words :—

V. 19. And another said : I have bought five yoke of oxen, and I go to try them ; I pray thee, hold me excused.

The business alleged in this case is less urgent than that mentioned by the first. There is no ἀνάγκη or necessity expressed here, but the fixed resolution not to change a plan. This man says : " I have bought five yoke of oxen, and I go to try them." It is still stronger in the Greek text which has : πορεύομαι δοκιμάσαι αὐτά = " I am now on my way to try them."

The third intended guest was still more rude in his reply, which is thus recorded :—

V. 20. And another said : I have married a wife, and therefore I cannot come.

St. Augustine and St. Prosper among the Fathers, and many modern commentators considered that in these instances, our Lord indicated the three great obstacles to eternal salvation which were afterwards thus described by St. John : " If any man love the world, the charity of the Father is not in him. For all that is in the world, is the concupiscence of the flesh, and the concupiscence of the eyes, and the pride of life "(1 John ii. 15, 16). We are not to imagine, indeed, that the possession of worldly honours on the part of the first, or the ownership of riches and the care of his goods on the part of the second, or the married state of the third could be bad in itself. What Christians are taught is this : that high worldly position, and the pursuit of gain, and the cares inseparable from married life are dangerous ; and that it is possible for one to become so occupied with these positions, pursuits, and cares, as to be deaf to the calls of God and indifferent to the duties essential for salvation. What were here alleged by the invited guests as impediments to the acceptance of the invitation, are very often the occasions of the three chief sins which sullied the lives of the pharisees, of the doctors of the law, and of the leaders of the Jews, and deprived them of the grace of conversion. These leaders of the people said truly of themselves : " Hath any one of the rulers or of the pharisees believed in him ? But this multitude that know not the law, are accursed " (John vii. 48, 49). For this cause the Messiah by the mouth of the prophet complains of the fruitlessness of his mission (see Isaias xlix. 4) ; and the knowledge of these impediments to its conversion caused Jesus to weep over Jerusalem.

Individuals may forfeit grace, but the designs of God for the salvation of man must be carried out. It was so in the circumstances here typified,

Vv. 21, 22. **And the servant returning, told these things to his lord. Then the master of the house being angry, said to his servant: Go out quickly into the streets and lanes of the city, and bring in hither the poor, and the feeble, and the blind, and the lame. And the servant said: Lord, it is done as thou hast commanded, and yet there is room.**

These would have been invited afterwards, even if the first had come ; but they were now brought in without previous notice in order to fill up the vacant places. In such a proceeding there is nothing foreign to the customs of the East. There it is usual for a chief to call on all passers-by to partake of his hospitality, and all classes are seen to sit down at the same entertainment. The persons typified by this second set of guests were the common people amongst the Jews—" the lost sheep of the house of Israel." These were called " the poor," because being bereft of true and zealous pastors (Mark vi. 34), they were without the gift of faith or of charity; they were called " the feeble," because they were destitute of spiritual strength to reject what is evil and to perform what is good ; they were called " the blind," because they had not yet received the full light of supernatural revelation ; and they were called " the lame," because of their halting gait in the way of the divine precepts.

Those hitherto called to the heavenly banquet were Jews. Now, although very many amongst the common people of that nation responded to the invitation of grace, especially after the Ascension, there still was room ;

V. 23. **And the lord said to the servant: Go out into the highways and hedges, and compel them to come in, that my house may be filled.**

" The highways and hedges " as contrasted with " the streets and lanes of the city," represent the nations of the Gentiles as contrasted with the commonwealth of the Jews ; and the condition of these Gentiles prior to their vocation to the faith is described by St. Paul as that of " aliens from the conversation of Israel, and strangers to the covenants, having no hope of the promise, and without God in this world " (Eph. ii. 12). Christ did not preach to them at all, nor did the apostles do so at first. Speaking of the work which he personally undertook and carried out, Christ said to the Syro-phœnician woman : " I was not sent except to the sheep that are lost of the house of Israel " (Matth. xv. 24) ; and of the first mission of the apostles it is recorded : " These twelve Jesus sent, commanding them, saying :

Go ye not into the way of the Gentiles, and into the cities of the Samaritans enter ye not; but go ye rather to the lost sheep of the house of Israel" (Matth. x. 5, 6). This dispensation was to be only for a time. Christ said indeed: "Suffer first the children to be filled; for it is not good to take the bread of the children and to cast it to the dogs" (Mark vii. 27). Still he was to give "himself a redemption for all" (1 Tim. ii. 6); and in due time the kingdom of God, rejected by the greater part of the Jews, was to have for its subjects the people of the Gentile race (Acts xiii. 47). This mercy, already foretold by the prophets (Isaias xlii. 6; xlix. 6, etc.), was predicted by Christ in the verse before us; the fulfilment of these predictions was provided for in the commission given by Christ to the apostles when on the day of his Ascension he said: "You shall receive the power of the Holy Ghost coming upon you; and you shall be witnesses unto me in Jerusalem, and in all Judæa and Samaria, and even to the uttermost part of the earth" (Acts i. 8); and this fulfilment actually took place when "they (the apostles) going forth, preached everywhere; the Lord working with them, and confirming the word with the signs that followed" (Mark xvi. 20). In this extract from St. Mark, we learn the nature of the means of conversion referred to in the words, "compel them to come in." These means were the assiduous preaching of the gospel truths rendered evidently credible by miracles, and the powerful internal workings of divine grace. They were not physical force which would deprive men of liberty, but the moral force of persuasion which was so strong that it infallibly though sweetly secured its purpose in the free assent of faith. "The weapons of our warfare," says St. Paul, "are not carnal, but mighty to God unto the pulling down of fortifications, destroying counsels and every height that exalteth itself against the knowledge of God, and bringing into captivity every understanding unto the obedience of Christ" (2 Cor. x. 4, 5).

The return of the servant is not recorded, for Christ, by his deputies the pastors and apostolic labourers of the Church, is still executing the commission of his Father in the conversion of the Gentile world. The parable terminates with the sentence:

V. 24. **But I say unto you, that none of these men that were invited, shall taste of my supper.**

The use of the expression "my supper" would seem at first sight to indicate that the sentence is to be taken as spoken by the master of the feast to the servant; but if this were so we should probably have had $\lambda\acute{\epsilon}\gamma\omega\ \gamma\grave{\alpha}\rho\ \sigma o\iota$ = "For I say to thee," and not $\lambda\acute{\epsilon}\gamma\omega\ \gamma\grave{\alpha}\rho\ \acute{\upsilon}\mu\hat{\iota}\nu$ = "For I say to you"—our Lord's usual form of address to his audience. We are, then, to understand that in this sentence, Christ, half continuing the parable and half explaining it, substitutes himself for the master of the feast, and indicates to those around him the unhappy lot of all who neglect the heavenly invitation of which he is the bearer to mankind. (See Knabenbauer, and McCarthy, and Alford, *in loco*). God " will have all men to be saved, and to come to the knowledge of the truth " (I Tim. ii. 4), and to all he gives at least sufficient grace for salvation. If therefore many are, and many will be lost, the fault is theirs, not his. " Destruction is thy own, O Israel : thy help is only in me " (Osee xiii. 9).

IV.—MORAL REFLECTIONS.

1. Man was created not for earth but for heaven, which was typified by the " great supper," and the Apostle says (Rom. vi. 22) : " Being now made free from sin, and having become servants to God, you have your fruit unto sanctification, and the end life everlasting." Our Creator who knows the value of eternal life, " will have all men to be saved, and to come to the knowledge of the truth " (I Tim. ii. 4) ; and to secure this end he gives to all those helps without which we should be powerless even to conceive a good thought. From our earliest years until our last hour he calls us to him by the voice of his ministers, by the good example of those around us, and by the interior whisperings of his grace ; but, like the invited guests of the parable, most men are drawn away by the pursuit of worldly gain, of empty honours, or of dangerous pleasures, and turn a deaf ear to the heavenly invitation. Of such as these was written the divine complaint : " I have spread forth my hands all the day to an unbelieving people, who walk in a way that is not good, after their own thoughts " (Isaias lxv. 2).

2. How miserable is the state of those who thus undervalue the things of God ! Notwithstanding that many have thus no care for their spiritual interests, and act as though the present life and its happiness were alone worthy of their consideration, it requires but little reflection to convince us that eternal salvation is our most important, or rather our only affair here below. If we succeed in this affair alone, and fail in all things else, we shall be completely and eternally happy : if in this matter alone we fail, though we prosper in all other undertakings, we shall be inconceivably and eternally miserable. Can the Son of God have exaggerated when he said (Matth. xvi. 26) : " What doth it profit a man, if he gain the whole world, and suffer the loss of his own soul ? Or what exchange shall a man give for his soul ? " We shall not gain the whole world ; and even if that were possible, it were better to sacrifice things which end with time, than to lose a happiness which never ends. If men did

not believe in a future life or in the present necessity of securing
a right to its joys by a meritorious use of grace, their conduct
would not be so unreasonable ; but they do believe in this,
and still they are so bewitched as to give up salvation for what is
worse than nothing. " O that they would be wise," says the
Sacred Scripture, " and would understand, and would provide
for their last end " (Deut. xxxii. 29). With truth does the
Psalmist thus compare to a dream the life of a worldling : " They
have slept their sleep ; and all the men of riches have found
nothing in their hands " (Ps. lxxv. 5). Well, too, does the Book
of Wisdom thus describe the last rude awakening of the wicked
at the sight of the just who have sacrificed all for the love of God
and to secure salvation : " These are they whom we had
sometime in derision and for a parable of reproach. We fools
esteemed their life madness, and their end without honour. Behold how they are numbered among the children of God, and
their lot is among the saints " (Wisdom v. 3-5). He was truly
wise of whom St. Liguori thus speaks (Sermons : Septuagesima
Sunday) : " St. Philip Neri said one day to a young man who
expected to gain a position in the world : ' Be of good heart,
my son. You may make a great fortune ; you may become an
eminent lawyer ; you may then be made a prelate ; then perhaps a cardinal ; then (who knows) perhaps a pope. And then ?
And then ? Go,' continued the saint, ' and reflect on these two
words.' The young man went his way, meditated on the two
words, abandoned all his worldly prospects, and gave himself
entirely to God. Leaving the world he entered into the Congregation of the Oratory, *and then* he died in the odour of sanctity."

3. A difficulty here presents itself. If our eternal salvation
is really our only business on earth, does it follow that we must
give up the duties of our position in life and occupy ourselves
solely with purely spiritual exercises ? If, to gain salvation, it
were necessary completely to renounce the world and to retire
to the desert or to shut ourselves up in a cloister, we should
indeed adopt these measures, because eternity is at stake ; but
these extraordinary means are necessary for only the few. For
us, who have not received such a special vocation, it is sufficient
to use the ordinary means which Divine Providence has placed
in the hands of all. Let us then fulfil the duties of our state ;
and let us sanctify the performance of these duties by a detachment from things of earth, by the frequentation of the
sacraments, by avoiding the occasions of sin, by recommending
ourselves to God in frequent prayer. Using these means, we
can give to the business of our state of life all the application
that is required without forgetting the business of eternity ;
we can watch over ourselves in the midst of our duties ; and
we can use the riches, and honours, and pleasures of the present

time as helps to reach those of heaven. Thus we shall do all that is ordinarily necessary to gain salvation, and we shall follow the admonition of the Apostle : " This therefore I say, brethren : The time is short. It remaineth that both they that have wives, be as if they had none ; and they that weep, as if they wept not ; and they that rejoice, as if they rejoiced not ; and they that buy, as if they possessed not ; and they that use this world, as if they used it not ; for the fashion of this world passeth away " (I Cor. vii. 29-31).

THIRD SUNDAY AFTER PENTECOST.

I.—TEXTS.

GREEK.

LUKE XV. 1-10.

¹ Ἦσαν δὲ αὐτῷ ἐγγίζοντες πάντες οἱ τελῶναι καὶ οἱ ἁμαρτωλοὶ, ἀκούειν αὐτοῦ. ² Καὶ διεγόγγυζον οἵ τε φαρεισαῖοι καὶ οἱ γραμματεῖς, λέγοντες· ὅτι οὗτος ἁμαρτωλοὺς προσδέχεται, καὶ συνεσθίει αὐτοῖς. ³ Εἶπεν δὲ πρὸς αὐτοὺς τὴν παραβολὴν ταύτην, λέγω.·. ⁴ Τίς ἄνθρωπος ἐξ ὑμῶν ἔχων ἑκατὸν πρόβατα, καὶ ἀπολέσῃ ἐξ αὐτῶν ἕν, οὐ καταλείπει τὰ ἐνενήκοντα ἐννέα ἐν τῇ ἐρήμῳ, καὶ πορεύεται ἐπὶ τὸ ἀπολωλὸς, ἕως εὕρῃ αὐτό; ⁵ Καὶ εὑρὼν ἐπιτίθησιν ἐπὶ τοὺς ὤμους αὐτοῦ χαίρων; ⁶ Καὶ ἐλθὼν εἰς τὸν οἶκον, συγκαλεῖ τοὺς φίλους καὶ τοὺς γείτονας, λέγων αὐτοῖς· Συγχάρητέ μοι, ὅτι εὗρον τὸ πρόβατόν μου τὸ ἀπολωλός. ⁷ Λέγω ὑμῖν, ὅτι οὕτως χαρὰ ἐν τῷ οὐρανῷ ἔσται ἐπὶ ἑνὶ ἁμαρτωλῷ μετανοοῦντι, ἢ ἐπὶ ἐνενήκοντα ἐννέα δικαίοις, οἵτινες οὐ χρείαν ἔχουσιν μετανοίας. ⁸ Ἢ τίς γυνὴ, δραχμὰς ἔχουσα δέκα, ἐὰν ἀπολέσῃ δραχμὴν μίαν, οὐχὶ ἅπτει λύχνον, καὶ σαροῖ τὴν οἰκίαν, καὶ ζητεῖ ἐπιμελῶς, ἕως οὗ εὕρῃ; ⁹ Καὶ εὑροῦσα συγκαλεῖ τὰς φίλας καὶ γείτονας, λέγουσα· Συγχάρητέ μοι, ὅτι εὗρον τὴν δραχμὴν ἣν ἀπώλεσα· ¹⁰ Οὕτως, λέγω ὑμῖν, γίνεται χαρὰ ἐνώπιον ἀγγέλων τοῦ θεοῦ ἐπὶ ἑνὶ ἁμαρτωλῷ μετανοοῦντι.

VULGATE.

LUKE XV. 1-10.

¹ Erant autem appropinquantes ei publicani et peccatores, ut audirent illum. ² Et murmurabant pharisæi et scribæ dicentes : Quia hic peccatores recipit, et manducat cum illis. ³ Et ait ad illos parabolam istam dicens : ⁴ Quis ex vobis homo, qui habet centum oves, et si perdiderit unam ex illis, nonne dimittit nonaginta novem in deserto, et vadit ad illam quæ perierat, donec inveniat eam? ⁵ Et cum invenerit eam, imponit in humeros suos gaudens. ⁶ Et veniens domum, convocat amicos et vicinos, dicens illis : Congratulamini mihi quia inveni ovem meam quæ perierat. ⁷ Dico vobis, quod ita gaudium erit in cœlo super uno peccatore pœnitentiam agente, quam super nonaginta novem justis qui non indigent pœnitentia. ⁸ Aut quæ mulier habens drachmas decem, si perdiderit drachmam unam, nonne accendit lucernam, et everrit domum, et quærit diligenter, donec inveniat? ⁹ Et cum invenerit, convocat amicas et vicinas, dicens : Congratulamini mihi quia inveni drachmam quam perdideram. ¹⁰ Ita dico vobis, gaudium erit coram angelis Dei super uno peccatore pœnitentiam agente.

II.—ENGLISH TRANSLATION.

LUKE XV. 1-10.

¹ Now, the publicans and sinners drew near unto him to hear him. ² And the pharisees and the scribes murmured, saying: " This man receiveth sinners, and eateth with them." ³ And he spoke to them this parable, saying: ⁴ " What man of you having a hundred sheep and having lost one of them, doth not leave the ninety-nine in the desert, and go after that which was lost until he find it ? ⁵ And when he hath found it, he layeth it upon his shoulders, rejoicing. ⁶ And coming home, he calleth together his friends and neighbours, saying to them : Rejoice with me, because I have found my sheep that was lost. ⁷ I say to you, that even so there shall be joy in heaven upon one sinner that doth penance, more than upon ninety-nine just who need not penance. ⁸ Or what woman having ten groats, if she lose one groat, doth not light a candle, and sweep the house, and seek diligently until she find it ? ⁹ And when she hath found it, she calleth together her friends and neighbours, saying : Rejoice with me, because I have found the groat which I had lost. ¹⁰ So I say to you, there shall be joy before the angels of God upon one sinner doing penance."

III.—NOTES.

Introductory. We learn from St. John (x. 22-40) that Christ, during the December before his death, celebrated in Jerusalem the Feast of the Dedication of the temple ; that on his declaring himself to be God, the Jews sought to stone him ; and that escaping from their hands, " he went again beyond the Jordan into that place where John was baptising first, and there he abode." The history of this residence in the district of Peræa beyond the Jordan is given almost exclusively by St. Luke. It would appear that this particular district was now chosen for his sojourn by Christ in order to remind his followers of the testimony borne to him on the spot by his Precursor. Attracted by the memory of the Baptist who had ministered there, and still more by the fame of Christ himself, " many resorted to him, and they said : John indeed did no sign ; but all things whatsoever John said of this man were true. And many believed in him " (John x. 41, 42). From the preceding and the present chapter of St. Luke we see that amongst the many who " re sorted to him " there were three classes. A large number were drawn by mere curiosity or by equally unworthy motives ; another large number, who were publicans and sinners, came

with a sincere desire to amend their lives ; and lastly there
were present scribes and pharisees who ever followed him to
"ensnare him in his speech" and to discredit him with the
people. To inspire the first class of hearers with more serious
thoughts, he pointed out in the parable of "the unfinished
tower" (Luke xiv. 28-30) and in that of "the king unprepared
for battle" (Luke xiv. 31, 32) the conditions and cost of becoming
his disciples. To reprove the scribes and pharisees he spoke
the parable of "the lost sheep" and that of "the lost groat."
As to the remaining class of hearers that were assembled around
Christ in this desert, St. Luke says :—

**V. 1. Now, the publicans and the sinners drew near unto
him to hear him.**

We should observe that the word "now" (Greek δέ) is not
an indication of time. It points out the connection between
this passage and the preceding chapter ; and it calls attention to
the contrast between the earnestness of the classes now to be described and the unworthy dispositions of the multitude previously
addressed (Luke xiv. 25-35). It is said that "the publicans
and sinners drew near unto him to hear him." This is more
forcibly expressed in the Greek text which has : Ἦσαν δὲ αὐτῷ
ἐγγίζοντες πάντες οἱ τελῶναι καὶ οἱ ἁμαρτωλοὶ, ἀκούειν αὐτοῦ = "Now all
the publicans (where he then was) were continually drawing
near unto him (*periphrastic imperfect*) to hear him." Moved
by our Lord's gentleness and yielding to the influence of grace,
these men were coming, one party after another without inter-
mission, to listen to his instructions as they had formerly come
to hear and to consult John the Baptist (Luke iii. 12, 13).

In sharp contrast with these, another portion of our Lord's
audience is now described by the evangelist, who says :—

**V. 2. And the pharisees and the scribes murmured, say-
ing : This man receiveth sinners, and eateth with them.**

The form of the Greek verb διεγόγγυζον with the particle and
in the imperfect, indicates the intensity of the feeling of dis-
approval exhibited and the repeated expression of this disap-
proval. Other instances are to be found in Luke v. 30 and vii.
30. *Cf.* Matth. ix. 11 ; Mark ii. 16. As St. Matthew records
(xii. 20), it had been foretold of Christ by the prophet Isaias,
that "the bruised reed he shall not break, and smoking flax
he shall not extinguish till he send forth judgment unto victory,"
i.e., till the divine law everywhere gloriously prevail. In this
prophecy, spoken 600 years before, it was announced that the
Messiah would by his clemency and mercy draw sinners to God,
and would cause the divine will to be victorious over corrupt
human nature. Now, whereas the scribes and pharisees ought

have recognised in Jesus the Messiah predicted by Isaias, ~~a~~d ought to have rejoiced that in him this prophecy was so ~~e~~arly fulfilled, they gave utterance to loud and indignant pro-~~te~~sts against the encouragement and help afforded to their once ~~si~~nful but now repentant brethren. They said in effect: " This ~~m~~an who professes to teach a higher degree of holiness, is him-~~se~~lf far from avoiding moral defilement. Forgetting that even ~~th~~e good are contaminated by intercourse with the wicked, he ~~no~~t only welcomes sinners to his presence (Gr. προσδέχεται), but ~~he~~ also shows them the highest mark of friendship by eating ~~wi~~th them."

For the sake of the people who might be led astray by these ~~hy~~pocrites, Christ wished to defend his own acts; he condemned ~~th~~e pharisaical contempt for the fallen, which was nothing else ~~th~~an a mask for pride;

V. 3. And he spoke to them this parable, saying:

Besides the errors introduced into their speculative teaching, ~~th~~e scribes and pharisees were known for three great moral ~~de~~fects. (See Ubaldi: *Introductio in S. S.*, vol. iii., page 649.) ~~In~~ the first place, being intent on their own material interests, ~~th~~ey were careless about sinners committed to their guidance. ~~"~~Woe to the shepherds of Israel, that fed themselves? Should ~~no~~t the flock be fed by the shepherds?" (Ezechiel xxxiv. 2). ~~A~~gain, in the incipient stages of repentance, they made no effort ~~to~~ second the action of divine grace. " The weak you have ~~no~~t strengthened; and that which was sick you have not healed; ~~th~~at which was broken you have not bound up" (Ezechiel ~~xx~~xiv. 4). Still further, when the call of God was listened to ~~an~~d the sinner entirely renounced his evil ways, this conversion ~~br~~ought no joy or change of manner to the hireling pastors. ~~"~~You ruled over them with rigour, and with a high hand " ~~(E~~zechiel xxxiv. 4).

It has been already said that to correct such a mode of dealing ~~w~~ith the fallen, Christ spoke the three parables of " the lost ~~sh~~eep," " the lost groat," and " the prodigal son." In these ~~il~~lustrations taken from the ordinary life of the people around ~~h~~im, he showed that true sanctity is accompanied by solicitude ~~in~~ seeking after sinners, by kindness and gentleness in receiving ~~th~~em on their return, and by a feeling of joy on beholding in ~~th~~eir conversion a glorious victory of divine grace.

Appealing to the experience of his audience, he says:—

V. 4. What man of you having a hundred sheep and having lost one of them, doth not leave the ninety-nine in the desert, and go after that which was lost until he find it?

The exact numbers mentioned in this and in the following

parable, have no special mystic significance. They are introduced to show that, compared with what remains, the loss appears small ; and we are thus enabled to form an estimate of
the value set by the shepherd on each individual sheep. (See
International Comm., *in loco*.)　Here and in other passages of
the New Testament (*e.g.*, Matth. xiv. 15 ; Mark vi. 32) the word
" desert "=Heb. מִדְבָּר=Gr. ἔρημος, signifies not a barren waste
in which the flock would perish, but an uninhabited tract of
pasture land.　The " man " spoken of in this parable, clearly
represents Jesus Christ himself, who as the great Pastor of
Souls, was to take the place of the shepherds of Israel denounced
by the prophet in these words : " Thus saith the Lord God,
Behold, I myself come upon the shepherds.　I will require
my flock at their hand ; and I will cause them to cease from
feeding the flock any more.　Neither shall the shepherds feed
themselves any more. . . .　And I will set up one shepherd
over them ; and he shall feed them, even my servant David.
He shall feed them, and he shall be their shepherd " (Ezechiel
xxxiv. 10 and 23).　The " hundred sheep " may represent
either the holy angels and mankind, or mankind only.　In the
former supposition the " ninety-nine " are the angels who per-
severed in large numbers, whilst the " one," the lost sheep, is
man who fell.　In the latter view, which is probably more
correct, the " ninety-nine " are the just, and the " one " is any
individual sinner. (McCarthy, *in loco*.)　Each such sinner is
described not as " a straying sheep," but as a " lost sheep " ;
and such he would be without hope, if Christ did not come on
earth to seek him, or if Christ did not continue to seek him by
the stings of conscience and the inspirations of grace.　" The
lost sheep," says St. Augustine, " returns not by its own strength,
but is carried back on the shepherd's shoulders : that which
could lose itself in wandering according to its own way and
pleasure, could not find itself nor be found at all, unless it had been
sought after by the tender mercy of the Shepherd " (St. August.
In Ps. lxxvii. 19).　Trench says well : " In the common things
of our daily experience, a sheep which could wander away
from, could also walk back to, the fold.　But it is not so with
the sheep of God's pasture ; this could lose, but it could not find
itself again ; there is in sin a *centrifugal* tendency ; and, of
necessity, the wanderings of this sheep could only be further and
further away.　Therefore, if it be found at all, this can only be
by its shepherd going to seek it ; without this, being once lost,
it must be lost for ever." (See Trench : *Parables*.)
　　In the Greek text the ἐπὶ after πορεύεται denotes the end for
which the shepherd leaves the larger number.　Πορεύεται itself
(in the present tense = " goes " or " continues to go ") being
united with the clause ἕως εὕρῃ αὐτό = " until he find it," indi-

cates that the search is not abandoned until the lost one is actually found.

Love is thus shown in the persevering character of the search for the lost sheep : it is not less strikingly manifested by the manner in which the lost sheep is treated on being recovered. Christ says of the shepherd :—

V. 5. And when he hath found it, he layeth it upon his shoulders, rejoicing.

On finding the wanderer, the shepherd neither shows anger nor utters complaint, but rejoices in the recovery of that which he loves.   This is not all.   He does not permit the sheep to return home on foot, or in charge of others : he takes it upon his shoulders (Greek ἐπὶ τοὺς ὤμους αὐτοῦ="upon *his own* shoulders"), and brings it back to the fold.   As may be seen in the explanation of the preceding verse, Christ is here describing himself and his action on the sinner's heart by means of graces which theologians call *preventing* and *concomitant*.   By these graces the sinner is first awakened to a knowledge of his danger ; he is invited to return ; and on consenting to return, he is brought to repentance and from repentance to justification.   Repentance and justification do not take place without the will and co-operation of him who is converted ; still so abundant is the help given, and so easy is the process made, that this return can be well described as a being carried back to the fold on the shoulders of the Divine Shepherd.   Should we wonder, then, that the first images painted on the walls of the catacombs and engraved on the sacred vessels of the early Christians, were suggested by reflections on this parable ?

Persons in great joy wish to have their feelings shared by others.   So is it with the shepherd here described ;

V. 6. And coming home, he calleth together his friends and neighbours, saying to them : Rejoice with me because I have found my sheep that was lost.

Here again does Christ describe himself.   The benefits that accrue from a return to God, are all on the side of the sinner who is converted ; but so great is the Redeemer's love for the human soul that this Divine Pastor calls his friends, namely the angels and saints in heaven and the just on earth, to share his happiness in the recovery of that which was lost.   It was easy for his audience to draw the conclusion.   It is as though he had said : "If each one of you around (" Which man of you," v. 4) would certainly rejoice thus on recovering with much labour a single sheep that had strayed from a large flock, would not he be inhuman in his cruelty who could take it ill when a lost fellow creature is led back by gentleness to the friendship of his loving Creator ? "

Not content with suggesting the conclusion to be drawn from the parable, Christ adds the remarkable words :—

V. 7. I say to you, that even so there shall be joy in heaven upon one sinner that doth penance, more than upon ninety-nine just who need not penance.

It has been well observed : " He seeks to shame the murmurers out of their murmurs, showing them how little sympathy those murmurs find in that higher heavenly world from whence he came. He holds up to them God and the angels of God rejoicing at the conversion of the sinner, and silently contrasts this the liberal joy and exultation of heaven with the envious repinings and narrow discontent that found place in their hearts " (Trench : *On the Parables*, p. 773). The clause " I say to you " being emphatic and equivalent to " *I who know it* say to you," our Lord here as elsewhere (see Matth. xviii. 10 ; John i. 51) puts before the audience his intimate knowledge of the unseen world of glory. The expression in the original text : " There shall be joy in heaven upon one sinner doing penance, *than* upon ninety-nine just who need not penance," is a reproduction of the Hebrew form of the comparative, and is equivalent to " there shall be *greater* joy in heaven on account of one sinner who is repentant, than on account of ninety-nine just men who need not repentance." But, it is asked, who are these that need not repentance ? Is it not written : " There is no just man upon earth that doth good and sinneth not " (Eccles. vii. 21) ; and are not all obliged to say daily : " Forgive us our debts, as we also forgive our debtors " ? (Matth. vi. 12 ; Luke xi. 4). In reply to this difficulty it is necessary to observe that there is not here any ironical censure of the pharisees who, although in sin, imagined themselves to have no need of penance, nor of the Jews generally who prided themselves on their *legal* justice (Trench). The comparison is instituted between one who is actually being justified by penance, and the large number who, though formerly in sin, have already been justified and have continued in the state of justification. This being so, it is asserted that the repentance of the former causes greater joy in heaven than the perseverance of the latter. But how can it be that there is greater joy over the conversion of the sinner than over the persevering obedience of the just ? To answer this difficulty we must closely examine the words of the text. Christ does not say that God *loves* more the one repentant sinner than the ninety-nine who have continued just ; nor is it said that God *rejoices* more. It is merely stated that there is more joy in heaven ; and as may be learned from the context (verse 10), this means that the angels rejoice more. Now, to the angels who are not omniscient, the conversion of any one sinner may not be known with certainty beforehand. This being the case, and the degree of intensity in *actual joy* being dependent as much on the unexpectedness of the success, or on the intensity of the anxiety dispelled, or on the vehemence of the desire satisfied, as it is on the greatness of the good obtained, it is not impossible that the angels in heaven are more intensely affected by the unlikely conversion of the one sinner than by the likely perseverance of the many just.

In the preceding parable our Lord pointed out the value which in heaven is set on the sinner's conversion : in the next, he shows the diligence to be employed in securing that conversion. He says :—

V. 8. Or what woman having ten groats, if she lose one groat, doth not light a candle, and sweep the house, and seek diligently until she find it ?

Of the three parables in this chapter that of " the lost sheep " is the only one recorded by any other evangelist. In each of these parables a different class of sinners is represented, and the order may have been arranged so as to illustrate by a climax the intensity of feeling occasioned by the loss. Thus in the parable of " the lost sheep " the reader learns the condition of him who is led away by *ignorance*, culpable indeed, but still by ignorance, and who wanders helplessly and hopelessly if not sought for by his Saviour ; in that of " the lost groat " there is a type of him who, *knowing* that he was stamped with the image of God, yields to the seductions of passion, and now lies hidden away, covered with the filth of sin and enveloped in the darkness which sin brings in its train ; lastly, in that of " the prodigal son " there is a figure of one who, with a *full knowledge* of the consequences and with a determined will, tears himself away from God his Father, and gives himself up to unbridled indulgence.

The particle $\check{\eta} = or$, indicates that in this second parable the same teaching is continued by means of another example. The δραχμή which is rendered *groat*, was a Greek coin equal to one-fourth of the Hebrew *sicle*, and it was of nearly the same value as the Roman *denarius, i.e.*, about $9\frac{1}{2}d$. of our money. (Introduction, pp. cxxi., cxxii.) Since coins were, and are, worn as ornaments by women in the East, and since the ten drachmas here mentioned were probably used for that purpose, the loss of even one, like the link of a chain, would be much felt, and the joy on finding it would be proportionately great. " It is quite common to see thousands of piastres, in various coins, around the forehead, suspended from the neck, and covering a system of network called *súffa* attached to the back of the head-dress, which spreads over the shoulders, and falls down to the waist. These jewels cannot be taken for the husband's debts "

(Thomson: *The Land and the Book*, p. 129). In the parable, the "groat" represents one in whose soul the image of God stamped by baptism, has been defaced or obscured by sin ; the " woman " is a figure of Christ in search of such a soul ; and the diligence of the woman is a type of the loving and persevering care with which our Redeemer seeks to recover such a lost but precious possession.

As was already remarked, joy is diffusive of itself. Thus is it with the woman who sought for " the lost groat " ;

V. 9. And when she hath found it, she calleth together her friends and neighbours, saying : Rejoice with me, because I have found the groat which I had lost.

As the woman is a figure of Christ, so the " friends and neighbours " now called to share her joy represent the angels in heaven, whom Christ invites to rejoice with him on the restoration of the sinner to a place among the just. The scope of this parable is the same as that of the parable of " the lost sheep," and it is here dwelt on with emphasis to thoroughly confound the murmuring pharisees and scribes. Manifesting his knowledge of the world invisible to these murmurers, Christ thus concludes :—

V. 10. So I say to you, there shall be joy before the angels of God upon one sinner doing penance.

Thus Christ revealed that in heaven the angels know what is passing here on earth ; that they interest themselves in man's salvation ; and that they are filled with gladness at the sinner's conversion. As he did in the former parable, so in this, our Divine Lord leaves it to his audience to make the application. If on the return of the sinner to the service of God, the angels rejoice exceedingly, and do so at the invitation of God himself, whom do those resemble that murmur at this victory of divine grace ? Surely not the inhabitants of heaven, but the devils in hell. But why do the angels rejoice, and why are they called upon to rejoice, at the conversion of a sinner in a world so far removed from theirs ? First, because this conversion redounds to the extrinsic glory of God, it being a victory gained by the grace of God whom the angels so intensely love ; again, because it is a great good for the sinner himself and secures the temporal and eternal happiness of a fellow-creature whom God infinitely loves ; still further, because by it the angels have one more companion prepared to fill the places left vacant by the fallen spirits ; and lastly, because in the justification of the wicked Christ's mission is accomplished. So dear indeed is this work to Christ, and so great is the value of the human soul, that he who cannot overrate things, would willingly die to rescue a *single sinner*, and did die for each one individually.

Each one can say with St. Paul: " I live in the faith of the Son of God, who loved *me* and delivered himself for *me* " (Gal. ii. 20).

IV.—MORAL REFLECTIONS.

The opening sentences of the present gospel passage afford us three important subjects for meditation—the eagerness of sinners to come to Jesus, his indulgent goodness towards them, and the evil-mindedness of the pharisees towards him because of this indulgence.

1. As the first step to be taken in order to be freed from bodily sickness, is to have recourse to the physician, so in order to be delivered from the diseases of the soul we must commence by having recourse to Jesus Christ, who alone can heal us. This is what was done by the publicans and sinners described here by St. Luke. They were in that state so common amongst men, in which one has lost his innocence, but not his faith ; in which he has lost the gift of sanctifying grace, but has not ceased to regret his loss ; in which he is no longer virtuous, but entertains the desire of once more becoming so. Such a religious feeling is the last bond by which the sinner holds on to God, and the means by which he may, if he will, retrace his steps and regain the paths of justice from which he has strayed. Happy are they who, in the midst of their crimes, are not dead to the stings of remorse, who have still this appreciation of better things, and who are thereby induced to approach their merciful Saviour. Sinners, therefore, ought to come to Jesus Christ, first by listening to the instructions which he gives in his Church, and then by practising the pious exercises which religion commands or counsels. These are prayer, meditation, spiritual reading, and devout attendance at the holy sacrifice of the Mass. The sweetness of God's presence and the power of his grace will dispel the charm of temptation which has seduced them ; their feeble desires will be changed into resolutions ; their efforts will be crowned with success ; and their remorse will lead them to salutary repentance.

2. What was the influence that drew around our Saviour these men whose conduct was so opposed to the principles he taught ? What attraction did they feel in a doctrine which condemned their mode of life ? It was the indulgent kindness of manner which tempered the rigour of his maxims. He introduced into the world the most austere moral code that had ever been preached ; but he found the means of making it acceptable by the gentleness with which he imposed it. Sinners naturally remarked the contrast between the pharisees whose disdainful pride was so repelling, and Jesus who, in seeking for them and

in speaking to them, had for them not anger, but pity and pardon.
" Such," says St. Gregory, " is the difference between true and
false virtue. The one inspires compassion, the other contempt :
the one detests only the sin, the other extends its hatred even
to the sinner." If, then, as parents or superiors we be placed
in charge of others, and if we would correct faults or errors with
success, we should imitate the conduct of our Divine Master ;
we should remember that, as long as the wayward objects of
our care are on earth, however criminal they may be, they are
the objects of his mercy, and that he does not cease to call them
by his exhortations, and to attract them to himself by his grace.
Acting otherwise than he did, and thus abusing the authority
conferred upon us, we should be opposing his beneficent intentions ;
we should be alienating those whom he seeks ; and we should be
driving to obstinate resistance those whom he labours to reconcile to his Father.

3. It would have been easy for Jesus to repel the charges
of the scribes and pharisees by drawing a parallel between these
classes and the much less culpable publicans and sinners whom
he was blamed for receiving with kindness. He could have told
his enemies that since he permitted themselves to approach him
notwithstanding their pride, hypocrisy, hardness of heart, and
other vices, they should not take it ill that he welcomed to his
presence men whose sins were much less grave. His gentleness
was far removed from such a course, and, though perpetually
attacked during his public life, he never once adopted recrimina-
tion as a defence. On this occasion he showed towards the
scribes and pharisees the indulgence they accused him of showing
towards the publicans and sinners ; he contented himself with
disabusing them of their erroneous principles ; and, to avoid all
that might savour of bitterness or reproach, he conveyed the
lesson he had to give in the beautiful parable of " the lost sheep "
and in that of " the lost groat." If, in correcting the sinful
we imitate the conduct of our Divine Master, we shall share in
the promise made to his disciples : " In your patience you shall
possess your souls " (Luke xxi. 19) ; and if he be our model
when we are subjected to the provocation of unjust accusation,
we shall be included in the prayer of his Apostle : " The peace of
God, which surpasseth all understanding, keep your hearts and
minds in Christ Jesus " (Phil. iv. 7).

FOURTH SUNDAY AFTER PENTECOST.

I.—TEXTS.

<table>
<tr><td>

GREEK.

LUKE V. 1-11.

¹ Ἐγένετο δὲ ἐν τῷ τὸν ὄχλον ἐπι-
κεῖσθαι αὐτῷ καὶ ἀκούειν τὸν λόγον
τοῦ θεοῦ, καὶ αὐτὸς ἦν ἑστὼς παρὰ τὴν
λίμνην Γεννησαρέτ. ² Καὶ εἶδεν πλοῖα
δύο ἑστῶτα παρὰ τὴν λίμνην· οἱ δὲ
ἁλιεῖς ἀπ᾽ αὐτῶν, ἀποβάντες ἔπλυνον
τὰ δίκτυα. ³ Ἐμβὰς δὲ εἰς ἓν τῶν
πλοίων, ὃ ἦν Σίμωνος, ἠρώτησεν αὐτὸν
ἀπὸ τῆς γῆς ἐπαναγαγεῖν ὀλίγον· καθί-
σας δὲ ἐκ τοῦ πλοίου ἐδίδασκεν τοὺς
ὄχλους. ⁴ Ὡς δὲ ἐπαύσατο λαλῶν,
εἶπεν πρὸς τὸν Σίμωνα· Ἐπανάγαγε εἰς
τὸ βάθος, καὶ χαλάσατε τὰ δίκτυα
ὑμῶν εἰς ἄγραν. ⁵ Καὶ ἀποκριθεὶς
Σίμων εἶπεν· Ἐπιστάτα, δι᾽ ὅλης νυκτὸς
κοπιάσαντες, οὐδὲν ἐλάβομεν· ἐπὶ δὲ
τῷ ῥήματί σου χαλάσω τὰ δίκτυα.
⁶ Καὶ τοῦτο ποιήσαντες, συνέκλεισαν
πλῆθος ἰχθύων πολύ· διερρήσσετο δὲ
τὰ δίκτυα αὐτῶν. ⁷ Καὶ κατένευσαν
τοῖς μετόχοις ἐν τῷ ἑτέρῳ πλοίῳ, τοῦ
ἐλθόντας συλλαβέσθαι αὐτοῖς· καὶ
ἦλθον, καὶ ἔπλησαν ἀμφότερα τὰ
πλοῖα, ὥστε βυθίζεσθαι αὐτά. ⁸ Ἰδὼν
δὲ Σίμων Πέτρος, προσέπεσεν τοῖς
γόνασιν Ἰησοῦ, λέγων· Ἔξελθε ἀπ᾽
ἐμοῦ, ὅτι ἀνὴρ ἁμαρτωλός εἰμι, κύριε.
⁹ Θάμβος γὰρ περιέσχεν αὐτὸν καὶ
πάντας τοὺς σὺν αὐτῷ, ἐπὶ τῇ ἄγρᾳ
τῶν ἰχθύων, ὧν συνέλαβον. ¹⁰ Ὁμοίως

</td><td>

VULGATE.

LUKE V. 1-11.

¹ Factum est autem, cum
turbæ irruerent in eum, ut au-
dirent verbum Dei, et ipse
stabat secus stagnum Genesa-
reth. ² Et vidit duas naves
stantes secus stagnum ; pisca-
tores autem descenderant, et
lavabant retia. ³ Ascendens
autem in unam navim, quæ
erat Simonis, rogavit eum a
terra reducere pusillum. Et
sedens docebat de navicula tur-
bas. ⁴ Ut cessavit autem lo-
qui, dixit ad Simonem : Duc
in altum, et laxate retia vestra
in capturam. ⁵ Et respondens
Simon dixit illi : Præceptor,
per totam noctem laborantes,
nihil cepimus ; in verbo autem
tuo laxabo rete. ⁶ Et cum hoc
fecissent, concluserunt piscium
multitudinem copiosam ; rum-
pebatur autem rete eorum.
⁷ Et annuerunt sociis qui erant
in alia navi ut venirent et ad-
juvarent eos. Et venerunt, et
impleverunt ambas naviculas,
ita ut pene mergerentur.
⁸ Quod cum videret Simon
Petrus, procidit ad genua Jesu,
dicens : Exi a me, quia homo
peccator sum, Domine. ⁹ Stu-
por enim circumdederat eum
et omnes qui cum illo erant, in
captura piscium quam cepe-
rant ; ¹⁰ Similiter autem Jaco-

</td></tr>
</table>

δὲ καὶ Ἰάκωβον καὶ Ἰωάνην, υἱοὺς
Ζεβεδαίου, οἱ ἦσαν κοινωνοὶ τῷ Σίμωνι·
καὶ εἶπεν πρὸς τὸν Σίμωνα Ἰησοῦς· Μὴ
φοβοῦ· ἀπὸ τοῦ νῦν ἀνθρώπους ἔσῃ
ζωγρῶν. ¹¹ Καὶ καταγαγόντες τὰ πλοῖα
ἐπὶ τὴν γῆν, ἀφέντες πάντα ἠκολού-
θησαν αὐτῷ.

bum et Joannem, filio, Zebe-
dæi, qui erant socii Simonis.
Et ait ad Simonem Jesus : Noli
timere : ex hoc jam homines
eris capiens. ¹¹ Et subductis
ad terram navibus, relictis
omnibus secuti sunt eum.

II.—ENGLISH TRANSLATION.

LUKE V. I-II.

¹ And it came to pass, that when the multitudes pressed upon
him to hear the word of God, he stood by the lake of Genesareth. ² And he saw two ships standing by the lake ; but the
fishermen had gone out of them, and were washing their nets.
³ And going into one of the ships, which was Simon's, he desired
him to draw back a little from the land. And sitting, he taught
the multitudes out of the ship. ⁴ Now when he had ceased to
speak, he said to Simon : " Launch out into the deep, and let
down your nets for a draught." ⁵ And Simon answering, said
to him : " Master, we have laboured all the night, and have
taken nothing ; but at thy word I will let down the net." ⁶ And
when they had done this, they enclosed a very great multitude
of fishes ; and their net broke. ⁷ And they beckoned to their
partners who were in the other ship, that they should come and
help them. And they came and filled both the ships, so that
they were almost sinking. ⁸ On seeing which, Simon Peter
fell down at Jesus' knees, saying : " Depart from me, for I
am a sinful man, O Lord." ⁹ For he was wholly astonished,
and all that were with him, at the draught of fishes which they
had taken. ¹⁰ And so were also James and John the sons of
Zebedee, who were Simon's partners. And Jesus saith to Simon :
" Fear not : henceforth thou shalt catch men." ¹¹ And having
brought their ships to land, leaving all things, they followed
him.

III.—NOTES.

Introductory. It was now nearly a year since our Lord had
worked his first miracle at Cana, and had thus confirmed the
faith of the disciples sent to him by John the Baptist. In the
interval he celebrated the Pasch in Jerusalem, and there converted Nicodemus with many others ; on his way back to
Galilee he preached to the Samaritans ; in Galilee itself his
teaching was despised ; and on being murderously attacked by
his townsmen of Nazareth, he came to reside in Capharnaum
which was henceforth to be " his own city." The event which

forms the subject matter of the present gospel passage, took place in this neighbourhood on the shore of Lake Genesareth. Amongst commentators there is a difference of opinion as to whether the calling of the apostles which is here recorded, be or be not the same as that which is mentioned in Matthew iv. 18-22, and Mark i. 16-20. Many (*e.g.*, Tostatus, Jansenius Gand., Bar., A Lapide, Lamy, Reischel, Grimm, Cornely, Fillion, etc.) think that the three accounts refer to one and the same event, and that circumstances omitted by one evangelist are supplied by another. It is more probable that the almost verbally identical narrations of SS. Matthew and Mark refer to a call different from that described by St. Luke ; and this opinion of St. Aug., Rab., Alb., St. Thomas, Caj., Maldonatus, Sylv., Men., Kilber, Calm., Patrizi, Coleridge, etc., is adopted in the following notes. It appears, indeed, that Peter, Andrew, James, and John were first invited to become disciples of Christ (John i. 35-42) ; that then after an absence of some months they were again invited to follow our Lord and to unite themselves more closely to him (Matthew iv. 18-22 ; Mark i. 16-20) ; that subsequently they were called to leave all things, and to devote themselves entirely to his service (Luke v. 10, 11) ; and that finally in the second year of Christ's public life, they were solemnly invested with the apostolic dignity (Matth. x. 1-4 ; Mark iii. 13-19 ; Luke vi. 13-16).

The circumstances which prepared the way for the renunciation of all things on the present occasion by the future apostles, are minutely described by St. Luke, who says :—

V. 1. **And it came to pass, that when the multitudes pressed upon him to hear the word of God, he stood by the lake of Genesareth.**

This sheet of water, called by St. Luke with characteristic accuracy a " lake," is elsewhere named a " sea," according to the custom of the Hebrews who thus designated every large expanse of water.

For a description of the lake, see Gospel of Fourth Sunday of Lent. St. Luke in the words ἐπικεῖσθαι αὐτῷ, strikingly illustrates the earnestness of the people who " pressed upon " Christ to hear his words not only in the synagogues, towns, and villages, but wherever he went.

This tumultuous eagerness of the crowd, though laudable in its purpose, was incompatible with the recollection and silence necessary for fruitful religious instruction ; but a remedy for the inconvenience was at hand. Christ looked around,

V. 2. **And he saw two ships standing by the lake ; but the fishermen had gone out of them, and were washing their nets.**

The ships were that of Simon and Andrew, and that of James and John, all of whom had already been called by Christ (Matth. iv. 18-22 ; Mark i. 16-20). Both ships had now come to land near where Christ stood ; and the fishermen, entertaining no hope of reward for further labour, had disembarked and were washing their nets, or, as the narrative suggests, had already washed their nets. The participle ἐστῶτα does not necessarily imply that the ships were drawn up on the beach. The verb στῆναι and its Latin equivalent *stare* are used in reference to vessels at anchor. (See Homer : Il. θ. 43 ; Virgil : Aen. vi. 902.)

Lest he should be overwhelmed by the crowd, and in order that his words might reach a larger number of persons, Christ availed himself of the means here presented ;

V. 3. **And going up into one of the ships, which was Simon's, he desired him to draw back a little from the land. And sitting, he taught the multitudes out of the ship.**

Such is the nature of the shelving shore of the lake of Genesareth, that one speaking from a boat a short distance off could be seen and heard by each member of a crowd standing on the beach, which rises from the water's edge like the tiers of an amphitheatre. Commentators remark here the gentleness and humility of Christ who, as Lord of all things, might have *commanded* Simon, whereas, according to the evangelist, he *requested* him or *besought* him (Greek ἠρώτησεν αὐτὸν, and not παρακάλεσεν αὐτῷ). They also draw attention to the striking prominence given to Simon amongst the apostles. It is Simon's ship Christ chooses ; it is from it he instructs the people ; it is of Simon individually the request is made to draw back from the shore ; to him direction is given to launch out into the deep ; and to him alone is addressed the first prediction : " Fear not : henceforth thou shalt catch men." We see that thus early Simon is distinguished from the other disciples ; and this distinction prepares these disciples to hear afterwards that on him was conferred the supreme authority and first place in the Church. St. Luke does not tell us the matter of the instruction given on this occasion ; but as there was always an intimate connection between the recorded discourses of our Divine Lord and the circumstances in which they were delivered, we may well suppose that it dealt with the beauty and glory of the spiritual kingdom whose rulers he was about to select, or the repose and joy of heaven which are to be the recompense of apparently fruitless labour here below.

It was customary with Christ to confirm his teaching by working a miracle (see Matth. viii. 1-3) ; and

V. 4. **Now when he had ceased to speak, he said to**

Simon : Launch out into the deep, and let down your nets for a draught.

The words " Launch out into the deep," or, as in the Greek ἐπανάγαγε = " put back again into the deep," are addressed to Simon, the owner and helmsman ; the remainder, as appears from the plural number, to Andrew and his companions or hired men.   The miracle was worked for various reasons.   In the first place, Christ wished by it to confirm the teaching in which he had just been engaged ; again, he desired to reward munificently the slight labour and generosity of Simon, who had given the use of his boat ; still further, he wished through their worldly avocation to reach the hearts of those from whom he was about to demand a generous sacrifice of all things earthly and a constant companionship with himself, poor as he was ; lastly he desired to foreshadow the success that awaited them after that sacrifice and in that companionship.

Our Lord knew the heart of the disciple whom he was addressing ;

V. 5. And Simon answering, said to him : Master, we have laboured all the night, and have taken nothing ; but at thy word I will let down the net.

In the gospels we find four titles given to Christ : Κύριος, διδάσκαλος, ραββί and ἐπιστάτης.   The name ραββί is never used by St. Luke, and ἐπιστάτης which is found here and which means not only a *teacher* but a *master* having authority, is peculiar to this evangelist.   Using this title, and so addressing our Divine Lord as one whose wish should be instantly obeyed, Simon declares that, though he and his companions had during the whole night been labouring (Greek κοπιάσαντες = *working with much effort* so as to become weary), still, on the strength of Christ's word (ἐπὶ δὲ τῷ ῥήματί σου) he would again commence.   On the lips of the future apostle these words did not exhibit any unwillingness to obey, but perfect faith in the implied promise of his Divine Master.   Although from his experience he knew well that with the night the favourable time for fishing was past, he did not hesitate to do as he was commanded.   Thus did he imitate Abraham of old " who against hope believed in hope, that he might be made the father of many nations, according to that which was said to him " (Rom. iv. 18).

The word of the Lord is efficacious, for it is written : " It shall not return to me void ; but it shall do whatsoever I please, and shall prosper in the things for which I sent it " (Isaias lv 11).   Simon and his companions obeyed therefore ;

V. 6. And when they had done this, they enclosed a very great multitude of fishes ; and their net broke.

The rendering "their net (or nets) broke" in our translation and in the Authorised Version, is correct if the reading in Codex B διερρήσσετο δὲ τὰ δίκτυα αὐτῶν be adopted. If the common and more probable reading διερρήγνυτο δὲ τὸ δίκτυον αὐτῶν be followed, the clause must be rendered: "their net was on the point of breaking." The latter appears to be the more probable of the two, inasmuch as it seems to be required by the context; for if the net actually broke, unless the rent was small, the fish which subsequently filled the two ships, would have escaped.

It is useless to inquire as to whether the miracle consisted in an act of the omnipotence of Christ by which he assembled in one place such a prodigious number of fishes, or is to be attributed to his omniscience by which he was aware of all that was passing in the depths of the lake. That the event was miraculous in itself or in its circumstances, is shown from the effects produced on the minds of the experienced fishermen who beheld it—effects minutely recorded by St. Luke in verses 8, 9, 10. To prove the quantity of the fish caught, the evangelist is not satisfied to remark that the "net was on the point of breaking": he implies that Simon and his companions were unable of themselves to draw the net on board. But they were now too far from the land to make their voices heard;

V. 7. And they beckoned to their partners who were in the other ship, that they should come and help them. And they came and filled both the ships, so that they were almost sinking.

As may be seen in verse 10, these partners were James and John, who had probably kept their ship anchored by the shore, when Simon was told to "draw back a little from the land." On being signalled to, they put off from the land, and being destined to the same vocation as Simon and Andrew, they too were made witnesses of the miracle. On the greatness of this miracle St. Luke again dwells when he states that, on account of the multitude of the fishes, the two ships were almost sinking, or, as in the Greek, ὥστε βυθίζεσθαι αὐτά = *so that they began to sink.*

Plummer remarks: "It is one of the inimitable touches of truthfulness in the narrative, that the instinct of work prevails at first over the sense that a miraculous power had been exerted." Soon they fully realised the divine character of that power,

Vv. 8, 9. On seeing which, Simon Peter fell down at Jesus' knees, saying: Depart from me, for I am a sinful man, O Lord. For he was wholly astonished, and all that were with him, at the draught of fishes which they had taken.

At his first interview with Simon (John i. 42), Christ had promised that the future apostle should be called Peter, and had thus indicated this apostle's office as the foundation stone of the Church. Up to the time of this miracle St. Luke uses the name, " Simon " ; on the present occasion he employs both names ; and after the final selection of the twelve (Luke vi. 13, etc. ; Matth. x. 1, etc. ; Mark iii. 13, etc.), he always gives the name of Peter to the Prince of the Apostles. Simon's prayer to Christ was not suggested by a mere dread of temporal calamity in punishment of his sins. As appears from the subsequent remark of the evangelist, it was an expression at once of wonder (Greek θάμβος= astonishment, not terror), of humility, and of reverential fear inspired by the consciousness that he was in the presence of his God, and that he was the unworthy host of a Divine Guest. This fact was brought home to him by the miracle he had witnessed ; and whereas he had previously addressed Christ as the " Master " whom he was bound to obey, he now salutes him as the supreme " Lord " to whom all nature is subject. Indeed he now recognised before him the Incarnate Word, the Messiah, the Great Being of whom the Psalmist said in prophecy (Psalm viii. 8, 9, 10) : " Thou hast put all things under his feet : . . . the birds of the air, and the fishes of the sea, that pass through the paths of the sea. O Lord, our Lord, how admirable is thy name in all the earth ! "

Not only Simon, but " all that were with him " were seized with this reverential fear ;

V. 10. And so were also James and John, the sons of Zebedee, who were Simon's partners. And Jesus saith to Simon: Fear not; henceforth thou shalt catch men.

This special reference to the effect produced on the sons of Zebedee by the miraculous draught of fishes, was inserted by St. Luke to prepare the reader for their sacrifice of all things which was about to be recorded. The words addressed to Simon whilst still in the ship make it clear that the miracle was worked to gain over the apostles to their vocation and to inspire them with confidence in their future work. The peculiar character of that work and its success were indicated by the verb and the tense of the verb here used. The verb is ζωγρεῖν which signifying " to capture alive," was employed in reference to game caught in nets ; and which being here in the periphrastic future, means : " Thou shalt be continually engaged in capturing alive." The sense of Christ's words, therefore, is : " Fear not. I have exercised my divine power not to fill you with fear or discouragement, but to make known to you your future occupation in my service. From the capture of fish which you thereby deprive of life, I am about to call you to the work of capturing men, who by your ministry will be freed from the death of sin and preserved in eternal life."

These words addressed to Simon were but a prophecy and had reference to him alone. They were not a formal invitation to enter into companionship with Christ and to share in his labours ; but that such a formal invitation was immediately afterwards given to him as well as to James and John, may be inferred from the following statement of the evangelist :—

V. 11. **And having brought their ships to land, leaving all things, they followed him.**

It was customary with the Jewish prophets and doctors to gather around them a body of disciples who lived in their company.   Thus in the Old Testament we read of the " sons of the prophets " (see 3 Kings xx. 35 ; 4 Kings ii. 3, 5, 7, 15 ; iv. 38 ; v. 22 ; vi. 1 ; Amos vii. 14), and in the New we are told of the disciples of St. John the Baptist who were so zealous for the honour of their master (John iii. 25).   Hence it could not have surprised Simon and the sons of Zebedee when Jesus who had already proved himself to be the Prince of Prophets, expressed his wish to gather around him in special intimacy a number of those who had already occasionally listened to his words and who believed in his divine mission.   Still the following of Christ involved more than the following of John the Baptist or of any amongst the ancient prophets.   Men came to John the Baptist and to the prophets to learn their doctrine ; men were to follow Christ not merely to hear his words, but also to imitate his life.   " If you know these things," said he, " you shall be blessed if you do them " (John xiii. 17).   As, therefore, Christ had not of his own whereon to lay his head (Luke ix. 58), and as he was accustomed to propose an imitation of his voluntary poverty to candidate apostles (Matth. xix. 21), he no doubt made known to those whom he now called, that in being invited into the circle of his special companions, they were being called upon to break asunder every earthly tie. Those invited understood the meaning of the invitation, but no one hesitated even for a moment ; for " having brought their ships to land, leaving all things they followed him."   If we regard only the material possessions given up, the sacrifices were indeed not very much ; but if we keep in mind the generous and whole-hearted spirit in which these possessions were abandoned and that for ever, the sacrifices must be admitted to be very great, and were proved to be very acceptable to God. When St. Peter some time afterwards reminded Christ of what had been done on the present occasion, and claimed a reward, the claim was admitted by that Just Judge, who promised a recompense of a hundred-fold in this life and unending happiness in the next (Matth. xix. 27-29 ; Mark x. 28-30 ; Luke xviii. 28-30). Truly, to serve God is to reign.

IV.—MORAL REFLECTIONS.

1. The condition of fallen man is one of labour, for it is written " In the sweat of thy face shalt thou eat bread, till thou return to the earth out of which thou wast taken " (Gen. iii. 19) ; and again, " Man is born to labour, and the bird to fly " (Job v. 7). How sad then is the lot of those who labour much, and find in the end that they have laboured in vain ! Such was the history of the apostles during their night-long fishing on this occasion : and such in the supernatural order is the history of many who, at the end of their lives, are obliged to make this sad confession : " Master, we have laboured all the night, and have taken nothing." As the apostles, in the absence of Jesus Christ, fruitlessly exerted themselves at the work of their calling, for a greater reason without his presence and concurrence the work of our eternal salvation will be undertaken in vain. Human pride recoils at this statement ; but still it is a fundamental truth of our religion revealed by our Divine Lord when he said : " Without me you can do nothing " (John xv. 5).

2. But who are those that work apart from Jesus Christ, and whose labours are consequently worthless for eternal life ?

In the first place they are those who live in mortal sin. Without sanctifying grace there is no merit ; and however good naturally may be our acts considered in themselves, they are of no value before the tribunal of God. " If," said St. Paul, " I speak with the tongues of men and of angels, and have not charity, I am become as sounding brass or a tinkling cymbal. And if I should have prophecy, and should know all mysteries and all knowledge, and if I should have all faith so that I could remove mountains, and have not charity, I am nothing. And if I should distribute all my goods to feed the poor, and if I should deliver my body to be burned, and have not charity, it profiteth me nothing " (1 Cor. xiii. 1-3). As long then as we remain enemies of God and bereft of sanctifying grace, however laborious our employments or glorious our achievements, we belong in the spiritual order to the number of those of whom the Holy Ghost has said : " He that rejecteth wisdom and discipline is unhappy ; and their hope is vain, and their labours without fruit, and their works unprofitable " (Wisd. iii. 11). If we pity the man who during the year has cultivated his farm with constant toil and receives in return a blighted crop, still more miserable is he who labours much but fails to render his labour fruitful for eternal life.

There is another condition of meritorious work and it is this, that whilst living in the state of grace, we perform our actions with the pure intention of pleasing our Creator. " Master," said St. Peter, " at thy word I will let down the net." Jesus Christ has said : " The light of thy body is thy eye. If thy eye be single, thy whole body shall be lightsome ; but if thy eye be evil, thy whole body shall be darksome " (Matth. vi. 22, 23). Our Divine Master meant to convey to his hearers, that if our intention, which is the eye of the soul, be free from defect and fixed on God alone, all our actions will be meritorious ; but that in proportion as our intention is vitiated by a desire to attain any other object than the performance of his will, our works must, in such proportion, be devoid of merit. God could not create us for any other end than for his own glory ; and he cannot be expected to reward with himself what is done for creatures. We have our existence for his service only, and are therefore bound in justice to obey, honour, and glorify him in all things. Christ said of himself : " I came down from heaven, not to do my own will, but the will of him that sent me " (John vi. 38). It is no less true of us that we have been sent into the world to do God's will ; and to omit the execution of this will is to frustrate the designs of our Creator and to oppose his dominion over his creatures. Since God, then, created us for his own glory and could not create us with any other purpose, how can he be expected to reward with the possession of himself what is not referred to him alone ?

3. If, then, without Jesus Christ, that is, without his grace and without the purpose of pleasing him, we have laboured all the night and taken nothing, we will endeavour at once to repair the past. " See, therefore, brethren," says St. Paul, " how you walk circumspectly : not as unwise, but as wise : redeeming the time, because the days are evil " (Ephes. v. 15, 16). Remembering that we are not " sufficient to think anything of ourselves, as of ourselves, but our sufficiency is from God " (2 Cor. iii. 5), we will daily pray to him to confirm us in his grace, to inspire us with the pure intention of promoting his glory, to direct us ever to the performance of his will, to render fruitful for eternity every effort of ours here below, and at last to crown his other gifts to us by bestowing on us the rewards of heaven.

FIFTH SUNDAY AFTER PENTECOST.

I.—TEXTS.

GREEK.

MATTHEW V. 20-24.

20 Λέγω γὰρ ὑμῖν, ὅτι ἐὰν μὴ περισσεύσῃ ὑμῶν ἡ δικαιοσύνη πλεῖον τῶν γραμματέων καὶ φαρεισαίων, οὐ μὴ εἰσέλθητε εἰς τὴν βασιλείαν τῶν οὐρανῶν. 21 Ἠκούσατε ὅτι ἐρρήθη τοῖς ἀρχαίοις, Οὐ φονεύσεις· ὅς δ' ἂν φονεύσῃ, ἔνοχος ἔσται τῇ κρίσει. 22 Ἐγὼ δὲ λέγω ὑμῖν, ὅτι πᾶς ὁ ὀργιζόμενος τῷ ἀδελφῷ αὐτοῦ, ἔνοχος ἔσται τῇ κρίσει· ὃς δ' ἂν εἴπῃ τῷ ἀδελφῷ αὐτοῦ Ῥακᾶ, ἔνοχος ἔσται τῷ συνεδρίῳ· ὃς δ' ἂν εἴπῃ Μωρέ, ἔνοχος ἔσται εἰς τὴν γέενναν τοῦ πυρός. 23 Ἐὰν οὖν προσφέρῃς τὸ δῶρόν σου ἐπὶ τὸ θυσιαστήριον, κἀκεῖ μνησθῇς ὅτι ὁ ἀδελφός σου ἔχει τι κατὰ σοῦ, 24 ἄφες ἐκεῖ τὸ δῶρόν σου ἔμπροσθεν τοῦ θυσιαστηρίου, καὶ ὕπαγε πρῶτον διαλλάγηθι τῷ ἀδελφῷ σου, καὶ τότε ἐλθὼν πρόσφερε τὸ δῶρόν σου.

VULGATE.

MATTHEW V. 20-24.

20 Dico enim vobis, quia nisi abundaverit justitia vestra plus quam scribarum et pharisæorum, non intrabitis in regnum cœlorum. 21 Audistis quia dictum est antiquis : Non occides; qui autem occiderit, reus erit judicio. 22 Ego autem dico vobis, quia omnis qui irascitur fratri suo, reus erit judicio ; qui autem dixerit fratri suo : Raca, reus erit concilio ; qui autem dixerit : Fatue, reus erit gehennæ ignis. 23 Si ergo offers munus tuum ad altare, et ibi recordatus fueris quia frater tuus habet aliquid adversum te, 24 relinque ibi munus tuum ante altare, et vade prius reconciliari fratri tuo ; et tunc veniens offeres munus tuum.

II.—ENGLISH TRANSLATION.

MATTHEW V. 20-24.

20 " For I tell you, that unless your justice abound more than that of the scribes and pharisees, you shall not enter into the kingdom of heaven. 21 You have heard that it was said to them of old : Thou shalt not kill, and whosoever shall kill shall be in danger of the Judgment. 22 But I say to you, that whosoever is angry with his brother, shall be in danger of the Judgment ; and whosoever shall say to his brother : Raca, shall be in danger of the Council ; and whosoever shall say : Thou fool,

shall be in danger of hell fire.   ²³ If therefore thou art offering
thy gift at the altar, and there thou rememberest that thy brother
hath anything against thee, ²⁴ leave there thy gift before the
altar, and go first to be reconciled to thy brother ; and then
coming thou shalt offer thy gift."

III.—NOTES.

Introductory. Towards the end of the first year of his public
life our Lord, surrounded by a crowd, ascended one of the hills
of Galilee, and there delivered the remarkable discourse which
St. Matthew has recorded in the fifth, sixth, and seventh chapters
of his gospel. Since the time of the Crusades the traditional
scene of this discourse has been called the " Mount of the Beatitudes," and the discourse itself is known as the " Sermon on
the Mount." From that epitome of Christian doctrine and
precept, the present brief extract is taken. Having opened his
address with a declaration of the blessedness of those who were
to be his disciples and citizens of the Messianic kingdom now
to be established, Christ proceeds to lay down the laws by which
that kingdom should be governed, and also his relation as a
Law-giver to the law of Moses, especially as interpreted according to the letter only. In this connection he said : " Do
not think that I come to destroy the law or the prophets,"
that is, the legislation of the Old Testament : " I am not come
to destroy, but to fulfil," that is (according to the Greek $\pi\lambda\eta\rho\hat{\omega}\sigma\alpha\iota$),
to fill out or expand, replacing the type by the reality, and an
incomplete legislation by the more perfect one for which the
former was but a preparation. Still further, I say unto you :
" Till heaven and earth pass away, one jot or one tittle of the
law shall not pass away till all be fulfilled. He, therefore, that
shall break one of these least commandments, and shall so teach
men, shall be called the least in the kingdom of heaven."
Having thus defined his position with regard to the Old Dispensation, and having condemned the knowledge and practice
of the law which had hitherto appeared to suffice, he now illustrates what he had just said :—

**V. 20. For I tell you, that unless your justice abound more
than that of the scribes and pharisees, you shall not enter
into the kingdom of heaven.**

The phrase " kingdom of heaven " occurs in the gospel of
St. Matthew only. In the parallel passages of SS. Mark and
Luke we have " the kingdom of God," or some equivalent.
St. Matthew, who wrote for the Jews, appears to have made
frequent use of the expression with a view to correct his country-
men's mistaken ideas regarding the temporal sovereignty of

the Messiah. The word " kingdom " has not always the same meaning. At times it is taken in its widest signification, and includes the *ruler*, the *subjects*, the *territory* or *chief city*, and the *form of government* (Matth. iii. 2 ; iv. 17 and 23 ; Mark xii. 34 ; xv. 43 ; Luke i. 33 ; iv. 43). The term is often used to designate some *one* of the constituent parts of a kingdom, and the limitation is suggested by the context. Thus, *e.g.*, in Matth. xvi. 28, and Mark viii. 39, it means " *the royal dignity* ; " in Matth. xiii. 24, 41, 47, the *subjects* ; in Matth. xiii. 43, and xxv. 34, the *territory* or *chief city* ; and in Matth. xiii. 31, and in Mark iv. 26, the *form of government*. When, as here, " the kingdom " is proposed as a prize to be gained or a place to be " entered," it means the *future abode of the blessed*. (See McCarthy, *in loco*.) The teaching and practice of the scribes and pharisees being such as they were, it is not surprising that everyone should be excluded from the kingdom of heaven who had no higher ideal of duty than they had. We may learn from what follows that here our Lord does not merely condemn the hypocrisy and false interpretations of these teachers so revered by the people ; nor does he merely supply the deficiencies of a law which sufficed for its own time. He asserts that in his kingdom about to be established there will be need of a higher order of justice (righteousness is here meant) than has been hitherto taught or practised by pharisee or scribe.

His hearers being thus prepared to receive his precepts, Christ, in what follows to the end of this chapter, makes good his promise of fulfilling, *i.e.*, of filling out or expanding the law ; and at the same time he indicates the greater abundance of righteousness to be demanded from his disciples. Thus he says :—

V. 21. You have heard that it was said to them of old : Thou shalt not kill, and whosoever shall kill shall be in danger of the Judgment.

In the Authorised Version, τοῖς ἀρχαίοις is incorrectly rendered " by them of old time." 1°. This is against the usage of the New Testament, where ἐῤῥήθη is always followed by ὑπό or διά with the gen. when it means : " was said by " (Matth. i. 22 ; iv. 14 ; xiii. 35), and it is followed by the dat. when it means : " was said to " (Rom. ix. 12 ; Apoc. vi. 11, etc.). 2°. This translation is excluded by the contrast expressed in the following clause : 'Εγὼ δὲ λέγω ὑμῖν = " But I say to you." 3°. This rendering is also opposed to the interpretation of the Greek Fathers. (See McCarthy, *in loco*.) Our Lord was speaking to those who were accustomed each sabbath to hear the law read by the scribes. Therefore the ἀρχαίοι = " men of old " are those to whom this precept was first given on Mount Sinai, or in other words, the Israelites who had just come out from Egypt.

The meaning of the clause is : " You have heard from your teachers the scribes, that to your fathers of old it was said in the law : Thou shalt not kill." The next clause : " And whosoever shall kill, shall be in danger of the Judgment," was not a threat added by the Jewish doctors. It was prescribed in Exodus (xxi. 12 ; Lev. xxiv. 17), and still more clearly in Numbers (xxxv. 11, 12), that a person accused of homicide should be brought to trial before the judges, and if found guilty of wilful murder, should be put to death. The establishment of such courts in every tribe and even in every city is provided for in Deuteronomy (xvi. 18), and a mode of procedure is laid down in Deuteronomy (xvii. 8-13 ; xix. 2-13). Thus the external act was forbidden explicitly and in express terms : thus was awarded the punishment of that act. This elementary, and in a certain sense imperfect, legislation was adapted to the condition of the Israelites coming out of the Egyptian bondage—a condition compared by St. Paul (Gal. iv. 3) to that of childhood : by this means it was intended that a rude and as yet unformed people should be restrained, and gradually led from the imperfect to the perfect, from the less perfect to the more perfect. " The law was our pedagogue in Christ," says St. Paul (Gal. iii. 24), and hence from Christ was to be expected not a contrary, but a more perfect discipline : not an abolition of the law, but a legislation more minute, more perfect, and more fully understood. This was granted in the preaching of Christ as appears from the following words :—

V. 22. **But I say to you, etc.**

With the law given to a people still undisciplined, and as it were, in the condition of childhood, the Legislator of the New Testament contrasts his own precepts already briefly announced in the Eight Beatitudes (St. Chrysostom). " Behold," says this same saint, " the fullness of power : behold the manner of address which was becoming in a legislator. Which of the prophets ever spoke after this fashion ? The prophet's words were : Thus saith the Lord ; but the words of the Son were not these. They laid down the law for their fellow-servants : he for those who owed obedience to himself." (See Knabenbauer, *in loco*.) As Suarez remarks, the force of the expression is in this that Christ virtually compares his moral law with the ancient moral law, and shows that he imposes this ancient moral law anew, and expounds it in a more perfect manner (De Legibus, x. 2. 3).

What addition does Christ make to this precept of the decalogue, or what exposition does he give regarding it ? He says that

Whosoever is angry with his brother, shall be in danger of the Judgment.

Since murder has its origin in anger, and since he who removes or cuts out the root, removes the branches or does not permit them even to spring forth, the prohibition of anger in this instance is the perfection and complement of the law proscribing murder. The righteousness taught and practised by the pharisees was limited to abstention from taking another's life : the righteousness of Christ's disciples was to exclude even a feeling of anger against a brother. It is to be noted that Christ forbids anger *against a brother* or, in other words, such anger as is incompatible with the love due to others. It follows, therefore, that Christ does not include in this condemnation the zeal which attacks not a brother, but a brother's failings. " Be angry and sin not " (Ps. iv. 5).

But what does our Lord signify here by the word " Judgment " ? The word " Judgment " has a meaning analogous to that of the same expression in the preceding verse where it designates the local court of justice established in each city and the punishment of death by the sword awarded in that court. Thus the clause " shall be in danger of the Judgment " is here equivalent to, " shall be liable to such punishment in the other world as may be parallel with that punishment of death by the sword which is awarded for murder in the local criminal courts." The future punishment of internal sins of anger is thus declared to be the death of the soul or eternal damnation ; and consequently, it is implied that such internal sins of anger are, in the language of theologians, mortal *ex genere suo.*

But there are higher grades of wickedness in anger ; and a higher grade is reached when the internal feeling manifests itself in opprobrious expressions. Thus our Lord adds :—

And whosoever shall say to his brother : Raca, shall be in danger of the Council.

The word " Raca," in Aramaic רֵיקָא, is equivalent to the Greek κενός, and signifies *empty, empty headed,* or *without intelligence.* It expresses an angry contempt for the absence of that intelligence by which man is distinguished from the brute. This openly expressed contempt being a greater crime than the mere internal sin of ill-feeling, Christ declares that it puts the offender " in danger of the Council." But what does Christ mean in saying that such a crime entails the punishment inflicted by the Council or Sanhedrim ? The Sanhedrim (Introduction, pp. cvi., cvii.) was the supreme Jewish court first mentioned in Numbers (xi. 16, 17) and permanently established about the time of the Machabees (2 Mach. i. 10). It consisted of seventy or seventy-two members, including the high-priest as president, two vice-presidents, the ex-high-priests, the heads of the twenty-four priestly families, the elders or heads of other families, and some of the scribes. The charges on which it decided were those of idolatry, those of false prophecy, those preferred against the high-priest, and those carried to it on appeal from the local courts. Before its powers were curtailed by a foreign authority, the punishment it inflicted was that of death by stoning or by burning. Christ's meaning is, therefore, that anger, vented in such contemptuous words as the one here mentioned, shall merit before God's tribunal a punishment greater than that inflicted on simple anger, angry feelings, nay, a punishment so much the greater by how much the more the Sanhedrim surpassed the local courts in dignity, and by how much the more the sentence of this tribunal exceeded theirs in rigorous severity.

There is a graver crime of anger than that which shows itself in the contemptuous word already mentioned. Our Lord indicates it thus :—

And whosoever shall say Thou fool, shall be in danger of hell-fire (*or more exactly*, the Gehenna of Fire).

The word " fool " in the Greek μωρὲ, was most probably the equivalent of the Hebrew נבל. It was a term expressive of the greatest contumely or abhorrence, and signified : " Thou impious wretch," or " thou atheist." One whose anger is expressed in such a word, is in danger of the " Gehenna of Fire." Gehenna, in Hebrew גיא הנום or גיא בן הנום (Josue xv. 8 ; xviii. 16), meant the " Valley of Hinnom " (Introduction, p. lxiii.). In this place at the south-east of Jerusalem (Jeremias vii. 31), the idolatrous Jews formerly sacrificed their children by fire to Moloch ; and for this reason it was " polluted " by Josias (4 Kings xxiii. 10). From that time it was held in such abomination that it became a receptacle for carcasses of beasts and corpses of criminals. As these were burned on account of the warm climate, and as fires were continually kept up for the purpose, the place received its name of " Gehenna of Fire," and became to the Jews a type of the place of eternal punishment. The meaning, therefore, of our Lord's words is : " The punishment of this last offence is so much greater than that of the former, by how much the being burned alive or the being cast out after death to be burned with the carcasses of beasts exceeds the punishment of being put to death even by stoning." (See Knabenbauer, Bloomfield, Alford, and McCarthy.)

The whole of this somewhat difficult passage may be paraphrased in the following manner : " I say to you, that besides the crime of murder there are lesser offences which render you amenable to eternal justice. As there are less serious acts which expose you to the investigation of an inferior earthly tribunal and to the lighter punishments it may inflict, as there are greater offences which expose you to a trial before the Sanhedrim or great Council of the nation and to the greater punishments it awards, as there are enormous crimes which bring upon you the greatest punishment which that earthly tribunal can impose, viz., the Gehenna of Fire, so it is in the matter of offences before the tribunal of God. If any man be angry (interiorly) with his brother, he shall be amenable to the divine justice and to its rigorous punishments ; if any man allow his anger to appear in uncharitable words, he shall be still more severely punished in eternity ; if any man say a very grievously hurtful or opprobrious word to his brother, he shall receive as his award a punishment corresponding to that of those who are executed at Gehenna. How imperfect, then, is the exposition of the law given by your teachers who, in this matter, pass over internal sins, and take account of murder alone ? "

Christ, having in this manner " fulfilled " the law, or having completed it by supplying what was wanting to the perfection and correct interpretation of the fifth precept of the decalogue, now proceeded to draw an inference from the guilt and danger of anger in thought or word. He said :—

Vv. 23, 24. **If therefore thou art offering thy gift at the altar, and there thou rememberest that thy brother hath anything against thee, leave there thy gift before the altar, and go first to be reconciled to thy brother ; and then coming thou shalt offer thy gift.**

These words are very emphatic. Christ does not say merely : " If thy brother hath anything against thee, be reconciled to him." He wished to show the extreme importance of this act of fraternal charity by the words in which this command is imposed, and by stating that even should the effort at reconciliation entail the interruption of a sacrifice which is the highest act of religious worship, the effort should be made. Valerius Maximus (Lib. iii. 2) narrates with much praise that whilst Alexander was once burning incense during this religious rite, some of the fire fell on the arms of a young man who was holding the brazier, and that the young man bore the intense pain without moving, lest he should incur the guilt of interrupting the sacred ceremony. Thus, amongst the Gentiles no less than amongst the Jews, it was not permitted to break off a sacrifice once begun. Notwithstanding a precept so rigorously enforced in ordinary circumstances, our Lord teaches that it is more necessary to seek reconciliation with an offended brother than to perfect this highest exercise of divine worship, and that an unrepaired injury inflicted on our fellow-man is an impediment to the acceptability of our service before God. If, then,

the most holy act of religion must be suspended until it can
be performed in peace and charity, with how much more reason
must all other affairs be put aside when there is question of the
essential duty of brotherly love ! We here see the extent to
which Jesus wishes the righteousness of his disciples to exceed
that taught and practised by the scribes and pharisees. These
doctors maintained that, murder excepted, all sins of anger,
hatred, and reviling, were offences very slight indeed and easily
condoned if sacrifices were offered and other external rites ac-
curately observed : Christ, on the contrary, made known that
brotherly love is preferred to sacrifice, and that without brotherly
love God will neither hear our prayers nor accept the offering
which we make. A prelude to this teaching is found in the
prayer of David : " I will wash my hands among the innocent ;
and I will compass thy altar, O Lord " (Psalm xxv. 6). It
is echoed in the warning of the Apostle of the Gentiles : " If
I speak with the tongues of men and of angels, and have not
charity, I am become as sounding brass or a tinkling cymbal. And
if I should have prophecy, and should know all mysteries and
all knowledge, and if I should have all faith so that I could
remove mountains, and have not charity, I am nothing "
(1 Cor. xiii. 1, 2).

IV.—MORAL REFLECTIONS.

In the points in which it was most admired, the piety of the
pharisees had its defects. Whilst these men were careful about
their external actions, they were undisturbed about the interior
condition of their souls ; whilst they attached great importance
to minute observances, they neglected the essential precepts
of the law ; and whilst they hypocritically sought the esteem of
men, they disregarded that of God.

1. In the first place, the pharisees made virtue consist in
their external observances ; they counted for nothing the motives of their observances ; and provided they were not wanting
in the ceremonies prescribed by custom, they believed themselves irreprehensible. Thus, to the works commanded by the
law they allied the vices which the law condemned ; to many
acts of humility they joined thoughts of pride ; to frequent fasts,
the indulgence of sensual desires ; to abundant alms-deeds,
secret rapine and injustice ; to deeds of charity, contempt of
others. This disposition is diametrically opposed to the religion
of Jesus Christ, and should be far removed from the hearts of
his disciples. " God is a spirit," said our Divine Master, " and
they that adore him, must adore him in spirit and in truth "
(John iv. 24). But if we condemn the worship of the pharisees,
does not this worship sometimes find imitators amongst our-

selves? How many are there not who pride themselves on their regularity in the performance of external duties which the law commands, whilst they do not control their temper, correct their vicious inclinations, or repress their passions? How many are there not who gain for themselves a reputation for devotion by frequent visits to the temple of God, and at other times are given to vanity, self-indulgence, bitterness and anger? Let us give up this delusion which, whilst leading souls astray, entails their continuance in error by the false sense of security which it produces. We should commence by rectifying the interior, and then our external duties of all kinds will be easily fulfilled. If we banish from our heart its many vices, and fill it with the virtues in which we are deficient, we shall then apply ourselves with fruit to all the outward observances of religion.

2. Again, the justice of the pharisees consisted in minute observances and frivolous practices of devotion. Whilst acting thus they could not have been in good faith, and they justly merited the severe condemnation of Jesus Christ. This should not surprise us; but what should surprise is, that amongst ourselves we find some truly pious souls falling into a similar error, and seeking perfection where it is not to be found. Despairing of success by direct temptation to sin, the devil makes use of their love of holiness to tempt such persons, and he suggests to them means of perfection which are apparent but not real. Since they find a pleasure in exercises of piety, he suggests that these be multiplied to excess; each day new devotions are added to those already in use; the warnings of authority are disregarded; and in order to indulge the suggestion of an ill-regulated imagination, essential duties are sometimes overlooked. Virtuous souls that are carried away by a desire for perfection so laudable in itself but in such need of direction, should fear the deception of the enemy and should fear themselves. Martha placed her perfection in the multitude of things she did for Jesus; but the Divine Master disabused her of her error. It is not in doing much that we become holy; but in doing excellently well that which we do. Within the circle of our obligations we are to seek for sanctity, and there may we find it.

3. The greatest defect in the pretended piety of the pharisees was their hypocrisy. They sought not merit before God, but a reputation with the people; and this reputation they wished to gain, not by practising virtue, but by appearing to practise it. Thus they hoped that by ostentatious alms-deeds and by long prayers in the public places, they might conceal the vices to which they were abandoned, and for which they were often reproached by Jesus Christ. We must avoid this sin which is so detested by both God and men; but at the same time we

must not fail to edify our neighbour in accordance with the command of Jesus Christ : " So let your light shine before men that they may see your good works, and glorify your Father who is in heaven " (Matth. v. 16). Hypocrisy and edification differ essentially ; and it is in the intention this difference is found. The pharisee wishes by his acts to attract the admiration of the world and to gain the first place in its esteem : the just man, according to the admonition of Christ, wishes to promote the honour of God. In the one the desire of publicity is the effect of pride : in the other this desire springs from charity. The one seeks his own advantage ; the other the benefit of his neighbour and the glory of his Creator. When, therefore, the Christian is inspired to do any good work in public, he should examine the motive on which he acts ; and by the purity of his intention he should save himself from this sentence pronounced against the hypocrites : " Amen I say to you, they have received their reward " (Matth. vi. 2).

SIXTH SUNDAY AFTER PENTECOST.

I.—TEXTS.

GREEK.

MARK VIII. 1-9.

1 Ἐν ἐκείναις ταῖς ἡμέραις, πάλιν πολλοῦ ὄχλου ὄντος, καὶ μὴ ἐχόντων τί φάγωσιν, προσκαλεσάμενος τοὺς μαθητὰς αὐτοῦ, λέγει αὐτοῖς· 2 Σπλαγχνίζομαι ἐπὶ τὸν ὄχλον, ὅτι ἤδη ἡμέραις τρισὶν προσμένουσιν, καὶ οὐκ ἔχουσιν τί φάγωσιν· 3 καὶ ἐὰν ἀπολύσω αὐτοὺς νήστεις εἰς οἶκον αὐτῶν, ἐκλυθήσονται ἐν τῇ ὁδῷ· καί τινες αὐτῶν ἀπὸ μακρόθεν εἰσίν. 4 Καὶ ἀπεκρίθησαν αὐτῷ οἱ μαθηταὶ αὐτοῦ· Ὅτι πόθεν τούτους δυνήσεταί τις ὧδε χορτάσαι ἄρτων ἐπ᾽ ἐρημίας. 5 Καὶ ἠρώτα αὐτούς· Πόσους ἔχετε ἄρτους; Οἱ δὲ εἶπαν· Ἑπτά. 6 Καὶ παραγγέλλει τῷ ὄχλῳ ἀναπεσεῖν ἐπὶ τῆς γῆς· καὶ λαβὼν τοὺς ἑπτὰ ἄρτους, εὐχαριστήσας ἔκλασεν, καὶ ἐδίδου τοῖς μαθηταῖς αὐτοῦ, ἵνα παρατιθῶσιν· καὶ παρέθηκαν τῷ ὄχλῳ. 7 Καὶ εἶχαν ἰχθύδια ὀλίγα· καὶ εὐλογήσας αὐτὰ, εἶπεν καὶ ταῦτα παρατιθέναι. 8 Καὶ ἔφαγον, καὶ ἐχορτάσθησαν· καὶ ἦραν περισσεύματα κλασμάτων, ἑπτὰ σπυρίδας. 9 Ἦσαν δὲ ὡς τετρακισχίλιοι· καὶ ἀπέλυσεν αὐτούς.

VULGATE.

MARK VIII. 1-9.

1 In diebus illis iterum quum turba multa esset, nec haberent quod manducarent, convocatis discipulis, ait illis: 2 Misereor super turbam, quia ecce jam triduo sustinent me, nec habent quod manducent; 3 et si dimisero eos jejunos in domum suam, deficient in via; quidam enim ex eis de longe venerunt. 4 Et responderunt ei discipuli sui: Unde illos quis poterit hic saturare panibus in solitudine? 5 Et interrogavit eos: Quot panes habetis? Qui dixerunt: Septem. 6 Et praecepit turbae discumbere super terram. Et accipiens septem panes, gratias agens, fregit et dabat discipulis suis ut apponerent; et apposuerunt turbae. 7 Et habebant pisciculos paucos; et ipsos benedixit, et jussit apponi. 8 Et manducaverunt, et saturati sunt; et sustulerunt quod superaverat de fragmentis, septem sportas. 9 Erant autem qui manducaverant, quasi quatuor millia; et dimisit eos.

II.—ENGLISH TRANSLATION, WITH PARALLEL PASSAGE FROM ST. MATTHEW.

MARK VIII. 1-9.

¹ In those days again, when there was a great multitude and they had nothing to eat, calling his disciples together, he saith to them : ² " I have compassion on the multitude ; for behold, they have now been with me three days, and have nothing to eat ; ³ and if I shall send them away fasting to their home, they will faint on the way ; for some of them came from afar off." ⁴ And his disciples answered him : " Whence can anyone fill them with bread here in the wilderness ? " ⁵ And he asked them : " How many loaves have you ? " And they said : " Seven." ⁶ And he commanded the multitude to sit down upon the ground. And taking the seven loaves, giving thanks, he broke and gave to his disciples to set before them ; and they set them before the people. ⁷ And they had a few little fishes ; and he blessed them, and commanded them to be set before them. ⁸ And they did eat and were filled ; and they took up that which was left of the fragments, seven baskets. ⁹ And they that had eaten were about four thousand ; and he sent them away.

MATTHEW XV. 32-39.

³² And Jesus called together his disciples, and said : " I have compassion on the multitude, because they continue with me now three days, and have nothing to eat, and I will not send them away fasting, lest they faint on the way." ³³ And the disciples say unto him : " Whence then should we have so many loaves in the desert as to fill so great a multitude ? " ³⁴ And Jesus said to them : " How many loaves have you ? " But they said " Seven, and a few little fishes." ³⁵ And he commanded the multitude to sit down upon the ground. ³⁶ And taking the seven loaves and the fishes, and giving thanks, he broke and gave to his disciples, and the disciples gave to the people. ³⁷ And they did all eat and had their fill. And they took up seven baskets full of what remained of the fragments. ³⁸ And they that did eat were four thousand men beside children and women. ³⁹ And having dismissed the multitude, he went up into a boat and came into the borders of Magedan.

III.—COMBINED NARRATIVE.

In those days again, when there was a great multitude [as sembled], and they had nothing to eat, calling his disciples together, Jesus saith to them : " I have compassion on the multitude ; for behold, they have now been with me three days, and have nothing to eat ; and if I shall send them away fasting to their home, they will faint on the way ; for some of them came from afar off. I will not send them away fasting, lest they faint on the way." And his disciples answered him : " Whence then should we have so many loaves as to fill so great a multitude with bread here in the wilderness ? " And he asked them : " How many loaves have you ? " And they said : " Seven." And he commanded the multitude to sit down upon the ground. And taking the seven loaves, and giving thanks, he broke and gave to his disciples to set before them ; and the disciples set them before the people. And they had a few little fishes ; and he blessed them, and commanded them to be set before them. And they did eat, and had their fill. And they took up that which was left of the fragments, seven baskets full. And they that had eaten were about four thousand men besides children and women. And he sent them away. And having dismissed the multitude, he went up into a boat, and came into the borders of Magedan.

IV.—NOTES.

Introductory. The event which is recorded in this gospel passage by St. Mark and in the corresponding passage by St. Matthew, took place during the third year of our Lord's public life. For some time Christ had withdrawn from Judæa and Lower Galilee (Introduction, p. xxxix.) in order to avoid the increasing hatred of the pharisees and the suspicions of Herod Antipas. Wishing to pass some time in seclusion, he had gone into the neighbourhood of Tyre (Introduction, p. lii.). Then, continuing his journey, he had passed into the region of Decapolis by the Sea of Galilee (Introduction, p. xlvii.). Our Divine Redeemer during his former visit to this district (Mark vi. 32-44 ; Matth. xiv. 14-21 ; Luke ix. 11-17 ; John vi. 2-13) had for the first time multiplied the loaves and fishes ; he had healed the demoniac of Gadara or Gerasa (Introduction, p. xxxviii.), and he had given to this demoniac the unusual order to publish his cure abroad. Notwithstanding our Lord's desire for privacy, during this second visit now recorded, exceptional circumstances called for the exercise of his miraculous power in the case of the deaf and dumb man and in those of many others (Mark vii. ; Matth. xv.). Thus it happened that the half-pagan inhabitants of Decapolis who had formerly asked him to retire from their midst, now followed him in large numbers, and Christ entered on his ministry amongst a people whose changed dispositions prepared them for his preaching. Such being the state of things, St. Mark says :—

V. 1. In those days again when there was a great multitude, and they had nothing to eat, calling his disciples together, he saith to them :

By using the word, "again," the evangelist alludes to the former visit to this region when, followed into the desert by five thousand men, Christ, as has been said, miraculously supplied their corporal wants. From the parallel passage in St Matthew we learn that now the circumstances were the same; there was a large crowd in want of food, and there were no natural means of supplying that want in the desert. St. Matthew supplements St. Mark's introductory account by saying that during the period of retirement in Decapolis, our Lord "came nigh the Sea of Galilee; and going up into a mountain, he sat there. And there came to him great multitudes, having with them the dumb, the blind, the lame, the maimed, and many others. And they cast them down at his feet, and he healed them; so that the multitudes marvelled on seeing the dumb speak, the lame walk, the blind see. And they glorified the God of Israel" (Matth. xv. 29-31).

In these circumstances Christ put before his apostles the condition of the people around him, and said—

Vv. 2, 3. I have compassion on the multitude; for behold, they have now been with me three days, and have nothing to eat; and if I shall send them away fasting to their home, they will faint on the way; for some of them came from afar off.

The present meaning and the form of σπλαγχνίζομαι are found only in the middle and late Hellenic. Σπλαγνεύω is the proper form, and its meaning is, to eat the entrails of a victim after sacrifice, or to obtain auguries from these entrails. (Gould: *Gospel of St. Mark, Int. Comm.*) The expression in the text signifies literally: "In my inmost heart or bowels I feel compassion." Our Lord had called his apostles that he might bring before them and all whom they should afterwards instruct, the persevering devotion of these people and the necessity for the miracle he was about to work. Some of these persons, like the boy with the five barley loaves and the two fishes on the former occasion, might have brought some provision with them; some, probably, came without any such preparation; but now all were without anything to eat. Moreover, "some of them came from afar off," and, on being dismissed fasting, would "faint on the way." Christ showed his love by giving three days of continual instruction for the relief of their spiritual necessities, and he was now about to prove his love still further by the miracle which supplied their corporal wants.

The Divine Master's exhibition of tender feeling for such devoted followers was coldly received;

V. 4. And his disciples answered him: Whence can anyone fill them with bread here in the wilderness?

The apostles having already seen a large number fed miracu-

lously in similar straits, this answer seems strange, and to
some rationalists it appears a sufficient reason for denying the
truthfulness or accuracy of the evangelists who record it. To
understand the matter, we should remember that throughout
the pages of the gospels we have abundant evidence of the weak
faith of these same apostles, who on this account were severely
reproved by Christ (Mark viii. 17-21) even after the second
Multiplication of the Loaves. Moreover, it is to be observed
that it did not belong to them to dictate to their Divine Master
the time or the manner in which he should manifest his power.
For this cause on the present occasion as on nearly every other,
the apostles abstained from suggesting the working of a miracle ;
and it is with remarkable and modest reserve that even the
Blessed Virgin made known to her Divine Son the failing of
the wine at the marriage feast of Cana.

The apostles having confessed their inability to supply by
natural means the food that was required, Christ wished to
make still more evident to them the miraculous nature of the
act he was about to perform ;

**V. 5. And he asked them : How many loaves have you?
And they said : Seven.**

In the former miracle of this kind (Mark vi. 32-44) our Lord
had fed a larger number of men with a smaller number of loaves,
and he thus showed that his divine power was independent
of the matter on which he deigned to work. Having called
the attention of the apostles to what he was about to do, Christ
sent through them a command ($\pi\alpha\rho\alpha\gamma\gamma\epsilon\lambda\lambda\epsilon\iota$) to the multitude,
and so prepared the minds of all for the miraculous favour now
to be conferred.

The evangelist says :

**Vv. 6, 7. And he commanded the multitude to sit down upon
the ground. And taking the seven loaves, giving thanks, he
broke and gave to his disciples to set before them ; and they
set them before the people. And they had a few little fishes ;
and he blessed them, and commanded them to be set before
them.**

How truly worthy of praise are the tenderness and mercy with
which Christ helps the needy, and with which in doing so, he
dwells lovingly on the long journey and acute suffering endured
for his sake ; how adorable is the divine power which he displays in the miracle itself ; how admirable is the piety with
which he thanks his Father, the Giver of all good gifts ; how
boundless is the liberality with which he provides for all ; and
how unceasing is the care with which he instructs his apostles
and fits them for the sublime mission that awaits them ! The
apostles were to bear witness to this manifestation of divine

power, and to be the future ministers of the Bread of Life to the spiritually famished children of men. For this reason it was ordained that before their very eyes this wonder should be accomplished, and that by their very touch this miracle should be worked to satisfy the bodily wants of the followers of Christ.

The evangelist recording the teaching of St. Peter who was one of those present, thus concludes:

Vv. 8, 9. And they did eat and were filled; and they took up that which was left of the fragments, seven baskets. And they that had eaten were about four thousand; and he sent them away.

In the Greek text St. Mark carefully distinguishes between the baskets (σπυρίδας) mentioned in the history of this miracle and those others (κοφίνους) referred to in the first Multiplication of the Loaves (John vi. 13; Matth. xiv. 20; Mark vi. 43; Luke ix. 17). The nature of the difference is not known, but that there *was* a difference is certain from Mark viii. 19, 20, where in Christ's allusion to the two miracles each kind of basket is mentioned with a different name. This much is clear that on each of these occasions the evangelist calls attention to the miraculous character of the event by showing that a greater quantity of food remained after the meal than had existed before the multitude " did eat and were filled."

V.—MORAL REFLECTIONS.

The tender goodness described in the present gospel passage is an instance of the providence which rules the destinies of all creatures, and provides for all their wants. The author of the book of Wisdom says to God: " Who shall resist the strength of thy arm ? For the whole world before thee is as the least grain of the balance, and as a drop of morning dew that falleth down upon the earth. But thou hast mercy upon all, because thou canst do all things. . . . For thou lovest all things that are, and hatest none of the things which thou hast made; for thou didst not appoint or make anything, hating it. And how could anything endure, if thou wouldst not, or be preserved, if not called by thee ? But thou sparest all because they are thine, O Lord " (Wisdom xi. 22-27). This providence manifests itself throughout the universe; but it is towards man, the masterpiece of creation, that it is shown in a special manner and with a wisdom of which it is written that it " reacheth . . . from end to end mightily, and ordereth all things sweetly " (Wisdom viii. 1). God knew all our needs from eternity as he knows them now; he saw from eternity all that does or will take place in the world; and all the events that men regard as the effect of chance, were foreknown and resolved on or permitted in the eternal decrees of his providence. To all of us he says, as he said to his apostles: " Are not two sparrows sold for a farthing ? And not one of them shall fall on the ground without your Father. But the very hairs of your head are all numbered. Fear not therefore : better are you than many sparrows " (Matth. x. 29-31). Nor does he merely know our wants. He has compassion on us as he had " compassion on the multitude " ; and to each one of us he says as he said to the people of Jerusalem : " Can a woman forget her infant so as not to have pity on the son of her womb ? And if she should forget, yet will not I forget thee " (Isaias xlix. 15). Nor is this a barren compassion for our miseries. As it was in the case of the multitude in the desert, his providence anticipates our desires, and even our knowledge of our necessities.

What should be the feelings aroused within us by these reflections on the providence of God ? In the first place, knowing that " the life of man upon earth is a warfare, and his days are like the days of a hireling " (Job vii. 1), we shall look on our present miseries, crosses, or misfortunes, as the will of a good God; and we shall receive them from his hands with patient resignation. It is written : " Wait on God with patience : join thyself to God, and endure, that thy life may be increased in thy last end. Take all that shall be brought upon thee, and in thy sorrow endure, and in thy humiliation keep patience. For gold and silver are tried in the fire, but acceptable men in the furnace of humiliation " (Ecclus. ii. 3-5).

Again, remembering that we are ever in the hands of our loving Father, we shall be filled with confidence as to the future. " God," says the Apostle, " is faithful, who will not suffer you to be tempted above that which you are able to endure ; but with temptation he will make also a way of escape, that you may be able to bear it " (1 Cor. x. 13). And St. Peter adds : " The God of all grace, who hath called us unto his eternal glory in Christ Jesus, after you have suffered a little, will himself perfect you, and confirm you, and establish you " (1 Peter v. 10).

Lastly, confessing our indebtedness to God's providence for all the blessings hitherto received or still to be obtained, we shall show to him a gratitude proportioned to his gifts. Gratitude is a duty which nature itself suggests, and which our Divine Benefactor imposes. The love, indeed, which we have for ourselves, makes us love those who do us good ; and the desire of a repetition of that goodness urges us to show our appreciation of what has been done for us in the past. Now, we have received all from God ; and to his providence we are indebted for all that we possess in body and soul, in the order of nature and in the order of grace. At the sight of such indebtedness we should share in the feelings of the Royal Prophet when he said : " Bless the Lord, O my soul ; and let all that is within me bless his holy name.   Bless the Lord, O my soul, and never forget all that he has done for thee.   .   .   .   He has not dealt with us according to our sins, nor rewarded us according to our iniquities ; for according to the height of the heaven above the earth, he hath strengthened his mercy towards them that fear him " (Ps. cii. 1, 2, 10, 11).   Such thanksgiving should never be omitted by the recipient of the divine bounty.   " As the rivers," says St. Bernard, " bring back the waters of the ocean from which they come, so does gratitude refer to God the blessings he has bestowed ; and as those waters again descend to refresh the parched earth, so does our fulfilment of this duty of gratitude secure for us a fresh outpouring of heavenly favours.

SEVENTH SUNDAY AFTER PENTECOST.

I.—TEXTS.

GREEK.

MATTHÉW VII. 15-21.

¹⁵ Προσέχετε ἀπὸ τῶν ψευδοπροφη-τῶν, οἵ τινες ἔρχονται πρὸς ὑμᾶς ἐν ἐνδύμασι προβάτων, ἔσωθεν δέ εἰσιν λύκοι ἅρπαγες· ¹⁶ Ἀπὸ τῶν καρπῶν αὐτῶν ἐπιγνώσεσθε αὐτούς· μήτι συλ-λέγουσιν ἀπὸ ἀκανθῶν σταφυλὰς, ἢ ἀπὸ τριβόλων σῦκα; ¹⁷ Οὕτως πᾶν δένδρον ἀγαθὸν καρποὺς ποιεῖ καλούς· τὸ δὲ σαπρὸν δένδρον καρποὺς πονη-ροὺς ποιεῖ. ¹⁸ Οὐ δύναται δένδρον ἀγα-θὸν καρποὺς πονηροὺς ἐνεγκεῖν, οὐδὲ δένδρον σαπρὸν καρποὺς καλοὺς ποιεῖν· ¹⁹ Πᾶν δένδρον μὴ ποιοῦν καρπὸν καλὸν ἐκκόπτεται, καὶ εἰς πῦρ βάλλεται. ²⁰ Ἄρα γε ἀπὸ τῶν κηρπῶν αὐτῶν ἐπιγ-νώσεσθε αὐτούς. ²¹ Οὐ πᾶς ὁ λέγων μοι· Κύριε, Κύριε, εἰσελεύσεται εἰς τὴν βασιλείαν τῶν οὐρανῶν· ἀλλ' ὁ ποιῶν τὸ θέλημα τοῦ πατρός μου τοῦ ἐν τοῖς οὐρανοῖς.

VULGATE.

MATTHEW VII. 15-21.

¹⁵ Attendite a falsis pro-phetis, qui veniunt ad vos in vestimentis ovium, intrinsecus autem sunt lupi rapaces. ¹⁶ A fructibus eorum cognoscetis eos. Numquid colligunt de spinis uvas, aut de tribulis ficus? ¹⁷ Sic omnis arbor bona fructus bonos facit ; mala au-tem arbor malos fructus facit. ¹⁸ Non potest arbor bona malos fructus facere, neque arbor mala bonos fructus facere. ¹⁹ Omnis arbor quæ non facit fructum bonum, excidetur, et in ignem mittetur. ²⁰ Igitur ex fructibus eorum cognos-cetis eos. ²¹ Non omnis qui dicit mihi : Domine, Domine, intrabit in regnum cœlorum ; sed qui facit voluntatem Patris mei qui in cœlis est, ipse intra-bit in regnum cœlorum.

II.—ENGLISH TRANSLATION.

MATTHEW VII. 15-21.

¹⁵ " Beware of false prophets, who come to you in the clothing of sheep but inwardly are ravening wolves. ¹⁶ By their fruits you shall know them. Do men gather grapes of thorns or figs of thistles ? ¹⁷ Even so every good tree bringeth forth

good fruit, but the evil tree bringeth forth evil fruit. [18] A good tree cannot bring forth evil fruit, neither can an evil tree bring forth good fruit. [19] Every tree that bringeth not forth good fruit, shall be cut down, and shall be cast into the fire. [20] Wherefore, by their fruits you shall know them. [21] Not every one that saith to me : ' Lord, Lord,' shall enter into the kingdom of heaven ; but he that doth the will of my Father who is in heaven, he shall enter into the kingdom of heaven."

III.—NOTES.

Introductory. The gospel extract put before us by the Church to-day is taken from the conclusion of a discourse which was delivered by Christ towards the end of the first year of his public life, and which, according to a probable opinion, was repeated next year in a condensed form immediately after the selection of his apostles (Luke vi. 17-49). The discourse as recorded by St. Matthew is called the " Sermon on the Mount " from the hill in Galilee where it was spoken by our Divine Lord. Commencing with the eight " Beatitudes " which laid down the conditions of citizenship in his kingdom, Christ showed the relation of superiority in which this kingdom stood when compared with the Old Dispensation ; he next enumerated the sacrifices to be made by his subjects together with the means to be used to secure the blessings which he offered to mankind ; and he terminated with the exhortation : " Enter ye in at the narrow gate ; for wide is the gate and broad is the way that leadeth to destruction, and many there are who go in thereat. How narrow is the gate and strait is the way that leadeth to life, and few there are who find it ! "

Christ having thus pointed out the two roads by which men may journey, and having under figurative expressions warned his hearers as to the supreme dangers of error in their choice which arise from the inherent weakness of human nature, he proceeds to reveal another danger to be met with in the selection of a guide. He says :—

V. 15. Beware of false prophets, who come to you in the clothing of sheep but inwardly are ravening wolves.

The word " prophet " (Introduction, p. cli.) does not always signify one who predicts the future. The name was used by both sacred and profane writers to designate one who out of the usual course, and with extraordinary powers, was commissioned to teach the people in God's name and to preserve, reform, or restore divine worship. Similarly a " false prophet " is, strictly speaking, one who pretending to an extraordinary mission from God to secure any of these ends, opposes the work of the true and divinely appointed ministers of religion. This is strictly the meaning in the eleven passages of the New Testament where the term occurs ; but in proportion, the name may be understood as referring to all who, without any divine commission to teach, assume that office for the purpose of leading into error the simple faithful. There are, then, two classes of these impostors. Some openly attack the doctrine of Christ handed down in the Church, and seeking to substitute their own, lay claim to the miraculous powers by which the teachings of Christ were commended to the world. Of these it is written : " There shall arise false Christs and false prophets, and they shall show great signs and wonders, in so much as to deceive (if possible) even the elect " (Matth. xxiv. 24). Others there are who, making a profession of Christianity and of giving honour to Christ, put forward stealthily a doctrine which is contrary to that of the Church, or advocate a discipline subversive of hers. Such are especially the heretics and evil-doers who were here described by our Divine Lord, and who were denounced by the Apostle when he wrote : " Now the Spirit manifestly saith, that in the last times some shall depart from the faith, giving heed to spirits of error and doctrines of devils, speaking lies in hypocrisy, and having their conscience seared, forbidding to marry, to abstain from meats which God hath created to be received with thanksgiving by the faithful and by them that have known the truth " (1 Tim. iv. 1-3). It is said that these come " in the clothing of sheep," i.e., they outwardly liken themselves to the members of Christ's fold in the practice of fasting, almsdeeds, prayer, chastity, the frequentation of the sacraments and the contempt of riches and pleasures. This is their outward appearance, but within their hearts, like ravenous wolves, they conceal the intention of entrapping the simple and unsuspecting. Now, it will be asked, if these false prophets be wolves hidden under the appearance of sheep, how is their true character to be known that their baneful guidance may be rejected ? Our Lord answers :—

V. 16. **By their fruits you shall know them. Do men gather grapes of thorns, or figs of thistles ?**

As has been observed, the false prophets referred to by Christ are not merely those teachers who, laying claim to an extraordinary mission and to extraordinary powers, seek to supersede the traditional teaching of the Church, but all who without pretension to such extraordinary powers, usurp the place of the legitimately constituted pastors, and endeavour to corrupt stealthily the Church's doctrine. The " fruits " by which these impostors may be discovered, are their works, or their doctrine, or both. However much the impostor may strive to conceal his character, it at times betrays itself to the attentive observer in acts of pride, cupidity, luxury, or other vices.   This fact is implied in the frequent references of St. Paul and of St. John to the sectaries of their age.   In almost the last verses of his epistle to the Romans, St. Paul thus writes, as it were, a paraphrase of the words of Christ : " Now I beseech you, brethren, to mark them that cause dissensions and offences contrary to the doctrine which you have learned, and to avoid them.   For they that are such serve not Christ our Lord, but their own belly, and by pleasing speeches and good words, seduce the hearts of the innocent " (Rom. xvi. 17, 18).   Again the Apostle says : " There are many disobedient, vain talkers, and seducers   .   .   .   who subvert whole houses, teaching the things which they ought not, for filthy lucre's sake.   .   .   . Both their mind and their conscience are defiled.   They profess that they know God ; but in their works they deny him, being abominable, and incredulous, and to every good work reprobate " (Titus i. 10, 11, 15, 16).   Sometimes the " false prophet " is betrayed in the character of his doctrine which, on being examined, is found to be opposed to that handed down from age to age in the Church.   This is the test recommended by St. John who wrote to the faithful of his own time regarding Cerinthus and that heretic's followers : " Dearly beloved, believe not every spirit, but try the spirits if they be of God ; because many false prophets are gone out into the world.   By this is the spirit of God known : Every spirit that confesseth that Jesus Christ is come in the flesh, is of God ; and every spirit that dissolveth Jesus, is not of God " (1 John iv. 1, 2, 3). Thus the " false prophets " or seducers of the faithful are ever sure to be discovered—in some cases sooner by their acts, in others sooner by the character of their teaching.   If their works and words be carefully examined, it will be found either that their doctrine condemns their deeds, however good these may be in appearance, or else their deeds will condemn their doctrine, however true at first sight this doctrine may seem to be.   The ruling principle of human acts being the will, it would be as unnatural for a hypocrite not to show himself at last in the character of his doctrines and evil deeds, as it would be for the thistle to deceive the eye with a crop of figs, or for a thorny shrub to bring forth a harvest of grapes.

This truth is so important that our Lord generalises the statement in the following words :—

Vv. 17, 18. **Even so every good tree bringeth forth good fruit, but the evil tree bringeth forth evil fruit.   A good tree cannot bring forth evil fruit, neither can an evil tree bring forth good fruit.**

It is to be observed in the first place, that the Greek word ὄντως = " even so " does not here introduce an *a pari* argument ; but it indicates a transition from the particular instances of the preceding verse to the general statement of the law. The word ὄντως, therefore, might be more correctly rendered by : " So too," or " So in all cases." Again, it is remarked that, according to the Hebrew idiom in these two verses, the same thought is expressed first affirmatively and then negatively, to give greater force to the statement. Lastly, to avoid a mis-understanding of this text so often perverted by heretics, it should be remembered that in comparisons a complete simi-larity is not to be expected to exist between the illustration and the person or thing illustrated. " Omnis comparatio claudicat." In the present case, although to some extent there is a likeness between the terms of the comparison, there exist at the same time very great differences. Thus, trees being by nature good or bad, and this nature being invariable, the tree which is good can bear only good fruit, and that which is bad can produce only bad fruit. Again, since a tree can be but of the *one species*, it can produce only the one kind of fruit—the good tree that which is valuable, the bad tree that which is worthless. It is not so with man. Even in his fallen state he is a free agent, and, as the dispositions of a free agent need not be immutable, he becomes good or bad according to the character and tendency of his will. Now, since the will is changeable, on account of this changeableness of will one who is now good may become bad and then commit bad actions, whilst a man now bad may subsequently become good and then practise acts of virtue. Nor is this all. Since in fallen man there is a two-fold inclina-tion—that of the spirit which ever tends to virtue, and that of the flesh which ever tends to vice—a man who deserves to be called good on account of his predominant inclination to virtue, may from time to time or even at the same time act ill through the inclination of the flesh, which even in the saints is never eradicated during life though it may be more or less controlled. Although, then, the words of our Lord are *simply* and *absolutely* true of the tree itself, they are to be taken not without limitation when applied to man, of whom the tree is *only to a certain extent* an image. The meaning of our Lord's words is, therefore, that we shall never find all or most of the acts of good men to be worthy of condemnation ; but on the contrary, if not all, the greater number and the more important of their acts are begun, carried on, and completed by the indwelling Spirit of God. Similarly it must come to pass that in the greater number and in the more important of his acts, the bad man will show the falsity of his teaching or the wickedness of his heart, however much he may attempt to conceal his character under the mask of truth and virtue. As the tree by *a physical necessity* indicates its nature by its fruits, so by a certain *moral necessity* the prophet or teacher manifests his disposition of mind and heart in his words, or in his works, or in both.

Recalling to the memory of his hearers the threat uttered by his Precursor, Christ says :—

V. 19. Every tree that bringeth not forth good fruit, shall be cut down, and shall be cast into the fire.

The sentence is more emphatically expressed in the Greek text where the present tense ἐκκόπτεται, καὶ ἐις πῦρ βάλλεται = " is cut down, and is cast into the fire," denotes the certainty and perhaps the nearness of the punishment. The meaning is that, as the useless and barren tree is already doomed to the fire, so those who by the absence of good works prove themselves to be " false prophets," shall be most certainly and quickly condemned to the punishment of hell.

Our Lord had already given a criterion by which false teachers might be known : he now repeated his admonition by saying :—

V. 20. Wherefore by their fruits you shall know them.

The " false prophets," as already stated, are those who, in opposition to the ordinary spiritual guides of the people, assume the office of teachers of religion and endeavour to lead astray the unwary. Christ affirms for the second time that the means by which the character of these impostors can be discovered, is the attentive consideration of their " fruits." That, morally speaking, this means may be relied on is indicated by the use of the particle Ἄρα γε, in which ἄρα marks the *inference* and γε the *certainty*.

To secure his disciples still more against deception, Christ adds :—

V. 21. Not every one that saith to me: Lord, Lord, shall enter into the kingdom of Heaven ; but he that doth the will of my Father who is in heaven, he shall enter into the kingdom of heaven.

According to some, *e.g.*, Jansenius Gand., Knabenbauer, etc., there is here a transition in the discourse, from the punishment of hypocritical teachers (verse 19) to that of the wicked in general. This opinion does not seem probable ; for in the succeeding verses the hypocritical teachers are still the subject of our Lord's warning. The repeated invocation of the divine name indicates the fervour outwardly shown by the " false prophets," and constitutes no small part of that external appearance of sanctity by means of which they wish to be taken as members of the fold. This should not impose upon the children of the Church : certainly it will not impose on Christ who here for the first time calls God *his* Father, attributes to himself absolutely the title of Lord, declares himself the Judge of mankind, and thus by implication affirms his divine nature. It is in vain to honour God with the lips, whilst the heart is far from him (Isaias xxix. 13 ; Matth. xv. 7, 8, 9 ; Mark vii. 6, 7) ; it is in vain to know and profess the truths of revelation, if they be not put into practice (John xiii. 17) ; it is in vain to prophesy or to work miracles in the name of Christ, if the use of these gifts be not accompanied by the practical love of God which Christ came to enkindle in the hearts of men. " If I speak with the tongues of men and of angels, and have not charity, I am become as sounding brass or a tinkling cymbal. And if I should have prophecy, and should know all mysteries and all knowledge, and if I should have all faith so that I could remove mountains, and have not charity, I am nothing. And if I should distribute all my goods to feed the poor, and if I should deliver my body to be burned, and have not charity, it profiteth me nothing " (I Cor. xiii. 1-3).

IV.—MORAL REFLECTIONS.

1. In this gospel passage our Divine Lord lays down the necessity of good works, and in the concluding words declares that without these good works, the belief in his teaching or the invocation of his name gives no title to a place in his kingdom. He says : " Not every one that saith to me : Lord, Lord, shall enter into the kingdom of heaven ; but he that doth the will of my Father who is in heaven, he shall enter into the kingdom of heaven." A mere speculative or abstract belief in the truths of revelation is not sufficient ; for it is written : " In Christ Jesus neither circumcision availeth anything, nor uncircumcision, but faith that worketh by charity " (Gal. v. 6). To be justified in the sight of God, two conditions are necessary— faith and obedience : we must believe what Christ has taught, and we must obey what he has commanded. " If you know these things," said our Divine Lord, " you shall be blessed if you do them " (John xiii. 17). As Christians we know the teaching of Christ, and understand that it is only by a practical and active faith we may hope to reap the benefit of Redemption. We are aware of this, and still how many there are whose lives are at variance with their belief ! As followers of Christ we should be true copies of that divine Model ; and our acts should be a public declaration of the sanctity of our profession. Of what use is it to know the truths which Christ has revealed, if we do not fulfil what he commands ? St. James says : " Receive the ingrafted word, which is able to save your souls. But be ye doers of the word and not hearers only, deceiving your

own selves. For if a man be a hearer of the word and not a doer, he shall be compared to a man beholding his own countenance in a glass. For he beheld himself, and went his way, and presently forgot what manner of man he was " (James i. 21-24). The unhappy fate of the slothful servant who was sentenced to the same place of darkness as he who was unfaithful to his trust, clearly shows that God will include in the same condemnation the Christians who neglect to improve the talents received from their Creator, and those who abuse or misapply them. The foolish virgins were accused of no other crime than that of neglecting to supply their lamps with the oil of charity; and still they were excluded from the marriage-feast. From this we learn that the obligation is incumbent on us to exercise ourselves in the practice of Christian virtues and to edify our neighbour by the shining light of our good example.

2. What are the good works of which Christ speaks? They may be included under three heads—mortification, alms-deeds, and prayer. Under the head of mortification is included not merely a restriction in the quantity and quality of food, but also every kind of voluntary self-denial or of suffering offered to God in a spirit of penance. When in this spirit we deny ourselves a delicacy at table, some lawful pleasure, or some other gratification of our will, we do a work very pleasing to God. When from the same motive we resign ourselves to sickness, reverse of fortune and other tribulations, or when we bear patiently the hardships of labour, hunger, thirst and fatigue, we bring forth good fruit; we are doing the will of our Father who is in heaven; and we are establishing for ourselves a right to " enter into the kingdom of heaven."

Again, by alms-deeds we are to understand every service or assistance rendered to our neighbour in a spirit of charity and in order to please God. Those who have it in their power, are bound to assist the poor by alms, and that, in proportion to their means; whilst those who are destitute of the world's goods, should gain the merit of the charitable by praying for the sinner, by consoling the afflicted, by instructing the ignorant, and by performing other spiritual or corporal works of mercy. Even here on earth how rich is the reward of those who thus show their love for God by their service to his creatures, and how unspeakable is the happiness that awaits them in heaven! The words of Christ are: " Whosoever shall give to drink to one of these little ones a cup of cold water only in the name of a disciple, amen I say to you, he shall not lose his reward " (Matth. x. 42). " Give, and it shall be given to you: good measure and pressed down and shaken together and running over shall they give into your bosom. For with the same measure with which you shall mete, it shall be measured to you again " (Luke vi. 38).

Lastly, there remains the duty of prayer, without which we shall not obtain the grace which is necessary to merit by our other works. Of prayer our Divine Master says that it should be continual; but his meaning is that whilst we attend the public offices of the Church, and address ourselves to God at frequent intervals, we should direct all our actions to his honour by a pure intention, and should do them in obedience to his holy will.

The performance of these works of mortification, alms-deeds, and prayer is not above our strength; for it is written: " This commandment which I command thee this day, is not above thee, nor far off from thee. . . . But the word is very nigh unto thee, in thy mouth and in thy heart, that thou mayest do it " (Deut. xxx. 11, 14). Let us then bless that heavenly Master who requires indeed the fulfilment of his will as a condition to enter heaven, but who has made this fulfilment so easy by the assistance of his holy grace.

EIGHTH SUNDAY AFTER PENTECOST.

I.—TEXTS.

GREEK

LUKE XVI. 1-9.

¹ Ἔλεγεν δὲ καὶ πρὸς τοὺς μαθητάς· Ἄνθρωπός τις ἦν πλούσιος, ὃς εἶχεν οἰκονόμον· καὶ οὗτος διεβλήθη αἰτῷ ὡς διασκορπίζων τὰ ὑπάρχοντα αὐτοῦ. ² Καὶ φωνήσας αὐτὸν, εἶπεν αὐτῷ· Τί τοῦτο ἀκούω περὶ σοῦ; ἀπόδος τὸν λόγον τῆς οἰκονομίας σου· οὐ γὰρ δύνῃ ἔτι οἰκονομεῖν· ³ Εἶπεν δὲ ἐν ἑαυτῷ ὁ οἰκονόμος. Τί ποιήσω, ὅτι ὁ κύριός μου ἀφαιρεῖται τὴν οἰκονομίαν ἀπ᾽ ἐμοῦ; Σκάπτειν οὐκ ἰσχύω, καὶ ἐπαιτεῖν αἰσχύνομαι. ⁴ Ἔγνων τί ποιήσω, ἵνα ὅταν μετασταθῶ τῆς οἰκονομίας, δέξωνταί με εἰς τοὺς οἴκους ἑαυτῶν. ⁵ Καὶ προσκαλεσάμενος ἕνα ἕκαστον τῶν χρεωφειλετῶν τοῦ κυρίου ἑαυτοῦ, ἔλεγεν τῷ πρώτῳ· Πόσον ὀφείλεις τῷ κυρίῳ μου; ⁶ Ὁ δὲ εἶπεν· Ἑκατὸν βάτους ἐλαίου· ὁ δὲ εἶπεν αὐτῷ· Δέξαι σου τὰ γράμματα, καὶ καθίσας γράψον ταχέως πεντήκοντα. ⁷ Ἔπειτα ἑτέρῳ εἶπεν· Σὺ δὲ πόσον ὀφείλεις; ὁ δὲ εἶπεν· Ἑκατὸν κόρους σίτου. Λέγει αὐτῷ· Δέξαι σου τὰ γράμματα, καὶ γράψον ὀγδοήκοντα. ⁸ Καὶ ἐπῄνεσεν ὁ κύριος τὸν οἰκονόμον τῆς ἀδικίας, ὅτι φρονίμως ἐποίησεν. ὅτι οἱ υἱοὶ τοῦ αἰῶνος τούτου φρονιμώτεροι ὑπὲρ τοὺς υἱοὺς τοῦ φωτὸς εἰς τὴν γενεὰν τὴν ἑαυτῶν εἰσίν. ⁹ Καὶ ἐγὼ ὑμῖν λέγω· Ἑαυτοῖς ποιήσατε φίλους ἐκ τοῦ μαμωνᾶ τῆς ἀδικίας, ἵνα ὅταν ἐκλείπῃ, δέξωνται ὑμᾶς εἰς τὰς αἰωνίους σκηνάς.

VULGATE.

LUKE XVI. 1-9.

¹ Dicebat autem et ad discipulos suos : Homo quidam erat dives qui habebat villicum; et hic diffamatus est apud illum quasi dissipasset bona ipsius. ² Et vocavit illum, et ait illi : Quid hoc audio de te? Redde rationem villicationis tuæ ; jam enim non poteris villicare. ³ Ait autem villicus intra se : Quid faciam, quia dominus meus aufert a me villicationem? Fodere non valeo, mendicare erubesco. ⁴ Scio quid faciam, ut, cum amotus fuero a villicatione, recipiant me in domos suas. ⁵ Convocatis itaque singulis debitoribus domini sui, dicebat primo : Quantum debes domino meo? ⁶ At ille dixit : Centum cados olei. Dixitque illi : Accipe cautionem tuam, et sede cito, scribe quinquaginta. ⁷ Deinde alii dixit : Tu vero quantum debes? Qui ait : Centum coros tritici. Ait illi : Accipe litteras tuas, et scribe octoginta. ⁸ Et laudavit dominus villicum iniquitatis, quia prudenter fecisset ; quia filii hujus sæculi prudentiores filiis lucis in generatione sua sunt. ⁹ Et ego vobis dico : Facite vobis amicos de mammona iniquitatis, ut, cum defeceritis, recipiant vos in æterna tabernacula.

II.—ENGLISH TRANSLATION.

LUKE XVI. 1-9.

1 And he said also unto his disciples : " There was a certain rich man who had a steward ; and the same was accused unto him, that he had wasted his goods.   2 And he called him, and said unto him : ' How is it that I hear this of thee ?   Give an account of thy stewardship, for now thou canst be steward no longer.'   3 And the steward said within himself : ' What shall I do, because my lord taketh away from me the stewardship ?   To dig I am not able : to beg I am ashamed.   4 I know what I will do, that when I shall be removed from the stewardship, they may receive me into their houses.'   5 Therefore, calling together every one of his lord's debtors, he said unto the first : ' How much dost thou owe my lord ? '   6 But he said : ' A hundred barrels of oil.'   And he said unto him : ' Take thy bill, and sit down quickly, and write fifty.'   7 Then he said unto another : ' And how much dost thou owe ? '   And he said : ' A hundred quarters of wheat.' He said unto him : ' Take thy bill, and write eighty.'   8 And the lord commended the unjust steward because he had done wisely ; for the children of this world are wiser in their generation than the children of light.   9 And I say unto you : Make to yourselves friends of the mammon of iniquity, that when you fail, they may receive you into everlasting dwellings."

III.—NOTES.

Introductory. When the Jews sought to stone our Divine Lord in Jerusalem at the Feast of the Dedication of the temple (Introduction, p. clxix.) during the last year of his public life, he withdrew to Peræa beyond the Jordan, and continued to preach there until recalled to Judæa at the death of Lazarus. The present passage of the gospel is an extract from the history of this period. Besides the apostles, Christ had at this time amongst his audience a large number of publicans and sinners, who were attracted by his kindness (Luke xv. 1) ; and he had also the scribes and pharisees, who were murmuring at his warm reception of these outcasts of Jewish society (Luke xv. 2). To defend his conduct in thus dealing so gently with fallen but repentant man, he spoke to his censurers three parables—that of " the lost sheep " (Luke xv. 4-7), that of " the lost groat " (Luke xv. 8-10), and that of " the prodigal son " (Luke xv. 11-32).

Having recorded this crushing reply, the evangelist thus continues :—

V. 1. And he said also unto his disciples, etc.

The present instruction was given in the presence of the pharisees (see v. 14), but was intended for Christ's followers including the publicans and sinners. In it, whilst recalling to their memory the foresight they might have exercised in providing for their temporal welfare, their Divine Master exhorted them to be no less diligent in securing their eternal happiness by using the means of salvation mercifully placed within their reach.

Christ's teaching took the form of a parable, and the parable was this:—

There was a certain rich man who had a steward ; and the same was accused unto him, that he had wasted his goods.

The Greek word οἰκονόμος = *an agent*, or *a manager of a master's household or goods*, is more correctly rendered by the English *steward* in the wide sense, than by the Vulgate *villicus* which means *an overseer of a farm* or a steward in the strict sense. The office of steward was often filled by a slave (Introduction, pp. lxxvi., lxxvii.) ; but in this instance the position is represented as being held by a freeman subject to dismissal from the establishment. The duties of such persons were formerly confined to the charge of *the house* and subsequently included the care of *the whole property*. The accusation against the steward in the parable was not only " that he had wasted " but also that he was still wasting (ὡς διασκορπίζων) his master's goods. For the purpose of the parable it does not matter in what spirit the accusation was made. The verb διεβλήθη does not *necessarily* imply a wrongful or false charge, but it does *generally* signify a malicious one. That the steward was really guilty, seems manifest from his own subsequent conduct as well as from the settled determination of his master to dismiss him.

This master having confided to his servant a position of great trust, and having had his confidence abused was now naturally indignant with him ;

V. 2. And he called him, and said unto him : How is it that I hear this of thee ? Give an account of thy stewardship ; for now thou canst be steward no longer.

In both parts of this verse the translation of the Greek is misleading. In the first part the master does not ask : " How is it that I hear this of thee ? " but " What is this that I hear of thee ? " He asks the steward to reflect on the serious nature of the offence with which he was charged and of which he had probably been convicted. In the second part the master does not say : " Give *an* account of thy stewardship " but " give up *the* account of thy stewardship " (ἀπόδος τὸν λόγον τῆς οἰκονομίας σου). It is not an apology or defence of his conduct that is required from the steward, as would appear from the English version, but what would now be called the accounts or office books. As has been suggested, the official's conduct had been previously inquired into ; and his dishonesty having been proved, he is now about to be dismissed.

The sentence " Thou canst be steward no longer " was absolute ; it excluded all hope of similar employment with the present or any other master ;

V. 3. **And the steward said within himself: What shall I do, because my lord taketh away from me the stewardship? To dig I am not able : to beg I am ashamed.**

The verb " to dig " (Greek, $\sigma\kappa\acute{a}\pi\tau\epsilon\iota\nu$) here signifies all hard, manual labour. For this the steward is *unfitted* ($o\grave{v}\kappa\ i\sigma\chi\acute{v}\omega = I$ *am not strong enough*). The verb $\dot{\epsilon}\pi a\iota\tau\epsilon\hat{\iota}\nu$ signifies to " ask again and again," " to ask importunately," and so, " to beg for alms " (*Int. Comm.*). As one hitherto occupying an honourable position, the steward is ashamed to adopt this means of subsistence. In his feelings are reflected these thoughts of Ecclesiasticus : " My son, in thy lifetime be not indigent ; for it is better to die than to want. The life of him that looketh toward another man's table is not to be counted a life ; for he feedeth his soul with another man's meat. . . . Begging will be sweet in the mouth of the unwise ; but in his belly there shall burn a fire " (Ecclus. xl. 29-32).

The steward while dissipating his master's property, had not been laying up a store even for himself ; and reflecting, as men do in such circumstances, he at first saw no prospect but that of helpless want or disgraceful mendicancy. After further consideration the outlook brightened, and he said :—

V. 4. **I know what I will do, that when I shall be removed from the stewardship, they may receive me into their houses.**

It is remarked (see Plummer, *Int. Comm.*, and Farrar) that the use of the aorist $\check{\epsilon}\gamma\nu\omega\nu$ indicates the suddenness of the idea, and is equivalent to " I know now," " I have just hit on a plan." The reader learns from the following verses the nature of the plan thus hit on, and the persons through whom it was to be worked out. The steward determined that while still in charge of the accounts, he would remit a portion of the debts due to his master, so that the persons thus freed from their obligations might remember his good services and afford him shelter.

In executing this scheme no time was to be lost, and

V. 5. **Therefore, calling together every one of his lord's debtors, he said unto the first : How much dost thou owe my lord?**

Christ describes the arrangement made by the steward with only two of the debtors ; but all were " called together " that, all being implicated, no one might inform on the rest. In the expression $\check{\epsilon}\nu a\ \check{\epsilon}\kappa a\sigma\tau o\nu\ \tau\hat{\omega}\nu\ \chi\rho\epsilon\omega\phi\epsilon\iota\lambda\epsilon\tau\hat{\omega}\nu\ \tauo\hat{\nu}\ \kappa\nu\rho\acute{\iota}o\nu\ \dot{\epsilon}a\nu\tauo\hat{\nu} =$

"each one of *his own* lord's debtors," the entire absence of fidelity and principle is emphatically noted. It is not certain whether these debtors had bought the goods about to be mentioned, or had contracted to pay the amount as rent. The latter supposition is the more probable. Since in the East payments, especially of rent, are made in kind, the steward had ample opportunity to appropriate the goods of his master. On former occasions, he received from the debtors more than he entered in his accounts : this time, by reducing the amount payable he makes that amount tally with the amount entered in the bond. Thus he seeks to gain favour with the debtors by a partial remission of their debt, and tries at the same time to conceal the number of his manifest frauds in the past. (See Farrar and *Int. Comm.*)

Although the original or duplicate copies of the bonds were kept by the steward, each debtor is questioned as to his obligation, so that the magnitude of the remission might be adverted to in each case. The first, then, was questioned as to what he owed ;

Vv. 6, 7. But he said : A hundred barrels of oil. And he said unto him : Take thy bill, and sit down quickly, and write fifty. Then he said unto another : And how much dost thou owe ? And he said : A hundred quarters of wheat. He said unto him : Take thy bill and write eighty.

"The debts over which the steward variously disposed, according as he wished to gain more or less favour, were considerable. In the first case they are stated as 'a hundred *Bath* (barrels) of oil,' in the second as 'a hundred *Cor* (quarters) of wheat.' In regard to these quantities we have the preliminary difficulty, that three kinds of measurement were in use in Palestine—that of the 'Wilderness,' or the original Mosaic ; that of 'Jerusalem,' which was more than a fifth larger ; and that of Sepphoris, probably the common Galilean measurement, which, in turn, was more than a fifth larger than the Jerusalem measure. To be more precise, one Galilean was equal to $\frac{3}{2}$ 'Wilderness' measures. Assuming the measurement to have been the Galilean, one *Bath* (barrel) would have been equal to an Attic *Metrêtês*, or, about 39 *litres*. On the other hand, the so-called 'Wilderness' measurement would correspond with the Roman measures, and, in that case, the *Bath* (barrel) would be the same as the *Amphora*, or amount to a little less than 26 *litres*. The latter is the measurement adopted by Josephus. In the parable, the first debtor was owing 100 of these '*Bath*' (barrels), or, according to the Galilean measurement, about 3,900 *litres* of oil (853 gallons and 1 pint) " (Edersheim : *Life and Times of Jesus the Messiah*, vol. ii., pp. 268, 269). The value of this was very probably about £10, and the remission of the debt about £5. The second debtor owed "a hundred quarters of wheat." The "quarter" (Heb. כֹּר and Gr. κόρος) was the largest Hebrew dry measure and was equal to 10 *Bath* or barrels. Following the Galilean computation and taking the average price of wheat at that time, the second debt would amount to something between £100 and £125, and the remission given by the steward would be one between £20 and £25. At first sight, the sums in these cases appear small ; but they were not really so. Account being taken of the cost of living and of labour, the value of money in Palestine at the time of our Lord was at least five times as great as it is here at present.

The materials for writing amongst the Jews were of various kinds, but those commonly in use, especially for acknowledgment of debts, were tablets of wood covered with wax, together with a *stylus* generally of iron. In documents prepared with these materials, it would, of course, have been easy to erase the Hebrew letters which were used as numerals. Still, inasmuch as the least suspicion of an erasure which was not explained and certified would deprive the document of all legal value, it is probable that the debtors were called upon in this case to draw up new bonds and not merely to change the numbers in the old ones. (See Edersheim : *Life and Times of Jesus the Messiah*, vol. ii., pp. 269-273.)

Without indicating the manner in which the fraud was discovered, Christ thus passes on to describe what followed on the discovery :—

V. 8. And the lord commended the unjust steward, because he had done wisely; for the children of this world are wiser in their generation than the children of light.

That the words of this verse are those of our Lord himself and not an observation of the evangelist, is clear from the fact that without any introductory clause the next verse commences with Christ's application of the parable : " And I say to you." It is to be understood in the first place, that " the lord " is the " rich man," the master of the steward. Again, the name " the steward of injustice " (τὸν οἰκονόμον τῆς ἀδικίας) is a He-braism meaning " the unjust steward," as in the next verse the words " of the mammon of iniquity " (τὸν μαμωνᾶ τῆς ἀδικίας) are equivalent to " of the iniquitous mammon." Still further, the word φρονίμως means " cunningly " or " cleverly," and not " wisely "—a term used always in a higher sense. The word υἱος = *son* or *child* is used in the Scripture to denote a great likeness, or intimate connection. Hence the " children of this world " and " the children of light " are respectively those who, adopting the habits and manners of the world of darkness, become like to it, and those who, obeying in all things the divine will manifested to them by reason and revelation, become like to that God whom they serve and love as their Father. Lastly, the clause " in their generation," or more correctly, " unto their own generation " (Gr., εἰς τὴν γενεὰν τὴν ἑαυτῶν) signifies most probably " for their own time." The meaning of the whole sentence is then : " The master praised not the fraud of the steward, but his cleverness and foresight in making use of the present opportunity to provide for the future." The master had reason to bestow this praise ; because those who care only for this world, show more prudence in securing their well-being for their time on earth, than the spiritually-minded do in safe-guarding their interests for eternity.

In the first application of the parable which is here implicitly given, the injustice of the steward is not excused, much less is it commended. The conclusion is merely drawn that if he and such as he wickedly and cunningly use their opportunity to provide for their future needs in this world, the Christian should prudently and holily make use of his earthly goods and of his other present means to secure the eternal well-being for which he is destined. Not satisfied with thus implying the lesson to be learned from the provident foresight of worldlings, Christ ex-plicitly lays down this lesson in the following words :—

V. 9. And I say unto you : Make to yourselves friends of the mammon of iniquity, that when you shall fail, they may receive you into everlasting dwellings.

It has already been stated that by a Hebraism " the mammon of iniquity " is put for " iniquitous mammon." Mammon is so described because the character of the acts by which sometimes men acquire it, or the wicked manner in which men spend it, is supposed by metonymy to adhere to the thing itself. It is almost certain that the reading of the Greek text should be not ἐκλείπητε in the plural, but ἐκλείπῃ in the singular, and that in our translation we should have not " when you shall fail," etc., but " when it (the mammon of iniquity) shall fail," etc. The " failure " referred to occurs at death, when the stewardship of each one ceases, and when the goods that a man possesses, or rather administers, pass into other hands. St. Paul says : " We brought nothing into this world, and certainly we can carry nothing out " (1 Tim. vi. 7). Laying down the moral applica-tion of the preceding story in the words : " I say to you," em-phatically marking the importance of this application by the position of the pronoun (ἑαυτοῖς ποιήσατε = " Make unto your-selves "), and contrasting the precarious hospitality looked for-ward to by the steward with the permanent abode in heaven, Christ admonishes his disciples so to use their earthly goods that at death they will have secured " friends " to help them in their necessity. These " friends " are the poor. Relieved by the alms of the rich, the poor repay the debt thus contracted, when in this life they offer to God prayers and the merits of good works, and in the next continuously intercede that their benefactors may obtain a happy death, a release from the pains of purgatory, and a speedy admission into the " everlasting dwellings " of the kingdom of heaven. Nor is anything lost if the *immediate* objects of our alms-deeds prove forgetful, indifferent, ungrateful, or unworthy. The *ultimate* object of true charity is Jesus Christ, who accepts as offered to himself whatever is done for any member of his mystical body. It is he who made the promise : " Amen I say to you, as long as you did it to one of these my least brethren, you did it to me " (Matth. xxv. 40). The benediction pronounced by the Psalmist on him who compassionates the sufferings of Christ himself, may then be confidently expected by all who compassionately devote their goods to alleviate the sufferings of Christ's poor. " Blessed is he that understandeth concerning the needy and the poor : the Lord will deliver him in the evil day " (Psalm xl. 2).

IV.—MORAL REFLECTIONS.

As the " rich man " of the parable is God, and as each of us is represented by " the steward," it is of importance that we know well the relation in which we stand to the Divine Being and that we reflect on the duties which are founded on this relation.

1. God being the Creator and preserver of all creatures, these belong to him entirely, exclusively, and on every title. Nothing which in our vanity we imagine we possess, is really ours ; and an absolute indigence is all we can call our own. That which the Apostle says of the gifts of grace is true of all our goods and even of ourselves. " What hast thou that thou hast not received ? And if thou hast received, why dost thou glory, as if thou hadst not received it ? " (1 Cor. iv. 7). God gave us our souls that we might give them back to him one day adorned with virtues, and our bodies that we might preserve them pure and fit to be his living temples. St. Paul says : " We brought nothing into this world, and certainly we can carry nothing out " (1 Tim. vi. 7). All the goods we enjoy in the interval between our birth and our death are held only temporarily, precariously, and after the manner of a trust. God does not give them absolutely, but lends them to us ; he does not abandon them but confides them to our care ; by an inalienable and imprescriptible right he retains the dominion of them in his hands ; he is the sole proprietor of them, whilst we are but the stewards charged

with the administration of them and accountable for that administration. This being understood, if we but consider the duty of a steward towards his master, we shall have the measure of our duty towards God in the management of all that he has committed to our keeping. We well know that a steward can dispose of his master's goods only in accordance with that master's order; that he can rule only according to the master's intentions; that he can apply nothing to any use of which the master may disapprove; and that if with his master's goods he serves his own interest or pleasure, he is an unfaithful servant and must submit to the punishment which it may please his master to inflict. Are we then in the condition of the servant mentioned in the parable? Does our conscience accuse us of having squandered or injured our heavenly Master's property, or of having devoted it to a use different from that for which it was intended? The powers of our body—our health and strength—were given that we might be able to carry on uninterruptedly the service of God; and have we not frequently used them to offend him? The endowments of our mind—our talents and our knowledge—while promoting our own sanctification, should have contributed to the edification of our neighbour; and must we not confess that instead they have been employed for vanity and disedification? The goods of fortune conferred by Providence in order that we might be the instruments of divine beneficence to the poor, have perhaps been spent in ministering to our luxury, our pleasure, or our passions. The interior and exterior graces, which should have sufficed to withdraw us from sin and to confirm us in virtue, have been perhaps neglected, rejected, and despised.

2. Like the steward in the parable we shall have one day to account for our stewardship. Imitating, then, the foresight of this man, let us provide for the future; let the gifts which God bestows on us be henceforth employed in God's service; and let that which has hitherto been to us "the mammon of iniquity," become now for us a treasure of salvation. By our material alms to the poor, by our spiritual alms of prayer for the sinner, by our consolation given to the afflicted, by our instruction of the ignorant, in a word, by our practice of the spiritual and corporal works of mercy, we shall satisfy for our past offences and secure for ourselves intercessors who, on our removal from the stewardship at death, will receive us "into everlasting dwellings."

NINTH SUNDAY AFTER PENTECOST.

I.—TEXTS.

GREEK.

LUKE XIX. 41-47.

⁴¹ Καὶ ὡς ἤγγισεν, ἰδὼν τὴν πόλιν, ἔκλαυσεν ἐπ᾽ αὐτήν, λέγων· ὅτι Εἰ ἔγνως ἐν τῇ ἡμέρᾳ ταύτῃ καὶ σὺ τὰ πρὸς εἰρήνην· νῦν δὲ ἐκρύβη ἀπὸ ὀφθαλμῶν σου· ⁴³ Ὅτι ἥξουσιν ἡμέραι ἐπὶ σέ, καὶ περιβαλοῦσιν οἱ ἐχθροί σου χάρακά σοι, καὶ περικυκλώσουσί σε, καὶ συνέξουσίν σε πάντοθεν, ⁴⁴ καὶ ἐδαφιοῦσίν σε, καὶ τὰ τέκνα σου ἐν σοί· καὶ οὐκ ἀφήσουσιν λίθον ἐπὶ λίθον ἐν σοί, ἀνθ᾽ ὧν οὐκ ἔγνως τὸν καιρὸν τῆς ἐπισκοπῆς σου. ⁴⁵ Καὶ εἰσελθὼν εἰς τὸ ἱερὸν, ἤρξατο ἐκβάλλειν τοὺς πωλοῦντας, λέγων αὐτοῖς· Γέγραπται· ⁴⁶ Καὶ ἔσται ὁ οἶκός μου οἶκος προσευχῆς· ὑμεῖς δὲ αὐτὸν ἐποιήσατε σπήλαιον λῃστῶν. ⁴⁷ Καὶ ἦν διδάσκων τὸ καθ᾽ ἡμέραν ἐν τῷ ἱερῷ·

VULGATE.

LUKE XIX. 41-47.

⁴¹ Et ut appropinquavit, videns civitatem, flevit super illam, dicens : ⁴² Quia si cognovisses et tu, et quidem in hac die tua, quæ ad pacem tibi ; nunc autem abscondita sunt ab oculis tuis. ⁴³ Quia venient dies in te, et circumdabunt te inimici tui vallo, et circumdabunt te, et coangustabunt te undique, ⁴⁴ et ad terram prosternent te et filios tuos qui in te sunt, et non relinquent in te lapidem super lapidem, eo quod non cognoveris tempus visitationis tuæ. ⁴⁵ Et ingressus in templum, cœpit ejicere vendentes in illo et ementes, ⁴⁶ dicens illis : Scriptum est : Quia domus mea domus orationis est ; vos autem fecistis illam speluncam latronum. ⁴⁷ Et erat docens quotidie in templo.

II.—ENGLISH TRANSLATION WITH PARALLEL PASSAGES FROM SS. MATTHEW AND MARK.

LUKE XIX. 41-47.

⁴¹ And when he drew near, seeing the city, he wept over it, saying : ⁴² "If thou also hadst known, and that in this thy day, the things that are to thy peace ; but now they are hidden

from thy eyes. ⁴³ For days shall come upon thee, and thy enemies shall cast a trench about thee, and compass thee round, and straiten thee on every side, ⁴⁴ and beat thee flat to the ground and thy children who are in thee and they shall not leave in thee a stone upon a stone ; because thou hast not known the time of thy visitation."

⁴⁵ And entering into the temple, he began to cast out them that sold therein and them that bought, ⁴⁶ saying to them : " It is written : *My house is the house of prayer.   But you have made it a den of thieves.*"   ⁴⁷ And he was teaching daily in the temple.

MATTHEW XXI. 10-19.

¹⁰ And when he was come into Jerusalem, the whole city was moved, saying : " Who is this ? "   ¹¹ And the people said : " This is Jesus the prophet, from Nazareth of Galilee."

¹² And Jesus went into the temple of God, and cast out all them that sold and bought in the temple, and overthrew the tables of the money changers and the chairs of them that sold doves. ¹³ And he saith to them : " It is written : *My house shall be called the house of prayer ; but you have made it a den of thieves.*"   ¹⁴ And the blind and the lame came to him in the temple ; and he healed them.   ¹⁵ And the chief-priests and scribes, seeing the wonderful things that he did, and the children crying in the temple and saying : *Hosanna to the son of David*, were moved with indignation, ¹⁶ and said to him : " Hearest thou what these say ? "   And Jesus said to them : " Yea, have you never read : *Out of the mouth of infants and of sucklings thou hast perfected praise ?* "   ¹⁷ And leaving them, he went out of the city to Bethany, and remained there.

¹⁸ And in the morning, returning into the city, he was hungry. ¹⁹ And seeing a certain fig-tree by the wayside, he came to it, and found nothing on it but leaves only, and he saith to it : " May no fruit grow on thee henceforward for ever."   And immediately the fig-tree withered away.

MARK XI. 11-19.

¹¹ And he entered into Jerusalem, into the temple ; and having viewed all things round about, when now the even-tide was come, he went out to Bethany with the twelve.

¹² And the next day when he came out from Bethany, he was hungry.   ¹³ And when he had seen afar off a fig-tree having leaves, he came if perhaps he might find any thing on it.   And when he was come to it, he found nothing but leaves ; for it was not the time for figs.   ¹⁴ And answering he said to it : " May no man eat fruit of thee hereafter any more for ever."   And his disciples heard it.

¹⁵ And they came to Jerusalem. And when he had entered into the temple, he began to cast out them that sold and bought in the temple, and overthrew the tables of the money changers and the chairs of them that sold doves. ¹⁶ And he suffered not that any man should carry a vessel through the temple. ¹⁷ And he taught, saying to them : " Is it not written, *My house shall be called the house of prayer to all nations ; but you have made it a den of thieves* ? " ¹⁸ Hearing this, the chief-priests and the scribes sought how they might destroy him ; for they feared him, because the whole multitude was astonished at his teaching. ¹⁹ And when evening was come, he went forth out of the city.

LUKE XIX. 47, 48.

⁴⁷ But the chief-priests and the scribes and the rulers of the people sought to destroy him. ⁴⁸ And they found not what to do to him ; because all the people were very attentive to hear him.

III.—COMBINED NARRATIVE.

And when he drew near, seeing the city, he wept over it, saying : " If thou hadst known, and that in this thy day, the things that are to thy peace ; but now they are hidden from thy eyes. For days shall come upon thee, and thy enemies shall cast a trench about thee, and compass thee around, and straiten thee on every side, and beat thee flat to the ground and thy children who are in thee ; and they shall not leave in thee a stone upon a stone ; because thou hast not known the day of thy visitation." And he entered into Jerusalem, into the temple ; and when he was come into Jerusalem, the whole city was moved, saying : " Who is this ? " And the people said : " This is Jesus the prophet, from Nazareth of Galilee." And the blind and the lame came to him in the temple ; and he healed them. And the chief-priests and the scribes seeing the wonderful things that he did, and the children crying in the temple and saying : " Hosanna to the son of David," were moved with indignation, and said to him : " Hearest thou what these say ? " And Jesus said to them : " Yea, have you never read : *Out of the mouths of infants and of sucklings thou hast perfected praise* ? " And having viewed all things round about, when now the even-tide was come, leaving them, he went out of the city to Bethany with the twelve, and remained there.

And the next day in the morning when they came out of Bethany, returning into the city, he was hungry. And when he had seen afar off a certain fig-tree by the way-side having leaves, he came to it, if perhaps he might find anything on it. And when he had come to it, he found nothing on it but leaves only ; for it was not the time for figs.   And answering, he said to it : " May no man eat fruit of thee hereafter any more for ever.   May no fruit grow on thee henceforward for ever."   And his disciples heard it.   And immediately the fig-tree withered away.

And they came to Jerusalem.   And Jesus went into the temple of God.   And when he had entered into the temple, he began to cast out all them that sold therein and them that bought, and overthrew the tables of the money changers and the chairs of them that sold doves.   And he suffered not that any man should carry a vessel through the temple.   And he taught, saying to them : " Is it not written : *My house shall be called the house of prayer to all nations ; but you have made it a den of thieves* ? "   Hearing this, the chief-priests and the scribes and the rulers of the people sought how they might destroy him.   And they found not what to do to him ; for they feared him, because all the people were very attentive to hear him, [and] the whole multitude was astonished at his teaching.   And when evening was come, he went forth out of the city.   And he was teaching daily in the temple.

IV.—NOTES.

Introductory.   This extract is taken from the history of the few days before the Passion—a history recorded with more or less detail by each of the four evangelists.   From a comparison of these sacred writers it is seen that the two events here brought together by St. Luke—the weeping over Jerusalem and the expulsion of the traders from the temple—occurred respectively on the first and on the second day of the last week of our Lord's life on earth.   When after the resurrection of Lazarus the Council (Introduction, pp. cvi., cvii.) had determined on Christ's death, our Redeemer was obliged to leave Judæa and he dwelt for some time secretly at Ephrem near the desert (John xi. 54).   As the Pasch approached, " the chief-priests and the pharisees had given a commandment that if any man knew where he was, he should tell, that they might apprehend him " (John xi. 56).   Notwithstanding this, now that his time was at hand, Christ returned to accomplish his sacrifice ; but to show that " he was offered because it was his own will " (Isaias liii. 7), he wished first to receive the public homage of that people by whom he was soon to be put to death.   According to St. John he arrived at Bethany (Introduction, p. lxiv.) on Mount Olivet six days before the Pasch and supped there with his friends Lazarus, Martha, and Mary.   The next morning he set out on his triumphal march from Bethany to Jerusalem, accompanied on his way by his apostles and an immense crowd who had come up to celebrate the feast in the Holy City.   This crowd preceded and followed him, holding palm branches in their hands, casting their garments before him, and saluting him with Hosannas as the son of David, the long-expected Messiah.

Continuing his account, St. Luke fills in the record of the other evangelists with a description of the touching scene which forms the chief matter of the present passage. He says of Christ :—

V. 41. **And when he drew near, seeing the city, he wept over it, saying : etc.**

On the road over which Jesus passed there is a point on the side of Mount Olivet where, bathed in the glorious Eastern sunshine, Jerusalem came at once in sight with its majestic marble and gilded temple, its splendid palaces, and its numerous population much increased by the strangers come up for the approaching solemnity. Our Lord was not moved by the acclamations of the crowd nor by the beauty of the scene before him. He was filled with sorrow on thinking of the incurable blindness of the people who in a few days, rejecting him their only hope, would fill up the measure of their iniquity by the crime of deicide, and would bring down upon themselves the most fearful chastisement ever inflicted on a nation. The intense grief of Christ at this foreknowledge is indicated by the Greek verb which is not ἐδάκρυσεν implying a *silent shedding of tears*, but ἔκλαυσεν which signifies a *weeping aloud with cries and sobs*. It is remarked that our Lord did neither of these during his Agony or Passion. His tears, therefore, were now caused not by the prospect of the sufferings he was soon to endure, but by the prospect of the misfortunes of his persecutors themselves ; and it is expressly stated that, " seeing the city, he wept *over it*."

This is still further shown by the following words of Christ :—

V. 42. **If thou also hadst known, and that in this thy day, the things that are to thy peace ; but now they are hidden from thy eyes.**

" If thou also hadst known " is equivalent to " If thou, too, hadst known as I do." The contrast is not between the culpable ignorance of the inhabitants of Jerusalem and the knowledge of the crowd who were receiving him in triumph ; for many members of this crowd belonged to the city. Christ contrasts the culpable ignorance of that city with the knowledge which he possessed and which he had desired to communicate to it. This was a knowledge of his Messianic character and of the danger of rejecting one who came to them in the name of the Lord. Such truths were to their " peace," that is, according to the Hebrew idiom, it was essential to their spiritual and temporal well-being to admit these truths ; but, having been once offered to them, this revelation was now denied them or hidden from their eyes.

Although the clauses, taken separately, are easily understood, still when combined as in this verse, they cause much difficulty to commentators.   Some consider that the sentence is elliptical, as happens in the discourse of those who speak under strong emotion, and that our Lord, whilst giving expression to the condition : " If thou hadst known," etc., omits the consequent clause by a figure called aposiopesis.   These writers are not very successful in their attempts to supply the omission.   One of the best of these attempts gives the following as the meaning : " If thou hadst known even this very day in the midst of thy triumph what is really conducive to thy well-being, thou also wouldst weep as I do over the fate in store for thee because of the sinful blindness of thy children."   To other interpreters it appears better to render the Greek εἰ not by si = if but by utinam = would that.   This use of εἰ for εἴθε is sometimes found in the LXX version and in the classical writers.   (See Josue vii. 7 ; Job x. 4 ; Isaias xlviii. 18 ; Iliad A. 135.   Cf. "O mihi praeteritos referat si Jupiter annos." Virgil : Aen. viii. 560.) Thus taking the words as the expression of a wish, the meaning is : "Would that thou also hadst known as I do, what is conducive and necessary to thy well-being, and that, even in this thy last opportunity for repentance !   But the reverse is the case ; since now with terrible consequences for thee these things are hidden from thy eyes."

If the verse be understood in the first way just indicated, our Lord next proceeds to explain why the city should weep with him ; if it be understood in the second way, he is about to give a reason for wishing that the inhabitants of Jerusalem had that necessary spiritual knowledge which, in consequence of their sins, is now denied them.   He says :—

V. 43. **For days shall come upon thee, and thy enemies shall cast a trench about thee, and compass thee around, and straiten thee on every side.**

In the Greek text there is no article prefixed to ἡμέραι = " days." Especially when without the article, this word is sometimes used like the Latin " tempora " to signify periods of misfortune ; and such is the meaning here required by the usual punctuation of the English translation.   The punctuation being amended and " days " being taken in the ordinary sense, the clause : " and thy enemies," etc., is a Hebrism for " in which thy enemies," etc.   Again, the word χάραξ meant at first, a single pointed stake or pole (vallus) ; then, a palisade or fence constructed with such stakes (vallum) ; and lastly, a palisaded mound (vallum agger).   From Isaias xxix. 1-3 in the LXX version, to which our Lord alludes, it is clear that the word has in this passage the last mentioned meaning, and that it should not be rendered " vallum " and " trench " as in the Vulgate and in the English translation respectively. When a town could not easily be taken by storm, it was customary to raise around it a mound of earth protected by a palisade. This secured the besiegers against sudden attacks from the besieged, and cut off communication with the country outside.

The fulfilment of this prophecy is described by Josephus (B. J., v. 6, 2, etc.), and in the same order of details as is here given. He says that the Roman legions under Titus began the siege by raising mounds against what seemed to be the weakest part of the wall, and by covering these with stakes and branches of trees. When the Jews destroyed the mounds, Titus proceeded to blockade the city by surrounding the place with a wall about five miles long, and by raising four palisaded mounds constructed like the first. The result was a complete isolation of the inhabitants and a famine of a fearful character.

Christ having described the operations of the future siege, foretold in the following verse what was to happen on the taking of the city :—

V. 44. And thy enemies shall beat thee flat to the ground and thy children who are in thee, and they shall not leave in thee a stone upon a stone ; because thou hast not known the time of thy visitation.

In the first part of this verse there is probably an example of the figure called syllepsis. The Greek verb ἐδαφίζειν signifies both to " lay flat with the ground " (A. V.), and to " dash down against the ground " (Rh. V.). Both senses appear to be intended here. In the former meaning the verb describes the destruction of the material buildings of the city, and in the latter the fate of the inhabitants. As to the buildings Josephus (B. J., vii. 11) says : " The whole circuit of the city was so thoroughly levelled and dug up, that no one visiting it would believe it had ever been inhabited." To show the greatness of the obstacles overcome in the siege, the Romans left a part of the wall and a few towers. These were overturned in the reign of Hadrian, after a rebellion of the Jews under Barcochba ; and in the time of Julian the Apostate, even the foundations of the temple were removed. On being rebuilt the city no longer occupied its ancient position ; and the site of even the chief places can only be guessed at with the help of the works of Josephus.

Not less remarkable was the lot of the people. As the siege took place when the Jews were assembled for the celebration of the Pasch, the number present in Jerusalem was about 3,000,000. According to Josephus (B. J., vi. 9, 3) 1,100,000 of these lost their lives by famine or the sword ; and 100,000 were sold as slaves or carried away to build the Coliseum in Rome. In the siege of the rebuilt city under Hadrian 580,000 lost their lives by the sword, and a larger number by famine and pestilence. The name of the place was changed to Aelia until the time of Constantine the Great ; and the Jews were not permitted to enter, or even to approach, the place before the middle of the fourth century. (See Smith s.v.)

Our Lord indicates the cause of this terrible chastisement when he adds : " Because thou hast not known the time of thy visitation." The word " visitation " may mean either a visit of mercy or one of punishment. Explained by the context, the term is here to be understood in the former sense ; and Christ declares that the Jews merited their punishment, because they did not know, or rather did not *appreciate*, the time, *i.e.*, the *favourable opportunity* (καιρὸν) when by the ministry of his Son, God in his mercy called them to repentance.

Having, in common with SS. Matthew and Mark, described the triumphal procession towards Jerusalem, and having filled in the accounts of the other evangelists with the pathetic history of Christ's weeping over the terrible fate in store for its inhabitants, St. Luke does not record our Lord's entry into the city nor his visit to the temple on this occasion. The visit of Christ to the temple which was his palace as the Son of God, had been already described by SS. Matthew and Mark. From these latter evangelists the reader learns the commotion (the verb in the original text indicates a convulsion or shaking as by an earthquake) caused by Christ's appearance in Jerusalem ; the miracles which he worked in the temple ; the indignation shown by the chief-priests and scribes at the popular joy ; and the departure to Bethany on the approach of night (see Parallel Passages and Combined Narrative).

The same two sacred writers mention the return to the city on the following morning, and the cursing of the barren fig-tree by the way. At this point the three evangelists continue their narrative, and St. Luke with greater brevity than the others proceeds to give the following account of the second cleansing of the temple :—

V. 45. **And entering into the temple, he began to cast out them that sold therein and them that bought.**

This is called the *second* cleansing of the sacred edifice because it is quite distinct from that which is described by St. John (ii. 14-16), and which occurred three years before, at the commencement of our Lord's public life. The place referred to in this verse was not the Holy of Holies, into which only the high-priest entered, and that only once a year ; neither was it the inner court into which the Jewish people came to pray and to offer sacrifice. Most probably the evangelist speaks of the outer court to which even the Gentiles and those legally unclean had access (Introduction, p. cxxxvii., *seq.*). Under the portico of this court was held a market for the sale of oxen, sheep, oil, wine, or other requisites for divine worship; and in the same place sat those who supplied the sacred tribute in exchange for foreign coins. This was ostensibly for the convenience of Jews coming from afar, and it seemed to promote the worship and honour of God. But inasmuch as the traders exacted unjust prices or received fees which were unlawful (Lightfoot), and the whole place had become a place of greedy and noisy traffic, Christ again expelled the traders themselves, and in a holy anger overturned the tables of the money changers and the chairs of those who sold doves. Nay more, as St. Mark adds, " he suffered not that any man should carry a vessel through the temple," or when engaged in worldly business should use the courts of the holy place as a passage.

Having driven forth the profaners of the temple, Christ justified his action by appealing to the Sacred Scriptures and by

V. 46. **Saying to them: It is written; My house is the house of prayer. But you have made it a den of thieves.**

The first part of the verse is a quotation from Isaias (lvi. 7) and is given thus more fully by St. Mark: " My house shall be called the house of prayer to all nations." In the concluding words there is an allusion to Jeremias (vii. 11): " Is this house, then, in which my name hath been invoked, become a den of robbers in your eyes? I, I am he: I have seen it, saith the Lord." It is remarked that on the former occasion Christ had charged the merchants with making the temple "a house of traffic"; he now more severely denounced their conduct, when saying that they had " made it a den of thieves." The temple had really become so when the pharisees, scribes, and priests, hiding their avarice and other vices under the appearance of piety, thought of nothing else than the spoliation of the poor who came to worship. From this passage we may infer the low condition to which religion and piety had fallen when those who should have been the guardians of the temple and the defenders of its honour, permitted such profanations, and even sanctioned or ordered them to take place within the sacred precincts. The time had come, therefore, when Christ should fulfil the prediction of the prophet: " Presently the Lord whom you seek, and the Angel of the Testament whom you desire, shall come to the temple. . . . He is like a refining fire, and like the fuller's herb. And he shall sit refining and cleansing the silver; and he shall purify the sons of Levi, and shall refine them as gold and as silver; and they shall offer sacrifices to the Lord in justice " (Malach. iii. 1-3). The weeping over Jerusalem and the cleansing of the temple described in the preceding verses, occurred respectively on the Monday and on the Tuesday of the last week of our Lord's life. St. Luke in the two following chapters records the instructions given to the people by Christ during the remaining days before the Passion ; and the evangelist prefaces this record with the brief summary :—

V. 47. And he was teaching daily in the temple.

The words ἦν διδάσκων = " was teaching " is the periphrastic imperfect tense, and it gives prominence to the fact that our Lord's work of preaching during this time was unceasing. " Daily " (τὸ καθ' ἡμέραν), as we read in St. Luke, and from morning till evening, as we may learn from SS. Matthew and Mark, Christ was to be heard in the courts of the temple giving his last lessons to the crowds that were come up for the Paschal solemnity. The spirit in which these instructions were heard is indicated in v. 48, where it is written that " all the people were very attentive to hear him," or much more emphatically in the Greek text which has : ὁ λαὸς γὰρ ἅπας ἐξεκρέματο ἀυτοῦ ἀκούωι = " all the people listening to him, were hanging from him," *i.e.*, were hanging on his words. See a similar expression in Virgil Æneid (iv. 79) : " Pendetque iterum narrantis ab ore " ; Ennapius in Aedisio : ἐξεκρέματο τῶν λογῶν. The ministers sent by the rulers and pharisees to arrest Jesus on one occasion (John vii. 32-46) were overpowered by the force of his words ; and without carrying out the command, they returned to their masters with the explanation : " Never did man speak like this man." Such were the feelings of Christ's audience during the last days of his life. St. Luke puts before the reader a sad contrast to all this when he says (vv. 47, 48) : " The chief-priests, and the scribes, and the rulers of the people sought to destroy him ; and they found not what to do to him." At the same time, then, whilst Christ was *continuously* preaching in the temple, and seeking the salvation of the inhabitants of Jerusalem, whilst these inhabitants were *continuously* receiving his words with an avidity which the evangelist so graphically describes, the rulers of the people were straining every nerve (Gr., ἐζήτουν) to bring about his death. For the moment, as St. Luke says, " they found not what to do to him " (Luke xix. 48). His hour had not yet come ; he did not yet deliver himself up to them ; and hence they were still powerless against him (see Matth. xxvi. 55 ; Mark xiv. 49 ; Luke xxii. 53 ; John x. 17, 18).

V.—MORAL REFLECTIONS.

1. In clothing himself with our humanity, the Son of God took upon himself the different feelings to which that humanity is subject. Since, however, all the emotions of Jesus Christ hitherto

described by the evangelists were aroused by the exercise of the spiritual ministry in which he was engaged, his intense sorrow at the future temporal calamities of the faithless city might be surprising to the reader of the gospel. It should be remembered, then, that sanctity is not incompatible with the emotions of joy, sadness, aversion, fear, love or indignation which we naturally feel. Virtue is not apathetic. Religion does not annihilate nature, but perfects it ; it does not deaden our natural feelings, but moderates and directs them ; it does not prohibit us to rejoice or to be afflicted, but makes known to us the true causes of our joy and of our sorrow.

2. Now what was the chief cause of the tears of Jesus ? He wept indeed over the temporal calamities of Jerusalem, but he did so principally because these calamities were to be merited by its sins. If we regard with eyes of faith the course of human affairs, we shall not cease to be affected at it, but we shall be affected otherwise than we are. We shall not cease to be touched at the temporal evils around us, but we shall be much more so at the spiritual evils of sin and its consequences to which we are now almost indifferent. We cannot be so exclusively occupied with the things of heaven as to become indifferent to those of earth. That which we can do, and should do, is to value eternal blessings more than those which are merely temporal ; to desire the former more ; to fear more to be deprived of them ; and to regret bitterly having lost them by our sins. If our affections cannot be concentrated on one object to the absolute exclusion of all others, let the primary and final objects of our love be God and his holy grace ; let us give to him the preference of our will ; and let that will, rising above the feelings of corrupt nature, prefer all other evils rather than commit even one venial sin. Our duty is then accomplished and God is pleased.

3. We should have first a profound regret for our own sins, and then, like Jesus Christ, a sincere compassion for those of others. Jesus Christ knew, as no one else could know, the enormity of the crime of deicide which Jerusalem was about to commit ; he felt the justice of the chastisement which he predicted ; but his compassion, far from being stifled, was all the more excited. Equity demands the punishment of the wicked, but charity forbids us to rejoice at it ; and whilst blaming sinners, the just man weeps for them still more. Indeed if we turn our thoughts upon ourselves, will not the sinner's fate make us tremble ? Are we entirely free from sin ? Have we been always so ? And if we now live in God's grace, are we sure that we shall always remain in that happy state ? Let us meditate on human frailty in general ; let us reflect well on our own ; let us not at any time confound wickedness with the wicked ; and whilst reserving for

sin our just severity, let us give to the sinner the assurance of our compassion and the assistance of our prayers.

4. In weeping over the punishment and disasters of his nation, Jesus Christ approves, and teaches, and consecrates, the interest we should take in the welfare of the country which gave us birth.   Religion, which extends our charity to all men, does not thereby make us cosmopolitans ; on the contrary, it reminds us of the special ties which bind us to the soil where God has placed us.   If Providence afflicts with any calamity a particular region, the Church calls its inhabitants around her altars to disarm by their prayers the anger of heaven ; and petitions for the prosperity of kingdoms, the peace of states, the safety of sovereigns, and the fertility of the earth form part of the ordinary devotions of the faithful.   They are unjust, then, who accuse Christianity of being indifferent to the good of society ; and such a reproach ill becomes those whose own principles are subversive of social order.   Compare the patriotism of the Christian with that of him who is without faith.   The one serves his country from a sense of duty, the other through a desire of gain ; the one is occupied with the public good, the other thinks of his own advantage only ; and whilst the one acts with disinterestedness, the other is moved by ambition.   There is not, then, any true patriotism except that which religion inspires ; because that alone is pure in its motive, assured in its effects, constant in its duration, and unchanged amid the varying circumstances brought round by time.

TENTH SUNDAY AFTER PENTECOST.

I.—TEXTS.

GREEK

LUKE XVIII. 9-14.

⁹ Εἶπεν δὲ καὶ πρός τινας τοὺς πεποι-
θότας ἐφ᾽ ἑαυτοῖς ὅτι εἰσὶν δίκαιοι, καὶ
ἐξουθενοῦντας τοὺς λοιποὺς, τὴν παραβολὴν ταύτην· ¹⁰ Ἄνθρωποι δύο ἀνέ-
βησαν εἰς τὸ ἱερὸν προσεύξασθαι· εἷς
φαρεισαῖος, καὶ ὁ ἕτερος τελώνης. ¹¹ Ὁ
φαρεισαῖος σταθεὶς, ταῦτα πρὸς ἑαυτὸν
προσηύχετο· Ὁ θεός, εὐχαριστῶ σοι,
ὅτι οὐκ εἰμὶ ὥσπερ οἱ λοιποὶ τῶν
ἀνθρώπων, ἅρπαγες, ἄδικοι, μοιχοί, ἢ
καὶ ὡς οὗτος ὁ τελώνης· ¹² Νηστεύω
δὶς τοῦ σαββάτου, ἀποδεκατεύω πάντα
ὅσα κτῶμαι· ¹³ Ὁ δὲ τελώνης μακρόθεν ἑστὼς οὐκ ἤθελεν οὐδὲ τοὺς ὀφθαλ-
μοὺς ἐπᾶραι εἰς τὸν οὐρανόν, ἀλλ᾽
ἔτυπτε τὸ στῆθος ἑαυτοῦ, λέγων· Ὁ
θεὸς, ἱλάσθητί μοι τῷ ἁμαρτωλῷ.
¹⁴ Λέγω ὑμῖν, κατέβη οὗτος δεδικαιωμέ-
νος εἰς τὸν οἶκον ἑαυτοῦ, παρ᾽ ἐκεῖνον·
ὅτι πᾶς ὁ ὑψῶν ἑαυτὸν, ταπεινωθήσεται·
ὁ δὲ ταπεινῶν ἑαυτὸν, ὑψωθήσεται.

VULGATE.

LUKE XVIII. 9-14.

⁹ Dixit autem et ad quosdam
qui in se confidebant tanquam
justi et aspernabantur cæteros,
parabolam istam : ¹⁰ Duo homines ascenderunt in templum
ut orarent : unus pharisæus, et
alter publicanus. ¹¹ Pharisæus
stans, hæc apud se orabat :
Deus, gratias ago tibi quia non
sum sicut cæteri hominum, rap-
tores, injusti, adulteri ; velut
etiam hic publicanus. ¹² Jejuno
bis in sabbato ; decimas do om-
nium quæ possideo. ¹³ Et publicanus a longe stans, nolebat
nec oculos ad cœlum levare ;
sed percutiebat pectus suum,
dicens : Deus, propitius esto
mihi peccatori. ¹⁴ Dico vobis,
descendit hic justificatus in domum suam ab illo ; quia omnis
qui se exaltat, humiliabitur, et
qui se humiliat, exaltabitur.

II.—ENGLISH TRANSLATION.

LUKE XVIII. 9-14.

⁹ And to some also who trusted in themselves as just and despised others, he spoke this parable : ¹⁰ " Two men went up into
the temple to pray : the one a pharisee, and the other a publican.
¹¹ The pharisee standing, prayed thus with himself : O God, I
give thee thanks that I am not as the rest of men, extortioners,
unjust, adulterers ; as is also this publican. ¹² I fast twice in the
week ; I give tithes of all that I possess. ¹³ And the publican

standing afar off, would not so much as lift up his eyes towards heaven, but struck his breast, saying : O God, be merciful to me a sinner. 14 I say to you, this man went down into his house justified rather than the other ; because every one that exalteth himself shall be humbled, and he that humbleth himself shall be exalted."

III.—NOTES.

Introductory. Some months before his Passion our Lord came from Peræa to Bethany near Jerusalem to restore his friend Lazarus to life. The chief-priests and pharisees, enraged at the effect of this miracle amongst the people, resolved to put Jesus to death ; but he withdrew to " a city that is called Ephrem, and there he abode with his disciples " (John xi. 54). Having lived in retirement at this place for a short period, he set out on his last journey to Jerusalem by a circuitous route through Samaria, Galilee, and Peræa beyond the Jordan. During this journey he was on one occasion asked by the pharisees as to the time at which he would establish that kingdom of God about which he had so often spoken (Luke xvii. 20). Having explained to the pharisees the spiritual nature of his kingdom so different from that which they expected (Luke xvii. 21), he turned to his disciples ; he foretold to these the tribulations which awaited them ; and he recommended to them the persevering prayer of faith as the means of securing God's protection in such external obstacles to salvation (Luke xvii. 22 ; xviii. 8). But since the obstacles to salvation are not merely those which come from without, he, in the present passage, completes his instruction when, addressing himself to all then present, both pharisees and disciples, he insists on the necessity of eliminating from the heart the spirit of pride, which is incompatible with God's love and renders man unworthy of God's grace.

In the first verse of this gospel extract St. Luke indicates the character of the audience to whom, besides the disciples, this second portion of Christ's instruction was addressed. The evangelist says :—

V. 9. And to some also who trusted in themselves as just and despised others, he spoke this parable.

The "some" to whom our Lord now spoke, were much in need of the lesson that followed. From the matter of the parable itself and from this observation of St. Luke, it is clear that on more than one head they were sadly wanting in moral rectitude or justice. In the first place, puffed up with the sight of their good works and disregarding the spirit in which these works were done, they felt over-confident of being in God's favour, and forgot the warning of Solomon : " There are just men and

wise men, and their works are in the hands of God ; and yet
man knoweth not whether he be worthy of love or hatred, but
all things are kept uncertain for the time to come " (Eccles.
ix. 1, 2). Again, " they trusted in themselves " as the source of
their justification, and ignored the fact that, whatever value
may be found in really good works, it is due to the grace of
God who, according to St. Augustine, in rewarding merit is
merely crowning his own gifts. " What hast thou," says the
Apostle, " that thou hast not received ? And if thou hast received, why dost thou glory as if thou hadst not received it ? "
(1 Cor. iv. 7). Lastly, from this unfounded confidence in their
justification, and from this reliance on themselves alone as the
source of their justification, sprang the greatest crime of all—
that utter contempt not for *some others*, nor for *most others*, but
for *all others*, which is described in the original text by the very
strong expression ἐξουθενοῦντας τοὺς λοιποὺς.

To bring out by comparison the wickedness of this state of
mind, to indicate its punishment, and to encourage the humble
penitent, Christ " spoke this parable " or history as it is regarded by some. He said :—

V. 10. **Two men went up into the temple to pray : the one
a pharisee, and the other a publican.**

The temple was built on Mount Moria, one of the highest
points in the city of Jerusalem (Introduction, p. cxxxvii.). Hence
the approach to the sacred edifice is so often mentioned in the
Scriptures as a " going up " or ascent (Acts iii. 1 ; John vii. 14 ;
2 Paralipomenon xxix. 20 ; 1 Machab. iv. 36, 37, etc.), and the
departure as a descent (Luke xviii. 14). It was customary with
the Jews to go there for private prayer at other hours besides
those set apart for the morning and the evening sacrifice ; and
the visit now referred to was probably one for private devotion.
In the judgment of those who listened to Christ, there could
not be found a greater contrast than that between the pharisee
and the publican. It will be useful, therefore, to keep in mind
what has been handed down regarding these two classes whose
representatives are here introduced to our notice.

The *pharisees* (Introduction, pp. clxxiii., clxxiv.) are said to
have derived their name from the Hebrew word פָּרַשׁ = *he separated*, because they were supposed to be separated from the rest
of men by their eminent degree of sanctity and great learning.
They possessed great influence with the people, included in
their body many distinguished men with not a few illustrious
women, and were formidable even to their rulers because of the
tumults which they often excited in the state. Puffed up with
their reputation for sanctity, for minute attention to ceremonial
observances, and for knowledge of the law, they held all others
in contempt ; and together with the scribes they were the con-

stant and determined enemies of our Lord.   In their speculative
teaching, they asserted (*a*) the existence of a divine providence,
although Josephus speaks of them as fatalists ; (*b*) the immortality
of the soul and the resurrection of the body ; (*c*) the transmigra-
tion of souls (Josephus : *Antiq.* xviii. 1-3 ; Matth. xiv. 2 ; xvi. 14 ;
John ix. 2, 3, 34) ; (*d*) the existence of both good and evil spirits ;
(*e*) the justifying power of the Mosaic law ; and (*f*) the impossibility of the damnation of any Jew (Josephus : *Bell. Jud.* ii. 8-14 ;
St. Justin : *Dialogue with Tryphon*).   Their moral teaching
was very defective and merited severe censure from Christ.
Thus, (*a*) they put human traditions on a par with the prescriptions of the divine law (Matth. xv. 2, 3 ; Mark vii. 3-8) ;
(*b*) they perverted the sense of the law in most important
points (Matth. xv. 3-6 ; xxiii. 16-22) ; (*c*) whilst interpreting
the law most rigidly, they neglected the spirit in which it should
be fulfilled (Matth. xxiii. 23-28) ; and (*d*) although they forbade
works which were permitted on the Sabbath, and cut themselves
off from all intercourse with sinners, they paid no attention to
interior purity of heart (Matth. xxiii. 26-28).

The *publicans* (Introduction, p. cxxx.), often mentioned in the
synoptic gospels but never in that of St. John, were the collectors
of the taxes in the provinces of the Roman Empire.   They
were of two classes.   The publicans proper (ἀρχιτελῶναι) were
the rich capitalists or companies of capitalists generally of the
equestrian order, who farmed the revenues of the state for a
certain sum to be paid into the public treasury (*in publicum*).
Zacheus very probably belonged to this class, for he is called
ἀρχιτελώνης = *a prince of the publicans* (Luke xix. 2).   A common
interest bound these together, and they formed a very powerful
body.   Thus Cæsar says of one of them, Dumnorix : "Complures
annos portoria reliquaque Aeduorum vectigalia parvo pretio
redempta habere, propterea quod illo licente contra liceri audeat
nemo.   His rebus et suam rem familiarem auxisse et facultates ad
largiendum magnas comparasse ; magnum numerum equitatus
suo sumptu semper alere et circum se habere, neque solum domi,
sed etiam apud finitimas civitates largiter posse," etc. (*B. G.*
i. 18).   The publicans of the second class (τελῶναι) were called
portitores from *portus* a sea-port where they carried on their business.   These were the agents or underlings of the publicans
proper, and were generally natives of the place where they were
stationed.   It was their personal duty to examine the goods
imported or exported, to assess the value of these, and to enforce
payment of the tax.   With the exception of Zacheus, it is to
these publicans that the gospels refer.   The injustice of both
classes was proverbial.   Of the first it was written : " Ubi publicanus est, ibi aut jus publicum vanum, aut libertas sociis nulla "
(Livy, xlv. 18) ; and the frauds of the τελῶναι or portitores gave

rise to the saying : Πάντες τελῶναι πάντες εἰσί ἅρπαγες = "All tax-gatherers are robbers." They were detested in every place, but especially in Palestine where many were of opinion that the chosen people of God could not conscientiously pay tribute to the Romans (Matth. xxii. 15-17). The office of tax-gatherer, therefore, was generally held by pagans ; and if a Jew entered into the service he was regarded as the willing slave of a foreign tyrant, was shunned as a spy or informer, was denied all social intercourse as an abandoned sinner, and was practically excluded from religious worship as an apostate (Matth. ix. 11 ; xi. 19). " A beautiful illustration of the feeling towards publicans is supplied in the life of St. Matthew. He was before his conversion ' a publican ' (Matth. ix. 9), and while he sets forth prominently in the gospel the horror with which his class was viewed by the people (Matth. v. 46, 47 ; ix. 10, 11 ; xi. 19, passim), he humbly calls himself ' Matthew, the *publican*,' even in the catalogue of the apostles (Matth. x. 2-4, and note the contrast there : Peter, the *chief;* Matthew, the *publican;* Judas, the *traitor*) ; whereas the other evangelists studiously avoid connecting the hated term ' publican ' with the name of Matthew " (McCarthy : *Gospels of the Sundays*, p. 367).

Our Lord says, then, that a pharisee and a publican went up into the temple to pray, and he graphically describes the acts of each of these worshippers. Of the first he says :—

V. 11. The pharisee standing, prayed thus with himself ; O God, I give thee thanks that I am not as the rest of men, extortioners, unjust, adulterers ; as is also this publican.

Amongst the Jews sovereigns alone were permitted to pray sitting (Introduction, p. clxii.) : all others ordinarily prayed standing, with arms extended and hands turned up, as it were to receive the blessings of heaven. The mention of the posture, then, in this case and the use of the word σταθεὶς not applied to the publican, seem to convey that the pharisee took up a conspicuous position and assumed a striking attitude to catch the eyes of the bystanders. The word ἑστὼς applied to the publican indicates less care for effect. The pharisee appeared to begin well with praise to God ; still his prayer was one of thanksgiving in form only, and was directed not to the glory of God but to his own. He soon threw off the mask by attributing to himself that for which he seemed to thank God. He did not thank God for having enabled him to keep the law ; but he asserted that he had kept it, and implied that this was due to his own strength. Still further, from taking complacency in his own supposed perfection, he proceeded to judge and to condemn all others. " I am not as the rest of men." " Quid est *sicut caeteri homines* nisi *sicut omnes praeter me* " (St. Aug.). Other members of his sect divided the human race into two classes : pharisees and the rest who were " accurst " (John vii. 48, 49). But this proud man will admit only himself into the class of the just (*Int. Comm.*). Nor is he satisfied with a general condemnation of his fellow-creatures : for seeing the publican praying at a distance, he singles him out for special reprobation. He does not think that the sinner of a short time since may be now reconciled with God. He does not pray to God for that sinner's conversion, but wishes, as it were, to remind God of the wickedness of the abandoned wretch before him. The sins which he lays to the charge of other men in general and of the publican in particular, are adultery (μοιχοί), violent seizing on a neighbour's goods (ἅρπαγες) and secret over-reaching by fraud (ἄδικοι). He declares himself free from these crimes ; but, at least of pharisees as a body, this statement was not true. Christ charged them with extortion (Matth. xxiii. 25), with injustice (Luke xx. 47), and with shameful laxity in the matter of divorce (Matth. xix. 3-9). Josephus, himself a pharisee, accused them of the crime of adultery. A prayer has been defined : " Conversio mentis ad Deum, per pium et humilem affectum " (St. Aug., Lib. de Spiritu et Anima, c. 50). The prayer of the pharisee, therefore, was unworthy of the name and was well described by Christ himself as being offered (πρὸς ἑαυτὸν) = *unto himself*, that is, unto his own glory. Very different was the confession of St. Paul, who said : " I am the least of the apostles, who am not worthy to be called an apostle, because I persecuted the Church of God. But by the grace of God I am what I am ; and his grace in me hath not been void ; but I have laboured more abundantly than all they ; yet not I, but the grace of God with me " (1 Cor. xv. 9, 10).

The pharisee thus glorified in the fact that he avoided the crimes of " the rest of men " ; he next boasted of the good works which he performed ; and he said :—

V. 12. **I fast twice in the week ; I give tithes of all that I possess.**

The first clause is literally rendered : " I fast twice in the sabbath." As this word " sabbath " meant either the day of rest (Mark xvi. 2), or the whole week commencing and ending with that day (Matth. xxviii. 1), the signification in any particular passage has to be sought for in the context or in the subject matter. Here the term, as is evident, applies to the whole week. In the written law of Moses there was only one day in the whole year set apart for fasting—the Day of Atonement, on the tenth of the seventh month (Lev. xvi. 29) ; in the time of the prophet Zachary there were four fast days (Zach. viii. 19) ; and during the Babylonian captivity some others were prescribed on account of the calamities which befell the nation (Introduction, pp. clxxi.-clxxiii.). The two fasts on Monday and Thursday of each week, which are here spoken of, were introduced by the pharisees themselves and continued to be voluntary. The mortification, then, which is mentioned in the parable, was boasted of as a work of supererogation. This was not enough. The payment of tithes (Introduction, p. clvii.), which existed among all nations of antiquity, was prescribed by the law of Moses (Exod. xxii. 29 ; Levit. xxvii. 30) for the maintenance of the priests and levites, who themselves were obliged to give a tithe to the high-priest (Numbers xviii. 26-28). A second tithe was contributed by the people towards the expenses of the feasts (Deut. xii. 5-18), and a third was expended every third year on a feast for slaves, orphans and widows. But inasmuch as the law of tithes re-ferred to corn, wine, oil, and cattle only, the pharisee here boasts of a second work of supererogation. Whilst all others are adulterers, he is not content with the prescriptions of the law, but mortifies his flesh by fasting twice in the week ; and whilst his fellow-men are unjust and extortioners, he gives more than is required by paying tithes on all he possesses, or rather gains (πάντα ὅσα κτῶμαι).

Such was the pharisee and such his spirit of prayer : another worshipper with another spirit is now to be described ; and of him our Lord says :—

V. 13. And the publican standing afar off, would not so much as lift up his eyes towards heaven, but struck his breast, saying, O God, be merciful to me a sinner.

This prayer having been proposed as a model, its character is to be closely examined. In it are found all the conditions re-quisite to secure pardon for sin, namely, a humble acknowledg-ment of unworthiness in God's sight, a sorrow for past trans-gressions, and a hope of pardon. Firstly, the publican acknow-ledged his unworthiness by standing " afar off " from the Holy Place, and by not even raising his hands and his eyes to heaven as was the custom of his race at prayer (Psalm cxxii. 1, 2). Again, he expressed his sorrow for his sins by striking his breast— the natural and customary sign of grief (Luke xxiii. 48)—and by this, as it were, punishing his heart, the seat of his affections and the source of his transgressions. Lastly, as confession and sorrow without hope of pardon, and hope of pardon without sorrow and admission of guilt would be equally useless, the publican secured the remission of his sins by the very brief but very full and efficacious prayer : " O God, be merciful to me, a sinner." With regard to this prayer it is useful to observe that the publican asks of God merely an act of mercy, and such an act of mercy as may secure his reconciliation. He does not speak of his merits in the past, nor does he put forward an excuse for his present crimes ; for he openly declares himself a sinner. Whilst imploring the divine pardon, he makes use of words which show that his mind is occupied with the one thought of the injury he has done to God, and that his heart is filled with the one desire of being again the friend of his Creator. This is the meaning of the Greek expression 'Ειλάσθητί μοι=" Propitius esto mihi," that is, " Approach me who am far removed from you, and be clement and forgiving to me." Moreover, it is to be remarked that the publican does not assert that others as well as he are transgressors and have need of pardon, but he directs his attention to his own sins only. He says : " Be propitious to me a sinner," or as it is still more forcibly put in the Greek : " Be propitious to me, *the* sinner " (τῷ ἁμαρτωλῷ). The pharisee considered himself alone in a class : he was *the* saint, and all others were sinners. On the contrary, with St. Paul, who named himself the " chief of sinners " (1 Tim i. 15), the publican in his appeal to God calls himself " *the* sinner," the transgressor by excellence, in comparison with whom all others are just.

The Psalmist (Ps. l. 19) had said : " A contrite and humble heart, O God, thou wilt not despise " ; and our Lord confirmed this statement of the prophet by the sentence :—

V. 14. **I say to you, this man went down into his house justified rather than the other.**

The Greek text here presents a great difficulty to interpreters. It is necessary to suppose an ellipsis of μᾶλλον before παρ' ἐκεῖνον. A similar ellipsis is found in Luke xv. 7, and in Matth. xviii. 8. The Greek might be thus rendered : " Descendit hic in domum suam justior quam ille "=" This man went down into his house, more just than that other." It is true the clause *taken by itself* does not necessarily imply that the publican, much less the pharisee, was just before God. (See Ezechiel xvi. 51 ; Gen. xxxviii. 26.) It is however, quite usual in the Sacred Scripture to express by a comparison a strong negation of the second member (John iii. 19 ; 1 Tim. i. 4 ; *cf.* Gen. xxxviii. 26 ; and Habacuc i. 13). That this usage is followed here is evident from the remaining words of the verse, where the design is to show that the humility of the publican was rewarded by God, and that the pride of the pharisee was punished. The full sense of the clause may be thus expressed : " I say to you, that the publican by his humility merited and obtained pardon of all his sins ; whilst the pride of the pharisee was followed by greater guilt and brought down on him a greater condemnation."

Christ, having passed judgment on the two worshippers, justified his sentence and gave the great spiritual lesson of the parable in these concluding words :—

Because everyone that exalteth himself shall be humbled, and he that humbleth himself shall be exalted.

Christ does not here promise that those are to be respectively exalted or humbled who occupy a humble or an exalted position in the sight of the world. What he does promise is this, that sometimes here and in every case hereafter, God will exalt the man who voluntarily humbles himself in spirit whatever may be his station, and that sometimes here and in every case hereafter, the same Just Judge will humble him who in a spirit of ambition aims at exaltation. Humility of mind and heart are requisite conditions for eternal glory ; and whilst this humility of mind and heart is compatible with the highest position on earth, it may be wanting in the lowest. The necessity of the interior spirit of humility was often made known to the Jews, who read in the book of Proverbs (iii. 34) cited by the Prince of the Apostles (1 Peter v. 5) and by St. James (iv. 6) : " He shall scorn the scorners ; and to the meek he will give grace," or, as it is in the Septuagint : " The Lord resists the proud ; but he gives his grace to the humble." The lesson was often repeated by Christ and by his apostles in words almost identical with those in the present passage (see Matth. xxiii. 12 ; Luke xiv. 11 ; 1 Peter v. 6) ; and pride was a vice condemned by every action of our Lord's life. Therefore did St. Leo say truly : " Tota christianæ sapientiæ disciplina non in abundantia verbi, non in astutia disputandi, neque in appetitu laudis et gloriæ, sed in vera et voluntaria humilitate consistit, quam Dominus Jesus ab utero matris usque ad supplicium crucis omni fortitudine et elegit et docuit."

IV.—MORAL REFLECTIONS.

Of all the parables in the gospels, that of " the pharisee and the publican " is perhaps the most generally known ; and in these characters so clearly drawn, all of us may find matter well worthy of careful consideration. Let us examine these two types of mankind, and let us see the extent to which we are ourselves portrayed in the description of either.

1. In the first place, by the prominent position he took up during his prayer no less than by the words he used, the pharisee sought to attract the esteem of men whilst he pretended to give honour to God. This hypocrisy is revolting to us ; but if we turn our eyes upon ourselves, we may find perhaps that sometimes we are chargeable with the same vice. Many of our acts and many of our religious exercises, which need but a pure intention to be pleasing to God, are vitiated or rendered entirely bad by the sentiments of vain glory with which they are done, and by the desire of human applause which is their motive. All the saints admonish us to be on our guard against vain glory, and they tell us that like a cunning thief it robs us of the merit of our good works almost before its presence is perceived. In the last chapter of his *Morals*, St. Gregory the Great declared that this was his own experience. " I confess," he says, " that on

examining my intention in writing this, it appears to me I have no other wish than to please God ; but while I am not on my guard, I find that a certain kind of desire of pleasing men enters in, and I feel some vain satisfaction at having performed my work well." Pride is so universal a passion that we all have need at all times to keep in mind the warning of our Divine Lord : " Take heed that you do not your justice before men to be seen by them ; otherwise you shall not have a reward of your Father who is in heaven " (Matth. vi. 1).

Again, the pharisee instituted a comparison between himself and others, not that he might take a warning from the weakness and crimes which he supposed he saw around him, but that he might exult in the contemplation of his own good deeds. Here was another phase of pride which we may behold in all who are subject to this vice, and which on close examination we may perhaps discover in ourselves. We take pleasure in comparing ourselves with those who seem to be inferior to us in perfection, that we may indulge our self-esteem ; but we avoid a comparison with those who clearly surpass us, lest we discover therein a cause for humiliation. How foolish is this ! If we compare ourselves with any of our fellow-creatures, let these be the elect whom the Church proposes for our homage and imitation. The example of these heroes of holiness will afford us instruction in our ignorance, remedies for our imperfections, a support in our weakness, encouragement in our faintheartedness, and an answer to the vain excuses put forward by our tepidity. In contemplating their greatness, we shall learn something of our own littleness ; and in considering the distance that separates us from them, we shall be moved to make that distance less. Let us, then, be filled with the noble emulation to be equal to great saints, and not rest in the base satisfaction of thinking ourselves better than great sinners.

Lastly, in the enumeration of his good deeds the pharisee did not mention the fulfilment of any duty that was really essential. Whilst he neglected serious obligations, he made his religion consist in works of supererogation—in fasts which were not prescribed, and in the payment of tithes beyond what was demanded. This sad defect is sometimes found amongst Christians who, for the exercise of virtues enjoined by the gospel, substitute practices which are indeed pious in themselves, but which are not necessary and are often incompatible with one's state of life. This subversion of the moral law arises from various causes. Amongst the simple, it proceeds from ignorance or from false zeal : amongst the better instructed, as in the case of the pharisee, it is due to hypocrisy or to the desire of securing the homage given to piety at the expense of piety itself. Let us ever remember that works of supererogation can sometimes supplement the full performance of our duties, but can never take the place of what is strictly commanded.

2. In contrast with the pharisee Christ proposes the publican, and what a contrast between this model of humility, and the example of pride which we have just been considering! Whilst the pharisee by his attitude and words insults his fellow-creatures and offends his Creator, the publican hides himself from the sight of men and fears even to look up to heaven. Judging himself unworthy to appear before God, he takes the last place amongst the worshippers assembled in the temple. If the contemplation of the divine mercy inspires him with hope, the feeling of his unworthiness makes him regard it as a favour to be admitted into the presence of God. He is not content to confess his sins: he wishes to expiate them by mortification, and he strikes his breast in testimony of his sorrow. His prayer is as humble as that of the pharisee is arrogant; and by sincerely acknowledging his crimes, he hopes to obtain their remission. Here is the model of our penance and prayer. Which of us can dare to say that he is without sin? We have all offended God, and some of us, perhaps, more grievously than the publican of the gospel. We have only one security against the divine justice which threatens us: it is the divine mercy which deigns to receive us again after our offences. Let us cast ourselves into the arms which this divine mercy holds out to us. Let us cast ourselves into them with confidence—not with the presumptuous confidence of the pharisee, but with the modest confidence of the publican founded on a knowledge of the divine goodness which promises never to despise the contrite and humble heart. Let us come to God with a sincere confession of our sins, a lively sorrow, an abundant satisfaction; and then let us hope for all things from him whose " tender mercies are over all his works " (Ps. cxliv. 9).

3. The different dispositions of the pharisee and of the publican brought about the different results announced by our Divine Lord. These men returned to their houses—the one free from the weight of his sins, and the other burthened with one sin more. Such are the effects respectively of humility and of pride. We are born for greatness, as we learn from the desires of our heart and from the teaching of our faith; and we here learn how to reach that greatness. It is a fundamental maxim of our religion that our humility will be recompensed with glory or our pride punished with degradation. It is for us, then, to make a choice between the glory of the present life, and that of the future; between a glory that passes away, and that which remains for ever; between the empty glory which is bestowed by men, and that with which God crowns his elect. In the natural as well as in the supernatural order, the words of Christ must be fulfilled: " Every one that exalteth himself, shall be humbled; and he that humbleth himself, shall be exalted."

ELEVENTH SUNDAY AFTER PENTECOST.

GREEK.

MARK VII. 31-37.

³¹ Καὶ πάλιν ἐξελθὼν ἐκ τῶν ὁρίων Τύρου ἦλθεν διὰ Σειδῶνος, εἰς τὴν θάλασσαν τῆς Γαλειλαίας, ἀνὰ μέσον τῶν ὁρίων Δεκαπόλεως. ³² Καὶ φέρουσιν αὐτῷ κωφὸν καὶ μογιλάλον, καὶ παρακαλοῦσιν αὐτὸν ἵνα ἐπιθῇ αὐτῷ τὴν χεῖρα. ³³ Καὶ ἀπολαβόμενος αὐτὸν ἀπὸ τοῦ ὄχλου κατ᾽ ἰδίαν, ἔβαλεν τοὺς δακτύλους αὐτοῦ εἰς τὰ ὦτα αὐτοῦ· καὶ πτύσας, ἥψατο τῆς γλώσσης αὐτοῦ. ³⁴ Καὶ ἀναβλέψας εἰς τὸν οὐρανὸν, ἐστέναξεν, καὶ λέγει αὐτῷ· Ἐφφαθά, ὅ ἐστιν, Διανοίχθητι. ³⁵ Καὶ ἠνοίγησαν αὐτοῦ αἱ ἀκοαί, καὶ ἐλύθη ὁ δεσμὸς τῆς γλώσσης αὐτοῦ, καὶ ἐλάλει ὀρθῶς. ³⁶ Καὶ διεστείλατο αὐτοῖς ἵνα μηδενὶ λέγωσιν· ὅσον δὲ αὐτοῖς διεστέλλετο, αὐτοὶ μᾶλλον περισσότερον ἐκήρυσσον. ³⁷ Καὶ ὑπερπερισσῶς ἐξεπλήσσοντο, λέγοντες· Καλῶς πάντα πεποίηκεν· ὡς καὶ τοὺς κωφοὺς ποιεῖ ἀκούειν, καὶ ἀλάλους λαλεῖν.

VULGATE.

MARK VII. 31-37.

³¹ Et iterum exiens de finibus Tyri, venit per Sidonem ad mare Galilææ, inter medios fines Decapoleos. ³² Et adducunt ei surdum et mutum ; et deprecabantur eum ut imponat illi manum. ³³ Et apprehendens eum de turba seorsum, misit digitos suos in auriculas ejus ; et exspuens, tetigit linguam ejus. ³⁴ Et suspiciens in cœlum, ingemuit, et ait illi : Ephphetha, quod est : Adaperire. ³⁵ Et statim apertæ sunt aures ejus, et solutum est vinculum linguæ ejus, et loquebatur recte. ³⁶ Et præcepit illis ne cui dicerent. Quanto autem eis præcipiebat, tanto magis plus prædicabant ; ³⁷ et eo amplius admirabantur, dicentes : Bene omnia fecit : et surdos fecit audire, et mutos loqui.

I.—ENGLISH TRANSLATION WITH PARALLEL PASSAGE FROM ST. MATTHEW.

MARK VII. 31-37.

³¹ And again, going out of the coasts of Tyre he came by Sidon to the Sea of Galilee, through the midst of the coasts of Decapolis. ³² And they bring to him one deaf and dumb ; and they besought him that he would lay his hand upon him. ³³ And

taking him apart from the multitude, he put his fingers into his ears ; and spitting, he touched his tongue. [34] And looking up to heaven, he groaned, and saith to him : " Ephphetha," which is : " Be thou opened." [35] And immediately his ears were opened, and the string of his tongue was loosed, and he spoke right. [36] And he charged them that they should tell no man. But the more he charged them, so much the more a great deal did they publish it ; [37] and so much the more did they wonder, saying : " He hath done all things well : he hath made both the deaf to hear, and the dumb to speak."

MATTHEW XV. 29-31.

[29] And when Jesus had passed away thence, he came nigh to the Sea of Galilee. And going up into a mountain, he sat there. [30] And there came to him great multitudes having with them the dumb, the blind, the lame, the maimed, and many others. And they cast them down at his feet ; and he healed them : [31] so that the multitudes marvelled on seeing the dumb speak, the lame walk, the blind see. And they glorified the God of Israel.

III.—COMBINED NARRATIVE.

And again, when Jesus had passed away thence, going out of the coasts (region) of Tyre, he came by Sidon nigh to the Sea of Galilee, through the midst of the coasts (region) of Decapolis. And going up into the mountain, he sat there. And there came to him great multitudes having with them the dumb, the blind, the lame, the maimed, and many others. And they cast them down at his feet ; and he healed them : so that the multitudes marvelled on seeing the dumb speak, the lame walk, the blind see. And they adored the God of Israel. And they bring to him one deaf and dumb ; and they besought him that he would lay his hand upon him. And taking him from the multitude apart, he put his fingers into his ears ; and spitting, he touched his tongue. And looking up to heaven, he groaned, and saith to him : " Ephphetha," which is : " Be thou opened." And immediately his ears were opened, and the string of his tongue was loosed, and he spoke right. And he charged them that they should tell no man. But the more he charged them, so much the more a great deal did they publish it ; and so much the more did they wonder, saying : " He hath done all things well : he hath made both the deaf to hear, and the dumb to speak.

IV.—NOTES.

Introductory. About the time of the Pasch in the third year of our Lord's public life, there came a crisis in his relations with the pharisees and with his disciples alike. The day after he had fed the five thousand men with the five loaves and two fishes in the desert, he announced his future gift of the Holy Eucharist, and was at once deserted by many of his followers (John vi. 61-72) ; about the same time the pharisees from Jerusalem became more violent in their opposition and hatred ; and the civil ruler, Herod Antipas, the murderer of John the Baptist, began to watch his movements with a sinister interest (Luke ix. 7-9). In these circumstances Jesus retired into Upper Galilee (Introduction, p. xxxix), to the neighbourhood of Tyre and Sidon (Introduction, pp. lii., liii.) ; and there he healed the daughter of the Syro-Phœnician woman, whose earnest prayer and lively faith foreshadowed the future conversion of the Gentiles. The continuation of this journey and the miracles that were worked during it are described by the two evangelists, SS. Matthew and Mark. St. Mark says of our Divine Lord :—

V. 31. **And again, going out of the coasts of Tyre, he came by Sidon to the Sea of Galilee through the midst of the coasts of Decapolis.**

The translation of the verse might be thus amended : " And again, going from the borderland (or region) of Tyre, he came through Sidon into the midst of the borderland (or region) of Decapolis to the Sea of Galilee." The word " coasts " is a misleading archaism standing for borderland, or region, or territory. Derived from the Latin *costa = a rib* or *a side*, it formerly signified a borderland or region in general, but it is now restricted in meaning to the border or shore of the sea. In the Greek text there is nothing to indicate that our Lord ever reached the seacoast at Tyre. The evangelist, then, wished to say that Jesus, who had desired to conceal himself in the part of Upper Galilee (Introduction, p. xxxix.) *bordering* on Tyre, but could not lie hidden (Mark vii. 24), again moved forward, and on his journey came through the territory of Sidon into the territory of Decapolis (Introduction, p. xxxviii.), and to the Sea of Galilee (Introduction, p. xlvii.). Christ, who is called by St. Paul " the Minister of the Circumcision " (Rom. xv. 8), confined his teaching almost exclusively to the Jews. Still, in this passing visit to the confines of Pagan Phœnicia, in his remarkable praise of the Gentile centurion at Capharnaum (Luke vii. 9 ; Introduction, pp. xlix. and l.), and in his gracious reception of the Greek proselytes at Jerusalem (John xii. 20-25), he indicated that all mankind would yet be called to the light of the Gospel. When, during a former visit to this country of Decapolis, he had healed the Gerasene demoniac (Matth. viii. 28-34 ; Mark v. 1-20 ; Luke viii. 26-39), he was requested to leave the place ; but this was not the case on the present occasion. St. Matthew records that now " there came to him great multitudes having with them the dumb, the blind, the lame, the maimed, and many others. And they cast them down at his feet ; and he healed them ; so that the multitude marvelled, on seeing the dumb speak, the lame walk, the blind see. And they glorified the God of Israel " (Matth. xv. 30, 31). Of these numerous cures, St. Mark mentions one in the following verses. He says :—

V. 32. **And they bring to him one deaf and dumb ; and they besought him that he would lay his hand upon him.**

This man, though entirely deaf (κωφός) was not perhaps entirely *deprived of the power of speech* (ἄλαλος), but was *labouring under an impediment of speech* (μογιλάλος) so great that he was looked upon as dumb by the witnesses of the miracle (verse 37). The bystanders or friends, moved by some particular circumstance of the case, implored with special earnestness (παρακαλοῦσιν) that our Lord, like the prophets of old (4 Kings v. 11), would remove the disease by his sacred touch.

Christ heard their petition.

V. 33. **And taking him apart from the multitude, he put his fingers into his ears ; and spitting, he touched his tongue.**

It has been remarked by Maldonatus that Christ did not appear willing to manifest his divinity and his omnipotence to the same extent on each occasion. Doubtless he did not judge it to be expedient, although the reason of the inexpediency is not known to us. At one time, by a word he cast out devils and raised the dead to life ; at another, by a touch, or by the application of saliva or of moistened dust, he healed the diseased. Thus he assimilated his mode of action to that of natural causes, and accommodated the exercise of his power to the circumstances of time and place in which he was. We have here an instance of this divine economy. At the period of his ministry now under review, Christ had departed from Galilee with his disciples, and had hidden himself as far as might be, because of the hostility of the pharisees and the dangerous suspicions of Herod. As was probably done with the others mentioned by St. Matthew, Christ now took the deaf and dumb man to himself apart from the crowd, lest the rumour of these miracles might cause any commotion amongst the Gentile population, and thus still further arouse the suspicions of Herod or inflame the anger of the pharisees who were already plotting their Redeemer's death. The necessity for precaution would account for the secrecy of the cure, and for the injunctions : " He charged them that they should tell no man " (verse 36), and that they should " beware of the leaven of the pharisees and of the leaven of Herod " (viii. 15).

The evangelist continues :—

V. 34. **And looking up to heaven, he groaned, and said to him : Ephphetha, which is : Be thou opened.**

As in the case of the blind man at Bethsaida (Mark viii. 22-26 ; Introduction, p. lii.), Christ made use of the ceremonies here mentioned to excite in the minds of the sufferer the necessary faith, and to indicate the heavenly source whence the relief was to come. He groaned over the misery of sin which brought with it disease and death into the world ; he looked up to heaven where alone help is to be found ; he put his fingers into the sick man's ears and touched his tongue with spittle, to show that no one can hear the saving truths of religion or confess the infinite goodness of God except through Jesus Christ, who in his sacred humanity is the fountain of all grace. Thus, according to St. Matthew, " he healed all that were sick, that this might be fulfilled which was spoken by the prophet Isaias, saying : He took our infirmities, and bore our diseases " (Matth. viii. 16, 17). Recording the personal recollections of St. Peter, who was an eye-witness of this miracle, St. Mark preserved the Aramaic word, " Ephphetha " (the imperative in ethpeel of the verb פְּתַח, Heb. פָּתַח) used by Christ on this occasion, and still employed by the ministers of the Church in the ceremonies of holy baptism.

It was God that spoke to the patient ;

V. 35. **And immediately his ears were opened, and the string of his tongue was loosed, and he spoke right.**

At the command of Jesus : " Ephphetha "=" Be thou opened " or " loosed," the deaf ears were unstopped and the silent tongue was loosed, as in the beginning the words : " Let there be light " were immediately followed by the effect, " and light was made " (Gen. i. 3).

Eternal Wisdom not only " reacheth from end to end mightily," but also " ordereth all things sweetly " (Wisdom viii. 1). Hence, for the same reason for which he took the infirm man " apart from the multitude," Christ imposed silence on those present ;

V. 36. **And he charged them that they should tell no man. But the more he charged them, so much the more a great deal did they publish it.**

It was only in the case of the greatest miracles that this injunction was laid on the witnesses (Maldonatus). As the evangelist states with an accumulation of comparatives, the injunction was not obeyed. Gould (*Int. Comm., in loco*) observes : " The conduct of the multitude is a good example of the way in which men treat Jesus, yielding him all homage except obedience." Such a judgment appears to be a little severe ; for in the gospel we never meet with a condemnation of those who thus published the works of Christ. It is clear indeed that the repetition of the prohibition on the part of our Lord was the very reason why it was disregarded ; but some explanation can be

given besides that of perversity on the part of the people in
question. It would appear that they regarded this order as an
evidence of their Benefactor's humility, and the repetition
of the command as a proof that he was more and more worthy
to have his praise proclaimed. (See McCarthy.) How true
it is that the applause of men is like the shadow, which ever
flies from those that follow it, and ever follows in the track of
those that fly from it !

The effect produced on the crowd by Christ's humility and
modesty is thus described with unusual emphasis by St. Mark :

V. 37. **And so much the more did they wonder, saying :
He hath done all things well : he hath made both the deaf to
hear, and the dumb to speak.**

In the Greek text we read the words : ὑπερπερισσῶς ἐξεπλήσσοντο,
which mean literally : " They were out of their senses with surprise." Accustomed to the vain glory and ostentation of the
pharisees, these people are unable to understand the modesty
of our Lord, who wished to conceal as far as possible the miraculous gifts he was conferring. Hence they confess that in
making the dumb to speak and the deaf to hear, " he hath
done all things well " ; and they express their admiration in
words similar to those in which the inspired writer described
the divine work of the first creation (Gen. i. 31).

V.—MORAL REFLECTIONS.

According to the Fathers of the Church, the miracles recorded
in this passage were worked for two purposes quite distinct—
the one principal and direct, the other secondary and allegorical.
The miracles of Jesus Christ were intended in the first place to
prove the truth of his divine mission, and then, to teach us the
moral law under figures easily understood and remembered. On
the present occasion it will be useful to consider them from this
latter point of view.

ı. The deaf and dumb man presented to Jesus Christ to be
cured is a figure of such as are spiritually bereft of speech and
hearing. These are unfortunately very numerous, and cannot
be freed from their infirmity except by the goodness and power
of the Redeemer. As those who are physically deaf cannot
hear the sounds around them, so the man who is afflicted with
spiritual deafness becomes unconscious of what God himself
says, and unconscious of what he causes to be said by the ministry
of others. This was the state in which, at his coming, our
Divine Lord found almost the whole human race. The law
which God had promulgated on Mount Sinai was received by
one people, and was unknown or misunderstood by almost all
others. The voice of the heavens which show forth the glory

of their Creator was scarcely anywhere heard, and men appeared to close their ears to this solemn proclamation of one only God, the Maker and Sovereign Ruler of all that exists. Because, then, we did not hear the voice by which God made known his existence and attributes together with our relations to him and to our fellow-men, Jesus Christ came to cure this almost universal deafness. By his own teaching and by that of his apostles, he accomplished his work ; all ears were opened to the words of salvation ; and St. Paul wrote regarding his fellow-labourers : " Verily, their sound hath gone forth into all the earth, and their words unto the ends of the whole world " (Rom. x. 18). The task was accomplished for the time ; but it has to be daily undertaken, and is daily undertaken, by Christ through the ministry of his Church on earth. As in the time of Christ, so now, there are many who do not hear the word of God, and who need at his hands the cure of their spiritual deafness. Some refuse to come to the instructions of the Church ; others come, but whilst the divine word reaches their ears, it does not penetrate into their soul. Nor is it to the preaching of the gospel only that they are deaf. Whatever may be the way in which God speaks, they do not hear. The inspirations he sends are rejected, the remorse with which he pursues them is disregarded ; the examples of virtue which he presents to them are forgotten ; the instances of chastisement which he shows them are unheeded ; the sickness which he sends them is murmured at. To many such amongst us we may apply the words spoken by the prophet regarding the Jews : " They would not hearken ; and they turned away the shoulder to depart ; and they stopped their ears not to hear ; and they made their heart as the adamant stone, lest they should hear the law and the words which the Lord of Hosts sent in his Spirit by the hands of the former prophets " (Zach. vii. 11, 12).

2. That this spiritual deafness which is so difficult to be cured may not fall upon us, we ought to attend carefully to its causes, which are two in number. In the first place, our ears are closed to the voice of God because they are occupied with other sounds. It is impossible at the same time to hear with attention two different discourses—to listen to the call of God, and to the seductions of the world. In vain God commands self-denial whilst the world preaches love of riches ; in vain he prescribes mortification whilst it invites to pleasure ; in vain he enjoins humility whilst it inspires us with vanity ; in vain he insists on love of our enemies whilst it incites to vengeance. We prefer what is agreeable to what is useful, flattering error to severe truth, a present momentary pleasure to future eternal happiness. " These are a people that provoke to wrath, and lying children, children that will not hear the law of God, who say

to the seers : See not ; and to them that behold : Behold not
for us those things that are right.   Speak unto us pleasant
things ; see errors for us ; take away from me the way ; turn away
the path from me ; let the Holy One of Israel cease from before
us " (Isaias xxx. 9-11).   The second cause of this spiritual
deafness is still more fatal than the first.   We cannot work out
our salvation without the divine assistance ; but God, in consequence of our refusing to listen to him, gradually withdraws
his grace, and ceases to make us hear his voice.   That which
was our crime becomes our punishment, and in us is fulfilled
this divine threat : " Because you have done all these works,
saith the Lord, and I have spoken to you, rising up early and
speaking, and you have not heard, and I have called you and
you have not answered, ...   I will cast you away from
before my face " (Jerem. vii. 13-15).

Knowing then the necessity of salutary admonitions and holy
inspirations, knowing the danger of rejecting the gifts of God
in whatever form they come, we should have recourse to him
who worked the miracle we read of to-day.   We should beg of
him to speak unceasingly to us the truths of faith, and to give
us at the same time the grace of ready ears to hear his law,
and of docile hearts to fulfil its precepts.

TWELFTH SUNDAY AFTER PENTECOST.

I.—TEXTS.

GREEK.

LUKE X. 23-37.

²³ Καὶ στραφεὶς πρὸς τοὺς μαθητὰς, κατ' ἰδίαν εἶπεν· Μακάριοι οἱ ὀφθαλμοὶ, οἱ βλέποντες ἃ βλέπετε. ²⁴ Λέγω γὰρ ὑμῖν, ὅτι πολλοὶ προφῆται καὶ βασιλεῖς ἠθέλησαν ἰδεῖν ἃ ὑμεῖς βλέπετε, καὶ οὐκ εἶδαν· καὶ ἀκοῦσαι μου ἃ ἀκούετε, καὶ οὐκ ἤκουσαν.

²⁵ Καὶ ἰδοὺ, νομικός τις ἀνέστη, ἐκπειράζων αὐτὸν, λέγων· Διδάσκαλε, τί ποιήσας ζωὴν αἰώνιον κληρονομήσω; ²⁶ Ὁ δὲ εἶπεν πρὸς αὐτόν· Ἐν τῷ νόμῳ τί γέγραπται; πῶς ἀναγινώσκεις; ²⁷ Ὁ δὲ ἀποκριθεὶς εἶπεν· Ἀγαπήσεις κύριον τὸν θεόν σου ἐξ ὅλης καρδίας σου, ἐν ὅλῃ τῇ ψυχῇ σου, καὶ ἐν ὅλῃ τῇ ἰσχύϊ σου, καὶ ἐν ὅλῃ τῇ διανοίᾳ σου· καί τὸν πλησίον σου ὡς σεαυτόν. ²⁸ Εἶπεν δὲ αὐτῷ· Ὀρθῶς ἀπεκρίθης· τοῦτο ποίει, καὶ ζήσῃ. ²⁹ Ὁ δὲ θέλων δικαιῶσαι ἑαυτόν, εἶπεν πρὸς τὸν Ἰησοῦν· Καὶ τίς ἐστίν μου πλησίον; ³⁰ Ὑπολαβὼν ὁ Ἰησοῦς εἶπεν· Ἄνθρωπός τις κατέβαινεν ἀπὸ Ἱερουσαλὴμ εἰς Ἱερειχὼ, καὶ λῃσταῖς περιέπεσεν· οἳ καὶ ἐκδύσαντες αὐτὸν, καὶ πληγὰς ἐπιθέντες, ἀπῆλθον, ἀφέντες ἡμιθανῆ· ³¹ Κατὰ συγκυρίαν δὲ ἱερεύς τις κατέβαινεν ἐν τῇ ὁδῷ

VULGATE.

LUKE X. 23-37.

²³ Et conversus ad discipulos suos, dixit : Beati oculi qui vident quæ vos videtis. ²⁴ Dico enim vobis quod multi prophetæ et reges voluerunt videre quæ vos videtis, et non viderunt ; et audire quæ auditis, et non audierunt.

²⁵ Et ecce quidam legisperitus surrexit tentans illum, et dicens : Magister, quid faciendo vitam æternam possidebo? ²⁶ At ille dixit ad eum : In lege quid scriptum est? Quomodo legis? ²⁷ Ille respondens dixit : Diliges Dominum Deum tuum ex toto corde tuo, et ex tota anima tua, et ex omnibus viribus tuis, et ex omni mente tua ; et proximum tuum sicut teipsum. ²⁸ Dixitque illi : Recte respondisti : hoc fac, et vives. ²⁹ Ille autem volens justificare seipsum, dixit ad Jesum : Et quis est meus proximus ? ³⁰ Suscipiens autem Jesus, dixit : Homo quidam descendebat ab Jerusalem in Jericho, et incidit in latrones, qui etiam despoliaverunt eum ; et plagis impositis abierunt, semivivo relicto. ³¹ Accidit autem ut sacerdos quidam descenderet

ἐκείνη· καὶ ἰδὼν αὐτὸν, ἀντιπαρῆλθεν.
³²Ὁμοίως δὲ καὶ λευείτης, κατὰ τὸν
τόπον ἐλθὼν, καὶ ἰδὼν, ἀντιπαρῆλθεν.
³³ Σαμαρείτης δέ τις ὁδεύων, ἦλθεν κατ᾽
αὐτὸν, καὶ ἰδὼν ἐσπλαγχνίσθη.   ³⁴ Καὶ
προσελθὼν κατέδησε τὰ τραύματα αὐτοῦ,
ἐπιχέων ἔλαιον καὶ οἶνον. ἐπιβιβάσας
δὲ αὐτὸν ἐπὶ τὸ ἴδιον κτῆνος, ἤγαγεν
αὐτὸν εἰς πανδοχεῖον, καὶ ἐπεμελήθη
αὐτοῦ. ³⁵ Καὶ ἐπὶ τὴν αὔριον ἐκβαλὼν
ἔδωκεν δύο δηνάρια τῷ πανδοχεῖ, καὶ
εἶπεν· Ἐπιμελήθητι αὐτοῦ· καὶ ὅ τί ἐὰν
προσδαπανήσῃς, ἐγὼ ἐν τῷ ἐπανέρχεσ-
θαί με ἀποδώσω σοι.   ³⁶ Τίς τούτων
τῶν τριῶν πλησίον δοκεῖ σοι γεγονέναι
τοῦ ἐμπεσόντος εἰς τοὺς λῃστάς; ³⁷ Ὁ
δὲ εἶπεν· Ὁ ποιήσας τὸ ἔλεος μετ᾽
αὐτοῦ. Εἶπεν δὲ αὐτῷ Ἰησοῦς· Πορεύου,
καί σὺ ποίει ὁμοίως.

eadem via ; et viso illo, præ-
terivit.   ³² Similiter et levita,
cum esset secus locum, et videret eum, pertransiit.   ³³ Sa-
maritanus autem quidam iter
faciens, venit secus eum ; et
videns eum, misericordia motus est ; ³⁴ et appropians alli-
gavit vulnera ejus, infundens
oleum et vinum ; et imponens
illum in jumentum suum, duxit
in stabulum, et curam ejus
egit.   ³⁵ Et altera die protulit
duos denarios, et dedit stabu-
lario, et ait : Curam illius
habe : et quodcumque supere-
rogaveris, ego, cum rediero,
reddam tibi.   ³⁶ Quis horum
trium videtur tibi proximus
fuisse illi qui incidit in latrones?   ³⁷ At ille dixit : Qui
fecit misericordiam in illum
Et ait illi Jesus : Vade, et tu
fac similiter.

II.—ENGLISH TRANSLATION.

LUKE X. 23-37.

²³ And turning to his disciples, he said : " Blessed are the
eyes that see the things that you see.   ²⁴ For I say to you,
that many prophets and kings have desired to see the things
that you see, and have not seen them ; and to hear the things
that you hear, and have not heard them."

²⁵ And behold, a certain lawyer stood up, tempting him, and
saying : " Master, what must I do to possess eternal life ? "
²⁶ But he said to him : " What is written in the law ? How
readest thou ? "   ²⁷ He answering, said : " Thou shalt love the
Lord thy God with thy whole heart, and with thy whole soul,
and with all thy strength, and with all thy mind ; and thy
neighbour as thyself."   ²⁸ And he said to him : " Thou hast
answered right : this do, and thou shalt live."   ²⁹ But wishing to
justify himself, he said to Jesus : " And who is my neighbour ? "
³⁰ And Jesus answering, said : " A certain man went down from
Jerusalem to Jericho, and fell among robbers, who both stripped
him, and having wounded him, went away leaving him half
dead.   ³¹ And it chanced that a certain priest went down the
same way, and seeing him, passed by.   ³² In like manner also

a levite, when he was near the place and saw him, passed by. [33] But a certain Samaritan being on his journey, came near him ; and seeing him, he was moved with compassion ; [34] and going up to him, bound up his wounds, pouring in oil and wine ; and setting him upon his own beast, he brought him to an inn, and took care of him. [35] And the next day he took out two pence, and gave to the host, and said : ' Take care of him ; and whatsoever thou shalt spend over and above, I at my return will repay thee.' [36] Which of these three in thy opinion was neighbour to him that fell among the robbers ? " [37] But he said : " He that showed mercy to him." And Jesus saith to him : " Go, and do thou in like manner."

III.—NOTES.

Introductory. Except during the great feasts, which he celebrated in Jerusalem, our Lord confined his preaching almost exclusively to Galilee. Towards October, however, in the last year of his public life, when going up to the Holy City for the Feast of Tabernacles (Introduction, p. clxix.), he passed through Judæa, and sent the seventy-two disciples into the towns and villages of that province to prepare the people for a visit from himself and his apostles. When these disciples rejoined him in Jerusalem they told him of the power which in his name they had been enabled to exercise over even the evil spirits. Although the gospel does not state that our Lord had previously and expressly communicated this power over demons to the seventy-two disciples (Luke x. 1-17) as he had to the twelve apostles (Luke ix. 1), it was not without his implied permission that they had acted as they did, and whilst they were exercising this power in his name, he was beholding in their partial victories over the devil an earnest of the total fall of Satan's kingdom. He therefore replied to them : " I beheld Satan like lightning falling from heaven," or more exactly : " I was watching Satan like lightning falling from heaven." (See *Speaker's Comm.*, *in loco.*) Jesus then confirmed the grant of the power they had recently exercised ; he manifested his joy at the success which had attended their preaching amongst the poor ; he thanked his Heavenly Father for what had been accomplished by them ; but he warned them against the spirit of pride which had begun to assert itself in their minds and to manifest itself in their words. All this had taken place in the presence of the crowd. Addressing himself then to the disciples alone, he said :—

V. 23. **Blessed are the eyes that see the things that you see.**

These words, with some few but important variations, were

spoken by our Lord on another occasion and in different circumstances (Matth. xiii. 13-17). When, after hearing the parable of the sower spoken to the multitude, the disciples asked
their Divine Master the question : " Why speakest thou to them
in parables ? " he quoted for them the prophecy of Isaias (vi. 9)
regarding the blindness of the Jews in general, and then declared the singular blessedness bestowed upon themselves in
seeing his miracles and in hearing and believing his words. He
now repeated the saying, and declared them singularly blessed
in beholding him bodily present, in hearing him speak to the
multitudes as man never spoke before, in witnessing his miracles, and in exercising by his delegation during their late mission the wonderful powers of which they had just spoken.

That this happiness of theirs was not only great in itself, but
specially reserved for them by Providence, Christ now proceeds
to prove when he adds :—

**V. 24. For I say to you, that many prophets and kings
have desired to see the things that you see, and have not
seen them ; and to hear the things that you hear, and have
not heard them.**

Amongst the " many " to whom Christ here refers, are Abraham, who was both prince and prophet (Gen. xxiii. 6, and xx.
7) ; Jacob, both prince and prophet (Gen. xlix. 1-4) ; Balaam,
a prophet (Numbers xxiv. 17) ; David, both king and prophet
(2 Kings xxiii. 1-3) ; Isaias, a prophet (Isaias ii. 2, xlv. 8). All
these and others had foretold and ardently desired the coming
of their Saviour ; but, as Christ now reminds his hearers, to
neither king nor prophet was given the joy of seeing on earth
the Desired of Nations. Of Abraham and of the other saints
of the Old Law, St. Paul says : " All these died according to
faith, not having received the promises, but beholding them
afar off, and saluting them, and confessing that they are pilgrims and strangers on the earth. . . . All these being approved
by the testimony of faith, received not the promise, God providing some better things for us, that they should not be perfected
without us " (Hebrews xi. 13, 39, 40). The statement of Christ
to the apostles which we are considering, is not contradicted by
his subsequent declaration in the temple (John viii. 56) ;
" Abraham your father rejoiced that he might see my day :
he *saw it*, and was glad." In the latter saying recorded by
St. John, there is question of seeing with the eyes of the soul by
a revelation granted to the holy patriarch in Limbo : in the
present passage there is reference to vision with the eyes of the
body whilst on earth—a blessing given only to the apostles, the
disciples, and other contemporaries of Christ during his life
here below.

As already said, the words in the two preceding verses were spoken by Christ on the return of the seventy-two disciples from their mission, and have no connection with the fact which is next described by St. Luke. Without giving any record as to time or place, the evangelist continues :—

V. 25. And behold, a certain lawyer stood up, tempting him, and saying : Master, what must I do to possess eternal life ?

The incidents and parable here recorded are peculiar to St. Luke ; and nearly all the circumstances are different from those found in St. Matthew xxii. 34-40 and in St. Mark xii. 28-34, who describe an event that occurred during the last week of our Lord's life.

The name " lawyer " (Greek, νομικός), often met with in St. Luke and only once elsewhere in the gospels (Matth. xxii. 35), signified an expounder of the law. Amongst the Jews this occupation and that of transcribing and preserving the sacred text were the offices of the scribes who, *as a rule*, were bitter enemies of our Lord. There is no reason, however, to suppose that the " lawyer " here mentioned shared the feelings of his class or asked this question from any bad motive (Introduction, p. cxxviii.). The word in the Greek text, ἐκπειράζων = *putting fully to the test*, has not necessarily the ordinary sense of the English word " tempting," but probably that of " trying " for himself if the report regarding our Lord's wisdom were well founded. The form of address, therefore, is respectful ; the question is a fair one ; and though to Christians it seems easy of solution, it was not so to a Jew of that time, when so much importance was attached to sacrifices, purifications, strict observance of the sabbath, and legal ceremonies of every kind.

In proposing this most important question, the " lawyer " most probably expected that the New Teacher would lay down some difficult work as essential to salvation ;

V. 26. But he said to him : What is written in the law ? How readest thou ?

Our Lord in the first part of the answer, refers the questioner to the text of the law itself (Ἐν τῷ νόμῳ τί γέγραπται ;) ; and in the second part, requires him to state the practical import of the precept there contained (Πῶς ἀναγινώσκεις ;). The aim of the " lawyer " though not perverse, was not practical ; and Jesus pointed out that knowledge intended for practical purposes, is of no avail when not reduced to practice.

From being an examiner the " lawyer " is now subjected to examination ; and

V. 27. He answering, said: Thou shalt love the Lord thy God with thy whole heart, and with thy whole soul, and with

**all thy strength, and with all thy mind; and thy neighbour
as thyself.**

This reply of the lawyer to the first portion of Christ's question is a compendium of the whole Mosaic legislation—love of
God and love of one's neighbour.   The summary of our duties
towards God is found in Deuteronomy vi. 4-9, 13, and was
recited in the daily morning prayer of the Jews.   The summary
of our duties towards our neighbour is from Leviticus xix. 18 :
" Seek not revenge, nor be mindful of the injury of thy citizens ;
thou shalt love thy friend as thyself." (Compare with this
Rom. xiii. 8-10 ; James ii. 8.)   Our Lord more than once referred to these two commandments as a compendium of all the
precepts of religion, and as a fulfilment of the whole law.   Thus,
in reply to the doctor of the law, who asked what was the " great
commandment," he said : " Thou shalt love the Lord thy God.
.   .   .   This is the greatest and the first commandment.   And
the second is like to this : Thou shalt love thy neighbour as
thyself " (Matth. xxii. 37-39).

The summary of the law contained in the quotation by the
lawyer in the present passage embraced man's whole being—
physical, intellectual, and moral : it called the whole man to the
service of God in himself and in his image—our neighbour.
(Compare *Int. Comm.*).   Our Lord, therefore, replied,

**V. 28. And he said to him : Thou hast answered right :
this do and thou shalt live.**

Afterwards Christ was himself to give the lawyer's answer to
another scribe (Mark xii. 29-31), and he admits the statement of
the lawyer to be correct.   As, however, he had not only asked
a statement of the law, but had also called attention to its
practical application in the affairs of life (πῶς ἀναγινώσκεις ;=
How readest thou ?), he appended to his approval of the answer
given, an implied admonition that knowledge of duty is not
sufficient for salvation unless this knowledge be very carefully
reduced to practice.   " Not the hearers of the law," said the
Apostle, " are just before God, but the doers of the law shall
be justified " (Rom. ii. 13).   Thus Christ showed that the original
question was fully answered, and that he had no fresh obligation
to impose as a condition for salvation, except the carrying out
in practice of what was already known in theory.

The lawyer, although realising the full force of Christ's reply,
was not yet satisfied,

**V. 29. But wishing to justify himself, he said to Jesus :
And who is my neighbour ?**

The meaning of the clause, " wishing to justify himself," depends on the spirit in which the lawyer may be supposed to have

acted from the beginning. In the opinion of those who consider him to have been in bad faith (Mald., Jans. Ypr., etc.),
his aim now was to *clear himself* from the charge of seeking to
entrap Christ by asking for information which he had himself
been able to give, and had actually given. Such commentators
think, therefore, that in his defence he endeavoured to *justify
himself before men*, and to show that he had a right to ask an
easily-answered question because of this more difficult one connected with it. As has been already stated, there are no grounds
for the suspicion of bad faith. It seems more probable, therefore, that, wishing to fulfil the second commandment and thus
to *justify himself before God*, the lawyer asked to be instructed
on a then much controverted point, namely, who should be regarded as our neighbour.

This second question gave occasion for the parable, or as is
more likely, the history of the good Samaritan ;

**V. 30. And Jesus answering, said: A certain man went
down from Jerusalem to Jericho, and fell among robbers, who
both stripped him, and having wounded him, went away
leaving him half dead.**

It has been remarked by Bloomfield that the Greek ὑπολαβὼν
which is rendered " answering," is really equivalent to " taking
him up." It means more than a mere reply, and indicates that
in the subsequent discourse the speaker takes exception to, or
objects to, an opinion held by another. This is really what
Christ did, not formally, but after the Oriental method, by
telling a story which supplied the material for forming a correct
view on the point under discussion. It is not expressly stated,
but it is implied, that the man spoken of in this story was a
Jew, and therefore of the same religion as the priest and the
levite, though of a different race and religion from those of the
Samaritan. Between the Jews and the Samaritans there had
been a long-continued and most intense hatred, for the origin of
which the reader is referred to McCarthy : *Gospels*, pp. 386,
387. The scene of the story is between Jerusalem and Jericho,
which were the two chief cities of Palestine, and which were
about eighteen miles apart. The road between these two cities
was at all times frequented by robbers ; and in one part it was
called *Adummim* or the *Bloody Way*, from the number of murders which were there committed. Near Jericho, Pompey
destroyed strongholds of robbers (Strabo, *Geog.* xvi. 2-41) :
Herod the Great succeeded in expelling them, but only for a
time (Thompson, *The Land and the Book*, p. 423) ; and subsequent Roman governors could not entirely free the country
from their depredations. These depredations still continue ;
and in 1820, Sir Frederick Heneker, an English Baronet, was

there stripped and murdered by Arabs. The appearance of the place is thus graphically described by a recent writer: " There we see the long descent of 3,000 feet, by which the traveller ' went *down* ' from Jerusalem on its high table-land to Jericho in the Jordan valley. There the last traces of cultivation and habitation, after leaving Bethany, vanish away, and leave him in a wilderness as bare and solitary as the Desert of Arabia. Up from the valley of the Jordan below, or from the caves in the overhanging mountains around him, issue the Bedouin robbers, who from a very early time gave this road a proverbial celebrity for its deeds of blood, and who now make it impossible even for the vast host of pilgrims to descend to the Jordan without a Turkish guard. Sharp turns of the road, projecting spurs of rock, everywhere facilitate the attack and escape of the plunderers. They seize upon the traveller and strip him, as is still the custom of their descendants in like case ; they beat him severely, and leave him naked and bleeding under the fierce sun reflected from the white glaring mountains, to die, unless some unexpected aid arrives." (Stanley's *Sinai and Palestine*, quoted in the *Speaker's Commentary*.)

Such was the scene where the unfortunate way-farer " fell among robbers," or as the Greek text has it, " fell into the midst of robbers," whose sudden appearance is well expressed by the use of the aorist περιέπεσεν. Every circumstance that is narrated aggravated the injury inflicted on their victim by these plunderers, " who both stripped him " (*i.e.*, despoiled or robbed him of all he had), and having wounded him, went away leaving him half dead.

That the traveller should have thus fared at the hands of evil-doers by profession was hard, but still harder was the cruel treatment received from members of his own race and ministers of his own religion. Our Lord continuing his description, says :

V. 31. **And it chanced that a certain priest went down the same way, and seeing him, passed by.**

Jericho was a great sacerdotal centre and one of the cities reserved to the priests (Introduction, pp. cxlvi., cxlvii.) and levites (Introduction, pp. cxlv., cxlvi.) by Josue in the distribution of the Land of Promise. The priest, then, was probably returning to his home there on the conclusion of his course of duty in the temple of Jersualem. Charity even towards one's enemy had been enjoined by Moses and the prophets (Exod. xxiii. 4, 5 ; Deut. xxii. 1-4 ; Isaias lviii. 7), and quoting from Osee vi. 6, our Lord declared that the practice of mercy is more pleasing to God than sacrifice (Matth. ix. 13 ; xii. 7). This must have been well known to the priest, but he did not heed it. He " passed by," or, according to the strong and rare expression in the Greek text (ἀντιπαρῆλθεν), " he passed by keeping the other side of the road," *i.e.*, he studiously avoided the robbed and wounded traveller. Thus did he wilfully throw away his opportunity of being merciful himself and of teaching others to be so. That such an opportunity and such a grace were offered him seems to be signified by the use of the uncommon expression, κατὰ συγκυρίαν. This clause, κατὰ συγκυρίαν, translated " by chance," really means " by coincidence," or " at the same time." The word " chance " = τύχη or συντυχία does not occur in the New Testament, and only once or twice in the Old. Bengel remarks (*in loco*) : " Many good opportunities are concealed under events which seem to happen by chance." It has been well said that what appears to us to be by accident, is to the inspired writers the effect of God's secret providence.

The unworthy descendant of Aaron was not alone in his neglect of grace and of the opportunity of doing an act of mercy towards the poor traveller. The wicked, indeed, find many imitators, and

V. 32. In like manner also a levite, when he was near the place and saw him, passed by.

As the priests, descendants of Aaron, were appointed to offer sacrifice to God, so the levites, the other descendants of Levi, were commissioned to assist the priests in their sacred duties. The levite here mentioned appears to have been accompanying the priest, and in default of his superior, should have shown charity to the distressed ; but this sacred minister acted worse than the former, as appears from the Greek text, κατὰ τὸν τόπον ἐλθών, καὶ ἰδών, ἀντιπαρῆλθεν = *coming up to the place and seeing him, passed by, keeping the far* (*or opposite*) *side of the road.* This heartless cruelty is noted in the Greek text by St. Luke's favourite expression of δὲ καὶ (*cf.* xiv. 12 ; xvi. 1, 22, etc.).

For the honour of humanity, all were not so unfeeling ;

V. 33. But a certain Samaritan being on his journey, came near him ; and seeing him, he was moved with compassion.

The emphatic position of the word " Samaritan " in the Greek text puts the conduct of this man in strong contrast with that of the two preceding travellers. He belonged to a race which was contemned by the Jews as heathen and idolatrous (Introduction, p. cxxxii. *seq.*). A Samaritan, indeed, was regarded as an alien by the Jews (Luke xvii. 18), who would have no dealings with him (John iv. 9) ; his testimony would not be admitted in a Jewish court of law ; no Jew would eat with him ; and the " lawyer " (Luke x. 37) would not name him. (See Farrar, *in loco*, where he quotes in substance from Josephus : *Antiq.* xx. 6, 1 ; xviii. 2, 2, *B. J.*, ii. 12, 3.) The two peoples, therefore, had no common origin, no common political or religious views, no social intercourse. They were strangers in blood,

in manners, in religion ; and were locally united only to bring
out more strongly their mutual and abiding hatred. (See
McCarthy, *in loco*.) Looking at the matter from a merely natural
point of view, there seemed to be no bond of union between
the two men now brought face to face ; and still our Lord selected
these as types of " neighbours," who were bound to discharge
towards each other the mutual offices of supernatural charity.

The manner in which these offices were now discharged on
the part of the Samaritan is indicated by the strong expression
ἐσπλαγχνίσθη = *was inwardly moved with compassion.* Nor was
this enough. Unlike the unworthy priest and still more unworthy levite, he did more than feel pity for the stranger ;

**V. 34. And going up to him, bound up his wounds, pouring
in oil and wine ; and setting him upon his own beast, he
brought him to an inn, and took care of him.**

It is to be remarked that " the most beloved physician "
(Coloss. iv. 14) St. Luke, whilst recording our Lord's words,
here dwells on the treatment of the sick which was then in vogue.
Oil is mentioned as a remedy for wounds in Isaias i. 6, and in
Plin., *Hist. Nat.*, xxxi. 17. The mixture of oil and wine is not
referred to as such in the Bible ; but it is in the Talmudic treatise
Shabbath, f. 133a. It is mentioned, too, in the history of the
army of Aelius Gallius. (See Farrar and McCarthy, quoting from
Smith, *B.D.*, art. *Oil*.) Again it is to be noted that the word
used to signify a refuge for travellers is generally κατάλυμα. The
place so designated was the same as the modern caravansary.
The word πανδοχεῖον which is here employed, signifies an inn
in our modern sense of the word—an hotel or hospice with a
host (see verse 35), who for payment supplied food and lodging
to all comers. From a show of pity which itself was a consolation, the Samaritan proceeded to afford such help as was at
hand, and to procure the further attention that was needed by
the robbed and wounded Jew. He approached with kindness,
bound up the bleeding wounds, applied the ordinary remedies
of the day, put the stranger on his own beast, walked by his
side to an inn, and himself acted as his nurse.

The Samaritan was obliged to continue his journey, but he
wished to provide for the further necessities of the invalid ;

**V. 35. And the next day he took out twopence, and gave to
the host, and said : Take care of him ; and whatsoever thou
shalt spend over and above, I, at my return, will repay thee.**

The " two pence " given to the host were two Roman
silver coins, called " denarii " (Introduction, p. cxxii.). In the
time of Christ the " denarius " or Roman silver penny was
equivalent to 9½d. of our money (Hastings). It was the ordinary day-wage of a labourer (see Matth. xx. 2), and had been

lately given as the pay of a Roman soldier (Tacitus, *Ann.* i. 17). The amount seems small ; but it was sufficient for the probable needs of the patient during the short absence of his benefactor. That this patient might not experience any want now unforeseen the Samaritan commissions the host to be unsparing in attention to him ; and he promises that full payment will be made not by the Jew, but by himself, and not at a distant or uncertain date, but on his return journey. That such is the meaning of the last words is clear from the emphatic position of the pronoun ἐγὼ in the Greek and in the Latin, and from the use of the pres. inf. in the Greek.

Having proposed to the doctor of the law these three types of men, and having so graphically described their several ways of dealing with their robbed and wounded fellow-creature, Christ asked :—

Vv. 36, 37. **Which of these three, in thy opinion, was neighbour to him that fell among the robbers ? But he said : He that showed mercy to him.**

These verses require careful attention. " It will be observed," says Alford (*in loco*), " that our Lord not only elicits the answer from the questioner himself, but that it comes *in an inverted form*. The lawyer had asked *to whom* he was to understand himself obliged to fulfil the duties of neighbourship ? but the answer has for its subject *one who fulfilled them to another*. The reason of this is to be found—partly in the relation of neighbourship being *mutual*, so that if this man is my neighbour, I am his also ;—but chiefly in the intention of our Lord to bring out a strong contrast by putting the hated and despised Samaritan in the *active* place, and thus to reflect back the ὁμοίως more pointedly."

Another difficulty requires solution. At first sight it would seem from Christ's question and the lawyer's answer that the Samaritan alone was neighbour to the wounded Jew. To answer this difficulty, some direct attention to the use of the clause πλησίον γεγονέναι, which signifies not " to have been a neighbour," but rather " to have become a neighbour," or " to have proved a neighbour." According to these commentators, then, it is implied that though all others were really neighbours to the Jew, our Lord wished to hear from the lawyer who it was that " became a neighbour," or " proved a neighbour " in the circumstances. (See *Int. Comm.*, *in loco*.) A simpler and better answer is given by others. It does not really follow from Christ's question and from the lawyer's answer that the Samaritan alone was neighbour to the wounded Jew. The lawyer, who out of intense hatred will not name the Samaritan, is first forced by Christ to admit that this detested stranger alone had acted as a neighbour to the Jew. Then, approving of this kindness and prescribing it as a duty, Christ showed indirectly that it was the only mode of fulfilling the law in question. From this our Lord allowed his interrogator to conclude that the most alien in religion and country, and therefore. all men are neighbours.

The theory had been fully unfolded, but the practical application was now to be proposed to the lawyer ;

And Jesus saith to him : Go, and do thou in like manner.

If this rendering were correct, the Greek should be Πορεύου, καὶ ποίει σὺ ὁμοίως. As the text stands, the meaning is rather : "Go, thou also do likewise." It is remarked that in these words the historical truth or likelihood of the narrative is implied, and imitation is prescribed. Nay more, the imitation prescribed is to take the form not merely of a single *act*, but of a life-long *practice*. This is the force of the present imperative.

Here we have the moral of the parable and the application made by Christ himself. The sense of our Lord's words is : " As the Samaritan recognised a neighbour in the unfortunate Jewish traveller, and, what is more, acted towards him as a neighbour notwithstanding differences of religion, country, and social customs, so do you adopt the life-long practice of recognising as neighbours all without exception, however alien to you in country, in religion, in social customs, or in feeling. Nor is this enough. If, while recognising all as your neighbours, you wish to fulfil the second precept of divine charity assist them in their necessities according to your power. Thus by relieving the necessitous after the example of the Samaritan, you shall perform a more pleasing act of religion than by those external sacrifices on which priests and levites lay such stress, whilst they treat with indifference the miseries of their fellow-creatures and turn a deaf ear to the voice of distress."

IV.—MORAL REFLECTIONS.

1. The question put by Jesus and the answer given by the lawyer are of supreme interest to us. All the discourses of our Divine Master have a deeper sense and an application much more extended than appears at first sight. In truth, whilst seeming to address himself to the people of his own time only, his eternal word is addressed to all generations ; and what ne said to this doctor regarding the knowledge of the divine law, he says to all mankind in all ages. The study of God's law should be the first and principal occupation of every Christian, for the divine hand that wrote it has inserted there all we need to know that we may be directed and sustained on our way to heaven. With precepts the most sublime it joins motives the most efficacious ; instructing the mind and touching

the heart, it leads us at once by reason and by sentiment ; and dictated for all men, it is adapted to the particular wants of each. So true is this, that ignorance finds there lessons for its instruction ; feebleness, supports to sustain it ; faint-hearted-ness, encouragement to excite it ; pusillanimity, examples to arouse it ; timidity, hope to invite it ; and presumption, warnings to keep it in check. The human mind can imagine nothing which the divine law has not provided for, nor can the human heart desire anything which is not there regulated. Whilst this is so, how many Christians there are who are ignorant of this law ; how many refuse to learn it, and still put forward their ignorance as an excuse for violating it ! How many there are who, having had the happiness of being instructed in it, neglect to observe it or allow it to be effaced from their hearts by crimi-nal habits ! Let us inquire if any one of these reproaches applies to ourselves ; and if this be the case, let us in future repair our faults by a careful study and exact fulfilment of our duty to God.

2. What is this law to which Christ draws the attention of the doctor, and to which he invites our own ? From the reply of the doctor, which was approved by our divine Master, the abridgment and substance of the law is the love of God and of our neighbour, or, in other words, divine charity. It is not that in the Christian religion there is no other virtue than that of charity. To believe such a statement would be a dangerous error formally opposed to the teaching of the Holy Spirit and the declaration of the Church. Charity is the first of virtues, but it is not the only one. It supposes all the others, but it does not replace them ; it is our motive in the fulfilment of all our duties, but it does not dispense us from these duties. It is so far the " fulfilling of the law " (Rom. xiii. 10), that its effect is to make us keep perfectly all the commandments. Such is the teaching of Jesus Christ, who says : " He that hath my commandments and keepeth them, he it is that loveth me " (John xiv. 21). Such too is the lesson repeated in almost identical words by " the disciple whom Jesus loved."

3. It is from heaven that charity comes ; it is in the bosom of God that it has its source ; and St. John has said that " God is charity " (1 John iv. 8). An eternal love unites the three Divine Persons ; and the love which the Father has for him, Jesus Christ has for us. He says : " As the Father hath loved me, I also have loved you " (John xv. 9) ; and he wills that this be the type of our love for our neighbour. " This," said he, " is my commandment, that you love one another, as I have loved you " (John xv. 12). As Jesus Christ loved his Father for his own sake, and loved us for his Father's sake, we should follow the same order in the exercise of charity. We cannot

indeed love for themselves all men, known and unknown, friends
and enemies ; but we can and must love them for God, and love
God in them.   In loving them even when they hate and injure
us, we love the images of God, the adopted children of our common Father, the brethren of Jesus Christ.   Such is the great
virtue of charity.   The love which the Father has for the Son,
that which the Son has for us, that which we have for God and
for each other, are but one love having its source in God and
finding its ultimate object in him.

4. Between the love of God for us and our love for our neighbour, there is another point of resemblance—it is the spirit of
self-sacrifice.   Behold the love of Jesus Christ !   It was it that
caused him to immolate himself for us when he had clothed
himself with our humanity.   St. John tells us that this was the
proof of divine love ; and he immediately adds that it should
be the mark of ours.   " In this," says he, " we have known
the charity of God, because he hath laid down his life for us ;
and we ought to lay down our lives for the brethren " (1 John
iii. 16).   All that can be of use to our neighbour is secured for
him by this virtue.   It does not think of any good which it does
not labour to procure him, nor know of any service which it
does not seek to render him.   When it cannot benefit him by
its alms, it does so by its prayers ; and invoking the divine
power for the objects of its solicitude, it draws down upon them
by its intercession the blessings of heaven.

5. Human charity resembles divine love in its duration.   As
this sublime virtue comes from heaven, it conducts us thither ;
and after having been in time the source of our merit, in eternity it will be our recompense.   The other virtues pass away
with this life : not so charity.   Faith can no longer exist in the
beatific vision ; hope will have ceased when we enter on the
possession of our reward ; but charity will triumph over time,
and the ruin of earthly things will but augment its purity and
intensify its force.   It is by charity, therefore, that we approach
to God and become truly his images.   Can we, then, be
astonished at the praise which St. Paul gives to this virtue, at
the necessity he finds for it, at the prerogatives he claims for it,
or at the marvellous effects he attributes to it ?   (See 1 Cor. xiii.)
It is, in truth, the completion of the moral edifice—an edifice
which it crowns and protects.

THIRTEENTH SUNDAY AFTER PENTECOST.

I.--TEXTS.

GREEK.

LUKE XVII. 11-19.

¹¹ Καὶ ἐγένετο ἐν τῷ πορεύεσθαι εἰς Ἰερουσαλήμ, καὶ αὐτὸς διήρχετο διὰ μέσου Σαμαρείας καὶ Γαλειλαίας. ¹² Καὶ εἰσερχομένου αὐτοῦ εἴς τινα κώμην, ἀπήντησαν δέκα λεπροὶ ἄνδρες, οἳ ἀνέστησαν πόρρωθεν. ¹³ Καὶ αὐτοὶ ἦραν φωνὴν, λέγοντες· Ἰησοῦ ἐπιστάτα, ἐλέησον ἡμᾶς. ¹⁴ Καὶ ἰδὼν εἶπεν αὐτοῖς· Πορευθέντες ἐπιδείξατε ἑαυτοὺς τοῖς ἱερεῦσιν. Καὶ ἐγένετο ἐν τῷ ὑπάγειν αὐτούς, ἐκαθαρίσθησαν. ¹⁵ Εἷς δὲ ἐξ αὐτῶν, ἰδὼν ὅτι ἰάθη, ὑπέστρεψεν, μετὰ φωνῆς μεγάλης δοξάζων τὸν θεόν. ¹⁶ Καὶ ἔπεσεν ἐπὶ πρόσωπον παρὰ τοὺς πόδας αὐτοῦ, εὐχαριστῶν αὐτῷ· καὶ αὐτὸς ἦν Σαμαρείτης. ¹⁷ Ἀποκριθεὶς δὲ ὁ Ἰησοῦς, εἶπεν· Οὐχὶ οἱ δέκα ἐκαθαρίσθησαν; Οἱ δὲ ἐννέα ποῦ; ¹⁸ Οὐχ εὑρέθησαν ὑποστρέψαντες δοῦναι δόξαν τῷ θεῷ, εἰ μὴ ὁ ἀλλογενὴς οὗτος. ¹⁹ Καὶ εἶπεν αὐτῷ· Ἀναστὰς πορεύου (* ἡ πίστις σου σέσωκέν σε).

* Omitted in Codex B, but found in other MSS. and in *Textus Receptus*, and translated in Vulgate.

VULGATE.

LUKE XVII. 11-19.

¹¹ Et factum est, dum iret in Jerusalem, transibat per mediam Samariam et Galilæam. ¹² Et cum ingrederetur quoddam castellum, occurrerunt ei decem viri leprosi, qui steterunt a longe, ¹³ et levaverunt vocem, dicentes : Jesu, præceptor, miserere nostri. ¹⁴ Quos ut vidit, dixit : Ite, ostendite vos sacerdotibus. Et factum est, dum irent, mundati sunt. ¹⁵ Unus autem ex illis, ut vidit quia mundatus est, regressus est, cum magna voce magnificans Deum. ¹⁶ Et cecidit in faciem ante pedes ejus, gratias agens ; et hic erat Samaritanus. ¹⁷ Respondens autem Jesus dixit : Nonne decem mundati sunt? Et novem ubi sunt? ¹⁸ Non est inventus qui rediret et daret gloriam Deo, nisi hic alienigena. ¹⁹ Et ait illi : Surge, vade, quia fides tua te salvum fecit.

II.—ENGLISH TRANSLATION.

LUKE XVII. 11-19.

¹¹ And it came to pass, as he was going to Jerusalem, he passed through the midst of Samaria and Galilee. ¹² And as

he entered into a certain town, there met him ten men that were lepers, who stood afar off, [13] and lifted up their voice, saying: "Jesus, Master, have mercy on us." [14] And when he saw them, he said: "Go, show yourselves to the priests." And it came to pass, as they went, they were made clean. [15] And one of them, when he saw that he was made clean, went back, with a loud voice glorifying God. [16] And he fell on his face before his feet, giving thanks; and this was a Samaritan. [17] And Jesus answering, said: "Were not ten made clean? And where are the nine? [18] There is no one found to return and give glory to God but this stranger." [19] And he said to him: "Arise, go thy way; for thy faith hath made thee whole."

III.—NOTES.

Introductory. It was the aim of St. Paul's preaching to declare the universality of Christ's redemption; and St. Luke, the companion of that apostle, included in his gospel such facts of Christ's life as brought into relief this all-embracing love of the Redeemer. Hence, as he was afterwards (Luke xviii. 35-xix. 9) to record side by side the blessing of sight bestowed on the Jewish blind man of Jericho, and the greater blessings of faith and justification granted to the heathen Zachaeus, prince of the publicans in the same city, so does he in the present passage record the healing of the mixed group of lepers and the special praise bestowed on the Samaritan who was found amongst them. This event took place in the last journey of Christ to Jerusalem, a short time before his Passion. As may be learned from the gospel of St. John (John xi. 1-3), Christ had been called from Peræa to Bethany on the death of Lazarus, and by restoring him to life he had aroused against himself the anger of the pharisees (John xi. 46-53). From Ephrem, to which he then retired for a time with his disciples (John xi. 54), he set out by a circuitous route through Samaria and Galilee on the west of the Jordan, and through Peræa on the east, and arrived in Jerusalem to celebrate the Passover before he suffered. The precise time and place at which this miracle occurred during the journey, are not recorded by St. Luke, who says merely:—

V. 11. And it came to pass, as he was going to Jerusalem, he passed through the midst of Samaria and Galilee.

It has been remarked that St. Luke does not give many geographical references in his gospel; and the one here found presents a great difficulty to commentators. According to some the clause, διὰ μέσου = "through the midst of," is inserted to make known the districts *through which* lay the direct road to

Jerusalem followed by Jesus when going up to the Holy City from the extreme north of Palestine. This is the opinion generally held ; but it is not free from serious objections. Another explanation is thus offered by Bloomfield (*in loco*) : " The only way of satisfactorily accounting for the mention of Samaria before Galilee (contrary to the true geographical position) is to suppose with many eminent expositors . . . that our Lord did not proceed by the *direct* way (namely, through Samaria) to Jerusalem, but that, upon coming to the confines of Samaria and Galilee, he diverged to the east, so as to have Samaria on the right, and Galilee on the left. Thus he seems to have passed the Jordan at Scythopolis (where there was a bridge), and to have descended along the left bank on the Peræan side, until he again crossed the river, when he came opposite to Jericho. A reason which induced him to take this circuitous route was probably to avoid any molestation from the Samaritans, and at the same time to impart to a greater number of Jews the benefits of the gospel."

Having thus indicated the scene of the miracle as far as was necessary to explain the different nationalities of the persons to be cured, St. Luke continues :—

Vv. 12, 13. And as he entered into a certain town, there met him ten men that were lepers, who stood afar off, and lifted up their voice saying: Jesus, Master, have mercy on us.

Leprosy (Introduction, p. xciii.) is a horrible disease, painful, disgusting, and most frequently incurable. At the commencement, it shows itself in little whitish spots on some part of the skin ; and these develop into a rash, then into ulcers, which gradually cover the whole body. When the disease reaches an acute stage, the hands and feet swell, are chapped, and burst open. At a later period the nails fall off ; the eyes become bleared and lose their lustre ; the nose pours forth a purulent watery matter ; the breath is fetid ; and the voice is hoarse and shrill. Throughout the whole illness, the patient is restless and melancholy even to despair ; his sufferings before death are aggravated by consumption and dropsy ; and even if death does not supervene, the sickness leaves its traces in a lifelong and ghastly whiteness from head to foot. Amongst the Jews those infected with leprosy were subjected to many restrictions, and sometimes were not permitted to enter the cities (Levit. x ii. 46). When they were permitted to assist at divine worship, they had a special place set apart in the synagogues ; and being generally forbidden all intercourse with others, they were accustomed to live in desert places far from the habitations of men.

Commentators remark the unusually large number of lepers that were here found together, and the most unlooked-for asso-

ciation of Jews and Samaritans.   Perhaps they had heard that
Christ was to pass along the road , and not being permitted to
enter the city, they assembled outside the gates and awaited
his approach.   Probably too, all being outcasts from every other
society, as happens between Mohammedans and Jews in the leper
houses of the East, in their common misery they laid aside for a
time the national antipathies which in other cirumstances would
have kept Jews and Samaritans apart.   But though excluded
from the society of men, and obliged to remain at a distance of
one hundred paces from the city gates, they knew that in Christ
they could find relief.   No doubt, moved by grace conferred
on them, they gave themselves to prayer ; they made their
petition in common ; although their disease scarcely permitted
the exertion, " they lifted up their voice " with earnest confi-
dence ; and they called on Jesus as the Master ($\epsilon\pi\iota\sigma\tau\acute{a}\tau a$) who
has in his hands the power of life and death.

According to the divine promise, such a prayer could not but
obtain from Christ relief for the lepers,

**V. 14. And when he saw them, he said: Go show your-
selves to the priests.   And it came to pass as they went, they
were made clean.**

Leprosy was a striking figure of the spiritual disease of sin
which Christ came on earth to heal.   Hence, it is remarked
that one of the miracles of the first year of our Lord's public
life (Matth. viii. 2-4 ; Mark i. 40-45 ; Luke v. 12-14) was the
cure of a leper, and that he was ever ready to give ear to the
petition of persons afflicted with this malady.   Such was the
case with the sufferers here described ; for " when he saw,"
or, as it is in the Greek, $\iota\delta\grave{\omega}\nu =$ " immediately that he saw " their
distress, he inspired them with hope.   According to the Mosaic
legislation (Levit. xiii., xiv. ; cf. Matth. viii. 4), only the priests
(not necessarily in Jerusalem) had authority to declare one affected
with leprosy, and to prescribe the rites for his purification on
recovery from the disease (Introduction, p. clix.).   The lepers
were now directed to comply with these requirements of the
law, which was binding on the Jews amongst them, and they
thus received an implied promise of restoration to health.
Unlike what took place on other occasions, these sufferers
were not cured before their departure ; but " it came to pass,
as they went, they were made clean," in order that the faith
and gratitude of all and especially of the Samaritan might be
tested and rewarded.   Alford remarks : " In this going away,
in the absence of Jesus they were healed ; what need to go back
and give him thanks ?   Here was a trial of their *love—faith*
they had, enough to go, and enough to be cleansed : but *love*
(with one exception)—gratitude, they had not."

The lepers were not wanting in the fulfilment of the command imposed on them ;

Vv. 15, 16. **And one of them, when he saw that he was made clean, went back, with a loud voice glorifying God. And he fell on his face before his feet, giving thanks; and this was a Samaritan.**

The cure took place on the journey to the priests (see preceding verse) ; and the use of the aorist ἰδὼν would seem to indicate that *immediately* without proceeding further, this man returned to Christ. It is much more probable, however, that he did not do so until he had fulfilled the precept imposed upon him, and had submitted to the prescribed purification. The reasons for this opinion are that 1°, of his own accord on his return he approached our Lord—an act not permitted to those who, though cured from leprosy, had not yet been pronounced clean by the competent authority ; and that 2°, the willingness to present himself to the priest appears to have been exacted from each leper as a condition in our Lord's implied promise of a cure. Having been restored to health, then, and having complied with the ceremony of legal purification, this man on his return showed by his loud voice the intensity of the joy with which he gave thanks to God, to whom he attributed the blessing just received.

Presenting himself before Jesus, he expressed his gratitude to him as a mediator with God. Nay more, it would seem that enlightened by faith he recognised in him the dignity of God made Man. Such a conclusion commends itself to us if we consider the form of expression used by the evangelist in describing the leper's acts and words. In that description there is a perfect parallelism between the sentence ὑπέστρεψε, . . . δοξάζων τὸν θεόν = "He went back . . . glorifying God" and the sentence, ἔπεσεν . . . . εὐχαριστῶν αὐτῷ = "He fell . . . giving thanks to him"; and this parallelism seems to indicate that the "giving glory" and the "giving thanks" had the same person for their object. As, therefore, it is expressly stated in the first sentence that he to whom the leper gave glory, was God, it follows that he before whose feet the leper fell, *i.e.*, Christ, was in the second sentence declared to be God.

And what was this man, whose exhibition of religious feeling is thus so minutely described? With great emphasis on the pronoun, St. Luke says: καὶ αὐτὸς ἦν Σαμαρείτης = "and *he* was a Samaritan." He was an "alien" (verse 18), a schismatic, a half heathen, from whom this gratitude and profession of gratitude could hardly have been expected. Already indeed, as it was the aim of the evangelist to show, Christ who would have been the glory of his people Israel, was beginning to shine as a " light to the revelation of the Gentiles " (Luke ii. 32).

That such was the lesson to be learned, is shown in the following words :—

Vv. 17, 18. And Jesus answering, said: Were not ten made clean ? And where are the nine ? There is no one found to return and give glory to God but this stranger.

The word ἀποκριθεὶς, here translated " answering, " has frequently in the New Testament the special meaning of " opening a conversation," and does not necessarily introduce a reply.   On the present occasion, the words which follow were spoken *about* the Samaritan and his companions, not *to* him.   The questions thus introduced were not asked by Christ in ignorance of the facts, but in order to publish the cure of all, which he had already known by his omniscience and had effected by his omnipotence. Then by the emphatic position at the end given to the ποῦ = " where," attention is very forcibly drawn to the absence of all except the Samaritan, who is contrasted with the nine others as a " stranger " or alien.   Unless he was a Jewish proselyte (Introduction, p. cxxx.), this man was partly a stranger in religion ; in any case, he was wholly a stranger in race or blood ; and he submitted himself to the judgment of the priests not in virtue of a previous obligation, but solely in compliance with Christ's command.   The nine others, indeed, were not wanting in faith, for Christ had submitted their faith to the test by sending them while still diseased to obtain from the priests a certificate of their cure.   Probably, too, they were grateful in their hearts for the benefit conferred ; but as they did not return to express this feeling, their conduct was censured by our Lord.   Man, composed of a body and soul, is required to give *outward expression* to his thankfulness for divine gifts, and to make an outward acknowledgment of his indebtedness to God.   St. Bernard observes that those who at first are not so highly favoured, are frequently the most faithful to this duty of gratitude, and thus earn for themselves new and greater blessings.

That some such additional blessings were conferred on the Samaritan in this case, would appear from the concluding words of Christ thus recorded by St. Luke :—

V. 19. And he said to him : Arise, go thy way; for thy faith hath made thee whole.

The Vatican codex B, from which our Greek text is generally copied, has not any expression corresponding to : " Thy faith hath made thee whole."   These words, however, are found in the Lewis Sinai palimpsest (Syriac) ; they have elsewhere sufficient MS. authority to support them ; and they are very probably authentic.

It is remarked that except in very few cases such as those of the dead (Matth. ix.; Mark v.; Luke vii.; viii.; John xi.) and that of the high-priest's servant (Luke xxii. 50, 51), Christ required in the subject of a miracle a belief in his divine power. This was required not as an efficient cause, but as a necessary condition of restoration to health. Not only the Samaritan, then, but also the nine others had faith in Christ's power. Nay more, there is no reason to think that they had all received from God's infinite goodness absolution from their sins as well as liberation from their corporal disease. Why, then, does our Lord here refer with emphasis to the faith of the Samaritan? By the words ἡ πίστις σου σέσωκέ σε = "thy faith hath made *thee* whole," he seems to have indicated that in reward for the faith which in the case of the Samaritan was not permitted to lie dormant, this "stranger" received with the cure of his corporal disease not only the first grace of justification, but also a higher grade of sanctity and the crowning blessing of perseverance therein.

IV.—MORAL REFLECTIONS.

In this gospel passage there are three points that afford us matter for useful reflection: the association of the lepers with each other, the earnest prayer offered in common, and the gratitude shown by the Samaritan.

1. In the first place, as corporal leprosy was a figure of the spiritual leprosy of sin, so the association of these unhappy men is a figure of what we see take place amongst the wicked. That one resembles his companions, is a proverb founded on nature, justified by experience, and consecrated by use in the Sacred Scripture. It is written: "He that walketh with the wise, shall be wise: a friend of fools shall become like to them" (Prov. xiii. 20). Conformity of tastes, of inclinations, of principles, is the most general cause of this fellowship. The just seek the society of the just and wish to derive instruction from their discourse, support from their exhortation, and encouragement from their example. On the other hand, the wicked ardently seek for evil companions in order to give themselves without shame to a dissolute life, to be encouraged by mutual approbation, and to fortify themselves against remorse by bad example. But if the association of the wicked with each other is brought about by their common corruption of heart, it also leads to that result. It is in such society that innocence is lost and depravity of morals is consummated. If the just man finds it difficult to persevere, if the apostle says: "Let him that thinketh he standeth, take heed lest he fall" (1 Cor. x. 12), if we have continual need of prayer and good example to support our weakness,

how can he escape a fall who joins to his own feebleness the inducements to evil that are to be found in bad companions? If it is not easy to resist the seduction of our corrupt nature within, how shall we succeed at the same time against multiplied assaults from without? It is not always possible to avoid the company of the wicked; but in this impossibility of retreat from danger, we should take such precautions as will assure our preservation from contagion. If it must be, let us see sinners, but not more frequently than is necessary; let us speak to them, but not with familiarity; let us live with them, but without imitation; and whilst taking care to suffer no injury from their example, we should endeavour to render our intercourse profitable to their souls.

2. In the second place, when the lepers raised their voices together to beseech their Saviour for their cure, they gave us a specimen of that prayer in common which Christ strongly recommends, and the power of which he expressly declares. His words are: " I say to you, that if two of you shall consent upon earth concerning anything whatsoever they shall ask, it shall be done to them by my Father who is in heaven; for where there are two or three gathered together in my name, there am I in the midst of them " (Matth. xviii. 19, 20). This union of petitions is agreeable to God, for in it is found the earnestness by which the kingdom of heaven is gained. Here we may *apply* the words: " The kingdom of heaven suffereth violence, and the violent bear it away " (Matth. xi. 12). The piety of some communicates ardour to the coldness of others; they mutually animate and aid each other; they receive and give edification; and the divine goodness deigns to accept in favour of the less perfect the dispositions of the more devout. Entering into the views of her Founder, the Church has made public prayer the external bond which unites us her children in the profession of our faith and in the offering of our worship; and accepting her invitation to contribute our part to devout exercises performed in common, we share in the rewards of the whole.

3. Not without a special significance the evangelist remarks that one of the lepers, on being healed, returned thanks to Jesus Christ, and at the same time glorified God as the author of his cure. It is very natural and just that we express our gratitude to those from whom immediately we receive a benefit, who assist us in our needs, who comfort us in our sufferings, who console us in our afflictions, who counsel us in our doubts, or who instruct us in our ignorance. Still, whilst performing this duty to our immediate benefactors, we should raise our thoughts to him from whom primarily and principally all our happiness proceeds. " Do not err, therefore, my dearest brethren," says St. James, " every best gift, and every perfect gift, is from

above, coming down from the Father of lights, with whom there is no change nor shadow of alteration " (James i. 16, 17). Creatures are but the instruments of God's munificence and the channels through which his graces flow to us. If men assist us, it is God who suggests the thought to them, inspires them with the will, and places the means in their hands. Whatever, then, may be the hand held out to us, it is to God we should first give thanks ; it is with him our gratitude should commence ; and it is with him it should terminate.

FOURTEENTH SUNDAY AFTER PENTECOST.

I.—TEXTS.

GREEK.

MATTHEW VI. 24-33.

²⁴ Οὐδεὶς δύναται δυσὶ κυρίοις δουλεύειν· ἢ γὰρ τὸν ἕνα μισήσει, καὶ τὸν ἕτερον ἀγαπήσει· ἢ ἑνὸς ἀνθέξεται, καὶ τοῦ ἑτέρου καταφρονήσει· οὐ δύνασθε θεῷ δουλεύειν καὶ μαμωνᾷ. ²⁵ Διὰ τοῦτο λέγω ὑμῖν· μὴ μεριμνᾶτε τῇ ψυχῇ ὑμῶν τί φάγητε ἢ τί πίητε, μηδὲ τῷ σώματι ὑμῶν τί ἐνδύσησθε. Οὐχὶ ἡ ψυχὴ πλεῖόν ἐστι τῆς τροφῆς, καὶ τὸ σῶμα τοῦ ἐνδύματος; ²⁶ Ἐμβλέψατε εἰς τὰ πετεινὰ τοῦ οὐρανοῦ, ὅτι οὐ σπείρουσιν, οὐδὲ θερίζουσιν, οὐδὲ συνάγουσιν εἰς ἀποθήκας, καὶ ὁ πατὴρ ὑμῶν ὁ οὐράνιος τρέφει αὐτά· οὐχ' ὑμεῖς μᾶλλον διαφέρετε αὐτῶν; ²⁷ Τίς δὲ ἐξ ὑμῶν μεριμνῶν δύναται προσθεῖναι ἐπὶ τὴν ἡλικίαν αὐτοῦ πῆχυν ἕνα; ²⁸ Καὶ περὶ ἐνδύματος τί μεριμνᾶτε; Καταμάθετε τὰ κρίνα τοῦ ἀγροῦ πῶς αὐξάνουσιν. Οὐ κοπιοῦσιν, οὐδὲ νήθουσιν· ²⁹ λέγω δὲ ὑμῖν, ὅτι οὐδὲ Σολομὼν ἐν πάσῃ τῇ δόξῃ αὐτοῦ περιεβάλετο ὡς ἓν τούτων. ³⁰ Εἰ δὲ τὸν χόρτον τοῦ ἀγροῦ σήμερον ὄντα καὶ αὔριον εἰς

VULGATE.

MATTHEW VI. 24-33.

24 Nemo potest duobus dominis servire ; aut enim unum odio habebit, et alterum diliget ; aut unum sustinebit, et alterum contemnet. Non potestis Deo servire et mammonæ. 25 Ideo dico vobis, ne solliciti sitis animæ vestræ quid manducetis, neque corpori vestro quid induamini. Nonne anima plus est quam esca, et corpus plus quam vestimentum ? 26 Respicite volatilia cœli, quoniam non serunt, neque metunt, neque congregant in horrea ; et Pater vester cœlestis pascit illa. Nonne vos magis pluris estis illis? 27 Quis autem vestrum cogitans potest adjicere ad staturam suam cubitum unum? 28 Et de vestimento quid solliciti estis? Considerate lilia agri quomodo crescunt : non laborant neque nent ; 29 dico autem vobis quoniam nec Salomon in omni gloria sua coopertus est sicut unum ex istis. 30 Si autem fœnum agri quod hodie est et cras in clibanum

κλίβανον βαλλόμενον, ὁ θεὸς οὕτως ἀμφιέννυσιν, οὐ πολλῷ μᾶλλον ὑμᾶς, ὀλιγόπιστοι; ³¹ Μὴ οὖν μεριμνήσητε, λέγοντες· Τί φάγωμεν, ἢ τι πίωμεν, ἢ τί περιβαλώμεθα; ³² Πάντα γὰρ ταῦτα τὰ ἔθνη ἐπιζητοῦσιν· οἶδεν γὰρ ὁ πατὴρ ὑμῶν ὁ οὐράνιος ὅτι χρῄζετε τούτων ἁπάντων. * ³³ Ζητεῖτε δὲ πρῶτον τὴν δικαιοσύνην, καὶ τὴν βασιλείαν αὐτοῦ, καὶ ταῦτα πάντα προστεθήσεται ὑμῖν·

mittitur, Deus sic vestit, quanto magis vos, modicæ fidei! ³¹ Nolite ergo solliciti esse, dicentes: Quid manducavimus, aut quid bibemus, aut quo operiemur? ³² Hæc enim omnia gentes inquirunt. Scit enim Pater vester quia his omnibus indigetis. ³³ Quærite ergo primum regnum Dei et justitiam ejus, et hæc omnia adjicientur vobis.

II.—ENGLISH TRANSLATION

MATTHEW VI. 24-33.

²⁴ No man can serve two masters. For either he will hate the one, and love the other; or he will sustain the one, and despise the other. You cannot serve God and mammon. ²⁵ Therefore I say to you, be not solicitous for your life, what you shall eat; nor for your body, what you shall put on. Is not the life more than the meat, and the body more than the raiment? ²⁶ Behold the birds of the air, for they neither sow, nor do they reap, nor gather into barns; and your heavenly Father feedeth them. Are not you of much more value than they? ²⁷ And which of you, by taking thought, can add to his stature one cubit? ²⁸ And for raiment why are you solicitous? Consider the lilies of the field, how they grow: they labour not, neither do they spin; ²⁹ but I say to you, that not even Solomon in all his glory was arrayed as one of these. ³⁰ And if God doth so clothe the grass of the field, which is to-day, and to-morrow is cast into the oven, how much more you, O ye of little faith! ³¹ Be not solicitous, therefore, saying: What shall we eat, or what shall we drink, or wherewith shall we be clothed? ³² For after all these things do the heathens seek. For your Father knoweth that you have need of all these things. ³³ Seek ye, therefore, first the kingdom of God and his justice; and all these things shall be added unto you.

III.—NOTES.

Introductory. During the first year of his public life, Christ addressed to his disciples the " Sermon on the Mount," so called from the hill in Galilee where it was delivered. In this discourse, which is intended as a summary of his moral precepts, our Lord made clear the relation in which his teaching stood to that of the Old Dispensation—a relation of greater perfection and of a

---

* Westcott and Hort, and Hetzenauer have Ζητεῖτε δὲ πρῶτον τὴν βασιλείαν καὶ τὴν δικαιοσύνην αὐτοῦ, καὶ ταῦτα πάντα προστεθήσεται ὑμῖν.

fuller accomplishment of the divine law. He then proceeded to show the spirit with which his followers should be imbued and the means on which they should rely, that they might be worthy citizens of his kingdom on earth and successful competitors for the rewards of heaven. It is from the latter portion of Christ's instruction that the present extract is taken. In the previous verses of this chapter, their Divine Master had taught his hearers not to seek for the praise of men lest they might be wanting in the singleness of mind which is required for the service of God. But there is a greater obstacle to salvation than the desire of human applause, and it is to be found in an inordinate love of riches, or in an engrossing solicitude for temporal possessions. To remove this obstacle from the path of his disciples, our Lord exhorted them to fix their hearts not on earthly treasures which pass away (verse 19), but on those which like heaven itself will last for ever (verses 20, 21), and to do this with that purity of intention which should be the guiding light of all their actions (verses 22, 23). It might be thought that an attachment to temporal possessions is compatible with a love for those which are eternal. To dissipate such a delusion Christ says :—

V. 24. **No man can serve two masters. For either he will hate the one, and love the other ; or he will sustain the one, and despise the other. You cannot serve God and mammon.**

" Mammon," in Gr. $\mu\alpha\mu\omega\nu\dot{\alpha}s$ and in Chaldee ממונא is a word used in the later stages of the Hebrew and in the Punic language to signify *riches*. " Mammona apud Hebraeos divitiae appellari dicuntur. Congruit et Punicum nomen ; nam *lucrum* Punice mammon dicitur " (St. Augustine). As our Lord was speaking of an entire service ($\delta o \upsilon \lambda \epsilon \acute{\iota} \epsilon \iota \nu$) such as a slave is bound to render to an owner, it is true that a divided obedience is impossible even if the commands imposed be not contradictory. And if this be true even when the commands imposed are not contradictory, how clearly is the proverb verified when, as in the present case, the masters—God and mammon—are essentially and mutually opposed, and their commands are contradictory. The incompatibility of a love of riches with the service of God is clearly stated by St. Paul, who says (Coloss. iii. 5, 6) : " Mortify . . . covetousness which is the service of idols, for which things the wrath of God cometh upon the children of unbelief." The same truth is insisted on in 1 Tim. vi. 9, 10, where the Apostle says : " They that will become rich, fall into temptation, and into the snare of the devil, and into many unprofitable and hurtful desires, which draw men into destruction and perdition. For the root of all evils is the desire of money, coveting which, some have wandered from the faith and have entangled themselves in many sorrows." On the one hand, we are to observe here that we are warned against the service not only of *unjust gain*, but also of *riches* even when justly sought for or acquired. This is declared to be incompatible with the service of God, who will have us so love himself that all things else may be loved only as a means of reaching him. On the other hand, we should remember it is the *service* and not the *possession* of earthly goods that is condemned. " Speak not to me of *rich* men, but of men that *served* riches. Job was, indeed, rich, but he did not serve mammon. He had wealth, but he was the master and not the slave of it. He had riches, but he acted as a steward over the goods of another. He never seized the property of his neighbour, but rather bestowed his own on the needy and poor. What is more, he did not boast of his possessions ; for he said : ' If I have rejoiced over my great riches and because my hand hath gotten much ' " (St. Chrysostom, *in loco*).

To serve God as becomes us, it is not enough to be free from that slavery to riches in themselves of which Christ had just spoken. There is a danger or an impediment to salvation in too great an eagerness to secure even the necessaries of life— an eagerness which indirectly and very soon brings about the same result as avarice itself. Hence it is that in connection with the principle already laid down, Christ adds the precept :—

V. 25. Therefore I say to you, be not solicitous for your life, what you shall eat ; nor for your body, what you shall put on.

Although the word ψυχή signifies primarily and usually the inferior part of the soul in contrast with the superior or intellectual principle (πνεῦμα), here it appears to mean all that which is immaterial in man as distinguished from that which is material, and which is designated by the word σῶμα = *the body*. Since, however, the soul is the principle of life, and since whatever tends to keep body and soul united, so far tends to prolong existence, ψυχή here and often elsewhere is rendered *life* (Matth. ii. 20 ; Mark iii. 4 ; Luke vi. 9 ; John x. 11). It follows that our Lord here instructs us not to be solicitous for even the *necessaries of life ;* and the kind of solicitude that is forbidden is clearly expressed in the Greek μὴ μεριμνᾶτε = " be not anxiously solicitous," so as to have your heart *divided* and your attention distracted from your last end. Very much to the point, then, is the remark of St. Jerome : " Labor exercendus est : sollicitudo tollenda." Man, indeed, at his fall incurred the sentence : " Cursed is the earth in thy work ; with labour and toil shalt thou eat thereof all the days of thy life " (Gen. iii. 17) ; and the Apostle knowing that labour is the lot of all in this world, wrote to his disciples : " Neither did we eat any man's bread for nothing ; but in labour and in toil we worked night and day, lest we should be chargeable to any of you. . . . When we were with you, this we declared to you : that if any man will not work, neither let him eat. For we have heard there are some among you who walk disorderly, working not at all" (2 Thess. iii. 8-11). A diligent attention then to temporal concerns is prescribed ; but this attention is ever to be tempered by a reliance on the providence of God, " casting all your care upon him, for he hath care of you " (1 Peter v. 7. See McCarthy).

Christ next gives seven arguments to show us how unworthy of us is this distracting and anxious solicitude for our material well-being. And first of all he says :—

Is not the life more than the meat, and the body more than the raiment ?

Anxious and distracting cares are out of place in all who have one able and willing to supply their wants. Our Lord shows in this argument that such is the case with man. It is as though he had said : " If God, without any merit of labour on your part, has been able and willing to bestow on you your body and soul, is he not able and willing to grant you those smaller gifts of food and raiment by which, in accordance with his providence, the union of body and soul is to be preserved? Because he wished you to exist, he created you ; and in his wish that you exist, there is included the wish to give you what is necessary for existence itself." This argument called by logicians, *a majore ad minus*, is followed by one *a minore ad majus*, which is thus proposed by Christ :—

V. 26. Behold the birds of the air, for they neither sow, nor do they reap, nor gather into barns; and your heavenly Father feedeth them. Are not you of much more value than they ?

The Euchites, idle monks condemned by the Church, sought in this passage a justification of their sloth, and as St. Augustine records, the Manicheans endeavoured to show that this statement contradicted and superseded the warning of Solomon : " Go to the ant, O sluggard, and consider her ways, and learn wisdom, which . . . provideth meat for herself in the summer, and gathereth her food in the harvest " (Proverbs vi. 6-8). In the words of Christ there is no prohibition of labour so much commended by the Wise Man, nor is there any justification of slothful negligence. Our Lord when directing our attention to the providence of God which supplies the birds of the air with food, wished us to lay aside all *anxious distrust* of that providence in supplying our needs. He wished us to rest assured that if God, who is merely their *Creator*, feeds the birds of the air when without labour they seek by instinct for food, he as our *Father* will more surely supply our wants when, in fulfilment of his ordinance, we by the labour of our hands seek for what is necessary. Nay more, he signifies to us that we ought not to fear lest that provident care fail us when, being occupied with higher duties, we are unable to apply ourselves to the occupations by which our daily bread is ordinarily secured. The force of the argument does not rest on a comparison between man endowed with intelligence and the birds of the air guided by mere instinct. It is founded principally on the different relation in which these two classes of creatures stand with regard to God, who is merely the Creator of the lower animals whilst he is both the Creator and the loving Father of mankind. Christ, then, implies that if God provides for the wants of the birds of the air because he is their Creator, much more certainly will he provide for our wants because he is not only our Creator but also our Father.

In the preceding argument, Christ had shown the unreasonableness of an anxious solicitude for even the necessaries of life, since God is both able and willing to supply our wants. He next draws the same conclusion from the fact that without God's assistance no solicitude on our part will secure the object of our desires. He says :—

V. 27. **And which of you, by taking thought, can add to his stature one cubit?**

St. Luke completes the argument when he records these words of Christ : " If then ye be not able to do so much as the least thing, why are you solicitous for the rest ? " (Luke xii. 26). The word ἡλικία is used in reference to both *stature* and *age ;* and the word πῆχυς though generally signifying a measure of *space*, is also employed with regard to *time*. The latter signification seems better adapted to the end Christ had here in view ; but whichever meaning is given to these terms, the argument is conclusive. Taking ἡλικία to refer to age or length of life, the meaning is : " The greatest care and forethought are unavailing to add in the smallest degree to the term of life appointed for you by God : much less can they aid in providing for your wants during the whole time of your existence. Since, then, anxious solicitude is to be put aside as useless in the former case, much more is it to be avoided in the latter." Taking ἡλικία to refer to stature, the argument according to Calmet is : " If you cannot add to your stature which appears to be so immediately your own, much less can you influence the succession of the seasons, the due action of the elements, and the other causes on which the supply of food depends. Since, then, anxious solicitude about the former is in vain and is to be avoided, much more is that which is felt about the latter."

Having proved that we should not be over anxious as to our supply of food, Christ passes on to show what should be our state of feeling with regard to clothing ; and as he had just taken an illustration from the animal kingdom, he now takes one from the flowers that grow around him as he speaks.   He thus continues :—

Vv. 28. 29. **And for raiment why are you solicitous ? Consider the lilies of the field, how they grow: they labour not, neither do they spin ; but I say to you, that not even Solomon in all his glory was arrayed as one of these.**

" The lilies of the field are identified by Doctor Thompson with a species of lily found in the neighbourhood of Hûlèh.   He speaks of having met with ' this incomparable flower, in all its loveliness . . . around the northern base of Thabor, and on the hills of Nazareth, where our Lord spent his youth ' " (*Cambridge Bible, in loco*).   " The plant . . . must have been a conspicuous object on the shores of the lake of Genesareth (Matth. vi. 28 ; Luke xii. 27) ; it must have flourished in the deep, broad valleys of Palestine (Cant. ii. 1) ; among the thorny shrubs (*ibid.* ii. 2) and pastures of the desert (*ibid.* ii. 16 ; iv. 5 ; vi. 3) ; and it must have been remarkable for its rapid and luxuriant growth (Osee xiv. 5 ; Ecclus. xxxix. 14).   That its flowers were brilliant in colour would seem to be indicated in Matth. vi. 28, where it is compared with the gorgeous robes of Solomon ; and that this colour was scarlet or purple was implied in Cant. v. 13 " (Smith, *B. D., s.v.*).   Solomon was possessed of such riches and surrounded with such magnificence that in these he surpassed all kings who had previously reigned.   Notwithstanding this, our Lord here declared that so great a monarch in his greatest glory " was not arrayed," or, according to the Greek, " arrayed not himself," as God arrays one of the flowers that grow wild on the hillsides and in the valleys of Galilee. These flowers " labour not " like men, " neither do they spin " like women, and still God clothes them with a marvellous and inimitable richness.   " What silk, what royal purple. what pattern wrought by men can be compared to various flowers ? What exceeds the rose in brilliancy of colours, or the lily in whiteness ?   And that the blue shade of the violet cannot be surpassed by any artificial dye, is plain rather to the eye than to the mind " (St. Jerome).

Christ completes his argument in the following words :—

V. 30. **And if the grass of the field, which is to-day. and to-morrow is cast into the oven, God doth so clothe, how much more you, O ye of little faith !**

By the " grass of the field " our Lord meant the lilies already mentioned The Hebrews divided the vegetable kingdom into two classes עֵץ and עֵשֶׂב = *trees* and *plants* or herbs, the former of which were called by Hellenists ξύλον, and the latter, χόρτος.

This latter class comprised grass, corn, and *flowers*, including the lilies just mentioned. From scarcity of fuel, all the withered stalks of the herbage are in the East employed for that purpose (see Bloomfield). "The Jewish oven was a vessel narrower at the top than at the bottom, made of baked clay. Sometimes the fuel was placed within, and the cakes laid against the sides. Sometimes the oven was heated by a fire kindled beneath or around it" (*Cambridge Bible, in loco*). Our Lord's argument, therefore, is equivalent to this: "If the lilies, reckoned but as grass and destined soon to wither and to be burned as fuel, are for the moment clothed by God with such incomparable beauty, how much more will he exert his power and show his love in supplying necessary raiment for you, for whom all earthly things are created and who are destined not for a brief or fading existence but for an eternity of glory !"

Having reproached his hearers for that want of faith from which undue solicitude arises ("O ye of little faith"), he repeated the injunction already given (verse 25), and he put forward an additional reason—the fifth—in these words :—

Vv. 31, 32. Be not solicitous therefore, saying : What shall we eat, or what shall we drink, or wherewith shall we be clothed ? For after all these things do the heathen seek.

The Jews were accustomed to look with horror on the habits of the pagan world. Hence, frequently in the Old Testament and already in this discourse (Matth. v. 47), these same pagans were mentioned with a view to shame the Jews into the practice of what is necessary to gain eternal life. It is, therefore, as if Christ had here said : "I have told you that 'unless your justice abound more than that of the scribes and pharisees, you shall not enter into the kingdom of heaven' (Matth. v. 20). What then will be your punishment if you do not excel even the heathens ? And is not this your condition of mind when you give yourselves up to an immoderate anxiety regarding food and raiment ? "

The same line of thought is followed in the sixth argument when Christ says :—

For your Father knoweth that you have need of all these things.

These words have great power to remove all distracting care with regard to the future. To bring about this effect nothing more is required than the knowledge that there is one who is aware of our necessities and has the power and the will to relieve them. Our Lord tells us that such a blessing is ours. It is said expressly that there is a Being who knows our wants ; this Being is called our "Father"—a name implying a love which will anticipate our feeling of distress; and according to the Greek text (ὁ πατὴρ ὑμῶν ὁ οὐράνιος) this Being is called our "*heavenly* Father," thus giving us to understand that with an almighty power he can have no difficulty in coming to our assistance. He it was who said of his providential care: "Can a woman forget her infant, so as not to have pity on the son of her womb? And if she should forget, yet will not I forget thee" (Isaias xlix. 15). Where, then, is there room for anxiety regarding the supply of wants already known to such a God?

As a preface to the last two arguments, our Lord had for the second time laid down a negative precept prohibiting a diffident and anxious solicitude for even food and clothing. He now adds a positive injunction, explaining at the same time the manner in which we should differ from the heathen in seeking for these necessaries of life, and indicating the means by which in God's providence we shall secure what we require here below. He says:—

V. 33. Seek ye, therefore, first the kingdom of God and his justice; and all these things shall be added unto you.

It is to be observed that in the Greek text, instead of ζητεῖτε οὖν = "seek ye therefore," our reading is ζητεῖτε δὲ = "but seek ye." The clause is thus in opposition to "after all these things do the heathen seek." It is as if Christ had said: "The heathens indeed seek these things only; but you, who call God your Father, should seek first the kingdom of God and his justice." The kingdom of God and his justice are the reign of God in our souls and the perfect practice of every virtue—a practice which will surely follow as the effect of the in-dwelling of the Divine Spirit. The striving after the kingdom of God and his justice is to be "first," not necessarily in the order of *time*, but in the order of *intention*. Hence, whilst we are not prohibited from promoting our temporal interests, this promotion of our temporal interests is ever to be subordinated and directed to the attainment of the one thing necessary—God's glory and the salvation of our souls. Maldonatus says well: "Christum non omnino vetuisse cætera quærere, sed ita quærere ut eorum sollicitudo a regno Dei quærendo nos avertat, ita quærere ut illis servire videamur; quærere autem secundo loco, id est propter regnum Dei, non vetuit sed docuit."

To those who thus seek "first the kingdom of God and his justice" and who desire temporal blessings only with a view to secure these spiritual possessions, Christ promises that temporal blessings shall not be wanting. And it is to be noted that he does not say "all these things shall be *given* unto you," but "all these things shall be *added* unto you," over and above the direct object of your wish. The promise is made in this form, lest we should suppose that worldly possessions are suitable to be our reward, or that they are at all worthy of being sought for except as an accessory and as a means of obtaining our eternal salvation. (See Jansenius Gand.) It may be said, and it has been said in contradiction to this promise, that many just and holy men have been in want of the necessaries of life, and that Lazarus, worthy of reposing in Abraham's bosom, was permitted to lie in his sores and hunger unheeded at the rich man's gate (Luke xvi. 20-22). The answer is easy. In the first place, we cannot judge as to internal dispositions from the data supplied in external appearances. Many whose extreme afflictions seem to us most undeserved, may have secret offences to atone for, and may be ready to acknowledge with the brethren of Joseph: "We deserve to suffer these things because we have sinned. . . . Therefore is this affliction come upon us" (Gen. xlii. 21). Moreover, even granting that there are exceptional cases like that of Lazarus, in which the just man is found in destitution, these cases do not falsify the promise of Christ, who speaks not of *extraordinary exceptions*, but of the *ordinary working of divine providence*. Regarding only the ordinary laws of that providence, and with more light as to the spiritual condition of individuals in the sight of God and of his saints, we might securely say with the holy David: "I have been young and now am old; and I have not seen the just forsaken, nor his seed seeking bread" (Ps. xxxvi. 25) (See McCarthy.)

IV.—MORAL REFLECTIONS.

The maxim placed at the head of the present passage is one of the most important of our religion; for it contains the fundamental principle, and embodies the substance, of all Christian morality. It is necessary, therefore, to understand well the meaning of the statement, that God wills to be exclusively served.

1. Is it forbidden in our religion to serve other men, or does the service of God demand that we shake off all other dependence and that we isolate ourselves from society before we are to hold commerce with him? This is not so. Reason and revelation teach that man was created for society; and as God has placed us in society, he wishes that we fulfil the duties without which society could not exist. Now society is maintained in existence by submission to legitimate earthly superiors, and therefore this submission forms an essential part of our fulfilment of the divine commandments. It was a divine law that St. Paul announced when he said: "Wives, be subject to your husbands, as it behoveth in the Lord" (Col. iii. 18); "Children,

obey your parents in all things ; for this is well pleasing to the Lord " (*ib*. ii. 20) ; " Servants, in all things obey your masters according to the flesh, not serving to the eye as pleasing men, but in simplicity of heart, fearing God " (*ib*. iii. 22) ; " Let every soul be subject to the higher powers ; for there is no power but from God, and those that are, are ordained of God. . . . Wherefore, be subject of necessity not only for wrath, but also for conscience' sake " (Rom. xiii. 1-5). Thus the service of our created masters, far from being opposed to the exclusive service of God, is an essential part of that divine service ; and in executing their commands we do not infringe his rights, but carry out his law.

2. In what, then, does the exclusive service of God consist ? We find that it includes two chief obligations. In the first place, the service of God should be so far our object, that to it all other service be subordinate ; and secondly, in thus directing all things to God's service, we must do so with the intention of obeying and pleasing him alone. It does not need a great effort of reason to know that since God is our first, and properly speaking our only, master, our first duty should be to serve him, and all other service should be directed to this. But although it is easy to arrive at this speculative truth, it requires a great effort of virtue to follow out in practice all the consequences to which this truth leads. He must indeed have shaken off all yoke of religion who dares to say : " The Lord shall not see ; neither shall the God of Jacob understand " (Ps. xciii. 7) ; but an error very common amongst Christians is that they seek to ally and put on a par the service of God and that of the world. We pretend to fulfil the duties which God imposes, and at the same time we are bent on enjoying the illicit pleasures which the world affords. Alternately recollected and dissipated, we pass from religious exercises to dangerous amusements. Charitable or ill-willed according to the circumstances of the hour, we now give alms, and then give utterance to calumny or detraction. We wish to acquire before God the merit of an exact devotion, and before the world a reputation of a too indulgent manner. Do we not see around us very many whose piety is of this nature ? And without examining our neighbour's conduct, may we not find that we have to make these accusations against ourselves ? How often has not the attraction of sinful pleasure gained the victory over the impulse of grace, the desire of being loved by the world over that of being dear to God, and the fear of human judgments over that of the judgment to come ? In all this we deceive ourselves ; and since " no man can serve two masters," we must select the service of the world with its punishments, or the service of God with its rewards.

3. The exclusive service of God requires not only that we have the fulfilment of God's commandments as the object at which we aim in all our works, but also that we do this through love of him and with the pure intention of pleasing his divine majesty. When telling us that " no man can serve two masters," Christ gives the reason, viz., that we cannot love both. God wishes to be served with love, and our love is an essential element, it is even a principal part of divine worship. Not to love God, is not to serve him ; and we do not love him, if there be any other object that is loved except *in* him and *for* him. There is no delusion more absurd, and at the same time more fatal, than to think we can divide our heart between what God commands and what the world suggests ; between self-denial and cupidity ; between mortification and indulgence ; between humility and pride. God will not accept a divided heart. Therefore, that which we would love with God, is the object of our predilection ; and in the object of our predilection we find our God. We are not to conclude from this that all earthly attachments are interdicted to us. The love of our neighbour is formally commanded ; and our affection for those connected with us by blood or friendship, far from being forbidden, is commended to us by the example of Jesus Christ himself (John xi. 3, 5, 35, 36). Amongst the greatest vices of the pagans denounced by St. Paul, was this that they were " without affection " (Rom. i. 31) ; and the same Apostle declared that : " If any man hath not a care of his own and especially of those of his house, he hath denied the faith, and is worse than an infidel " (1 Tim. v. 8). The love of creatures is not culpable in itself : it becomes culpable only when it rivals, and thus excludes, the love of the Creator.

4. Not only should God be the Master whom we serve in all we do, and the Being in whom and for whom we love all things else, but also the promotion of his glory should be the intention that directs all our conscious acts. The reference of all our acts to God is not merely a counsel ; it is a precept. Still, to fulfil this precept a formal offering and advertence to God at all times is not required ; for such a continual attention is not now possible to human nature. But although we cannot now refer to God formally and in particular each of our actions, we can make a general offering of them : we cannot repeat this offering at each instant, but we can make it each morning at our rising and can renew it frequently throughout the day. Thus without relinquishing the occupations of our state of life, we shall render to God a service very pleasing to him ; we shall in the first place seek the kingdom of God and his justice ; and whilst we await our eternal reward in heaven, even here on earth all other things necessary " shall be added " unto us.

FIFTEENTH SUNDAY AFTER PENTECOST.

I.—TEXTS.

GREEK.

LUKE VII. 11-16.

11 Καὶ ἐγένετο ἐν τῷ ἐξῆς, ἐπορεύθη εἰς πόλιν καλουμένην Ναῒν· καὶ συνεπορεύοντο αὐτῷ οἱ μαθηταὶ αὐτοῦ, καὶ ὄχλος πολύς. 12 Ὡς δὲ ἤγγισεν τῇ πύλῃ τῆς πόλεως, καὶ ἰδοὺ, ἐξεκομίζετο τεθνηκὼς μονογενὴς υἱὸς τῇ μητρὶ αὐτοῦ, καὶ αὕτη ἦν χήρα· καὶ ὄχλος τῆς πόλεως ἱκανὸς ἦν σὺν αὐτῇ. 13 Καὶ ἰδὼν αὐτὴν ὁ κύριος ἐσπλαγχνίσθη ἐπ' αὐτῇ, καὶ εἶπεν αὐτῇ· Μὴ κλαῖε. 14 Καὶ προσελθὼν ἥψατο τῆς σοροῦ· οἱ δὲ βαστάζοντες ἔστησαν· καὶ εἶπεν· Νεανίσκε, σοὶ λέγω, Ἐγέρθητι. 15 Καὶ ἐκάθισεν ὁ νεκρός, καὶ ἤρξατο λαλεῖν· καὶ ἔδωκεν αὐτὸν τῇ μητρὶ αὐτοῦ. 16 Ἔλαβεν δὲ φόβος πάντας, καὶ ἐδόξαζον τὸν Θεόν, λέγοντες· ὅτι προφήτης μέγας ἠγέρθη ἐν ἡμῖν, καὶ ὅτι ἐπεσκέψατο ὁ θεὸς τὸν λαὸν αὐτοῦ.

VULGATE.

LUKE VII. 11-16.

11 Et factum est deinceps, ibat in civitatem quæ vocatur Naim ; et ibant cum eo discipuli ejus, et turba copiosa. 12 Cum autem appropinquaret portæ civitatis, ecce defunctus efferebatur filius unicus matris suæ, et hæc vidua erat ; et turba civitatis multa cum illa. 13 Quam cum vidisset Dominus, misericordia motus super eam, dixit illi : Noli flere. 14 Et accessit, et tetigit loculum. (Hi autem qui portabant, steterunt.) Et ait : Adolescens, tibi dico : Surge. 15 Et resedit qui erat mortuus, et cœpit loqui. Et dedit illum matri suæ. 16 Accepit autem omnes timor ; et magnificabant Deum, dicentes : Quia propheta magnus surrexit in nobis, et quia Deus visitavit plebem suam.

II.—ENGLISH TRANSLATION.

LUKE VII. 11-16.

11 And it came to pass afterwards, that he went into a city that is called Naim ; and there went with him his disciples, and a great multitude. 12 And when he came nigh to the gate of

the city, behold, a dead man was carried out, the only son of his mother, and she was a widow ; and a great multitude of the city was with her. ¹³ And when the Lord had seen her, being moved with mercy towards her, he said to her : " Weep not." ¹⁴ And he drew nigh and touched the bier. And they that carried it stood still. And he said : " Young man, I say to thee, Arise." ¹⁵ And he that was dead, sat up and began to speak. And he gave him to his mother. ¹⁶ And there came a fear on them all ; and they glorified God, saying : " A great prophet is risen up among us, and God hath visited his people."

III.—NOTES.

Introductory. The miracle which is here described, and which is one of the greatest mentioned by the evangelists, is recorded by St. Luke alone. It took place during the second year of our Lord's public life. As may be gathered from a comparison of the gospels, Christ had already selected from his now numerous disciples the chosen twelve, whom he named apostles. In their presence at Capharnaum (Introduction, p. liii.) where he principally resided, he had graciously listened to the prayer and praised the faith of the Gentile centurion, and he had healed that centurion's servant by a single word. St. Luke follows up this account with the history of the restoration to life of the Jewish widow's son, a fact in which every circumstance of time, place, and witnesses is described. The evangelist says :—

V. 11. **And it came to pass afterwards, that he went into a city that is called Naim; and there went with him his disciples, and a great multitude.**

Critics are here divided in opinion as to the correct reading. Codices A, B, and R have ἐν τῷ ἑξῆς (scil. χρόνῳ) = *afterwards :* whilst codices ℵ, C, and D have ἐν τῇ ἑξῆς (scil. ἡμέρᾳ) = *the day after.* From a consideration of intrinsic and extrinsic evidence, the former reading appears to be the more probable.

Capharnaum on account of its large population, its great trade, and the influx of strangers, afforded such a field for our Lord's preaching that at this time it became his chief place of residence and was even called " his own city " (Matth. ix. 1). Still, his ministrations were not confined to it alone. Amongst the places visited was Naim (Introduction, p. lvii.), a village not elsewhere referred to in the Sacred Scriptures, but mentioned by Eusebius and by St. Jerome, the latter of whom spoke of it as still existing in his time. Travellers have recently identified it with the village at the foot of the Little Hermon, a short distance to the south of Nazareth. Stanley speaks of it in the following extract : " On the northern slope of the rugged and barren ridge of Little Hermon, immediately west of Endor which lies in a further recess of the same range, is the ruined village of *Nain*. No convent, no tradition marks the spot. But, under these circumstances, the name is sufficient to guarantee its authenticity. One entrance alone it could have had—that which opens on the rough hill-side in its downward slope to the plain. It must have been in this deep descent, as, according to Eastern custom, they ' carried out the dead man,' that nigh to the gate of the village, the bier was stopped, and the long procession of mourners stayed, and the young man delivered back to his mother."

From Capharnaum to that place, a distance of about twenty-five miles, Jesus went on his errand of mercy ; " and there went with him his disciples," who were afterwards to bear witness to the miracle, " and a great multitude " ;

V. 12. **And when he came nigh to the gate of the city, behold, a dead man was carried out, the only son of his mother, and she was a widow ; and a great multitude of the city was with her.**

Except in the case of kings of the House of David who were buried in the City of David, it was the custom of the Jews, as of other nations of antiquity, to inter the dead in gardens or in unfrequented places outside the towns (Introduction, pp. c., ci.). Such a funeral ceremony was about to be performed when Jesus arrived ; and all the circumstances are noted by St. Luke with a simplicity and conciseness that render his account a masterpiece of description. It was usual for friends to follow the dead to the last resting-place, and to show their sympathy with the survivors ; but the evangelist specially dwells on the number of those who attended the obsequies in this case. The reasons for such a concourse were to be found in the circumstances of both the son and the mother. He was snatched away in the flower of his youth ; and it seemed that his name and that of his family were to be henceforth unknown in Israel. Nor was this all. By his death his mother, a widow, was left without consolation or resource on earth. In him she was deprived of an only child on whom was expended all her maternal love, and with whom vanished all her hope of posterity and all her prospect of support in her declining years. Widowhood alone was looked on as a type of desolation (see Ruth i. 20, 21 ; 1 Tim. v. 5) ; and the mourning of those who were rendered childless, became proverbial. Hence Jeremias (vi. 26) says : " Gird thee with sackcloth, O daughter of my people, and sprinkle thee with ashes : make thee mourning as for an only son, a bitter lamentation, because the destroyer shall suddenly come upon us." (*Cf.* Zach.

xii. 10 ; 2 Kings xiv. 5-7, etc.)   These causes for grief when
taken singly—much more when taken together—appealed to the
sympathy and secured the presence of fellow-citizens at the
funeral of the widow's son.   Still, on such occasions the sympathy
and presence of men can do but little : it is Christ alone who can
bring true comfort to the sorrowing heart.   In him, to use the
words of the Apostle, " we have not a high-priest who cannot
have compassion on our infirmities ; but one tempted in all
things like as we are, without sin " (Heb. iv. 15).

Divine consolation was at hand for the widow ;

**V. 13. And when the Lord had seen her, being moved with
mercy towards her, he said to her: Weep not.**

As Jesus wept at the death of Lazarus (John xi. 35), so did
he now show the strong feeling of compassion which the evangelist describes by the emphatic verb, ἐσπλαγχνίσθη = *was moved
to the very heart with compassion*.   Nay more, he addressed the
afflicted widow in the words : " Weep not."   On his lips this
was no idle or conventional phrase ; for whilst he spoke such
words to her ear, he filled her heart with resignation and with
hope.   He was the Lord of life and of death ; and he had come
on earth that, partially here, and fully hereafter, he might
bring to pass the promise of the Apocalypse : " God shall wipe
away all tears from their eyes ; and death shall be no more ;
neither shall there be mourning, nor crying, nor sorrow any more ;
for the former things are passed away " (Apoc. xxi. 4).

In their efforts to reconcile the widow to what they considered her hopeless fate, her friends had probably many times
repeated to her the same expressions as did our Lord.   Our Lord,
however, exhorted her to cease weeping not because her case
was hopeless, but because he was about to remove the cause
of her sorrow.   This he at once proceeded to do ;

**V. 14. And he drew nigh and touched the bier.   And they
that carried it, stood still.   And he said : Young man, I say
to thee, Arise.**

The σορός of the Greek text generally signified an open vessel,
a cinerary urn, or a coffin of marble or other material in which
the dead were laid.   Such coffins were not in use amongst the
Jews.   Hence the word here refers to the " bier " or framework
on which the body, wrapped in linen bands, was carried forth
for burial.   Something in our Lord's manner indicated his
wish that the bearers should stand still ; and when they had
done so, he addressed to the dead man the command : " Arise."
To give such a command implied that he was the Lord of life
and of death.   When he raised to life the " ruler's " daughter
who had just died, when he restored life to this young man
who was already being borne to the grave, and when he called

forth Lazarus who had been already four days in the tomb, Christ did not pray for heavenly aid ; he did not use a lengthened form of words ; nor did he enter on any struggle with death. Unlike Elias with the widow's son (3 Kings xvii. 19-21), unlike Eliseus with the son of the Sunamitess (4 Kings iv. 29-35), unlike even St. Peter (Acts ix. 40, 41) who knelt down and prayed when Tabitha was being restored to life, our Lord used his own divine power, and raised the dead by a word addressed to the subject of the miracle.

As in the case of the " ruler's " daughter and in that of Lazarus, the Creator had here commanded his creature ;

V. 15. And he that was dead, sat up and began to speak. And he gave him to his mother.

The verb ἐκάθισεν, rendered "sat up," is almost exclusively a medical term when used in the intransitive sense which it has here.   Taken in connection with the clause " began to speak," it expresses a fact which proved the supernatural and miraculous character of our Lord's action.   It has been well said : " The supporters of natural interpretation pretend that the young man was merely overtaken by a lethargic sleep.   In that case, the miracle of power would only disappear to make room for a miracle of knowledge equally difficult to understand. For how should Jesus know that the supposed dead man was still alive, and that the moment of his awakening was at hand ? " (Godet, quoted in the *Speaker's Comm.*)

Christ's immediate purpose on this occasion was to console the desolate widow, for whose sorrow he had felt such deep compassion.   (See verse 13.)   Hence, it is recorded of our Lord that having restored the son to life, " he gave him to his mother." The ultimate end, however, of all our Lord's acts on earth was the honour of his Eternal Father.   This was promoted among the witnesses on the present occasion ;

V. 16. And there came a fear on them all ; and they glorified God, saying : A great prophet is risen up among us, and God hath visited his people.

The evangelist does not record the joyful feelings of the mother, which may be imagined ; but he passes on to relate the effects produced on the witnesses of this marvellous exhibition of divine power.   On all " there came a great fear."   This was not a feeling like that of the Gerasenes who, when our Lord had cast out the legion of devils, anticipated some temporal evils as the result of his presence, and " besought him to depart from them " (Luke viii. 37).   The feeling of which the evangelist now speaks was a holy fear (φόβος = *a reverential awe mixed with admiration*). This was the first result of the miracle.   The second was that the inhabitants of Naim " glorified God," that is, turning to the Lord of life and of death they gave to him such honour as is due to the Supreme Being alone (ἐδόξαζον τὸν θεὸν). In doing so, they proclaimed that after many centuries there again appeared amongst them a great prophet who, like Elias and Eliseus, was able to raise the dead to life ; and they confessed that God had thus once more visited them not *in judgment* but as the *physician* of their ills (ἐπεσκέψατο ὁ θεὸς τὸν λαὸν αὐτοῦ). That this is the meaning of the last clause appears from the medical term ἐπεσκέψατο, which is here used by the evangelist, and which has always this signification in the New Testament (*cf.* Luke i. 68, 78 ; Acts xv. 14 ; Hebr. ii. 6 ; Matth. xxv. 36-43 ; James i. 27 ; Acts vi. 3 ; vii. 23 ; xv. 36). When restoring life to the dead man by his own authority and with a word (" I say to thee : Arise "), Jesus had exercised a power beyond that of all other prophets. Hence, in the next verse, St. Luke mentions the third effect of the miracle when he says that the people sent abroad the report even beyond the confines of Galilee. " This rumour concerning him went forth through all Judæa and through all the surrounding country." Nor was this all. " John's disciples told him of all these things " (Luke vii. 18), and afforded the now imprisoned Precursor the opportunity of sending these same disciples to see with their eyes and to hear with their ears the greatness of the new Master whom he himself had been commissioned to announce to the world.

IV.—MORAL REFLECTIONS.

1. We are accustomed to the sight described in the first part of this gospel passage, but what are the thoughts suggested by such a spectacle ? We often behold the dead carried out for burial, but what effect has this upon our conduct ? Most men fail to take in the lesson which it teaches, viz., the certainty of their own passage to another world ; or, if a practical application of this lesson forces itself upon them, they hasten to drive away a thought which disturbs, afflicts, or affrights them. Those who are given up to dissipation, vanity, and pleasure, do not wish to reflect on the end of all things here below. Nevertheless, the more we are averse to occupy ourselves with this thought, the more we should keep it before our minds ; and the more terrors this meditation has for us, the more useful it will prove itself to be. It is, indeed, a great grace that God so often reminds us of the certainty of death. Death is the school of life ; for there we learn what we are, what we should be, and what we shall become. The contemplation of the corruption to which our bodies must one day be reduced, enables us to see the uselessness of the excessive care we often bestow upon them ; whilst the recollection of our unending state in the next

world leads us to the conclusion that we should here labour for the future happiness of our souls. What thought can bring more vividly before us the worthlessness of earthly goods than the consideration that all must be surrendered on the bed of death ; and where is there a greater source of encouragement in the exercise of virtue and in the practice of good deeds than the knowledge that whilst death deprives us of all things else, it confirms us for ever in the possession of the rewards acquired by the service of God ? It is not surprising that unbelievers whose desires and hopes are fixed on the things of this perishable life, endeavour to forget that it will not last for ever ; but it is surprising that this is done by Christians whose faith teaches that their present state is but a passage to another. What is the result of efforts to ignore the approach of death ? These efforts cannot avert the fate which is in store for all mankind and may entail the loss of eternal salvation. Unlike the lovers of this world, then, we will keep before us the certainty of death ; and in this meditation we will form the practical resolution of preparing well for that which we are powerless to avoid.

2. When shall we die ? We know not. Though the fact that we shall die is certain, the time and other circumstances of our death are quite hidden from us all. Consider the case of the dead man described in the present gospel passage. In the flower of his youth, an only son, the hope of his family, he might naturally have expected a long life ; but he is cut off and carried forth for burial. Youth, strength, health, and devotion of friends are but poor defences against death, which in a moment scatters them before its face. What, then, is the conclusion to be drawn from our conviction regarding the uncertainty of the hour when death will come ? The conclusion is drawn for us by Jesus Christ. " Take ye heed," he says, " watch and pray, for ye know not when the time is. . . . Watch ye, therefore (for you know not when the lord of the house cometh : at even, or at midnight, or at the cock-crowing, or in the morning), lest coming on a sudden, he find you sleeping. And what I say to you, I say to all: Watch " (Mark xiii. 33, 35, 36, 37). Wisely taking this admonition to heart, we will think each morning that the present day may be our last ; at evening we will reflect that before another sunrise we may awaken in eternity ; each act of ours will be performed as if immediately to be judged ; each prayer, each fast, each work of mercy, will be made a preparation for our departure hence. Thus and thus only shall we be secure. There is no sudden death for him who is always ready ; and death has neither danger nor terror for him whose conscience testifies that he is in a condition to meet his Judge. " In all thy works," says the Holy Ghost, " remember thy last end. and thou shalt never sin " (Ecclus. vii. 40).

SIXTEENTH SUNDAY AFTER PENTECOST.

I.—TEXTS.

GREEK.

LUKE XIV. 1-11.

¹ Καὶ ἐγένετο ἐν τῷ ἐλθεῖν αὐτὸν εἰς οἶκόν τινος τῶν ἀρχόντων φαρεισαίων σαββάτῳ φαγεῖν ἄρτον, καὶ αὐτοὶ ἦσαν παρατηρούμενοι αὐτόν. ² Καὶ ἰδοὺ, ἄνθρωπός τις ἦν ὑδρωπικὸς ἔμπροσθεν αὐτοῦ. ³ Καὶ ἀποκριθεὶς ὁ Ἰησοῦς εἶπεν πρὸς τοὺς νομικοὺς καὶ φαρεισαίους, λέγων· Ἔξεστιν τῷ σαββάτῳ θεραπεῦσαι, ἢ οὔ; ⁴ Οἱ δὲ ἡσύχασαν. Καὶ ἐπιλαβόμενος ἰάσατο αὐτὸν, καὶ ἀπέλυσεν. ⁵ Καὶ πρὸς αὐτοὺς εἶπεν· Τίνος ὑμῶν υἱὸς ἢ βοῦς εἰς φρέαρ πεσεῖται, καὶ οὐκ εὐθέως ἀνασπάσει αὐτὸν ἐν ἡμέρᾳ τοῦ σαββάτου; ⁶ Καὶ οὐκ ἴσχυσαν ἀνταποκριθῆναι πρὸς ταῦτα. ⁷ Ἔλεγεν δὲ πρὸς τοὺς κεκλημένους παραβολήν, ἐπέχων πῶς τὰς πρωτοκλισίας ἐξελέγοντο, λέγων πρὸς αὐτούς· Ὅταν κληθῇς ὑπό τινος εἰς γάμους, μὴ ἱατακλιθῇς εἰς τὴν πρωτοκλισίαν· μήποτε ἐντιμότερός σου ᾖ κεκλημένος ὑπ' αὐτοῦ, ⁹ καὶ ἐλθὼν ὁ σὲ καὶ αὐτὸν καλέσας, ἐρεῖ σοι· Δὸς τούτῳ τόπον· καὶ τότε ἄρξῃ μετὰ αἰσχύνης τὸν ἔσχατον τόπον κατέχειν. ¹⁰ Ἀλλ' ὅταν κληθῇς, πορευθεὶς ἀνάπεσε εἰς τὸν

VULGATE.

LUKE XIV. 1-11.

1 Et factum est cum intraret Jesus in domum cujusdam principis pharisæorum sabbato manducare panem, et ipsi observabant eum. 2 Et ecce homo quidam hydropicus erat ante illum. 3 Et respondens Jesus, dixit ad legisperitos et pharisæos, dicens : Si licet sabbato curare ? 4 At illi tacuerunt. Ipse vero apprehensum sanavit eum, ac dimisit. 5 Et respondens ad illos dixit : Cujus vestrum asinus aut bos in puteum cadet, et non continuo extrahet illum die sabbati ? 6 Et non poterant ad hæc respondere illi. 7 Dicebat autem et ad invitatos parabolam, intendens quomodo primos accubitus eligerent, dicens ad illos : 8 Cum invitatus fueris ad nuptias, non discumbas in primo loco, ne forte honoratior te sit invitatus ab illo, 9 et veniens is qui te et illum vocavit, dicat tibi : Da huic locum ; et tunc incipias cum rubore novissimum locum tenere. 10 Sed cum vocatus fueris, vade, recumbe in novissimo loco ; ut, cum venerit qui te invitavit, dicat

ἔσχατον τόπον· ἵνα ὅταν ἔλθῃ ὁ κεκληκώς σε, ἐρεῖ σοι· Φίλε, προσανάβηθι
ἀνώτερον. Τότε ἔσται σοι δόξα ἐνώπιον
πάντων τῶν συνανακειμένων σοι. ¹¹Ὅτι
πᾶς ὁ ὑψῶν ἑαυτὸν, ταπεινωθήσεται·
καὶ ὁ ταπεινῶν ἑαυτὸν ὑψωθήσεται.

tibi : Amice, ascende supe-
rius. Tunc erit tibi gloria
coram simul discumbentibus.
11 Quia omnis qui se exaltat,
humiliabitur ; et qui se humiliat, exaltabitur.

II.—ENGLISH TRANSLATION.

LUKE XIV. 1-11.

1 And it came to pass that, when Jesus went into the house of
one of the chief of the pharisees on the sabbath-day to eat bread,
they watched him. 2 And behold, there was before him a certain
man who had the dropsy. 3 And Jesus answering, spoke to the
lawyers and pharisees, saying : " Is it lawful to heal on the
sabbath-day ? " 4 But they held their peace. He, however,
taking him, healed him, and sent him away. 5 And answering
them, he said : " Which of you shall have an ass or an ox fall
into a pit, and will not immediately draw him out on the sabbath-
day ? " 6 And they could not answer him as to these things.
7 And he spoke a parable to them also that were invited, when
he observed how they chose the first seats at the table, saying
to them : 8 " When thou art invited to a wedding, sit not down
in the first place, lest perhaps one more honourable than thou
be invited by him, 9 and he that invited thee and him, come and
say to thee : ' Give this man place ' ; and then thou begin with
shame to take the lowest place. 10 But when thou art invited,
go, sit down in the lowest place ; that when he who invited thee
cometh, he may say to thee : ' Friend, go up higher.' Then
shalt thou have glory before them that sit at table with thee.
11 Because everyone that exalteth himself, shall be humbled ;
and he that humbleth himself, shall be exalted."

III.—NOTES.

Introductory. The miracle and the discourse which form the
subject-matter of this chapter, took place a few months before
the Passion. In the preceding December, Christ had assisted
at the Feast of the Dedication of the Temple ; on his openly
declaring his divinity, the Jews sought to stone him ; and he
escaping miraculously out of their hands, went to reside in
Peræa, which lay to the east of the Jordan (John x. 22-42).
His missionary journeys through this district until his return
to Bethany on the death of Lazarus (John xi. 1), are described
by St. Luke alone. It was now a long time since the pharisees
and the lawyers, smarting under his reproaches, " began to urge
him vehemently and to ply him with questions about many
things, lying in wait for him, and seeking to catch something

from his mouth that they might accuse him " (Luke xi. 53, 54) ; but in the present passage the reader has a striking illustration of the manner in which these attacks were renewed. Although our Lord was well aware of the pharisees' insincerity, he did not disdain to accept their invitations to table, in order that by his divine grace and by his instructions he might enlighten the minds and soften the hearts of his bitter enemies.

V. 1. And it came to pass that, when Jesus went into the house of one of the chief of the pharisees on the sabbath-day to eat bread, they watched him.

Contrary to what the Greek text would seem to imply, the pharisees as such had neither rulers nor even grades of rank ; but they had amongst them chief men and eminent doctors, like the learned rabbis Hillel, Schammai, Gamaliel, and distinguished members of the Sanhedrim, like Nicodemus. Our Lord, being invited by one such as these, entered the house as the evangelist says, " to eat bread "—a Hebrew phrase signifying " to partake of any meal however sumptuous." The food being cooked on the previous day, entertainments were given on the sabbath and on feasts ; and they even formed a part of the religious ceremony at least from the time of the Captivity. (*Cf.* 2 Esdras viii. 8-12 ; Tobias ii. 1, 2.) These entertainments, at first very frugal and simple, were subsequently remarkable for their expensive and luxurious character. St. Augustine (Enarr. in Ps. xci. 2) warned the Christians of his day against imitating the Jews in this respect. " Ecce et hodiernus dies sabbati est ; hunc in presenti tempore otio quodam corporaliter languido et fluxo et luxurioso celebrant Judaei. Vacant enim ad nugas ; et cum Deus praeceperit sabbatum, illi in his quae Deus prohibet, exercent sabbatum." The occupation of our Lord's host and of his fellow-guests is not well described in our version, which has simply that " they watched him." The Greek periphrastic imperfect καὶ αὐτοὶ ἦσαν παρατηρούμενοι αὐτόν instead of the simple imperfect, is equivalent to : " and they themselves (*i.e.*, the pharisees) were closely and continuously watching him." Their evil disposition is shown in the subsequent remarks of our Lord (verse 3), and in the very use of the verb παρατηρεῖσθαι, which means not merely to watch but to *spy after* with an interested and sinister purpose. The opportunity for indulging their spirit of calumny was, as they thought, just at hand ;

V. 2. And behold, there was before him a certain man who had the dropsy.

These words *taken by themselves* do not enable us to decide whether the sick man came of his own accord, or was brought there by the pharisees to entrap our Lord. The remark of the evangelist, however, in the preceding verse and the question of Christ in that which follows, make it very probable that the invitation itself and the acts of the guests were all inspired by the desire to ensnare Christ which was now become the settled purpose of his enemies.   (See St. Luke xi. 53, 54 ; xx. 20 ; Mark xii. 13.)   Farrar says truly that the verse represents with inimitable vividness the flash of recognition with which our Lord at once grasped the whole meaning of the scene.   The dropsical man was not one of the guests : he stood as *though by accident* in the promiscuous throng which may always enter an Oriental house during a meal.   But his presence was no accident.   The dropsy is an unsightly, and was regarded generally as an incurable, disease.   The pharisees' plot had, therefore, been concocted with that complex astuteness which in other instances also (*vid.* xx. 19-38 ; John viii. 3-6) marks the deadliness of their purpose.   They argued that he could not ignore the presence of a man conspicuously placed before him ; that on the one hand perhaps he might fail in the cure of a disease generally incurable ; or that, on the other hand, if he *did* heal the man on the sabbath-day there would be room for another charge before the Sanhedrim.   One element which kindled our Lord's indignation against the pharisees for these crafty schemes was the way in which they had made a mere tool of human misery and human shame.   The scheme had been well thought out ; but it is written : " Wisdom shall perish from their wise men, and the understanding of their prudent men shall be hid " (Isaias xxix. 14).

Indeed " there is no wisdom, there is no prudence, there is no counsel against the Lord " (Proverbs xxi. 30) ;

V. 3. And Jesus answering, spoke to the lawyers and pharisees, saying: Is it lawful to heal on the sabbath-day?

Although the word " answering," in Greek, ἀποκριθεὶς, in addition to its ordinary meaning, sometimes signifies in Sacred Scripture, " commencing an address," the context shows that on this occasion our Lord was replying to the thoughts passing in the minds of his audience.   In that audience there were with the pharisees some " lawyers."   These were members of the same class of officials who are elsewhere named " scribes " ; and though not necessarily pharisees, they were generally members of that sect.   They were called " lawyers " because it belonged to them to study and to interpret the Mosaic law ; and they received the name of " scribes " because it was their duty to watch over the transcription of the Sacred Scriptures and of the public records.   Their hostility to Christ is frequently noted in the gospels ; and of this hostility we have here an instance.   As was remarked in dealing with verse 2, they had endeavoured to put our Lord in a dilemma ; but he turned their schemes against themselves by proposing the question here recorded. If, in answer to this question, they said : " It is lawful to cure on the sabbath-day," their plot should be allowed to fail, and their repeated accusation on the head of non-observance of the sabbath should be admitted to be groundless. If they answered : " It is not lawful," they should be prepared for a rebuke given in similar circumstances on other occasions (Luke vi. 9 ; xiii. 11-17), and for a refutation of their teaching implied in the succeeding verses of this passage.

They were not disposed to accept either alternative ;

V. 4. But they held their peace. He, however, taking him, healed him and sent him away.

They tried to escape from their difficulty by an ignoble silence ; and this silence on the part of the lawyers able and bound to answer the question, was a complete though tacit justification of the cure. (See *International Comm.* and Farrar, *in loco.*) It has been well said : " Doctores illi suo silentio se misere gerunt ; non audent negare, quia Domini confutationem timent et sentiunt ab ipso populo ejusmodi negationem repudiari ; nolunt affirmare ne suae auctoritati derogent, cum sanationes sabbato factas saepius antea, reprehenderint. Et tamen cum sint doctores legis, rogati liceatne sabbato, respondere debebant. Quare hic omnino valet : Qui tacet consentire videtur." (See Knabenbauer : *In Lucam*, p. 427.)

Christ healed the dropsical man ; and the terms in which this miracle is described are worthy of notice. These words, ἐπιλαβόμενος ἰάσατο αὐτὸν, which are rendered : " he taking him, healed him," really signify that Christ took the sick man kindly by the hand, and healed him by the very touch. Such is the meaning of the verb ἐπιλαμβάνεσθαι here as well as in Romans xiv. 1, where the Apostle writes : " Now him that is weak in faith, take unto you," *i.e.*, " Take him by the hand and treat him tenderly." Nor did Christ's consideration for the poor sufferer end with the miraculous cure. To shield him from such persecution as had overtaken the blind man healed during the previous Feast of Tabernacles in Jerusalem (John ix.), our Lord provided for his safety by immediately sending him away.

The pharisees and the lawyers had remained silent ; but Christ knew that in spite of the evidence of the miracle they condemned him. He then condescended to justify his action by a proof drawn from their own experience.

Vv. 5, 6. And answering them, he said : Which of you shall have an ass or an ox fall into a pit, and will not immediately draw him out on the sabbath-day ? And they could not answer him as to these things.

There is a dispute as to whether the correct reading of the

Greek text is υἱὸς ἢ βοῦς = " a son or an ox," or ὄνος ἢ βοῦς = " an ass or an ox." According to the present Greek text, which is unquestionably correct if MSS. authority alone be regarded, the reading should be υἱὸς ἢ βοῦς = " a son or an ox." The unusual collocation probably suggested a change from the original to the present reading of the Vulgate and of the English version—a reading borrowed from Luke xiii. 15, or from Deut. xxii. 4. When a choice is to be made between two readings, the rule is that *caeteris paribus* the more difficult is to be preferred, it being probable that for dogmatic or for other reasons a change of reading has taken place.

The argument *a minori ad majus* in either reading is perfectly conclusive. In it our Lord says, as it were : " Which of you yourselves (τίνος ὑμῶν) shall have his son or even his ox fall into a pit, and will not immediately, without scruple, and without fear of reprehension, extricate him by much labour (ἀνασπάσει αὐτὸν) on the sabbath-day ? " He leaves it to themselves to draw this evident conclusion : " If, then, as you admit by your practice, so much labour may be lawfully expended on the sabbath-day in a work of rescue undertaken from a motive of merely natural and paternal affection for one's children or of care for one's property, it surely cannot be unlawful on that day to perform a most easy act from a motive of pure charity towards others." The force of the argument was so overwhelming that the pharisees and lawyers, who before (verse 3) found it *inconvenient to answer*, were now left *without the power to reply* (οὐκ ἴσχυσαν ἀνταποκριθῆναι).

Having thus healed the bodily disease of the dropsical man, and having justified his action performed on the sabbath-day, our Lord now proceeds to apply a remedy to the more fatal spiritual disease of the assembled guests ;

V. 7. And he spoke a parable to them also that were invited when he observed how they chose the first seats at the table, saying to them: etc.

In the Greek text we have here an instance of an ellipsis which frequently occurs. The word ἐπέχων has τὸν νοῦν or τοὺς ὀφθάλμους understood ; and the whole clause thus completed is equivalent to : " fixing his attention (or his eyes) on them as they were picking out for themselves the chief places at the table." At meals (Introduction, pp. lxxxvi.-lxxxviii.) the Jews reclined on couches or pillows, each of which generally accommodated three persons. The couch on which the host lay, was the first or centre one, and the others were arranged in order of precedence around three sides of a low table. On each couch the middle place was the position of honour, that on the left was for the second in dignity, and that on the right, for the third. The desire of distinction at table was so general that it was found amongst the apostles during the Last Supper, and was there silently rebuked by Christ when he washed their feet. As our Lord observed each of the guests at the present entertainment eagerly contending for a recognition of his supposed right of precedence, he wished to inspire them with sentiments of humility. With this object he spoke to them a " parable " not in the usual sense of the word, but in the wider sense of a maxim (*cf.* Luke v. 36-39 ; Mark iii. 23) conveyed in somewhat figurative language. He spoke this parable, " saying to them " :—

V. 8. When thou art invited to a wedding, sit not down in the first place, lest perhaps one more honourable than thou be invited by him.

In order to convey the lesson with more delicacy, and not to offend his hearers by any personal allusions, our Lord speaks here of a marriage feast, not of an entertainment like that at which the pharisees and lawyers are now present. As Christ points out, no one should on such an occasion thrust himself unbidden into a place of honour before others, but should modestly await the directions of the host, who has invited all, and to whom it belongs to assign his position to each. Christ says, as it were : " Not only humility, but even prudence suggests this course to thee, lest thou mistake the arrangements made for another guest,

V. 9. And he that invited thee and him, come and say to thee : Give this man place, and then thou begin with shame to take the lowest place.

It is probable that there is here an allusion to Proverbs xxv. 6, 7 : " Appear not glorious before the king ; and stand not in the place of great men. For it is better that it should be said to thee : ' Come up hither,' than that thou shouldst be humbled before the prince." The words of Christ ($ἄρξῃ$ . . . $κατέχει$) give a striking picture of the humiliation of the proud. The self-assumed importance that unbidden at once takes the highest position, is followed by a lingering withdrawal and a reluctant descent to the lowest. Under the influence of such a spirit of ambition, a man prefers himself to all ; but he is in turn despised by all, until with shame he is compelled to take the lowest place. It should not be so with the humble man or even with the prudent man, who wishes to escape possible confusion. Whether, then, a man is actuated by true humility or by the less spiritual but legitimate motive of a prudent avoidance of confusion and shame, he should lay aside the arrogance of ambition, since this is the only means to escape humiliation. Truly worthy of attention is the advice of the Apostle : " Let nothing be done through contention, nor through vain glory ; but in humility, let each esteem others better than themselves, each one not considering the things that are his own, but those that are other men's. For let this mind be in you, which was also in Christ Jesus : Who being in the form of God, thought it not robbery to be equal with God, but he emptied himself, taking the form of a servant " (Phil. ii. 3-7).

Such was the admonition of our Divine Master himself who said in continuation :—

V. 10. **But when thou art invited, go, sit down in the lowest place ; that when he who invited thee cometh, he may say to thee : Friend, go up higher. Then shalt thou have glory before them that sit at table with thee.**

" If you endeavour to be truly humble," says Rodriguez, " you will undoubtedly gain esteem even though you seek it not ; and the more you avoid being esteemed and honoured, the greater account will be made of you ; for glory is like a shadow, which follows always when you fly from it, and is never to be caught when you run after it." (*Christian Perfection. Treatise on Humility*, vol. ii., c. ii., p. 197.)

The reader should be careful not to mistake the meaning of Christ's admonition. As the word ἵνα sometimes introduces *the result* rather than *the purpose,* and as the former meaning is here suggested by the character of the speaker and by the context, it follows that our Lord does not teach his hearers to seek the lowest place *in order that* they may be raised to one higher ; but that if they seek the lowest, *it will come to pass that* they will be invited to a higher position (ἵνα ὅταν ἔλθῃ ὁ κεκληκώς σε, ἐρεῖ σοι, κ.τ.λ). It was not Christ's purpose merely to teach the rules which should govern our conduct in our social relations with our fellow-men. He points out what happens to the presumptuous and ambitious in human intercourse, so that the practice of a prudent modesty before men may at least ultimately lead his disciples to the exercise of true humility before God. Therefore it is that he adds this moral lesson which he has been aiming at throughout :—

V. 11. **Because every one that exalteth himself, shall be humbled ; and he that humbleth himself, shall be exalted.**

This most salutary truth, often on the lips of our Lord and of his apostles (Matth. xxiii. 12 ; Luke xviii. 14 ; 1 Peter v. 6), had been made known to the Gentiles by the light of reason, and to the Jews by the Sacred Scriptures. Thus pagan philosophers, especially Thales, the first amongst the seven sages, adopted as a worldly maxim the saying : " He that humbleth himself shall be exalted." The book of Proverbs, too, insists on it in more than one passage. " Humiliation," says Solomon, " followeth the proud, and glory shall uphold the humble of spirit " (Proverbs xxix. 23). The same lesson is taught in examples recorded by sacred writers of the Old and of the New Testament. Thus we learn that Lucifer said in his pride : " I will ascend above the height of the clouds, I will be like the most High " ; but he was " brought down to hell, into the depth of the pit " (Isaias xiv. 14, 15 in the mystic sense). Of Antiochus it is written : " He who, being filled with pride beyond the condition of a man, supposed that he had even the waves of the sea at his bidding and that he weighed the heights of the mountains in a balance, being now cast down to the ground, was carried in a litter, bearing witness in himself to the manifest power of God. . . . And because of the intolerable stench, no one could endure to carry the man that a little before thought he touched the stars of heaven. Hereupon, therefore, being brought down from his great pride, being admonished by the scourge of God as his pains increased every minute, he began to come to a knowledge of himself. And as not even he himself could now endure his stench, he said these words : ' It is right to be subject to God, and that one who is mortal should not put himself on a par with God ' " (1 Mach. ix. 8, 10, 11, 12). On the other hand, the Precursor declared himself unworthy to loose the shoes of the Messiah (John i. 27), and the Messiah honoured him with this testimony : " There hath not risen among them that are born of women, a greater than John the Baptist " (Matth. xi. 11). Again, the Blessed Virgin called herself the handmaid of the Lord, and she became the Mother of God (Luke i. 38-48, and Luke i. 31-35). Lastly, Christ " humbled himself, becoming obedient unto death, even to the death of the cross. Wherefore also God hath exalted him, and hath given him a name which is above every name, that in the name of Jesus every knee should bow, of those that are in heaven and on earth and under the earth, and that every tongue should confess that the Lord Jesus Christ is in the glory of God the Father " (Phil. ii. 8-11. See McCarthy, *in loco*).

IV.—MORAL REFLECTIONS.

The chief lesson taught us in the present gospel passage, is the practice of humility—a practice which our Divine Master commended unceasingly from his birth in the stable until his death on the cross. We shall do well, then, to consider this virtue in its different kinds, or rather, from the different points of view from which it is presented to us by the masters of the spiritual life.

1. Humility of mind, as it is called, is the first and most essential element in the character of the Christian. It is founded on self-knowledge, and is nothing else than the admission of

our frailty, of our passions, of our evil inclinations, and of our
vices.   In the sight of our corruption and nothingness, revealed
to us by our experience and still more certainly by our faith,
how can we entertain any other than a lowly estimate of ourselves considered either in relation to God or to our neighbour ?
In vain should we try to conceive the infinite distance that
separates us from the perfection of our Creator ; and if we reflect on what we are in his sight, we cannot but be ashamed
of our misery, of our weakness, of our worthlessness, of our
ingratitude, and of our sins.   When we stand in his presence,
even what he has done to exalt us should humble us in our
estimate of ourselves.   " O Lord, our Lord," said the Psalmist,
" how admirable is thy name in the whole earth ; for thy magnificence is elevated above the heavens ! . . .   What is man
that thou art mindful of him, or the son of man that thou
visitest him ? "   (Ps. viii. 2, 5).   The knowledge of ourselves
should likewise regulate our thoughts regarding our neighbour :
it should exclude all contempt for him, and all idea of superiority to him.   If our contempt for our neighbour is occasioned
by our greater temporal advantages, by our riches, by our birth,
by our dignity, by our intelligence, by our acquired knowledge,
how small is the distance which these distinctions place between
man and man !   If this contempt arises from a supposed larger
share of virtue and good works than our neighbour can claim,
our judgment is censured in advance by the Apostle, who
says : " Wherein thou judgest another, thou condemnest thyself ; for thou dost the same things which thou judgest ? "
(Rom. ii. 1).   But it will be asked : " In order to practise humility
of mind, must the hero believe himself a coward, or is the clever
man to think himself a fool, or is the saint always to consider
himself as culpable as the wretch whose existence is a menace
to society ? "   Certainly this is not the meaning of the law
of Christ ; for humility is not untruth.   What the humble man
must, and does believe, is that if he has any good quality or
practises any virtue, this is due to God's unmerited bounty ;
that " every best gift, and every perfect gift, is from above,
coming down from the Father of lights " (James i. 17) ; that
if he were placed in other circumstances without greater grace,
he might be worse than the worst he sees around him ; and
that, consequently, in himself he can find no cause to glory.
Thus, humility of mind consists not in denying what we are
or what we have above others, but in recognising to the full
our natural as well as our supernatural endowments, and in
then attributing them to the Great Giver of all.   This was
the humility of Mary, the most exalted of all beings after God.
When St. Elizabeth proclaimed her greatness in the well-known
words : " Blessed art thou among women, and blessed is the

fruit of thy womb," Mary acknowledged the justice of this praise,
and even added to it in the exclamation : " Behold, henceforth,
all generations shall call me blessed." Still, to whom did she
attribute all ? Not to herself, but to him who showed the
might of his arm in raising her from her lowliness. " My soul,"
said she, " doth magnify the Lord, and my spirit hath rejoiced
in God my Saviour ; because he hath regarded the humility
of his handmaid. . . . He that is mighty hath done great things
to me, and holy is his name " (Luke i. 42-49).

2. Humility of mind or an acknowledgment of our nothingness is not enough : it must be supplemented by humility of
heart, which consists in shunning the esteem and applause of
the world, and in voluntarily embracing occasions of humiliation. In the saints this goes so far that they desire to be
humbled ; they are pleased at affronts ; they rejoice at being
contemned and despised. Such was the example set us by our
Lord himself. He could not practise the first kind of humility
by despising himself ; for " being in the form of God, [he]
thought it not robbery to be equal with God " (Philipp. ii. 6) ;
but to give us a much needed instruction he did practise the
second and " emptied himself, taking the form of a servant,
being made in the likeness of men, and in habit found as a man.
He humbled himself, becoming obedient unto death : even to
the death of the cross " (Philipp. ii. 7, 8). Such, too, was the
humility of the Apostle, who declared to his disciples that he
was not worthy to be called an apostle, because he persecuted
the Church of God (1 Cor. xv. 9), and who said of himself :
" Though I should have a mind to glory, I shall not be foolish ;
for I will say the truth. But I forbear, lest any man should
think of me above that which he seeth in me or anything he
heareth from me. . . . Gladly, therefore, will I glory in my infirmities, that the power of Christ may dwell in me. For which
cause I take pleasure in my infirmities, in reproaches, in necessities, in persecutions, in distresses, for Christ " (2 Cor. xii. 6,
9, 10).

3. Interior humility of mind and of heart, however perfect
in itself, is not sufficient : it must manifest itself exteriorly in
our intercourse with others. It is to this especially that Christ
referred in saying to each of the assembled guests : " When
thou art invited to a wedding, go, sit down in the lowest place ";
for the precept is not limited in its application to repasts, but
should govern our conduct in every circumstance of life. An
infinitely wise Providence has distributed men into classes ;
and it is this graduated difference of rank from the sovereign
to the humblest subject, that secures the harmony, prosperity,
and stability of society. In opposition to these beneficent
intentions, the proud man is discontented with his position ;

and aiming at one higher, he seeks to surpass his equals and to rival his superiors. How different is the spirit of Jesus Christ, and how great the peace of mind which, even in this world, the practice of Christian humility is sure to bring! But is it forbidden to maintain our rank, or must the superior yield his place to his subordinates and expose his dignity to contempt? To think so would be to misunderstand the words of our Divine Master; for the maintenance of social distinction, so necessary to public order, cannot be contrary to the precepts of the gospel. The object of our Saviour is to repress the ambition of those who would aim at distinction or honours not belonging to their state of life; to condemn the spirit of jealous rivalry amongst equals; and to impress upon superiors the wisdom and utility of bridging over by modesty and discreet condescension, the interval that separates them from their inferiors. Dignity and affability are not opposed, but give to each other a true value. Dignity makes itself beloved by becoming affable; and affability is reverenced when it modestly maintains its dignity. We should ever remember the inspired precept: " In proportion to thy greatness, humble thyself in all things; and thou shalt find grace before God. For great is the power of God alon and he is honoured by the humble " (Ecclus. iii. 20, 21).

SEVENTEENTH SUNDAY AFTER PENTECOST.

I.—TEXTS.

GREEK.

MATTHEW XXII. 34-46.

³⁴ Οἱ δὲ φαρεισαῖοι ἀκούσαντες ὅτι ἐφίμωσε τοὺς σαδδουκαίους, συνήχθησαν ἐπὶ τὸ αὐτό. ³⁵ Καὶ ἐπηρώτησεν εἷς ἐξ αὐτῶν νομικὸς, πειράζων αὐτόν· ³⁶ Διδάσκαλε, ποία ἐντολὴ μεγάλη ἐν τῷ νόμῳ; ³⁷ Ὁ δὲ ἔφη αὐτῷ· Ἀγαπήσεις κύριον τὸν θεόν σου ἐν ὅλῃ καρδίᾳ σου, καὶ ἐν ὅλῃ ψυχῇ σου, καὶ ἐν ὅλῃ τῇ διανοίᾳ σου. ³⁸ Αὕτη ἐστὶν ἡ μεγάλη καὶ πρώτη ἐντολή. ³⁹ Δευτέρα, Ὁμοίως ἀγαπήσεις τὸν πλησίον σου, ὡς σεαυτόν. ⁴⁰ Ἐν ταύταις ταῖς δυσὶν ἐντολαῖς ὅλος ὁ νόμος κρέμαται, καὶ οἱ προφῆται.

⁴¹ Συνηγμένων δὲ τῶν Φαρεισαίων, ἐπηρώτησεν αὐτοὺς ὁ Ἰησοῦς, ⁴² λέγων· Τί ὑμῖν δοκεῖ περὶ τοῦ Χριστου; Τίνος υἱός ἐστιν; Λέγουσιν αὐτῷ· Τοῦ Δαυείδ. ⁴³ Λέγει αὐτοῖς· Πῶς οὖν Δαυεὶδ ἐν πνεύματι καλεῖ αὐτὸν κύριον, λέγων· ⁴⁴ Εἶπεν ὁ κύριος τῷ κυρίῳ μου· Κάθου ἐκ δεξιῶν μου, ἕως ἂν θῶ τοὺς ἐχθρούς σου ὑποκάτω τῶν ποδῶν σου. ⁴⁵ Εἰ οὖν Δαυεὶδ καλεῖ αὐτὸν κύριον, πῶς υἱὸς αὐτοῦ ἐστιν; ⁴⁶ Καὶ οὐδεὶς ἐδύνατο ἀποκριθῆναι αὐτῷ λόγον· οὐδὲ ἐτόλμησέν τις ἀπ᾽ ἐκείνης τῆς ἡμέρας ἐπερωτῆσαι αὐτὸν οὐκέτι.

VULGATE.

MATTHEW XXII. 34-46.

³⁴ Pharisæi autem, audientes quod silentium imposuisset sadducæis, convenerunt in unum ; ³⁵ et interrogavit eum unus ex eis legis doctor, tentans eum : ³⁶ Magister, quod est mandatum magnum in lege? ³⁷ Ait illi Jesus : Diliges Dominum Deum tuum ex toto corde tuo, et in tota anima tua, et in tota mente tua. ³⁸ Hoc est maximum et primum mandatum. ³⁹ Secundum autem simile est huic : Diliges proximum tuum sicut teipsum. ⁴⁰ In his duobus mandatis universa lex pendet, et prophetæ. ⁴¹ Congregatis autem pharisæis, interrogavit eos Jesus, ⁴² dicens : Quid vobis videtur de Christo? Cujus filius est? Dicunt ei : David. ⁴³ Ait illis : Quomodo ergo David in spiritu vocat eum Dominum, dicens : ⁴⁴ Dixit Dominus Domino meo : Sede a dextris meis, donec ponam inimicos tuos scabellum pedum tuorum? ⁴⁵ Si ergo David vocat eum Dominum, quomodo filius ejus est? ⁴⁶ Et nemo poterat ei respondere verbum ; neque ausus fuit quisquam ex illa die eum amplius interrogare.

II.—ENGLISH TRANSLATION WITH PARALLEL PASSAGES FROM SS. MARK AND LUKE.

MATTHEW XXII. 34-46.

34 But hearing that he had silenced the sadducees, the pharisees came together ; 35 and one of them, a doctor of the law, asked him, tempting him : 36 " Master, which is the great commandment in the law ? " 37 Jesus said to him : " Thou shalt love the Lord thy God with thy whole heart, and with thy whole soul, and with thy whole mind. 38 This is the greatest and the first commandment. 39 And the second is like to this : Thou shalt love thy neighbour as thyself. 40 On these two commandments dependeth the whole law, and the prophets." 41 And the pharisees being gathered together, Jesus asked them, 42 saying : " What think you of Christ ? Whose son is he ? " They say to him : " David's." 43 He saith to them : " How, then, doth David in spirit call him Lord, saying : 44 The Lord said to my Lord, Sit on my right hand, until I make thy enemies thy footstool ? 45 If David then call him Lord, how is he his son ? " 46 And no man was able to answer him a word ; neither durst any man from that day forth ask him any more questions.

MARK XII. 28-37.

28 And of the scribes there came one that had heard them reasoning together ; and seeing that he had answered them well, he asked him : " Which is the first commandment of all ? " 29 And Jesus answered him : " The first commandment of all is : Hear, O Israel : The Lord thy God is one God ; 30 and thou shalt love the Lord thy God, with thy whole heart, and with thy whole soul, and with thy whole mind, and with thy whole strength. This is the first commandment. 31 And the second is like to it : Thou shalt love thy neighbour as thyself. There is no other commandment greater than these." 32 And the scribe said to him : " Well, master, thou hast said in truth, that there is one God, and there is no other besides him. 33 And that he be loved with the whole heart, and with the whole understanding, and with the whole soul, and with the whole strength, and that one's neighbour be loved as oneself, is a greater thing than all holocausts and sacrifices." 34 And Jesus seeing that he had answered wisely, said to him : " Thou art not far from the kingdom of God." And no man after that durst ask him any question. 35 And Jesus answering, said, while teaching in the temple : " How do the scribes say, that Christ is the son of David ; 36 for David himself saith by the Holy Ghost : The Lord said to my Lord : Sit on my right hand, until I make thy enemies thy footstool ? 37 David, therefore, himself calleth

him Lord ; and whence is he, then, his son ? " And a great multitude heard him gladly.

LUKE XX. 41-44.

41 But he said to them : " How say they that Christ is the son of David, 42 and David himself saith in the book of Psalms : The Lord said to my Lord : Sit thou on my right hand, 43 until I make thy enemies thy footstool ? 44 David, then, calleth him Lord ; and how is he his son ? "

III.—COMBINED NARRATIVE.

PART I.

But hearing that he had silenced the sadducees, the pharisees came together ; and there came one of them, one of the scribes, a doctor of the law, that had heard them reasoning together. And seeing that he had answered them well, he tempting him, asked him : " Master, which is the great commandment in the law ?   Which is the first commandment of all ? "   And Jesus answered him : " The first commandment of all is : Hear, O Israel : The Lord thy God is one God ; and thou shalt love the Lord thy God with thy whole heart, and with thy whole soul, and with thy whole mind, and with thy whole strength.   This is the greatest and the first commandment.   And the second is like to it : Thou shalt love thy neighbour as thyself.   There is no other commandment greater than these : on these two commandments dependeth the whole law, and the prophets." And the scribe said to him : " Well, Master, thou hast said in truth, that there is one God, and there is no other besides him. And that he be loved with the whole heart, and with the whole understanding, and with the whole soul, and with the whole strength, and that one's neighbour be loved as oneself, is a greater thing than all holocausts and sacrifices."   And Jesus seeing that he had answered wisely, said to him : " Thou art not far from the kingdom of God."

PART II.

And the pharisees being gathered together, Jesus answering, said, while teaching in the temple : " What think you of Christ ? Whose son is he ? "   They say to him : " David's."   He saith to them : " How do the scribes say that Christ is the son of David ; for David himself saith by the Holy Ghost in the book of Psalms : The Lord said to my Lord : Sit on my right hand, until I make thy enemies thy footstool ?   David, therefore, himself calleth him Lord ; and whence is he, then, his son ? " And no man was able to answer him a word ; neither durst any man from that day forth ask him any more questions. And a great multitude heard him gladly.

IV.—NOTES.

Introductory. The gospel passages read in the Mass of the 17th, 19th, and 22nd Sundays after Pentecost are taken from St. Matthew's account of our Lord's discourses in the temple on the Wednesday before the Passion. This was the last occasion on which Christ appeared in the sacred edifice (John xii. 36) ; and the day was spent in a prolonged effort to convert those enemies who had already determined on his death (John xi. 47-53). On that morning, as soon as he had returned from Bethany to the city and was engaged in the instruction of the people, there came to him a number of the chief-priests and the scribes, and the ancients (Matth. xxi. 23 ; Mark xi. 27, 28 ; Luke xx. 1, 2), who were intent on finding in his words the matter for a formal accusation before the Council or before the Roman governor. Christ declined to answer directly their question regarding the authority on which he acted (Matth. xxi. 24-27 ; Mark xi. 29-33 ; Luke xx. 3-8) ; in the parable of " the obedient and the disobedient son," he put before them a picture of their insincerity (Matth. xxi. 28-32) ; in the parable of " the wicked husbandmen " and in that of " the marriage-feast," he foretold their reprobation, the destruction of their nation, and the calling of the Gentiles (Matth. xxi. 33-xxii. 14 ; Mark xii. 1-12 ; Luke xx. 9-19) ; and he dismissed them in wonder at the superhuman wisdom of his answer regarding the payment of tribute to Cæsar (Matth. xxii. 15-22 ; Mark xii. 13-17 ; Luke xx. 20-26). The sadducees (Introduction, p. clxxiii.) met with a similar humiliation in Christ's reply to their insidious question regarding the possibility of the resurrection (Matth. xxii. 23-32 ; Mark xii. 18-27 ; Luke xx. 27-40). St. Matthew adds (verse 33) that " the multitudes hearing it, were in admiration at his doctrine " ;

Vv. 34, 35. But hearing that he had silenced the sadducees, the pharisees came together ; and one of them, a doctor of the law, asked him, tempting him.

This statement does not necessarily signify that the " doctor of the law," or " scribe " (Introduction, p. cxxviii.) as he is called by St. Mark, wished to ensnare our Lord, or to provoke him by hypocrisy. The expression πειράζων αὐτὸν, which is rendered " tempting him," may equally be rendered " testing him " as to his knowledge of the law and his skill in its exposition. The signification of the words in each passage where they occur, is to be determined by the context ; and the context here seems to exclude any bad motive from the question. Although the pharisees (Introduction, p. clxxiii.), as a class, were ill-disposed towards our Lord, and although this " doctor of the law " or " scribe " was " one of them " and appears to have been put forward by them as their spokesman, he seems not to have shared their spirit. In the first place it may be inferred from a comparison of the gospels that it was one of those that praised our Lord's answer to the sadducees who also asked this question (Luke xx. 39). St. Mark says of him in the Parallel Passage: "Of the scribes there came one that had heard them (Christ and the sadducees) reasoning together, and seeing that he (Christ) had answered them well, he asked him: Which is the first commandment of all?" (Mark xii. 28). Moreover this "doctor of the law" afterwards expressed his admiration for Christ's reply to himself (Mark xii. 32), and was in turn spoken of with high approval by our Divine Lord, who said: "Thou art not far from the kingdom of God" (Mark xii. 34).

The question of the sadducees regarding the possibility of the resurrection (Matth. xxii. 23-28; Mark xii. 18-23; Luke xx. 27-33) was speculative and proposed in bad faith: that of the "doctor of the law" was practical and asked with a sincere desire of knowing the truth. Addressing Christ he said:—

V. 36. **Master, which is the great commandment in the law?**

Jewish theologians distinguished the human precepts or traditions from the divine; and these latter to the number of 613, were divided into "the great" and "the small." As may be seen in the Parallel Passage of St. Mark, it was the object of the scribe to learn from our Lord, which was the first commandment of all. The question is one that presents no difficulty to the well-instructed Christian; but it was not so even to learned Jews in the time of Christ. Having only imperfect notions of God and of his attributes, many then attached too much importance to the offering of sacrifice, to the rigid observance of the sabbath, and to outward purifications, whilst they bestowed comparatively but little attention on the practice of interior virtue. In the controversy regarding the relative importance of the ceremonial, and of the moral, precepts of the law, they overlooked the necessity of what must be the soul of all acceptable worship; for they had not yet learned the lesson taught to the Samaritan woman: "The hour cometh, and now is, when the true adorers shall adore the Father in spirit and in truth; for the Father also seeketh such to adore him. God is a spirit; and they that adore him, must adore him in spirit and in truth (John iv. 23, 24).

That the "doctor of the law" had a fairly correct conception of his obligations, is shown in his approval of our Lord's reply; but that he was not quite sure of his ground, is clear from the question he proposed. He needed instruction from the Divine Teacher ; and

Vv. 37, 38. Jesus said to him: Thou shalt love the Lord :hy God with thy whole heart, and with thy whole soul, and with thy whole mind. This is the greatest and the first commandment.

The reply is taken from Deuteronomy (vi. 4, 5) as may be seen in St. Mark's gospel, where the preceding verse is quoted and a fourth member is added to the commandment. Probably we should be able to reconstruct the first part of our Lord's answer in its entirety, if we thus combined the records of the two evangelists : " The first commandment of all is : Hear, O Israel : The Lord thy God is one God ; and thou shalt love the Lord thy God with thy whole heart, and with thy whole soul, and with thy whole mind, and with thy whole strength. This is the greatest and the first commandment." It is not easy, perhaps, to point out the distinction between the several clauses of this precept ; but still we cannot accept the view of Maldonatus who says : " Sunt qui hæc nimis subtiliter, meo judicio, distinguunt : mihi omnia hæc videntur significare, ut Deum quantum possumus diligamus, et omnia quæ habemus, illi impendamus." In the opinion of this commentator and of those who follow him, the construction is similar to that of Plautus, c. ii. 3 : " Id petam, idque persequar, *corde, et animo, atque viribus,*" where for emphasis the expression of the same idea is repeated in different words. Much more probable is the opinion of those who consider that a distinct part of the precept is expressed in each clause. In such an exposition the " heart " ($\kappa\alpha\rho\delta\iota\alpha$) is the will or seat of the affections ; the " soul " ($\psi\upsilon\chi\eta$) is the vital principle, the sphere of the inferior appetites, the lower faculty in man's spiritual nature ; the " mind " ($\delta\iota\alpha\nu o\iota\alpha$) is the higher faculty of thought ; and the " strength " ($\iota\sigma\chi\upsilon s$) comprises all the bodily powers. All these together, namely, the *will,* the *inferior appetites* of the soul, the *intellect,* the *members of the body,* go to form the human being, and each of these has assigned to it a special function. To fulfil the commandment laid upon him, man must devote each of the constituents of his being to the love of his Creator, and must employ them in the service of that Creator, so that, whatever the will desires, whatever the intellect apprehends, whatever the appetite relishes, whatever the senses perceive, may be all directed to God. (See Sporer Tract. ii. in 1 Decal. Praecept. c. v., quoted by McCarthy.)

The " doctor of the law " was told, then, that " the great commandment " was one which prescribed the love of God with our whole being ; but what is the character of the love by which the precept may be fulfilled ? In the explanation of

John xi. 5, it has been well observed that " the loss involved . . . in translating both ἀγαπᾶν and φιλεῖν by ' love,' cannot be remedied satisfactorily.   Φιλεῖν (*amare*) denotes a passionate, emotional warmth, which loves and does not care to ask why ; the affection which is based on natural relationship, as of parents, brothers, lovers, and the like.   Ἀγαπᾶν (*diligere*) denotes a calm, discriminating attachment, which loves because of the excellence of the loved object ; the affection which is based on esteem, as of friends.   Φιλεῖν is the stronger, but less reasoning ; ἀγαπᾶν the more earnest, but less intense.   The sisters of Lazarus naturally use the more emotional word (v. 3), describing their own feeling towards their brother ; the evangelist equally naturally uses the loftier and less impulsive word. . . . Both words are used of the love of the Father to the Son ; φιλεῖν (v. 20), because the love is founded on relationship ; ἀγαπᾶν (iii. 35 ; x. 17 ; xv. 9 ; xvii. 23, 24, 26), because of the character of the love " (Cambridge *Greek Testament*).   There are, then, two kinds of love—that which belongs to man as a thinking being, and that affection which is felt by him in common with other animals.   The former is expressed in Greek by the verb ἀγαπᾶν, and in Latin by *diligere* or *magni facere* : the latter by the Greek φιλεῖν and by the Latin *amare* or *affectum amoris corde et sensu percipere*.   As is clear from the Greek text, the former and more spiritual kind of love is what is here prescribed to the " doctor of the law " and to us, as the fulfilment of " the greatest and the first commandment."

But why is this called " the greatest and the first commandment " ?   It is so called because 1° it has for its object the most perfect Being, a God infinitely good and perfect in himself ; 2° because it tends to that object in the most perfect manner, by a *love of appreciation* above all things ; and 3° because it is in itself the object of all other divine precepts, which are imposed on man for no other purpose than to secure the observance of this, and so to bring about a union with God. St. Augustine (Tract. v. *in* 1 *Joann.*) says well : " Charity is that without which nothing avails, but the possession of which makes up for all things else."   It is no wonder, then, that having laid many grave injunctions on the faithful of Colossae, the Apostle concludes with the words : " But above all these things, have charity, which is the bond of perfection " (Col. iii. 14).

When Christ had given this as the commandment which is " first " in dignity and " greatest " in the extent of the duties it imposes, he added :—

V. 39. And the second is like to this : Thou shalt love thy neighbour as thyself.

It is to be observed that as the first precept of the law of love is taken from Deuteronomy, so is the second a reproduction of Leviticus xix. 18, not according to the rendering of the Vulgate, but according to that of the Septuagint. Again, we should remark that this latter precept is not said to be *equal* to the first ; because, although the ultimate object is the same in each, the immediate object in the love of God infinitely surpasses the immediate object in the love of our neighbour. Still, it is *like* to the first ; because as God is to be loved above *all* created things on account of his *own infinite perfection*, so our neighbour is to be loved above *all other* visible things, inasmuch as in his natural, and still more in his supernatural, gifts he is *the image of God*. Thus the commandments are " like " for this reason that although the immediate object is not the same, the ultimate object of each love is identical and the motive is the same. The manner in which this commandment should be fulfilled will be afterwards explained under the head of " Moral Reflections."

St. Mark says that having announced the two great precepts of the law of love, our Lord subjoined : " There is no other commandment greater than these." He then gave the reason of their supreme importance when, according to St. Matthew, he said :—

V. 40. On these two commandments dependeth the whole law, and the prophets.

The prescriptions of " the whole law and the prophets depend " on these two commandments 1° " because all the moral precepts found elsewhere in the Sacred Scriptures are virtually contained in these, and are reducible to these, as conclusions to their principles ; 2° because all the virtuous acts taught by revealed religion must be elicited from the spirit fostered by these precepts ; and 3° because, like mere means to an end, all the prescriptions of every other law must be observed, or omitted, or modified, as circumstances require in order that this supreme law of charity may be kept inviolate. That all other precepts depend on these two commandments, is true whether the two be taken together, or taken singly. It is true if they be taken together, because, whilst the first urges us to perform perfectly all our duties to God, the fulfilment of the second supposes a spirit which will neglect no obligation to our neighbour. It is true also if these commandments be taken singly, because the observance of the one is included in the observance of the other, or at least presupposes the observance of that other. He who loves God truly and from his heart, is prepared to fulfil God's commands in the performance of the duties towards himself and his neighbour which the divine law imposes. On the other hand, he who for a right motive truly loves his neighbour as himself, necessarily loves God on account of whom both he himself and his neighbour are to be loved.

Hence the words of St. Paul, who did not hesitate to say to the Romans: " Love, therefore, is the fulfilling of the law " (Rom. xiii. 10).

The effect of our Lord's answer is thus described by St. Mark: " The scribe said to him: ' Well, master, thou hast said in truth, that there is one God, and there is no other besides him. And that he be loved with the whole heart, and with the whole understanding, and with the whole soul, and with the whole strength, and that one's neighbour be loved as oneself is a greater thing than all holocausts and sacrifices.' And Jesus seeing that he had answered wisely, said to him: ' Thou art not far from the kingdom of God.' And no man after that durst ask him any question " (Mark xii. 32-34).

The scribe merited the commendation he received, for no one is " far from the kingdom of God " who clearly sees and heartily approves of what God requires to be done. Still we are not yet in the way of salvation until we fully know and submissively receive what God requires to be believed ; for the Apostle has written : " Without faith, it is impossible to please God " (Hebrew xi. 6). Hence, having given to this man a summary of the moral law, Christ proceeded to complete the lesson by proving to him and to those who had put him forward, the fundamental truth of his divinity.

Vv. 41, 42. **And the pharisees being gathered together, Jesus asked them, saying: What think you of Christ? Whose son is he? They say to him: David's.**

SS. Mark and Luke omit this interrogation and answer ; but in giving Christ's subsequent objection to the answer, both evangelists imply that the question recorded by St. Matthew was put by our Lord and replied to by the scribes, who no doubt formed a large contingent of the pharisees present on this occasion. Nothing gave so much offence to the heads of the Jewish religion as that Jesus had attributed to himself the divine nature and had taught that he was the Son of God. In this discussion, therefore, which was to be his last with the pharisees, he wished to prove that he was really God. He did so by calling their attention to the prophecies regarding the Christ or Messiah whom his words and works during the last three years had proved him to be. To his question on the teaching of the Scripture, they answered that the Messiah was to be a descendant of David. Now, whilst the sacred writers had foretold the human nature of the Messiah and his descent from David, they not less clearly announced his divinity ; but the meaning of these latter prophecies was lost sight of by the greater number, who looked forward to their fulfilment in the establishment of a temporal kingdom. To correct this false idea, our Lord quotes for his hearers a psalm which was admitted by all to have David for its author, and the dignity of the Messiah for its subject-matter. Therefore

V. 43. He saith to them: How, then, doth David in spirit call him Lord, saying: etc.

As we may learn from the context, the word " Lord " in this verse corresponds to the Hebrew אדון which signifies a *sovereign master*. It was a term implying an acknowledgment of *superiority* in the person to whom it was addressed, and, therefore, was never given as a title to *inferiors*, though sometimes, out of courtesy perhaps, to equals. This, then, is our Lord's argument : " An independent monarch such as David, would acknowledge no lord or master but God, and would not bestow the title of ' Lord ' (אדון) upon an ordinary son or descendant. Hence, when David, under the influence of the Holy Ghost, thus designated the Messiah, he acknowledged the superiority, and implied the divinity of the Messiah." The testimony to the dignity of his descendant, the Messiah, is thus given by the Royal Prophet :—

V. 44. The Lord said to my Lord: Sit on my right hand until I make thy enemies thy footstool.

An examination of the 109th Psalm (Heb. 110th), from which these words are taken, shows the suitability of the quotation for the purpose Christ had in view. As has been observed, the reference to the Messiah was admitted by the ancient Jews, and neither was, nor could be denied by the pharisees on this occasion. In the first place, the opening words of the original Hebrew are rendered : " The oracle (or saying) of Jehovah to my supreme Lord (נאם יהוה לאדני) : Sit on my right hand "— an introductory formula which is not elsewhere found in the Psalms, and which invites the reader's attention to the sublime character of him whose glory is here to be set forth. Then again, the person here invited to sit on the right hand of Jehovah is himself declared to be Supreme God. The reason is because " my Lord " in verse 1 is identified with " the Lord " in verse 5. Now " the Lord " in verse 5 is the Supreme Being (*a*) because the title given him in verse 5 is אֲדֹנָי—a title which, *when pointed in this manner*, is never given to a creature ; and (*b*) because to him in verse 6, is attributed the power to judge all nations—a power which implies that he has redeemed all nations, and consequently that he is not only Man, but God (St. Thomas, *Summa*, Suppl. Quæst. 90, art. 1, *ad tertium*). Still further the same truth may be inferred from verse 3. If in that verse we follow the most generally received Hebrew text, we find the *infinite power* of this " Lord " thus described by Jehovah : " As the dew from the womb of the morning, so is the dew of thy youth," *i.e.*, " many as are the dewdrops at the dawn of the morning, so many are the hosts at thy service in thy contest with Satan." If, on the other hand, we prefer the reading of the Septuagint and of the Vulgate, his infinite power, his divine generation, and his eternal existence are set forth in these words : " With thee is *the* principality in the day of thy strength, . . . from the womb, *before the day-star I begot thee*." Thus in every line of the psalm it is expressly stated or clearly implied, that the Messiah, here addressed as the " Lord " and invited to sit on the right hand of the great God, is himself not merely Man, but God as well : that he is one who, as God, has existed before all creatures, and who, as Man, is to sit on the right hand of God in the undisturbed possession of more than royal power until, in token of their complete defeat, his prostrate enemies become his " footstool." (See McCarthy.,

But if this be so, and, as Christ urged,

V. 45. If David, then, call him Lord, how is he his son ?

Those who admit the two natures in the Messiah, find it easy to reply that in his humanity he was truly David's son, whilst in his divinity he was David's Supreme Lord. It was not so with the pharisees who, blinded by their prejudices, would not make use of the light offered them by Christ, and who thus rendered themselves unworthy of further help. They remained in their voluntary ignorance ;

V. 46. And no man was able to answer him a word ; neither durst any man from that day forth ask him any more questions.

On many occasions before, and more than once that very day, these wicked men had sought to entrap the infinite wisdom of Jesus, but they had on each occasion met with an ignominious defeat, and that in the presence of the people whose teachers and models they were supposed to be. For the short time that remained until the Passion, they desisted from these contests *in words*, but took *other means* to bring about the death of the Redeemer.

V.—MORAL REFLECTIONS.

1. Unlike the " doctor of the law " no Christian is uncertain as to the first and greatest commandment ; for the first lesson given us in childhood is, that we were sent on earth to know our Creator and to love him. How reasonable is this precept since all that gains our love for our fellow-men is found in God in an eminent manner ! We love those dear to us for their qualities of mind and heart, but these created qualities are not comparable to the attributes of God ; we love our friends for

the kindness they show us, but there is no friendship so tender
or constant as that of which God ceaselessly gives us testimony
even after our repeated offences ; we love our benefactors for
the good they do us, but the blessings which we receive from
God are out of all proportion above what men can bestow ;
we cherish the parents to whom we owe our birth, but it is to
God we primarily owe our existence (2 Mach. vii. 22, 23) ; we
are filled with gratitude to those who make sacrifices for us,
but God has sacrificed himself on the cross for our redemption.
Everything without us, then, preaches the necessity of the love
of God ; and everything within us urges the fulfilment of this
duty.

2. This love of God is not of the same nature as that which
we have for friends, relatives, benefactors, or parents ; it is
not an effusion of tender feeling ; but it is what theologians call
a love of appreciation or a love of preference.   The feeling we
experience for those bound to us by kinship or by other ties is
good, it is inspired by nature, and it comes from our Creator ;
but it is not what he demands from us when he calls on us to
give him our heart.   To love him as he wills, is to prefer him
to all creatures ; to prefer his immense blessings to all they
can procure for us ; to prefer the certain, infinite, eternal happiness which he promises in the possession of himself, to the
frivolous pleasures held out to us by the world ; and to be
prepared to lose all things else rather than the least of his
graces.   This is the love above all things or the love of preference, which God requires.

3. This love of God, superior to all other attachments, is not
confined to a mere speculation of the mind, but must manifest itself in its effects.   The first and principal of these effects
is that all our actions proceed from the love of God and be
directed to it.   When there exists in the soul a ruling passion,
from it spring almost all our sentiments, and to the object of
that passion tend almost all our actions.   This is not always
the end we actually and distinctly put before our mind ; but
it is continually our secret and habitual motive.   If the love
of God be in us as it ought to be, if it be the principal and
dominant feeling of our heart, it must produce the same effect.
To think on God actually in all our actions is not possible for
us in this life ; but the general disposition of referring to him
all we do, is possible, just and necessary ; and such an habitual
disposition should be kept alive by repeated and frequently
repeated acts.   The reference of all our works to God is followed by another effect of divine love, viz., the keeping of the
commandments.   Jesus Christ has said : If you love me keep my
commandments. . . .   He that hath my commandments, and
keepeth them, he it is that loveth me " (John xiv. 15-21).   If

divine love is our dominant sentiment, if it is the principle of our actions, it should inspire us to do that which is pleasing to God, and to turn aside from that which offends him. Let us apply this rule to ourselves; let us judge ourselves by it; and from the manner in which we observe God's law, let us ascertain if we have for him the love with which he wishes that we be penetrated.

4. The fulfilment of the divine law, which is the test of this divine love, includes the performance of our duties both to God and to our neighbour. Hence this second portion of the answer which Jesus gave to the scribe: " The second [commandment] is like to this: Thou shalt love thy neighbour as thyself." The two commandments cannot be separated, and St. John has written: " If any man say: I love God, and hateth his brother, he is a liar; for he that loveth not his brother whom he seeth, how can he love God whom he seeth not " (1 John iv. 20). The extent to which we should love our neighbour is thus described by our Divine Master: " This is my commandment: That you love one another *as I have loved you.* Greater love than this no man hath, that a man lay down his life for his friends " (John xv. 12, 13). We owe our life to our brethren, not, as a rule, that we must give it up in their service, but that we must ever employ it for their good. The occasions are rare in which we should die for our neighbour; but those in which we are obliged to make other sacrifices are very common. These sacrifices will sometimes be very painful to nature, but will be rendered sweet by grace; and in the practice of fraternal charity we shall find that it is enriched by the privations which it imposes, that it rejoices in the troubles which it meets, and that it feels itself honoured in the humiliations which it entails.

EIGHTEENTH SUNDAY AFTER PENTECOST.

I.—TEXTS.

GREEK.

MATTHEW IX. 1-8.

¹ Καὶ ἐμβὰς εἰς πλοῖον, διεπέρασεν, καὶ ἦλθεν εἰς τὴν ἰδίαν πόλιν. ² Καὶ ἰδοὺ προσέφερον αὐτῷ παραλυτικὸν ἐπὶ κλίνης βεβλημένον· Καὶ ἰδὼν ὁ Ἰησοῦς τὴν πίστιν αὐτῶν, εἶπεν τῷ παραλυτικῷ· Θάρσει, τέκνον, ἀφίενταί σου αἱ ἁμαρτίαι. ³ Καὶ ἰδοὺ τινὲς τῶν γραμματέων εἶπαν ἐν ἑαυτοῖς· Οὗτος βλασφημεῖ. ⁴ Καὶ εἰδὼς ὁ Ἰησοῦς τὰς ἐνθυμήσεις αὐτῶν, εἶπεν· Ἱνατί ἐνθυμεῖσθε πονηρὰ ἐν ταῖς καρδίαις ὑμῶν; ⁵ Τί γὰρ ἐστιν εὐκοπώτερον, εἰπεῖν· Ἀφίενταί σου αἱ ἁμαρτίαι, ἢ εἰπεῖν· Ἔγειραι καὶ περιπάτει; ⁶ Ἵνα δὲ εἰδῆτε, ὅτι ἐξουσίαν ἔχει ὁ υἱὸς τοῦ ἀνθρώπου ἐπὶ τῆς γῆς ἀφιέναι ἁμαρτίας, τότε λέγει τῷ παραλυτικῷ· Ἔγειρε, ἀρόν σου τὴν κλίνην, καὶ ὕπαγε εἰς τὸν οἶκόν σου. ⁷ Καὶ ἐγερθεὶς ἀπῆλθεν εἰς τὸν οἶκον αὐτοῦ. ⁸ Ἰδόντες δὲ οἱ ὄχλοι ἐφοβήθησαν, καὶ ἐδόξασαν τὸν θεὸν τὸν δόντα ἐξουσίαν τοιαύτην τοῖς ἀνθρώποις.

VULGATE.

MATTHEW IX. 1-8.

¹ Et ascendens in naviculam, transfretavit, et venit in civitatem suam. ² Et ecce offerebant ei paralyticum jacentem in lecto. Et videns Jesus fidem illorum, dixit paralytico : Confide, fili, remittuntur tibi peccata tua. ³ Et ecce quidam de scribis dixerunt intra se : Hic blasphemat. ⁴ Et cum vidisset Jesus cogitationes eorum, dixit : Ut quid cogitatis mala in cordibus vestris? ⁵ Quid est facilius, dicere : Dimittuntur tibi peccata tua, an dicere : Surge, et ambula? ⁶ Ut autem sciatis quia Filius hominis habet potestatem in terra dimittendi peccata, (tunc ait paralytico) : Surge : tolle lectum tuum, et vade in domum tuam. ⁷ Et surrexit, et abiit in domum suam. ⁸ Videntes autem turbæ timuerunt, et glorificaverunt Deum, qui dedit potestatem talem hominibus.

II.—ENGLISH TRANSLATION, WITH PARALLEL PASSAGES FROM SS. MARK AND LUKE.

MATTHEW IX. 1-8.

¹ And entering into a boat, he passed over the water and came into his own city. ² And behold, they brought to him one sick of the palsy, lying in a bed. And Jesus seeing their faith, said to the man sick of the palsy : " Be of good heart,

son, thy sins are forgiven thee." ³ And behold, some of the scribes said within themselves : " He blasphemeth." ⁴ And Jesus seeing their thoughts, said : " Why do you think evil in your hearts ? ⁵ Which is easier, to say : Thy sins are forgiven thee, or to say : Arise and walk ? ⁶ But that you may know that the Son of Man hath power on earth to forgive sins, (then saith he to the man sick of the palsy) : Arise, take up thy bed, and go into thy house." ⁷ And he arose, and went into his house. ⁸ And the multitudes seeing it, feared, and glorified God, who gave such power to men.

MARK II. 1-12.

¹ And he entered again into Capharnaum after some days. ² And it was heard that he was in the house ; and many came together, so that there was no room, no, not even at the door. And he spoke the word to them. ³ And they came to him, bringing one sick of the palsy, who was carried by four. ⁴ And when they could not offer him unto him on account of the multitude, they uncovered the roof where he was ; and opening it, they let down the bed wherein the man sick of the palsy lay. ⁵ And when Jesus had seen their faith, he saith to the man sick of the palsy : " Son, thy sins are forgiven thee." ⁶ And there were some of the scribes sitting there, and thinking in their hearts : ⁷ " Why doth this man speak thus ? He blasphemeth. Who can forgive sins, but God only ? " ⁸ And Jesus presently knowing in his spirit that they so thought within themselves, saith to them : " Why think you these things in your hearts ? ⁹ Which is easier, to say to the man sick of the palsy : Thy sins are forgiven thee, or to say : Arise, take up thy bed, and walk ? ¹⁰ But that you may know that the Son of Man hath power on earth to forgive sins, (he saith to the man sick of the palsy) : ¹¹ I say to thee : Arise, take up thy bed, and go into thy house." ¹² And immediately he arose, and taking up his bed, he went his way in the sight of all ; so that all wondered and glorified God, saying : " We never saw the like."

LUKE V. 17-26.

¹⁷ And it came to pass on a certain day as he sat teaching, that there were also sitting by pharisees and doctors of the law, who were come out of every town of Galilee, and Judæa and Jerusalem ; and the power of the Lord was to heal them. ¹⁸ And behold, men brought in a bed a man who had the palsy ; and they sought means to bring him in, and to lay him before him. ¹⁹ And when they could not find by what way they might bring him in on account of the multitude, they went up on the roof, and let him down through the tiles with his bed into the midst before Jesus. ²⁰ And when he saw their faith, he

said : " Man, thy sins are forgiven thee." ²¹ And the scribes and pharisees began to think, saying : Who is this that speaketh blasphemies ? Who can forgive sins, but God only ? " ²² And when Jesus knew their thoughts, answering, he said to them : " What is it you think in your hearts ? ²³ Which is easier, to say : Thy sins are forgiven thee, or to say : Arise and walk ? ²⁴ But that you may know that the Son of Man hath power on earth to forgive sins, (he saith to the man sick of the palsy) : I say to thee : Arise, take up thy bed, and go into thy house." ²⁵ And immediately rising up before them, he took up the bed on which he lay ; and he went away to his own house glorifying God. ²⁶ And all were astonished ; and they glorified God ; and they were filled with fear, saying : " We have seen wonderful things to-day."

III.—COMBINED NARRATIVE.

And entering into a boat, he (Jesus) passed over the water, and came again into his own city, Capharnaum, after some days. And it came to pass on a certain day, that it was heard he was in the house (*literally*, at home) ; and many came together, so that there was no room, no, not even at the door. And he spoke the word to them. [And] as he sat teaching, there were also sitting by pharisees and doctors of the law, that were come out of every town of Galilee, and Judæa, and Jerusalem ; and the power of the Lord was to heal them. And behold, men brought to him one sick of the palsy, who was carried by four [and] lying on a bed ; and they sought means to bring him (the sick man) in and to lay him before him (Jesus). And when they could not find by what way they might bring him (the sick man) in [and] offer him unto him (Jesus) on account of the multitude, they went up upon the roof ; and they uncovered the roof where he (Jesus) was ; and opening it, they let down through the tiles into the midst before Jesus the bed whereon the man sick of the palsy lay. And Jesus seeing their faith, said to the man sick of the palsy : " Be of good heart, son, thy sins are forgiven thee." And there were some of the scribes sitting there. And behold, some of the scribes and pharisees said within themselves : " Why doth this man speak thus ? He blasphemeth. Who can forgive sins but God only ?" And Jesus presently knowing in his spirit that they so thought within themselves, said to them : " Why do you think these things ? Why do you think evil in your hearts ? Which is easier, to say to the man sick of the palsy : Thy sins are forgiven thee, or to say : Arise, take up thy bed, and walk. But that you may know that the Son of Man hath power on earth to forgive sins, (then saith he to the man sick of the palsy) : I say to thee : Arise, take up thy bed, and go into thy house." And immediately he arose, and taking up the bed on which he lay, he went away in the sight of all into his own house, glorifying God. And all were astonished. And the multitudes seeing it, feared [and] wondered, saying: "We have seen wonderful things to-day: we never saw the like." And they glorified God who gave such power to men.

IV.—NOTES.

Introductory. This miracle is recorded by SS. Matthew, Mark and Luke; and from a comparison of the Parallel Passages in these evangelists, it appears to have been wrought at Capharnaum, a city of Galilee, towards the close of the first year of our Lord's public life. It is generally admitted that, whilst SS. Matthew and Mark classified the facts of the gospel history without much regard to the sequence of events, St. Luke followed very exactly the chronological order. Taking, then, this last evangelist as his guide on the present occasion, the reader will find that the miracles here described did not take place after, but sometime before, the cure of the Gerasene demoniac which is narrated by St. Matthew towards the end of the last chapter. From St. Mark (i. 45), and still more from St. Luke (v. 15), it is seen that after the miraculous draught of fishes (Luke v. 1-10), the calling of Peter, Andrew, James and John (Matthew iv. 18-22; Mark i. 16-20; Luke v. 11), the Sermon on the Mount (Matthew v.-vii.), and the healing of the leper (Matthew viii. 2-4; Mark i. 40-44; Luke v. 12-14), the fame of Christ "went abroad the more, and great multitudes came together to hear; . . . and he retired (as it would appear, from the western shore of the Sea of Galilee, across the lake) into the desert, and prayed" (Luke v. 16).

Having spent some time in retirement, as was his custom after a series of miracles, then

V. 1. Entering into a boat, he passed over the water, and came into his own city.

The place is not named by St. Luke; it is merely designated "his own city" by St. Matthew; but in the Parallel Passage St. Mark removes all doubt by stating that it was at Capharnaum the miracle was worked. This was called "his own city," because some time before, on his being rejected at Nazareth where he had been reared, Christ took up his residence at Capharnaum, and thenceforth made it his head-quarters when he preached in Galilee. During his absence from this place after the cure of the leper, the report of the miracle had been spread abroad so that on his return he could not "openly go into the city, but was without in desert places" (Mark i. 45). However, "again he entered into Capharnaum after some days and it was heard that he was in the house (Gr. ἐν οἴκῳ = *at home*);

and many came together, so that there was no room, no, not even at the door. And he spoke the word to them " (Mark ii. 1, 2). The expression used by St. Mark (ἐλάλει αὐτοῖς τὸν λόγον = *He was accustomed to speak the word to them*) indicates that the instructions were frequently given in the circumstances referred to. Now, as we learn from St. Luke (v. 17), during the time our Lord was thus engaged, " it came to pass on a certain day as he sat teaching, that there were also sitting by pharisees and doctors of the law, that were come out of every town of Galilee, and Judæa, and Jerusalem ; and the power of the Lord was to heal them."

Christ was addressing this assembly ;

V. 2. And behold, they brought to him one sick of the palsy lying in a bed.

In order to fully appreciate St. Matthew's subsequent reference to " their faith," it is necessary to keep in mind the more minute accounts given by the other evangelists in the Parallel Passages—accounts which may be thus combined : " Behold, men came to him [and] brought to him a man sick of the palsy, who was lying in a bed [and] carried by four. And when they could not find by what way they might bring him in on account of the multitude, they went up on the roof ; and they uncovered the roof where he (Jesus) was ; and opening it, they let him (the sick man) down with his bed through the tiles into the midst before Jesus." In the first place, we must observe that from St. Matthew's use of the word ἰδοὺ = " behold," it does not follow that this event occurred immediately on Christ's return across the lake, or even immediately on his entering "his own city," Capharnaum. The sense is : " He came into his own city, and while he was there these events took place." Again, though difficult to accomplish, what is told regarding the bearers of the sick man will not appear impossible if we recollect the customs and circumstances of the place. As is implied in Livy xxxix. 14 with respect to Roman houses, we know that in the East it was customary to have a stairs on the exterior of a dwelling in addition to that in the interior ; and by either means of ascent, persons could reach the roof. The roof itself was flat or nearly so, and consisted of a slight covering of material easily removed. Underneath was the principal chamber, often used for family gatherings or for such purposes as the present. (Introduction, pp. lxxix.-lxxxi.)

On account of the crowd (see Parallel Passages), the task before the bearers of the sick man was not easy ; but the determination to overcome the difficulty showed these men's firm belief in our Lord's power.

And Jesus seeing their faith, said to the man sick of the palsy : Be of good heart, son, thy sins are forgiven thee.

Although it is not likely that without the sick man's faith the appeal for his restoration to health would have been made, still the faith of which the evangelist speaks, appears to have been that of the four bearers, and not that of the invalid himself. This seems clear, especially from St. Mark's words: "*They* uncovered the roof, . . . *they* let down the bed, . . . and when Jesus had seen *their* faith," etc. St. Jerome holds the same opinion when he writes: "Videns autem Jesus non ejus fidem qui afferebatur, sed eorum qui afferebant," etc. It is probable, then, that to the faith of his friends the sick man owed his cure (St. Jerome and Maldonatus). Pleased with this manifestation of faith on the part of the bearers, Christ inspired the paralytic with confidence by the sweetness of his address which is thus given *substantially* by St. Luke: " Man, thy sins are forgiven thee," but which probably is thus recorded *verbatim* by SS. Matthew and Mark: " Be of good heart, son, thy sins are forgiven thee." Still, since it appears to be restoration to bodily health that was sought for, why did Christ answer the petition thus? He did so (1) to show that in this case bodily disease was the temporal punishment of sin—a punishment from which the paralytic was not to be freed without a remission of the guilt itself; (2) to indicate and to remove the cause of sickness, which is often the effect as well as the penalty of sin; (3) to show what the paralytic should have sought in the first place; and (4) to provide an occasion for proving his own divinity before the doctors of the law. (See Schouppe.) It may well be supposed that the paralytic, as he lay before our Divine Redeemer, was burdened rather with the memory of his spiritual destitution than with the thought of his corporal infirmities. It is likely, too, that in saying to him: " Be of good heart," Christ at the same time brought before his mind the full enormity of his sins, and then, infusing into the guilty soul a spirit of supernatural sorrow, responded to that soul's secret wishes with an assurance of pardon. None of the prophets had thus spoken; and Jesus by such words showed that he exercised the office attributed to him by St. John the Baptist, saying: " Behold the Lamb of God; behold him who taketh away the sin of the world " (John i. 29. See Knabenbauer).

Although this testimony of the Precursor had been publicly and repeatedly given, and although the number of Jesus' miracles had already established his claim to a dignity more than human, the heads of the Jewish community there present closed their eyes to the evidence;

V. 3. **And behold, some of the scribes said within themselves : He blasphemeth.**

SS. Mark and Luke give the reason with which these men endeavoured to justify their conclusion: " Who can forgive sins, but God only?" The word "blaspheme" has various meanings in the Sacred Scriptures. Sometimes it signifies "to curse," or "to speak opprobriously," and then it indicates an offence committed not only against God, but also against a fellow-man. In this sense St. Paul says of himself and his companions: "We are *blasphemed*, and we entreat; we are made as the refuse of this world, the off-scouring of all even until now" (1 Cor. iv. 13). Again, in his exhortation to the Ephesians the Apostle writes: "Let all bitterness, and anger, and indignation, and clamour, and *blasphemy* be put away from you, with all malice" (Ephesians iv. 31). Of blasphemy against God, two kinds are mentioned by the inspired writers. One kind is committed when men attribute to God what is unbecoming the divine dignity, or deny any of the divine attributes. Thus when the king of the Assyrians had denied the power of the Lord to deliver Jerusalem, Ezechias received the answer: "Be not afraid for the words which thou hast heard, with which the servants of the king of the Assyrians have *blasphemed* me" (4 Kings xix. 6). Another kind of blasphemy against God is committed when a man claims for himself or for another the performance of any divine work or the possession of any divine attribute. It was of this last kind of blasphemy that the scribes were guilty when, attributing the miracles of Christ to Beelzebub, they heard their sentence of reprobation in the fearful words: "He that shall *blaspheme* against the Holy Ghost, shall never have forgiveness, but shall be guilty of an everlasting sin" (Mark iii. 29). This, too, was the crime now laid to the charge of Jesus by the scribes and pharisees. They did not make the accusation openly; but, as we learn from St. Mark, they entertained the rash judgment in their hearts that he, in their eyes a mere man, was arrogating to himself the divine power of forgiving sins. That there might be no excuse for this error, two arguments are now to be brought forward;

V. 4. And Jesus seeing their thoughts, said: Why do you think evil in your hearts?

Christ here established his claim to the divine power of forgiving sin by showing that he had the other divine power of knowing the secrets of hearts; for the knowledge of the secrets of hearts is set forth in the Scriptures as a special attribute of God. Thus it is written: "Thou alone knowest the hearts of the children of men" (2 Paral. vi. 30); still further: "Man seeth those things that appear, but the Lord beholdeth the heart" (1 Kings xvi. 7); and again: "The searcher of hearts and reins is God" (Ps. vii. 9). The "evil," then, which the scribes and pharisees thought in their heart, consisted not in attributing the power of forgiving sins to God alone, but in denying that power to Christ, and in accusing him of blasphemy when he had already given so many proofs that he was the Son of God.   Our Lord might have said of his enemies on this occasion as he said of them later on to his apostles : " If I had not done among them the works which no other man hath done, they would not have sin : but now they have both seen and hated both me and my Father " (John xv. 24).

Although by the revelation of their secret thoughts, Christ had sufficiently confuted the charge of the scribes, and had vindicated his claim to the divine power of forgiving sins, he did not disdain to give another and more manifest proof of his authority.   He prepared his audience for this proof by asking the question :—

V. 5. Which is easier, to say : Thy sins are forgiven thee, or to say : Arise and walk ?

It was equally easy merely to utter either of these sentences ; but it was not of this mere utterance that Christ spoke.   He demanded which was the easier when there was question of producing at the same time the effect indicated by these words. There can be, indeed, no other such opposition as that between God and sin—the Infinite Good and the infinite evil.   Hence the forgiveness of sin—an effect in the supernatural order—is raised far above all miraculous cures of disease ; and whilst St. Gregory said well that the conversion of St. Paul was a greater manifestation of divine power than the raising of Lazarus to life, St. Augustine had asserted before him that the remission of sin is a greater work than the creation of the world (St. Aug., Tract. 72 in Joannem).   But in this question there was not an invitation to examine the relative greatness of the work in the two cases. " Unde signanter Christus non ait, quid est facilius, *remittere peccata* an *sanare paralyticum*, sed DICERE : *Remittuntur tibi peccata*, an DICERE : *Surge et ambula* " (A Lapide). This observation is repeated by another writer who says : " It must be carefully noted, that he does not ask, which is easier, to forgive sins or to raise a sick man—for it could not be affirmed that that of forgiving was easier than that of healing—but, which is easier, to claim this power or that ; *to say* : Thy sins be forgiven thee, or to *say* : Arise and walk " (Trench, *Parables*). Christ meant to prepare his hearers to appreciate the proof he was about to give by showing that whatever danger of imposition there might be in the case of one claiming to forgive sins, there was no danger of imposition in the case of one claiming the power of healing the paralytic before them.   " Utrum sint paralytico peccata demissa, solus noverat qui dimittebat. *Surge* autem et *ambula*, tam ille qui consurgebat, quam hi qui consurgentem videbant, approbare poterant " (St. Jerome).

After this introduction, Christ thus continued :—

Vv. 6, 7. But that you may know that the Son of Man hath power on earth to forgive sins, (then saith he to the man sick of the palsy): Arise, take up thy bed, and go into thy house.   And he arose and went into his house.

The words enclosed in brackets are so marked off to show that they are not our Lord's, but the evangelist's ; and St. Matthew here combines the direct with the indirect mode of narration. In the usual form, the words would stand thus : " That you may know that the Son of Man hath power on earth to forgive sins, *I say* to the man sick of the palsy : ' Arise,' etc.," or : " That you may know that I can forgive sin, witness this work. Then saith he to the man sick of the palsy : ' Arise,' etc." (McCarthy).

The title " Son of Man " is met with thirty-eight times in Matthew, twenty-six times in Luke, eleven times in John, once in the Acts, and once in the Apocalypse ; but in all these instances it is given to our Lord only, and if we except Acts vii. 55, Apoc. i. 13, and perhaps John xii. 34, it is given to him by himself alone. According to A Lapide it indicated not merely the human nature of Christ—for that human nature might have been created anew as it was in Adam—but it implied descent from Adam the father of the human race.   In assuming this title, therefore, Christ showed his humility by declaring that he was not merely a man, but descended from sinful man. He showed his condescension and love by thus presenting himself as a brother amongst brethren, and as a child amongst children, that all might approach him as a brother and as a child.   " Secundum hanc (carnem) Christus filius hominis est, quod etiam se ipse saepissime appellat, commendans nobis quid misericorditer dignatus sit esse pro nobis " (St. Augustine : *De Consensu Evang.*, lib. 2, cap. 1).

It has been already remarked that the forgiveness of sins is a greater work than the healing of the paralytic.   If this be so, how did Christ prove that he had the power to do the former, because he did the latter ?   Some answer with Maldonatus that Christ, who had attributed both powers to himself, left his audience to conclude that he was not deceiving in the first case, since he proved from evidence before their eyes that he was not deceiving in the second.   A better solution of the difficulty is given by A Lapide, who says that there is here a question of a miracle wrought in *proof of a revealed doctrine*.   Now, although it is not impossible that a miracle may be worked by those who are wanting in personal sanctity, it is impossible that God in his providence would permit any such display of divine power in support of what is untrue.   By the miraculous cure, therefore, of the paralytic the seal of God's approval was set on the declaration made by Christ, viz., that he had the greater power of forgiving sins.

The means by which the paralytic had been carried into the presence of Christ is called by St. Matthew, κλίνη, by St. Mark, κράββατος, and by St. Luke, κλινίδιον; the last two evangelists thus describing more distinctly the *pallet* or mat generally used in the East for the purpose of repose, and enabling us to understand how the command given by our Lord was feasible for one person. There are, indeed, numerous indications that in the houses of the wealthy and in palaces, there were bedsteads highly ornamented, and that the richness and magnificence of the beds and bedsteads amongst the Asiatics were at least equal to what obtained among the Greeks and Romans. Still, among the poorer classes, bedsteads when used were probably light portable frames for keeping the bedding off the ground, and for carrying sick persons as on a litter. The ordinary bedding used throughout the East at the present day is probably similar in character to that which has been in use for centuries, and consists of (1) a mat of rushes or straw; (2) skins, or a cloak, or a quilt stuffed with dry herbs, hair, or a vegetable fibre to lie upon; (3) a covering of light stuff in summer, or of skins or quilted stuff in winter. The bed, indeed, was essentially an article that could be moved about readily from place to place as we learn from 1 Kings xix. 15. (See Hastings: *Dictionary of the Bible*, s.v. Bed.)

To render the cure more evident to all, he who, being unable to move, had been carried into the house, is now ordered to take the " mat " or " pallet " on which he lay, and to return to his home. From the Combined Narrative we learn that " immediately he arose, and taking up the bed on which he lay, he went away in the sight of all into his own house, glorifying God."

With the exception probably of the scribes and pharisees, all were struck by this clear manifestation of divine power;

V. 8. And the multitudes seeing it, feared, and glorified God who gave such power to men.

In addition to what is stated by St. Matthew, some more particulars are recorded by SS. Mark and Luke. The Combined Narrative reads thus: " And the multitudes seeing it, feared [and] wondered, saying: ' We have seen wonderful things to-day: we never saw the like.' And they glorified God who gave such power to men." Three effects of the miracle are here expressly noted. (1) Although the multitude did not yet recognise the divinity of Christ, they were filled with that reverential fear of God, which " is the beginning of wisdom "; (2) they were carried away with wonder at the miraculous cure of the paralytic; and (3) recognising Christ's purpose in working the miracle, they glorified the merciful Lord who gave power on earth to forgive sins. In the midst of this thanksgiving on the part of the poor and simple, it was sad to behold the obdurate unbelief of the scribes and pharisees—an unbelief implied in the ominous silence of the evangelists regarding these unworthy leaders of the people. Their infidelity to lesser graces was being punished by their culpable blindness; and their condition reminds us of the subsequent declaration of Christ about such as they: " If they hear not Moses and the prophets, neither will they believe if one rise again from the dead " (Luke xvi. 31).

Y.—MORAL REFLECTIONS.

In this gospel passage there are certain facts that supply us with material for very useful reflection. They are: the perseverance of the friends of the paralytic, the dispositions of the paralytic himself, and the effects of the miracle on the crowd.

1. The friends of the paralytic here described by the Holy Spirit had a difficulty in coming to Christ, for, as may be seen in the Parallel Passages, they were stopped at the door of the house by a crowd which rendered an entrance impossible. Their determination was not thereby abated; for their ingenious charity found out another way, or rather, he whom they sought suggested to them another means of reaching his presence. The sinner who wishes to return to Jesus, must expect to meet with obstacles. The temptations of the world, the seduction of pleasure, the influence of bad example, the fear of men's judgments, the dread of raillery, the enemy of salvation himself will oppose our progress. The devil, indeed, will multiply his attacks in proportion to the earnestness of our desire of justification; but we shall find within ourselves the most powerful means to keep us in sin. The arms of which he will make most use are unruly passions which must be controlled, inclinations which must be reformed, tastes which must be abandoned, cherished attachments which must be broken off, inveterate habits which must be overcome. The imagination which exaggerates our difficulties, will be affrighted at the sight of these difficulties. Often the thought of the effort to be made, arrests us in taking the first step. This fatal fear of combats with ourselves has caused holy thoughts to be rejected, pious desires to vanish, and good resolutions to be given up. How many conversions, happily begun and sometimes almost completed, have come to nothing in presence of a temptation, of an evil companion, or of an imaginary impossibility. The paralytic would have continued in his infirmity and would have died in his sins, if his friends had been deterred by the first difficulties they met; and such is the fate of those whom cowardice with-

holds from entering on the road of penance, or whom feebleness overcomes when they have made some advance. We should, indeed, be very distrustful of ourselves ; but we should confide very much in God. He invites us to himself ; he promises his help ; and if we listen lovingly to him, " he who hath begun a good work . . . will perfect it unto the day of Christ Jesus " (Philipp. i. 6).

2. It is very probable (see note on verse 2) that with the cure of his corporal disease, the remission of his sins was merited for the paralytic by the faith of his friends ; but before he received this grace it was necessary that he himself should have the preparatory dispositions of faith and hope in his Heavenly Physician and of sorrow for the past. The same is necessary for all who are in the same spiritual condition. With St. Thomas (*Summa*, I, 2, q. 114, art. 6), theologians commonly hold that the just can merit (*merito de congruo fallibili*) even an efficacious grace of conversion for sinners ; and in virtue of the grace thus merited for him by others, an adult, according to the Council of Trent (Sess. 6, cap. 6), disposes himself for justification by faith in God, by fear of him, by hope in him, by an initial love of him as the source of all justice, by a hatred of past offences, and by a determination to observe the divine law in future. These dispositions were infused into the soul of the paralytic at the words of Christ, and they will be infused into the souls of all who ask them from that merciful Redeemer. If, then, we be estranged from God by sin, let us seek for our justification through the merits and intercession of our friends who are also the friends of God, and let us secure the dispositions necessary for justification by our own fervent prayer.

3. The sacred text notes the effects which the miracle produced on the assembled crowd. The first were fear and wonder which naturally accompany the sight of such an astonishing prodigy ; and to these sudden and involuntary feelings succeeded another ·—that of thankfulness to God who placed at our service a power capable of healing not only the ills of the body, but also the more serious and more incurable diseases of the soul. The visible miracles of corporal cures are become comparatively rare since their evidence is no longer necessary for the establishment of Christ's kingdom ; but the invisible wonder of the forgiveness of sins is still, and ever will be, worked by the power of the Church. Imitating the crowd described in the gospel, let us return thanks to God for so great a blessing ; and let us show our appreciation of it by our perseverance in the holy state which it has enabled us to reach.

NINETEENTH SUNDAY AFTER PENTECOST.

I.—TEXTS.

GREEK.

MATTHEW XXII. 1-14.

1 Καὶ ἀποκριθεὶς ὁ Ἰησοῦς, πάλιν εἶπεν ἐν παραβολαῖς αὐτοῖς, λέγων· 2 Ὡμοιώθη ἡ βασιλεία τῶν οὐρανῶν ἀνθρώπῳ βασιλεῖ, ὅστις ἐποίησεν γάμους τῷ υἱῷ αὐτοῦ· 3 Καὶ ἀπέστειλεν τοὺς δούλους αὐτοῦ, καλέσαι τοὺς κεκλημένους εἰς τοὺς γάμους· καὶ οὐκ ἤθελον ἐλθεῖν. 4 Πάλιν ἀπέστειλεν ἄλλους δούλους, λέγων· Εἴπατε τοῖς κεκλημένοις· Ἰδοὺ τὸ ἄριστόν μου ἡτοίμακα, οἱ ταῦροί μου καὶ τὰ σιτιστὰ τεθυμένα, καὶ πάντα ἕτοιμα· δεῦτε εἰς τοὺς γάμους. 5 Οἱ δὲ ἀμελήσαντες, ἀπῆλθον, ὃς μὲν εἰς τὸν ἴδιον ἀγρόν, ὃς δὲ ἐπὶ τὴν ἐμπορίαν αὐτοῦ· 6 οἱ δὲ λοιποὶ κρατήσαντες τοὺς δούλους αὐτοῦ, ὕβρισαν καὶ ἀπέκτειναν. 7 Ὁ δέ βασιλεὺς ὠργίσθη· καὶ πέμψας τὰ στρατεύματα αὐτοῦ, ἀπώλεσεν τοὺς φονεῖς ἐκείνους, καὶ τὴν πόλιν αὐτῶν ἐνέπρησεν. 8 Τότε λέγει τοῖς δούλοις αὐτοῦ· Ὁ μὲν γάμος ἕτοιμός ἐστιν, οἱ δὲ κεκλημένοι οὐκ ἦσαν ἄξιοι. 9 Πορεύεσθε οὖν ἐπὶ τὰς διεξόδους τῶν ὁδῶν, καὶ ὅσους ἐὰν εὕρητε, καλέσατε εἰς τοὺς γάμους. 10 Καὶ ἐξελθόντες οἱ δοῦλοι ἐκεῖνοι εἰς

VULGATE.

MATTHEW XXII. 1-14.

1 Et respondens Jesus, dixit iterum in parabolis eis, dicens : 2 Simile factum est regnum cœlorum homini regi qui fecit nuptias filio suo. 3 Et misit servos suos vocare invitatos ad nuptias, et nolebant venire. 4 Iterum misit alios servos, dicens : Dicite invitatis : Ecce prandium meum paravi ; tauri mei et altilia occisa sunt, et omnia parata : venite ad nuptias. 5 Illi autem neglexerunt, et abierunt, alius in villam suam, alius vero ad negotiationem suam ; 6 reliqui vero tenuerunt servos ejus, et contumeliis affectos occiderunt. 7 Rex autem cum audisset, iratus est ; et missis exercitibus suis, perdidit homicidas illos, et civitatem illorum succendit. 8 Tunc ait servis suis : Nuptiæ quidem paratæ sunt, sed qui invitati erant, non fuerunt digni. 9 Ite ergo ad exitus viarum, et quoscumque inveneritis, vocate ad nuptias. 10 Et egressi servi ejus in vias, congregaverunt omnes quos inve-

τὰς ὁδοὺς, συνήγαγον πάντας ὅσους εὗρον, πονηρούς τε καὶ ἀγαθούς· καὶ ἐπλήσθη ὁ νυμφὼν ἀνακειμένων. ¹¹ Εἰσελθὼν δὲ ὁ βασιλεὺς θεάσασθαι τοὺς ἀνακειμένους, εἶδεν ἐκεῖ ἄνθρωπον οὐκ ἐνδεδυμένον ἔνδυμα γάμου· ¹² Καὶ λέγει αὐτῷ· Ἑταῖρε, πῶς εἰσῆλθες ὧδε μὴ ἔχων ἔνδυμα γάμου; Ὁ δὲ ἐφιμώθη· ¹³ Τότε ὁ βασιλεὺς εἶπεν τοῖς διακόνοις· Δήσαντες αὐτοῦ πόδας καὶ χεῖρας, ἐκβάλετε αὐτὸν εἰς τὸ σκότος τὸ ἐξώτερον· ἐκεῖ ἔσται ὁ κλαυθμὸς καὶ ὁ βρυγμὸς τῶν ὀδόντων. ¹⁴ Πολλοὶ γάρ εἰσιν κλητοὶ, ὀλίγοι δὲ ἐκλεκτοί.

nerunt, malos et bonos ; et impletæ sunt nuptiæ discumbentium. ¹¹ Intravit autem rex ut videret discumbentes, et vidit ibi hominem non vestitum veste nuptiali. ¹² Et ait illi : Amice, quomodo huc intrasti non habens vestem nuptialem? At ille obmutuit. ¹³ Tunc dixit rex ministris : Ligatis manibus et pedibus ejus, mittite eum in tenebras exteriores ; ibi erit fletus, et stridor dentium. ¹⁴ Multi enim sunt vocati, pauci vero electi.

II.—ENGLISH TRANSLATION.
MATTHEW XXII. 1-14.

¹ And Jesus answering, spoke again in parables to them, saying : ² " The kingdom of heaven is likened to a king, who made a marriage for his son. ³ And he sent his servants, to call them that were invited to the marriage ; and they would not come. ⁴ Again he sent other servants, saying : ' Tell them that were invited : Behold, I have prepared my dinner ; my beeves and fatlings are killed, and all things are ready : come ye to the marriage.' ⁵ But they neglected, and went their ways, one to his farm, and another to his merchandise ; ⁶ and the rest laid hands on his servants, and having treated them contumeliously, put them to death. ⁷ But when the king had heard of it, he was angry ; and sending his armies, he destroyed those murderers, and burned their city. ⁸ Then he saith to his servants : ' The marriage indeed is ready ; but they that were invited were not worthy. ⁹ Go ye, therefore, unto the partings of the highways ; and as many as you shall find, call to the marriage.' ¹⁰ And his servants going forth into the highways, gathered together all that they found, both bad and good ; and the marriage was filled with guests. ¹¹ And the king went in to see the guests ; and he saw there a man that had not on a wedding-garment. ¹² And he saith to him : ' Friend, how camest thou in hither not having on a wedding-garment ? ' But he was silent. ¹³ Then the king said to the waiters : ' Bind his hands and feet, and cast him into the exterior darkness : there shall be weeping and gnashing of teeth.' ¹⁴ For many are called, but few are chosen."

III.—NOTES.

Introductory. As was remarked in the explanation of the

gospel for the seventeenth Sunday after Pentecost, the present
extract is taken from St. Matthew's account of our Lord's last
visit to the temple on the Wednesday before the Passion. The
Sanhedrim or Council of the Jews had determined on Christ's
death (John xi. 53) ; and early in the morning when he was
teaching the people, emissaries of this body were already around
him, and were endeavouring to seize upon some statement which
might secure his condemnation in the court of the high-priest, or
in that of Pontius Pilate the Roman governor. Seeing their
hypocrisy and the fixity of their evil purpose, our Lord, in the
parable of " the wicked husbandmen," foretold the punishment
that awaited them personally for their resistance to grace, their
violence towards the messengers of the gospel, and the crime of
deicide which they were about to commit. Then, whilst they
were enraged at this parable, the application of which was
drawn from their own lips (Matth. xxi. 40, 41), he announced in
the present passage, the calling of the Gentiles to the faith,
the rejection of the Jews as a nation, the destruction of their city,
the very manner in which that destruction would be brought
about, and the punishment of those who, although accepting the
call to the faith, do not live as becomes believers.

As a preface to his record of this prediction, St. Matthew
says : " When the chief-priests and pharisees had heard his
parables, they knew that he spoke of them ; and seeking to lay
hands on him, they feared the multitudes, because they held
him as a prophet."

V. 1. **And Jesus answering, spoke again in parables to
them, saying, etc.**

It has been already stated that, like the Hebrew עָנָה, the
Greek ἀποκριθεὶς which is here rendered " answering," may
either introduce a reply properly so called, or may mark the
commencement of a discourse not preceded by any question ;
and the meaning of the word in each passage must be determined by the context. The latter use of the word is frequent in
the New Testament (cf. Matth. xi. 25 ; xii. 38 ; xv. 15 ; Mark
xi. 14 ; Luke xiv. 3 ; Acts iii. 12) ; and unless an answer to *the
thoughts* of the pharisees be intended here, the whole clause is
equivalent to : " Jesus began to speak again in parables to
them."

The parable which follows must be carefully distinguished
from that recorded by St. Luke (xiv. 16-24). Though the two
are alike in some respects, there is a difference in the circumstances of place and occasion, which are stated in each case
with precision, and a difference in the style of the parables
corresponds to the two periods at which they were spoken.
That in St. Luke was spoken earlier in our Lord's ministry,

when the enmity of the pharisees had not yet fully manifested itself. There the refusal of the guests is *more courteous,* and their only penalty is *exclusion*; here they *maltreat the servants,* and are *utterly destroyed.* (See Alford, *in loco.*) It may be added that the purpose in the two parables is not the same. The parable of St. Luke, in which *a certain man* makes a great *supper,* the last meal of the day when labour is over, and sends *one servant* to some of the guests, is intended as a denunciation of the vices that exclude from the banquet of the next life, to which we are invited by Christ : the parable of St. Matthew, in which *a king* sends *many servants* to invite to a *dinner,* is intended as a warning to those who refuse to enter the Church on earth, to which the messengers of the gospel were sent to call them.

The parable is thus given by St. Matthew :—

V. 2. The kingdom of heaven is likened to a king, who made a marriage for his son.

St. Matthew wrote his gospel to remove the prejudices of the Jews, and to prove that the dominion of their Messiah was to be of a spiritual, not of a temporal nature. This is why the first evangelist, and he alone, so frequently uses the term " kingdom of heaven," which in the parallel passages of the gospels is exchanged for the expression " the kingdom of God," " the kingdom of Christ," or simply " the kingdom " (*cf.* Matth. iv. 17 with Mark i. 15 ; Matth. xi. 11 with Luke vii. 28). The " kingdom " is sometimes taken in the widest acceptation, including ruler, subjects, realm, form of government, etc. (*cf.* Matth. iii. 2 ; iv. 17-23 ; Mark xii. 34 ; xv. 43 ; Luke i. 33 ; iv. 43) ; at other times it designates one of these constituents (Luke ix. 27 ; Matth. xiii. 24-50 ; Mark ix. 46) ; and in these several instances the precise meaning of the term is to be learned from the context. In some passages the expression refers to the dominion of God over the Church Triumphant in heaven ; in others, to that which he exercises over the Church Militant on earth. When the " kingdom " is proposed as a *reward,* or *possession,* or *place of rest,* into which we are to enter, it signifies the society of the angels and saints in heaven ; but when it is " likened " to some person or thing, it means the congregation of the faithful here below. The latter is the case in the present instance ; and so, Christ here says that the Church on earth is like to a king who prepared a marriage for his son. His meaning is that the same thing happens in the Church on earth as that which took place when, under circumstances afterwards to be described, a king made a marriage for his son, *i.e.,* a feast on the occasion of his son's marriage. To solemnise the nuptial union and to hold a nuptial feast were so necessarily associated in practice, that in biblical as well as in classical language, the one expression ποιεῖν γάμον was used for both.   It is, however, the feast that is here referred to ; for according to the most common opinion of commentators following SS. Augustine and Gregory the Great, our Lord in this figurative language wished to tell us that the " king," *i.e.*, his Heavenly Father, on the union of the divine and the human nature which had already taken place in the mystery of the Incarnation, prepared to celebrate this union by a spiritual banquet of grace in his Church on earth.

Christ thus continues :—

V. 3. And he sent his servants, to call them that were invited to the marriage ; and they would not come.

A previous notice of the approaching entertainment is here implied.   Indeed the issuing of an invitation followed by a verbal summons to the guests was, and is still, the custom in the East. (*Cf.* Esther v. 8 and vi. 14.   Trench : *Parables*. Introduction, p. lxxxviii.)   When, therefore, the time for the feast had arrived, the " king " sent his servants to call those that *had previously been invited* (τοὺς κεκλημένους) ; " and they would not come." The intended guests were a type of the Jewish race, who from the time of Abraham their father had been selected out of all nations, and had been called on to prepare for the mystic marriage-feast of the Messiah.   This first invitation was ever kept before them by the messengers of God, and especially by the long line of prophets who, from age to age, in clearer and clearer terms depicted to them the privileges, and the glory, and the happiness to be theirs on the coming of the " Just One."   When " in the fulness of time " the mystic marriage of the Incarnation had taken place, God sent his servants to summon the Jewish people to the feast.   These servants were John the Baptist (Luke iii. 2-18 ; Mark i. 6-8 ; Matth. iii. 1-12 ; John i. 23-36), the apostles (Matth. x. 1-42 ; Mark iii. 13-19 ; Luke vi. 12-16), and the seventy-two disciples (Luke x. 1-20).   With these must be joined Christ himself who, " taking the form of a servant, being made in the likeness of men, and in habit found as a man " (Philipp. ii. 7), carried his Father's summons to the guests.   " His own share in this work, inviting them, that is, unto himself (Matth. iv. 17 ; Mark i. 14, 15), his ' Come unto me,' naturally in the parable falls out of sight.   It would have disturbed its proprieties had the king's son been himself a bearer of the invitation.   A condescension so infinite would have seemed unnatural ; for it is only the Son of the *heavenly* king who has ever stooped so far.   He indeed was content, even while the marriage was made for himself, to be as one of those sent forth to call the guests thereunto.   It is not implied that on this first occasion the servants had any positive ill usage to endure.   They found, indeed, a general indifference to the message, and alienation from the messengers ; but nothing worse.   In agreement with this we have no record of any displays of active enmity against the apostles or disciples during the life-time of the Lord, nor at first against the Lord himself.   It was simply ' they would not come ' " (Trench : *Parables*, p. 226).

Although such an occasion as this has always a political significance, and although the rejection of the royal invitation implies ordinarily a spirit of disloyalty and rebellion, the king attributed the conduct of the guests to ignorance or to want of reflection.   He did not desist from his gracious purpose ; and

V. 4. Again he sent other servants, saying : Tell them that were invited : Behold I have prepared my dinner, my beeves and fatlings are killed, and all things are ready : come ye to the marriage.

The ἄριστον (*cf. Iliad*, xxiv. 124) in early Greek is the *morning meal* or breakfast ; but in later Greek (*cf.* Thuc. iv. 90) and here, it is the *mid-day refreshment* or luncheon, the same as the Roman *prandium*.   In Luke xiv. 16, the feast is called δεῖπνον μέγα=*a great dinner*, like the Roman *coena* which was the chief meal of the day taken in the evening when all work was over. It is thus clear, as has been already remarked, that the parable in St. Luke refers to the last and great banquet of glory in heaven, which awaits us at the end of this life, but which many will be found unworthy to enjoy.   The present parable regards the abundant spiritual feast of grace which is offered to all in the Church on earth, but which many refuse to avail themselves of.   The richness of the viands and the unstinted supply at the royal feast are denoted in the message sent by the king.   As it was one of the characteristics of great banquets (Introduction, pp. lxxxiv.-lxxxv.) to bring to table fatted calves and birds of various kinds, so these are here mentioned under the name of τὰ σιτιστὰ =*altilia*=*fatted animals*.   The sending forth of the messengers   signified that after the Resurrection and Ascension " other servants," *i.e.*, the same apostles and disciples who themselves had become other men by the gifts of the Holy Ghost, were to be joined by such preachers as SS. Paul, and Barnabas, and Stephen in their second appeal to the Jews.   They were commanded (Matth. xxviii. 19, 20 ; Acts i. 8 ; iv. 19, 20 ; xiii. 46, 47) by God to announce that the Messiah, " crucified and slain " by the hands of wicked men, had arisen from the dead ; that all things requisite for the spiritual nourishment and salvation of man were prepared in the teaching and sacraments of the Church ; and that according to the prophets, the gifts of the Holy Ghost were now to be poured out upon all flesh (Isaias xliv. 3 ; Joel ii.

28; Acts ii. 17). The apostles and the apostolic preachers obeyed the command of God and delivered the divine invitation; the Jews needed only to enter the Church that they might inherit the blessings promised to their race since the call of Abraham ;

Vv. 5, 6. **But they neglected, and went their ways, one to his farm, and another to his merchandise ; and the rest laid hands on his servants, and having treated them contumeliously, put them to death.**

Short of interfering with the freedom of the human will, every means had now been tried by the " king " to assemble the guests for the feast ; but in proportion as he showed more kindness, they became more hardened in their indifference or more unbridled in their anger (Euthym.). Some being content with the possessions they had already acquired in their " farm," or being covetous of greater gain by their " merchandise," turned a deaf ear to the bearers of the royal summons : others, impatient at the repetition of an invitation which they had already declined, allowed violence to take the place of their previous contempt.

The murder of the king's servants might at first sight seem strange and even improbable ; but what was thus foretold in the parable, was carried out to the letter in the early days of the Christian Church. Of the two classes referred to by our Divine Lord—the irreligious or careless, and those violent in their opposition—the former were represented in the audience thus described by St. Luke : " When they agreed not among themselves, they departed, Paul speaking this one word : Well did the Holy Ghost speak to our fathers by Isaias the prophet, saying : Go to this people, and say to them : With the ear you shall hear, and shall not understand ; and seeing you shall see, and shall not perceive. For the heart of this people is grown gross, and with their ears they have been dull of hearing, and their eyes they have shut ; lest perhaps they should see with their eyes, and hear with their ears, and understand with their heart, and should be converted, and I should heal them " (Acts xxviii. 25-27). That the deeds of the second class who ill-treated and slew the king's messengers, typified the conduct of the Jews after the Resurrection, need not be proved for a reader of the New Testament. They imprisoned and scourged the apostles (Acts v. 18 and 40) ; they excited the passions of the Gentiles against them (Acts xiv. 2-6) ; they ceaselessly harassed St. Paul (Acts xvii. 5-14) ; they secured his imprisonment (Acts xxi. 11, 13, 27-36 ; xxiii. 24, etc.), and were perhaps responsible for his death ; they stoned St. Stephen (Acts vii. 56-60) ; to please them, James, the brother of John, was beheaded (Acts xii. 1-3) ; they cast down from the temple James the " brother of the

Lord " (Hegesippus) ; and they raised such a persecution against the Church in Jerusalem, that the faithful of that city were all dispersed through the countries of Judæa and Samaria (Acts viii. 1).

As the " children of Ammon " had done an injury to David himself in the persons of his ambassadors (2 Kings x. 2-6), so had the intended guests of our parable insulted the majesty of the king by slaying the servants who conveyed his invitation. The criminals hoped to escape the consequences of their treason ;

V. 7. But when the king had heard of it, he was angry ; and sending his armies, he destroyed those murderers and burned their city.

Alford (*in loco*) says : " This is a startling introduction of the *interpretation into the parable*. We knew not before that they had a city." The city was no longer *his* city but theirs, just as the temple was no longer *his* house (Luke xix. 46) but *theirs* (Matth. xxiii. 38).

In the interpretation all writers are agreed that our Lord referred here to the final overthrow of the Jewish nation which took place on the destruction of the city and temple of Jerusalem —a destruction already fully described in the notes on the gospel for the ninth Sunday after Pentecost. In that catastrophe, the Roman forces under Titus were the instruments of divine vengeance, and hence they are called the " armies " of the king, *i.e.*, of God, as the Medes in the overthrow of Babylon were named the " sanctified ones " of the Lord (Isaias xiii. 3), and as Nabuchodonosor and his army were said to have rendered great service to the Lord in the expedition undertaken against Tyre (Ezechiel xxix. 18-20). Titus himself, the pagan general, confessed that the destruction of Jerusalem was the work of God. Nor was this without reason. According to Josephus (B. J. vi. 93 ; vii. 1), eleven hundred thousand Jews lost their lives during the siege ; one hundred thousand more were reduced to slavery ; and the whole space within the city walls was so thoroughly levelled and dug up, that no one visiting the place could believe that it had ever been inhabited. In the parable our Lord first described the crime of the Jews ; he next indicated the punishment to be inflicted at the destruction of Jerusalem ; and lastly he foretold the admission of the Gentiles to the mystic banquet.

The admission of the Gentiles into the Church took place long before the fall of the Holy City ; but this disregard of chronological order is easily justified. " The ' then ' (v. 8) must not be pressed. The parable is not an historical enumeration of the several facts according to their chronological order, but an imaginary narration in which the several stages of the action are bound together according to their essential connection " (Kiel, quoted by Trench : *Parables*, p. 231, note).

Moreover, the words of Christ were a prophecy ; and in the language of prophecy, the matter is arranged not in the chronological, but in the logical order of cause and effect existing between the several events foretold. Now in the present case the wilful blindness of the Jews was the cause of their rejection ; and though their rejection was a punishment immediately determined on, and therefore immediately mentioned in the parable, it was deferred for a time, whilst a minor punishment was being inflicted on them by the transference of their privileges to the Gentiles. (See Knabenbauer, *in loco*.)

The king thus judges the delinquents and awards their chastisement ;

V. 8. **Then he saith to his servants : The marriage indeed is ready ; but they that were invited, were not worthy.**

In this figurative language, it is said that whilst God on his part had done all that was necessary to enable the Jews to be present at the mystic banquet in the Church, these were not worthy of the efficacious grace which would have secured their being present thereat. So much indeed is *said* ; but, as Jansenius of Ghent remarks, much more is *signified*. Not only did those who were first invited possess no *positive merits* giving them a right to these efficacious graces of conversion, but in addition they rendered themselves *positively unworthy*. On the other hand, can we assert that the Gentiles were worthy ? Few of them, indeed, had merited these graces *de congruo*, and none *de condigno*. Still there was not amongst them the Jewish spirit of self-confidence arising from descent from Abraham—a confidence which was condemned by St. John the Baptist ; they were not guilty of that wilful contempt for lesser graces which was reproved on more than one occasion by Christ himself (Luke xi. 35 ; John xii. 35, 36) ; and they had not that feeling of self-righteousness regarding which the Apostle wrote : " They not knowing the justice of God, and seeking to establish their own, have not submitted themselves to the justice of God " (Rom. x. 3).

Although the first guests thus excluded themselves from the feast, it was the settled purpose of the king that the feast should be held. Then he said to the servants :—

V. 9. **Go ye, therefore, into the partings of the highways ; and as many as you shall find, call to the marriage.**

The servants of the king are now not to make any distinction amongst those to whom the invitation is to be addressed : all whom they find are to be called.   That the summons may reach all, it is to be given at what are named in the Greek text διεξόδοι τῶν ὁδῶν. This phrase, not elsewhere found in the New Testament, is here rendered in the Vulgate " exitus viarum," and in the English version " partings of the highways " ; but it may equally mean the places where the streets meet in a city, the outlets of the streets into the country at the city gates, or the distant points in the country with which the roads communicate.   If the phrase be taken to mean the places where the streets meet, or the outlets of the streets into the country, the king's wish was to have his message delivered where the greatest concourse of hearers was likely to be found : if the phrase means the distant points in the country to which the roads lead, the parable signifies that the king intended his invitation to be carried even to those who were most remote and least likely to be thought of or taken into consideration.

The king's command was obeyed ;

V. 10. **And his servants going forth into the highways, gathered together all that they found, both bad and good ; and the marriage was filled with guests.**

In the last verse " the marriage " was the rendering of the Gr. τοὺς γάμους, and the term there signified the *nuptial feast* here, too, " the marriage" is the rendering of the Gr. ὁ νυμφὼ; but it means the " *banquet hall* " where the nuptial feast was held.   To this banquet hall the servants called all without distinction—the only bar to admission being an unwillingness to come.   Christ thus foretold the world-wide preaching of the gospel ; and to secure the fulfilment of his prophecy, he, on the day of his Ascension said to his apostles and through them to their helpers and successors : " You shall be witnesses unto me in Jerusalem, and in all Judæa, and Samaria, and even to the uttermost part of the earth " (Acts i. 8).   The apostles executed his orders ; " they going forth, preached everywhere " (Mark xvi. 20) ; they visited such centres of civilisation as Corinth, Athens, Alexandria, and Rome ; they penetrated into the trackless wilderness, the barbarian inhabitants of which had never been subjected to the imperial authority ; they proclaimed that " the same is Lord over all, rich unto all that call upon him " (Rom. x. 12) ; and as the servants of the parable invited everyone without discrimination, so the apostles recognised no distinction between Jew and Greek, between bond and free, for henceforth all were to be one in Christ Jesus (Gal. iii. 28).

The diligence of the king's servants met with success : the banquet-hall was filled.

Vv. 11, 12. **And the king went in to see the guests; and he saw there a man that had not on a wedding-garment.   And**

he saith to him: Friend how camest thou in hither not having on a wedding-garment? But he was silent.

The expression ἔνδυμα γάμου, which is rendered "wedding-garment," and which means literally "the garment of the wedding," marks emphatically by its construction the character of the robe in question, namely, that it was *one suited for marriage feasts and used at these only.* (See McCarthy.) Where this garment was to be procured is not mentioned; but the generally entertained supposition that the king provided one for each guest, seems improbable for the following reasons: (1°) though there was such a custom amongst the Persians, it was unknown amongst the Jews; (2°) as has been remarked, the providing of the garments is not mentioned in the parable, where a reference to this fact would have served to explain the anger of the king and to emphasise the wickedness of the guest; (3°) the fact that this provision was made would render inexplicable the conduct of the servants, whose duty of distributing the garments would have implied the obligation of excluding from the feast all who refused to appear suitably attired (Knabenbauer). Whatever value may be set on this reasoning, and whatever opinion we may hold on the question itself, it is clear that in appearing without the wedding-garment the guest had committed a grave offence. Indeed, on being asked to defend himself he was powerless to reply (ἐφιμώθη = *he was gagged*). The truth conveyed in this incident of the parable, is that for adults membership in the Church by faith and baptism does not suffice. "God who created us without ourselves, will not save us without ourselves"; he demands our co-operation; he requires that before his all-seeing eyes we be ever clothed in the wedding-garment of charity or sanctifying grace, which is received at our entrance into the Church by baptism and is to be preserved unsullied through a life spent in the practice of good works. For failure in this we have no excuse. "Nam Deus impossibilia non jubet, sed jubendo monet, et facere quod possis, et petere quod non possis; et adjuvat, ut possis. Cujus mandata gravia non sunt, cujus jugum suave est et onus leve" (Council of Trent, sess. vi., c. 11).

The guilt of the guest being evident and even tacitly admitted by himself,

V. 13. Then the king said to the waiters: Bind his hands and feet, and cast him into the exterior darkness: there shall be weeping and gnashing of teeth.

The binding of the hands and feet indicated the impossibility of escape from the punishment; the casting "into the exterior darkness"—an allusion to the profusion of lights at an Eastern banquet—signified the extinction of all hope of pardon or reprieve; and the "weeping and gnashing of teeth"—an expression in which in the Greek each noun takes the article—made known emphatically to the culprit the extreme suffering and intense pain he was to endure.   By all this our Lord foretold the punishment of hell in which a place is found *immediately* after the particular judgment, not only for infidels who refuse to enter the Church, but also for those whether Jews or Gentiles who, having become Christians, are found at death to have led unworthy lives.

Christ concludes with this application of the parable :—

V. 14. **For many are called, but few are chosen.**

It might appear at first sight that this moral, however true in itself, was not warranted by what had been just laid down ; for whereas it was said in the parable that one only was excluded from the full banquet-hall, whilst many were permitted to remain, it is now asserted that from the mystic feast there typified, many will be excluded, whilst only a few are chosen to remain.   The incorrectness of this conclusion will be seen by those who keep in view not only the words of the parable, but also its scope.   It was not the scope of the parable to indicate the relative numbers of the saved and the lost in the next world, or even of the worthy and the unworthy members of the Church on earth typified by the marriage feast.   Our Lord intended rather to foretell that, though God is so good as to invite all into his Church, all will not come ; nay more, that the number who *fittingly* respond to the invitation is small in comparison with the number of those who receive that invitation.   When we understand this to be our Lord's purpose the logical sequence of the conclusion is evident.   The invited were (1°) those who rejected the invitation and would not come ; (2°) the unworthy guest who accepted the invitation and came, but was expelled ; and (3°) the guests who accepted the invitation, came, and were found worthy to remain.   The " chosen " were the last class only, and they were few in number compared with all who were " called."

By this announcement Christ, in the first place, humbled the pride of the pharisees, who thought that as children of Abraham, the Jews and especially they themselves had an indefeasible right to a place in the kingdom of the Messiah (*cf*. Matth. iii. 9 ; John viii. 39) ; again, by the use of the word " chosen " he showed that whilst all who are invited get sufficient grace to be saved, those who come, owe their coming and acceptance of the invitation to an additional or efficacious grace of God ; and lastly, he predicted that, though God wills " many " (that is *all*, see 1 Tim. ii. 4) to be saved, " few " comparatively will attain salvation.

IV.—MORAL REFLECTIONS.

1. All who are members of the Church are called to the marriage-feast which the king prepared for his Son ; and what is more, all Christians are invited to become the spouses of this Son, and to enter into a spiritual union with him here on earth, whilst awaiting that of the beatific vision in heaven. This union commences by faith, is perfected by charity, is rendered fruitful by good works, and can be dissolved by mortal sin alone. Thus the invitation to " the marriage-feast " is the vocation to the faith—a sublime vocation, an inestimable benefit, the forerunner of all other blessings in the supernatural order, and one which, if corresponded with, will procure for us all others. Is it wonderful, then, that the Apostle so earnestly implored the people of Ephesus, and with them ourselves, to fully correspond with the grace of faith ? " I, therefore," said he, " a prisoner in the Lord, beseech you that you walk worthy of the vocation in which you are called : with all humility and mildness, with patience, supporting one another in charity, careful to keep the unity of the Spirit in the bond of peace " (Ephes. iv. 1-3). We should fear lest many who have the misfortune of not receiving this wonderful and efficacious grace bestowed on us and who would have used it better than we have, may be compared with us in the day of judgment, and may receive a more indulgent sentence than we. Addressing some cities which had not corresponded with his merciful efforts for their conversion, Christ exclaimed : " Wo to thee, Corozain ! wo to thee, Bethsaida ! for if in Tyre and Sidon had been wrought the miracles that have been wrought in you, they had long ago done penance in sackcloth and ashes. But I say unto you, it shall be more tolerable for Tyre and Sidon in the Day of Judgment than for you " (Matth. xi. 21, 22).

2. The reasons with which those first invited endeavoured to excuse their absence from the marriage-feast, represent the causes which prevented the Jews from embracing the truth, and which still prevent many Christians from accepting the invitation to a living faith animated by charity and fruitful in good works. In the case of many amongst us, these impediments to salvation are principally of two kinds.

The intended guests who went to their farm or country-house, represent those who, amidst the dissipations and pleasures of the present life, think not of the future. Their only purpose is to enjoy the world ; they pass from one amusement to another ; they are ever flying from the ennui which pursues them and sometimes seizes on them in the midst of their distractions ; according to their own expression, they are ever seeking to pass the time, or more correctly, to lose it. Thus in a useless and idle life, they pay no attention to the calls of God, and they squander the precious treasure of grace with which they might merit a happy eternity. The intended guests who went to their merchandise, represent those who neglect their salvation not from idleness or dissipation, but from too great a devotion to worldly business. They have a fortune to amass, a position to secure, a name to make, a family to provide for. These temporal cares absorb all their attention to the exclusion of any care for their eternal welfare ; and the mind, completely occupied with these concerns, has no time for the concerns of salvation. All other affairs are looked to with an indefatigable activity and perseverance ; but the principal affair, the essential affair, the only affair, is neglected and forgotten. " What," says our Divine Master, " shall it profit a man if he gain the whole world, and suffer the loss of his soul " (Mark viii. 36). For all of us the moment of death approaches—that moment which we so often forget, but which we should ever have before our eyes. What will then avail our possessions, or our merchandise, or our traffic ? The worldling must present himself for judgment, despoiled of the material possessions which he has been gathering, and void of the spiritual goods which he has failed to acquire ; and he will find written over the supreme tribunal what Balthassar saw traced by the divine hand on the wall of his palace : " Thou art weighed in the balance, and art found wanting " (Daniel v. 27).

3. And how shall we avoid this fate, accept the invitation of Jesus Christ, and be included amongst the guests at the heavenly marriage-feast ? Must our care of heavenly things cause us to neglect entirely those of earth ? This would be a dangerous error. God has sent us into the world ; he has placed us in a certain state of life which brings us into relations with our fellow-men ; and these relations impose upon us duties which religion does not condemn, but counsels or commands. What religion forbids is to prefer temporal affairs to that of our salvation, or to devote ourselves with such ardour to temporal interests that our eternal interests may be thereby neglected. What religion demands is that we subordinate the things of earth to those of heaven, that we use the things of earth to procure for ourselves and for others the things of heaven, and that we do this because God wills it and as far as he wills it. The Christian sanctifies his ordinary actions by the intention with which he does them ; and these ordinary actions are really pious deeds, when they are done for God and in conformity with God's will. Thus the same occupation becomes for the worldling an occasion of reprobation, and for the just man a means of acquiring merit and a help to salvation.

TWENTIETH SUNDAY AFTER PENTECOST.

I.—TEXTS.

GREEK.

JOHN IV. 46-53.

⁴⁶Ἦλθεν οὖν πάλιν ἐν Κανᾶ τῆς Γαλειλαίας, ὅπου ἐποίησεν τὸ ὕδωρ οἶνον. Καὶ ἦν τίς βασιλικὸς, οὗ ὁ υἱὸς ἠσθένει ἐν Καφαρναούμ. ⁴⁷ Οὗτος ἀκούσας ὅτι Ἰησοῦς ἥκει ἐκ τῆς Ἰουδαίας εἰς τὴν Γαλειλαίαν, ἀπῆλθεν πρὸς αὐτὸν, καὶ ἠρώτα ἵνα καταβῇ καὶ ἰάσηται αὐτοῦ τὸν υἱόν· ἤμελλεν γὰρ ἀποθνήσκειν. ⁴⁸ Εἶπεν οὖν ὁ Ἰησοῦς πρὸς αὐτόν· Ἐὰν μὴ σημεῖα καὶ τέρατα ἴδητε, οὐ μὴ πιστεύσητε. ⁴⁹ Λέγει πρὸς αὐτὸν ὁ βασιλικὸς· Κύριε, κατάβηθι πρὶν ἀποθανεῖν τὸ παιδίον μου. ⁵⁰ Λέγει αὐτῷ ὁ Ἰησοῦς· Πορεύου· ὁ υἱός σου ζῇ. Ἐπίστευσεν ὁ ἄνθρωπος τῷ λόγῳ ὃν εἶπεν αὐτῷ ὁ Ἰησοῦς, καὶ ἐπορεύετο· ⁵¹ Ἤδη δὲ αὐτοῦ καταβαίνοντος, οἱ δοῦλοι αὐτοῦ ὑπήντησαν αὐτῷ, λέγοντες· ὅτι ὁ παῖς αὐτοῦ ζῇ. ⁵² Ἐπύθετο οὖν τὴν ὥραν ἐκείνην, ἐν ᾗ κομψότερον ἔσχεν. Εἶπον οὖν αὐτῷ· Ὅτι χθὲς ὥραν ἑβδόμην ἀφῆκεν αὐτὸν ὁ πυρετός. ⁵³ Ἔγνω οὖν ὁ πατὴρ ὅτι ἐκείνῃ τῇ ὥρᾳ, ἐν ᾗ εἶπεν αὐτῷ ὁ Ἰησοῦς· Ὁ υἱός σου ζῇ· καὶ ἐπίστευσεν αὐτὸς καὶ ἡ οἰκία αὐτοῦ ὅλη.

VULGATE.

JOHN IV. 46-53.

⁴⁶ Venit ergo iterum in Cana Galilææ, ubi fecit aquam vinum. Et erat quidam regulus, cujus filius infirmabatur Capharnaum. ⁴⁷ Hic cum audisset quia Jèsus adveniret a Judæa in Galilæam, abiit ad eum, et rogabat eum ut descenderet, et sanaret filium ejus; incipiebat enim mori. ⁴⁸ Dixit ergo Jesus ad eum : Nisi signa et prodigia videritis, non creditis. ⁴⁹ Dicit ad eum regulus : Domine, descende priusquam moriatur filius meus. ⁵⁰ Dicit ei Jesus : Vade, filius tuus vivit. Credidit homo sermoni quem dixit ei Jesus, et ibat. ⁵¹ Jam autem eo descendente, servi occurrerunt ei, et nuntiaverunt dicentes, quia filius ejus viveret. ⁵² Interrogabat ergo horam ab eis in qua melius habuerit. Et dixerunt ei : Quia heri hora septima reliquit eum febris. ⁵³ Cognovit ergo pater quia illa hora erat in qua dixit ei Jesus : Filius tuus vivit; et credidit ipse, et domus ejus tota.

II.—ENGLISH TRANSLATION.

JOHN IV. 46-53.

⁴⁶ He came again, therefore, into Cana of Galilee, where he made the water wine. And there was a certain ruler, whose son was sick at Capharnaum. ⁴⁷ He having heard that Jesus was come from Judæa into Galilee, went to him, and prayed him to come down and heal his son ; for he was at the point of death. ⁴⁸ Jesus therefore said to him : " Unless you see signs and wonders, you believe not." ⁴⁹ The ruler saith to him : " Lord, come down ere my son die." ⁵⁰ Jesus saith to him : "Go thy way ; thy son liveth." The man believed the word that Jesus said to him, and went his way. ⁵¹ And as he was going down, his servants met him ; and they brought word, saying that his son lived. ⁵² He asked, therefore, of them the hour at which he grew better. And they said to him : " Yesterday at the seventh hour, the fever left him." ⁵³ The father knew, therefore, that it was at the same hour at which Jesus said to him : " Thy son liveth " ; and he himself believed, and his whole house.

III.—NOTES.

Introductory. The event that forms the subject matter of this passage, took place during the first year of our Lord's public life ; and it is to be carefully distinguished from the healing of the centurion's servant which, with many marked points of difference, is recorded by St. Matthew (viii. 5-13) and by St. Luke (vii. 1-10). The circumstances in the present case are these. Jesus had celebrated the Pasch in Jerusalem (John ii. 13 ; Introduction, pp. lxi. *seq.*) ; he had there worked many miracles (John ii. 23) ; he had cleansed the temple (Introduction, pp. cxxxvii. *seq.*) by driving forth the money-changers and buyers and sellers from the sacred edifice (John ii. 14-16) ; and he had instructed Nicodemus who came to him by night (John iii. 1-21). Retiring from Judæa (Introduction, p. xxxix.) where the anger of the pharisees was being aroused against him (John iv. 1-4), he passed into Samaria (Introduction, p. xxxix.). Spending two days at Sichar (Introduction, p. lviii.), a city of that province, he converted the woman of Samaria and many of her fellow-citizens (John iv. 5-42) ; and entering into Galilee (Introduction, p. xxxix.), he continued his work in the district where his childhood and early manhood had been spent (John iv. 43, 44). To prepare us for the account he is about to give, the evangelist tells us (John iv. 45, 46) that " when he (Christ) was come again into Galilee, the Galileans received him, having seen all the things he had done at Jerusalem on the festival day. . . .

He came again, therefore, into Cana of Galilee (Introduction,
p. lvi.), where he made the water wine."

St. John, having described the time and place of the miracle,
continues thus :

**V. 46. And there was a certain ruler whose son was sick
at Capharnaum.**

The Greek τίς βασιλικός is variously and not very well translated.   Thus the Authorised Version has : " a certain nobleman "
—a meaning too limited, since the word has no reference to
birth.   The Vulgate and our Douay Version have respectively
" quidam regulus " and " a certain ruler "—a translation
founded on the erroneous reading βασιλίσκος = *a petty king*,
instead of βασιλικός.   According to the usage of Josephus (*B. J.*
vii. 5, 2, and *Antiq.* xv. 8, 4), the word βασιλικός signified a soldier,
courtier, or other officer *in the service of the king* as contrasted
with *those in the service of Rome.*   This man, then, was probably
a civil or a military *officer* of Herod Antipas, tetrarch of Galilee ;
and it is conjectured that he was Chusa, Herod's steward
referred to in Luke viii. 3.   He resided in Capharnaum, a prosperous centre of trade on the shore of Lake Genesareth, and
within a journey of seven hours from Cana.   From the reproof
subsequently given by our Divine Lord, he appears to have
been a Jew in religion.   This royal officer had a son—an only
son as appears from the use of the article (ὁ υἱὸς)—who was at
the time attacked by a dangerous fever.

The report of the miracles worked in Cana and in Jerusalem
had reached the ears of the father ; and, as the evangelist says,

**V. 47. He having heard that Jesus was come from Judæa
into Galilee, went to him and prayed him to come down and
heal his son ; for he was at the point of death.**

Cana was situated amidst the hills of Galilee, at a very considerable elevation above Capharnaum, so that the seven hours'
journey from the former city to the latter on Lake Genesareth is a continual descent.   Hence the request made to Jesus
to " come down."   Commentators are not of one opinion with
regard to the first dispositions of this officer.   According to
St. Augustine, he came to our Lord without any real hope or
faith, and was urged to adopt this course as a last and des-
perate remedy.   Such a supposition seems to be incompatible
with the repeated and urgent prayer to heal the sick child.
Equally improbable is the supposition of others, viz., that the
officer fully and perfectly believed from the beginning ; for
then Christ's reproof in the next verse would be uncalled for.
The truth seems to be that the man's prayer was accompanied
by faith, but by faith that was at first very imperfect.   It was
probably in consequence of this weakness of faith that Christ's

aid was not sought for until all other remedies were found to be useless, that this aid was invoked solely for the temporal necessities of the sick child, and that the corporal presence of our Lord was regarded as an essential condition that any cure might be effected.

Our Divine Lord wished, indeed, to heal the corporal disease of the son ; but having come on earth chiefly to save souls, he desired first to cure the spiritual blindness of the father. With apparent severity

V. 48. Jesus, therefore, said to him : Unless you see signs and wonders, you believe not.

It is clear that each of the words σημεῖα and τέρατα = *signs and wonders*, has a distinct application ; but writers are not agreed as to the nature of the distinction here intended. According to some the words refer to different classes of miraculous effects—the σημεῖα = *signs* being effects that do not *in themselves* exceed the powers of nature, but only *in the circumstances* in which they are produced ; whilst the τέρατα = *wonders* are effects that, not only in the circumstances in which they are produced, but also in themselves, transcend the power of every created cause. The former are known to theologians as *miracula quoad modum* : the latter as *miracula quoad substantiam*. An example of the former kind of miracle would be met with when, instantaneously and without medical appliances, a cure is brought about in a sick person who, with medical appliances and great care, might slowly regain his health. An example of the second kind is the changing of water into wine, or the raising of the dead to life. This distinction between " signs " and " wonders " was first laid down by Ammonius, whose opinion is quoted and approved of by Maldonatus, A Lapide, and others ; but their interpretation is not borne out by an appeal to parallel passages of the Sacred Scriptures. That the Blessed Virgin gave birth to Christ was an effect transcending all the powers of created nature ; and still it was called " a sign " by Isaias (vii. 14). Again in 2 Paralip. xxxii. 24, 31, the turning back of the shadow on the sun-dial, which is called a " sign " in the former verse, is called a " wonder " in the latter (*cf.* 4 Kings xx. 9-11). Other interpreters, amongst whom are Estius and McCarthy, rightly say, then, that the words " signs " and " wonders " are the different names of any one class of miraculous works when regarded from different points of view. Thus, inasmuch as a miracle tends to excite awe or astonishment, it is called a " wonder," but inasmuch as it is an indication of God's will, it receives the name of a " sign." On this subject Westcott (*in loco*) says : " The two words (σημεῖα καὶ τέρατα) are combined in Matth. xxiv. 24 ; Mark xiii. 22 ; Acts (ii. 19), ii. 22, 43, iv. 30, v. 12, vi. 8, vii. 36, viii. 13, xiv. 3, xv. 12 ; Rom. xv. 19 ; 2 Cor. xii. 12 ;

(2 Thes. ii. 9) ; Hebr. ii. 4. They severally mark the two chief aspects of miracles : the spiritual aspect, whereby they suggest some deeper truth than meets the eye, of which they are in some sense symbols and pledges ; and the external aspect, whereby their strangeness arrests attention. ' Sign ' and ' work ' (see v. 20) are the characteristic words for miracles in St. John. The word here translated ' wonders ' is never used by itself in the New Testament."

The officer is addressed as one of the class of men who, without the evidence of miracles will not believe, or (as in the Greek, with the strong negative οὐ μὴ πιστεύσητε) *will in no wise believe.* As the Gentiles of a later date sought for wisdom (1 Cor. i. 22), so the Jews, of whom this was one, were ever seeking for signs and wonders, without believing the more when their request was granted. Elsewhere (Matth. xii. 39 ; xvi. 4) Christ reproached them for this constant search after the miraculous through a spirit of curiosity or a desire to appear as the nation most favoured by God. Our Divine Lord wished in the present instance to repress that vice ; and in the words of our verse, he pointed out the imperfection of the faith of the officer and of his fellow-countrymen as compared with that of the Samaritans, who, under the secret influence of grace ever accompanying the divine word, showed a ready obedience to his teaching without the testimony of any miracle. " When the Samaritans were come to him," wrote St. John, " they desired him that he would tarry there. And he abode there two days. And many more believed in him because of his own word. And they said to the [Samaritan] woman : ' We now believe, not for thy saying ; for we ourselves have heard him, and know that this is indeed the Saviour of the world ' " (John iv. 40-42).

Urging his request,

V. 49. The ruler said to him : Lord, come down ere my son die.

To the rebuke administered by Christ no reply was given by the father, who was wholly occupied with the danger of his son, and who thought that any reply would be a loss of time when the disease required an immediate remedy. The terms in which the request is repeated are more respectful in tone, but still reveal the imperfection of this man's faith. He had before shown his unbelief in the power of Christ to heal when absent : he now equivalently declares it impossible for Christ to recall the dead to life. The prophet Isaias (xlii. 3), who is quoted by St. Matthew (xii. 20), had foretold of the Messiah that " the bruised reed he shall not break, and smoking flax he shall not extinguish." As our Divine Lord fulfilled the first portion of the prediction in his mode of dealing with the incipient penitence of the Samaritan woman (John iv. 7-26), so did he fulfil the remainder in his treatment of the afflicted father, whose little spark of faith was to be fanned into a bright and enduring flame (Alford).

Having thus prepared the officer for the gift to be conferred,

V. 50. Jesus saith to him : Go thy way : thy son liveth. The man believed the word that Jesus said to him, and went his way.

The word *life* in place of *health* or *cure* is a Hebraism very frequently met in the Psalms, in which *vivificare* is put for *sanare*. (See Ps. lxx. 20 ; lxxix. 19 ; lxxxiv. 7.) Thus in our passage the word ζῆ, translated " liveth," is the equivalent of the Hebrew היה in Josue v. 8, and conveys the idea of liberation from the evil or danger of death by sickness. Christ does not *pray* for the cure, but with all the power and majesty of the Master of nature he wills the effect, and it takes place. He does not proceed to the bed-side of the patient ; but working at a distance, he both heals the bodily illness of the child and strengthens the faith of the father. As Alford observes, there is a marked difference between our Lord's action in the case of this man and in that of the centurion (Matth. viii. 7). In the case of the centurion, who humbly requested him to " speak only the word," he offers to go to the house : here, he is urgently requested to go to the house, and he merely speaks the word. He wished thus in a different manner to honour the humility of the pagan and to perfect the faith of the Jew, whilst doing in each instance more than had been asked or hoped for.

He who had hitherto believed that Christ when corporally present could restore his son to health, now believed that the corporal presence of the Heavenly Physician was not necessary for the purpose. Touched by that interior grace which, in a greater or in a lesser measure ever accompanies the hearing of God's voice, " the man believed the word that Jesus said to him, and went his way ; "

V. 51. And as he was going down his servants met him ; and they brought word, saying that his son lived.

The growth of the officer's faith was gradual like that of the Samaritan woman (John iv.). Believing that Christ was at least a prophet, this man felt assured that his son was now out of danger of death, and he looked forward with confidence to a speedy and complete restoration to health. Whilst he was journeying from Cana to Capharnaum, his servants were hastening in the opposite direction to bring him the joyful news of his son's unexpected and instantaneous recovery. The distance from Cana to Capharnaum was only twenty-five miles ; but the heat of the early summer and the roughness of the roads in that hilly country rendered travelling painfully slow. Thus, it was not until the next day (see v. 52) that he met his servants. Having been informed by them "that his son lived,"

V. 52. He asked, therefore, of them the hour at which he grew better. And they said to him : Yesterday at the seventh hour the fever left him.

The clause κομψότερον ἔσχεν, a colloquial expression found in Arrian. Dissert. iii. 10, signifies "was somewhat better "; and it shows that on the part of the father, only a gradual improvement was understood to have taken place. It is in strong contrast with the expression ἀφῆκεν αὐτὸν ὁ πυρετός which was used by the servants, and which indicated a complete and instantaneous recovery.

"The seventh hour" might stand for 7 a.m. or for 7 p.m., according to our mode of reckoning; but most of the ancient and very many of the modern commentators consider that St. John follows the Jewish method of computation, and that the time of the cure was *the seventh hour from sunrise* or 1 p.m.—a time when the heat was greatest and when a cessation of the fever was most unlikely. Their reason for this conclusion is that the other writers in the New Testament follow this method of computation, and that there is no reason to suppose that St. John here differs from them.

As has been already remarked the officer did not meet his servants until the day after the miracle. Confident that an amendment in his son's condition was taking place, he appears to have gone leisurely away ; for if he left at once on having his interview with our Lord, the hour (1 p.m.) was early enough to permit of his reaching Capharnaum the same evening after a journey of twenty-five miles (see Alford). Most likely, he and his servants started on their respective journeys not in the heat of the day, but in the cool of the evening ; they stopped on the way for necessary repose ; and they met early on the following forenoon.

The effect of the servants' words is thus described by the evangelist :—

V. 53. The father knew, therefore, that it was at the same hour at which Jesus said to him: Thy son liveth ; and he himself believed, and his whole house.

St. John here describes the last stage in the growth of the father's faith. This father had not hitherto fully realised Christ's power : he now learns that his son was not merely rescued from danger of death, but was instantly restored to full health and vigour at the moment when Jesus spoke, and by the power over nature which Jesus wielded. Yielding, therefore, to grace, he believed not merely " the word which Jesus spoke," but he " believed " absolutely in Jesus himself. Still further, "his whole house," that is his whole family, wife, children, and servants became disciples of Christ. So important is this event in itself and in its consequences, that St. John comments upon the matter in the following words : " This is again the second miracle that Jesus did, when he was come out of Judæa into Galilee " (John iv. 54).

IV.—MORAL REFLECTIONS.

1. The illness of a son was the cause that brought the officer to the presence of Jesus Christ ; and if that temporal affliction had not befallen him, he would not have sought for relief from his Saviour, nor obtained it together with the great gift of faith. Thus does God commonly deal with those whom he wishes to draw to himself. It is not ordinarily in temporal prosperity that we are inspired to work out our salvation : on the contrary, the ordinary effect of worldly happiness is to withdraw us from God, and the enjoyment of created goods produces an attachment to them which lessens the love we should have for our Creator. The love of God and the love of the world being so opposed as they are, what the one gains in our hearts the other loses. The conversions, then, are few that are brought about by prosperity ; but adversity is the season when grace most frequently and most powerfully calls us to the ways of justice. In separating us from the objects of our affections, God makes us feel the instability of our present state ; in depriving us of the false goods in which we placed our happiness, he leads us to desire a happiness more solid ; in afflicting us by the death of those we cherish, he induces us to seek the consolations of religion. How many are there not amongst the saints whom a reverse of fortune or a temporal loss has been the cause of bringing wholly to God, and who now rejoice in heaven at what once seemed to them an unmixed evil ! It required the coming of Christ to teach us the value of affliction ; and it is from his Apostle that we hear the words : " We glory also in tribulations ; knowing that tribulation worketh patience, and patience trial, and trial hope. And hope confoundeth not ; because the charity of God is poured forth in our hearts, by the Holy Ghost who is given to us " (Rom. v. 3-5).

2. The conduct of the officer when Christ appeared to disregard his petition, teaches us the necessity of perseverance in prayer. Our Divine Master tells us that what may not be secured by a single request is to be gained by importunity in asking. Speaking of one whose necessities were at first unheeded by a friend, he declared : " If he shall continue knocking, I say to you, that although he will not rise and give to him because he is his friend, yet because of his importunity he will rise and give

to him as many as he needeth. And I say to you : Ask, and it shall be given to you ; seek, and you shall find ; knock, and it shall be opened to you " (Luke xi. 8, 9). God promises to grant in itself or equivalently all that which we ask in prayer made with the proper dispositions (Mark xi. 24) ; but he does not promise to grant it at the moment when we ask. Men fear to be importuned or are angered thereat ; but it is not so with God. God is pleased at our repeated solicitation, and when he appears sometimes not to hear our prayers, this is to increase our fervour, and to excite our desires the more, by delaying to satisfy them.

3. The evangelist notices as a result of the miracle, that the officer not only himself believed, but also brought his whole house to the faith. This man was not content that he alone should know, honour, and obey his Saviour ; he communicated this happiness to all his dependants. His zeal teaches all who are invested with authority the care they should take of the salvation of their subordinates ; but it is especially to heads of families that this lesson is addressed. They should consider themselves in their homes not only as masters, but also as apostles ; and they should provide not merely for the temporal well-being of their children and domestics, but also, and much more, for the spiritual interests of all subject to them. This is an obligation imposed on superiors by the law of God, by their state, and by their interest. The great Apostle prescribes this duty with an energy which would seem exaggerated if it were not inspired. He declares that " if any man have not a care of his own, and especially of those of his house, he hath denied the faith, and is worse than an infidel " (1 Tim. v. 8). How is this ? We practically deny our religion and are more culpable than the unbeliever, when we suffer the faith to be unknown to, or outraged by, those whom we are bound to lead to God. Let us, then, imitate the zeal of this officer, and we shall share in his reward. By giving good example to those under our charge, by giving to them or procuring for them religious instruction, and by patiently correcting their defects or shortcomings, we shall use aright the authority with which God has invested us ; and as according to our state we thus assist in the work of the Church's pastors, when the Prince of Pastors shall appear he will give us a never-fading crown of glory (1 Peter v. 4).

TWENTY-FIRST SUNDAY AFTER PENTECOST.

I.—TEXTS.

GREEK.

MATTHEW XVIII. 23-35.

²³ Διὰ τοῦτο ὡμοιώθη ἡ βασιλεία τῶν οὐρανῶν ἀνθρώπῳ βασιλεῖ ὃς ἠθέλησεν συνᾶραι λόγον μετὰ τῶν δούλων αὐτοῦ. ²⁴ Ἀρξαμένου δὲ αὐτοῦ συναίρειν, προσήχθη εἷς αὐτῷ ὀφειλέτης μυρίων ταλάντων. ²⁵ Μὴ ἔχοντος δὲ αὐτοῦ ἀποδοῦναι, ἐκέλευσεν αὐτὸν ὁ κύριος πραθῆναι, καὶ τὴν γυναῖκα, καὶ τὰ τέκνα, καὶ πάντα ὅσα ἔχει, καὶ ἀποδοθῆναι. ²⁶ Πεσὼν οὖν ὁ δοῦλος προσεκύνει αὐτῷ, λέγων· Μακροθύμησον ἐπ' ἐμοί, καὶ πάντα ἀποδώσω σοι. ²⁷ Σπλαγχνισθεὶς δὲ ὁ κύριος τοῦ δούλου, ἀπέλυσεν αὐτὸν, καὶ τὸ δάνειον ἀφῆκεν αὐτῷ. ²⁸ Ἐξελθὼν δὲ ὁ δοῦλος, εὗρεν ἕνα τῶν συνδούλων αὐτοῦ, ὃς ὤφειλεν αὐτῷ ἑκατὸν δηνάρια· καὶ κρατήσας αὐτὸν ἔπνιγε, λέγων· Ἀπόδος, εἴ τι ὀφείλεις. ²⁹ Πεσὼν οὖν ὁ σύνδουλος αὐτοῦ, παρεκάλει αὐτὸν, λέγων· Μακροθύμησον ἐπ' ἐμοί, καὶ ἀποδώσω σοι. ³⁰ Ὁ δὲ οὐκ ἤθελεν· ἀλλὰ ἀπελθὼν ἔβαλεν αὐτὸν εἰς φυλακήν, ἕως ἀποδῷ τὸ ὀφειλόμενον. ³¹ Ἰδόντες οὖν αὐτοῦ οἱ σύνδουλοι τὰ γενόμενα, ἐλυπήθησαν σφόδρα· καὶ ἐλθόντες διεσάφησαν τῷ κυρίῳ ἑαυτῶν πάντα τὰ γενόμενα. ³² Τότε προσκαλεσάμενος αὐτὸν ὁ κύριος

VULGATE.

MATTHEW XVIII. 23-35.

23 Ideo assimilatum est regnum cœlorum homini regi qui voluit rationem ponere cum servis suis. 24 Et quum cœpisset rationem ponere, oblatus est ei unus qui debebat ei decem millia talenta. 25 Cum autem non haberet unde redderet, jussit eum dominus ejus venumdari, et uxorem ejus, et filios, et omnia quæ habebat, et reddi. 26 Procidens autem servus ille, orabat eum, dicens : Patientiam habe in me, et omnia reddam tibi. 27 Misertus autem dominus servi illius, dimisit eum, et debitum dimisit ei. 28 Egressus autem servus ille invenit unum de conservis suis, qui debebat ei centum denarios ; et tenens suffocabat eum, dicens : Redde quod debes. 29 Et procidens conservus ejus, rogabat eum, dicens : Patientiam habe in me, et omnia reddam tibi. 30 Ille autem noluit ; sed abiit, et misit eum in carcerem, donec redderet debitum. 31 Videntes autem conservi ejus quæ fiebant, contristati sunt valde ; et venerunt, et narraverunt domino suo omnia quæ facta fue-

αὐτοῦ λέγει αὐτῷ· Δοῦλε πονηρέ, πᾶ-
σαν τὴν ὀφειλὴν ἐκείνην ἀφῆκά σοι,
ἐπεὶ παρεκάλεσάς με. ³³ Οὐκ ἔδει καὶ
σὲ ἐλεῆσαι τὸν σύνδουλόν σου, ὡς
κᾀγώ σε ἠλέησα ; ³⁴ Καὶ ὀργισθεὶς ὁ
κύριος αὐτοῦ παρέδωκεν αὐτὸν τοῖς
βασανισταῖς, ἕως ἀποδῷ πᾶν τὸ ὀφειλόμενον. ³⁵ Οὕτως καὶ ὁ πατήρ μου ὁ
οὐράνιος ποιήσει ὑμῖν, ἐὰν μὴ ἀφῆτε
ἕκαστος τῷ ἀδελφῷ αὐτοῦ ἀπὸ τῶν
καρδιῶν ὑμῶν.

rant. ³² Tunc vocavit illum
dominus suus, et ait illi : Serve
nequam, omne debitum dimisi
tibi, quoniam rogasti me.
³³ Nonne ergo oportuit et te
misereri conservi tui, sicut et
ego tui misertus sum? ³⁴ Et
iratus dominus ejus tradidit
eum tortoribus, quoadusque
redderet universum debitum.
³⁵ Sic et Pater meus cœlestis
faciet vobis, si non remiseritis
unusquisque fratri suo de cordibus vestris.

II.—ENGLISH TRANSLATION.

MATTHEW XVIII. 23-35.

²³ " Therefore is the kingdom of heaven likened to a king
who would take an account of his servants. ²⁴ And when he had
begun to take the account, one was brought to him, that owed
him ten thousand talents. ²⁵ And as he had not wherewith to
pay it, his lord commanded that he should be sold, and his
wife, and children, and all that he had, and that payment should
be made. ²⁶ But that servant falling down, besought him
saying : ' Have patience with me, and I will pay thee all.' ²⁷ And
the lord of that servant being moved with pity, let him go,
and forgave him the debt. ²⁸ But when that servant was gone
out, he found one of his fellow-servants that owed him a hundred
pence ; and laying hold of him, he throttled him, saying : ' Pay
what thou owest.' ²⁹ And his fellow-servant falling down,
besought him, saying : ' Have patience with me, and I will pay
thee all.' ³⁰ And he would not ; but went and cast him into
prison, till he should pay the debt. ³¹ Now his fellow-servants
seeing what was done, were very much grieved ; and they came
and told their lord all that was done. ³² Then his lord called
him, and said to him : ' Thou wicked servant, I forgave thee all
the debt, because thou besoughtest me. ³³ Shouldst not thou
also, then, have had compassion on thy fellow-servant, even as I
had compassion on thee ? ' ³⁴ And his lord being angry, delivered
him to the torturers until he should pay all the debt. ³⁵ So also
shall my heavenly Father do to you, if you forgive not every
one his brother from your hearts."

III.—NOTES.

Introductory. This parable, recorded by St. Matthew only,
was spoken by our Lord towards the end of the third year of

his public life, a little before he raised Lazarus from the dead. At that time Christ was preaching in Peræa, on the east of the Jordan, a district to which he had retired when the Jews at the previous Feast of the Dedication of the Temple, attempted to stone him as a blasphemer (John x. 22-42). As he was one day instructing his disciples on the duty of fraternal charity, he said : " If thy brother sin against thee, reprove him ; and if he do penance, forgive him. And if he sin against thee seven times in a day, and seven times in a day be converted unto thee, saying : ' I repent,' forgive him " (Luke xvii. 3, 4). The Jewish doctors mistaking the meaning of Amos i. 3 ; ii. 6, and of Job xxxiii. 29, had laid it down that an enemy should be pardoned three times, but no more ; and St. Peter, probably remembering this restriction of his teachers, considered as excessive the indulgence prescribed by Christ. This apostle, therefore, to assure himself that he correctly understood the command just given, came to his divine Master and said : " Lord, how often shall my brother offend against me and I forgive him ?   Till seven times ? " Jesus said to him : " I say not to thee till seven times ; but till seventy times seven times " (Matth. xviii. 21, 22).   Commenting on this answer, St. Chrysostom (*in loco*) says well : " What then saith Christ, the good God, who is loving towards man ?   *I say not unto thee : Until seven times, but : Until seventy times seven times*, setting not a number here, but what is infinite, and perpetual, and for ever."

Our Lord, having thus prescribed a spirit of forgiveness which should be unrestricted in its exercise, proceeded according to the Eastern custom to enforce the necessity of this precept by a parable.   He said :—

V. 23. Therefore is the kingdom of heaven likened to a king who would take an account of his servants.

As has been already fully explained in dealing with other parables (see verse 9 in the gospel for the Seventeenth Sunday after Pentecost), this opening sentence means that " the same thing happens in the Church on earth, as when, under circumstances afterwards to be described, a king takes an account of his servants."   Although, as appears from the concluding words (verse 35) of this parable, the lesson is that each man must expect to be called to account by God the Supreme Ruler of all, the illustration is taken from the dealings of a king with his ministers of state or the officers of his court.   Alford (*in loco*) says : " The δοῦλοι here are not *slaves*, but ministers or stewards.   By the πραθῆναι of verse 25, they could not be slaves in the literal sense. But in Oriental language (see Herodotus *passim*) all the subjects of the king, even the great ministers of state, are called δοῦλοι. The individual example is one in *high trust*, or his debt could never have reached the enormous sum mentioned."   In figurative language, the dealings of the earthly king with his servants are made to shadow forth the dealings of God with us his creatures, and especially with us the members of his Church on earth. To us he has permitted the use of great treasures—blessings of nature and of grace ; and even during our lifetime he will visit us and enter into a reckoning with us. " To this he brings us by the preaching of the law,—by the setting of our sins before our face,—by awakening and alarming our conscience that was asleep before,—by bringing us into adversities (2 Par. xxxiii. 11-13)—by casting us into sore sicknesses (Job xxxiii. 19-30), into perils of death ; so that there is not a step between us and it (4 Kings xx. 4) ; he takes account with us, when he makes us feel that we could not answer him one thing in a thousand, that our trespasses are more than the hairs of our heads ; when by one means or another he brings our careless carnal security to an end " (Psalm xlix. 21 ; Acts xvi. 30). (Trench : *Parables*, page 152. The changes in the references are made to suit the Douay Bible.)

The king, then, called on his servants to render an account of their stewardship ;

V. 24. And when he had begun to take the account, one was brought to him, that owed him ten thousand talents.

As money (Introduction, pp. cxx.-cxxiii.) was reckoned by weight, the " talent," originally a measure of weight, came to signify among both Jews and Greeks a certain sum of gold or of silver. It differed in value in different states. In our monetary system the Attic silver talent would be equal to £240 ; the Jewish talent in silver would be £353 ; and the same in gold was equivalent to £5,075. We do not know to which of these our Lord referred ; and thus the ten thousand talents due by the servant may have been £2,400,000, or £3,530,000, or £50,750,000. Even the first mentioned computation reveals an enormous debt ; but it will not surprise those who remember (1°) that the " servant " may have been one of the chief officers in charge of the royal revenues (see note on preceding verse), and (2°) that in the despotic monarchies of the East, rulers were, and are, masters of the property and person of each of their subjects. Trench says : " Harpalus, satrap of Babylonia and Syria, besides the enormous sums which he had squandered, carried off with him five thousand talents when he fled to Athens from the wrath of Alexander (Grote : *Hist. of Greece*, vol. viii., page 496). It was with exactly ten thousand talents that Darius sought to buy off Alexander, that he should not prosecute his conquests in Asia (Plutarch : *Reg. et Imp. Apoph.*) ; being the same sum with which Haman would have purchased of the Persian king permission to destroy all the Jews in the kingdom (Esth. iii. 9). The same was the fine imposed by the Romans on Antiochus

the Great, after his defeat by them." (Trench : *Parables*, page
153, note 3.)   Still, although the sum due by the servant was
almost incredibly great, probably exceeding the whole revenue
of Palestine at that time, and equal to the revenue of Norway,
Denmark, or Greece at present (see Cambridge Bible, *in loco*),
it but imperfectly represents that of which it is here a figure—
man's sinful indebtedness to the divine justice for even one
mortal transgression.

The servant's debt was clearly proved ;

**V. 25. And as he had not wherewith to pay it, his lord
commanded that he should be sold, and his wife, and children,
and all that he had, and that payment should be made.**

It was laid down in Exodus xxii. 3 that insolvent debtors
should be sold, and the existence of this law is implied in Leviticus xxv. 39, 47 ; 4 Kings iv. 1, together with many other passages
of the Old Testament ; but if the Jews had ever the right to
reduce the whole of the debtor's family to bondage, it does not
appear that such a right was exercised in the time of Christ.
This latter act of severity referred to in the parable, appears
then to have been borrowed from the manners of Eastern nations
amongst whom, as well as amongst the ancient Romans, even
greater rigour in the punishment of offenders is known to have
been customary (*cf.* Dan. vi. 24 ; Esth. xvi. 18 ; Herodotus iii. 9).
Our Lord's design here is to show that if *human* laws give to a
creditor such an absolute power, much more justly may God proceed to extremes in demanding satisfaction from his offending
creatures.

The sentence was passed by the king, and would soon have
been carried into execution ;

**V. 26. But that servant falling down, besought him, say-
ing : Have patience with me, and I will pay thee all.**

The first clause πεσὼν οὖν ὁ δοῦλος προσεκύνει αὐτῷ may be better
rendered : " But that servant falling down, was worshipping
him." The urgent, persistent, and repeated request is indicated
by the use of the imperfect tense in the Greek. Terror suggested
a promise of what was already (verse 25) said to be impossible.
The debtor asked his lord to " have patience " with him, or
literally, to " wait a little time longer " for payment (μακροθύμησον
ἐπ' ἐμοί). More was granted than was asked ;

**V. 27. And the lord of that servant being moved with pity,
let him go, and forgave him the debt.**

Here again the reader is introduced to the customs of those
Eastern monarchs who, at one time inexorably severe in the
infliction of punishment, are at another time lavish in the extent
of their gifts. Examples of this are handed down in history.

(See Knabenbauer ; *In Isaiam*, vol. ii. pages 173, 174 ; *In Matth.*, vol. ii. page 133 ; Suetonius ; Tacitus.)   But though this act of the king was one of almost incredible generosity, it only imperfectly typifies the goodness of God in dealing with man's offences. When, like the steward in the parable, we cast ourselves at God's feet and ask for pardon, he remits the debt of punishment, temporal or eternal, which we have incurred ; he undoes the injury we have inflicted on our souls ; he restores us to our place in his favour ; and he gives back to us our former right to eternal happiness. He does more. Before repentance, God, like the father of " the prodigal son," is looking for us from afar ; with a love greater than that of any earthly father, he is desiring our return ; and with a power exceeding that of any earthly sovereign, he is drawing us to himself by his preventing grace, and is infusing into our souls the dispositions required as a preparation for our justification.

The servant's debt having been remitted, the experience of such generous treatment imposed the duty of imitation ;

Vv. 28, 29, 30. But when that servant was gone out, he found one of his fellow-servants that owed him a hundred pence : and laying hold of him, he throttled him, saying : Pay what thou owest. And his fellow-servant falling down, besought him saying : Have patience with me and I will pay thee all. And he would not ; but went and cast him into prison till he should pay the debt.

The *denarius*, or Roman *silver penny*, being equivalent to about 9½ pence of our money (Hastings), the debt due in this second case was not quite £4—a sum so small when compared with ten thousand talents, that apparently out of shame the creditor did not name it ($εἴ τι ὀφείλεις =$ " if thou owest anything "). Still, behold the heartlessness of his exaction. At the very first moment, he resorted to violence ($κρατήσας αὐτὸν ἔπνιγε =$ " laying hold on him, he at once dragged him violently by the throat ") ; having had his own debt freely and entirely remitted by the king, he would not listen to the prayer of a fellow-servant for time to pay in full ; he was not moved by a supplication expressed in precisely the same form of words which had excited compassion and obtained mercy for himself ; he did not regard the disparity between the debts—his own of ten thousand talents and his companion's of a hundred pence ; and he did not hesitate to inflict a most rigorous and life-long punishment from which he himself had so narrowly escaped. (See Euthym., quoted by Knabenbauer, *in loco*.) In these verses is comprised the second part of the story ; and whilst in the first part there is a figure or type of God's merciful dealings with men, here there is an illustration of men's harsh dealings with each other. How great is the ingratitude and cruelty of him who, having experienced the infinite goodness of his Creator in remitting the enormous debt of even one sin, will not pardon the comparatively small offences committed against himself by a fellow-creature ! The difference between the injury done to man by these offences, however grave or however frequently repeated, and that done to God by even one sin, cannot be expressed fully in human language. It finds, indeed, but a poor illustration in the proportion between the hundred denarii and the ten thousand talents.

Having thus pictured to some extent the wickedness of the unforgiving heart, our Lord next proceeds, so far as the audience can understand, to typify the consequences of that wickedness in the well-deserved punishment of the unmerciful servant. It is said that

V. 31. Now his fellow-servants seeing what was done, were very much grieved ; and they came and told their lord all that was done.

The original text well expresses the feelings of the " fellow-servants " by the verb ἐλυπήθησαν, which, with the idea of sorrow for the offence, often includes, according to Bengel, that of righteous indignation against the offender. The original text indicates, too, that these companions of the poor debtor went *at once* (ἐλθόντες) and made an *accurate* and *full statement* of the revolting cruelty they had witnessed (διεσάφησαν . . . πάντα τὰ γενόμενα).

The unfeeling creditor had forgotten the maxim that to press our legal rights to extremes is often most opposed to what is right, and he had no anticipation that the equity of his action might be questioned; but

Vv. 32, 33. Then his lord called him, and said to him: Thou wicked servant, I forgave thee all the debt because thou besoughtest me. Shouldst not thou also, then, have had compassion on thy fellow-servant, even as I had compassion on thee.

In the former interview this man was dealt with as it was customary to deal with insolvent debtors ; but now for the first time the king charges him with crime, reminds him of the benefits he had received, and declares the obligation under which he lay of doing to others what he had wished to be done to himself. Cajetan remarks that the king does not say : " You ought to have *remitted your fellow-servant's debt*, as I remitted yours," but rather : " Shouldst not thou also, then, *have had compassion* on thy fellow-servant, even as I had compassion on thee." It is as if the king had said : " If you were unwilling to follow me in my *liberality*, you should at least have imitated me in *mercy* by acceding to your debtor's request for time." There was not any question here of a legal, but of a moral, obligation of a strict nature. " Sicut honestas moralis non admittit hominem impotentem solvere vexari in persona et libertate, ita non admittit vexari in iisdem impotentem pro tunc, suppliciter rogantem dilationem cum promissione solvendi omnia ; rursus in nonnullam injuriam communis domini redundat tractare sic conservum statim post acceptum tantum beneficium." (See Cajetan, quoted by Knabenbauer *in loco*.)

The servant could offer no defence ;

V. 34. And his lord being angry, delivered him to the tormenters until he should pay all the debt.

" Grotius makes the βασανισταί (*tormentors*) merely = δεσμοφύλακες (*jailers*) ; and so Kuinoel, who observes that debtors are given to safe keeping, but not to tortures.   This is not accurate. Thus in early times there were certain legal tortures, a chain weighing fifteen pounds, a pittance of food barely sufficient to sustain life (see Arnold, *Hist. of Rome*, vol. i., p. 136 ; Livy ii. 23), which the Roman creditor might apply to the debtor for the bringing him to terms.   In the East, too, where no depth of apparent poverty excludes the suspicion that there may be some-where a hidden store, where too it is almost a point of honour not to pay but on hardest compulsion, the torture would be often used to wring something from the sufferings of the debtor himself, or from the compassion of his friends.   In all these cases the jailer would be naturally the ' tormentor ' as well " (Trench, *Parables*, p. 161, *note*).   It should be borne in mind, too, in the present case, that the unmerciful servant, who as a debtor had previously been condemned to slavery, was now for his recent crime to be punished most severely.   As it is said that the punishment was to last until the whole debt would have been paid, and as it was plainly impossible to fulfil this condition, the sentence was one of perpetual imprisonment and torture.   Thus ends the third part of the parable.   In it the reader receives a warning that the conduct of all who do not forgive their fellow-men is most offensive to the angels and saints, to the just on earth, and to God himself.   Indeed, although God is a Being of infinite clemency, he shows an extraordinary anger against sinners such as these ; he deals with them so rigorously that St. James had written : " Judgment without mercy to him that hath not done mercy " (James ii. 13) ; he inflicts on them a punishment as great as if their former debts to the divine justice had not been remitted ; and since their former debts could never have been discharged by any efforts of the sinners themselves, the duration of the punishment is that of eternity itself.

Lest we should mistake this meaning, or substitute any other for it, our Lord himself makes the application of the parable when he says :—

V. 35. **So also shall my heavenly Father do to you, if you forgive not every one his brother from your hearts.**

Again Christ puts into our own hands the shaping of our destiny for eternity, and repeats a command already given in these words of the Sermon on the Mount : " Thus therefore shall you pray : ' Our Father who art in heaven, . . . forgive us our debts as we also forgive our debtors.' . . . For if you will forgive men their offences, your heavenly Father will forgive you also your offences ; but if you will not forgive men, neither will your father forgive you your offences " (Matth. vi. 9, 12, 14, 15).

Here, however, we meet with a difficulty.   It may be asked : " Does it not seem, on the one hand, to follow from the parable that he who is unfaithful to this precept, becomes again responsible for his sins which are already pardoned ; and is not this interpretation borne out by the warning of the Holy Ghost : ' Be not without fear about sin forgiven, and add not sin upon sin' (Ecclus. v. 5) ? On the other hand, do we not hear from St. Paul that ' the gifts and the calling of God are without repentance ' (Rom. xi. 29) ?   Is it not still more clearly promised that on repentance the guilt of our offences will be blotted out for ever and the corresponding punishment condoned, where the prophet says of God : ' He will put away our iniquities ; and he will cast all our sins *into the depths of the sea* ' " (Micheas vii. 19) ?   It is easy to reconcile these apparently conflicting statements if we remember that when remitted, a debt to the divine justice may be contracted anew either *substantially* or *virtually*.   This debt may be contracted substantially by a *fresh fall* into the sin already forgiven—a fall with which according to Vasquez and De Lugo, God often punishes the crime of harshness towards an offending but repentant brother.   The same debt may be contracted virtually in that harshness itself which because of the ingratitude it implies, God detests and punishes as much as the former offence already forgiven (see McCarthy *in loco*).   With reason, then, has St. Jerome (*in loco*) written on this matter : " Formidolosa sententia, si juxta nostram mentem sententia Dei flectitur atque mutatur. Si parva fratribus non dimittimus, magna nobis a Deo non dimittentur."

IV.—MORAL REFLECTIONS.

In reading this parable we applaud the justice of the master ; we approve of his severity ; and we are pleased to see him mete out to the merciless servant a punishment richly deserved by inhuman cruelty.   This is in accordance with the instincts of our nature.   Still, whilst such feelings naturally take possession of our hearts, we should apply the parable to ourselves, and should consider the reasons we ourselves have for pardoning from our hearts all those who have offended or injured us.

1. Our first reason is the example of Christ our Lord. Christ knew our weakness and the difficulty of the duty he laid upon us in this branch of the law of charity. Hence in giving his commandment, he also assisted us to fulfil it by putting before us his own example ; in dictating his law, he commenced by submitting to it ; and to lighten the yoke he imposed, he first bore it himself. It was love of his enemies and the desire to forgive them that drew him down from heaven and clothed him with a mortal body ; it was this that during his whole life caused him to bestow his blessings on a people who ceaselessly persecuted and reviled him ; it was this that nailed him to the cross and made him with his last breath pray for his executioners. The master in the parable pointed to his own forgiving spirit as a type which should have been followed by his servant ; and in the same manner does Christ call on us to imitate the charity of which he himself is the Divine Model. In this sense he might have addressed to us the words spoken at his Last Supper : " I have given you an example, that as I have done to you, so you do also " (John xiii. 15).

2. Again, we are called to be the adopted children of God ; but the condition on which this adoption depends is that we deal with our brethren as God has dealt with us. " You have heard that it hath been said : Thou shalt love thy neighbour and hate thy enemy. But I say to you : Love your enemies ; do good to them that hate you ; and pray for them that persecute and calumniate you, that you may be the children of your Father who is in heaven, who maketh his sun to rise upon the good and the bad, and raineth upon the just and the unjust " (Matth. v. 43-45). To estimate our obligations by this standard and to learn what we owe to others, we have only to remember the many sins forgiven us and the many graces conferred on us, notwithstanding our repeated infidelity. At the thought of God's goodness, we are filled with a holy fervour, and cry out in the words of David : " What shall I render to the Lord for all the things that he hath rendered to me ? " (Ps. cxv. 12). We have not far to seek for the answer to our question. The sacrifice of our angry feelings in forgiving our enemies is the most agreeable return we can make, because it is the greatest we can make. By this sacrifice we shall at once most perfectly express our gratitude for the divine bounty ; and imitating that divine bounty, we shall prove ourselves true children of him " who maketh his sun to rise upon the good and the bad, and raineth upon the just and the unjust " (Matth. v. 45).

3. Still further, the spirit of forgiveness of injuries is not only

a suitable act of thanksgiving for the pardon of our offences, but it is also a means of securing that pardon itself ; and the remission of sins which holy penitents feared they had not obtained after years of prayer, contrition, and mortification, can be gained by this one act. Jesus Christ has said : " Forgive, and you shall be forgiven " (Luke vi. 37). If, therefore, over-coming ourselves, we be reconciled with our enemies and then present ourselves before our God, we may confidently claim the fulfilment of his promise, and may ask him to do for us in his mercy what we have done for others by his grace. We must not think, indeed, that forgiveness of injuries has the same power of obtaining remission of sin, or has it in the same way, as has an act of perfect charity or the reception of the sacra-ment of penance. It has not this power directly ; but an act so heroic as the love of our enemies, either emanates from perfect charity, which at once disarms the anger of God, or it brings with it the feeling of compunction, which suffices in the sacrament of penance for the remission of our offences. Either in its source then, or in its effects, it works our justification : he who makes such a sacrifice must be already the friend of God, or in making this sacrifice, he merits to become the friend of God.

4. Lastly, the pardon of injuries is not only a sure means of obtaining justification, but it is also a necessary condition for that end. Such is the teaching of Jesus Christ, who says in this passage : " So also shall my heavenly Father do to you, if you forgive not every one his brother from your hearts." Every day we recite the prayer : " Forgive us our trespasses, as we forgive those that trespass against us." Do we reflect on what we say, or do we know what we ask ? In these words we lay down the conditions of our salvation, and we measure for our-selves the grace we are to receive : in these words the vindictive and unforgiving cut themselves off from mercy. If it is not in this sense we understand the prayer, it is in this sense God hears it. On the lips of the unmerciful, therefore, a petition which is so touching and which is intended to obtain mercy, becomes an imprecation ; and God will remember this imprecation one day when pronouncing their sentence at his dread tribunal.

TWENTY-SECOND SUNDAY AFTER PENTECOST.

I. —TEXTS.

GREEK.

MATTHEW XXII. 15-21.

¹⁵ Τότε πορευθέντες οἱ φαρεισαῖοι, συμβούλιον ἔλαβον, ὅπως αὐτὸν παγιδεύσωσιν ἐν λόγῳ. ¹⁶ Καὶ ἀποστέλλουσιν αὐτῷ τοὺς μαθητὰς αὐτῶν μετὰ τῶν Ἡρωδιανῶν λέγοντας· Διδάσκαλε, οἴδαμεν ὅτι ἀληθὴς εἶ, καὶ τὴν ὁδὸν τοῦ θεοῦ ἐν ἀληθείᾳ διδάσκεις, καὶ οὐ μέλει σοι περὶ οὐδενός· οὐ γὰρ βλέπεις εἰς πρόσωπον ἀνθρώπων. ¹⁷ Εἰπὲ οὖν ἡμῖν, τί σοι δοκεῖ· Ἔξεστιν δοῦναι κῆνσον Καίσαρι, ἢ οὔ; ¹⁸ Γνοὺς δὲ ὁ Ἰησοῦς τὴν πονηρίαν αὐτῶν, εἶπεν· Τί με πείράζετε, ὑποκριταί; ¹⁹ Ἐπιδείξατέ μοι τὸ νόμισμα τοῦ κήνσου. Οἱ δὲ προσήνεγκαν αὐτῷ δηνάριον. ²⁰ Καὶ λέγει αὐτοῖς· Τίνος ἡ εἰκὼν αὕτη καὶ ἡ ἐπιγραφή; ²¹ Λέγουσιν· Καίσαρος. Τότε λέγει αὐτοῖς· Ἀπόδοτε οὖν τὰ Καίσαρος Καίσαρι, καὶ τὰ τοῦ θεοῦ τῷ θεῷ.

VULGATE.

MATTHEW XXII. 15-21.

¹⁵ Tunc abeuntes pharisæi, consilium inierunt ut caperent eum in sermone. ¹⁶ Et mittunt ei discipulos suos cum Herodianis dicentes : Magister, scimus quia verax es, et viam Dei in veritate doces, et non est tibi cura de aliquo ; non enim respicis personam hominum. ¹⁷ Dic ergo nobis quid tibi videtur : Licet censum dare Cæsari, an non? ¹⁸ Cognita autem Jesus nequitia eorum, ait : Quid me tentatis, hypocritæ? ¹⁹ Ostendite mihi numisma census. At illi obtulerunt ei denarium. ²⁰ Et ait illis Jesus : Cujus est imago hæc, et superscriptio? ²¹ Dicunt ei : Cæsaris. Tunc ait illis : Reddite ergo quæ sunt Cæsaris, Cæsari ; et quæ sunt Dei, Deo.

II.—ENGLISH TRANSLATION WITH PARALLEL PASSAGES FROM SS. MARK AND LUKE.

MATTHEW XXII. 15-21.

¹⁵ Then the pharisees going, consulted among themselves how they might ensnare him in his speech. ¹⁶ And they send to him their disciples with the Herodians, saying : " Master, we know that thou art a true speaker, and teachest the way of God in truth, neither carest thou for any man ; for thou dost not regard the

person of men.   17 Tell us, therefore, what dost thou think : Is it lawful to give tribute to Cæsar, or not ? "   18 But Jesus knowing their wickedness, saith : " Why do ye tempt me, ye hypocrites ?   19 Show me the coin of the tribute."   And they offered him a penny.   20 And Jesus saith to them : " Whose is this image and the inscription ? "   21 They say to him : " Cæsar's." Then he saith to them : " Render, therefore, to Cæsar the things that are Cæsar's ; and to God, the things that are God's."

MARK XII. 13-17.

13 And they send to him some of the pharisees and of the Herodians that they might catch him in his words.   14 And they coming, say to him : " Master, we know that thou art a true speaker, and carest not for any man ; for thou regardest not the person of men, but teachest the way of God in truth.   Is it lawful to give tribute to Cæsar ; or shall we not give it ? "   15 And he knowing their wiliness, saith to them : " Why do ye tempt me ?   Bring me a penny that I may see it."   16 And they brought it to him.   And he saith to them : " Whose is this image and the inscription ? "   They say to him : " Cæsar's." 17 And Jesus answering, said to them : " Render, therefore, to Cæsar, the things that are Cæsar's ; and to God, the things that are God's."   And they marvelled at him.

LUKE XX. 20-26.

20 And being upon the watch, they sent spies, who should feign themselves just, that they might take hold of him in his words, that they might deliver him up to the authority and power of the governor.   21And they asked him, saying : " Master, we know that thou speakest and teachest rightly, and thou dost not respect any person, but teachest the way of God in truth.   22 Is it lawful for us to give tribute to Cæsar, or not ?" 23 But he, considering their guile, said to them : " Why do ye tempt me ?   24 Show me a penny.   Whose image and inscription hath it ? "   They answering, said to him : " Cæsar's."   25 And he saith to them : " Render, therefore, to Cæsar, the things that are Cæsar's ; and to God, the things that are God's."   26 And they could not reprehend his word before the people ; and wondering at his answer, they held their peace.

III.—COMBINED NARRATIVE.

Then the pharisees going, consulted among themselves how they might ensnare him in his speech.   And being upon the watch, they sent to him spies, who should feign themselves just, some of the pharisees their disciples, with the Herodians, that they might catch him in his words, [and] that they might deliver him up to the authority and power of the governor.   And they coming, asked him, saying to him : " Master, we know that thou art a true speaker, and that thou speakest and teachest rightly, and carest not for any man ; for thou regardest not the person of men, but teachest the way of God in truth. Tell us, there- fore, what dost thou think : Is it lawful for us to give tribute to Cæsar, or not ? " But Jesus knowing their wickedness [and] considering their guile, said to them : " Why do ye tempt me, ye hypocrites ? Show me a penny, the coin of the tribute, that I may see it." And they offered him a penny. And Jesus saith to them : " Whose is this image and the inscription ? " They answering, said to him : " Cæsar's." And then Jesus answering, said to them : " Render, therefore, to Cæsar, the things that are Cæsar's ; and to God, the things that are God's." And they could not reprehend his word before the people ; and wondering at his answer, they held their peace.

IV.—NOTES.

Introductory. The circumstances in which this interview took place, have already been described in the explanation of the gospel assigned for the Seventeenth Sunday after Pentecost, and in that for the Nineteenth. It has been said that, when Christ, on the Wednesday morning before his death, " was teaching the people in the temple, and preaching the gospel, the chief-priests and the scribes with the ancients met together " (Luke xx. 1) around him. They were clearly delegates from each order of the Sanhedrim or Council ; and they were sent in order that, challenging Christ's authority (Matth. xxi. 23), they might interrupt his work, or in order that by their pre- tended difficulties, they might draw from him some expression to be afterwards used in evidence against him. Throughout the day they returned again and again to the charge ; and one of these efforts is recorded in the present passage by St. Matthew and in the Parallel Passages by SS. Mark and Luke.

In the parable of " the wicked husbandmen " (Matth. xxi. 33-44 ; Mark xii. 1-11 ; Luke xx. 9-18), and in that of " the marriage of the king's son " (Matth. xxii. 2-14), Christ had warned his enemies of the ruin of their country and of the repro- bation of their race—the well-deserved punishment of wilful blindness and abuse of grace. The Heavenly Physician was seeking to heal the spiritual diseases of these wicked men ; but, like patients in a violent fever, they were enraged against their Saviour ; and

V. 15. Then the pharisees going, consulted among them- selves, how they might ensnare him, in his speech.

The verb employed by the evangelist, *i.e.*, παγιδεύειν is from παγίς = a *net*, or *snare*, or covert means of destruction. used for catching wild animals in the chase. It is, therefore, very expressive, and indicates clearly the insidious and deadly purpose of Christ's enemies who were " seeking to lay hands on him," but " feared the multitudes " (Matth. xxi. 46). " Omnis quidem malitia confunditur aliquoties ratione veritatis, corrigitur autem nunquam, maxime eorum qui proposito malo et non ignorantia peccant. Eorum malignitas ex una parte confusa aliunde sibi aditum adinvenit ; animus enim malus, quanto magis veritatem audierit, eo amplius in malitiam excitatur " (Op. Imp., quoted by Knabenbauer, *in loco*).

The pharisees held their council ;

V. 16. And they send to him their disciples with the Herodians, saying: Master, we know that thou art a true speaker, and teachest the way of God in truth, neither carest thou for any man ; for thou dost not regard the person of men.

These words of St. Matthew are supplemented by SS. Mark and Luke ; and the Combined Narrative of the three evangelists may be constructed thus : " And being upon the watch, they sent to him spies, who should feign themselves just, some of the pharisees their disciples, with the Herodians, that they might catch him in his words, [and] that they might deliver him up to the authority and power of the governor. And they coming, asked him, saying to him : ' Master, we know that thou art a true speaker, and that thou speakest and teachest rightly, and carest not for any man ; for thou regardest not the person of men, but teachest the way of God in truth.' "

The pharisees, aware that their hypocritical character had been often denounced by Christ, sent to him on this occasion others whom they thought to be unknown to him and able to deceive him. These delegates of the pharisees are called by St. Matthew, " their disciples," by St. Mark, " some of the pharisees," by St. Luke, " spies, who should feign themselves just," that is, who should pretend that their question was inspired by a love of justice and a desire to know their obligations. It is added that with these delegates of the pharisees there were associated " Herodians " (Introduction, p. clxxvi.). This is a class of men which is not mentioned except in the gospels, and whose principles are little known. " Their political position, and consequent relation to the pharisees in the present case, has been variously explained. According to the common opinion (which, however, is put forward only as a conjecture by Origen), the Herodians as supporters of the family of Herod, who held their dominions by the grant of the Roman emperor, would be in favour of tribute to the supreme power, while the pharisees, as the rigid supporters of the law and the theocracy, and the enemies, as appears from Josephus (*Antiq*. xvii. 2, 4), of the

Herodian dynasty, would be opposed to it.   On this supposition, an affirmative reply to the question would give the latter a handle for accusing our Lord to the people as one who could not be their expected deliverer from a foreign yoke ; while a negative answer would give an opportunity to the former of accusing him before the Roman governor.   But it may be doubted whether the above conjecture respecting the Herodians is correct.   According to some critics, the name may be better explained by supposing them to have been supporters of the Herodian family as the last hope of retaining for the Jews a fragment of national government as distinguished from absolute dependence upon Rome as a province of the empire.   This view is advanced by Grotius, and supported by Meyer in this place, and by Ewald, *Die drei ersten Evangelien*, p. 196.   According to this supposition, the pharisees and the Herodians, however differing in other respects, were united in antagonism to the absolute dominion of Rome.   Whichever hypothesis be adopted, we learn from St. Luke (xx. 20) that their object was to take hold of our Lord's words that they might deliver him up to the Roman governor ; and the statement of the same evangelist that they ' feigned themselves just men ' seems to imply that they assumed a false character for this purpose.   Such a deception might be more easily attempted, if we suppose that both parties were ostensibly opponents of the Roman rule, though covertly acting in this instance in support of it " (*Speaker's Comm., in loco*).

In order to hide their malice and to lead our Lord into some declaration offensive to the civil rulers or to the people, these delegates of the pharisees praised the truthfulness of his teaching ; and they laid stress on the independence and equity of his decisions as a judge.   Thus when they said : " Neither carest thou for any man ; for thou dost not regard the person of men," they implied that he was free from that " respect of persons " so often denounced in the New Testament.   The idiom was Hebrew in its origin (פנים נשׂא = *to accept faces*), and referred to the crime of a judge who in his decision regards the *faces* or *external circumstances* of the litigants and not the *intrinsic* merits of the case.   The meaning is then : " Thou art always a fair and upright judge, uninfluenced by considerations of kindred, station, wealth, or power ; thou dost not dread either the anger of the civil authority or the indignation of the people, so as to swerve in the least from what is just and true."   (See Jansenius and McCarthy.)

With this guileful introduction they proposed the question :—

V. 17. Tell us, therefore, what dost thou think : Is it lawful to give tribute to Cæsar, or not ?

The diabolical hypocrisy of these men is manifested in the

terms used; for they do not ask: " Is there an obligation *of any kind* with regard to this matter ? " but, " Is it *permitted in conscience* ? " ($\check{\epsilon}\xi\epsilon\sigma\tau\iota\nu\ \delta o\hat{v}\nu a\iota\ \kappa\hat{\eta}\nu\sigma o\nu\ \ldots\ \hat{\eta}\ o\check{v};$). (Introduction, pp. cxix., cxx.) They pretend to consult for their eternal wel-fare and for the honour due to God, and not to care for the pecuniary loss or for the degradation of submission to a foreign government. When Pompey, after the capture of Jerusalem, made Judæa a Roman province, he imposed on the Jews an obliga-tion of contributing, *if required,* a certain sum for the expenses of the Republic; Julius Cæsar insisted on the right to collect this tribute; and Augustus, in a second census of Syria and Judæa under Quirinus, changed the occasional contribution into a fixed and annual poll-tax. Such a mark of subjection was borne with great reluctance by the Jews. Proud of their dignity as " the people of God," they said to Christ : " We are the seed of Abraham, and we have never been slaves to any man " (John viii. 33) ; and zealous for the laws, they considered themselves still bound by the command given to their fathers : " Thou shalt set up him [as king] whom the Lord thy God shall choose out of the number of thy brethren. Thou mayest not make a man of another nation king, who is not thy brother " (Deut. xvii. 15). It was forgotten that now the circumstances were changed ; that even in former times, God had commanded them to accept as the punishment of their sins the dominion of the Chaldeans ; and that he had declared them to be the subjects of Sesac, the king of Egypt (2 Paralipomenon xii. 8). Influenced by this rebellious disposition, the people rose in revolt under fanatical leaders, such as Theodas, before the time of Christ (Acts v. 36), and Judas of Galilee, a few years before the interview here recorded (Acts v. 37 ; Josephus : *Antiq. Jud.* Lib. xviii., cap. 2 ; Eusebius : *Hist.* Lib. i., cap. 5). Because, therefore, the pharisees with their strict views on the law favoured this resistance to Roman authority, and had with them the followers of Herod, who was the servant of Rome, they felt assured that in any reply to their questions, Jesus would be ensnared. If he denied the right to pay tribute, he could on the evidence of the Herodians be accused before Pilate as a fomenter of sedition : if he admitted that right he could be accused before the people as one who would violate the law by subjecting the chosen nation of God to a foreign and pagan ruler.

Although either answer would have served their purpose, we learn from the words of St. Luke (" that they might deliver him up to the power and authority of the governor ") that the pharisees expected a prohibition of the hateful tax ;

Vv. 18, 19. **But Jesus knowing their wickedness, said : Why do ye tempt me, ye hypocrites ? Show me the coin of the tribute. And they offered him a penny.**

According to St. Luke, the pharisees, with the intention of deceiving Jesus, had sent to him "spies who should feign themselves just." Our Lord showed that he was aware of "their wickedness" ($\pi o\nu\eta\rho\acute{\iota}a\nu = malice$) concealed with such care; and he could have declined to reply. In order, however, to show that they could not ensnare him, but were rather laying a snare for themselves, he asked for the "coin of the tribute." From the last words of verse 18, we learn that this was the *denarius*—a small silver Roman coin, equal in value to the Attic *drachma* and to about 9½d. of our money (Introduction, p. cxxii.). Some commentators, such as Jansenius of Ghent, find a difficulty in reconciling the present passage with Matthew xvii. 23, where it is said that a tax of two drachmas was required from each person. This difficulty is easily solved; for, as the tax here referred to was certainly a *civil* tax paid to the emperor, so that spoken of in Matth. xvii. 23 was certainly the *religious* contribution paid annually at this period by each Jew of twenty years of age for the support of the temple at Jerusalem, and exacted later on for that of the temple of Jupiter Capitolinus. (See Knabenbauer, *In Matth.* xvii. 23; Josephus, *Antiq.* xviii. 9, 1; *Bell. Jud.* vii. 6.)

The pharisees show the *denarius* or penny;

V. 20. And Jesus saith to them: Whose is this image and the inscription?

In ancient times when a man's possessions consisted in the number of his flocks, coins amongst the Romans bore the image of a sheep (*pecus*), hence the Latin name for money (*pecunia*); afterwards, according to Pliny (Lib. 23), that people used symbolical figures, *e.g.*, Janus, two-horse chariots, four-horse chariots, and arms; still later, their coins bore the images of the consuls; and last of all came the effigy of the emperors with an appropriate inscription. It is probable that there was no coinage amongst the Hebrews until the Babylonian Captivity. When there was, the Jewish rulers did not at first follow this custom of the Romans; but Herod Philip is said to have stamped his money with the image of his imperial master (Ratti, *Gospels of the Sundays*, etc., and Cambridge Bible, *in loco*).

To our Lord's question the pharisees and Herodians could give but one reply; and so

V. 21. They say to him: Cæsar's. Then he saith to them: Render, therefore, to Cæsar the things that are Cæsar's; and to God the things that are God's.

The effigy on the coin presented to Christ was probably that of Tiberius Cæsar, now in the fifteenth year of his reign from the death of Augustus; and according to Bloomfield (*in loco*),

the inscription was :   ΚΑΙΣΑΡ ΑΥΓΟΥΣΤ :   ΙΟΥΔΑΙΑΣ ΕΑΛΩΚΥΙΑΣ =
Cæsar Augustus : [ruler] of conquered Judæa.   According to
Hastings (*Dictionary of the Bible*, art. *Money*) the following is
the inscription of a *denarius* of the reign of Tiberius :—

> *Obv.*—TI. CÆSAR DIVI AUG. F[ILIUS] AUGUSTUS. Head of
> Tiberius, right, laureated.

> *Rev.*—PONTIF. MAXIM.   Livia seated, r., holding sceptre and
> flower.

Christ was well aware of the reply which would be given by
the pharisees ; but he asked his question that he might the more
effectually confound these hypocrites by their own confession.
In the first part of his answer, then, he said equivalently : " Since
this coin bears the image of the Roman emperor, and is current
amongst yourselves, you acknowledge your subjection to that
emperor as your ruler, and you should, therefore, pay the taxes
he imposes.   You cannot accept the coin and deny the authority of him who issues it."   The principle on which the argument
rests is one admitted by all ; and according to Maimonides, a
maxim of the Jewish rabbins was : " Wherever a king's money
is current, there the people acknowledge that king for their
lord " (McCarthy).   The principle is confirmed by the fact
that in token of their autonomy the Jews received from
Antiochus leave to coin money in the time of the Machabees
(I Mach. xv. 6, 7), and that the exercise of this right was attempted
by them in the rebellion of Bar-Cochba.

Against the validity of the argument it is said that, before
the Jews were conquered by Rome, they had current amongst
them both Roman and Greek money.   It should be remembered,
however, that there is a difference between this latter case and
that of the Jews in the time of Christ.   In Judæa before the
Roman conquest, the money of other nations was freely used
for convenience in commercial transactions ; but in the time
of Christ, the use of the Roman money in payment of tribute was
an obligation imposed by the imperial authority.   The word
νόμισμα being derived from νόμος = " *a law*," this νόμισμα τὸυ κήνσου
was not merely the coin *used for convenience* in paying the tax :
it was a coin which, *as determined by law*, would *alone* be accepted
for that purpose.   Because, then, on the one hand, St. Matthew
tells us that the piece of money produced for our Lord's inspection
was the small silver Roman *denarius* or *silver penny*, and because
on the other, we learn from Pliny (Lib. 23, cap. 3) that the tribute
imposed by the Romans on conquered nations had to be paid in
this silver coin, it follows that by the very production of the
denarius as their *tax-money*, the pharisees acknowledged themselves to be subject to the authority of Rome.

With regard to both parts of Christ's answer it has been well said : " Our Lord defeats the designs of his enemies by appealing to their own admission.   By accepting the coinage of Cæsar, they had themselves acknowledged his supremacy in temporal things, and consequently his claim to tribute.   But the answer goes further.   The followers of Judas of Galilee regarded the authority of Cæsar as incompatible with that of God.   Our Lord distinguishes between temporal and spiritual sovereignty, and shows that the two are not opposed to each other.   God was no longer, as of old, the civil Ruler of his people.   They had rejected his authority, and he had given them over to a foreign power, who reigned and claimed tribute by his ordinance (*cf.* Rom. xiii. 1-7).   But God was still, and must ever be the spiritual Ruler of the world, and to him now as ever worship and obedience were due.   It was a striking comment on this answer when, three days afterwards, Christ declared before Pilate : ' My kingdom is not of this world,' and the chief-priests, in demanding his death, declared : ' We have no king but Cæsar.'   The interpretation of those commentators who understand by ' the things that are God's ' the tribute for the service of the temple (ch. xvii. 24) seems altogether inadequate."   (*Speaker's Comm., in loco.*)

The three evangelists record the utter discomfiture of the enemies of our Lord ; and the combined statement of these sacred writers may be thus presented : " Hearing this, they wondered at him ; and they could not reprehend his word before the people ; and wondering at his answer, they held their peace ; and leaving him, they went their ways."

V.—MORAL REFLECTIONS.

1. No man, however holy, can hope to escape from calumny and detraction, when Jesus Christ was constantly assailed by malice.   Our Divine Master permitted these attacks that he might give us instruction on two important points.   In the first place, he teaches us to be neither astonished nor cast down when we are the objects of this form of uncharitableness : in the second, he indicates the mildness and self-restraint with which we should act in such painful circumstances.   How different is our conduct from that of Jesus Christ !   If we consider the effects produced on us by the malice of enemies, we shall see that these effects are ordinarily discouragement and distress of mind, often impatience and anger.   When we learn that others have attacked our character, or circulated evil reports about us, our first effort is to discover the authors of this wickedness.   How blind we are in this, and how much better would it be not to know the name of the enemy !   We should thus avoid on the

one hand the temptation to avenge ourselves, and on the other, the danger of making for ourselves an irreconcilable foe. Ordinarily it matters little to know the source of the detraction or calumny; but it is of great importance to examine with care if the accusation may have any apparent foundation in our conduct. The charges against us can in three ways be made to promote our salvation—if we support them with patience, if we offer to God the pain they cause us, and if we reform the defects which they bring under our notice. Detraction and calumny are vices which render odious the person who is guilty of them; but too great a susceptibility under detraction or calumny is a defect which renders very unhappy him who is thus attacked. Often the charge against us might have been forgotten if we did not call attention to it by our defence. We complain that evil reports are spread abroad; but frequently it is we who assist our enemy by our reference to these reports. Our self-love represents as manifest injustice all criticism of our conduct; but with a little attention and impartiality, we may nearly always see that we have drawn upon ourselves what at first sight we think we have not merited. The charge made against us appears a calumny, and may be such; but is it not possible that we have given to it an appearance of truth by our imprudence, or aroused the ill-feeling of our enemy by unfriendly acts? The certain means of living in peace may be included under two heads: not to give offence to others by our own words or actions, and not to be lightly offended at those of others. Of these two duties, the one is suggested by charity, and the other by humility. Let us love our neighbour, and we shall carefully avoid what may wound him: let us recognise our weakness and defects, and we shall feel the justice of the humiliations we have to endure.

2. If in one respect the answer of Jesus Christ to the insidious question of the pharisees did not contain all they had hoped to hear him say, on the other hand it gave them more instruction than they had asked for. In his reply, our Divine Master made submission to supreme rulers a precept of his religion, and gave to secular authority the sanction of his own: he commanded us to give our rulers without exception all that is their due, whilst we render to God all that belongs to the divine service. Hitherto nations were subject to their kings through fear; and kings on their side were in terror lest this bond of servitude should be broken. Mutual suspicions and reciprocal dread tormented both monarch and subjects; and this state of things was the occasion of harrowing oppression and of revolts. Jesus Christ re-established confidence between the ruler and the subject, by banishing the jealousies of the one and removing the unrest of the other. Religion rendered submission absolute, and security ensured moderation in the exercise of authority

How noble is the obedience of the Christian who learns from St. Paul. " There is no power but from God ; and those that are, are ordained of God. . . . Wherefore, be subject of necessity, not only for wrath, but also for conscience' sake " (Rom. xiii. 1, 5). As it is not founded on temporal motives but on the divine law, this obedience is not venal nor degrading ; and being independent of human favours, all passive as it is, it bears the noble character of true liberty.

TWENTY-THIRD SUNDAY AFTER PENTECOST.

I.—TEXTS.

GREEK.

MATTHEW IX. 18-26

¹⁸ Ταῦτα αὐτοῦ λαλοῦντος αὐτοῖς, ἰδοὺ ἄρχων εἷς προσελθὼν προσεκύνει αὐτῷ, λέγων· ὅτι ἡ θυγάτηρ μου ἄρτι ἐτελεύτησεν· ἀλλὰ ἐλθὼν ἐπίθες τὴν χεῖρά σου ἐπ᾽ αὐτήν, καὶ ζήσεται. ¹⁹ Καὶ ἐγερθεὶς ὁ Ἰησοῦς ἠκολούθησεν αὐτῷ, καὶ οἱ μαθηταὶ αὐτοῦ. ²⁰ Καὶ ἰδοὺ γυνὴ αἱμορροοῦσα δώδεκα ἔτη, προσελθοῦσα ὄπισθεν, ἥψατο τοῦ κρασπέδου τοῦ ἱματίου αὐτοῦ. ²¹ Ἔλεγεν γὰρ ἐν ἑαυτῇ· Ἐὰν μόνον ἅψωμαι τοῦ ἱματίου αὐτοῦ, σωθήσομαι. ²² Ὁ δὲ Ἰησοῦς στραφεὶς, καὶ ἰδὼν αὐτήν, εἶπεν· Θάρσει, θύγατερ· ἡ πίστις σου σέσωκέν σε. Καὶ ἐσώθη ἡ γυνὴ ἀπὸ τῆς ὥρας ἐκείνης. ²³ Καὶ ἐλθὼν ὁ Ἰησοῦς εἰς τὴν οἰκίαν τοῦ ἄρχοντος, καὶ ἰδὼν τοὺς αὐλητὰς, καὶ τὸν ὄχλον θορυβούμενον, ἔλεγεν· ²⁴ Ἀναχωρεῖτε· οὐ γὰρ ἀπέθανεν τὸ κοράσιον, ἀλλὰ καθεύδει. Καὶ κατεγέλων αὐτοῦ. ²⁵ Ὅτε δὲ ἐξεβλήθη ὁ ὄχλος, εἰσελθὼν ἐκράτησεν τῆς χειρὸς αὐτῆς, καὶ ἠγέρθη τὸ κοράσιον. ²⁶ Καὶ ἐξῆλθεν ἡ φήμη αὕτη εἰς ὅλην τὴν γῆν ἐκείνην.

VULGATE.

MATTHEW IX. 18-26.

¹⁸ Hæc illo loquente ad eos, ecce princeps unus accessit, et adorabat eum dicens : Domine, filia mea modo defuncta est ; sed veni, impone manum tuam super eam, et vivet. ¹⁹ Et surgens Jesus, sequebatur eum, et discipuli ejus. ²⁰ Et ecce mulier quæ sanguinis fluxum patiebatur duodecim annis, accessit retro, et tetigit fimbriam vestimenti ejus. ²¹ Dicebat enim intra se : Si tetigero tantum vestimentum ejus, salva ero. ²² At Jesus conversus et videns eam, dixit : Confide, filia, fides tua te salvam fecit. Et salva facta est mulier ex illa hora. ²³ Et cum venisset Jesus in domum principis, et vidisset tibicines et turbam tumultuantem, dicebat : ²⁴ Recedite ; non est enim mortua puella, sed dormit. Et deridebant eum. ²⁵ Et cum ejecta esset turba, intravit, et tenuit manum ejus. Et surrexit puella. ²⁶ Et exiit fama hæc in universam terram illam.

II.—ENGLISH TRANSLATION WITH PARALLEL PASSAGES FROM SS. MARK AND LUKE.

MATTHEW IX. 18-26.

18 As he was speaking these things unto them, behold, a certain ruler came up, and adored him, saying : " Lord, my daughter is even now dead ; but come, lay thy hand upon her, and she shall live." 19 And Jesus rising up, followed him with his disciples. 20 And behold, a woman who was troubled with an issue of blood twelve years, came behind him, and touched the hem of his garment. 21 For she said within herself : " If I shall touch only his garment, I shall be healed." 22 But Jesus turning and seeing her, said : " Be of good heart, daughter, thy faith hath made thee whole." And the woman was healed from that hour. 23And when Jesus was come into the house of the ruler, and saw the minstrels and the multitude making a tumult, he said : 24 " Give place ; for the maiden is not dead, but sleepeth." And they laughed him to scorn. 25 And when the multitude had been put out, he went in, and took her by the hand. And the maiden arose. 26 And the fame of this went abroad into all that country.

MARK V. 22-43.

22 And there cometh one of the rulers of the synagogue named Jairus ; and seeing him, he falleth down at his feet. 23 And he besought him much, saying " My daughter is at the point of death. Come, lay thy hand upon her that she may be safe and may live." 24 And he went with him, and a great multitude followed him, and they thronged him. 25 And a woman who was under an issue of blood for twelve years, 26 and had suffered many things from many physicians, and had spent all that she had, and was nothing the better, but rather worse, 27 when she had heard of Jesus, came in the crowd behind him, and touched his garment. 28 For she said : " If I shall touch only his garment, I shall be healed." 29 And forthwith the fountain of her blood was dried up, and she felt in her body that she was healed of the evil. 30 And immediately Jesus knowing in himself the virtue that had proceeded from him, turning to the multitude, said : " Who hath touched my garments ? " 31 And his disciples said to him : " Thou seest the multitude thronging thee, and sayest thou : ' Who hath touched me ? ' " 32 And he looked about to see her who had done this. 33 But the woman fearing and trembling, knowing what was done in her, came and fell down before him, and told him all the truth. 34 And he said to her : " Daughter, thy faith hath made thee whole . go in peace, and be thou healed of thy disease." 35 While he was yet speaking,

some come from the house of the ruler of the synagogue, saying :
" Thy daughter is dead : why dost thou trouble the Master any
further ? "   ³⁶ But Jesus having heard the word that was spoken,
saith to the ruler of the synagogue : " Fear not : only believe."
³⁷ And he suffered not any man to follow him, but Peter, and
James, and John the brother of James.   ³⁸ And they come to
the house of the ruler of the synagogue and he seeth a tumult,
and people weeping and wailing much.   ³⁹ And going in, he saith to
them : " Why make you this tumult, and weep ?   The maiden
is not dead, but sleepeth."   ⁴⁰ And they laughed him to scorn.
But he having put them all out, taketh the father and the mother
of the maiden and them that were with him, and entereth in
where the maiden was lying.   ⁴¹ And taking the maiden by the
hand, he saith to her · " Talitha cumi," which, being interpreted,
is : " Maiden, I say to thee : ' Arise.' "   ⁴² And immediately the
maiden arose and walked.   And she was twelve years old.   And
they were astonished with a great astonishment.   ⁴³ And he
charged them strictly that no man should know it ; and he commanded that something should be given her to eat.

LUKE VIII. 41-56.

⁴¹ And behold, there came a man whose name was Jairus, and
he was a ruler of the synagogue.   And he fell down at the feet
of Jesus, beseeching him that he would come into his house ;
⁴² for he had an only daughter almost twelve years old, and
she was dying.   And it happened as he went, that he was
thronged by the multitudes.   ⁴³ And there was a certain woman
having an issue of blood twelve years, who had spent all her
substance on physicians, and could not be healed by any.   ⁴⁴ She
came behind him, and touched the hem of his garment ; and
immediately the issue of her blood stopped.   ⁴⁵ And Jesus
said : " Who is it that touched me ? "   And all denying, Peter
and they that were with him said : " Master, the multitudes
throng and press thee, and dost thou say : ' Who touched me ? ' "
⁴⁶ And Jesus said : " Somebody hath touched me ; for I know
that virtue is gone out from me."   ⁴⁷ And the woman seeing
that she was not hid, came trembling, and fell down before his
feet, and declared before all the people for what cause she had
touched him, and how she was immediately healed.   ⁴⁸ But he
said to her : " Daughter, thy faith hath made thee whole.   Go
thy way in peace."   ⁴⁹ As he was yet speaking, there cometh
one to the ruler of the synagogue, saying to him : " Thy daughter
is dead : trouble him not."   ⁵⁰ And Jesus hearing this word,
answered the father of the maiden : Fear not : believe only,
and she shall be safe."   ⁵¹ And when he was come to the house
he suffered not any man to go in with him, but Peter, and James,

and John, and the father and mother of the maiden. [52] And all wept and mourned for her. But he said : " Weep not ; the maiden is not dead, but sleepeth." [53] And they laughed him to scorn, knowing that she was dead. [54] But he taking her by the hand, cried out, saying : " Maiden, arise," [55] And her spirit returned, and she arose immediately. And he bid them give her to eat. [56] And her parents were astonished, and these he charged to tell no man what was done.

III.—COMBINED NARRATIVE.

As he was speaking these things unto them, behold, a certain ruler of the synagogue named Jairus came up, and seeing him, he fell down at the feet of Jesus, and adored him, beseeching him that he would come into his house ; for he had an only daughter almost twelve years old, and she was dying. And he besought him much, saying : " Lord, my daughter is at the point of death, [or] is even now dead ; but come, lay thy hand upon her that she may be safe and may live." And Jesus rising up, followed him with his disciples. And it happened as he went, that a great multitude followed him ; and they thronged him. And behold, there was a certain woman who was troubled with an issue of blood twelve years ; and she had suffered many things from many physicians, and had spent all that she had, and was nothing the better, but rather worse. When she had heard of Jesus, she came in the crowd behind him, and touched the hem of his garment ; for she said within herself : " If I shall touch only his garment, I shall be healed." And forthwith the fountain of her blood was dried up ; and she felt in her body that she was healed. And immediately Jesus, knowing in himself the virtue that had proceeded from him, turning to the multitude, said : " Who hath touched my garments ? Who is it that touched me ? " And all denying, Peter and his disciples that were with him said : " Master, thou seest the multitude throng and press thee, and sayest thou : ' Who hath touched me ? ' " And Jesus said : " Somebody hath touched me ; for I know that virtue is gone out from me." And he looked about to see her who had done this. And the woman, seeing that she was not hid, fearing and trembling, [and] knowing what was done to her, came and fell down before his feet, and told him all the truth, and declared before all the people for what cause she had touched him, and how she was immediately healed. But Jesus turning and seeing her, said to her : " Be of good heart, daughter, thy faith hath made thee whole. Go thy way in peace, and be thou healed of thy disease." And the woman was healed from that hour. As he was yet speaking, some come from the house of the ruler of the synagogue, saying to him : " Thy daughter is dead. Why dost thou trouble the Master any further ? Trouble him not." But Jesus having heard the word that was spoken, said to the ruler of the synagogue, the father of the maiden : " Fear not : only believe, and she shall be safe." And they come into the house of the ruler of the synagogue. And when Jesus was come into the house of the ruler he admitted not any man to follow him, but Peter, and James, and John the brother of James, and the father and mother of the maiden. And all wept and mourned for her. And he saw the minstrels and the multitude making a tumult, and people weeping and wailing much. But he going in, said to them : " Why make this tumult and weep ? Weep not. Give place ; for the maiden is not dead, but sleepeth." And they laughed him to scorn, knowing that she was dead. And when the multitude had been put out, he taketh the father and the mother of the maiden and them that were with him, and entereth in where the maiden was lying. And taking the maiden by the hand, he cried out, saying to her : " Talitha cumi," which, being interpreted, is : " Maiden, I say to thee : Arise." And immediately her spirit returned ; and the maiden arose immediately and walked. And her parents were astonished with a great astonishment. And he charged them strictly to tell no man what was done, [and] that no man should know it. And he commanded that something should be given her to eat. And the fame of this went abroad into all that country.

IV.—NOTES.

Introductory. These two miracles were wrought towards the end of the second year of our Lord's public life, and are recorded by the three evangelists, SS. Matthew, Mark, and Luke. Having spoken in the neighbourhood of Capharnaum the many parables narrated in the 13th chapter of St. Matthew, Christ passed over the lake of Genesareth to the country of the Gerasenes (Introduction, p. xxxviii.), and during the journey calmed a storm which had suddenly sprung up (Matth. viii. 23-27 ; Mark iv. 36-40 ; Luke viii. 22-25). When he had freed the Gerasene demoniac from a legion of devils, the people of that district requested him to depart (Matth. viii. 28-34 ; Mark v. 1-20 ; Luke viii. 26-39). He returned across the lake to Capharnaum (Mark v. 21 ; Luke viii. 40), and there in an interview with some disciples of John the Baptist, heard the charge against his followers : " Why do we and the pharisees fast often, but thy disciples do not fast ? " (Matth. ix. 14).

The evangelist gives Christ's defence of this apparent absence of mortification (Matth. ix. 15-17), and then says that

Vv. 18, 19. **As he was speaking these things unto them, behold, a certain ruler came up, and adored him, saying: Lord, my daughter is even now dead; but come, lay thy hand upon her, and she shall live. And Jesus rising up, followed him with his disciples.**

St. Matthew, who dwells so much on the discourses of Christ, is remarkable for brevity when narrating the miracles; but the scope of St. Luke's gospel, and still more that of St. Mark's, required a fuller description of these divine works. Hence, as may be gathered from the Parallel Passages, many details which are omitted by the first evangelist on this occasion, are supplied by the two other sacred writers. The three narratives may be thus combined: " As he was speaking these things unto them, behold, a certain ruler of the synagogue named Jairus came up, and seeing him, he fell down at the feet of Jesus, and adored him, beseeching him that he would come into his house; for he had an only daughter almost twelve years old, and she was dying. And he besought him much, saying: ' Lord, my daughter is at the point of death, [or] is even now dead; but come, lay thy hand upon her that she may be safe, and may live.' And Jesus rising up, followed him with his disciples. And it happened as he went, that a great multitude followed him."

Amongst the Jews it was not permitted to offer sacrifice except in the temple of Jerusalem, but other religious exercises, *e.g.*, the reading of the Sacred Scriptures, the singing of hymns, and prayer could be, and often were, performed in common both in the temple itself and in the private houses of the Jews. It appears that from the time of the Machabees buildings were specially erected for this latter purpose in the different cities (Introduction, pp. cxli.-cxliii.). By the Hellenist Jews, these were called *synagogues* or *oratories*; whilst amongst the Jews in Palestine, they were known as בתי הכנסת or *houses of assembly*. In each synagogue, there were four classes of officers: 1° the *servants of the synagogue*, to whom were committed the menial duties; 2° the *legates* or *deputies*, who recited the public prayers, and communicated with other similar communities abroad; 3° the *ancients*, who consulted on every grave matter affecting the Jewish body; and 4° the *rulers* or *directors* of the public religious service, amongst whom one received the name of Nazan or head of the synagogue. Although it is likely that the office of ruler was in nearly every instance held by the pharisees, now for some time the declared enemies of Christ (Mark iii. 6), still the dignitary who on this occasion approached our Lord, fell at his feet, adored him, and besought him " that he would come into his house." St. Luke tells us graphically the reason of this man's grief and of his earnest prayer, namely, that " he had an only daughter about twelve years old, and she was dying."

But a difficulty here presents itself; for in recording the prayer of the ruler, St. Matthew has the words: "My daughter is even now dead." This appears at first sight to be irreconcilable with the statement of the other evangelists, according to whose account the child "was dying" (St. Luke), or was "at the point of death" (St. Mark). Remembering, however, that the man did not address Christ once only, but that, according to St. Mark, "he besought him much," we may accept as quite satisfactory the answer of Trench, who says: "When the father left his child, she was at the latest gasp; he knew not whether to regard her now as alive or dead; he only knew that life was ebbing so fast when he quitted her side, that she could scarcely be living still; and yet, having no certain notices of her death, he was perplexed whether to speak of her as departed or not, and thus at one moment would express himself in one language, at the next in another. Strange that a circumstance like this, so drawn from the life, so testifying to the reality of the things recorded, should be urged by some as a contradiction between one gospel and another!" (Trench: *Miracles*, p. 192.)

The prayer was heard. He who was yet to say: "Come to me all you that labour and are burdened, and I will refresh you" (Matth. xi. 28), acceded to the desire of the ruler. Jesus rising up, followed him, and was accompanied by his disciples and by a great multitude, who having heard the request, were anxious to see the result.

Vv. 20, 21. **And behold, a woman who was troubled with an issue of blood twelve years, came behind him, and touched the hem of his garment. For she said within herself: If I shall touch only his garment, I shall be healed.**

As in the history of the other miracle, so here, too, St. Matthew passes over many circumstances mentioned by SS. Mark and Luke. The words of the three evangelists may be thus combined: "And it happened as he went, that a great multitude followed him; and they thronged him. And behold, there was a certain woman who was troubled with an issue of blood twelve years; and she had suffered many things from many physicians, and had spent all that she had, and was nothing the better, but rather worse. When she had heard of Jesus, she came in the crowd behind him, and touched the hem of his garment; for she said within herself: "If I shall touch only his garment, I shall be healed."

The miserable condition of this poor woman is here graphically described by the evangelists, especially by St. Mark and by St. Luke. In the first place, she suffered from a disease so very dreadful that amongst the Jews it entailed a legal unclean-

ness ; secondly, in her case this disease had now lasted twelve
years ; thirdly, in seeking relief she " had suffered many things
from many physicians " (Introduction, p. xcvii.) ; fourthly, in
these efforts to recover her health she had spent all her substance,
thus adding poverty to physical pain ; and lastly, the effect of
all the remedies was not a recovery of health, but an aggravation
of her disorder.   All this is narrated by St. Mark to manifest
the goodness and power of Christ, who showed that he alone
can, and will, come to the succour of the afflicted when created
means have been tried in vain.   The woman had not seen any of
our Lord's miracles ; but, as St. Mark says, " she had heard of
Jesus."   Filled, then, with that wonderful faith which, according
to St. Paul, " cometh by hearing," she made her way through
the dense crowd up to Christ.   She did not come before him and
address him, as did the ruler, but she approached him from
behind, and secretly.   Shame and fear forbade any other course.
Labouring under an ailment which, according to the law (Lev.
xv. 25-28), excluded from intercourse with others and rendered
unclean all those who might come in contact with her, she felt
on the one hand, ashamed to make known her disease to Christ ;
whilst on the other, she feared lest she should be repelled by the
people as one who, by her presence, had defiled the whole multitude.   How wonderful was her faith !   Although her case was
despaired of by her medical attendants, and although she had
never seen any of Christ's miraculous cures, she said : " If I
shall touch only his garment, I shall be healed."   In other words,
she thought within herself : " I hear indeed that by the touch of
his hand he heals the other sick.   I cannot dare to wish that
with his hand he touch me, unclean as I am ; but such is my
belief in his power and in his holiness, that if I can touch only the
hem of his garment, I am confident that I shall recover the health
which hitherto, with much pain and expense, I have sought
for in vain."   From SS. Mark and Luke we learn that she carried
out her pious purpose ; and the former evangelist adds that
" forthwith the fountain of her blood was dried up, and she felt
in her body that she was healed of the evil."

The " hem of the garment " was a blue fringe which God
ordered to be worn by the Jews (Num. xv. 38-40 ; Deut. xxii. 12),
that, as by the sign of circumcision in their flesh, so by this
distinctive mark in their dress, they might be singled out from
all other peoples.   It was, then, a symbol of the wearer's holiness
of life, and, as the woman hoped to obtain her cure not only by the
exercise of Christ's power but also through a communication
of his sanctity, she wished to touch the symbol of his holiness
and acceptableness before God.

The miracle had been secretly wrought, and the woman would
have retired at once on finding herself healed ;

V. 22. But Jesus turning and seeing her, said : Be of good heart, daughter, thy faith hath made thee whole. And the woman was healed from that hour.

Here again, St. Matthew gives a mere summary, and his brief account must be thus completed from what is narrated by St. Mark and by St. Luke : " Immediately Jesus, knowing in himself the virtue that had proceeded from him, turning to the multitude, said : ' Who hath touched my garments ?   Who is it that touched me ? '   And all denying, Peter and his disciples that were with him said : ' Master, thou seest the multitude throng and press thee, and sayest thou : Who hath touched me ? '   And Jesus said · ' Somebody hath touched me ; for I know that virtue is gone out from me.'   And he looked about to see her who had done this.   And the woman, seeing that she was not hid, fearing and trembling, [and] knowing what was done to her, came and fell down before his feet, and told him all the truth, and declared before all the people for what cause she had touched him, and how she was immediately healed.   But Jesus turning and seeing her, said to her ·: ' Be of good heart, daughter, thy faith hath made thee whole.   Go thy way in peace, and be thou healed of thy disease.'   And the woman was healed from that hour."

When according to one evangelist Christ knew in himself the virtue that had gone out from him, and when another declares that Christ asserted this of himself, we are not to understand that the power of healing went forth locally from our Lord, but that this power which he had within him produced its external effect in the miraculous cure of the woman, and that he, not by any bodily change, but by his divine knowledge, was fully aware of the miracle which had taken place.

In the form of expression which he uses, the evangelist copies the words of Christ, whilst Christ accommodates his words to the capacity of an audience which looked upon his body as a vessel full of the power of healing and giving forth of that fullness to those in disease.   But if Christ was aware that the miracle had been wrought, and knew the person on whom it had been wrought, why did he make the inquiries which the evangelist records ?   He did so that, by the confession of all the circumstances made by the woman herself in the presence of the crowd, the fact of the miracle and its greatness might be rendered more evident.   But why did Christ in this instance depart from his custom of avoiding publicity and of even enjoining silence with regard to his miraculous cures ?   Why is it that he wished this healing to be heard of by the multitude, whilst on raising the daughter of Jairus to life, " he charged them (her parents) strictly that no man should know it " ?   According to Jansenius, he wished this miracle to be known for four reasons : *firstly*, because the glory of God which was the end of all Christ's work, would have been promoted but little were this altogether secret cure not to be made manifest ; *secondly*, that the imperfect faith of the ruler might be strengthened as a preparation for the blessing he was about to receive ; *thirdly*, to perfect the faith of the woman herself, who was so wanting in a true idea of Christ that she had hoped to escape his notice whilst she secured her liberation from disease ; *lastly*, our Lord wished thus to assure the woman of the permanence of her restoration to health.   Who this woman was, we do not know.   Sozomen, *Hist. Eccl.* l. v. 21, confirms the account of Eusebius, *Hist. Eccl.* l. vii. cap. 14, that she was a native of Cæsarea Philippi.   Sozomen adds that in his time, *i.e.*, at the beginning of the fourth century, her house was still shown in that city, and that before the entrance to the house there was a group of bronze statues representing, it was said, this woman in prayer before our Lord.   As we learn from the evangelist that the woman was reduced to poverty in seeking a cure at the hands of the physicians, the statues can hardly have been erected by herself.   They were subsequently destroyed by Julian the Apostate out of hatred for Christ, with whose miraculous work they were connected by tradition.

St. Matthew, whose narrative of the two miracles is very brief throughout, passes on to describe our Lord's arrival at the house of Jairus.   From the other two evangelists we learn that " as he (Christ) was yet speaking, some come from the house of the ruler of the synagogue, saying to him : ' Thy daughter is dead.   Why dost thou trouble the Master any further ?   Trouble him not.' But Jesus having heard the word that was spoken, said to the ruler of the synagogue, the father of the maiden : ' Fear not · only believe, and she shall be safe.'   And they come into the house of the ruler of the synagogue."

St. Matthew thus continues :—

V. 23. And when Jesus was come into the house of the ruler, and saw the minstrels and the multitudes making a tumult, he said, etc.

From the Parallel Passages we learn that, as at the Transfiguration on Mount Thabor and at the Agony in the Garden, three of the apostles were chosen to be present on this occasion in the chamber of death.   These three, " the most elect of the elected " (St. Chrys.), were : Peter, the Prince of the Apostles and ardent lover of our Lord ; James, the first of the twelve destined to seal his faith with his blood ; and John, the virgin " disciple whom Jesus loved."   The parents too (see Parallel Passages) were graciously permitted to behold a miracle in which they were so deeply interested (McCarthy).   This same author says : " It was the custom among the Jews to employ hired minstrels, who joined the friends in mourning over the dead. Among those hired for the purpose of mourning were wailing women 'skilful in lamentation' (Amos v. 16 ; Jeremias ix. 17), and 'singing men,' and 'flute players' (2 Par. xxxv. 25 ; Josephus, *Bell. Jud.* iii. 9, § 5). Indeed, among all the nations of antiquity the same usage prevailed (Herodotus ii. 85 ; Ovid, *Fast.* vi. 660) ; and according to the best informed modern travellers, it is still the practice in the East to employ professional mourners."

Speaking of those in the house of the dead maiden, St. Luke tells us that " all wept and mourned for her " (Introduction, p. ci.); and on combining the account of St. Mark with that of St. Matthew, we find that Christ at his entry " saw the minstrels and the multitude making a tumult, and people weeping and wailing much." As this scene of disturbance ill accorded with the solemnity of the occasion, our Lord said :

V. 24. Give place, for the maiden is not dead, but sleepeth. And they laughed him to scorn.

St. Luke adds the words : " Knowing that she was dead." " Paid mourners would not be called or assembled before death ; nor would people be seen 'weeping and wailing much' ; nor would the bystanders have laughed our Lord to scorn when he said : ' The maiden is not dead, but sleepeth ' (Matth., Mark). The very reason why they laughed him to scorn is explicitly stated by St. Luke (viii. 53) : ' And they laughed him to scorn, knowing that she was dead.' How *know* she was dead, if she was not ? St. Luke adds also that at the command of Christ ' her spirit returned,' implying surely previous death" (McCarthy). The bystanders understood our Lord to mean that death had not taken place in *any* sense ; but he, for the consolation especially of the parents, wished to make known that death had not now come *with its ordinary consequence* of no further awaking in this world. In the presence of him who had the power and intention of immediately raising the maiden to life, her death, like that of Lazarus, was but as a sleep. He, however, who had so often read the inmost thoughts of men, could not be ignorant of what had come to pass ; and that the maiden had really died is proved from the circumstances narrated by the evangelists.

When the death had been thus made certain to all, when the approaching resurrection had been obscurely but sufficiently promised by our Divine Lord,

V. 25. And when the multitude had been put out, he went in, and took her by the hand. And the maid arose.

As elsewhere in the cure of the sick, Christ here touched the dead body of the maiden, to make known the vivifying power of that sacred humanity by which, united as it was personally to the divinity, he was to restore all to the life of grace. St. Mark records the vernacular Aramaic expression "Talitha cumi," *i.e.*, " Maiden, arise," which Christ used on this occasion and which this evangelist doubtless had heard from St. Peter his master, one of the witnesses. According to St. Luke, Christ, in saying these words, " cried out," in order to signify that death to which all else must yield, was subject to him.

The dead maiden obeyed this voice of the Creator ; and, as St. Luke says, " her spirit returned," *i.e.*, the same soul and body that had been just separated, were once more united. In the Parallel Passages we read that, as a proof of restored life and vigour, " the damsel arose immediately and walked, and he (Christ) bid them (her parents) give her to eat. And her parents were astonished with great astonishment." Thus, too, in the resurrection of Lazarus Jesus " cried with a loud voice : ' Lazarus, come forth ' ; and presently he that had been dead, came forth " (John xi. 43, 44) ; and at a supper given to our Lord in the house of Martha and Mary, " Lazarus was one of them that were at table with him " (John xii. 2).

This was one of the three greatest miracles worked by Christ during his public life ;

V. 26. **And the fame of this went abroad into all that country.**

In St. Mark and St. Luke combined we read that Christ " charged them strictly to tell no man what was done, [and] that no man should know it." The reason of this command was the same as that for which our Lord excluded from the house all but the five witnesses—the parents of the child and the three apostles. He wished in the first place, not to arouse the envy of the pharisees ; again, he wished to guard against exciting a populace ever prone to sedition (John vi. 14, 15) ; lastly and most especially, he imposed this silence and caused his command to be recorded in the gospel as a lesson to his followers, that they should avoid vanity and ostentation even in circumstances where publicity would at first sight appear to be useful for the promotion of God's glory.

V.—MORAL REFLECTIONS.

1. The history of the ruler's young daughter brings to our mind the thought of death. More than any other, this thought is unwelcome to the greater part of mankind. We banish it as effectually as we can ; and when from time to time it forces itself upon us, it is, especially to the worldling, a source of affliction, of disturbance, and even of exasperation. " O death,"

says Ecclesiasticus, " how bitter is the remembrance of thee
to a man that hath peace in his possessions, to a man that is
at rest, and whose ways are prosperous in all things, and that
is yet able to take meat ! " (Ecclus. xli. 1, 2). Notwithstanding
all this, the thought of death was more than once commended
to the consideration of his disciples by their Divine Master ;
and the Holy Ghost has said : " In all thy works, remember
thy last end, and thou shalt never sin " (Ecclus. vii. 40).

2. What then have we to learn regarding death ? In the
first place, we must remember that death is inevitable ; for the
Apostle has written : " It is appointed unto men once to die,
and after this, the judgment " (Hebr. ix. 27). It is possible for
us to choose and to secure either a good or a bad death ; but
a power to which we must submit, will force us one day to undergo
this sentence passed on all mankind in the person of our first
father : " Thou shalt die " (Gen. ii. 17). Of all men who have
lived on earth, only two, Enoch and Elias, have not passed into
eternity through the gates of death ; but death still awaits them.
Each day we see around us men like to us—men who are leaving
our company to present themselves at the dread tribunal of
Christ. As, therefore, our turn must one day come, as we can
by no means escape this fate, should we not prepare ourselves
while time is given us ; and should not each of us apply to himself
the words spoken by the prophet Isaias to Ezechias : " Take
order with thy house ; for thou shalt die, and not live " (Isaias
xxxviii. 1) ?

3. Whilst we are certain that death awaits us, we are absolutely uncertain as to the time at which we shall die. This
moment will be known only when it is already come ; and until
then, it is a secret which God reserves for himself alone. What
God reveals on this subject, what he repeats in several passages
of the Sacred Scriptures, and what experience teaches us in the
history of others, is this, that however long deferred may be
the day of our death, it will be unexpected when it comes. We
know not the year, nor the week, nor the day, nor the hour.
As, therefore, we should prepare for death because we are sure
that it *will come*, so we should prepare immediately and be always
prepared because we know not *when it will come*. This is the
teaching of reason and of prudence ; but in revelation we have
a higher teacher than reason or prudence. Our Divine Master
while describing our uncertain tenure of life, draws the conclusion : " Watch ye, therefore, because ye know not at what
hour your Lord will come. But this know ye, that if the house-
holder knew at what hour the thief would come, he would certainly watch, and would not suffer his house to be broken open.
Wherefore be you also ready, because at what hour you know not,
the Son of Man will come. . . . . Blessed is that servant

whom when his lord shall come, he shall find so doing. **Amen** I say to you, he shall place him over all his goods. But if that evil servant shall say in his heart: My lord delayeth his coming and shall begin to strike his fellow-servants, and shall eat and drink with drunkards, the lord of that servant shall come in a day that he hopeth not, and at an hour that he knoweth not, and shall separate him, and appoint his portion with the hypocrites. There shall be weeping and gnashing of teeth" (Matth. xxiv 42-44 and 46-51).

4. Now if the fact that we shall die is certain, and if the time, place, and other circumstances of death are hidden from us, why is it that even amongst Christians the great majority do not live in preparation for this most important event? It is not because they fear their departure hence, and fearing it, fear to undertake anything that might bring it before their mind. The fear of death being implanted in our breast by nature and coming therefore from our Creator, cannot be in all circumstances reprehensible; but it becomes excessive and reprehensible if it be not moderated by love. According to St. Augustine, we should deal with death as we act with God. As God must be loved as well as feared, nay even, as he must be loved more than he is feared, so too, although on the one hand we should fear death, because on its character will depend our eternal lot, on the other hand, enlightened by faith and strengthened by grace, we should love and desire it, because God wills that by it we enter into the possession of our true life and eternal glory. The same St. Paul who said that "it is a fearful thing to fall into the hands of the living God" (Hebr. x. 31), has recorded his "desire to be dissolved and to be with Christ, a thing by far the better" (Philipp. i. 23).

Let us then prepare for death; and that we may do so continually, let us keep the thought of our last end ever before our eyes. This thought alone is an efficacious preservative against the sins to which we may be tempted; and it is a powerful incentive to repentance for those into which we may have fallen. "In all thy works remember thy last end, and thou shalt never sin" (Ecclus. vii. 40).

TWENTY-FOURTH SUNDAY AFTER PENTECOST.

I.—TEXTS.

GREEK.

MATTHEW XXIV. 15-35.

15 Ὅταν οὖν ἴδητε τὸ βδέλυγμα τῆς ἐρημώσεως, τὸ ῥηθὲν διὰ Δανιὴλ τοῦ προφήτου, ἑστὸς ἐν τόπῳ ἁγίῳ, ὁ ἀναγινώσκων νοείτω. **16** Τότε οἱ ἐν τῇ Ἰουδαίᾳ, φευγέτωσαν εἰς τὰ ὄρη. **17** Ὁ ἐπὶ τοῦ δώματος, μὴ καταβάτω ἆραί τι ἐκ τῆς οἰκίας αὐτοῦ. **18** Καὶ ὁ ἐν τῷ ἀγρῷ, μὴ ἐπιστρεψάτω ὀπίσω ἆραι τὸ ἱμάτιον αὐτοῦ. **19** Οὐαὶ δὲ ταῖς ἐν γαστρὶ ἐχούσαις, καὶ ταῖς θηλαζούσαις ἐν ἐκείναις ταῖς ἡμέραις. **20** Προσεύχεσθε δὲ ἵνα μὴ γένηται ἡ φυγὴ ὑμῶν χειμῶνος, μηδὲ σαββάτῳ. **21** Ἔσται γὰρ τότε θλίψις μεγάλη, οἵα οὐ γέγονεν ἀπ᾽ ἀρχῆς κόσμου ἕως τοῦ νῦν, οὐδ᾽ οὐ μὴ γένηται. **22** Καὶ εἰ μὴ ἐκολοβώθησαν αἱ ἡμέραι ἐκεῖναι, οὐκ ἂν ἐσώθη πᾶσα σάρξ· διὰ δὲ τοὺς ἐκλεκτοὺς κολοβωθήσονται αἱ ἡμέραι ἐκεῖναι. **23** Τότε ἐάν τις ὑμῖν εἴπῃ· Ἰδού, ὧδε ὁ Χριστός, ἢ ὧδε, μὴ πιστεύητε. **24** Ἐγερθήσονται γὰρ ψευδόχριστοι καὶ ψευδοπροφῆται, καὶ δώσουσιν σημεῖα μεγάλα καὶ τέρατα, ὥστε πλανῆσαι, εἰ δυνατὸν, καὶ τοὺς ἐκλεκτούς. **25** Ἰδού, προείρηκα ὑμῖν **26** Ἐὰν οὖν εἴπωσιν ὑμῖν· Ἰδού, ἐν τῇ ἐρήμῳ ἐστίν· μὴ ἐξέλθητε· Ἰδού, ἐν τοῖς ταμείοις· μὴ πιστεύσητε. **27** Ὥσ-

VULGATE.

MATTH. XXIV. 15-35.

15 Cum ergo videritis abominationem desolationis, quæ dicta est a Daniele propheta, stantem in loco sancto, qui legit, intelligat. **16** Tunc qui in Judæa sunt, fugiant ad montes; **17** et qui in tecto, non descendat tollere aliquid de domo sua; **18** et qui in agro, non revertatur tollere tunicam suam. **19** Væ autem prægnantibus, et nutrientibus in illis diebus! **20** Orate autem ut non fiat fuga vestra in hieme, vel sabbato; **21** erit enim tunc tribulatio magna, qualis non fuit ab initio mundi usque modo, neque fiet. **22** Et nisi breviati fuissent dies illi, non fieret salva omnis caro; sed propter electos breviabuntur dies illi. **23** Tunc si quis vobis dixerit: Ecce hic est Christus, aut illic, nolite credere. **24** Surgent enim pseudochristi et pseudoprophetæ, et dabunt signa magna et prodigia, ita ut in errorem inducantur (si fieri potest) etiam electi. **25** Ecce prædixi vobis. **26** Si ergo dixerint vobis: Ecce in deserto est, nolite exire:

περ γὰρ ἡ ἀστραπὴ ἐξέρχεται ἀπὸ
ἀνατολῶν καὶ φαίνεται ἕως δυσμῶν,
οὕτως ἔσται ἡ παρουσία τοῦ υἱοῦ τοῦ
ἀνθρώπου. ²⁸ ⁷Ὅπου ἐὰν ᾖ τὸ πτῶμα,
ἐκεῖ συναχθήσονται οἱ ἀετοί·

²⁹ Εὐθέως δὲ μετὰ τὴν θλίψιν τῶν
ἡμερῶν ἐκείνων ὁ ἥλιος σκοτισθήσε-
ται, καὶ ἡ σελήνη οὐ δώσει τὸ φέγγος
αὐτῆς, καὶ οἱ ἀστέρες πεσοῦνται ἀπὸ
τοῦ οὐρανοῦ, καὶ αἱ δυνάμεις τῶν οὐρανῶν σαλευθήσονται. ³⁰ Καὶ τότε
φανήσεται τὸ σημεῖον τοῦ υἱοῦ τοῦ
ἀνθρώπου ἐν οὐρανῷ· καὶ τότε κόψον-
ται πᾶσαι αἱ φυλαὶ τῆς γῆς, καὶ ὄψονται
τὸν υἱὸν τοῦ ἀνθρώπου ἐρχόμενον ἐπὶ
τῶν νεφελῶν τοῦ οὐρανοῦ, μετὰ δυ-
νάμεως καὶ δόξης πολλῆς. ³¹ Καὶ
ἀποστελεῖ τοὺς ἀγγέλους αὐτοῦ μετὰ
σάλπιγγος φωνῆς μεγάλης, καὶ ἐπισυ-
νάξουσιν τοὺς ἐκλεκτοὺς αὐτοῦ ἐκ τῶν
τεσσάρων ἀνέμων, ἀπ' ἄκρων οὐρανῶν
ἕως τῶν ἄκρων αὐτῶν.

³² Ἀπὸ δὲ τῆς συκῆς μάθετε τὴν
παραβολήν· Ὅταν ἤδη ὁ κλάδος αὐτῆς
γένηται ἀπαλὸς, καὶ τὰ φύλλα ἐκφύῃ,
γινώσκετε ὅτι ἐγγὺς τὸ θέρος. ³³ Οὕτως
καὶ ὑμεῖς, ὅταν ἴδητε πάντα ταῦτα,
γινώσκετε ὅτι ἐγγύς ἐστιν ἐπὶ θύραις.
³⁴ Ἀμὴν λέγω ὑμῖν, ὅτι οὐ μὴ παρέλθῃ
ἡ γενεὰ αὕτη, ἕως ἂν πάντα ταῦτα γένη-
ται· ³⁵ Ὁ οὐρανὸς καὶ ἡ γῆ παρελεύσε-
ται, οἱ δὲ λόγοι μου οὐ μὴ παρέλθωσιν.

Ecce in penetralibus, nolite credere. ²⁷ Sicut enim fulgur exit ab Oriente et paret usque in Occidentem, ita erit et adventus Filii hominis. ²⁸ Ubicumque fuerit corpus, illic congregabuntur et aquilæ.

²⁹ Statim autem post tribulationem dierum illorum, sol obscurabitur ; et luna non dabit lumen suum ; et stellæ cadent de cœlo ; et virtutes cœlorum commovebuntur. ³⁰ Et tunc parebit signum Filii hominis in cœlo ; et tunc plangent omnes tribus terræ ; et videbunt Filium hominis venientem in nubibus cœli cum virtute multa et majestate. ³¹ Et mittet angelos suos cum tuba et voce magna ; et congregabunt electos ejus a quatuor ventis, a summis cœlorum usque ad terminos eorum.

³² Ab arbore autem fici discite parabolam : Cum jam ramus ejus tener fuerit, et folia nata, scitis quia prope est æstas. ³³ Ita et vos quum videritis hæc omnia, scitote quia prope est in januis. ³⁴ Amen dico vobis, quia non præteribit generatio hæc, donec omnia hæc fiant. ³⁵ Cœlum et terra transibunt ; verba autem mea non præteribunt.

II.—ENGLISH TRANSLATION WITH PARALLEL PASSAGES FROM SS. MARK AND LUKE.

MATTHEW XXIV. 15-35.

15 " When, therefore, you shall see the abomination of desolation, which was spoken of by Daniel the prophet, standing in the holy place, let him that readeth, understand. **16** Then let them that are in Judæa, flee to the mountains ; **17** and let him that is on the house-top, not come down to take anything out of his house ; [18] and let him that is in the field not go back to take his coat.   [19] And woe to them that are with child, and that give suck in those days !   [20] But pray that your flight be not in the winter, nor on the sabbath ; [21] for there shall be then great tribulation, such as there hath not been from the beginning of the world until now, neither shall there be.   [22] And unless those days had been shortened, no flesh should be saved ; but for the sake of the elect those days shall be shortened. [23] Then if any man shall say to you : ' Lo, here is Christ, or there,' do not believe him.   [24] For false Christs and false prophets shall arise ; and they shall show great signs and wonders, insomuch as to deceive (if it be possible) even the elect.   [25] Behold, I have told it to you beforehand.   [26] If, therefore, they shall say to you : ' Behold, he is in the desert,' go ye not out ; ' Behold, he is in the closets,' believe it not.   [27] For as lightning cometh out of the East, and appeareth even unto the West, so shall also the coming of the Son of Man be.   [28] Wheresoever the body shall be, there shall the eagles also be gathered together.

[29] " And immediately after the tribulation of those days, the sun shall be darkened ; and the moon shall not give her light ; and the stars shall fall from heaven ; and the powers of heaven shall be moved.   [30] And then shall appear the sign of the Son of Man in heaven ; and then shall all the tribes of the earth mourn ; and they shall see the Son of Man coming in the clouds of heaven with much power and majesty.   [31] And he shall send his angels with a trumpet and a great voice ; and they shall gather together his elect from the four winds, from the farthest parts of the heavens to the utmost bounds of them.

[32] " But learn ye a parable from the fig-tree . When the branch thereof is now tender, and the leaves come forth, you know that summer is nigh   [33] So likewise, when ye shall see all these things, know that it is nigh, even at the doors.   [34] Amen I say to you, that this generation shall not pass away, till all these things be done.   [35] Heaven and earth shall pass away ; but my words shall not pass away."

MARK XIII. 14-31.

[14] " And when you shall see the abomination of desolation standing where it ought not : let him that readeth understand. Then let them that are in Judæa, flee to the mountains ; [15] and let him that is on the housetop, not go down into the house, nor enter therein, to take anything out of the house ; [16] and let him that shall be in the field, not turn back to take up his garment. [17] And woe to them that are with child, and that give suck in those days !   [18] But pray ye that these things happen not in winter. [19] For in those days there shall be such tribulations as were not from the beginning of the creation which God created until now,

neither shall there be.   20 And unless the Lord had shortened the days, no flesh should be saved ; but for the sake of the elect whom he hath chosen, he hath shortened the days.   21 And then, if any man shall say to you : ' Lo, here is Christ ' ; ' lo, he is there,' do not believe.   22 For false Christs and false prophets shall arise ; and they shall show signs and wonders, to seduce (if it be possible) even the elect.   23 Take you heed, therefore : behold, I have foretold all things to you.

24 " But in those days, after that tribulation, the sun shall be darkened ; and the moon shall not give her light ; 25 and the stars of heaven shall be falling down ; and the powers that are in heaven, shall be moved.   26 And then they shall see the Son of Man coming in the clouds with great power and glory.   27 And then shall he send his angels, and shall gather together his elect from the four winds, from the uttermost part of the earth to the uttermost part of heaven.

28 " But learn ye a parable from the fig-tree : When the branch thereof is now tender, and the leaves are come forth, you know that summer is very near.   29 So likewise, when ye shall see these things come to pass, know ye that it is very nigh, even at the doors.   30 Amen I say to you, that this generation shall not pass away, until all these things be done.   31 Heaven and earth shall pass away ; but my word shall not pass away."

Luke xxi. 20-33.

20 " And when you shall see Jerusalem compassed about with an army, then know that the desolation thereof is at hand. 21 Then let those who are in Judæa flee to the mountains ; and let them that are in the midst thereof depart out and let them that are in the countries, not enter into it.   22 For these are the days of vengeance, that all things which are written may be fulfilled. 23 But woe to them that are with child, and give suck in those days !   For there shall be great distress in the land, and wrath upon this people.   24 And they shall fall by the edge of the sword, and shall be led away captives into all nations ; and Jerusalem shall be trodden down by the Gentiles till the times of the nations be fulfilled.

25 " And there shall be signs in the sun, and in the moon, and in the stars ; and upon the earth distress of nations, by reason of the confusion of the roaring of the sea and of the waves ; 26 men withering away for fear, and expectation of what shall come upon the whole world.   For the powers of heaven shall be moved.   27 And then they shall see the Son of Man coming in a cloud with great power and majesty.   28 But when these things begin to come to pass, look up, and lift up your heads ; because your redemption is at hand."

29 And he spoke to them a similitude : " See the fig-tree, and

all the trees. ³⁰ When they now shoot forth their fruit, you know that summer is nigh. ³¹ So likewise, when you shall see these things come to pass, know that the kingdom of God is at hand. ³² Amen I say to you, this generation shall not pass away, till all things be done. ³³ Heaven and earth shall pass away ; but my words shall not pass away."

III.—COMBINED NARRATIVE.

" When, therefore, you shall see Jerusalem compassed about with an army, then know that the desolation thereof is at hand. And when you shall see the abomination of desolation, which was spoken of by Daniel the prophet, standing where it ought not, in the holy place, let him that readeth understand. Then let them that are in Judæa, flee unto the mountains ; and let them that are in the midst thereof, depart out ; and let them that are in the countries, not enter into it ; and let him that is on the house-top, not go down into the house, nor enter therein, to take any-thing out of the house ; and let him that shall be in the field, not turn back to take up his garment. And woe to them that are with child, and that give suck in those days. But pray ye that these things [and] your flight be not in the winter, nor on the sabbath ; for these are the days of vengeance, that all things which are written may be fulfilled. There shall be then great tribulation, such as hath not been from the beginning of the world which God created until now, neither shall there be ; and they shall fall by the edge of the sword, and shall be led away captives into all nations ; and Jerusalem shall be trodden down by the Gentiles till the times of the nations be fulfilled. And unless [by] the Lord those days had been shortened, no flesh should be saved ; but for the sake of the elect whom he hath chosen, those days shall be shortened. And then if any man shall say to you : ' Lo, here is Christ,' or, ' Lo, he is there,' do not believe him. For false Christs and false prophets shall arise ; and they shall show great signs and wonders insomuch as to deceive (if it be possible) even the elect. Take you heed, there-fore : behold, I have told all things to you beforehand. If, therefore, they shall say to you : ' Behold, he is in the desert,' go ye not out ; ' Behold, he is in the closets,' believe it not. For as lightning cometh out of the East and appeareth even unto the West, so shall also the coming of the Son of Man be. Where-soever the body shall be, there shall the eagles also be gathered together.

" And immediately after the tribulation of those days, there shall be signs in the sun, and in the moon, and in the stars ; and upon the earth distress of nations, by reason of the confusion of the roaring of the sea and of the waves ; men withering away

for fear, and expectation of what shall come upon the whole
world.   For the sun shall be darkened; and the moon shall not
give her light; and the stars of heaven shall fall down from
heaven ; and the powers of heaven shall be moved.   And then
shall appear the sign of the Son of Man in heaven ; and then shall
all the tribes of the earth mourn ; and then they shall see the
Son of Man coming in the clouds of heaven with much power and
majesty.   And he shall send his angels with a trumpet and a
great voice ; and they shall gather together his elect from the
four winds, from the uttermost part of the earth to the uttermost
part of heaven, from the furthest parts of the heavens to
the utmost bounds of them.   But when these things begin to
come to pass, look up, and lift up your heads ; because your
redemption is at hand.''
And he spoke to them a similitude : " But learn ye a parable
from the fig-tree.   See the fig-tree and all the trees.   When the
branch thereof is now tender and the leaves come forth, [and]
when they now shoot forth their fruit, you know that summer
is very nigh.   So you also, when you shall see all these things
come to pass, know ye that the kingdom of God is very nigh,
even at the doors.   Amen I say to you, that this generation shall
not pass away, till all these things be done.   Heaven and earth
shall pass away ; but my word shall not pass away.''

IV.—NOTES.

Introductory.   The circumstances under which these words
were spoken, may be learned from the introductory note on the
Gospel for the First Sunday of Advent.   Preaching in the temple
of Jerusalem for the last time, on the Wednesday morning before
his death, Christ had predicted to his enemies that this house,
no longer his but theirs, should be left desolate ; passing out of
the city, he had more explicitly foretold to his disciples, that of
the sacred edifice not a stone should be left upon a stone ; and afterwards sitting on the opposite eminence of Mount Olivet (Introduction, p. lxiv.), he delivered the long prophetic discourse on
the same subject, which is recorded by SS. Matthew, Mark, and
Luke.   The occasion was this.   SS. Peter, James, John, and
Andrew going apart from the other apostles, said to him : " Tell
us when shall these things be, and what shall be the sign of thy
coming and of the consummation of the world ? "   To the former
question Christ did not *clearly* reply ; to the latter he did.   In
the first part of his address (Matth. xxiv. 4-14 ; Mark xiii. 5-13 ;
Luke xxi. 8-19), he revealed to his disciples the persecutions and
temptations that must ever be the lot of his followers upon
earth, and the means by which these obstacles to salvation may
be overcome ; then in the second part (Matth. xxiv. 15-22 ;

Mark xiii. 14-20 ; Luke xxi. 20-24), he foretold the events that were to precede the ruin of Jerusalem ; and finally in the third part (Matth. xxiv. 23-51 ; Mark xiii. 21-37 ; Luke xxi. 25-36), he enumerated the signs that are to indicate the near approach of the Last Day and of his second coming to judge the world. The present extract includes the second, and portion of the third, section of this prophecy.

Having warned his apostles and us as to the difficulties in which salvation must be worked out, Christ approached the first question proposed to him and said :—

V. 15. **When therefore you shall see the abomination of desolation, which was spoken of by Daniel the prophet, standing in the holy place, let him that readeth, understand.**

The concluding words of the verse, found as they are in every manuscript both uncial and cursive, most certainly belong to the text, notwithstanding the contrary unsupported assertion of Alford If they are a clause parenthetically introduced by the evangelist, they draw attention to the importance of what is to follow ; and if, as is most probable, they were spoken by our Lord himself, they admonished the hearers to weigh well the importance of the angel's prediction recorded by Daniel. In order to understand Christ's words, it is necessary to keep certain facts before our mind.   In the first place it is to be observed that the expression, $\tau\grave{o}\ \beta\delta\acute{\epsilon}\lambda\upsilon\gamma\mu\alpha\ \tau\hat{\eta}s\ \acute{\epsilon}\rho\eta\mu\acute{\omega}\sigma\epsilon\omega s$=*the abomination of desolation*, with slight variations of number and case occurs three times in the prophecy of Daniel, *i.e.*, chap, ix. 27 ; chap. xi. 31, etc. ; and chap. xii. 11.   Christ here alludes neither to the second nor to the third of these predictions, but to the first.   All agree that the second foretells the afflictions of the Jews under Antiochus Epiphanes (see 1 Mach. i. 46-64 ; 2 Mach. vi. 1-9) ; and that the third deals with the same matter, is clear from the almost verbal identity of expression in the two passages of the prophet (*cf*. Dan. xi. 31-35, with Dan. xii. 10, 11).   Since, then, our Lord refers to Dan. ix. 27, and since in that passage it is said that there shall be in the *temple* " the abomination of desolation " ($\acute{\epsilon}\pi\grave{\iota}\ \tau\grave{o}\ \acute{\iota}\epsilon\rho\grave{o}\nu$ $\beta\delta\acute{\epsilon}\lambda\upsilon\gamma\mu\alpha\ \tau\hat{\omega}\nu\ \acute{\epsilon}\rho\eta\mu\acute{\omega}\sigma\epsilon\omega\nu$), it cannot be doubted that, notwithstanding the omission of the article in the Greek, the same sacred edifice is referred to in St. Matthew under the title of " the holy place." The scene, therefore, of " the abomination of desolation " was to be the temple itself, and not the whole country of Judæa, nor even the city of Jerusalem.   In the second place, it is to be noted that Christ did not indicate the nature of this " abomination " ; and interpreters are divided in opinion on this subject.   Some have thought that this abomination was the presence of the Roman army with idolatrous ensigns under Cestius Gallus, or of that under Titus, or that it was the garrison of Roman soldiers placed in the citadel of Antonia beside the temple.   Others

consider it was the statue of the emperor Adrian, or that of
Cæsar which Pilate ordered to be brought into the city.   Others,
in fine, think it will be the presence of Antichrist, who will seek
to have himself worshipped instead of God, and who by his persecution will desolate the Church.   To judge of these opinions
we should remember 1° that, as already stated, the scene of this
" abomination " was to be the temple itself, and not the country
of Judæa, nor even the city of Jerusalem, and that, therefore,
nothing happening outside the temple in the city of Jerusalem
or in the country of Judæa could be a fulfilment of the prophecy ;
2° that Christ's reference to the prophecy of Daniel being itself
a prophecy (" Behold I have told it to you beforehand "), therefore the " abomination of desolation " was something still to
come when Christ spoke ; 3° that the scene of the " abomination "
being the sacred edifice itself, the desecration was to take place
whilst the temple was still standing.   Having these facts before
us, we cannot accept any of the opinions just mentioned.   It is
clear that " the abomination of desolation " was not the Roman
garrison in the fort beside the temple, because it had been placed
there long before Christ spoke this prophecy ; nor was it the
Roman army under Cestius Gallus in the first siege of Jerusalem,
A.D. 66, for that army withdrew without entering the city, much
less the temple ; nor was it the army under Titus, which did
not reach the site of the temple until the building had been burned ;
it was not the image of Cæsar, which was never placed in the
temple ; nor was it the statue of Adrian, which was not erected
until many years after the temple and city had been destroyed.
A reason similar to this last excludes the idea of any reference to
Antichrist and his times.   There appears, indeed, to be but one
satisfactory explanation.   According to Jansenius Ypr., Hessel,
Baronius, Barad., and others, the " abomination of desolation "
is nothing else than the bloody excesses of the party of " zealots,"
who, between the siege of Jerusalem by Cestius Gallus, A.D. 66,
and that by Titus, A.D. 69-70, got possession of the temple,
made it a fortress, and there violated all rights human and
divine.   Hug (*Einleitung*, P. ii. § 5) says : " The wildest of the
zealots, a band of robbers who assumed the appellation of zealots
for their country, took possession of the temple, and made the
sanctuary a store for arms, and the seat of their tyranny and
murderous deeds. . . .   Thus was the holy place defiled by
detestable deeds : the abomination of desolation was in its
midst. . . .   They had not long held the temple, when in
order to make sure of its continued possession, and of superiority
over those who were peaceably disposed, they called to their aid
the Idumæans, a heathen people, who not only profaned the
place by their unholy presence, but even perpetrated a horrible
massacre within it, so that the outer courts streamed with blood."

(See description of the zealots' crimes given by Jansenius Ypr., *in loco*.)

Combining the gospel narratives, it is found that Christ gave to his followers two signs of the approaching ruin of Jerusalem : one mentioned by St. Matthew, and the other by St. Luke. The sign recorded by St. Matthew—" the abomination of desolation standing in the holy place "—was the desecration of the temple in the murders, robberies, and sacrileges committed by the zealots ; and that spoken of in the gospel of St. Luke—" when you shall see Jerusalem compassed about with an army "—was the unsuccessful siege by Cestius Gallus, A.D. 66, on whose departure there was still time for flight before Titus had invested and completely hemmed in the place.

As Christ had instructed his disciples how to deal with the evils foretold in the preceding part of this chapter, so he now pointed out the course of action to be adopted when they should first see Jerusalem surrounded by the army mentioned by St. Luke, and should behold the " abomination of desolation standing in the holy place," which was spoken of by St. Matthew. Our Lord said :—

V. 16. Then let them that are in Judæa flee to the mountains.

There is no probability that by " Judæa " more was meant than the former territories of Juda and Benjamin, *i.e.*, Judæa proper as distinguished from the provinces of Samaria and Galilee. It is true that these latter provinces were devastated in the Jewish wars ; but it is to be remembered that our Lord was speaking of the ruin of Jerusalem, and wished to warn those who might be living in the vicinity against crowding into the city as into a stronghold and place of refuge. Persons living at a distance in Samaria or in Galilee were not likely to look to Jerusalem for safety in the devastation which suddenly overtook themselves. Those in Judæa including Jerusalem are warned " to depart out " from that province ; and those in the neighbouring " countries " are commanded not to enter into it (Luke xxi. 21).

It is enjoined to flee to the mountains, " not only as being natural strongholds, often used as such (see Josephus, *B. J.* vii. 4, 3), but because they abounded in large caverns wherein the Jews, at times of public danger, took refuge. In this view Wetstein cites Gen. xix. 17 ; Jer. iv. 29 ; 1 Mach. ii. 28 ; ix. 15 ; Flor. iv. 10 ; Virg. *Æn.* ii. ult. ; Pausan. *Ach.* 15 ; Thucyd. viii. 41 ; Ammian. Marcell. xxvii. 12 ; Lucian *Zeux* " (Bloomfield, *in loco*).

We learn from Eusebius *H. E.* iii. 5, and from Epiphanius *Hær.* xxix., c. 7, that during the siege of Jerusalem many Christians took refuge in Pella, a city in the north of Peræa. " The

site of this city has been identified by Robinson ('Later
Researches,' p. 320 ; *cf.* Stanley, ' Sinai and Palestine,' p. 330)
with the ruins of Fahil, among the hills of Gilead, and the road
to it from Jerusalem lay across the chain of hills which form the
western boundary of the plain of the Jordan.   Epiphanius, *l.c.*,
speaks of the flight to Pella as having been commanded by Christ
himself, and apparently places it shortly before the siege of
Jerusalem. (*Cf.* De Mens. et Pond. c. 15.)   But Eusebius
assigns the cause of the flight to a revelation ($\kappa\alpha\tau\acute{\alpha}$ $\tau\iota\nu\alpha$ $\chi\rho\eta\sigma\mu\grave{o}\nu$ $\delta\iota$
$\mathring{\alpha}\pi o\kappa\alpha\lambda\acute{\upsilon}\psi\epsilon\omega\varsigma$) given to some distinguished members of the Church
at Jerusalem, and apparently places it before the war." (*Speakers'
Commentary, in loco.*)   Josephus refers to this flight of the
Jewish Christians to Pella when he states (*Bell. Jud.* ii. 20, 1)
that, on the departure of the defeated Cestius Gallus, many of
the Jews left the city of Jerusalem as one escapes from a sinking
ship.

Wishing to impress on his hearers the inevitable and fearful
ruin of the doomed city, Christ added :—

Vv. 17, 18. **And let him that is on the house-top, not
come down to take anything out of his house.   And let him
that is in the field, not go back to take his coat.**

" In this and the two following verses we have some proverbial (and perhaps hyperbolical) forms of expression, denoting
the imminence of the danger, and the necessity of the speediest
flight.   To understand these words, $\mathring{\epsilon}\pi\grave{\iota}$ $\tau o\hat{\upsilon}$ $\delta\acute{\omega}\mu\alpha\tau o\varsigma$ $\mu\grave{\eta}$ $\kappa\alpha\tau\alpha\beta\acute{\alpha}\tau\omega$,
we must remember that it was always customary in the East to
build the houses with flat roofs provided with a staircase both
inside and outside, *i.e.*, in the street.   By the latter way (or, as
others suppose, over the roofs of the neighbouring houses, and
so to the city wall) their flight is recommended to be taken. . . .
By $\tau\grave{\alpha}$ $\mathring{\iota}\mu\acute{\alpha}\tau\iota\alpha$ are meant the upper garments (the cloak and coat),
which husbandmen of the Southern countries have ever, when
at work, laid aside or left at home ; who are then said to be
$\gamma\upsilon\mu\nu o\acute{\iota}$=*naked.*   So Hesiod, Op. ii. 9, $\Gamma\upsilon\mu\nu\grave{o}\nu$ $\sigma\pi\epsilon\acute{\iota}\rho\epsilon\iota\nu$, $\gamma\upsilon\mu\nu\grave{o}\nu$ $\delta\grave{\epsilon}$
$\beta o\omega\tau\epsilon\hat{\iota}\nu$, $\Gamma\upsilon\mu\nu\grave{o}\nu$ δ' $\mathring{\alpha}\mu\hat{\alpha}\sigma\theta\alpha\iota$ " (Bloomfield, *in loco*).

Such being the necessity of instant removal on the appearance of the signs already indicated, our Lord says :—

V. 19. **And woe to them that are with child, and that give
suck in those days !**

Those bearing or nursing children would be unprepared for
instant flight ; and their anxiety for the safety of their offspring
would increase their own sufferings.   The fate of the mothers
and children who remained in the city during the siege is
described by Josephus ; and the harrowing description given by
that historian amply demonstrated the truth of our Saviour's
prophecy.

Two other possible difficulties in the escape are implied in the following words :—

V. 20. But pray that your flight be not in the winter, nor on the sabbath.

The meaning of this injunction is : " Pray that in your flight from these impending calamities, you meet with no impediment either physical such as the inclemency of the season, or moral such as the too strict observance of the sabbath-rest on your own part or on that of others." The allusion to the winter (Introduction, pp. xli., xlii.) is easily understood ; for then a journey, especially in " the mountains " of Palestine, would be very difficult if not impossible in consequence of the snow, the ice, and the badness of the roads. To understand the reference to " the sabbath " (Introduction, pp. clxiii., clxiv.), it is necessary to remember that in the later periods of Jewish history it was considered unlawful to go beyond a short distance on the day of rest. The custom is supposed to have owed its origin to the precept in Exod. xvi. 29 : " Let each man stay at home ; and let no one go forth out of his place on the seventh day." This injunction, which directly regarded the gathering of the manna in the desert, was subsequently so modified in Palestine, that a journey of 2,000 cubits, or about 6 furlongs was permitted. Such was the extent of the " sabbath-day's journey " mentioned in Acts i. 12. However, as the rabbins permitted a longer journey in case of danger to life (*cf.* Schoettgen i., p. 212), and as it was considered lawful in the time of the Machabees to march and to engage in battle on the sabbath-day (1 Mach. ii. 41 ; Josephus, *Antiq.* xii. 6, 2 ; xiv. 4, 2 ; xviii. 9, 2), it might be fairly asked, what had this strict injunction to do with any persons seeking to save their lives from fire or famine in a besieged city ; and especially, what had this Jewish legislation to do with Christians emancipated from obedience to the ceremonial precepts of that legislation ? It is answered, that Christ was looking forward to cases in which a superstitious regard for the Jewish customs would still linger in the minds of Christians of the Jewish race and might present a difficulty in taking to flight on the day of rest. Josephus records instances in which the religious observance of that day, even during the time of war, was the occasion of various misfortunes (*cf. Antiq.* xiii. 12, 4 ; xiv. 4, 2). We know, too, that the Jewish Christians, especially in Palestine, were accustomed to observe the seventh day of the week as their chief festival long after the preaching of the gospel. Christ, then, in the words of this verse, admonished those who would be living at the time of the fall of Jerusalem, to pray that the time of their flight be not *inopportune* ; he implied that this alone, if prayed for, would be granted ; and he declared that all the other evils mentioned could be neither averted nor lessened. (See McCarthy and Knabenbauer.)

Christ next states concisely the extent of the evils to be expected during the siege of the city.

V. 21. For there shall be then great tribulation, such as there hath not been from the beginning of the world until now, neither shall there be.

The triple Greek negative is very emphatic here, as it is in Hebr. xiii. 5, Οὐ μή σε ἀνῶ, οὐδ' οὐ μή σε ἐγκαταλίπω = " I will not leave thee, neither will I forsake thee " (Bloomfield). Still, that these words were no hyperbole, but a faithful description of what was actually to occur, may be learned from the history of Josephus who was himself an eye-witness of the siege. Using almost the same words as Christ, this Jewish priest and pharisee says : " It appears to me that the misfortunes of all men from the beginning of the world, if compared with the misfortunes of the Jews, were not so great as these " (*Bell. Jud. Proem* § 4). Again : " To put the matter briefly, no other city suffered so much " (*Bell. Jud.* v. 10, 5). Still further, he adds that those who, being pressed by hunger, went forth from the city at night to seek for food, on falling into the hands of the Romans, were scourged (Introduction, pp. cxii., cxiii.), tortured and crucified (Introduction, pp. cxvii., cxviii.) before the walls. Some days, five hundred were thus treated ; other days, more ; and so great was the multitude who met this fate that at last neither was there room for the crosses, nor were there crosses for the condemned (*Bell. Jud.* v. 11, 1). The number of Jews who lost their lives during the siege was eleven hundred thousand, whilst nearly one hundred thousand were led away as slaves to build the Flavian amphitheatre in Rome (*Bell. Jud.* vi. 9, 3). Jerusalem itself was so completely levelled with the ground that no one on seeing the site, would have believed that it had ever been inhabited (*Bell. Jud.* vii. 17. See Knabenbauer and McCarthy, *in loco*). True indeed was this more explicit prophecy recorded by St. Luke : " They shall fall by the edge of the sword ; and Jerusalem shall be trodden down by the Gentiles till the times of the nations be fulfilled."

Christ adds :—

V. 22. And unless those days had been shortened, no flesh should be saved : but for the sake of the elect those days shall be shortened.

As McCarthy observes, the " elect " here mentioned were not the *pious* Jews, that is Jews warmly attached to the faith of their fathers, nor those predestined *ante praevisa merita* (Jans. Ypr.), but such of the Jewish race as were then believers, or were destined to be afterwards members of the true Church.

As St. Augustine says, we cannot doubt that there were then among the Jews some who believed already, others who were to be brought to the faith by the manifest Judgment of God which was about to fall upon their nation, and others still whose descendants were to be converted before the second coming of Christ, when " all Israel should be saved, as it is written ' The Deliverer shall come out of Sion, and he shall turn away ungodliness from Jacob.' " (Rom. xi. 26. *Cf.* Isaias lix. 20.) On account, then, of the believing Jews—" a remnant saved according to the election of grace " (Rom. xi. 5)—and in order that the prophecy regarding the conversion of the unbelievers' descendants might be fulfilled, " those days had been shortened " ; for we are told by Christ that otherwise " no flesh (a Hebraism for no single person) should be saved," and Josephus confesses that if the siege had lasted a little longer, the whole nation must have been destroyed. Indeed this author says it was a proverbial expression in the mouths of all who escaped : Εἰ μὴ ταχέως ἀπωλόμεθα, οὐκ ἂν ἐσώθημεν (Bloomfield, *in loco*).

But how was this time of suffering brought to an end ? According to Alford, quoting from Gresswell, various causes combined to shorten the siege. (1) Herod Agrippa had begun to strengthen the walls of Jerusalem in a way which, if finished, would have rendered them impregnable ; but he was stopped by orders from Claudius, A.D. 42, or 43 (Jos. *Antiq.* xix. 7, 2). (2) The Jews, being divided into factions among themselves, had totally neglected any preparations to stand a siege. (3) The magazines of corn and provisions were burned just before the arrival of Titus. The words of Josephus on this subject are remarkable, and are as follows : Συνέβη γοῦν . . . κατακαῆναι δὲ πλὴν ὀλίγου πάντα τὸν σῖτον, ὃς ἂν αὐτοῖς οὐκ ἐπ᾽ ὀλίγα διήρκεσεν ἔτη πολιορκουμένοις. Λιμῷ γοῦν ἑάλωσαν, ὅπερ ἥκιστα δυνατόν ἦν, εἰ μὴ τοῦτον αὐτοῖς προπαρεσκεύασαν = " Accordingly it so came to pass, that . . . almost all that corn was burned, which would have been sufficient for a siege of many years. So they were taken eventually by means of famine—a thing which would have been impossible if they had not prepared the way for it by this act " (*Bell. Jud.* v. 1, 4). (4) Titus arrived suddenly, and the Jews voluntarily abandoned parts of the fortifications (*Bell. Jud.* vi. 8, 4). (5) Titus himself confessed : Σὺν θεῷ γ᾽ ἐπολεμήσαμεν, καὶ θεὸς ἦν ὁ τῶνδε τῶν ἐρυμάτων Ἰουδαίους καθελών, ἐπεὶ χεῖρές τε ἀνθρώπων ἢ μαχαναὶ τί πρὸς τούτους τοὺς πύργους δύνανται ; = " We have certainly had God for our helper in this war ; and it was no other than God that ejected the Jews out of these fortifications. For what could the hands of men or any engines do towards overthrowing these towers ? " (*Bell. Jud.* vi. 9, 1).

According to St. Chrysostom, St. Jerome, Theophylactus, Euthymius, Maldonatus, A Lapide, and nearly all Catholic commentators, our Lord, having predicted the horrors of the fall of Jerusalem and the signs by which the approach of that catastrophe might be recognised, passes on at this point to indicate the events which are to precede his second coming to judge the world. The transition was probably marked by a pause, after which Christ said :—

Vv. 23, 24. Then if any man shall say to you: Lo, here is Christ, or there, do not believe him. For false Christs and false prophets shall arise, and they shall show great signs and wonders, insomuch as to deceive (if it be possible) even the elect.

The time referred to in the word " then " was not the period immediately following the destruction of Jerusalem, nor that immediately preceding the Last Day, but the whole space between these events, which are very closely related to each other as type and antitype. The parallelism between the prophecies regarding the two is thus set forth in the Cambridge Bible :—

THE FALL OF JERUSALEM	THE SECOND ADVENT
(vv. 5-22).	(vv. 23-31).
(1) False Christs and false prophets (vv. 5-11).	(1) False Christs and false prophets (vv. 23, 24).
(2) Persecution and apostasy (vv. 9, 10, 12).	(2) Dangers even to the elect (v. 24).
(3) Wars, famine, pestilence (vv. 6, 7).	(3) Distress of nations (v. 29).
(4) Great tribulation (v. 21).	(4) The sun and moon darkened (v. 29).
(5) The abomination of desolation (v. 15).	(5) The sign of the Son of Man (v. 30).
(6) The escape of the Christians (vv. 16-18).	(6) The salvation of the elect (v. 31).

During this interval, and especially at the *beginning* and at the *end* of the Christian era, impostors were to appear. These are the precursors of Antichrist ; their efforts to deceive will be continued from time to time until the great apostasy at the end of the world ; the means adopted will be the working of pretended miracles ; and by such means they will endeavour to ensnare all, " even the elect," that is, even those predestined to eternal life. This is especially true of Antichrist himself, " whose coming," says the Apostle, " is according to the working of Satan, in all power and signs, and lying wonders " (2 Thess. ii. 9).   Many will be deceived by him ; for it is written : " All that dwell upon the

earth adored him, whose names are not written in the book
of life of the Lamb " (Apoc. xiii. 8). Chosen souls, however,
though sorely tried particularly in the time of Antichrist, will not
fail ; for again of the elect it is written : " My sheep hear my
voice ; and I know them ; and they follow me ; and I give them
life everlasting ; and they shall not perish forever ; and *no man
shall pluck them out of my hand* " (John x. 27, 28).
The remembrance of this prophecy together with the interior
light of grace is sufficient to secure the elect from deception.
Hence Christ adds :—

**Vv. 25, 26. Behold, I have told it to you beforehand. If,
therefore, they shall say to you : Behold, he is in the desert,
go ye not out : Behold, he is in the closets, believe it not.**

The last words repeat in a more explicit form the warning
already given in verse 23.   Our Lord's meaning is that whether
the impostors go forth into the desert to attract disciples by
an apparently ascetic life, or whether they invite persons to a
private consultation, no heed is to be given to their deceitful
words or acts.   Maldonatus says : " Proposuit duo pro omnibus
loca contraria : desertum et penetralia, id est conclave et intimam
maximeque reconditam domus partem, ut significaret qua-
cumque ratione, quocumque habitu, quocumque loco alius
Christus veniret, credendum illi non esse."

Passing from a negative, to a positive, description of his
second appearance on earth, Christ declared that, whereas this
coming will be at once made evident to all, it will differ much
from the first ;

**V. 27. For as lightning cometh out of the East, and ap-
peareth even unto the West, so shall also the coming of the
Son of Man be.**

At his first coming Christ had appeared in a particular city ;
he was born and he lived in obscurity ; and this obscure and
hidden visit had to be made known to the shepherds by an
angel, and to the Gentiles by a star.   His second advent, like
the lightning flash, will be sudden, unexpected, and visible to
the whole world.   How does the lightning appear ?   It needs
no messenger, no herald to announce its approach ; but at the
same moment it is seen throughout the world by all, even by
those who sit in their houses and by those who repose in their
bedchambers.   So shall the coming of Christ be visible at once
and everywhere, because of the splendour of his glory (St.
Chrysostom).   " Quasi sol in sua majestate praefulgens ubique
apparebit, ubique lucebit ; cunctis, etiam nolentibus, revelabi-
tur " (St. Bernard).

Christ thus declared to his disciples that his second and

glorious appearance on earth will be known to all, and this
independently of any announcement from man or angel. The
same thought is expressed in the following words :—

V. 28. **Wheresoever the body shall be, there shall the
eagles also be gathered together.**

The word here translated " body," and in the Vulgate
" corpus," is in the Greek text πτῶμα = " a dead body "
or " carcass." The whole sentence appears to have been proverbial, and is found in Job xxxix. 27-30 : " Will the eagle mount up
at thy command and make her nest in high places ? . . .
Thence she looketh for the prey, and her eyes behold afar off.
Her young ones shall suck up blood ; and *wheresoever the carcass
shall be, she is immediately there.*" The meaning of the saying
considered in itself, is quite clear ; but the sense in which it is
applied in the present passage, is not so easily determined. Some
understand by " the body " the body of Christ now glorious,
but once torn by nails and likened to a carcass, whilst " the
eagles " are the just of every age and country, who are to be
gathered around Christ on the Last Day (A Lap., Tirin., etc.).
Maldonatus interprets " the body " in this sense, but takes " the
eagles " to be all mankind just and unjust, who must come
before Christ for sentence. Others think " the body " to be the
city of Jerusalem already virtually dead when Christ spoke, and
the eagles to be the Romans who surrounded and destroyed it
(Lightfoot, Kuinoel, Kenrick). In reply to the question as to
where this will take place, Alford says : " The answer is,—first,
at Jerusalem ; where the corrupting body lies, thither shall the
vultures (literally) gather themselves together, coming as they
do from far on the scent of prey. Secondly, in its final fulfilment,
—*over the whole world* ;—for that is the πτῶμα now, and the ἀετοί
the angels of vengeance."

According to Knabenbauer (*in loco*), we cannot accept any of
these explanations as satisfactory, inasmuch as, other considerations apart, they all appear to be out of harmony with the context.
Unless we be prepared to admit a sudden and unaccountable
break in the discourse, this verse 28 must be connected with the
preceding verse 27 ; and the connection can consist only in this,
that in the two, Christ gave reasons for not believing the false
prophets who after the fall of Jerusalem were to announce the
fact of his second coming. The characteristics of that coming
are (1) that it will need no announcement when it takes place
(verse 27), and (2) an interiorly felt attraction by which the faithful will be drawn to Christ (verse 28)—an attraction so strong as
to render unnecessary any external guidance or help. By an
example, then, taken from nature, our Lord illustrated and
vividly pictured for his hearers what will happen in the supernatural order when he comes to judge the world. On filling

in the ellipsis, therefore, the true meaning of verse 28 which is under consideration may be expressed in the following paraphrase : " As the eagle, without any other guidance than natural instinct, knows from afar where its prey awaits it, so without any other admonition than the supernatural light which shines within them, the faithful will become aware of the advent of their Saviour ; and as the eagle on seeing its prey, flies towards that prey with astonishing rapidity, so on beholding Christ, the faithful, with an irrepressible desire and in an instant of time, will be drawn into his presence."   " The dead that are in Christ," says the Apostle, " shall rise first.   Then we that are alive, that are left, shall be taken up (ἁρπαγησόμεθα = *rapiemur* = *shall be snatched up*) together with them in the clouds to meet Christ " (1 Thess. iv. 16, 17).

The remaining verses of this passage of St. Matthew, which coincide almost word for word with those of the extract from St. Luke xxi. 25-33, are already explained in the notes on the Gospel for the first Sunday of Advent.

V.—MORAL REFLECTIONS.

One of the titles merited by Christ is that of Judge of the human race ; " for neither doth the Father judge any man, but he hath given all judgment to the Son " (John v. 22).   In the case of each one of us, our Redeemer exercises this office twice— in the Particular Judgment which, according to the *certain* teaching of theologians (*de fide certa*) takes place immediately after death, and in the General·Judgment, to which the latter part of the present passage refers.   There are several reasons for this second examination of our lives ; and the attentive consideration of each of these reasons cannot fail to promote our progress in virtue.

1. The first reason for the General Judgment is the glory of God, who will then reveal before all mankind those attributes of his which so many now refuse to recognise, and especially his providence in the disposition of things here below.   We see around us the wicked abounding in wealth and honours, and the just suffering in poverty and contempt.   This sight was a mystery to the saints themselves ; and their wonder is recorded in the Sacred Scriptures.   The Royal Prophet says : " My feet were almost moved, my steps had well-nigh slipped ; because I was envious of the wicked, when I saw the peace of sinners." A little afterwards he exclaims : " Behold, these are sinners, and still, prospering in the world, they have obtained riches !   And I said : Then in vain have I justified my heart, and washed my hands among the innocent, and I have been scourged all the day " (Ps. lxxii. 2, 3, 12-14).   At the General Judgment God's

providence in this will be vindicated before the whole world : it will then be seen that with afflictions God purifies his elect from their venial faults, or weans them from the love of earthly goods, whilst, in temporal prosperity he gives to the reprobate a passing reward for those merely natural good works of theirs which cannot be recompensed in the world to come. Awaiting the light which the great accounting day of God's justice will bring us, we must humble ourselves and say with the Apostle : " O the depth of the riches of the wisdom and of the knowledge of God ! How incomprehensible are his judgments, and how unsearchable are his ways ! . . . For of him, and by him, and in him, are all things. To him be glory for ever " (Rom. xi. 33, 36).

2. Another reason for the General Judgment is the manifestation of the glory of Christ. At his first coming, our Lord hid his greatness, lived a life of poverty, was overwhelmed with ignominy, and was at last condemned and crucified as a malefactor. At his second coming, he will appear surrounded with unspeakable glory and majesty, will cite all nations before his tribunal, and will receive from all the confession of which the Apostle speaks, when he says that " the Lord Jesus Christ is in the glory of God the Father " (Philipp. ii. 11). How worthy of adoration is this Divine Saviour who on the Last Day is to receive the homage of an assembled world ! How worthy of our love is he who, when on earth, concealed his greatness that he might gain our hearts ! How worthy of imitation is that humility and self-abnegation which merited such exaltation !

3. The third reason for the General Judgment is the glory of the elect, to whom God made this promise : " Whosoever shall glorify me, him will I glorify " (1 Kings ii. 30). In the Particular Judgment, indeed, the just are to receive their reward ; but it is necessary that before the whole world their merit be made known to those who now despise them, and that their sanctity be vindicated against their adversaries. Hence the promise of the Apostle : " Your life is hidden with Christ in God. When Christ your life shall appear, then you also shall appear with him in glory " (Col. iii. 3, 4). Should not this prospect encourage us in the practice of virtue and fill us with a contempt of all things earthly ? Should it not inspire us with the feelings of the Apostle who said : " The things that were gain to me, the same I have counted loss for Christ, . . . for whom I have suffered the loss of all things, and count them but as dung, that I may gain Christ, . . . that I may know him, and the power of his resurrection, and the fellowship of his sufferings, being made conformable to his death, if by any means I may attain to the resurrection which is from the dead " (Philipp. iii. 7, 8, 10, 11).

4. The fourth reason for the General Judgment is the greater confusion of the reprobate, regarding whom, as enemies of Christ, Isaias wrote : " Behold, all that fight against thee shall be confounded and ashamed. They shall be as nothing ; and the men that strive against thee shall perish " (Isaias xli. 11). This prophecy is not always fulfilled in the present life ; and many are now held in honour as just men, who in the sight of God are stained with crime. It is God's will, therefore, that in the General Judgment the sins of the wicked shall be manifested before all ; that when the sentence of damnation is pronounced against the reprobate, the reason of the divine decree shall be known to all ; and that in that day all shall confess : " Thou art just, O Lord, and thy judgment is right " (Ps. cxviii. 137). As then, " there is not anything secret, that shall not be made manifest ; nor hidden, that shall not be known and come abroad " (Luke viii. 17), we should have ever in our heart and on our lips the prayer of holy David : " Turn away thy face from my sins, and blot out all my iniquities. Create a clean heart in me, O God ; and renew a right spirit within mv bowels " (Ps. l. 11, 12).

5. The fifth reason for the General Judgment regards both the reprobate and the elect alike. The Catechism of the Council of Trent says : " As good and bad men performed all their actions through life not without the co-operation of their bodies, it follows by all means that good and bad actions appertain also to the bodies, which were the instruments of those actions. It was, therefore, most fitting that their bodies should participate with their souls in due rewards of eternal glory or in punishments ; and this could not be accomplished without a General Resurrection and a General Judgment." The knowledge that in the final award before the tribunal of Christ, our bodies are to share in the eternal happiness or misery of our souls, should be an efficacious incentive to the purity and holiness of life which will make us like to Christ and fit for the company of the angels. " If there be a natural body," said the Apostle, " there is also a spiritual body, as it is written : ' The first man Adam was made into a living soul ' : the last Adam was made into a quickening spirit. . . . The first man was of the earth, earthly: the second man from heaven, heavenly. As is the earthly, such also are those that are earthly ; and as is the heavenly, such also are those that are heavenly. Therefore, as we have borne the image of the earthly, let us bear the image of the heavenly. Now this I say, brethren, that flesh and blood cannot possess the kingdom of God ; neither shall corruption possess incorruption " (1 Cor. xv. 44, 45, 47-50). The certainty of a future resurrection should allay, if it does not prevent, our sorrow at the death of relatives or friends, and our

tear at the prospect of our own, since faith teaches that, if we shall have lived in God's service and shall have died in his love, our bodies on the Day of Judgment are to be once more united to our souls in an immortal life, and are to be endowed with qualities like those of the glorified body of Christ. This was the consoling thought of St. Paul, who said : " Our conversation is in heaven ; whence also we look for the Saviour, our Lord Jesus Christ, who will reform the body of our lowness made like to the body of his glory, according to the operation whereby he is able even to subdue all things unto himself " (Philipp. ii. 20, 21)

END OF VOL. II.

INDEX OF SUBJECTS.

Peter, St., Pre-eminent position amongst the Apostles, II., 36.
Pharisees—Denunciation of, I.,274 ; II., 60.
Derivation of name, etc., II., 251.
Enmity to Jesus, II., 311.
Faults of, II., 250.
History of the Sect, clxxiii.
John the Baptist questioned by, I., 35.
Moral Defects, II., 183.
Parables to reprove, II., 182 seq.
Piety of, defective, II., 208 seq.
Righteousness of condemned, II., 202-208.
Sins of, II., 257 seq.
Teaching, etc., clxxiv. ; II., 252.
Try to ensnare Jesus in his speech, II., 383 seq.
Phasga, Mount, xlv.
Philip, Apostle, character of, I., 290.
Philip, Tetrarch of Ituræa, etc., cv. ; I., 47, 110.
Physicians, mention of, in Scriptures, xcvii.
Pinnacle of the Temple, cxxxix.
Plains of Palestine, xlvi.
Pontius Pilate, rule and fate, I., 46.
Portitores, cxxxi.
Prætorium, Site of, lxiii.
Prayer—Characteristics of, I., 172.
Duty of, II., 227.
Efficacious, conditions of, II., 103-105.
" In the name of Jesus," II., 96 seq.
Jewish Customs, clxii.
Perseverance in, II., 368.
Pharisee's and Publican's, II., 253 seq.
Power of, II., 102.
Prayer in common, benefit of, II., 289.
Why sometimes unanswered, II., 98, 103.
Precipitation, Punishment by, cxvi.
Presentation in the Temple, Why submitted to, I., 90.
Pride, Sin of, II., 257, 317, 318.
Priests, cxlvi.
Chief Priests, cvi., cvii., I., 115.
High Priest, cxlviii.-cl.
Vestments, cxlvii.
" Prince of this world," II., 135.
Prisons rarely mentioned in early Scriptures, cix.
Prophets, cli.
" Art thou the Prophet," meaning of, I., 21.

Prophets—continued.
Meanings of word, I., 22, 95 ; II., 220.
False Prophets, II., 220, 224.
" Proselyte of Justice," cxxx.; I., 35.
" Proselyte of the Gate," cxxx. ; I., 158.
Propter Patrem, II., 164.
Proverb, Meaning of word, II., 98, 101.
Providence of God, I., 65 ; II., 216.
Publicans, cxxx.-cxxxii.
Publicans and Sinners, II., 182 seq., 252.
Purification of Blessed Virgin Mary, Why submitted to, I., 90.
Purifications, Legal, among the Jews, clix.
Quarantania or Quarentaria, xlv. ; I., 242, 248.
Quarter Measure, Value of, II., 233.
Quintilius Varus, When Governor of Syria, I., 58, 59.
Quirinius, Poll Tax imposed on Jews, I., 59 ; II., 386.
" Rabbi," Meaning of word, II., 195.
" Raca," Meaning of, II., 205.
Rama, lx.
" Redemption of Israel," Meaning of, I., 97.
Regeneration, Divine, Meaning of, I., 84.
" Rejoice greatly, O Daughter of Sion," Explanation, II., 19.
Resurrection, II., 25 seq.
Appearance of Jesus after, II., 42, 43, 109.
Great importance of, II., 36.
Lessons of, II., 36 seq.
Predictions concerning, I., 232.
Proofs of, II., 42, 43 seq.
Women's visit to the tomb, II., 31 seq.
Retaliation, Punishment of, cxiv.
Revised Version of the Bible, xxxii.
Reynolds, Dr. William, Douay Version of Bible, Translator, xxxi.
Rheims, Version of New Testament, xxx.
Riches, Love of, dangerous, II., 293.
Rivers of Palestine, xlix.-li.
Robbers in Palestine, II., 274.
Roman soldiers' pay, I., 195; II. 277.
Romans—Jewish Tribute, II., 386, State of Jews under, cv.
Rulers, Duty of submission to, II., 390.

INDEX OF TEXTS.

(NOTE: *I., II.,* signify *Volume I.* and *Volume II.*; *Int.* means the *Introduction in Volume I.*)

THE OLD TESTAMENT BOOKS.

THE NEW TESTAMENT BOOKS.

PRINTED BY M. H. GILL AND SON, LTD., DUBLIN